ALL GLORY TO ŚRĪ GURU AND GAURĀṄGA

ŚRĪMAD BHĀGAVATAM

of

KṚṢṆA-DVAIPĀYANA VYĀSA

कृष्णे स्वधामोपगते धर्मज्ञानादिभिः सह ।
कलौ नष्टदृशामेष पुराणार्कोऽधुनोदितः ॥

kṛṣṇe sva-dhāmopagate
dharma-jñānādibhiḥ saha
kalau naṣṭa-dṛśām eṣa
purāṇārko 'dhunoditaḥ

(p. 177)

BOOKS BY HIS DIVINE GRACE
A. C. BHAKTIVEDANTA SWAMI PRABHUPĀDA

Bhagavad-gītā As It Is
Śrīmad-Bhāgavatam (completed by disciples)
Śrī Caitanya-caritāmṛta
Kṛṣṇa, the Supreme Personality of Godhead
Teachings of Lord Caitanya
The Nectar of Devotion
The Nectar of Instruction
Śrī Īśopaniṣad
Light of the Bhāgavata
Easy Journey to Other Planets
Teachings of Lord Kapila, the Son of Devahūti
Teachings of Queen Kuntī
Message of Godhead
The Science of Self-Realization
The Perfection of Yoga
Beyond Birth and Death
On the Way to Kṛṣṇa
Rāja-vidyā: The King of Knowledge
Elevation to Kṛṣṇa Consciousness
Kṛṣṇa Consciousness: The Matchless Gift
Kṛṣṇa Consciousness: The Topmost Yoga System
Perfect Questions, Perfect Answers
Life Comes from Life
The Nārada-bhakti-sūtra (completed by disciples)
The Mukunda-mālā-stotra (completed by disciples)
Geetār-gān (Bengali)
Vairāgya-vidyā (Bengali)
Buddhi-yoga (Bengali)
Bhakti-ratna-boli (Bengali)
Back to Godhead magazine (founder)

BOOKS COMPILED FROM THE TEACHINGS OF HIS DIVINE GRACE
A. C. BHAKTIVEDANTA SWAMI PRABHUPĀDA AFTER HIS LIFETIME

Search for Liberation
A Second Chance
The Journey of Self-Discovery
Civilization and Transcendence
The Laws of Nature
Renunciation Through Wisdom
The Quest for Enlightenment
Dharma, the Way of Transcendence
Spiritual Yoga
Bhakti-Yoga, the Art of Eternal Love
Beyond Illusion and Doubt
The Hare Kṛṣṇa Challenge

ŚRĪMAD BHĀGAVATAM

First Canto
"Creation"

(Chapters 1–8)

With a Short Life Sketch
of Lord Śrī Caitanya Mahāprabhu,
the Ideal Preacher of Bhāgavata-dharma,
and with the Original Sanskrit Text,
Its Roman Transliteration, Synonyms,
Translation and Elaborate Purports

by

HIS DIVINE GRACE
A.C. BHAKTIVEDANTA SWAMI PRABHUPĀDA
Founder-*Ācārya* of the International Society for Krishna Consciousness

THE BHAKTIVEDANTA BOOK TRUST
LOS ANGELES • STOCKHOLM • MUMBAI • SYDNEY

Readers interested in the subject matter of this book are invited by the International Society for Krishna Consciousness to correspond with its Secretary at one of the following addresses:

The Bhaktivedanta Book Trust
P.O. Box 341445, Los Angeles, California 90034, USA
Phone: +1-800-927-4152 • Fax: +1-310-837-1056
E-mail: bbt.usa@krishna.com
web: www.krishna.com

The Bhaktivedanta Book Trust
P. O. Box 380, Riverstone, NSW 2765, Australia
Phone: +61-2-96276306 • Fax: +61-2-96276052
E-mail: bbtaustralia@gmail.com

Printed in China

Previous printings: 535,000
Current printing, 2016: 90,000

Library of Congress Cataloging in Publication Data (Revised)

Śrīmad-Bhāgavatam

In English and Sanskrit
Translation of Bhāgavatpurāṇa by His Divine Grace A. C. Bhaktivedanta Swami Prabhupāda. Los Angeles. Bhaktivedanta Book Trust
Includes index.
Contents: 1st Canto, Creation—Chapters 1–8

1. Purāṇas. Bhāgavatpurāṇa—Criticism, interpretation, etc.
I. A. C. Bhaktivedanta Swami Prabhupāda, 1896–1977.
II. Title.

BL1140.4.B4322E5 1987 294.5'925 87-25585

ISBN 0-912776-27-7

To
Śrīla Prabhupāda
Bhaktisiddhānta Sarasvatī
Gosvāmī Mahārāja

MY SPIRITUAL MASTER

On the 26th Annual Ceremony of His
Disappearance Day

He lives forever by his divine instructions
and
the follower lives with him.

EXPLANATION OF THE COVER

Note: See corresponding numbers on cover illustration.

1. The original spiritual planet, which resembles the whorl of a huge lotus flower, is called Goloka Vṛndāvana. It is the abode of Lord Kṛṣṇa, the original Personality of Godhead.

2. This original planet Goloka throws off a spiritual effulgence called the *brahma-jyoti*, which is the ultimate goal of the impersonalists.

3. Within this unlimited *brahma-jyoti* are unlimited numbers of spiritual planets, as there are innumerable material planets within the sun rays of the material universes. These spiritual planets are dominated by plenary expansions of Lord Kṛṣṇa, and the inhabitants there are ever-liberated living beings. They are all four-handed. The Lord is known there as Nārāyaṇa, and the planets are known as Vaikuṇṭhas.

4. Sometimes a spiritual cloud covers a corner of the spiritual sky's *brahma-jyoti*, and the covered portion is called the *mahat-tattva*. The Lord's plenary portion Mahā-Viṣṇu then lies down in the water within the *mahat-tattva*. The water is called the Causal Ocean (*kāraṇa-jala*).

5. As Mahā-Viṣṇu sleeps within the Causal Ocean, innumerable universes are generated with His breathing. These floating universes are scattered over the Causal Ocean. They stay during a breath of Mahā-Viṣṇu.

6. In every universal globe the same Mahā-Viṣṇu enters again as Garbhodakaśāyī Viṣṇu and lies on the Garbha Ocean, on the serpentine Śeṣa incarnation. From Garbhodakaśāyī Viṣṇu's navel sprouts a lotus stem, and on the lotus atop that stem Brahmā, the lord of the universe, is born. Within the universe Brahmā creates all living beings of different shapes in terms of their desires. He also creates the sun, the moon and other planets with their respective demigods.

7. The sun is situated almost in the center of every universe, and it distributes profuse light and heat all over the universe. There are millions and billions of suns in all the millions and billions of universes within the *mahat-tattva*. The suns and moons are required within the universes because they are dark by nature. The *Vedas* instruct us to go out of the dark universes and reach the glowing effulgence, the *brahma-jyoti*.

8. The *brahma-jyoti* is due to the illuminating Vaikuṇṭha planets, which need no sun or moon or power of electricity.

Śrīmad-Bhāgavatam helps us reach the supreme Vaikuṇṭha planet, Goloka Vṛndāvana. The door is open for everyone. Human life is meant for this particular aim, for it is the highest perfection.

Contents

Preface

We must know the present need of human society. And what is that need? Human society is no longer bounded by geographical limits to particular countries or communities. Human society is broader than in the Middle Ages, and the world tendency is toward one state or one human society. The ideals of spiritual communism, according to *Śrīmad-Bhāgavatam,* are based more or less on the oneness of the entire human society, nay, of the entire energy of living beings. The need is felt by great thinkers to make this a successful ideology. *Śrīmad-Bhāgavatam* will fill this need in human society. It begins, therefore, with the aphorism of Vedānta philosophy *janmādy asya yataḥ* to establish the ideal of a common cause.

Human society, at the present moment, is not in the darkness of oblivion. It has made rapid progress in the field of material comforts, education and economic development throughout the entire world. But there is a pinprick somewhere in the social body at large, and therefore there are large-scale quarrels, even over less important issues. There is need of a clue as to how humanity can become one in peace, friendship and prosperity with a common cause. *Śrīmad-Bhāgavatam* will fill this need, for it is a cultural presentation for the respiritualization of the entire human society.

Śrīmad-Bhāgavatam should be introduced also in the schools and colleges, for it is recommended by the great student-devotee Prahlāda Mahārāja in order to change the demoniac face of society.

kaumāra ācaret prājño dharmān bhāgavatān iha
durlabhaṁ mānuṣaṁ janma tad apy adhruvam arthadam
(*Bhāgavatam* 7.6.1)

Disparity in human society is due to lack of principles in a godless civilization. There is God, or the Almighty One, from whom everything emanates, by whom everything is maintained and in whom everything is merged to rest. Material science has tried to find the ultimate source of creation very insufficiently, but it is a fact that there is one ultimate source of everything that be. This ultimate source is explained rationally and authoritatively in the beautiful *Bhāgavatam*, or *Śrīmad-Bhāgavatam*.

Śrīmad-Bhāgavatam is the transcendental science not only for knowing the ultimate source of everything but also for knowing our relation with Him and our duty toward perfection of the human society on the basis of this perfect knowledge. It is powerful reading matter in the Sanskrit language, and it is now rendered into English elaborately so that simply by a careful reading one will know God perfectly well, so much so that the reader will be sufficiently educated to defend himself from the onslaught of atheists. Over and above this, the reader will be able to convert others to accepting God as a concrete principle.

Śrīmad-Bhāgavatam begins with the definition of the ultimate source. It is a bona fide commentary on the *Vedānta-sūtra* by the same author, Śrīla Vyāsadeva, and gradually it develops into nine cantos up to the highest state of God realization. The only qualification one needs to study this great book of transcendental knowledge is to proceed step by step cautiously and not jump forward haphazardly as with an ordinary book. It should be gone through chapter by chapter, one after another. The reading matter is so arranged with its original Sanskrit text, its English transliteration, synonyms, translation and purports so that one is sure to become a God-realized soul at the end of finishing the first nine cantos.

The Tenth Canto is distinct from the first nine cantos because it deals directly with the transcendental activities of the Personality of Godhead Śrī Kṛṣṇa. One will be unable to capture the effects of the Tenth Canto without going through the first nine cantos. The book is complete in twelve cantos, each independent, but it is good for all to read them in small installments one after another.

I must admit my frailties in presenting *Śrīmad-Bhāgavatam*, but still I am hopeful of its good reception by the thinkers and leaders of society on the strength of the following statement of *Śrīmad-Bhāgavatam* (1.5.11):

tad-vāg-visargo janatāgha-viplavo
yasmin prati-ślokam abaddhavaty api
nāmāny anantasya yaśo 'ṅkitāni yat
śṛṇvanti gāyanti gṛṇanti sādhavaḥ

"On the other hand, that literature which is full with descriptions of the transcendental glories of the name, fame, form and pastimes of the unlimited Supreme Lord is a transcendental creation meant to bring about a revolution in the impious life of a misdirected civilization. Such transcendental literatures, even though irregularly composed, are heard, sung and accepted by purified men who are thoroughly honest."

Oṁ tat sat

A.C. Bhaktivedanta Swami

Dated at Delhi
December 15, 1962

Introduction

The conception of God and the conception of Absolute Truth are not on the same level. The *Śrīmad-Bhāgavatam* hits on the target of the Absolute Truth. The conception of God indicates the controller, whereas the conception of the Absolute Truth indicates the *summum bonum* or the ultimate source of all energies. There is no difference of opinion about the personal feature of God as the controller because a controller cannot be impersonal. Of course modern government, especially democratic government, is impersonal to some extent, but ultimately the chief executive head is a person, and the impersonal feature of government is subordinate to the personal feature. So without a doubt whenever we refer to control over others we must admit the existence of a personal feature. Because there are different controllers for different managerial positions, there may be many small gods. According to the *Bhagavad-gītā* any controller who has some specific extraordinary power is called a *vibhūtimat sattva,* or controller empowered by the Lord. There are many *vibhūtimat sattvas,* controllers or gods with various specific powers, but the Absolute Truth is one without a second. This *Śrīmad-Bhāgavatam* designates the Absolute Truth or the *summum bonum* as the *paraṁ satyam.*

The author of *Śrīmad-Bhāgavatam,* Śrīla Vyāsadeva, first offers his respectful obeisances unto the *paraṁ satyam* (Absolute Truth), and because the *paraṁ satyam* is the ultimate source of all energies, the *paraṁ satyam* is the Supreme Person. The gods or the controllers are undoubtedly persons, but the *paraṁ satyam* from whom the gods derive powers of control is the Supreme Person. The Sanskrit word *īśvara* (controller) conveys the import of God, but the Supreme Person is called the *parameśvara,* or the supreme *īśvara.* The Supreme Person, or *parameśvara,* is the supreme conscious personality, and because He does not derive any power from any other source, He is supremely independent. In the Vedic literatures Brahmā is described as the supreme god or the head of all other gods like Indra, Candra and Varuṇa, but the *Śrīmad-Bhāgavatam* confirms that even Brahmā is not independent as far as his power and knowledge are concerned. He received knowledge in the form of the *Vedas* from the Supreme Person who resides within the heart of every living being. That Supreme Personality knows everything directly and indirectly. Individual infinitesimal persons, who are parts and parcels of the Supreme Personality, may know directly and indirectly everything about their bodies or external features, but the Supreme Personality knows everything about both His external and internal features.

The words *janmādy asya* suggest that the source of all production, maintenance or destruction is the same supreme conscious person. Even in our present experience we can know that nothing is generated from inert matter, but inert matter can be generated from the living entity. For instance, by contact with the living entity, the material body develops into a working machine. Men with a poor fund of knowledge mistake the bodily machinery to be the living being, but the fact is that the living being is the basis of the bodily machine. The bodily machine is useless as soon as the living spark is away from it. Similarly, the original source of all material energy is the Supreme Person. This fact is expressed in all the Vedic literatures, and all the exponents of spiritual science have accepted this truth. The living force is called Brahman, and one of the greatest *ācāryas* (teachers), namely Śrīpāda Śaṅkarācārya, has preached that Brahman is substance whereas the cosmic world is category. The original source of all energies is the living force, and He is logically accepted as the Supreme Person. He is therefore conscious of everything past, present and future, and also of each and every corner of His manifestations, both material and spiritual. An imperfect living being does not even know what is happening within his own personal body. He eats his food but does not know how this food is transformed into energy or how it sustains his body. When a living being is perfect, he is aware of everything that happens, and since the Supreme Person is all-perfect, it is quite natural that He knows everything in all detail. Consequently the perfect personality is addressed in the *Śrīmad-Bhāgavatam* as Vāsudeva, or one who lives everywhere in full consciousness and in full possession of His complete energy. All of this is clearly explained in the *Śrīmad-Bhāgavatam*, and the reader has ample opportunity to study this critically.

In the modern age Lord Śrī Caitanya Mahāprabhu preached the *Śrīmad-Bhāgavatam* by practical demonstration. It is easier to penetrate into the topics of the *Śrīmad-Bhāgavatam* through the medium of Śrī Caitanya's causeless mercy. Therefore a short sketch of His life and precepts is inserted herein to help the reader understand the real merit of *Śrīmad-Bhāgavatam*.

It is imperative that one learn the *Śrīmad-Bhāgavatam* from the person *Bhāgavatam*. The person *Bhāgavatam* is one whose very life is *Śrīmad-Bhāgavatam* in practice. Since Śrī Caitanya Mahāprabhu is the Absolute Personality of Godhead, He is both Bhagavān and *Bhāgavatam* in person and in sound. Therefore His process of approaching the *Śrīmad-Bhāgavatam* is practical for all people of the world. It was His wish that the *Śrīmad-Bhāgavatam* be preached in every nook and corner of the world by those who happened to take their birth in India.

The *Śrīmad-Bhāgavatam* is the science of Kṛṣṇa, the Absolute Personality of Godhead of whom we have preliminary information from the text of the *Bhagavad-gītā*. Śrī Caitanya Mahāprabhu has said that anyone, regardless of what he is, who is well versed in the science of Kṛṣṇa (*Śrīmad-Bhāgavatam* and *Bhagavad-gītā*) can become an authorized preacher or preceptor in the science of Kṛṣṇa.

There is a need for the science of Kṛṣṇa in human society for the good of all suffering humanity of the world, and we simply request the leaders of all nations to pick up this science of Kṛṣṇa for their own good, for the good of society and for the good of all the world's people.

A short sketch of the life and teachings of Lord Caitanya, the Preacher of Śrīmad-Bhāgavatam

Lord Śrī Caitanya Mahāprabhu, the great apostle of love of God and the father of the congregational chanting of the holy name of the Lord, advented Himself at Śrīdhāma Māyāpura, a quarter in the then city of Navadvīpa in Bengal, on the Phālgunī Pūrṇimā evening in the year 1407 Śakābda (corresponding to February 18, 1486, by the Christian calendar).

His father, Śrī Jagannātha Miśra, a learned *brāhmaṇa* from the district of Sylhet, came to Navadvīpa as a student because at that time Navadvīpa was considered to be the center of education and culture. He domiciled on the banks of the Ganges after marrying Śrīmatī Śacīdevī, a daughter of Śrīla Nīlāmbara Cakravartī, the great learned scholar of Navadvīpa.

Jagannātha Miśra had a number of daughters by his wife, Śrīmatī Śacīdevī, but they all expired at an early age. The two surviving sons, Śrī Viśvarūpa and Viśvambhara, became at last the object of their parental affection. The tenth child and youngest son, Viśvambhara, later became known as Nimāi Paṇḍita and then, after accepting the renounced order of life, Lord Śrī Caitanya Mahāprabhu.

Lord Śrī Caitanya Mahāprabhu exhibited His transcendental activities for forty-eight years and then disappeared from this mortal world in the year 1455 Śakābda at Purī.

For His first twenty-four years He remained at Navadvīpa as a student and householder. His first wife was Śrīmatī Lakṣmīpriyā, who died at an early age when the Lord was away from home. When He returned from East Bengal He was requested by His mother to accept a second wife, and He agreed. His second wife was Śrīmatī Viṣṇupriyā Devī, who bore the separation of the Lord throughout her life because the Lord took the order of *sannyāsa* at the age of twenty-four, when Śrīmatī Viṣṇupriyā was barely sixteen years old.

After taking *sannyāsa,* the Lord made His headquarters at Jagannātha Purī due to the request of His mother, Śrīmatī Śacīdevī. The Lord remained for twenty-four years at Purī. For six years of this time He traveled continuously all over India (and especially throughout southern India) preaching the *Śrīmad-Bhāgavatam.*

Lord Caitanya not only preached the *Śrīmad-Bhāgavatam* but propagated the teachings of the *Bhagavad-gītā* as well in the most practical way. In the *Bhagavad-gītā* Lord Śrī Kṛṣṇa is depicted as the Absolute Personality of Godhead, and His last teachings in that great book of transcendental knowledge instruct that one should give up all other modes of religious activities and accept Him (Lord Śrī Kṛṣṇa) as the *only* worshipable Lord. The Lord then assured that all His devotees would be protected from all sorts of sinful acts and that for them there would be no cause for anxiety.

Unfortunately, despite Lord Śrī Kṛṣṇa's direct order and the teachings of the *Bhagavad-gītā,* less intelligent people misunderstand Him to be nothing but a great historical personality, and thus they cannot accept Him as the original Personality of Godhead. Such men with a poor fund of knowledge are misled by many nondevotees. Thus the teachings of the *Bhagavad-gītā* were misinterpreted even by great scholars. After the disappearance of Lord Śrī Kṛṣṇa there were hundreds of commentaries on the *Bhagavad-gītā* by many erudite scholars, and almost every one of them was motivated by self-interest.

Lord Śrī Caitanya Mahāprabhu is the selfsame Lord Śrī Kṛṣṇa. This time, however, He appeared as a great devotee of the Lord in order to preach to the people in general, as well as to religionists and philosophers, about the transcendental position of Śrī Kṛṣṇa, the primeval Lord and the cause of all causes. The essence of His preaching is that Lord Śrī Kṛṣṇa, who appeared at Vrajabhūmi (Vṛndāvana) as the son of the King of Vraja (Nanda Mahārāja), is the Supreme Personality of Godhead and is therefore worshipable by all. Vṛndāvana-dhāma is nondifferent from the Lord because the name, fame, form and place where the Lord manifests Himself are all identical with the Lord as absolute knowledge. Therefore Vṛndāvana-dhāma is as worshipable as the Lord. The highest form of transcendental worship of the Lord was exhibited by the damsels of Vrajabhūmi in the form of pure affection for the Lord, and Lord Śrī Caitanya Mahāprabhu recommends this process as the most excellent mode of worship. He accepts the *Śrīmad-Bhāgavata Purāṇa* as the spotless literature for understanding the Lord, and He preaches that the ultimate goal of life for all human beings is to attain the stage of *prema,* or love of God.

Many devotees of Lord Caitanya like Śrīla Vṛndāvana dāsa Ṭhākura, Śrī Locana dāsa Ṭhākura, Śrīla Kṛṣṇadāsa Kavirāja Gosvāmī, Śrī Kavikarṇapūra, Śrī Prabodhānanda Sarasvatī, Śrī Rūpa Gosvāmī, Śrī Sanātana Gosvāmī, Śrī Raghunātha Bhaṭṭa Gosvāmī, Śrī Jīva Gosvāmī, Śrī Gopāla Bhaṭṭa Gosvāmī, Śrī Raghunātha dāsa Gosvāmī and in this latter age within two hundred years, Śrī Viśvanātha Cakravartī, Śrī Baladeva Vidyābhūṣana, Śrī Śyāmānanda Gosvāmī, Śrī Narottama dāsa Ṭhākura, Śrī Bhaktivinoda Ṭhākura and at last Śrī Bhaktisiddhānta Sarasvatī Ṭhākura (our spiritual master) and many other great and renowned scholars and devotees of the Lord have prepared voluminous books and literatures on the life and precepts of the Lord. Such literatures are all based on the *śāstras* like the *Vedas, Purāṇas, Upaniṣads, Rāmāyaṇa, Mahābhārata* and other histories and authentic literatures approved by the recognized *ācāryas.* They are unique in composition and unrivaled in presentation, and they are full of transcendental knowledge. Unfortunately the people of the world are still ignorant of them, but when these literatures, which are mostly in Sanskrit and Bengali, come to light the world and when they are presented before thinking people, then India's glory and the message of love will overflood this morbid world, which is vainly searching after peace and prosperity by various illusory methods not approved by the *ācāryas* in the chain of disciplic succession.

The readers of this small description of the life and precepts of Lord Caitanya will profit much to go through the books of Śrīla Vṛndāvana dāsa Ṭhākura (*Śrī Caitanya-bhāgavata*) and Śrīla Kṛṣṇadāsa Kavirāja Gosvāmī (*Śrī Caitanya-caritāmṛta*). The early life of the Lord is most fascinatingly expressed by the author of *Caitanya-bhāgavata,* and as far as the teachings are concerned, they are more vividly explained in the *Caitanya-caritāmṛta.* Now they are available to the English-speaking public in our *Teachings of Lord Caitanya.*

The Lord's early life was recorded by one of His chief devotees and contemporaries, namely Śrīla Murāri Gupta, a medical practitioner of that time, and the latter part of the life of Śrī Caitanya Mahāprabhu was recorded by His private secretary Śrī Dāmodara Gosvāmī, or Śrīla Svarūpa Dāmodara, who was practically a constant companion of the Lord at Purī. These two devotees recorded practically all the incidents of the Lord's activities, and later on all the books dealing with the Lord, which are above mentioned, were composed on the basis of the *kaḍacās* (notebooks) by Śrīla Dāmodara Gosvāmī and Murāri Gupta.

So the Lord advented Himself on the Phālgunī Pūrṇimā evening of 1407 Śakābda, and it was by the will of the Lord that there was a lunar eclipse on that evening. During the hours of eclipse it was the custom of the Hindu public to take bath in the Ganges or any other sacred river and chant the Vedic *mantras* for purification. When Lord Caitanya was born during the lunar eclipse, all India was roaring with the holy sound of Hare Kṛṣṇa, Hare Kṛṣṇa, Kṛṣṇa Kṛṣṇa, Hare Hare/ Hare Rāma, Hare Rāma, Rāma Rāma, Hare Hare. These sixteen names of the Lord are mentioned in many *Purāṇas* and *Upaniṣads,* and they are described as the *Tāraka-brahma nāma* of this age. It is recommended in the *śāstras* that offenseless chanting of these holy names of the Lord can deliver a fallen soul from material bondage. There are innumerable names of the Lord both in India and outside, and all of them are equally good because all of them indicate the Supreme Personality of Godhead. But because these sixteen are especially recommended for this age, people should take advantage of them and follow the path of the great *ācāryas* who attained success by practicing the rules of the *śāstras* (revealed scriptures).

The simultaneous occurrence of the Lord's appearance and the lunar eclipse indicated the distinctive mission of the Lord. This mission was to preach the importance of chanting the holy names of the Lord in this Age of Kali (quarrel). In this present age quarrels take place even over trifles, and therefore the *śāstras* have recommended for this age a common platform for realization, namely chanting the holy names of the Lord. People can hold meetings to glorify the Lord in their respective languages and with melodious songs, and if such performances are executed in an offenseless manner, it is certain that the participants will gradually attain spiritual perfection without having to undergo more rigorous methods. At such meetings everyone, the learned and the foolish, the rich and the poor, the Hindus and the Muslims, the Englishmen and the Indians, and the *caṇḍālas* and the *brāhmaṇas,* can all hear the transcendental sounds and thus cleanse the dust of material association from the mirror of the heart. To confirm the Lord's mission, all the people of the world will accept the holy name of the Lord as the common platform for the universal religion of mankind. In other words, the advent of the holy name took place along with the advent of Lord Śrī Caitanya Mahāprabhu.

When the Lord was on the lap of His mother, He would at once stop crying as soon as the ladies surrounding Him chanted the holy names and clapped their hands. This peculiar incident was observed by the neighbors with awe and veneration. Sometimes the young girls took pleasure in making the Lord cry and then stopping Him by chanting the holy name. So from His very childhood the Lord began to preach the importance of the holy name. In His early age Lord Śrī Caitanya was known as Nimāi. This name was given by His beloved mother because the Lord took His birth beneath a *nimba* tree in the courtyard of His paternal house.

When the Lord was offered solid food at the age of six months in the *anna-prāśana* ceremony, the Lord indicated His future activities. At this time it was customary to offer the child both coins and books in order to get some indication of the future tendencies of the child. The Lord was offered on one side coins and on the other the *Śrīmad-Bhāgavatam*. The Lord accepted the *Bhāgavatam* instead of the coins.

When He was a mere baby crawling in the yard, one day a snake appeared before Him, and the Lord began to play with it. All the members of the house were struck with fear and awe, but after a little while the snake went away, and the baby was taken away by His mother. Once He was stolen by a thief who intended to steal His ornaments, but the Lord took a pleasure trip on the shoulder of the bewildered thief, who was searching for a solitary place in order to rob the baby. It so happened that the thief, wandering hither and thither, finally arrived just before the house of Jagannātha Miśra and, being afraid of being caught, dropped the baby at once. Of course the anxious parents and relatives were glad to see the lost child.

Once a pilgrim *brāhmaṇa* was received at the house of Jagannātha Miśra, and when he was offering food to the Godhead, the Lord appeared before him and partook of the prepared food. The eatables had to be rejected because the child touched them, and so the *brāhmaṇa* had to make another preparation. The next time the same thing happened, and when this happened repeatedly for the third time, the baby was finally put to bed. At about twelve at night when all the members of the house were fast asleep within their closed rooms, the pilgrim *brāhmaṇa* offered his specially prepared foods to the Deity, and, in the same way, the baby Lord appeared before the pilgrim and spoiled his offerings. The *brāhmaṇa* then began to cry, but since everyone was fast asleep, no one could hear him. At that time the baby Lord appeared before the fortunate *brāhmaṇa* and disclosed His identity as Kṛṣṇa Himself. The *brāhmaṇa* was forbidden to disclose this incident, and the baby returned to the lap of His mother.

There are many similar incidents in His childhood. As a naughty boy He sometimes used to tease the orthodox *brāhmaṇas* who used to bathe in the Ganges. When the *brāhmaṇas* complained to His father that He was splashing them with water instead of attending school, the Lord suddenly appeared before His father as though just coming from school with all His school clothes and books. At the bathing *ghāṭa* He also used to play jokes on the neighboring girls who engaged in worshiping Śiva in hopes of getting good husbands. This is a common practice amongst unmarried girls in Hindu families. While they were engaged in such worship, the Lord naughtily appeared before them and said, "My dear sisters, please give Me all the offerings you have just brought for Lord Śiva. Lord Śiva is My devotee, and Pārvatī is My maidservant. If you worship Me, then Lord Śiva and all the other demigods will be more satisfied." Some of them refused to obey the naughty Lord, and He would curse them that due to their refusal they would be married to old men who had seven children by their previous wives. Out of fear and sometimes out of love the girls would also offer Him various goods, and then the Lord would bless them and assure them that they would have very good young husbands and that they would be mothers of dozens of children. The blessings would enliven the girls, but they used often to complain of these incidents to their mothers.

In this way the Lord passed His early childhood. When He was just sixteen years old He started His own *catuṣpāṭhī* (village school conducted by a learned *brāhmaṇa).* In this school He would simply explain Kṛṣṇa, even in readings of grammar. Śrīla Jīva Gosvāmī, in order to please the Lord, later composed a grammar in Sanskrit, in which all the rules of grammar were explained with examples that used the holy names of the Lord. This grammar is still current. It is known as *Hari-nāmāmṛta-vyākaraṇa* and is prescribed in the syllabus of schools in Bengal.

During this time a great Kashmir scholar named Keśava Kāśmīrī came to Navadvīpa to hold discussions on the *śāstras.* The Kashmir *paṇḍita* was a champion scholar, and he had traveled to all places of learning in India. Finally he came to Navadvīpa to contest the learned *paṇḍitas* there. The *paṇḍitas* of Navadvīpa decided to match Nimāi Paṇḍita (Lord Caitanya) with the Kashmir *paṇḍita,* thinking that if Nimāi Paṇḍita were defeated, they would have another chance to debate with the scholar, for Nimāi Paṇḍita was only a boy. And if the Kashmir *paṇḍita* were defeated, then they would even be more glorified because people would proclaim that a mere boy of Navadvīpa had defeated a champion scholar who was famous throughout India. It so happened that Nimāi Paṇḍita met Keśava Kāśmīrī while strolling on the banks of the Ganges. The Lord requested him to compose a Sanskrit verse in praise of the Ganges, and the *paṇḍita* within a short time composed a hundred *ślokas,* reciting the verses like a storm and showing the strength of his vast learning. Nimāi Paṇḍita at once memorized all the *ślokas* without an error. He quoted the sixty-fourth *śloka* and pointed out certain rhetorical and literary irregularities. He particularly questioned the *paṇḍita's* use of the word *bhavānī-bhartuḥ.* He pointed out that the use of this word was redundant. *Bhavānī* means the wife of Śiva, and who else can be her *bhartā,* or husband? He also pointed out several other discrepancies, and the Kashmir *paṇḍita* was struck with wonder. He was astonished that a mere student of grammar could point out the literary mistakes of an erudite scholar. Although this matter was ended prior to any public meeting, the news spread like wildfire all over Navadvīpa. But finally Keśava Kāśmīrī was ordered in a dream by Sarasvatī, the goddess of learning, to submit to the Lord, and thus the Kashmir *paṇḍita* became a follower of the Lord.

The Lord was then married with great pomp and gaiety, and at this time He began to preach the congregational chanting of the holy name of the

Lord at Navadvīpa. Some of the *brāhmaṇas* became envious of His popularity, and they put many hindrances on His path. They were so jealous that they finally took the matter before the Muslim magistrate at Navadvīpa. Bengal was then governed by Pathans, and the governor of the province was Nawab Hussain Shah. The Muslim magistrate of Navadvīpa took up the complaints of the *brāhmaṇas* seriously, and at first he warned the followers of Nimāi Paṇḍita not to chant loudly the name of Hari. But Lord Caitanya asked His followers to disobey the orders of the Kazi, and they went on with their *saṅkīrtana* (chanting) party as usual. The magistrate then sent constables who interrupted a *saṅkīrtana* and broke some of the *mṛdaṅgas* (drums). When Nimāi Paṇḍita heard of this incident He organized a party for civil disobedience. He is the pioneer of the civil disobedience movement in India for the right cause. He organized a procession of one hundred thousand men with thousands of *mṛdaṅgas* and *karatālas* (hand cymbals), and this procession passed over the roads of Navadvīpa in defiance of the Kazi who had issued the order. Finally the procession reached the house of the Kazi, who went upstairs out of fear of the masses. The great crowds assembled at the Kazi's house displayed a violent temper, but the Lord asked them to be peaceful. At this time the Kazi came down and tried to pacify the Lord by addressing Him as his nephew. He pointed out that Nīlāmbara Cakravartī referred to him as an uncle, and consequently, Śrīmatī Śacīdevī, the mother of Nimāi Paṇḍita, was his sister. He asked the Lord whether his sister's son could be angry at His maternal uncle, and the Lord replied that since the Kazi was His maternal uncle he should receive his nephew well at his home. In this way the issue was mitigated, and the two learned scholars began a long discussion on the Koran and Hindu *śāstras*. The Lord raised the question of cow-killing, and the Kazi properly answered Him by referring to the Koran. In turn the Kazi also questioned the Lord about cow sacrifice in the *Vedas,* and the Lord replied that such sacrifice as mentioned in the *Vedas* is not actually cow-killing. In that sacrifice an old bull or cow was sacrificed for the sake of receiving a fresh younger life by the power of Vedic *mantras*. But in the Kali-yuga such cow sacrifices are forbidden because there are no qualified *brāhmaṇas* capable of conducting such a sacrifice. In fact, in Kali-yuga all *yajñas* (sacrifices) are forbidden because they are useless attempts by foolish men. In Kali-yuga only the *saṅkīrtana yajña* is recommended for all practical purposes. Speaking in this way, the Lord finally convinced the Kazi, who became the Lord's follower. The Kazi thenceforth declared that no one should hinder the *saṅkīrtana* movement which was started by the Lord, and the Kazi left this order in his will for the sake of progeny. The Kazi's tomb still exists in the area of Navadvīpa, and Hindu pilgrims go there to show their respects. The Kazi's descendants are residents, and they never objected to *saṅkīrtana,* even during the Hindu-Muslim riot days.

This incident shows clearly that the Lord was not a so-called timid Vaiṣṇava. A Vaiṣṇava is a fearless devotee of the Lord, and for the right cause he can take any step suitable for the purpose. Arjuna was also a Vaiṣṇava devotee of Lord Kṛṣṇa, and he fought valiantly for the satisfaction of the Lord. Similarly, Vajrāṅgajī, or Hanumān, was also a devotee of Lord Rāma, and he gave lessons to the nondevotee party of Rāvaṇa. The principles of Vaiṣṇavism are to satisfy the Lord by all means. A Vaiṣṇava is by nature a nonviolent, peaceful living being, and he has all the good qualities of God, but when the nondevotee blasphemes the Lord or His devotee, the Vaiṣṇava never tolerates such impudency.

After this incident the Lord began to preach and propagate His *Bhāgavata-dharma,* or *saṅkīrtana* movement, more vigorously, and whoever stood against this propagation of the *yuga-dharma,* or duty of the age, was properly punished by various types of chastisement. Two *brāhmaṇa* gentlemen named Cāpala and Gopāla, who also happened to be maternal uncles of the Lord, were inflicted with leprosy by way of chastisement, and later, when they were repentant, they were accepted by the Lord. In the course of His preaching work, He used to send daily all His followers, including Śrīla Nityānanda Prabhu and Ṭhākura Haridāsa, two chief whips of His party, from door to door to preach the *Śrīmad-Bhāgavatam.* All of Navadvīpa was surcharged with His *saṅkīrtana* movement, and His headquarters were situated at the house of Śrīvāsa Ṭhākura and Śrī Advaita Prabhu, two of His chief householder disciples. These two learned heads of the *brāhmaṇa* community were the most ardent supporters of Lord Caitanya's movement. Śrī Advaita Prabhu was the chief cause for the advent of the Lord. When Advaita Prabhu saw that the total human society was full of materialistic activities and devoid of devotional service, which alone could save mankind from the threefold miseries of material existence, He, out of His causeless compassion for the age-worn human society, prayed fervently for the incarnation of the Lord and continually worshiped the Lord with water of the Ganges and leaves of the holy *tulasī* tree. As far as preaching work in the *saṅkīrtana* movement was concerned, everyone was expected to do his daily share according to the order of the Lord.

Once Nityānanda Prabhu and Śrīla Haridāsa Ṭhākura were walking down a main road, and on the way they saw a roaring crowd assembled. Upon inquiring from passers-by, they understood that two brothers, named Jagāi and Mādhāi, were creating a public disturbance in a drunken state. They also heard that these two brothers were born in a respectable *brāhmaṇa* family, but because of low association they had turned into debauchees of the worst type. They were not only drunkards but also meat-eaters, woman-hunters, dacoits and sinners of all description. Śrīla Nityānanda Prabhu heard all of these stories and decided that these two fallen souls must be the first to be delivered. If they were delivered from their sinful life, then the good name of Lord Caitanya would be even still more glorified. Thinking in this way, Nityānanda Prabhu and Haridāsa pushed their way through the crowd and asked the two brothers to chant the holy name of Lord Hari. The drunken brothers became enraged upon this request and attacked Nityānanda Prabhu with filthy language. Both brothers chased them a considerable distance. In the evening the report of the preaching work was submitted to the Lord, and He was glad to learn that Nityānanda and Haridāsa had attempted to deliver such a stupid pair of fellows.

The next day Nityānanda Prabhu went to see the brothers, and as soon as He approached them one of them threw a piece of earthen pot at Him. This struck Him on the forehead, and immediately blood began to flow. But Nityānanda Prabhu was so kind that instead of protesting this heinous act, He said, "It does not matter that you have thrown this stone at Me. I still request you to chant the holy name of Lord Hari."

One of the brothers, Jagāi, was astonished to see this behavior of Nityānanda Prabhu, and he at once fell down at His feet and asked Him to pardon his sinful brother. When Mādhāi again attempted to hurt Nityānanda Prabhu, Jagāi stopped him and implored him to fall down at His feet. In the meantime the news of Nityānanda's injury reached the Lord, who at once hurried to the spot in a fiery and angry mood. The Lord immediately invoked His Sudarśana *cakra* (the Lord's ultimate weapon, shaped like a wheel) to kill the sinners, but Nityānanda Prabhu reminded Him of His mission. The mission of the Lord was to deliver the hopelessly fallen souls of Kali-yuga, and the brothers Jagāi and Mādhāi were typical examples of these fallen souls. Ninety-nine percent of the population of this age resembles these brothers, despite high birth and mundane respectability. According to the verdict of the revealed scriptures, the total population of the world in this age will be of the lowest *śūdra* quality, or even lower. It should be noted that Śrī Caitanya Mahāprabhu never acknowledged the stereotyped caste system by birthright; rather, He strictly followed the verdict of the *śāstras* in the matter of one's *svarūpa,* or real identity.

When the Lord was invoking His Sudarśana *cakra* and Śrīla Nityānanda Prabhu was imploring Him to forgive the two brothers, both the brothers fell down at the lotus feet of the Lord and begged His pardon for their gross behavior. The Lord was also asked by Nityānanda Prabhu to accept these repenting souls, and the Lord agreed to accept them on one condition, that they henceforward completely give up all their sinful activities and habits of debauchery. Both the brothers agreed and promised to give up all their sinful habits, and the kind Lord accepted them and did not again refer to their past misdeeds.

This is the specific kindness of Lord Caitanya. In this age no one can say that he is free from sin. It is impossible for anyone to say this. But Lord Caitanya accepts all kinds of sinful persons on the one condition that they promise not to indulge in sinful habits after being spiritually initiated by the bona fide spiritual master.

There are a number of instructive points to be observed in this incident of the two brothers. In this Kali-yuga practically all people are of the quality of Jagāi and Mādhāi. If they want to be relieved from the reactions of their misdeeds, they must take shelter of Lord Caitanya Mahāprabhu and after spiritual initiation thus refrain from those things which are prohibited in the *śāstras.* The prohibitory rules are dealt with in the Lord's teachings to Śrīla Rūpa Gosvāmī.

During His householder life, the Lord did not display many of the miracles which are generally expected from such personalities, but He did once perform a wonderful miracle in the house of Śrīnivāsa Ṭhākura while *saṅkīrtana* was in full swing. He asked the devotees what they wanted to eat, and when He was informed that they wanted to eat mangoes, He asked for a seed of a mango, although this fruit was out of season. When the seed was brought to Him He sowed it in the yard of Śrīnivāsa, and at once a creeper began to grow out of the seed. Within no time this creeper became a full-grown mango tree heavy with more ripened fruits than the devotees could eat. The tree remained in Śrīnivāsa's yard, and from then on the devotees used to take as many mangoes from the tree as they wanted.

The Lord had a very high estimation of the affections of the damsels of Vrajabhūmi (Vṛndāvana) for Kṛṣṇa, and in appreciation of their unalloyed service to the Lord, once Śrī Caitanya Mahāprabhu chanted the holy names of the *gopīs* (cowherd girls) instead of the names of the Lord. At this time some of His students, who were also disciples, came to see Him, and when they saw that the Lord was chanting the names of the *gopīs,* they were astonished. Out of sheer foolishness they asked the Lord why He was chanting the names of the *gopīs* and advised Him to chant the name of Kṛṣṇa. The Lord, who was in ecstasy, was thus disturbed by these foolish students. He chastised them and chased them away. The students were almost the same age as the Lord, and thus they wrongly thought of the Lord as one of their peers. They held a meeting and resolved that they would attack the Lord if He dared to punish them again in such a manner. This incident provoked some malicious talks about the Lord on the part of the general public.

When the Lord became aware of this, He began to consider the various types of men found in society. He noted that especially the students, professors, fruitive workers, *yogīs,* nondevotees, and different types of atheists were all opposed to the devotional service of the Lord. "My mission is to deliver all the fallen souls of this age," He thought, "but if they commit offenses against Me, thinking Me to be an ordinary man, they will not benefit. If they are to begin their life of spiritual realization, they must some way or another offer obeisances unto Me." Thus the Lord decided to accept the renounced order of life (*sannyāsa*) because people in general were inclined to offer respects to a *sannyāsī.*

Five hundred years ago the condition of society was not as degraded as it is today. At that time people would show respects to a *sannyāsī,* and the *sannyāsī* was rigid in following the rules and regulations of the renounced order of life. Śrī Caitanya Mahāprabhu was not very much in favor of the renounced order of life in this Age of Kali, but that was only for the reason that very few *sannyāsīs* in this age are able to observe the rules and regulations of *sannyāsa* life. Śrī Caitanya Mahāprabhu decided to accept the order and become an ideal *sannyāsī* so that the general populace would show Him respect. One is duty-bound to show respect to a *sannyāsī,* for a *sannyāsī* is considered to be the master of all *varṇas* and *āśramas.*

While He was contemplating accepting the *sannyāsa* order, it so happened that Keśava Bhāratī, a *sannyāsī* of the Māyāvādī school and resident of Katwa (in Bengal), visited Navadvīpa and was invited to dine with the Lord. When Keśava Bhāratī came to His house, the Lord asked him to award Him the *sannyāsa* order of life. This was a matter of formality. The *sannyāsa* order is to be accepted from another *sannyāsī.* Although the Lord was independent in all respects, still, to keep up the formalities of the *śāstras,* He accepted the *sannyāsa* order from Keśava Bhāratī, although Keśava Bhāratī was not in the Vaiṣṇava-sampradāya (school).

After consulting with Keśava Bhāratī, the Lord left Navadvīpa for Katwa to formally accept the *sannyāsa* order of life. He was accompanied by Śrīla Nityānanda Prabhu, Candraśekhara Ācārya, and Mukunda Datta. Those three assisted Him in the details of the ceremony. The incident of the Lord's accepting the *sannyāsa* order is very elaborately described in the *Caitanya-bhāgavata* by Śrīla Vṛndāvana dāsa Ṭhākura.

Thus at the end of His twenty-fourth year the Lord accepted the *sannyāsa* order of life in the month of Māgha. After accepting this order He became a full-fledged preacher of the *Bhāgavata-dharma.* Although He was doing the same preaching work in His householder life, when He experienced some obstacles to His preaching He sacrificed even the comfort of His home life for the sake of the fallen souls. In His householder life His chief assistants were Śrīla Advaita Prabhu and Śrīla Śrīvāsa Ṭhākura, but after He accepted the *sannyāsa* order His chief assistants became Śrīla Nityānanda Prabhu, who was deputed to preach specifically in Bengal, and the Six Gosvāmīs (Rūpa Gosvāmī, Sanātana Gosvāmī, Jīva Gosvāmī, Gopāla Bhaṭṭa Gosvāmī, Raghunātha dāsa Gosvāmī and Raghunātha Bhaṭṭa Gosvāmī), headed by Śrīla Rūpa and Sanātana, who were deputed to go to Vṛndāvana to excavate the present places of pilgrimage. The present city of Vṛndāvana and the importance of Vrajabhūmi were thus disclosed by the will of Lord Śrī Caitanya Mahāprabhu.

The Lord, after accepting the *sannyāsa* order, at once wanted to start for Vṛndāvana. For three continuous days He traveled in the Rāḍha-deśa (places where the Ganges does not flow). He was in full ecstasy over the idea of going to Vṛndāvana. However, Śrīla Nityānanda diverted His path and brought Him instead to the house of Advaita Prabhu in Śāntipura. The Lord stayed at Śrī Advaita Prabhu's house for a few days, and knowing well that the Lord was leaving His hearth and home for good, Śrī Advaita Prabhu sent His men to Navadvīpa to bring mother Śacī to have a last meeting with her son. Some unscrupulous people say that Lord Caitanya met His wife also after taking *sannyāsa* and offered her His wooden slipper for worship, but the authentic sources give no information about such a meeting. His mother met Him at the house of Advaita Prabhu, and when she saw her son in *sannyāsa* dress, she lamented. By way of compromise, she requested her son to make His headquarters in Purī so that she would easily be able to get information about Him. The Lord granted this last desire of His beloved mother. After this incident the Lord started for Purī, leaving all the residents of Navadvīpa in an ocean of lamentation over His separation.

The Lord visited many important places on the way to Purī. He visited the temple of Gopīnāthajī, who had stolen condensed milk for His devotee Śrīla Mādhavendra Purī. Since then Deity Gopīnāthajī is well known as Kṣīra-corā-gopīnātha. The Lord relished this story with great pleasure. The propensity of stealing is there even in the absolute consciousness, but because this propensity is exhibited by the Absolute, it loses its perverted nature and thus becomes worshipable even by Lord Caitanya on the basis of the absolute consideration that the Lord and His stealing propensity are one and identical. This interesting story of Gopīnāthajī is vividly explained in the *Caitanya-caritāmṛta* by Kṛṣṇadāsa Kavirāja Gosvāmī.

After visiting the temple of Kṣīra-corā-gopīnātha of Remuṇā at Balasore in Orissa, the Lord proceeded towards Purī and on the way visited the temple of Sākṣi-gopāla, who appeared as a witness in the matter of two *brāhmaṇa* devotees' family quarrel. The Lord heard the story of Sākṣi-gopāla with great pleasure because He wanted to impress upon the atheists that the worshipable Deities in the temples approved by the great *ācāryas* are not idols, as alleged by men with a poor fund of knowledge. The Deity in the temple is the *arcā* incarnation of the Personality of Godhead, and thus the Deity is identical with the Lord in all respects. He responds to the proportion of the devotee's affection for Him. In the story of Sākṣi-gopāla, in which there was a family misunderstanding by two devotees of the Lord, the Lord, in order to mitigate the turmoil as well as to show specific favor to His servitors, traveled from Vṛndāvana to Vidyānagara, a village in Orissa, in the form of His *arcā* incarnation. From there the Deity was brought to Cuttack, and thus the temple of Sākṣi-gopāla is even today visited by thousands of pilgrims on the way to Jagannātha Purī. The Lord stayed overnight there and began to proceed toward Purī. On the way, His *sannyāsa* rod was broken by Nityānanda Prabhu. The Lord became apparently angry with Him about this and went alone to Purī, leaving His companions behind.

At Purī, when He entered the temple of Jagannātha, He became at once saturated with transcendental ecstasy and fell down on the floor of the temple unconscious. The custodians of the temple could not understand the transcendental feats of the Lord, but there was a great learned *paṇḍita* named Sārvabhauma Bhaṭṭācārya, who was present, and he could understand that the Lord's losing His consciousness upon entering the Jagannātha temple was not an ordinary thing. Sārvabhauma Bhaṭṭācārya, who was the chief appointed *paṇḍita* in the court of the King of Orissa, Mahārāja Pratāparudra, was attracted by the youthful luster of Lord Śrī Caitanya Mahāprabhu and could understand that such a transcendental trance was only rarely exhibited and only then by the topmost devotees who are already on the transcendental plane in complete forgetfulness of material existence. Only a liberated soul could show such a transcendental feat, and the Bhaṭṭācārya, who was vastly learned, could understand this in the light of the transcendental literature with which he was familiar. He therefore asked the custodians of the temple not to disturb the unknown *sannyāsī*. He asked them to take the Lord to his home so He could be further observed in His unconscious state. The Lord was at once carried to the home of Sārvabhauma Bhaṭṭācārya, who at that time had sufficient power of authority due to his being the *sabhā-paṇḍita,* or the state dean of faculty in Sanskrit literatures. The learned *paṇḍita* wanted to scrutinizingly test the transcendental feats of Lord Caitanya because often unscrupulous devotees imitate physical feats in order to flaunt transcendental achievements just to attract innocent people and take advantage of them. A learned scholar like the Bhaṭṭācārya can detect such imposters, and when he finds them out he at once rejects them.

In the case of Lord Caitanya Mahāprabhu, the Bhaṭṭācārya tested all the symptoms in the light of the *śāstras*. He tested as a scientist, not as a foolish sentimentalist. He observed the movement of the stomach, the beating of the heart and the breathing of the nostrils. He also felt the pulse of the Lord and saw that all His bodily activities were in complete suspension. When he put a small cotton swab before the nostrils, he found that there was a slight breathing as the fine fibers of cotton moved slightly. Thus he came to know that the Lord's unconscious trance was genuine, and he began to treat Him in the prescribed fashion. But Lord Caitanya Mahāprabhu could only be treated in a special way. He would respond only to the resounding of the holy names of the Lord by His devotees. This special treatment was unknown to Sārvabhauma Bhaṭṭācārya because the Lord was still unknown to him. When the Bhaṭṭācārya saw Him for the first time in the temple, he simply took Him to be one of many pilgrims.

In the meantime the companions of the Lord, who reached the temple a little after Him, heard of the Lord's transcendental feats and of His being carried away by the Bhaṭṭācārya. The pilgrims at the temple were still gossiping about the incident. But by chance, one of these pilgrims had met Gopīnātha Ācārya, who was known to Gadādhara Paṇḍita, and from him it was learned that the Lord was lying in an unconscious state at the residence of Sārvabhauma Bhaṭṭācārya, who happened to be the brother-in-law of Gopīnātha Ācārya. All the members of the party were introduced by Gadādhara Paṇḍita to Gopīnātha Ācārya, who took them all to the house of the Bhaṭṭācārya where the Lord was lying unconscious in a spiritual trance. All the members then chanted loudly the holy name of the Lord Hari as usual, and the Lord regained His consciousness. After this, the Bhaṭṭācārya received all the members of the party, including Lord Nityānanda Prabhu, and asked them to become his guests of honor. The party, including the Lord, went for a bath in the sea, and the Bhaṭṭācārya arranged for their residence and meals at the house of Kāśī Miśra. Gopīnātha Ācārya, his brother-in-law, also assisted. There were some friendly talks about the Lord's divinity between the two brothers-in-law, and in this argument Gopīnātha Ācārya, who knew the Lord before, now tried to establish the Lord as the Personality of Godhead, and the Bhaṭṭācārya tried to establish Him as one of the great devotees. Both of them argued from the angle of vision of authentic *śāstras* and not on the strength of sentimental *vox populi*. The incarnations of God are determined by authentic *śāstras* and not by popular votes of foolish fanatics. Because Lord Caitanya was an incarnation of God in fact, foolish fanatics have proclaimed so many so-called incarnations of God in this age without referring to authentic scriptures. But Sārvabhauma Bhaṭṭācārya or Gopīnātha Ācārya did not indulge in such foolish sentimentalism; on the contrary, both of them tried to establish or reject His divinity on the strength of authentic *śāstras*.

Later it was disclosed that the Bhaṭṭācārya also came from the Navadvīpa area, and it was understood from him that Nīlāmbara Cakravartī, the maternal grandfather of Lord Caitanya, happened to be a class fellow of the father of Sārvabhauma Bhaṭṭācārya. In that sense, the young *sannyāsī* Lord Caitanya evoked paternal affection from the Bhaṭṭācārya. The Bhaṭṭācārya was the professor of many *sannyāsīs* in the order of the Śaṅkarācārya-sampradāya, and he himself also belonged to that cult. As such, the Bhaṭṭācārya desired that the young *sannyāsī* Lord Caitanya also hear from him about the teachings of Vedānta.

Those who are followers of the Śaṅkara cult are generally known as Vedāntists. This does not, however, mean that Vedānta is a monopoly study of the Śaṅkara-sampradāya. Vedānta is studied by all the bona fide *sampradāyas*, but they have their own interpretations. But generally only those in the Śaṅkara-sampradāya are known as Vedāntists, and people have no knowledge of the Vaiṣṇava Vedāntists. For this reason the Bhaktivedanta title was first offered to the author by the Vaiṣṇavas.

The Lord agreed to take lessons from the Bhaṭṭācārya on the Vedānta, and they sat together in the temple of Lord Jagannātha. The Bhaṭṭācārya went on speaking continually for seven days, and the Lord heard him with all attention and did not interrupt. The Lord's silence raised some doubts in the Bhaṭṭācārya's heart, and he asked the Lord how it was that He did not ask anything or comment on his explanations of Vedānta.

The Lord posed Himself before the Bhaṭṭācārya as a foolish student and pretended that He heard the Vedānta from him because the Bhaṭṭācārya felt that this was the duty of a *sannyāsī*. But the Lord did not agree with his lectures. By this the Lord indicated that the so-called Vedāntists amongst the Śaṅkara-sampradāya, or any other *sampradāya* who do not follow the instructions of Śrīla Vyāsadeva, are mechanical students of the Vedānta. They are not fully aware of that great knowledge. The explanation of the *Vedānta-sūtra* is given by the author himself in the text of *Śrīmad-Bhāgavatam*. One who has no knowledge of the *Bhāgavatam* will hardly be able to know what the Vedānta says.

The Bhaṭṭācārya, being a vastly learned man, could follow the Lord's sarcastic remarks on the popular Vedāntist. He therefore asked Him why He did not ask about any point which He could not follow. The Bhaṭṭācārya could understand the purpose of His dead silence for the days He heard him. This showed clearly that the Lord had something else in mind; thus the Bhaṭṭācārya requested Him to disclose His mind.

Upon this, the Lord spoke as follows: "My dear sir, I can understand the meaning of the *sūtras* like *janmādy asya yataḥ, śāstra-yonitvāt,* and *athāto brahma jijñāsā* of the *Vedānta-sūtra,* but when you explain them in your own way it becomes difficult for Me to follow them. The purpose of the *sūtras* is already explained in them, but your explanations are covering them with something else. You do not purposely take the direct meaning of the *sūtras* but indirectly give your own interpretations."

The Lord thus attacked all Vedāntists who interpret the *Vedānta-sūtra* fashionably, according to their limited power of thinking, to serve their own purpose. Such indirect interpretations of the authentic literatures like the *Vedānta-sūtra* are hereby condemned by the Lord.

The Lord continued: "Śrīla Vyāsadeva has summarized the direct meanings of the *mantras* in the *Upaniṣads* in the *Vedānta-sūtra.* Unfortunately you do not take their direct meaning. You indirectly interpret them in a different way.

"The authority of the *Vedas* is unchallengeable and stands without any question of doubt. And whatever is stated in the *Vedas* must be accepted completely, otherwise one challenges the authority of the *Vedas.*

"The conchshell and cow dung are bone and stool of two living beings. But because they have been recommended by the *Vedas* as pure, people accept them as such because of the authority of the *Vedas.*"

The idea is that one cannot set his imperfect reason above the authority of the *Vedas.* The orders of the *Vedas* must be obeyed as they stand, without any mundane reasoning. The so-called followers of the Vedic injunctions make their own interpretations of the Vedic injunctions, and thus they establish different parties and sects of the Vedic religion. Lord Buddha directly denied the authority of the *Vedas,* and he established his own religion. Only for this reason, the Buddhist religion was not accepted by the strict followers of the *Vedas.* But those who are so-called followers of the *Vedas* are more harmful than the Buddhists. The Buddhists have the courage to deny the *Vedas* directly, but the so-called followers of the *Vedas* have no courage to deny the *Vedas,* although indirectly they disobey all the injunctions of the *Vedas*. Lord Caitanya condemned this.

The examples given by the Lord of the conchshell and the cow dung are very much appropriate in this connection. If one argues that since cow dung is pure, the stool of a learned *brāhmaṇa* is still more pure, his argument will not be accepted. Cow dung is accepted, and the stool of a highly posted *brāhmaṇa* is rejected. The Lord continued:

"The Vedic injunctions are self-authorized, and if some mundane creature adjusts the interpretations of the *Vedas,* he defies their authority. It is foolish to think of oneself as more intelligent than Śrīla Vyāsadeva. He has already expressed himself in his *sūtras,* and there is no need of help from personalities of lesser importance. His work, the *Vedānta-sūtra,* is as dazzling as the midday sun, and when someone tries to give his own interpretations on the self-effulgent sunlike *Vedānta-sūtra,* he attempts to cover this sun with the cloud of his imagination.

"The *Vedas* and *Purāṇas* are one and the same in purpose. They ascertain the Absolute Truth, which is greater than everything else. The Absolute Truth is ultimately realized as the Absolute Personality of Godhead with absolute controlling power. As such, the Absolute Personality of Godhead must be completely full of opulence, strength, fame, beauty, knowledge and renunciation. Yet the transcendental Personality of Godhead is astonishingly ascertained as impersonal.

"The impersonal description of the Absolute Truth in the *Vedas* is given to nullify the mundane conception of the absolute whole. Personal features of the Lord are completely different from all kinds of mundane features. The living entities are all individual persons, and they are all parts and parcels of the supreme whole. If the parts and parcels are individual persons, the source of their emanation must not be impersonal. He is the Supreme Person amongst all the relative persons.

"The *Vedas* inform us that from Him [Brahman] everything emanates, and on Him everything rests. And after annihilation, everything merges in Him only. Therefore, He is the ultimate dative, causative and accommodating cause of all causes. And these causes cannot be attributed to an impersonal object.

"The *Vedas* inform us that He alone became many, and when He so desires He glances over material nature. Before He glanced over material nature there was no material cosmic creation. Therefore, His glance is not material. Material mind or senses were unborn when the Lord glanced over material nature. Thus evidence in the *Vedas* proves that beyond a doubt the Lord has transcendental eyes and a transcendental mind. They are not material. His impersonality therefore is a negation of His materiality, but not a denial of His transcendental personality.

"Brahman ultimately refers to the Personality of Godhead. Impersonal Brahman realization is just the negative conception of the mundane creations. Paramātmā is the localized aspect of Brahman within all kinds of material bodies. Ultimately the Supreme Brahman realization is the realization of the Personality of Godhead. Lord Śrī Kṛṣṇa is that Supreme Personality of Godhead according to all evidence of the revealed scriptures. He is the ultimate source of *viṣṇu-tattvas.*

"The *Purāṇas* are also supplementary to the *Vedas*. The Vedic *mantras* are too difficult for an ordinary man. Women, *śūdras* and the so-called twice-born higher castes are unable to penetrate into the sense of the *Vedas*. And thus the *Mahābhārata* as well as the *Purāṇas* are made easy to explain the truths of the *Vedas*. In his prayers before the boy Śrī Kṛṣṇa, Brahmā said that there is no limit to the fortune of the residents of Vrajabhūmi headed by Śrī Nanda Mahārāja and Yaśodāmayī because the eternal Absolute Truth has become their intimate relative.

"The Vedic *mantra* maintains that the Absolute Truth has no legs and no hands and yet goes faster than all and accepts everything that is offered to Him in devotion. The latter statements definitely suggest the personal features of the Lord, although His hands and legs are distinguished from mundane hands and legs or other senses.

"Brahman, therefore, is never impersonal, but when such *mantras* are indirectly interpreted, it is wrongly thought that the Absolute Truth is impersonal. The Absolute Truth Personality of Godhead is full of all opulences, and therefore He has a transcendental form of full existence, knowledge and bliss. How then can one establish that the Absolute Truth is impersonal?

"Brahman, being full of opulences, is understood to have manifold energies, and all these energies are classified under three headings under the authority of *Viṣṇu Purāṇa* [6.7.61], which says that the transcendental energies of Lord Viṣṇu are primarily three. His spiritual energy and the energy of the living entities are classified as superior energy, whereas the material energy is an inferior one, which is sprouted out of ignorance.

"The energy of the living entities is technically called *kṣetra-jña* energy.

This *kṣetrajña-śakti,* although equal in quality with the Lord, becomes overpowered by material energy out of ignorance and thus suffers all sorts of material miseries. In other words, the living entities are located in the marginal energy between the superior (spiritual) and inferior (material) energies, and in proportion to the living being's contact with either the material or spiritual energies, the living entity is situated in proportionately higher and lower levels of existence.

"The Lord is beyond the inferior and marginal energies as above mentioned, and His spiritual energy is manifested in three different phases: as eternal existence, eternal bliss and eternal knowledge. As far as eternal existence is concerned, it is conducted by the *sandhinī* potency; similarly, bliss and knowledge are conducted by the *hlādinī* and *saṁvit* potencies respectively. As the supreme energetic Lord, He is the supreme controller of the spiritual, marginal and material energies. And all these different types of energies are connected with the Lord in eternal devotional service.

"The Supreme Personality of Godhead is thus enjoying in His transcendental eternal form. Is it not astounding that one dares to call the Supreme Lord nonenergetic? The Lord is the controller of all energies, and the living entities are parts and parcels of one of the energies. Therefore there is a gulf of difference between the Lord and the living entities. How then can one say that the Lord and the living entities are one and the same? In the *Bhagavad-gītā* also the living entities are described as belonging to the superior energy of the Lord. According to the principles of intimate correlation between the energy and the energetic, both of them are nondifferent also. Therefore, the Lord and the living entities are nondifferent as the energy and the energetic.

"Earth, water, fire, air, ether, mind, intelligence and ego are all inferior energies of the Lord, but the living entities are different from all as superior energy. This is the version of *Bhagavad-gītā* [7.4–5].

"The transcendental form of the Lord is eternally existent and full of transcendental bliss. How then can such a form be a product of the material mode of goodness? Anyone, therefore, who does not believe in the form of the Lord is certainly a faithless demon and as such is untouchable, a not-to-be-seen *persona non grata* fit to be punished by the Plutonic king.

"The Buddhists are called atheists because they have no respect for the *Vedas,* but those who defy the Vedic conclusions, as above mentioned, under the pretense of being followers of the *Vedas,* are verily more dangerous than the Buddhists.

"Śrī Vyāsadeva very kindly compiled the Vedic knowledge in his *Vedānta-sūtra,* but if one hears the commentation of the Māyāvāda school (as represented by the Śaṅkara-sampradāya) certainly he will be misled on the path of spiritual realization.

"The theory of emanations is the beginning subject of the *Vedānta-sūtra.* All the cosmic manifestations are emanations from the Absolute Personality of Godhead by His inconceivable different energies. The example of the touchstone is applicable to the theory of emanation. The touchstone can convert an unlimited quantity of iron into gold, and still the touchstone remains as it is. Similarly, the Supreme Lord can produce all manifested worlds by His inconceivable energies, and yet He is full and unchanged. He is *pūrṇa* [complete], and although an unlimited number of *pūrṇas* emanate from Him, He is still *pūrṇa.*

"The theory of illusion of the Māyāvāda school is advocated on the ground that the theory of emanation will cause a transformation of the Absolute Truth. If that is the case, Vyāsadeva is wrong. To avoid this, they have skillfully brought in the theory of illusion. But the world or the cosmic creation is not false, as maintained by the Māyāvāda school. It simply has no permanent existence. A nonpermanent thing cannot be called false altogether. But the conception that the material body is the self is certainly wrong.

"*Praṇava* [*oṁ*], or the *oṁkāra* in the *Vedas,* is the primeval hymn. This transcendental sound is identical with the form of the Lord. All the Vedic hymns are based on this *praṇava oṁkāra. Tat tvam asi* is but a side word in the Vedic literatures, and therefore this word cannot be the primeval hymn of the *Vedas.* Śrīpāda Śaṅkarācārya has given more stress on the side word *tat tvam asi* than on the primeval principle *oṁkāra.*"

The Lord thus spoke on the *Vedānta-sūtra* and defied all the propaganda of the Māyāvāda school.* The Bhaṭṭācārya tried to defend himself and his Māyāvāda school by jugglery of logic and grammar, but the Lord defeated him by His forceful arguments. He affirmed that we are all related with the Personality of Godhead eternally and that devotional service is our eternal function in exchanging the dealings of our relations.

---

*In our *Teachings of Lord Caitanya* we have more elaborately explained all these philosophical intricacies. *Śrīmad-Bhāgavatam* clarifies them all.

The result of such exchanges is to attain *prema,* or love of Godhead. When love of Godhead is attained, love for all other beings automatically follows because the Lord is the sum total of all living beings.

The Lord said that but for these three items—namely, eternal relation with God, exchange of dealings with Him and the attainment of love for Him—all that is instructed in the *Vedas* is superfluous, and that any other explanation of the *Vedas* is concocted.

The Lord further added that the Māyāvāda philosophy taught by Śrīpāda Śaṅkarācārya is an imaginary explanation of the *Vedas,* but it had to be taught by him (Śaṅkarācārya) because he was ordered to teach it by the Personality of Godhead. In the *Padma Purāṇa* it is stated that the Personality of Godhead ordered His Lordship Śiva to deviate the human race from Him (the Personality of Godhead). The Personality of Godhead was to be so covered so that people would be encouraged to generate more and more population. His Lordship Śiva said to Devī: "In the Kali-yuga, I shall preach the Māyāvāda philosophy, which is nothing but clouded Buddhism, in the garb of a *brāhmaṇa.*"

After hearing all these speeches of the Lord Śrī Caitanya Mahāprabhu, the Bhaṭṭācārya was struck with wonder and awe and regarded Him in dead silence. The Lord then encouraged him with assurance that there was no cause to wonder. "I say that *devotional service unto the Personality of Godhead is the highest goal of human life.*" He then quoted the "*ātmārāma*" *śloka* from the *Bhāgavatam* (1.7.10), thus assuring him that even the liberated souls who are absorbed in the spirit and spiritual realization also take to the devotional service of the Lord Hari because the Personality of Godhead has such transcendental qualities that He attracts the heart of the liberated soul too.

Then the Bhaṭṭācārya desired to listen to the explanation of this *śloka.* The Lord first of all asked the Bhaṭṭācārya to explain it, and after that He would explain it. The Bhaṭṭācārya then explained the *śloka* in a scholarly way with special reference to logic. He explained the *śloka* in nine different ways chiefly based on logic because he was the most renowned scholar of logic of the time.

The Lord, after hearing the Bhaṭṭācārya, thanked him for the scholarly presentation of the *śloka,* and then, at the request of the Bhaṭṭācārya, the Lord explained the *śloka* in sixty-four different ways without touching the nine explanations given by the Bhaṭṭācārya.

Thus after hearing the explanation of the *ātmārāma śloka* from the Lord, the Bhaṭṭācārya was convinced that such a scholarly presentation is impossible for an earthly creature.* Before this, Śrī Gopīnātha Ācārya had tried to convince him of the divinity of the Lord, but at the time he could not so accept Him. But the Bhaṭṭācārya was astounded by the Lord's exposition of the *Vedānta-sūtra* and explanations of the *ātmārāma śloka,* and thus he began to think that he had committed a great offense at the lotus feet of the Lord by not recognizing Him to be Kṛṣṇa Himself. He then surrendered unto Him, repenting for his past dealings with Him, and the Lord was kind enough to accept the Bhaṭṭācārya. Out of His causeless mercy, the Lord manifested before him first as four-handed Nārāyaṇa and then again as two-handed Lord Kṛṣṇa with a flute in His hand.

The Bhaṭṭācārya at once fell down at the lotus feet of the Lord and composed many suitable *ślokas* in praise of the Lord by His grace. He composed one hundred *ślokas* in praise of the Lord. The Lord then embraced him, and out of transcendental ecstasy the Bhaṭṭācārya lost consciousness of the physical state of life. Tears, trembling, throbbing of the heart, perspiration, emotional waves, dancing, singing, crying and all the eight symptoms of trance were manifested in the body of the Bhaṭṭācārya. Śrī Gopīnātha Ācārya became very glad and astonished by this marvelous conversion of his brother-in-law by the grace of the Lord.

Out of the hundred celebrated *ślokas* composed by the Bhaṭṭācārya in praise of the Lord, the following two are most important, and these two *ślokas* explain the mission of the Lord in gist.

1. Let me surrender unto the Personality of Godhead who has appeared now as Lord Śrī Caitanya Mahāprabhu. He is the ocean of all mercy and has now come down to teach us material detachment, learning and devotional service to Himself.

2. Since pure devotional service of the Lord has been lost in the oblivion of time, the Lord has appeared to renovate the principles, and therefore I offer my obeisances unto His lotus feet.

The Lord explained the word *mukti* to be equivalent to the word Viṣṇu, or the Personality of Godhead. To attain *mukti,* or liberation from the bondage of material existence, is to attain to the service of the Lord.

---

*The complete text of the explanation given by the Lord will form a booklet itself, and therefore we have presented it as a chapter in our *Teachings of Lord Caitanya.*

The Lord then proceeded towards South India for some time and converted all He met on the way to become devotees of Lord Śrī Kṛṣṇa. Such devotees also converted many others to the cult of devotional service, or to the *Bhāgavata-dharma* of the Lord, and thus He reached the bank of the Godāvarī, where He met Śrīla Rāmānanda Rāya, the governor of Madras on behalf of Mahārāja Pratāparudra, the King of Orissa. His talks with Rāmānanda Rāya are very important for higher realization of transcendental knowledge, and the conversation itself forms a small booklet. We shall, however, give herewith a summary of the conversation.

Śrī Rāmānanda Rāya was a self-realized soul, although outwardly he belonged to a caste lower than the *brāhmaṇa* in social status. He was not in the renounced order of life, and besides that he was a high government servant in the state. Still, Śrī Caitanya Mahāprabhu accepted him as a liberated soul on the strength of the high order of his realization of transcendental knowledge. Similarly, the Lord accepted Śrīla Haridāsa Ṭhākura, a veteran devotee of the Lord coming from a Mohammedan family. And there are many other great devotees of the Lord who came from different communities, sects and castes. The Lord's only criterion was the standard of devotional service of the particular person. He was not concerned with the outward dress of a man; He was concerned only with the inner soul and its activities. Therefore all the missionary activities of the Lord are to be understood to be on the spiritual plane, and as such the cult of Śrī Caitanya Mahāprabhu, or the cult of *Bhāgavata-dharma,* has nothing to do with mundane affairs, sociology, politics, economic development or any such sphere of life. *Śrīmad-Bhāgavatam* is the purely transcendental urge of the soul.

When He met Śrī Rāmānanda Rāya on the bank of the Godāvarī, the *varṇāśrama-dharma* followed by the Hindus was mentioned by the Lord. Śrīla Rāmānanda Rāya said that by following the principles of *varṇāśrama-dharma,* the system of four castes and four orders of human life, everyone could realize Transcendence. In the opinion of the Lord, the system of *varṇāśrama-dharma* is superficial only, and it has very little to do with the highest realization of spiritual values. The highest perfection of life is to get detached from the material attachment and proportionately realize the transcendental loving service of the Lord. The Personality of Godhead recognizes a living being who is progressing in that line. Devotional service, therefore, is the culmination of the culture of all knowledge. When Śrī Kṛṣṇa, the Supreme Personality of Godhead, appeared for the deliverance of all fallen souls, He advised the deliverance of all living entities as follows. The Supreme Absolute Personality of Godhead, from whom all living entities have emanated, must be worshiped by all their respective engagements, because everything that we see is also the expansion of His energy. That is the way of real perfection, and it is approved by all bona fide *ācāryas* past and present. The system of *varṇāśrama* is more or less based on moral and ethical principles. There is very little realization of the Transcendence as such, and Lord Śrī Caitanya Mahāprabhu rejected it as superficial and asked Rāmānanda Rāya to go further into the matter.

Śrī Rāmānanda Rāya then suggested renunciation of fruitive actions unto the Lord. The *Bhagavad-gītā* (9.27) advises in this connection: "Whatever you do, whatever you eat and whatever you give, as well as whatever you perform in penance, offer to Me alone." This dedication on the part of the worker suggests that the Personality of Godhead is a step higher than the impersonal conception of the *varṇāśrama* system, but still the relation of the living being and the Lord is not distinct in that way. The Lord therefore rejected this proposition and asked Rāmānanda Rāya to go further.

Rāya then suggested renunciation of the *varṇāśrama-dharma* and acceptance of devotional service. The Lord did not approve of this suggestion also for the reason that all of a sudden one should not renounce his position, for that may not bring in the desired result.

It was further suggested by Rāya that attainment of spiritual realization freed from the material conception of life is the topmost achievement for a living being. The Lord rejected this suggestion also because on the plea of such spiritual realization much havoc has been wrought by unscrupulous persons; therefore all of a sudden this is not possible. The Rāya then suggested sincere association of self-realized souls and, from any worldly position, hearing submissively the transcendental message of the pastimes of the Personality of Godhead. This suggestion was welcomed by the Lord. This suggestion was made following in the footsteps of Brahmājī, who said that the Personality of Godhead is known as *ajita*, or the one who cannot be conquered or approached by anyone. But such *ajita* also becomes *jita* (conquered) by one method, which is very simple and easy. The simple method is that one has to give up the arrogant attitude of declaring oneself to be God Himself. One must be very meek and submissive and try to live peacefully by lending the ear to the speeches of the transcendentally self-realized soul who speaks on the message of *Bhāgavata-dharma,* or the religion of glorifying the Supreme Lord and His devotees. To glorify a great man is a natural instinct for living beings, but they have not learned to glorify the Lord. Perfection of life is attained simply by glorifying the Lord in association with a self-realized devotee of the Lord.* The self-realized devotee is he who surrenders unto the Lord fully and who does not have attachment for material prosperity. Material prosperity and sense enjoyment and their advancement are all activities of ignorance in human society. Peace and friendship are impossible for a society detached from the association of God and His devotees. It is imperative, therefore, that one sincerely seek the association of pure devotees and hear them patiently and submissively from any position of life. The position of a person in the higher or lower status of life does not hamper one in the path of self-realization. The only thing one has to do is to hear from a self-realized soul with a routine program. The teacher may also deliver lectures from the Vedic literatures, following in the footsteps of the bygone *ācāryas* who realized the Absolute Truth. Lord Śrī Caitanya Mahāprabhu recommended this simple method of self-realization generally known as *Bhāgavata-dharma. Śrīmad-Bhāgavatam* is the perfect guide for this purpose.

Above these topics discussed by the Lord and Śrī Rāmānanda Rāya, there were still more elevated spiritual talks between the two great personalities, and we purposely withhold those topics for the present because one has to come to the spiritual plane before further talks with Rāmānanda Rāya can be heard. We have presented further talks of Śrīla Rāmānanda Rāya with the Lord in another book (*Teachings of Lord Caitanya*).

At the conclusion of this meeting, Śrī Rāmānanda Rāya was advised by the Lord to retire from service and come to Purī so that they could live together and relish transcendental talks. Some time later, Śrī Rāmānanda Rāya retired from the government service and took a pension from the King. He returned to his residence in Purī, where he was one of the most confidential devotees of the Lord. There was another gentleman at Purī of the name Śikhi Māhiti, who was also a confidant like Rāmānanda Rāya.

*The International Society for Krishna Consciousness has been formed for this purpose.

The Lord used to hold confidential talks on spiritual values with three or four companions at Purī, and He passed eighteen years in that way in spiritual trance. His talks were recorded by His private secretary Śrī Dāmodara Gosvāmī, one of the four most intimate devotees.

The Lord extensively traveled all over the southern part of India. The great saint of Mahārāṣṭra known as Saint Tukārāma was also initiated by the Lord. Saint Tukārāma, after initiation by the Lord, overflooded the whole of the Mahārāṣṭra Province with the *saṅkīrtana* movement, and the transcendental flow is still rolling on in the southwestern part of the great Indian peninsula.

The Lord excavated from South India two very important old literatures, namely the *Brahmā-saṁhitā** and *Kṛṣṇa-karṇāmṛta,* and these two valuable books are authorized studies for the person in the devotional line. The Lord then returned to Purī after His South Indian tour.

On His return to Purī, all the anxious devotees of the Lord got back their life, and the Lord remained there with continued pastimes of His transcendental realizations. The most important incident during that time was His granting audience to King Pratāparudra. King Pratāparudra was a great devotee of the Lord, and he considered himself to be one of the servants of the Lord entrusted with sweeping the temple. This submissive attitude of the King was very much appreciated by Śrī Caitanya Mahāprabhu. The King requested both the Bhaṭṭācārya and Rāya to arrange his meeting with the Lord. When, however, the Lord was petitioned by His two stalwart devotees, He flatly refused to grant the request, even though it was put forward by personal associates like Rāmānanda Rāya and Sārvabhauma Bhaṭṭācārya. The Lord maintained that it is dangerous for a *sannyāsī* to be in intimate touch with worldly money-conscious men and with women. The Lord was an ideal *sannyāsī.* No woman could approach the Lord even to offer respects. Women's seats were accommodated far away from the Lord. As an ideal teacher and *ācārya,* He was very strict in the routine work of a *sannyāsī.* Apart from being a divine incarnation, the Lord was an ideal character as a human being. His behavior with other persons was also above suspicion. In His dealing as *ācārya,* He was harder than the thunderbolt and softer than the rose. One of His associates, Junior Haridāsa, committed a great mistake by lustfully glancing at a young woman. The Lord as Supersoul could detect

*Summary of *Śrīmad-Bhāgavatam.*

this lust in the mind of Junior Haridāsa, who was at once banished from the Lord's association and was never accepted again, even though the Lord was implored to excuse Haridāsa for the mistake. Junior Haridāsa afterwards committed suicide due to being disassociated from the company of the Lord, and the news of his suicide was duly related to the Lord. Even at that time the Lord was not forgetful of the offense, and He said that Haridāsa had rightly met with the proper punishment.

On the principles of the renounced order of life and discipline, the Lord knew no compromise, and therefore even though He knew that the King was a great devotee, He refused to see the King, only because the King was a dollar-and-cents man. By this example the Lord wanted to emphasize the proper behavior for a transcendentalist. A transcendentalist has nothing to do with women and money. He must always refrain from such intimate relations. The King was, however, favored by the Lord by the expert arrangement of the devotees. This means that the beloved devotee of the Lord can favor a neophyte more liberally than the Lord. Pure devotees, therefore, never commit an offense at the feet of another pure devotee. An offense at the lotus feet of the Lord is sometimes excused by the merciful Lord, but an offense at the feet of a devotee is very dangerous for one who actually wants to make progress in devotional service.

As long as the Lord remained at Purī, thousands of His devotees used to come to see Him during the Ratha-yātrā car festival of Lord Jagannātha. And during the car festival, the washing of the Guṇḍicā temple under the direct supervision of the Lord was an important function. The Lord's congregational *saṅkīrtana* movement at Purī was a unique exhibition for the mass of people. That is the way to turn the mass mind towards spiritual realization. The Lord inaugurated this system of mass *saṅkīrtana*, and leaders of all countries can take advantage of this spiritual movement in order to keep the mass of people in a pure state of peace and friendship with one another. This is now the demand of the present human society all over the world.

After some time the Lord again started on His tour towards northern India, and He decided to visit Vṛndāvana and its neighboring places. He passed through the jungles of Jhārikhaṇḍa (Madhya Bhārata), and all the wild animals also joined His *saṅkīrtana* movement. The wild tigers, elephants, bears and deer all together accompanied the Lord, and the

Lord accompanied them in *saṅkīrtana*. By this He proved that by the propagation of the *saṅkīrtana* movement (congregational chanting and glorifying of the name of the Lord) even the wild animals can live in peace and friendship, and what to speak of men who are supposed to be civilized. No man in the world will refuse to join the *saṅkīrtana* movement. Nor is the Lord's *saṅkīrtana* movement restricted to any caste, creed, color or species. Here is direct evidence of His great mission: He allowed even the wild animals to partake in His great movement.

On His way back from Vṛndāvana He first came to Prayāga, where He met Rūpa Gosvāmī along with his younger brother, Anupama. Then He came down to Vārāṇasī (Benares), where he became the guest of Śrī Tapana Miśra and Candraśekhara, assisted by a Mahārāṣṭra *brāhmaṇa*. At that time Vārāṇasī was headed by a great *sannyāsī* of the Māyāvāda school named Śrīpāda Prakāśānanda Sarasvatī. When the Lord was at Vārāṇasī, the people in general became more attracted to Lord Caitanya Mahāprabhu on account of His mass *saṅkīrtana* movement. Wherever He visited, especially the Viśvanātha temple, thousands of pilgrims would follow Him. Some were attracted by His bodily features, and others were attracted by His melodious songs glorifying the Lord.

The Māyāvādī *sannyāsīs* designate themselves as Nārāyaṇa. Vārāṇasī is still overflooded with many Māyāvādī *sannyāsīs*. Some people who saw the Lord in His *saṅkīrtana* party considered Him to be actually Nārāyaṇa, and this report reached the camp of the great *sannyāsī* Prakāśānanda.

In India there is always a kind of spiritual rivalry between the Māyāvāda and *Bhāgavata* schools, and thus when the news of the Lord reached Prakāśānanda he knew that the Lord was a Vaiṣṇava *sannyāsī*, and therefore he minimized the value of the Lord before those who brought him the news. He deprecated the activities of the Lord because of His preaching the *saṅkīrtana* movement, which was in his opinion nothing but religious sentiment. Prakāśānanda was a profound student of the Vedānta, and he advised his followers to give attention to the Vedānta and not to indulge in *saṅkīrtana*.

One devotee *brāhmaṇa*, who became a devotee of the Lord, did not like the criticism of Prakāśānanda, and he went to the Lord to express his regrets. He told the Lord that when he uttered the Lord's name before the *sannyāsī* Prakāśānanda, the latter strongly criticized the Lord, although the *brāhmaṇa* heard Prakāśānanda uttering several times the name Caitanya. The *brāhmaṇa* was astonished to see that the *sannyāsī* Prakāśānanda could not vibrate the sound Kṛṣṇa even once, although he uttered the name Caitanya several times.

The Lord smilingly explained to the devotee *brāhmaṇa* why the Māyāvādī cannot utter the holy name of Kṛṣṇa. "The Māyāvādīs are offenders at the lotus feet of Kṛṣṇa, although they utter always *brahma, ātmā,* or *caitanya,* etc. And because they are offenders at the lotus feet of Kṛṣṇa, they are actually unable to utter the holy name of Kṛṣṇa. The name Kṛṣṇa and the Personality of Godhead Kṛṣṇa are identical. There is no difference in the absolute realm between the name, form or person of the Absolute Truth because in the absolute realm everything is transcendental bliss. There is no difference between the body and the soul for the Personality of Godhead, Kṛṣṇa. Thus He is different from the living entity who is always different from his outward body. Because of Kṛṣṇa's transcendental position, it is very difficult for a layman to actually know the Personality of Godhead, Kṛṣṇa, His holy name and fame, etc. His name, fame, form and pastimes are all one and the same transcendental identity, and they are not knowable by the exercise of the material senses.

"The transcendental relationship of the pastimes of the Lord is the source of still more bliss than one can experience by realization of Brahman or by becoming one with the Supreme. Had it not been so, then those who are already situated in the transcendental bliss of Brahman would not have been attracted by the transcendental bliss of the pastimes of the Lord."

After this, a great meeting was arranged by the devotees of the Lord in which all the *sannyāsīs* were invited, including the Lord and Prakāśānanda Sarasvatī. In this meeting both the scholars (the Lord and Prakāśānanda) had a long discourse on the spiritual values of the *saṅkīrtana* movement, and a summary is given below.

The great Māyāvādī *sannyāsī* Prakāśānanda inquired from the Lord as to the reason for His preferring the *saṅkīrtana* movement to the study of the *Vedānta-sūtra*. Prakāśānanda said that it is the duty of a *sannyāsī* to read the *Vedānta-sūtra*. What caused the Lord to indulge in *saṅkīrtana*?

After this inquiry, the Lord submissively replied: "I have taken to the *saṅkīrtana* movement instead of the study of Vedānta because I am a great fool." The Lord thus represented Himself as one of the numberless fools of this age who are absolutely incapable of studying the Vedānta philosophy. The fools' indulgence in the study of Vedānta has caused so much havoc in society. The Lord thus continued: "And because I am a great fool, My spiritual master forbade Me to play with Vedānta philosophy. He said that it is better that I chant the holy name of the Lord, for that would deliver Me from material bondage.

"In this Age of Kali there is no other religion but the glorification of the Lord by utterance of His holy name, and that is the injunction of all the revealed scriptures. And My spiritual master has taught Me one *śloka* [from the *Bṛhan-nāradīya Purāṇa*]:

harer nāma harer nāma harer nāmaiva kevalam
kalau nāsty eva nāsty eva nāsty eva gatir anyathā

"So on the order of My spiritual master, I chant the holy name of Hari, and I am now mad after this holy name. Whenever I utter the holy name I forget Myself completely, and sometimes I laugh, cry and dance like a madman. I thought that I had actually gone mad by this process of chanting, and therefore I asked My spiritual master about it. He informed Me that this was the real effect of chanting the holy name, which produces a transcendental emotion that is a rvare manifestation. It is the sign of love of God, which is the ultimate end of life. Love of God is transcendental to liberation [*mukti*], and thus it is called the fifth stage of spiritual realization, above the stage of liberation. By chanting the holy name of Kṛṣṇa one attains the stage of love of God, and it was good that fortunately I was favored with the blessing."

On hearing this statement from the Lord, the Māyāvādī *sannyāsī* asked the Lord what was the harm in studying the Vedānta along with chanting the holy name. Prakāśānanda Sarasvatī knew well that the Lord was formerly known as Nimāi Paṇḍita, a very learned scholar of Navadvīpa, and His posing as a great fool was certainly to some purpose. Hearing this inquiry by the *sannyāsī*, the Lord smiled and said, "My dear sir, if you do not mind, I will answer your inquiry."

All the *sannyāsīs* there were very much pleased with the Lord for His honest dealings, and they unanimously replied that they would not be offended by whatever He replied. The Lord then spoke as follows:

"*Vedānta-sūtra* consists of transcendental words or sounds uttered by the transcendental Personality of Godhead. As such, in the Vedānta there cannot be any human deficiencies like mistake, illusion, cheating or inefficiency. The message of the *Upaniṣads* is expressed in the *Vedānta-sūtra,* and understanding the direct meaning of what is said there is certainly glorious. Whatever interpretations have been given by Śaṅkarācārya have no direct bearing on the *sūtra,* and therefore such commentation spoils everything.

"The word Brahman indicates the greatest of all, which is full with transcendental opulences, superior to all. Brahman is ultimately the Personality of Godhead, and He is covered by indirect interpretations and established as impersonal. Everything that is in the spiritual world is full of transcendental bliss, including the form, body, place and paraphernalia of the Lord. All are eternally cognizant and blissful. It is not the fault of the Ācārya Śaṅkara that he has so interpreted Vedānta, but if someone accepts it, then certainly he is doomed. Anyone who accepts the transcendental body of the Personality of Godhead as something mundane certainly commits the greatest blasphemy."

The Lord thus spoke to the *sannyāsī* almost in the same way that He spoke to the Bhaṭṭācārya of Purī, and by forceful arguments He nullified the Māyāvāda interpretations of the *Vedānta-sūtra.* All the *sannyāsīs* there claimed that the Lord was the personified *Vedas* and the Personality of Godhead. All the *sannyāsīs* were converted to the cult of *bhakti,* all of them accepted the holy name of the Lord Śrī Kṛṣṇa, and they dined together with the Lord in the midst of them. After this conversion of the *sannyāsīs,* the popularity of the Lord increased at Vārāṇasī, and thousands of people assembled to see the Lord in person. The Lord thus established the primary importance of *Śrīmad-Bhāgavata-dharma,* and He defeated all other systems of spiritual realization. After that everyone at Vārāṇasī was overwhelmed with the transcendental *saṅkīrtana* movement.

While the Lord was camping at Vārāṇasī, Sanātana Gosvāmī also arrived after retiring from office. Formerly known as Sākara Mallika, he had been one of the state ministers in the government of Bengal, then under the regime of Nawab Hussain Shah. He had had some difficulty in getting relief from the state service, for the Nawab was reluctant to let him leave. Nonetheless he came to Vārāṇasī, and for two months the Lord taught him the principles of devotional service. He taught him about the constitutional position of the living being, the cause of his bondage under material conditions, his eternal relation with the Personality of Godhead, the transcendental position of the Supreme Personality of Godhead, His expansions in different plenary portions of incarnations, His control of different parts of the universe, the nature of His transcendental abode, devotional activities, their different stages of development, the rules and regulations for achieving the gradual stages of spiritual perfection, the symptoms of different incarnations in different ages, and how to detect them with reference to the context of revealed scriptures.

The Lord's teachings to Sanātana Gosvāmī form a big chapter in the text of *Śrī Caitanya-caritāmṛta,* and to explain the whole teachings in minute details will require a volume in itself. These are treated in detail in our book *Teachings of Lord Caitanya.*

At Mathurā, the Lord visited all the important places; then He reached Vṛndāvana. Lord Caitanya appeared in the family of a high-caste *brāhmaṇa,* and over and above that as a *sannyāsī* He was the preceptor for all the *varṇas* and *āśramas.* But He used to accept meals from all classes of Vaiṣṇavas. At Mathurā the Sanoḍiyā *brāhmaṇas* are considered to be in the lower status of society, but the Lord accepted meals in the family of such a *brāhmaṇa* also because His host happened to be a disciple of the Mādhavendra Purī family.

At Vṛndāvana the Lord took bath in twenty-four important bathing places, or ghāṭas. He traveled to all the twelve important *vanas* (forests). In these forests all the cows and birds welcomed Him, as if He were their very old friend. The Lord also began to embrace all the trees of those forests, and by doing so He felt the symptoms of transcendental ecstasy. Sometimes He fell unconscious, but He was made to regain consciousness by the chanting of the holy name of Kṛṣṇa. The transcendental symptoms that were visible on the body of the Lord during His travel within the forest of Vṛndāvana were all unique and inexplicable, and we have just given a synopsis only.

Some of the important places that were visited by the Lord in Vṛndāvana were Kāmyavana, Ādīśvara, Pāvana-sarovara, Khadiravana, Śeṣaśāyī, Khela-tīrtha, Bhāṇḍīravana, Bhadravana, Śrīvana, Lauhavana, Mahāvana, Gokula, Kāliya-hrada, Dvādaśāditya, Keśī-tīrtha, etc. When He saw the place where the *rāsa* dance took place, He at once fell down in trance. As long as He remained at Vṛndāvana, He made His headquarters at Akrūra-ghāṭa.

From Vṛndāvana His personal servitor Kṛṣṇadāsa Vipra induced Him to go back to Prayāga to take bath during the Māgha-melā. The Lord acceded to this proposal, and they started for Prayāga. On the way they met with some Pathans, amongst whom there was a learned Moulana. The Lord had some talks with the Moulana and his companions, and the Lord convinced the Moulana that in the Koran also there are descriptions of *Bhāgavata-dharma* and Kṛṣṇa. All the Pathans were converted to His cult of devotional service.

When He returned to Prayāga, Śrīla Rūpa Gosvāmī and his youngest brother met Him near the Bindu-mādhava temple. This time the Lord was welcomed by the people of Prayāga more respectfully. Vallabha Bhaṭṭa, who resided on the other bank of Prayāga in the village of Āḍāila, was to receive Him at his place. But while going there the Lord jumped in the river Yamunā. With great difficulty He was picked up in an unconscious state. Finally He visited the headquarters of Vallabha Bhaṭṭa. This Vallabha Bhaṭṭa was one of His chief admirers, but later on he inaugurated his own party, the Vallabha-sampradāya.

On the bank of the Daśāśvamedha-ghāṭa at Prayāga for ten days continually the Lord instructed Rūpa Gosvāmī in the science of devotional service to the Lord. He taught the Gosvāmī the divisions of the living creatures in the 8,400,000 species of life. Then He taught him about the human species. Out of them He selected the followers of the Vedic principles, out of them the fruitive workers, out of them the empiric philosophers, and out of them the liberated souls. He said that among liberated souls there are only a few who are actually pure devotees of Lord Śrī Kṛṣṇa.

Śrīla Rūpa Gosvāmī was the younger brother of Sanātana Gosvāmī, and when he retired from service he brought with him two boats full of gold coins. This means that he brought with him some hundreds of thousands of rupees accumulated by the labor of his service. And before leaving home for Lord Caitanya Mahāprabhu, he divided the wealth as follows: fifty percent for the service of the Lord and His devotees, twenty-five percent for relatives and twenty-five percent for his personal needs in case of emergency. In that way he set an example for all householders.

The Lord taught the Gosvāmī about devotional service, comparing it to a creeper, and advised him to protect the *bhakti* creeper most carefully against the mad elephant offense against the pure devotees. In addition, the creeper has to be protected from the desires of sense enjoyment, monistic liberation and perfection of the *haṭha-yoga* system. They are all detrimental on the path of devotional service. Similarly, violence against living beings, and desire for worldly gain, worldly reception and worldly fame are all detrimental to the progress of *bhakti,* or *Bhāgavata-dharma.*

Pure devotional service must be freed from all desires for sense gratification, fruitive aspirations and culture of monistic knowledge. One must be freed from all kinds of designations, and when one is thus converted to transcendental purity, one can then serve the Lord by purified senses.

As long as there is the desire to enjoy sensually or to become one with the Supreme or to possess the mystic powers, there is no question of attaining the stage of pure devotional service.

Devotional service is conducted under two categories, namely primary practice and spontaneous emotion. When one can rise to the platform of spontaneous emotion, he can make further progress by spiritual attachment, feeling, love, and many higher stages of devotional life for which there are no English words. We have tried to explain the science of devotional service in our book *The Nectar of Devotion,* based on the authority of *Bhakti-rasāmṛta-sindhu* by Śrīla Rūpa Gosvāmī.

Transcendental devotional service has five stages of reciprocation:

1. The self-realization stage just after liberation from material bondage is called the *śānta,* or neutral stage.

2. After that, when there is development of transcendental knowledge of the Lord's internal opulences, the devotee engages himself in the *dāsya* stage.

3. By further development of the *dāsya* stage, a respectful fraternity with the Lord develops, and above that a feeling of friendship on equal terms becomes manifest. Both these stages are called the *sakhya* stage, or devotional service in friendship.

4. Above this is the stage of parental affection toward the Lord, and this is called the *vātsalya* stage.

5. And above this is the stage of conjugal love, and this stage is called the highest stage of love of God, although there is no difference in quality in any of the above stages. The last stage, conjugal love of God, is called the *mādhurya* stage.

Thus He instructed Rūpa Gosvāmī in devotional science and deputed him to Vṛndāvana to excavate the lost sites of the transcendental pastimes of the Lord. After this, the Lord returned to Vārāṇasī and delivered the *sannyāsīs* and instructed the elder brother of Rūpa Gosvāmī. We have already discussed this.

The Lord left only eight *ślokas* of His instructions in writing, and they are known as the *Śikṣāṣṭaka*. All other literatures of His divine cult were extensively written by the Lord's principal followers, the Six Gosvāmīs of Vṛndāvana, and their followers. The cult of Caitanya philosophy is richer than any other, and it is admitted to be the living religion of the day with the potency for spreading as *viśva-dharma*, or universal religion. We are glad that the matter has been taken up by some enthusiastic sages like Bhaktisiddhānta Sarasvatī Gosvāmī Mahārāja and his disciples. We shall eagerly wait for the happy days of *Bhāgavata-dharma*, or *prema-dharma*, inaugurated by the Lord Śrī Caitanya Mahāprabhu.

The eight *ślokas* completed by the Lord are:

1

Glory to the Śrī Kṛṣṇa saṅkīrtana, *which cleanses the heart of all the dust accumulated for years and extinguishes the fire of conditional life, of repeated birth and death. This* saṅkīrtana *movement is the prime benediction for humanity at large because it spreads the rays of the benediction moon. It is the life of all transcendental knowledge, it increases the ocean of transcendental bliss, and it enables us to fully taste the nectar for which we are always anxious.*

2

O my Lord, Your holy name alone can render all benediction to living beings, and thus You have hundreds and millions of names like Kṛṣṇa and Govinda. In these transcendental names You have invested all Your transcendental energies. There are not even hard and fast rules for chanting these names. O my Lord, out of kindness You enable us to easily approach You by chanting Your holy names, but I am so unfortunate that I have no attraction for them.

3

One should chant the holy name of the Lord in a humble state of mind, thinking oneself lower than the straw in the street; one should be more tolerant than a tree, devoid of all sense of false prestige, and ready to offer all respect to others. In such a state of mind one can chant the holy name of the Lord constantly.

4

O almighty Lord, I have no desire to accumulate wealth, nor do I desire beautiful women, nor do I want any number of followers. I only want Your causeless devotional service birth after birth.

5

O son of Mahārāja Nanda [Kṛṣṇa], I am Your eternal servitor, yet somehow or other I have fallen into the ocean of birth and death. Please pick me up from this ocean of death and place me as one of the atoms of Your lotus feet.

6

O my Lord, when will my eyes be decorated with tears of love flowing constantly when I chant Your holy name? When will my voice choke up, and when will the hairs of my body stand on end at the recitation of Your name?

7

O Govinda! Feeling Your separation, I am considering a moment to be like twelve years or more. Tears are flowing from my eyes like torrents of rain, and I am feeling all vacant in the world in Your absence.

8

I know no one but Kṛṣṇa as my Lord, and He shall remain so even if He handles me roughly in His embrace or makes me brokenhearted by not being present before me. He is completely free to do anything and everything, for He is always my worshipful Lord unconditionally.

CHAPTER ONE

Questions by the Sages

ॐ नमो भगवते वासुदेवाय

TEXT 1

जन्माद्यस्य यतोऽन्वयादितरतश्चार्थेष्वभिज्ञः स्वराट्
तेने ब्रह्म हृदा य आदिकवये मुह्यन्ति यत्सूरयः ।
तेजोवारिमृदां यथा विनिमयो यत्र त्रिसर्गोऽमृषा
धाम्ना स्वेन सदा निरस्तकुहकं सत्यं परं धीमहि ॥ १ ॥

oṁ namo bhagavate vāsudevāya
janmādy asya yato 'nvayād itarataś cārtheṣv abhijñaḥ svarāṭ
tene brahma hṛdā ya ādi-kavaye muhyanti yat sūrayaḥ
tejo-vāri-mṛdāṁ yathā vinimayo yatra tri-sargo 'mṛṣā
dhāmnā svena sadā nirasta-kuhakaṁ satyaṁ paraṁ dhīmahi

oṁ—O my Lord; *namaḥ*—offering my obeisances; *bhagavate*—unto the Personality of Godhead; *vāsudevāya*—unto Vāsudeva (the son of Vasudeva), or Lord Śrī Kṛṣṇa, the primeval Lord; *janma-ādi*—creation, sustenance and destruction; *asya*—of the manifested universes; *yataḥ*—from whom; *anvayāt*—directly; *itarataḥ*—indirectly; *ca*—and; *artheṣu*—purposes; *abhijñaḥ*—fully cognizant; *sva-rāṭ*—fully independent; *tene*—imparted; *brahma*—the Vedic knowledge; *hṛdā*—consciousness of the heart; *yaḥ*—one who; *ādi-kavaye*—unto the original created being; *muhyanti*—are illusioned; *yat*—about whom; *sūrayaḥ*—great sages and demigods; *tejaḥ*—fire; *vāri*—water; *mṛdām*—earth; *yathā*—as much as; *vinimayaḥ*—action and reaction; *yatra*—whereupon; *tri-sargaḥ*—three modes of creation, creative faculties; *amṛṣā*—almost factual; *dhāmnā*—along with all transcendental paraphernalia; *svena*—self-sufficiently; *sadā*—always; *nirasta*—negation by absence; *kuhakam*—illusion; *satyam*—truth; *param*—absolute; *dhīmahi*—I do meditate upon.

O my Lord, Śrī Kṛṣṇa, son of Vasudeva, O all-pervading Personality of Godhead, I offer my respectful obeisances unto You. I meditate

upon Lord Śrī Kṛṣṇa because He is the Absolute Truth and the primeval cause of all causes of the creation, sustenance and destruction of the manifested universes. He is directly and indirectly conscious of all manifestations, and He is independent because there is no other cause beyond Him. It is He only who first imparted the Vedic knowledge unto the heart of Brahmājī, the original living being. By Him even the great sages and demigods are placed into illusion, as one is bewildered by the illusory representations of water seen in fire, or land seen on water. Only because of Him do the material universes, temporarily manifested by the reactions of the three modes of nature, appear factual, although they are unreal. I therefore meditate upon Him, Lord Śrī Kṛṣṇa, who is eternally existent in the transcendental abode, which is forever free from the illusory representations of the material world. I meditate upon Him, for He is the Absolute Truth.

PURPORT Obeisances unto the Personality of Godhead, Vāsudeva, directly indicate Lord Śrī Kṛṣṇa, who is the divine son of Vasudeva and Devakī. This fact will be more explicitly explained later in the text of this work, when Śrī Vyāsadeva directly asserts that Śrī Kṛṣṇa is the original Personality of Godhead and all others are His direct or indirect plenary portions or portions of the portion. Śrīla Jīva Gosvāmī has even more explicitly explained the subject matter in his *Kṛṣṇa-sandarbha*. And Brahmā, the original living being, has explained the subject of Śrī Kṛṣṇa substantially in his treatise named *Brahma-saṁhitā*. In an *Upaniṣad* in the *Sāma-veda*, it is also stated that Lord Śrī Kṛṣṇa is the divine son of Devakī. Therefore, in this prayer, the first proposition holds that Lord Śrī Kṛṣṇa is the primeval Lord, and if any transcendental nomenclature is to be understood as belonging to the Absolute Personality of Godhead, it must be the name indicated by the word Kṛṣṇa, which means the all-attractive. In *Bhagavad-gītā*, in many places, the Lord asserts Himself to be the original Personality of Godhead, and this is confirmed by Arjuna, who also cites great sages like Nārada, Vyāsa, and many others. In the *Padma Purāṇa*, it is also stated that out of the innumerable names of the Lord, the name of Kṛṣṇa is the principal one. Although Vāsudeva indicates the plenary portion of the Personality of Godhead, and although all the different forms of the Lord, being identical with Vāsudeva, are thus indicated in this text, the name Vāsudeva particularly indicates Kṛṣṇa, the divine son of Vasudeva and Devakī. Śrī Kṛṣṇa is always meditated upon by the *paramahaṁsas,* who are the perfected ones among those in the renounced order of life.

Vāsudeva, or Lord Śrī Kṛṣṇa, is the cause of all causes. Everything that exists emanates from the Lord. How this is so is explained in later chapters of this work. This work is described by Mahāprabhu Śrī Caitanya as the spotless *Purāṇa* because it contains the transcendental narration of the Personality of Godhead Śrī Kṛṣṇa. The history of the *Śrīmad-Bhāgavatam* is also very glorious. It was compiled by Śrī Vyāsadeva after he had attained maturity in transcendental knowledge. He wrote this under the instructions of Śrī Nāradajī, his spiritual master. Vyāsadeva compiled all Vedic literatures, containing the four divisions of the *Vedas,* the *Vedānta-sūtras* (or the *Brahma-sūtras*), the *Purāṇas,* the *Mahābhārata,* and so on. But nevertheless he was not satisfied. His dissatisfaction was observed by his spiritual master, and thus Nārada advised him to write on the transcendental activities of Lord Śrī Kṛṣṇa. These transcendental activities are described specifically in the *Bhāgavatam's* Tenth Canto, which is considered its substance. But in order to reach the very substance one must proceed gradually by developing knowledge of the categories.

It is natural that a philosophical mind wants to know about the origin of the creation. At night he sees the stars in the sky, and he naturally speculates about their inhabitants. Such inquiries are natural for man because man has a developed consciousness which is higher than that of the animals. The author of *Śrīmad-Bhāgavatam* gives a direct answer to such inquiries. He says that the Lord Śrī Kṛṣṇa is the origin of all creations. He is not only the creator of the universe, but the destroyer as well. The manifested cosmic nature is created at a certain period by the will of the Lord. It is maintained for some time, and then it is annihilated by His will. Therefore, the supreme will is behind all cosmic activities. Of course, there are atheists of various categories who do not believe in a creator, but that is due to a poor fund of knowledge. The modern scientist, for example, has created space satellites, and by some arrangement or other, these satellites are thrown into outer space to fly for some time at the control of the scientist who is far away. Similarly, all the universes with innumerable stars and planets are controlled by the intelligence of the Personality of Godhead.

In Vedic literatures, it is said that the Absolute Truth, Personality of Godhead, is the chief amongst all living personalities. All living beings, beginning from the first created being, Brahmā, down to the smallest ant, are individual living beings. And above Brahmā, there are even other living beings with individual capacities, and the Personality of Godhead is also a similar living being. And He is an individual as are the other living beings. But the Supreme Lord, or the supreme living being, has the greatest intelligence, and He possesses supermost inconceivable energies of all different varieties. If a man's brain can produce a space satellite, one can very easily imagine how brains higher than man can produce similarly wonderful things which are far superior. The reasonable person will easily accept this argument, but there are stubborn atheists who would never agree. Śrīla Vyāsadeva, however, at once accepts the supreme intelligence as the *parameśvara*. He offers his respectful obeisances unto the supreme intelligence addressed as the *para* or the *parameśvara* or the Supreme Personality of Godhead. And that *parameśvara* is Śrī Kṛṣṇa, as admitted in *Bhagavad-gītā* and other scriptures delivered by Śrī Vyāsadeva and specifically in this *Śrīmad-Bhāgavatam*. In *Bhagavad-gītā*, the Lord says that there is no other *para-tattva* (*summum bonum*) than Himself. Therefore, Śrī Vyāsadeva at once worships the *para-tattva*, Śrī Kṛṣṇa, whose transcendental activities are described in the Tenth Canto.

Unscrupulous persons go immediately to the Tenth Canto and especially to the five chapters which describe the Lord's *rāsa* dance. This portion of the *Śrīmad-Bhāgavatam* is the most confidential part of this great literature. Unless one is thoroughly accomplished in the transcendental knowledge of the Lord, one is sure to misunderstand the Lord's worshipable transcendental pastimes called *rāsa* dance and His loving affairs with the *gopīs*. This subject matter is highly spiritual, and only the liberated persons who have gradually attained to the stage of *paramahaṁsa* can transcendentally relish this *rāsa* dance. Śrīla Vyāsadeva therefore gives the reader the chance to gradually develop spiritual realization before actually relishing the essence of the pastimes of the Lord. Therefore, he purposely invokes a Gāyatrī *mantra, dhīmahi*. This Gāyatrī *mantra* is meant for spiritually advanced people. When one is successful in chanting the Gāyatrī *mantra*, he can enter into the transcendental position of the Lord. One must therefore acquire brahminical qualities or be perfectly situated in the quality of goodness in order to chant the Gāyatrī *mantra* successfully and then attain to the stage of transcendentally realizing the Lord, His name, His fame, His qualities and so on.

Śrīmad-Bhāgavatam is the narration of the *svarūpa* of the Lord manifested by His internal potency, and this potency is distinguished from the external potency which has manifested the cosmic world, which is within our experience. Śrīla Vyāsadeva makes a clear distinction between the two in this *śloka*. Śrī Vyāsadeva says herein that the manifested internal potency is real, whereas the external manifested energy in the form of material existence is only temporary and illusory like the mirage in the desert. In the desert mirage there is no actual water. There is only the appearance of water. Real water is somewhere else. The manifested cosmic creation appears as reality. But reality, of which this is but a shadow, is in the spiritual world. Absolute Truth is in the spiritual sky, not the material sky. In the material sky everything is relative truth. That is to say, one truth depends on something else. This cosmic creation results from interaction of the three modes of nature, and the temporary manifestations are so created as to present an illusion of reality to the bewildered mind of the conditioned soul, who appears in so many species of life, including the higher demigods, like Brahmā, Indra, Candra, and so on. In actuality, there is no reality in the manifested world. There appears to be reality, however, because of the true reality which exists in the spiritual world, where the Personality of Godhead eternally exists with His transcendental paraphernalia.

The chief engineer of a complicated construction does not personally take part in the construction, but he knows every nook and corner because everything is done under his direction. He knows everything about the construction, both directly and indirectly. Similarly, the Personality of Godhead, who is the supreme engineer of this cosmic creation, knows every nook and corner, although affairs are apparently being carried out by demigods. Beginning from Brahmā down to the insignificant ant, no one is independent in the matter of material creation, for the hand of the Lord is seen everywhere. All material elements as well as all spiritual sparks emanate from Him only. And whatever is created in this material world is but the interaction of two energies, the material and the spiritual, which emanate from the Absolute Truth, the Personality of Godhead, Śrī Kṛṣṇa. A chemist can manufacture water in the chemical laboratory by mixing hydrogen and oxygen. But, in reality, the living entity works in the laboratory under the direction of the Supreme Lord. And the materials with which he works are also supplied by the Lord.

The Lord knows everything directly and indirectly, and He is cognizant of all minute details, and He is fully independent. He is compared to a mine of gold, and the cosmic creations in so many different forms are compared to objects made from the gold, such as gold rings, necklaces and so on. The gold ring and the gold necklace are qualitatively one with the gold in the mine, but quantitatively the gold in the mine is different. Therefore, the Absolute Truth is simultaneously one and different. Nothing is absolutely equal with the Absolute Truth, but at the same time, nothing is independent of the Absolute Truth.

Conditioned souls, beginning from Brahmā, who engineers the entire universe, down to the insignificant ant, are all creating, but none of them are independent of the Supreme Lord. The materialist wrongly thinks that there is no creator other than his own self. This is called *māyā,* or illusion. Because of his poor fund of knowledge, the materialist cannot see beyond the purview of his imperfect senses, and thus he thinks that matter automatically takes its own shape without the aid of a superior intelligence. This is refuted in this *śloka* by Śrīla Vyāsadeva: "Since the complete whole or the Absolute Truth is the source of everything, nothing can be independent of the body of the Absolute Truth." Whatever happens to the body quickly becomes known to the embodied. Similarly, the creation is the body of the absolute whole. Therefore, the Absolute knows everything directly and indirectly that happens in the creation.

In the *śruti-mantra,* it is also stated that the absolute whole or Brahman is the ultimate source of everything. Everything emanates from Him, and everything is maintained by Him. And at the end, everything enters into Him. That is the law of nature. In the *smṛti-mantra,* the same is confirmed. It is said there that the source from which everything emanates at the beginning of Brahmā's millennium and the reservoir to which everything ultimately enters, is the Absolute Truth or Brahman. Material scientists take it for granted that the ultimate source of the planetary system is the sun, but they are unable to explain the source of the sun. Herein, the ultimate source is explained. According to the Vedic literature, Brahmā is the creator of this universe. Yet he had to meditate to get inspiration for such creation. Therefore, neither Brahmā nor the sun is the ultimate creator. It is stated in this *śloka* that Brahmā was taught Vedic knowledge by the Personality of Godhead. One may argue that Brahmā, being the original living being, could not be inspired because there was no other being living at that time. Herein it is stated that the Supreme Lord inspired the secondary creator, Brahmā, in order that Brahmā could carry out his creative functions. So, the supreme intelligence behind all creations is the Absolute Godhead, Śrī Kṛṣṇa. In *Bhagavad-gītā,* Lord Śrī Kṛṣṇa states that it is He only who superintends the creative energy, *prakṛti,* which constitutes the totality of matter. Therefore, Śrī Vyāsadeva does not worship Brahmā, but the Supreme Lord, who guides Brahmā in his creative activities.

In this *śloka,* the particular words *abhijñaḥ* and *svarāṭ* are significant. These two words distinguish the Supreme Lord from all the other living entities. No other living entity is either *abhijñaḥ* or *svarāṭ.* That is, no one is either fully cognizant or fully independent. Even Brahmā has to meditate upon the Supreme Lord in order to create. Then what to speak of great scientists like Einstein! The brains of such a scientist are certainly not the products of any human being. Scientists cannot manufacture such a brain, and what to speak of foolish atheists who defy the authority of the Lord? Even Māyāvādī impersonalists who flatter themselves that they can become one with the Lord are neither *abhijñaḥ* nor *svarāṭ.* Such impersonalists undergo severe austerities to acquire knowledge to become one with the Lord. But ultimately they become dependent on some rich disciple who supplies them with money to build monasteries and temples. Atheists like Rāvaṇa or Hiraṇyakaśipu had to undergo severe penances before they could flout the authority of the Lord. But ultimately, they were rendered helpless and could not save themselves when the Lord appeared before them as cruel death. This is also the case with the modern atheists who also dare to flout the authority of the Lord. Such atheists will be dealt with similarly, for history repeats itself. Whenever men neglect the authority of the Lord, nature and her laws are there to penalize them. This is confirmed in *Bhagavad-gītā* in the well-known verse *yadā yadā hi dharmasya glāniḥ.* "Whenever there is a decline of *dharma* and a rise of *adharma,* O Arjuna, then I incarnate Myself." (Bg. 4.7)

That the Supreme Lord is all-perfect is confirmed in all *śruti-mantras.* It is said in the *śruti-mantras* that the all-perfect Lord threw a glance over matter and thus created all living beings. The living beings are parts and parcels of the Lord, and He impregnates the vast material creation with seeds of spiritual sparks, and thus the creative energies are set in motion to enact so many wonderful creations. An atheist may argue that God is no more expert than a watchmaker, but of course God is greater because He can create machines in duplicate male and female forms. The male and female forms of different types of machineries go on producing innumerable similar machines without God's further attention. If a man could manufacture such a set of machines that could produce other machines without his attention, then he could approach the intelligence of God. But that is not possible, for each machine has to be handled individually. Therefore, no one can create as well as God. Another name for God is *asamordhva,* which means that no one is equal to or greater than Him. *Paraṁ satyam,* or the Supreme Truth, is He who has no equal or superior. This is confirmed in the *śruti-mantras.* It is said that before the creation of the material universe there existed the Lord only, who is master of everyone. That Lord instructed Brahmā in Vedic knowledge. That Lord has to be obeyed in all respects. Anyone who wants to get rid of the material entanglement must surrender unto Him. This is also confirmed in *Bhagavad-gītā.*

Unless one surrenders unto the lotus feet of the Supreme Lord, it is certain that he will be bewildered. When an intelligent man surrenders unto the lotus feet of Kṛṣṇa and knows completely that Kṛṣṇa is the cause of all causes, as confirmed in *Bhagavad-gītā,* then only can such an intelligent man become a *mahātmā,* or great soul. But such a great soul is rarely seen. Only the *mahātmās* can understand that the Supreme Lord is the primeval cause of all creations. He is *parama* or ultimate truth because all other truths are relative to Him. He is omniscient. For Him, there is no illusion.

Some Māyāvādī scholars argue that *Śrīmad-Bhāgavatam* was not compiled by Śrī Vyāsadeva. And some of them suggest that this book is a modern creation written by someone named Vopadeva. In order to refute such meaningless arguments, Śrī Śrīdhara Svāmī points out that there is reference to the *Bhāgavatam* in many of the oldest *Purāṇas.* This first *śloka* of the *Bhāgavatam* begins with the Gāyatrī *mantra.* There is reference to this in the *Matsya Purāṇa,* which is the oldest *Purāṇa.* In that *Purāṇa* it is said about the *Bhāgavatam* that in it there are many narrations of spiritual instructions, that it begins with the Gāyatrī *mantra,* and that it contains the history of Vṛtrāsura. Anyone who makes a gift of this great work on a full moon day attains to the highest perfection of life by returning to Godhead. There is reference to the *Bhāgavatam* in other *Purāṇas* also, where it is clearly stated that this work was finished in twelve cantos, which include eighteen thousand *ślokas*. In the *Padma Purāṇa* also there is reference to the *Bhāgavatam* in a conversation between Gautama and Mahārāja Ambarīṣa. The king was advised therein to read regularly *Śrīmad-Bhāgavatam* if he desired liberation from material bondage. Under the circumstances, there is no doubt about the authority of the *Bhāgavatam*. Within the past five hundred years, many erudite scholars and *ācāryas* like Jīva Gosvāmī, Sanātana Gosvāmī, Viśvanātha Cakravartī, Vallabhācārya, and many other distinguished scholars even after the time of Lord Caitanya made elaborate commentaries on the *Bhāgavatam*. And the serious student would do well to attempt to go through them to better relish the transcendental messages.

Śrīla Viśvanātha Cakravartī Ṭhākura specifically deals with the original and pure sex psychology (*ādi-rasa*), devoid of all mundane inebriety. *The whole material creation is moving under the principle of sex life*. In modern civilization, sex life is the focal point for all activities. Wherever one turns his face, he sees sex life predominant. Therefore, sex life is not unreal. Its reality is experienced in the spiritual world. The material sex life is but a perverted reflection of the original fact. The original fact is in the Absolute Truth, and thus the Absolute Truth cannot be impersonal. It is not possible to be impersonal and contain pure sex life. Consequently, the impersonalist philosophers have given indirect impetus to the abominable mundane sex life because they have overstressed the impersonality of the ultimate truth. Consequently, man without information of the actual spiritual form of sex has accepted perverted material sex life as the all in all. There is a distinction between sex life in the diseased material condition and spiritual sex life.

This *Śrīmad-Bhāgavatam* will gradually elevate the unbiased reader to the highest perfectional stage of transcendence. It will enable him to transcend the three modes of material activities: fruitive actions, speculative philosophy, and worship of functional deities as inculcated in Vedic verses.

TEXT 2

धर्मः प्रोज्झितकैतवोऽत्र परमो निर्मत्सराणां सतां
वेद्यं वास्तवमत्र वस्तु शिवदं तापत्रयोन्मूलनम् ।
श्रीमद्भागवते महामुनिकृते किं वा परैरीश्वरः
सद्यो हृद्यवरुध्यतेऽत्र कृतिभिः शुश्रूषुभिस्तत्क्षणात् ॥ २ ॥

dharmaḥ projjhita-kaitavo 'tra paramo nirmatsarāṇāṁ satāṁ
vedyaṁ vāstavam atra vastu śivadaṁ tāpa-trayonmūlanam
śrīmad-bhāgavate mahā-muni-kṛte kiṁ vā parair īśvaraḥ
sadyo hṛdy avarudhyate 'tra kṛtibhiḥ śuśrūṣubhis tat-kṣaṇāt

dharmaḥ—religiosity; *projjhita*—completely rejected; *kaitavaḥ*—covered by fruitive intention; *atra*—herein; *paramaḥ*—the highest; *nirmatsarāṇām*—of the one-hundred-percent pure in heart; *satām*—devotees; *vedyam*—understandable; *vāstavam*—factual; *atra*—herein; *vastu*—substance; *śivadam*—well-being; *tāpa-traya*—threefold miseries; *unmūlanam*—causing uprooting of; *śrīmat*—beautiful; *bhāgavate*—the *Bhāgavata Purāṇa; mahā-muni*—the great sage (Vyāsadeva); *kṛte*—having compiled; *kim*—what is; *vā*—the need; *paraiḥ*—others; *īśvaraḥ*—the Supreme Lord; *sadyaḥ*—at once; *hṛdi*—within the heart; *avarudhyate*—becomes compact; *atra*—herein; *kṛtibhiḥ*—by the pious men; *śuśrūṣubhiḥ*—by culture; *tat-kṣaṇāt*—without delay.

Completely rejecting all religious activities which are materially motivated, this Bhāgavata Purāṇa propounds the highest truth, which is understandable by those devotees who are fully pure in heart. The highest truth is reality distinguished from illusion for the welfare of all. Such truth uproots the threefold miseries. This beautiful Bhāgavatam, compiled by the great sage Vyāsadeva [in his maturity], is sufficient in itself for God realization. What is the need of any other scripture? As soon as one attentively and submissively hears the message of Bhāgavatam, by this culture of knowledge the Supreme Lord is established within his heart.

PURPORT Religion includes four primary subjects, namely pious activities, economic development, satisfaction of the senses, and finally liberation from material bondage. Irreligious life is a barbarous condition. Indeed, human life begins when religion begins. Eating, sleeping, fearing, and mating are the four principles of animal life. These are common both to animals and to human beings. But religion is the extra function of the human being. Without religion, human life is no better than animal life. Therefore, in human societies there is some form of religion which aims at self-realization and which makes reference to man's eternal relationship with God.

In the lower stages of human civilization, there is always competition to lord it over the material nature or, in other words, there is a continuous rivalry to satisfy the senses. Driven by such consciousness, man turns to religion. He thus performs pious activities or religious functions in order to gain something material. But if such material gains are obtainable in other ways, then so-called religion is neglected. This is the situation in modern civilization. Man is thriving economically, so at present he is not very interested in religion. Churches, mosques or temples are now practically vacant. Men are more interested in factories, shops, and cinemas than in religious places which were erected by their forefathers. This practically proves that religion is performed for some economic gains. Economic gains are needed for sense gratification. Often when one is baffled in the pursuit of sense gratification, he takes to salvation and tries to become one with the Supreme Lord. Consequently, all these states are simply different types of sense gratification.

In the *Vedas,* the above-mentioned four activities are prescribed in the regulative way so that there will not be any undue competition for sense gratification. But *Śrīmad-Bhāgavatam* is transcendental to all these sense gratificatory activities. It is purely transcendental literature which can be understood only by the pure devotees of the Lord who are transcendental to competitive sense gratification. In the material world there is keen competition between animal and animal, man and man, community and community, nation and nation. But the devotees of the Lord rise above such competitions. They do not compete with the materialist because they are on the path back to Godhead where life is eternal and blissful. Such transcendentalists are nonenvious and pure in heart. In the material world, everyone is envious of everyone else, and therefore there is competition. But the transcendental devotees of the Lord are not only free from material envy, but are well-wishers to everyone, and they strive to establish a competitionless society with God in the center. The contemporary socialist's conception of a competitionless society is artificial because in the socialist state there is competition for the post of dictator. From the point of view of the *Vedas* or from the point of view of common human activities, sense gratification is the basis of material life. There are three paths mentioned in the *Vedas.* One involves fruitive activities to gain promotion to better planets. Another involves worshiping different demigods for promotion to the planets of the demigods, and another involves realizing the Absolute Truth and His impersonal feature and becoming one with Him.

The impersonal aspect of the Absolute Truth is not the highest. Above the impersonal feature is the Paramātmā feature, and above this is the personal feature of the Absolute Truth, or Bhagavān. *Śrīmad-Bhāgavatam* gives information about the Absolute Truth in His personal feature. It is higher than impersonalist literatures and higher than the *jñāna-kāṇḍa* division of the *Vedas*. It is even higher than the *karma-kāṇḍa* division, and even higher than the *upāsanā-kāṇḍa* division, because it recommends the worship of the Supreme Personality of Godhead, Lord Śrī Kṛṣṇa. In the *karma-kāṇḍa,* there is competition to reach heavenly planets for better sense gratification, and there is similar competition in the *jñāna-kāṇḍa* and the *upāsanā-kāṇḍa*. The *Śrīmad-Bhāgavatam* is superior to all of these because it aims at the Supreme Truth which is the substance or the root of all categories. From *Śrīmad-Bhāgavatam* one can come to know the substance as well as the categories. The substance is the Absolute Truth, the Supreme Lord, and all emanations are relative forms of energy.

Nothing is apart from the substance, but at the same time the energies are different from the substance. This conception is not contradictory. *Śrīmad-Bhāgavatam* explicitly promulgates this simultaneously-one-and-different philosophy of the *Vedānta-sūtra,* which begins with the "*janmādy asya*" *sūtra*.

This knowledge that the energy of the Lord is simultaneously one with and different from the Lord is an answer to the mental speculators' attempt to establish the energy as the Absolute. When this knowledge is factually understood, one sees the conceptions of monism and dualism to be imperfect. Development of this transcendental consciousness grounded in the conception of simultaneously-one-and-different leads one immediately to the stage of freedom from the threefold miseries. The threefold miseries are (1) those miseries which arise from the mind and body, (2) those miseries inflicted by other living beings, and (3) those miseries arising from natural catastrophes over which one has no control. *Śrīmad-Bhāgavatam* begins with the surrender of the devotee unto the Absolute Person. The devotee is fully aware that he is one with the Absolute and at the same time in the eternal position of servant to the Absolute. In the material conception, one falsely thinks himself the lord of all he surveys, and therefore he is always troubled by the threefold miseries of life. But as soon as one comes to know his real position as transcendental servant, he at once becomes free from all miseries. As long as the living entity is trying to master material nature, there is no possibility of his becoming servant of the Supreme. Service to the Lord is rendered in pure consciousness of one's spiritual identity; by service one is immediately freed from material encumbrances.

Over and above this, *Śrīmad-Bhāgavatam* is a personal commentation on the *Vedānta-sūtra* by Śrī Vyāsadeva. It was written in the maturity of his spiritual life through the mercy of Nārada. Śrī Vyāsadeva is the authorized incarnation of Nārāyaṇa, the Personality of Godhead. Therefore, there is no question as to his authority. He is the author of all other Vedic literatures, yet he recommends the study of *Śrīmad-Bhāgavatam* above all others. In other *Purāṇas* there are different methods set forth by which one can worship the demigods. But in the *Bhāgavatam* only the Supreme Lord is mentioned. The Supreme Lord is the total body, and the demigods are the different parts of that body. Consequently, by worshiping the Supreme Lord, one does not need to worship the demigods. The Supreme Lord becomes fixed in the heart of the devotee immediately. Lord Caitanya Mahāprabhu has recommended the *Śrīmad-Bhāgavatam* as the spotless *Purāṇa* and distinguishes it from all other *Purāṇas*.

The proper method for receiving this transcendental message is to hear it submissively. A challenging attitude cannot help one realize this transcendental message. One particular word is used herein for proper guidance. This word is *śuśrūṣu*. One must be anxious to hear this transcendental message. The desire to sincerely hear is the first qualification.

Less fortunate persons are not at all interested in hearing this *Śrīmad-Bhāgavatam*. The process is simple, but the application is difficult. Unfortunate people find enough time to hear idle social and political conversations, but when invited to attend a meeting of devotees to hear *Śrīmad-Bhāgavatam* they suddenly become reluctant, or they indulge in hearing the portion of the *Bhāgavatam* they are unfit to hear. Sometimes professional readers of the *Bhāgavatam* immediately plunge into the confidential topics of the pastimes of the Supreme Lord, which they interpret as sex literature. *Śrīmad-Bhāgavatam* is meant to be heard from the beginning. Those who are fit to assimilate this work are mentioned in this *śloka:* "One becomes qualified to hear *Śrīmad-Bhāgavatam* after many pious deeds." The intelligent person, with thoughtful discretion, can be assured by the great sage Vyāsadeva that he can realize the Supreme Personality directly by hearing

Śrīmad-Bhāgavatam. Without undergoing the different stages of realization set forth in the *Vedas,* one can be lifted immediately to the position of *paramahaṁsa* simply by agreeing to receive this message.

TEXT 3

निगमकल्पतरोर्गलितं फलं
शुकमुखादमृतद्रवसंयुतम् ।
पिबत भागवतं रसमालयं
मुहुरहो रसिका भुवि भावुकाः ॥ ३ ॥

nigama-kalpa-taror galitaṁ phalaṁ
śuka-mukhād amṛta-drava-saṁyutam
pibata bhāgavataṁ rasam ālayaṁ
muhur aho rasikā bhuvi bhāvukāḥ

nigama—the Vedic literatures; *kalpa-taroḥ*—the desire tree; *galitam*—fully matured; *phalam*—fruit; *śuka*—Śrīla Śukadeva Gosvāmī, the original speaker of *Śrīmad-Bhāgavatam; mukhāt*—from the lips of; *amṛta*—nectar; *drava*—semisolid and soft and therefore easily swallowable; *saṁyutam*—perfect in all respects; *pibata*—do relish it; *bhāgavatam*—the book dealing in the science of the eternal relation with the Lord; *rasam*—juice (that which is relishable); *ālayam*—until liberation, or even in a liberated condition; *muhuḥ*—always; *aho*—O; *rasikāḥ*—those who are full in the knowledge of mellows; *bhuvi*—on the earth; *bhāvukāḥ*—expert and thoughtful.

O expert and thoughtful men, relish Śrīmad-Bhāgavatam, the mature fruit of the desire tree of Vedic literatures. It emanated from the lips of Śrī Śukadeva Gosvāmī. Therefore this fruit has become even more tasteful, although its nectarean juice was already relishable for all, including liberated souls.

PURPORT In the two previous *ślokas* it has been definitely proved that the *Śrīmad-Bhāgavatam* is the sublime literature which surpasses all other Vedic scriptures due to its transcendental qualities. It is transcendental to all mundane activities and mundane knowledge. In this *śloka* it is stated that *Śrīmad-Bhāgavatam* is not only a superior literature but is the ripened fruit of all Vedic literatures. In other words, it is the cream of all Vedic knowledge. Considering all this, patient and submissive hearing is definitely essential. With great respect and attention, one should receive the message and lessons imparted by the *Śrīmad-Bhāgavatam.*

The *Vedas* are compared to the desire tree because they contain all things knowable by man. They deal with mundane necessities as well as spiritual realization. The *Vedas* contain regulated principles of knowledge covering social, political, religious, economic, military, medicinal, chemical, physical and metaphysical subject matter and all that may be necessary to keep the body and soul together. Above and beyond all this are specific directions for spiritual realization. Regulated knowledge involves a gradual raising of the living entity to the spiritual platform, and the highest spiritual realization is knowledge that the Personality of Godhead is the reservoir of all spiritual tastes, or *rasas.*

Every living entity, beginning from Brahmā, the first-born living being within the material world, down to the insignificant ant, desires to relish some sort of taste derived from sense perceptions. These sensual pleasures are technically called *rasas*. Such *rasas* are of different varieties. In the revealed scriptures the following twelve varieties of *rasas* are enumerated: (1) *raudra* (anger), (2) *adbhuta* (wonder), (3) *śṛṅgāra* (conjugal love), (4) *hāsya* (comedy), (5) *vīra* (chivalry), (6) *dayā* (mercy), (7) *dāsya* (servitorship), (8) *sakhya* (fraternity), (9) *bhayānaka* (horror), (10) *bībhatsa* (shock), (11) *śānta* (neutrality), (12) *vātsalya* (parenthood).

The sum total of all these *rasas* is called affection or love. Primarily, such signs of love are manifested in adoration, service, friendship, parental affection, and conjugal love. And when these five are absent, love is present indirectly in anger, wonder, comedy, chivalry, fear, shock and so on. For example, when a man is in love with a woman, the *rasa* is called conjugal love. But when such love affairs are disturbed there may be wonder, anger, shock, or even horror. Sometimes love affairs between two persons culminate in ghastly murder scenes. Such *rasas* are displayed between man and man and between animal and animal. There is no possibility of an exchange or *rasa* between a man and an animal or between a man and any other species of living beings within the material world. The *rasas* are exchanged between members of the same species. But as far as the spirit souls are concerned, they are one qualitatively with the Supreme Lord. Therefore, the *rasas* were originally exchanged between the spiritual living being and the spiritual whole, the Supreme Personality of Godhead. The spiritual exchange or *rasa* is fully exhibited in spiritual existence between living beings and the Supreme Lord.

The Supreme Personality of Godhead is therefore described in the *śruti-mantras,* Vedic hymns, as "the fountainhead of all *rasas.*" When one associates with the Supreme Lord and exchanges one's constitutional *rasa* with the Lord, then the living being is actually happy.

These *śruti-mantras* indicate that every living being has its constitutional position, which is endowed with a particular type of *rasa* to be exchanged with the Personality of Godhead. In the liberated condition only, this primary *rasa* is experienced in full. In the material existence, the *rasa* is experienced in the perverted form, which is temporary. And thus the *rasas* of the material world are exhibited in the material form of *raudra* (anger) and so on.

Therefore, one who attains full knowledge of these different *rasas,* which are the basic principles of activities, can understand the false representations of the original *rasas* which are reflected in the material world. The learned scholar seeks to relish the real *rasa* in the spiritual form. In the beginning he desires to become one with the Supreme. Thus, less intelligent transcendentalists cannot go beyond this conception of becoming one with the spirit whole, without knowing of the different *rasas.*

In this *śloka,* it is definitely stated that spiritual *rasa,* which is relished even in the liberated stage, can be experienced in the literature of the *Śrīmad-Bhāgavatam* due to its being the ripened fruit of all Vedic knowledge. By submissively hearing this transcendental literature, one can attain the full pleasure of his heart's desire. But one must be very careful to hear the message from the right source. *Śrīmad-Bhāgavatam* is exactly received from the right source. It was brought by Nārada Muni from the spiritual world and given to his disciple Śrī Vyāsadeva. The latter in turn delivered the message to his son Śrīla Śukadeva Gosvāmī, and Śrīla Śukadeva Gosvāmī delivered the message to Mahārāja Parīkṣit during the seven days before the King's death. Śrīla Śukadeva Gosvāmī was a liberated soul from his very birth. He was liberated even in the womb of his mother, and he did not undergo any sort of spiritual training after his birth. At birth no one is qualified, neither in the mundane nor in the spiritual sense. But Śrī Śukadeva Gosvāmī, due to his being a perfectly liberated soul, did not have to undergo an evolutionary process for spiritual realization. Yet despite his being a completely liberated person situated in the transcendental position above the three material modes, he was attracted to this transcendental *rasa* of the Supreme Personality of Godhead, who is adored by liberated souls who sing Vedic hymns. The Supreme Lord's pastimes are more attractive to liberated souls than to mundane people. He is of necessity not impersonal because it is only possible to carry on transcendental *rasa* with a person.

In the *Śrīmad-Bhāgavatam* the transcendental pastimes of the Lord are narrated, and the narration is systematically depicted by Śrīla Śukadeva Gosvāmī. Thus the subject matter is appealing to all classes of persons, including those who seek liberation to relish the mellow of becoming one with the supreme whole.

In Sanskrit the parrot is also known as *śuka*. When a ripened fruit is cut by the red beaks of such birds, its sweet flavor is enhanced. The Vedic fruit which is mature and ripe in knowledge is spoken through the lips of Śrīla Śukadeva Gosvāmī, who is compared to the parrot not for his ability to recite the *Bhāgavatam* exactly as he heard it from his learned father, but for his ability to present the work in a manner that would appeal to all classes of men.

The subject matter is so presented through the lips of Śrīla Śukadeva Gosvāmī that any sincere listener that hears submissively can at once relish transcendental tastes which are distinct from the perverted tastes of the material world. The ripened fruit is not dropped all of a sudden from the highest planet of Kṛṣṇaloka. Rather, it has come down carefully through the chain of disciplic succession without change or disturbance. Foolish people who are not in the transcendental disciplic succession commit great blunders by trying to understand the highest transcendental *rasa* known as the *rāsa* dance without following in the footsteps of Śukadeva Gosvāmī, who presents this fruit very carefully by stages of transcendental realization. One should be intelligent enough to know the position of *Śrīmad-Bhāgavatam* by considering personalities like Śukadeva Gosvāmī, who deals with the subject so carefully. This process of disciplic succession of the *Bhāgavata* school suggests that in the future also, for all time, *Śrīmad-Bhāgavatam* has to be understood from a person who is factually a representative of Śrīla Śukadeva Gosvāmī. A professional man who makes a business out of reciting the *Bhāgavatam* illegally is certainly not a representative of Śukadeva Gosvāmī. Such a man's business is only to earn his livelihood. Therefore one should refrain from hearing the lectures of such professional men. Such men usually go to the most confidential part of the literature without undergoing the gradual process of understanding this grave subject. They usually plunge into the subject matter of the *rāsa* dance, which is misunderstood by the foolish class of men. Some of them take this to be immoral, while others try to cover it up by their own stupid interpretations. They have no desire to follow in the footsteps of Śrīla Śukadeva Gosvāmī.

One should conclude, therefore, that the serious student of the *rasa* should receive the message of *Bhāgavatam* in the chain of disciplic succession from Śrīla Śukadeva Gosvāmī, who describes the *Bhāgavatam* from its very beginning and not whimsically to satisfy the mundaner who has very little knowledge in transcendental science. *Śrīmad-Bhāgavatam* is so carefully presented that a sincere and serious person can at once enjoy the ripened fruit of Vedic knowledge simply by drinking the nectarean juice through the mouth of Śukadeva Gosvāmī or his bona fide representative.

TEXT 4

नैमिषेऽनिमिषक्षेत्रे ऋषयः शौनकादयः ।
सत्रं स्वर्गाय लोकाय सहस्रसममासत ॥ ४ ॥

naimiṣe 'nimiṣa-kṣetre ṛṣayaḥ śaunakādayaḥ
satraṁ svargāya lokāya sahasra-samam āsata

naimiṣe—in the forest known as Naimiṣāraṇya; *animiṣa-kṣetre*—the spot which is especially a favorite of Viṣṇu (who does not close His eyelids); *ṛṣayaḥ*—sages; *śaunaka-ādayaḥ*—headed by the sage Śaunaka; *satram*—sacrifice; *svargāya*—the Lord who is glorified in heaven; *lokāya*—and for the devotees who are always in touch with the Lord; *sahasra*—one thousand; *samam*—years; *āsata*—performed.

Once, in a holy place in the forest of Naimiṣāraṇya, great sages headed by the sage Śaunaka assembled to perform a great thousand-year sacrifice for the satisfaction of the Lord and His devotees.

PURPORT The prelude of the *Śrīmad-Bhāgavatam* was spoken in the previous three *ślokas*. Now the main topic of this great literature is being presented. *Śrīmad-Bhāgavatam,* after its first recitation by Śrīla Śukadeva Gosvāmī, was repeated for the second time at Naimiṣāraṇya.

In the *Vāyavīya Tantra,* it is said that Brahmā, the engineer of this particular universe, contemplated a great wheel which could enclose the universe. The hub of this great circle was fixed at a particular place known as Naimiṣāraṇya. Similarly, there is another reference to the forest of Naimiṣāraṇya in the *Varāha Purāṇa,* where it is stated that by performance of sacrifice at this place, the strength of demoniac people is curtailed. Thus *brāhmaṇas* prefer Naimiṣāraṇya for such sacrificial performances.

The devotees of Lord Viṣṇu offer all kinds of sacrifices for His pleasure. The devotees are always attached to the service of the Lord, whereas fallen souls are attached to the pleasures of material existence. In *Bhagavad-gītā,* it is said that anything performed in the material world for any reason other than for the pleasure of Lord Viṣṇu causes further bondage for the performer. It is enjoined therefore that all acts must be performed sacrificially for the satisfaction of Viṣṇu and His devotees. This will bring everyone peace and prosperity.

The great sages are always anxious to do good to the people in general, and as such the sages headed by Śaunaka and others assembled at this holy place of Naimiṣāraṇya with a program of performing a great and continuous chain of sacrificial ceremonies. Forgetful men do not know the right path for peace and prosperity. However, the sages know it well, and therefore for the good of all men they are always anxious to perform acts which may bring about peace in the world. They are sincere friends to all living entities, and at the risk of great personal inconvenience they are always engaged in the service of the Lord for the good of all people. Lord Viṣṇu is just like a great tree, and all others, including the demigods, men, Siddhas, Cāraṇas, Vidyādharas and other living entities, are like branches, twigs and leaves of that tree. By pouring water on the root of the tree, all the parts of the tree are automatically nourished. Only those branches and leaves which are detached cannot be so satisfied. Detached branches and leaves dry up gradually despite all watering attempts. Similarly, human society, when it is detached from the Personality of Godhead like detached branches and leaves, is not capable of being watered, and one attempting to do so is simply wasting his energy and resources.

The modern materialistic society is detached from its relation to the Supreme Lord. And all its plans which are being made by atheistic leaders are sure to be baffled at every step. Yet they do not wake up to this.

In this age, the congregational chanting of the holy names of the Lord is the prescribed method for waking up. The ways and means are most scientifically presented by Lord Śrī Caitanya Mahāprabhu, and intelligent persons may take advantage of His teachings in order to bring about real peace and prosperity. *Śrīmad-Bhāgavatam* is also presented for the same purpose, and this will be explained more specifically later in the text.

TEXT 5

त एकदा तु मुनयः प्रातर्हुतहुताग्नयः ।
सत्कृतं सूतमासीनं पप्रच्छुरिदमादरात् ॥ ५ ॥

ta ekadā tu munayaḥ prātar huta-hutāgnayaḥ
sat-kṛtaṁ sūtam āsīnaṁ papracchur idam ādarāt

te—the sages; *ekadā*—one day; *tu*—but; *munayaḥ*—sages; *prātaḥ*—morning; *huta*—burning; *huta-agnayaḥ*—the sacrificial fire; *sat-kṛtam*—due respects; *sūtam*—Śrī Sūta Gosvāmī; *āsīnam*—seated on; *papracchuḥ*—made inquiries; *idam*—on this (as follows); *ādarāt*—with due regards.

One day, after finishing their morning duties by burning a sacrificial fire and offering a seat of esteem to Śrīla Sūta Gosvāmī, the great sages made inquiries, with great respect, about the following matters.

PURPORT Morning is the best time to hold spiritual services. The great sages offered the speaker of the *Bhāgavatam* an elevated seat of respect called the *vyāsāsana*, or the seat of Śrī Vyāsadeva. Śrī Vyāsadeva is the original spiritual preceptor for all men. And all other preceptors are considered to be his representatives. A representative is one who can exactly present the viewpoint of Śrī Vyāsadeva. Śrī Vyāsadeva impregnated the message of *Bhāgavatam* unto Śrīla Śukadeva Gosvāmī, and Śrī Sūta Gosvāmī heard it from him (Śrī Śukadeva Gosvāmī). All bona fide representatives of Śrī Vyāsadeva in the chain of disciplic succession are to be understood to be *gosvāmīs*. These *gosvāmīs* restrain all their senses, and they stick to the path made by the previous *ācāryas.* The *gosvāmīs* do not deliver lectures on the *Bhāgavatam* capriciously. Rather, they execute their services most carefully, following their predecessors who delivered the spiritual message unbroken to them.

Those who listen to the *Bhāgavatam* may put questions to the speaker in order to elicit the clear meaning, but this should not be done in a challenging spirit. One must submit questions with a great regard for the speaker and the subject matter. This is also the way recommended in *Bhagavad-gītā.* One must learn the transcendental subject by submissive aural reception from the right sources. Therefore these sages addressed the speaker Sūta Gosvāmī with great respect.

ऋषय ऊचुः

TEXT 6

त्वया खलु पुराणानि सेतिहासानि चानघ ।
आख्यातान्यप्यधीतानि धर्मशास्त्राणि यान्युत ॥ ६ ॥

ṛṣaya ūcuḥ
tvayā khalu purāṇāni setihāsāni cānagha
ākhyātāny apy adhītāni dharma-śāstrāṇi yāny uta

ṛṣayaḥ—the sages; *ūcuḥ*—said; *tvayā*—by you; *khalu*—undoubtedly; *purāṇāni*—the supplements to the *Vedas* with illustrative narrations; *sa-itihāsāni*—along with the histories; *ca*—and; *anagha*—freed from all vices; *ākhyātāni*—explained; *api*—although; *adhītāni*—well read; *dharma-śāstrāṇi*—scriptures giving right directions to progressive life; *yāni*—all these; *uta*—said.

The sages said: Respected Sūta Gosvāmī, you are completely free from all vice. You are well versed in all the scriptures famous for religious life, and in the Purāṇas and the histories as well, for you have gone through them under proper guidance and have also explained them.

PURPORT A *gosvāmī,* or the bona fide representative of Śrī Vyāsadeva, must be free from all kinds of vices. The four major vices are (1) illicit connection with women, (2) animal slaughter, (3) intoxication, (4) speculative gambling of all sorts. A *gosvāmī* must be free from all these vices before he can dare sit on the *vyāsāsana.* No one should be allowed to sit on the *vyāsāsana* who is not spotless in character and who is not freed from the above-mentioned vices. He not only should be freed from all such vices, but must also be well versed in all revealed scriptures or in the *Vedas*. The *Purāṇas* are also parts of the *Vedas*. And histories like the *Mahābhārata* or *Rāmāyaṇa* are also parts of the *Vedas*. The *ācārya* or the *gosvāmī* must be well acquainted with all these literatures. To hear and explain them is more important than reading them. One can assimilate the knowledge of the revealed scriptures only by hearing and explaining. Hearing is called *śravaṇa*, and explaining is called *kīrtana*. The two processes of *śravaṇa* and *kīrtana* are of primary importance to progressive spiritual life. Only one who has properly grasped the transcendental knowledge from the right source by submissive hearing can properly explain the subject.

TEXT 7

यानि वेदविदां श्रेष्ठो भगवान् बादरायणः ।
अन्ये च मुनयः सूत परावरविदो विदुः ॥ ७ ॥

yāni veda-vidāṁ śreṣṭho bhagavān bādarāyaṇaḥ
anye ca munayaḥ sūta parāvara-vido viduḥ

yāni—all that; *veda-vidām*—scholars of the *Vedas; śreṣṭhaḥ*—seniormost; *bhagavān*—incarnation of Godhead; *bādarāyaṇaḥ*—Vyāsadeva; *anye*—others; *ca*—and; *munayaḥ*—the sages; *sūta*—O Sūta Gosvāmī; *parāvara-vidaḥ*—amongst the learned scholars, one who is conversant with physical and metaphysical knowledge; *viduḥ*—one who knows.

Being the eldest learned Vedāntist, O Sūta Gosvāmī, you are acquainted with the knowledge of Vyāsadeva, who is the incarnation of Godhead, and you also know other sages who are fully versed in all kinds of physical and metaphysical knowledge.

PURPORT The *Śrīmad-Bhāgavatam* is a natural commentation on the *Brahma-sūtra,* or the *Bādarāyaṇi Vedānta-sūtras.* It is called natural because Vyāsadeva is author of both the *Vedānta-sūtras* and *Śrīmad-Bhāgavatam,* or the essence of all Vedic literatures. Besides Vyāsadeva, there are other sages who are the authors of six different philosophical systems, namely Gautama, Kaṇāda, Kapila, Patañjali, Jaimini and Aṣṭāvakra. Theism is explained completely in the *Vedānta-sūtra,* whereas in other systems of philosophical speculations, practically no mention is given to the ultimate cause of all causes. One can sit on the *vyāsāsana* only after being conversant in all systems of philosophy so that one can present fully the theistic views of the *Bhāgavatam* in defiance of all other systems. Śrīla Sūta Gosvāmī was the proper teacher, and therefore the sages at Naimiṣāraṇya elevated him to the *vyāsāsana.* Śrīla Vyāsadeva is designated herein as the Personality of Godhead because he is the authorized empowered incarnation.

TEXT 8

वेत्थ त्वं सौम्य तत्सर्वं तत्त्वतस्तदनुग्रहात् ।
ब्रूयुः स्निग्धस्य शिष्यस्य गुरवो गुह्यमप्युत ॥ ८ ॥

vettha tvaṁ saumya tat sarvaṁ tattvatas tad-anugrahāt
brūyuḥ snigdhasya śiṣyasya guravo guhyam apy uta

vettha—you are well conversant; *tvam*—Your Honor; *saumya*—one who is pure and simple; *tat*—those; *sarvam*—all; *tattvataḥ*—in fact; *tat*—their; *anugrahāt*—by the favor of; *brūyuḥ*—will tell; *snigdhasya*—of the one who is submissive; *śiṣyasya*—of the disciple; *guravaḥ*—the spiritual masters; *guhyam*—secret; *api uta*—endowed with.

And because you are submissive, your spiritual masters have endowed you with all the favors bestowed upon a gentle disciple. Therefore you can tell us all that you have scientifically learned from them.

PURPORT The secret of success in spiritual life is in satisfying the spiritual master and thereby getting his sincere blessings. Śrīla Viśvanātha Cakravartī Ṭhākura has sung in his famous eight stanzas on the spiritual master as follows: "I offer my respectful obeisances unto the lotus feet of my spiritual master. Only by his satisfaction can one please the Personality of Godhead, and when he is dissatisfied there is only havoc on the path of spiritual realization." It is essential, therefore, that a disciple be very much obedient and submissive to the bona fide spiritual master. Śrīla Sūta Gosvāmī fulfilled all these qualifications as a disciple, and therefore he was endowed with all favors by his learned and self-realized spiritual masters such as Śrīla Vyāsadeva and others. The sages of Naimiṣāraṇya were confident that Śrīla Sūta Gosvāmī was bona fide. Therefore they were anxious to hear from him.

TEXT 9

तत्र तत्राञ्जसायुष्मन् भवता यद्विनिश्चितम् ।
पुंसामेकान्ततः श्रेयस्तन्नः शंसितुमर्हसि ॥ ९ ॥

tatra tatrāñjasāyuṣman bhavatā yad viniścitam
puṁsām ekāntataḥ śreyas tan naḥ śaṁsitum arhasi

tatra—thereof; *tatra*—thereof; *añjasā*—made easy; *āyuṣman*—blessed with a long duration of life; *bhavatā*—by your good self; *yat*—whatever; *viniścitam*—ascertained; *puṁsām*—for the people in general; *ekāntataḥ*—absolutely; *śreyaḥ*—ultimate good; *tat*—that; *naḥ*—to us; *śaṁsitum*—to explain; *arhasi*—deserve.

Please, therefore, being blessed with many years, explain to us, in an easily understandable way, what you have ascertained to be the absolute and ultimate good for the people in general.

PURPORT In *Bhagavad-gītā,* worship of the *ācārya* is recommended. The *ācāryas* and *gosvāmīs* are always absorbed in thought of the well-being of the general public, especially their spiritual well-being. Spiritual well-being is automatically followed by material well-being. The *ācāryas* therefore give directions in spiritual well-being for people in general. Foreseeing the incompetencies of the people in this age of Kali, or the iron age of quarrel, the sages requested that Sūta Gosvāmī give a summary of all revealed scriptures because the people of this age are condemned in every respect. The sages, therefore, inquired of the absolute good, which is the ultimate good for the people. The condemned state of affairs of the people of this age is described as follows.

TEXT 10

प्रायेणाल्पायुषः सभ्य कलावस्मिन् युगे जनाः ।
मन्दाः सुमन्दमतयो मन्दभाग्या ह्युपद्रुताः ॥ १० ॥

prāyeṇālpāyuṣaḥ sabhya kalāv asmin yuge janāḥ
mandāḥ sumanda-matayo manda-bhāgyā hy upadrutāḥ

prāyeṇa—almost always; *alpa*—meager; *āyuṣaḥ*—duration of life; *sabhya*—member of a learned society; *kalau*—in this age of Kali (quarrel); *asmin*—herein; *yuge*—age; *janāḥ*—the public; *mandāḥ*—lazy; *sumanda-matayaḥ*—misguided; *manda-bhāgyāḥ*—unlucky; *hi*—and above all; *upadrutāḥ*—disturbed.

O learned one, in this iron age of Kali men almost always have but short lives. They are quarrelsome, lazy, misguided, unlucky and, above all, always disturbed.

PURPORT The devotees of the Lord are always anxious for the spiritual improvement of the general public. When the sages of Naimiṣāraṇya analyzed the state of affairs of the people in this age of Kali, they foresaw that men would live short lives. In Kali-yuga, the duration of life is shortened not so much because of insufficient food but because of irregular habits. By keeping regular habits and eating simple food, any man can maintain his health. Overeating, over–sense gratification, overdependence on another's mercy, and artificial standards of living sap the very vitality of human energy. Therefore the duration of life is shortened.

The people of this age are also very lazy, not only materially but in the matter of self-realization. The human life is especially meant for self-realization. That is to say, man should come to know what he is, what the world is, and what the supreme truth is. Human life is a means by which the living entity can end all the miseries of the hard struggle for life in material existence and by which he can return to Godhead, his eternal home. But, due to a bad system of education, men have no desire for self-realization. Even if they come to know about it, they unfortunately become victims of misguided teachers.

In this age, men are victims not only of different political creeds and parties, but also of many different types of sense-gratificatory diversions, such as cinemas, sports, gambling, clubs, mundane libraries, bad association, smoking, drinking, cheating, pilfering, bickerings, and so on. Their minds are always disturbed and full of anxieties due to so many different engagements. In this age, many unscrupulous men manufacture their own religious faiths which are not based on any revealed scriptures, and very often people who are addicted to sense gratification are attracted by such institutions. Consequently, in the name of religion so many sinful acts are being carried on that the people in general have neither peace of mind nor health of body. The student (*brahmacārī*) communities are no longer being maintained, and householders do not observe the rules and regulations of the *gṛhastha-āśrama.* Consequently, the so-called *vānaprasthas* and *sannyāsīs* who come out of such *gṛhastha-āśramas* are easily deviated from the rigid path. In the Kali-yuga the whole atmosphere is surcharged with faithlessness. Men are no longer interested in spiritual values. Material sense gratification is now the standard of civilization. For the maintenance of such material civilizations, man has formed complex nations and communities, and there is a constant strain of hot and cold wars between these different groups. It has become very difficult, therefore, to raise the spiritual standard due to the present distorted values of human society. The sages of Naimiṣāraṇya are anxious to disentangle all fallen souls, and here they are seeking the remedy from Śrīla Sūta Gosvāmī.

TEXT 11

भूरीणि भूरिकर्माणि श्रोतव्यानि विभागशः ।
अतः साधोऽत्र यत्सारं समुद्धृत्य मनीषया ।
ब्रूहि भद्राय भूतानां येनात्मा सुप्रसीदति ॥ ११ ॥

bhūrīṇi bhūri-karmāṇi śrotavyāni vibhāgaśaḥ
ataḥ sādho 'tra yat sāraṁ samuddhṛtya manīṣayā
brūhi bhadrāya bhūtānāṁ yenātmā suprasīdati

bhūrīṇi—multifarious; *bhūri*—many; *karmāṇi*—duties; *śrotavyāni*—to be learned; *vibhāgaśaḥ*—by divisions of subject matter; *ataḥ*—therefore; *sādho*—O sage; *atra*—herein; *yat*—whatever; *sāram*—essence; *samuddhṛtya*—by selection; *manīṣayā*—to the best of your knowledge; *brūhi*—please tell us; *bhadrāya*—for the good of; *bhūtānām*—the living beings; *yena*—by which; *ātmā*—the self; *suprasīdati*—becomes fully satisfied.

There are many varieties of scriptures, and in all of them there are many prescribed duties, which can be learned only after many years

of study in their various divisions. Therefore, O sage, please select the essence of all these scriptures and explain it for the good of all living beings, that by such instruction their hearts may be fully satisfied.

PURPORT *Ātmā,* or self, is distinguished from matter and material elements. It is spiritual in constitution, and thus it is never satisfied by any amount of material planning. All scriptures and spiritual instructions are meant for the satisfaction of this self, or *ātmā.* There are many varieties of approaches which are recommended for different types of living beings in different times and at different places. Consequently, the numbers of revealed scriptures are innumerable. There are different methods and prescribed duties recommended in these various scriptures. Taking into consideration the fallen condition of the people in general in this age of Kali, the sages of Naimiṣāraṇya suggested that Śrī Sūta Gosvāmī relate the essence of all such scriptures because in this age it is not possible for the fallen souls to understand and undergo all the lessons of all these various scriptures in a *varṇa* and *āśrama* system.

The *varṇa* and *āśrama* society was considered to be the best institution for lifting the human being to the spiritual platform, but due to Kali-yuga it is not possible to execute the rules and regulations of these institutions. Nor is it possible for the people in general to completely sever relations with their families as the *varṇāśrama* institution prescribes. The whole atmosphere is surcharged with opposition. And considering this, one can see that spiritual emancipation for the common man in this age is very difficult. The reason the sages presented this matter to Śrī Sūta Gosvāmī is explained in the following verses.

TEXT 12

सूत जानासि भद्रं ते भगवान् सात्वतां पतिः ।
देवक्यां वसुदेवस्य जातो यस्य चिकीर्षया ॥ १२ ॥

sūta jānāsi bhadraṁ te bhagavān sātvatāṁ patiḥ
devakyāṁ vasudevasya jāto yasya cikīrṣayā

sūta—O Sūta Gosvāmī; *jānāsi*—you know; *bhadram te*—all blessings upon you; *bhagavān*—the Personality of Godhead; *sātvatām*—of the pure devotees; *patiḥ*—the protector; *devakyām*—in the womb of

Devakī; *vasudevasya*—by Vasudeva; *jātaḥ*—born of; *yasya*—for the purpose of; *cikīrṣayā*—executing.

All blessings upon you, O Sūta Gosvāmī. You know for what purpose the Personality of Godhead appeared in the womb of Devakī as the son of Vasudeva.

PURPORT *Bhagavān* means the Almighty God who is the controller of all opulences, power, fame, beauty, knowledge and renunciation. He is the protector of His pure devotees. Although God is equally disposed to everyone, He is especially inclined to His devotees. *Sat* means the Absolute Truth. And persons who are servitors of the Absolute Truth are called *sātvatas*. And the Personality of Godhead who protects such pure devotees is known as the protector of the *sātvatas*. *Bhadraṁ te*, or "blessings upon you," indicates the sages' anxiety to know the Absolute Truth from the speaker. Lord Śrī Kṛṣṇa, the Supreme Personality of Godhead, appeared to Devakī, the wife of Vasudeva. Vasudeva is the symbol of the transcendental position wherein the appearance of the Supreme Lord takes place.

TEXT 13

तन्नः शुश्रूषमाणानामर्हस्यङ्गानुवर्णितुम् ।
यस्यावतारो भूतानां क्षेमाय च भवाय च ॥ १३ ॥

tan naḥ śuśrūṣamāṇānām arhasy aṅgānuvarṇitum
yasyāvatāro bhūtānāṁ kṣemāya ca bhavāya ca

tat—those; *naḥ*—unto us; *śuśrūṣamāṇānām*—those who are endeavoring for; *arhasi*—ought to do it; *aṅga*—O Sūta Gosvāmī; *anuvarṇitum*—to explain by following in the footsteps of previous *ācāryas; yasya*—whose; *avatāraḥ*—incarnation; *bhūtānām*—of the living beings; *kṣemāya*—for good; *ca*—and; *bhavāya*—upliftment; *ca*—and.

O Sūta Gosvāmī, we are eager to learn about the Personality of Godhead and His incarnations. Please explain to us those teachings imparted by previous masters [ācāryas], for one is uplifted both by speaking them and by hearing them.

PURPORT The conditions for hearing the transcendental message of the Absolute Truth are set forth herein. The first condition is that the audience must be very sincere and eager to hear. And the speaker must be in the line of disciplic succession from the recognized *ācārya.* The transcendental message of the Absolute is not understandable by those who are materially absorbed. Under the direction of a bona fide spiritual master, one becomes gradually purified. Therefore, one must be in the chain of disciplic succession and learn the spiritual art of submissive hearing. In the case of Sūta Gosvāmī and the sages of Naimiṣāraṇya, all these conditions are fulfilled because Śrīla Sūta Gosvāmī is in the line of Śrīla Vyāsadeva, and the sages of Naimiṣāraṇya are all sincere souls who are anxious to learn the truth. Thus the transcendental topics of Lord Śrī Kṛṣṇa's superhuman activities, His incarnation, His birth, appearance or disappearance, His forms, His names and so on are all easily understandable because all requirements are fulfilled. Such discourses help all men on the path of spiritual realization.

TEXT 14

आपन्नः संसृतिं घोरां यन्नाम विवशो गृणन् ।
ततः सद्यो विमुच्येत यद्बिभेति स्वयं भयम् ॥ १४ ॥

āpannaḥ saṁsṛtiṁ ghorāṁ yan-nāma vivaśo gṛṇan
tataḥ sadyo vimucyeta yad bibheti svayaṁ bhayam

āpannaḥ—being entangled; *saṁsṛtim*—in the hurdle of birth and death; *ghorām*—too complicated; *yat*—what; *nāma*—the absolute name; *vivaśaḥ*—unconsciously; *gṛṇan*—chanting; *tataḥ*—from that; *sadyaḥ*—at once; *vimucyeta*—gets freedom; *yat*—that which; *bibheti*—fears; *svayam*—personally; *bhayam*—fear itself.

Living beings who are entangled in the complicated meshes of birth and death can be freed immediately by even unconsciously chanting the holy name of Kṛṣṇa, which is feared by fear personified.

PURPORT Vāsudeva, or Lord Kṛṣṇa, the Absolute Personality of Godhead, is the supreme controller of everything, and as such He is feared by all others. There is no one in creation who is not afraid of the rage of the

Almighty. Great *asuras* like Rāvaṇa, Hiraṇyakaśipu, Kaṁsa, and others who were very powerful living entities were all killed by the Personality of Godhead. And the almighty Vāsudeva has empowered His name with the powers of His personal Self. Everything directly related to Him is identical with Him. It is stated herein that the name of Kṛṣṇa is feared even by fear personified. This indicates that the name of Kṛṣṇa is nondifferent from Kṛṣṇa. Therefore, the name of Kṛṣṇa is as powerful as Lord Kṛṣṇa Himself. There is no difference at all. Anyone, therefore, can take advantage of the holy names of Lord Śrī Kṛṣṇa even in the midst of the greatest dangers. The transcendental name of Kṛṣṇa, even though uttered unconsciously or by force of circumstances, can help one obtain freedom from the hurdle of birth and death.

TEXT 15

यत्पादसंश्रयाः सूत मुनयः प्रशमायनाः ।
सद्यः पुनन्त्युपस्पृष्टाः स्वर्धुन्यापोऽनुसेवया ॥ १५ ॥

yat-pāda-saṁśrayāḥ sūta munayaḥ praśamāyanāḥ
sadyaḥ punanty upaspṛṣṭāḥ svardhuny-āpo 'nusevayā

yat—whose; *pāda*—lotus feet; *saṁśrayāḥ*—those who have taken shelter of; *sūta*—O Sūta Gosvāmī; *munayaḥ*—great sages; *praśamāyanāḥ*—absorbed in devotion to the Supreme; *sadyaḥ*—at once; *punanti*—sanctify; *upaspṛṣṭāḥ*—simply by association; *svardhunī*—of the sacred Ganges; *āpaḥ*—water; *anusevayā*—bringing into use.

O Sūta, those great sages who have completely taken shelter of the lotus feet of the Lord can at once sanctify those who come in touch with them, whereas the waters of the Ganges can sanctify only after prolonged use.

PURPORT Pure devotees of the Lord are more powerful than the waters of the sacred river Ganges. One can derive spiritual benefit out of prolonged use of the Ganges waters. But one can be sanctified at once by the mercy of a pure devotee of the Lord. In *Bhagavad-gītā* it is said that any person, regardless of birth as *śūdra*, woman, or merchant, can take shelter of the lotus feet of the Lord and by so doing can return to Godhead. To take shelter of the lotus feet of the Lord means to take shelter of the pure devotees. The pure devotees whose only business is serving are honored by the names Prabhupāda and Viṣṇupāda, which indicate such devotees to be representatives of the lotus feet of the Lord. Anyone, therefore, who takes shelter of the lotus feet of a pure devotee by accepting the pure devotee as his spiritual master can be at once purified. Such devotees of the Lord are honored equally with the Lord because they are engaged in the most confidential service of the Lord, for they deliver out of the material world the fallen souls whom the Lord wants to return home, back to Godhead. Such pure devotees are better known as vicelords according to revealed scriptures. The sincere disciples of a pure devotee consider him equal with the Lord, but the pure devotee always considers himself to be a humble servant of the servant of the Lord. This is the pure devotional path.

TEXT 16

को वा भगवतस्तस्य पुण्यश्लोकेड्यकर्मणः ।
शुद्धिकामो न शृणुयाद्यशः कलिमलापहम् ॥ १६ ॥

ko vā bhagavatas tasya puṇya-ślokeḍya-karmaṇaḥ
śuddhi-kāmo na śṛṇuyād yaśaḥ kali-malāpaham

kaḥ—who; *vā*—rather; *bhagavataḥ*—of the Lord; *tasya*—His; *puṇya*—virtuous; *śloka-īḍya*—worshipable by prayers; *karmaṇaḥ*—deeds; *śuddhi-kāmaḥ*—desiring deliverance from all sins; *na*—not; *śṛṇuyāt*—does hear; *yaśaḥ*—glories; *kali*—of the age of quarrel; *mala-apaham*—the agent for sanctification.

Who is there, desiring deliverance from the vices of the age of quarrel, who is not willing to hear the virtuous glories of the Lord?

PURPORT The age of Kali is the most condemned age due to its quarrelsome features. Kali-yuga is so saturated with vicious habits that there is a great fight at the slightest misunderstanding. Those who are engaged in the pure devotional service of the Lord, who are without any desire for self-aggrandizement and who are freed from the effects of fruitive actions and dry philosophical speculations are capable of getting out of the estrangements of this complicated age. The leaders of the people are very much anxious to live in peace and friendship, but they have no information of the simple method of hearing the glories of the Lord. On the contrary, such leaders are opposed to the propagation of the glories of the Lord. In other words, the foolish leaders want to completely deny the existence of the Lord. In the name of secular state, such leaders are enacting various plans every year. But by the insurmountable intricacies of the material nature of the Lord, all these plans for progress are being constantly frustrated. They have no eyes to see that their attempts at peace and friendship are failing. But here is the hint to get over the hurdle. If we want actual peace, we must open the road to understanding of the Supreme Lord Kṛṣṇa and glorify Him for His virtuous activities as they are depicted in the pages of *Śrīmad-Bhāgavatam*.

TEXT 17

तस्य कर्माण्युदाराणि परिगीतानि सूरिभिः ।
ब्रूहि नः श्रद्दधानानां लीलया दधतः कलाः ॥ १७ ॥

tasya karmāṇy udārāṇi parigītāni sūribhiḥ
brūhi naḥ śraddadhānānāṁ līlayā dadhataḥ kalāḥ

tasya—His; *karmāṇi*—transcendental acts; *udārāṇi*—magnanimous; *parigītāni*—broadcast; *sūribhiḥ*—by the great souls; *brūhi*—please speak; *naḥ*—unto us; *śraddadhānānām*—ready to receive with respect; *līlayā*—pastimes; *dadhataḥ*—advented; *kalāḥ*—incarnations.

His transcendental acts are magnificent and gracious, and great learned sages like Nārada sing of them. Please, therefore, speak to us, who are eager to hear, about the adventures He performs in His various incarnations.

PURPORT The Personality of Godhead is never inactive as some less intelligent persons suggest. His works are magnificent and magnanimous. His creations both material and spiritual are all wonderful and contain all variegatedness. They are described nicely by such liberated souls as Śrīla Nārada, Vyāsa, Vālmīki, Devala, Asita, Madhva, Śrī Caitanya, Rāmānuja, Viṣṇu Svāmī, Nimbārka, Śrīdhara, Viśvanātha, Baladeva, Bhaktivinoda, Siddhānta Sarasvatī and many other learned and self-realized souls. These creations, both material and spiritual, are full of opulence, beauty and knowledge, but the spiritual realm is more magnificent due to its being full of knowledge, bliss and eternity. The material creations are manifested for some time as perverted shadows of the spiritual kingdom and can be likened to cinemas. They attract people of less intelligent caliber who are attracted by false things. Such foolish men have no information of the reality, and they take it for granted that the false material manifestation is the all in all. But more intelligent men guided by sages like Vyāsa and Nārada know that the eternal kingdom of God is more delightful, larger, and eternally full of bliss and knowledge. Those who are not conversant with the activities of the Lord and His transcendental realm are sometimes favored by the Lord in His adventures as incarnations wherein He displays the eternal bliss of His association in the transcendental realm. By such activities He attracts the conditioned souls of the material world. Some of these conditioned souls are engaged in the false enjoyment of material senses and others in simply negating their real life in the spiritual world. These less intelligent persons are known as *karmīs,* or fruitive workers, and *jñānīs,* or dry mental speculators. But above these two classes of men is the transcendentalist known as *sātvata,* or the devotee, who is busy neither with rampant material activity nor with material speculation. He is engaged in the positive service of the Lord, and thereby he derives the highest spiritual benefit unknown to the *karmīs* and *jñānīs.*

As the supreme controller of both the material and spiritual worlds, the Lord has different incarnations of unlimited categories. Incarnations like Brahmā, Rudra, Manu, Pṛthu and Vyāsa are His material qualitative incarnations, but His incarnations like Rāma, Narasiṁha, Varāha and Vāmana are His transcendental incarnations. Lord Śrī Kṛṣṇa is the fountainhead of all incarnations, and He is therefore the cause of all causes.

TEXT 18

अथाख्याहि हरेर्धीमन्नवतारकथाः शुभाः ।
लीला विदधतः स्वैरमीश्वरस्यात्ममायया ॥ १८ ॥

athākhyāhi harer dhīmann avatāra-kathāḥ śubhāḥ
līlā vidadhataḥ svairam īśvarasyātma-māyayā

atha—therefore; *ākhyāhi*—describe; *hareḥ*—of the Lord; *dhīman*—O sagacious one; *avatāra*—incarnations; *kathāḥ*—narratives; *śubhāḥ*—auspicious; *līlā*—adventures; *vidadhataḥ*—performed; *svairam*—pastimes; *īśvarasya*—of the supreme controller; *ātma*—personal; *māyayā*—energies.

O wise Sūta, please narrate to us the transcendental pastimes of the Supreme Godhead's multi-incarnations. Such auspicious adventures and pastimes of the Lord, the supreme controller, are performed by His internal powers.

PURPORT For the creation, maintenance and destruction of the material worlds, the Supreme Lord Personality of Godhead Himself appears in many thousands of forms of incarnations, and the specific adventures found in those transcendental forms are all auspicious. Both those who are present during such activities and those who hear the transcendental narrations of such activities are benefited.

TEXT 19

वयं तु न वितृप्याम उत्तमश्लोकविक्रमे ।
यच्छृण्वतां रसज्ञानां स्वादु स्वादु पदे पदे ॥ १९ ॥

vayaṁ tu na vitṛpyāma uttama-śloka-vikrame
yac-chṛṇvatāṁ rasa-jñānāṁ svādu svādu pade pade

vayam—we; *tu*—but; *na*—not; *vitṛpyāmaḥ*—shall be at rest; *uttama-śloka*—the Personality of Godhead, who is glorified by transcendental prayers; *vikrame*—adventures; *yat*—which; *śṛṇvatām*—by continuous hearing; *rasa*—humor; *jñānām*—those who are conversant with; *svādu*—relishing; *svādu*—palatable; *pade pade*—at every step.

We never tire of hearing the transcendental pastimes of the Personality of Godhead, who is glorified by hymns and prayers. Those who have developed a taste for transcendental relationships with Him relish hearing of His pastimes at every moment.

PURPORT There is a great difference between mundane stories, fiction, or history and the transcendental pastimes of the Lord. The histories of the whole universe contain references to the pastimes of the incarnations of the Lord. The *Rāmāyaṇa,* the *Mahābhārata,* and the *Purāṇas* are histories of bygone ages recorded in connection with the pastimes of the incarnations of the Lord and therefore remain fresh even after repeated readings. For example, anyone may read *Bhagavad-gītā* or the *Śrīmad-Bhāgavatam* repeatedly throughout his whole life and yet find in them new light of information. Mundane news is static whereas transcendental news is dynamic, inasmuch as the spirit is dynamic and matter is static. Those who have developed a taste for understanding the transcendental subject matter are never tired of hearing such narrations. One is quickly satiated by mundane activities, but no one is satiated by transcendental or devotional activities. *Uttama-śloka* indicates that literature which is not meant for nescience. Mundane literature is in the mode of darkness or ignorance, whereas transcendental literature is quite different. Transcendental literature is above the mode of darkness, and its light becomes more luminous with progressive reading and realization of the transcendental subject matter. The so-called liberated persons are never satisfied by the repetition of the words *ahaṁ brahmāsmi.* Such artificial realization of Brahman becomes hackneyed, and so to relish real pleasure they turn to the narrations of the *Śrīmad-Bhāgavatam.* Those who are not so fortunate turn to altruism and worldly philanthropy. This means the Māyāvāda philosophy is mundane, whereas the philosophy of *Bhagavad-gītā* and *Śrīmad-Bhāgavatam* is transcendental.

TEXT 20

कृतवान् किल कर्माणि सह रामेण केशवः ।
अतिमर्त्यानि भगवान् गूढः कपटमानुषः ॥ २० ॥

kṛtavān kila karmāṇi saha rāmeṇa keśavaḥ
atimartyāni bhagavān gūḍhaḥ kapaṭa-mānuṣaḥ

kṛtavān—done by; *kila*—what; *karmāṇi*—acts; *saha*—along with; *rāmeṇa*—Balarāma; *keśavaḥ*—Śrī Kṛṣṇa; *atimartyāni*—superhuman; *bhagavān*—the Personality of Godhead; *gūḍhaḥ*—masked as; *kapaṭa*—apparently; *mānuṣaḥ*—human being.

Lord Śrī Kṛṣṇa, the Personality of Godhead, along with Balarāma,

played like a human being, and so masked He performed many superhuman acts.

PURPORT The doctrines of anthropomorphism and zoomorphism are never applicable to Śrī Kṛṣṇa, or the Personality of Godhead. The theory that a man becomes God by dint of penance and austerities is very much rampant nowadays, especially in India. Since Lord Rāma, Lord Kṛṣṇa and Lord Caitanya Mahāprabhu were detected by the sages and saints to be the Personality of Godhead as indicated in revealed scriptures, many unscrupulous men have created their own incarnations. This process of concocting an incarnation of God has become an ordinary business, especially in Bengal. Any popular personality with a few traits of mystic powers will display some feat of jugglery and easily become an incarnation of Godhead by popular vote. Lord Śrī Kṛṣṇa was not that type of incarnation. He was actually the Personality of Godhead from the very beginning of His appearance. He appeared before His so-called mother as four-armed Viṣṇu. Then, at the request of the mother, He became like a human child and at once left her for another devotee at Gokula, where He was accepted as the son of Nanda Mahārāja and Yaśodā Mātā. Similarly, Śrī Baladeva, the counterpart of Lord Śrī Kṛṣṇa, was also considered a human child born of another wife of Śrī Vasudeva. In *Bhagavad-gītā,* the Lord says that His birth and deeds are transcendental and that anyone who is so fortunate as to know the transcendental nature of His birth and deeds will at once become liberated and eligible to return to the kingdom of God. So knowledge of the transcendental nature of the birth and deeds of Lord Śrī Kṛṣṇa is sufficient for liberation. In the *Bhāgavatam,* the transcendental nature of the Lord is described in nine cantos, and in the Tenth Canto His specific pastimes are taken up. All this becomes known as one's reading of this literature progresses. It is important to note here, however, that the Lord exhibited His divinity even from the lap of His mother, that His deeds are all superhuman (He lifted Govardhana Hill at the age of seven), and that all these acts definitely prove Him to be actually the Supreme Personality of Godhead. Yet, due to His mystic covering, He was always accepted as an ordinary human child by His so-called father and mother and other relatives. Whenever some herculean task was performed by Him, the father and mother took it otherwise. And they remained satisfied with unflinching parental love for their son. As such, the sages of Naimiṣāraṇya describe Him as apparently resembling a human being, but actually He is the supreme almighty Personality of Godhead.

TEXT 21

कलिमागतमाज्ञाय क्षेत्रेऽस्मिन् वैष्णवे वयम् ।
आसीना दीर्घसत्रेण कथायां सक्षणा हरेः ॥ २१ ॥

kalim āgatam ājñāya kṣetre 'smin vaiṣṇave vayam
āsīnā dīrgha-satreṇa kathāyāṁ sakṣaṇā hareḥ

kalim—the age of Kali (iron age of quarrel); *āgatam*—having arrived; *ājñāya*—knowing this; *kṣetre*—in this tract of land; *asmin*—in this; *vaiṣṇave*—specially meant for the devotee of the Lord; *vayam*—we; *āsīnāḥ*—seated; *dīrgha*—prolonged; *satreṇa*—for performance of sacrifices; *kathāyām*—in the words of; *sa-kṣaṇāḥ*—with time at our disposal; *hareḥ*—of the Personality of Godhead.

Knowing well that the age of Kali has already begun, we are assembled here in this holy place to hear at great length the transcendental message of Godhead and in this way perform sacrifice.

PURPORT This age of Kali is not at all suitable for self-realization by the methods practiced in Satya-yuga, the golden age, or Tretā- or Dvāpara-yugas, the silver and copper ages. For self-realization, the people in Satya-yuga, living a lifetime of a hundred thousand years, were able to perform prolonged meditation. And in Tretā-yuga, when the duration of life was ten thousand years, self-realization was attained by performance of great sacrifice. And in the Dvāpara-yuga, when the duration of life was one thousand years, self-realization was attained by worship of the Lord. But in the Kali-yuga, the maximum duration of life being one hundred years only and that combined with various difficulties, the recommended process of self-realization is that of hearing and chanting of the holy name, fame, and pastimes of the Lord. The sages of Naimiṣāraṇya began this process in a place meant specifically for the devotees of the Lord. They prepared themselves to hear the pastimes of the Lord over a period of one thousand years. By the example of these sages one should learn that regular hearing and recitation of the *Bhāgavatam* is the only way for self-realization. Other attempts are simply a waste of time, for they do not give any tangible results. Lord Śrī Caitanya Mahāprabhu preached this system of *Bhāgavata-dharma*, and He recommended that all those who were born in India should take the responsibility of broadcasting the messages of Lord Śrī Kṛṣṇa, primarily the message of *Bhagavad-gītā*. And when one is well established in the teachings of *Bhagavad-gītā*, he can take up the study of *Śrīmad-Bhāgavatam* for further enlightenment in self-realization.

TEXT 22

त्वं नः सन्दर्शितो धात्रा दुस्तरं निस्तितीर्षताम् ।
कलिं सत्त्वहरं पुंसां कर्णधार इवार्णवम् ॥ २२ ॥

tvaṁ naḥ sandarśito dhātrā dustaraṁ nistitīrṣatām
kaliṁ sattva-haraṁ puṁsāṁ karṇa-dhāra ivārṇavam

tvam—Your Goodness; *naḥ*—unto us; *sandarśitaḥ*—meeting; *dhātrā*—by providence; *dustaram*—insurmountable; *nistitīrṣatām*—for those desiring to cross over; *kalim*—the age of Kali; *sattva-haram*—that which deteriorates the good qualities; *puṁsām*—of a man; *karṇa-dhāraḥ*—captain; *iva*—as; *arṇavam*—the ocean.

We think that we have met Your Goodness by the will of providence, just so that we may accept you as captain of the ship for those who desire to cross the difficult ocean of Kali, which deteriorates all the good qualities of a human being.

PURPORT The age of Kali is very dangerous for the human being. Human life is simply meant for self-realization, but due to this dangerous age, men have completely forgotten the aim of life. In this age, the life span will gradually decrease. People will gradually lose their memory, finer sentiments, strength, and better qualities. A list of the anomalies for this age is given in the Twelfth Canto of this work. And so this age is very difficult for those who want to utilize this life for self-realization. The people are so busy with sense gratification that they completely forget about self-realization. Out of madness they frankly say that there is no need for self-realization because they do not realize that this brief life is but a moment on our great journey towards self-realization. The whole system of education is geared to sense gratification, and if a learned man thinks it over, he sees that the children of this age are being intentionally sent to the slaughterhouses of so-called education. Learned men, therefore, must be cautious of this age, and if they at all want to cross over the dangerous ocean of Kali, they must follow the footsteps of the sages of Naimiṣāraṇya and accept Śrī Sūta Gosvāmī or his bona fide representative as the captain of the ship. The ship is the message of Lord Śrī Kṛṣṇa in the shape of *Bhagavad-gītā* or the *Śrīmad-Bhāgavatam.*

TEXT 23

ब्रूहि योगेश्वरे कृष्णे ब्रह्मण्ये धर्मवर्मणि ।
स्वां काष्ठामधुनोपेते धर्मः कं शरणं गतः ॥ २३ ॥

brūhi yogeśvare kṛṣṇe brahmaṇye dharma-varmaṇi
svāṁ kāṣṭhām adhunopete dharmaḥ kaṁ śaraṇaṁ gataḥ

brūhi—please tell; *yoga-īśvare*—the Lord of all mystic powers; *kṛṣṇe*—Lord Kṛṣṇa; *brahmaṇye*—the Absolute Truth; *dharma*—religion; *varmaṇi*—protector; *svām*—own; *kāṣṭhām*—abode; *adhunā*—nowadays; *upete*—having gone away; *dharmaḥ*—religion; *kam*—unto whom; *śaraṇam*—shelter; *gataḥ*—gone.

Since Śrī Kṛṣṇa, the Absolute Truth, the master of all mystic powers, has departed for His own abode, please tell us to whom the religious principles have now gone for shelter.

PURPORT Religion consists of the prescribed codes enunciated by the Personality of Godhead Himself. Whenever there is gross misuse or neglect of the principles of religion, the Supreme Lord appears Himself to restore religious principles. This is stated in *Bhagavad-gītā* (4.8). Here the sages of Naimiṣāraṇya are inquiring about these principles. The reply to this question is given later. The *Śrīmad-Bhāgavatam* is the transcendental sound representation of the Personality of Godhead, and thus it is the full representation of transcendental knowledge and religious principles.

Thus end the Bhaktivedanta purports of the First Canto, First Chapter, of the Śrīmad-Bhāgavatam, *entitled "Questions by the Sages."*

CHAPTER TWO

Divinity and Divine Service

व्यास उवाच

TEXT 1
इति सम्प्रश्नसंहृष्टो विप्राणां रौमहर्षणिः ।
प्रतिपूज्य वचस्तेषां प्रवक्तुमुपचक्रमे ॥ १ ॥

vyāsa uvāca
iti sampraśna-saṁhṛṣṭo viprāṇāṁ raumaharṣaṇiḥ
pratipūjya vacas teṣāṁ pravaktum upacakrame

vyāsaḥ uvāca—Vyāsa said; *iti*—thus; *sampraśna*—perfect inquiries; *saṁhṛṣṭaḥ*—perfectly satisfied; *viprāṇām*—of the sages there; *raumaharṣaṇiḥ*—the son of Romaharṣaṇa, namely Ugraśravā; *pratipūjya*—after thanking them; *vacaḥ*—words; *teṣām*—their; *pravaktum*—to reply to them; *upacakrame*—attempted.

Ugraśravā [Sūta Gosvāmī], the son of Romaharṣaṇa, being fully satisfied by the perfect questions of the brāhmaṇas, thanked them and thus attempted to reply.

PURPORT The sages of Naimiṣāraṇya asked Sūta Gosvāmī six questions, and so he is answering them one by one.

सूत उवाच

TEXT 2
यं प्रव्रजन्तमनुपेतमपेतकृत्यं
द्वैपायनो विरहकातर आजुहाव ।
पुत्रेति तन्मयतया तरवोऽभिनेदुस्
तं सर्वभूतहृदयं मुनिमानतोऽस्मि ॥ २ ॥

sūta uvāca
yaṁ pravrajantam anupetam apeta-kṛtyaṁ
dvaipāyano viraha-kātara ājuhāva

putreti tan-mayatayā taravo 'bhinedus
taṁ sarva-bhūta-hṛdayaṁ munim ānato 'smi

sūtaḥ—Sūta Gosvāmī; *uvāca*—said; *yam*—whom; *pravrajantam*—while going away for the renounced order of life; *anupetam*—without being reformed by the sacred thread; *apeta*—not undergoing ceremonies; *kṛtyam*—prescribed duties; *dvaipāyanaḥ*—Vyāsadeva; *viraha*—separation; *kātaraḥ*—being afraid of; *ājuhāva*—exclaimed; *putra iti*—O my son; *tat-mayatayā*—being absorbed in that way; *taravaḥ*—all the trees; *abhineduḥ*—responded; *tam*—unto him; *sarva*—all; *bhūta*—living entities; *hṛdayam*—heart; *munim*—sage; *ānataḥ asmi*—offer obeisances.

Śrīla Sūta Gosvāmī said: Let me offer my respectful obeisances unto that great sage [Śukadeva Gosvāmī] who can enter the hearts of all. When he went away to take up the renounced order of life [sannyāsa], leaving home without undergoing reformation by the sacred thread or the ceremonies observed by the higher castes, his father, Vyāsadeva, fearing separation from him, cried out, "O my son!" Indeed, only the trees, which were absorbed in the same feelings of separation, echoed in response to the begrieved father.

PURPORT The institution of *varṇa* and *āśrama* prescribes many regulative duties to be observed by its followers. Such duties enjoin that a candidate willing to study the *Vedas* must approach a bona fide spiritual master and request acceptance as his disciple. The sacred thread is the sign of those who are competent to study the *Vedas* from the *ācārya,* or the bona fide spiritual master. Śrī Śukadeva Gosvāmī did not undergo such purificatory ceremonies because he was a liberated soul from his very birth.

Generally, a man is born as an ordinary being, and by the purificatory processes he is born for the second time. When he sees a new light and seeks direction for spiritual progress, he approaches a spiritual master for instruction in the *Vedas.* The spiritual master accepts only the sincere inquirer as his disciple and gives him the sacred thread. In this way a man becomes twice-born, or a *dvija.* After qualifying as a *dvija* one may study the *Vedas,* and after becoming well versed in the *Vedas* one becomes a *vipra.* A *vipra,* or a qualified *brāhmaṇa,* thus realizes the Absolute and makes further progress in spiritual life until he reaches the Vaiṣṇava stage.

The Vaiṣṇava stage is the postgraduate status of a *brāhmaṇa*. A progressive *brāhmaṇa* must necessarily become a Vaiṣṇava, for a Vaiṣṇava is a self-realized, learned *brāhmaṇa*.

Śrīla Śukadeva Gosvāmī was a Vaiṣṇava from the beginning; therefore, there was no need for him to undergo all the processes of the *varṇāśrama* institution. Ultimately the aim of *varṇāśrama-dharma* is to turn a crude man into a pure devotee of the Lord, or a Vaiṣṇava. Anyone, therefore, who becomes a Vaiṣṇava accepted by the first-class Vaiṣṇava, or *uttama-adhikārī* Vaiṣṇava, is already considered a *brāhmaṇa,* regardless of his birth due to his past deeds. Śrī Caitanya Mahāprabhu accepted this principle and recognized Śrīla Haridāsa Ṭhākura as the *ācārya* of the holy name, although Ṭhākura Haridāsa appeared in a Mohammedan family. In conclusion, Śrīla Śukadeva Gosvāmī was born a Vaiṣṇava, and, therefore, brahminism was included in him. He did not have to undergo any ceremonies. Any lowborn person—be he a Kirāta, Hūṇa, Āndhra, Pulinda, Pulkaśa, Ābhīra, Śumbha, Yavana, Khasa or even lower—can be delivered to the highest transcendental position by the mercy of Vaiṣṇavas. Śrīla Śukadeva Gosvāmī was the instructing spiritual master of Śrī Sūta Gosvāmī, who therefore offers his respectful obeisances unto Śrīla Śukadeva Gosvāmī before he begins his answers to the questions of the sages at Naimiṣāraṇya.

TEXT 3

यः स्वानुभावमखिलश्रुतिसारमेकम्
अध्यात्मदीपमतितितीर्षतां तमोऽन्धम् ।
संसारिणां करुणयाह पुराणगुह्यं
तं व्याससूनुमुपयामि गुरुं मुनीनाम् ॥ ३ ॥

yaḥ svānubhāvam akhila-śruti-sāram ekam
adhyātma-dīpam atititīrṣatāṁ tamo 'ndham
saṁsāriṇāṁ karuṇayāha purāṇa-guhyaṁ
taṁ vyāsa-sūnum upayāmi guruṁ munīnām

yaḥ—he who; *sva-anubhāvam*—self-assimilated (experienced); *akhila*—all around; *śruti*—the *Vedas; sāram*—cream; *ekam*—the only one; *adhyātma*—transcendental; *dīpam*—torchlight; *atititīrṣatām*—desiring to overcome; *tamaḥ andham*—deeply dark material existence; *saṁsāriṇām*—of the materialistic men; *karuṇayā*—out of causeless mercy; *āha*—said; *purāṇa*—supplement to the *Vedas; guhyam*—very confidential; *tam*—unto him; *vyāsa-sūnum*—the son of Vyāsadeva; *upayāmi*—let me offer my obeisances; *gurum*—the spiritual master; *munīnām*—of the great sages.

Let me offer my respectful obeisances unto him [Śuka], the spiritual master of all sages, the son of Vyāsadeva, who, out of his great compassion for those gross materialists who struggle to cross over the darkest regions of material existence, spoke this most confidential supplement to the cream of Vedic knowledge, after having personally assimilated it by experience.

PURPORT In this prayer, Śrīla Sūta Gosvāmī practically summarizes the complete introduction of *Śrīmad-Bhāgavatam. Śrīmad-Bhāgavatam* is the natural supplementary commentary on the *Vedānta-sūtras.* The *Vedānta-sūtras,* or the *Brahma-sūtras,* were compiled by Vyāsadeva with a view to presenting just the cream of Vedic knowledge. *Śrīmad-Bhāgavatam* is the natural commentary on this cream. Śrīla Śukadeva Gosvāmī was a thoroughly realized master of the *Vedānta-sūtra,* and consequently he also personally realized the commentary, *Śrīmad-Bhāgavatam.* And just to show his boundless mercy upon bewildered materialistic men who want to cross completely over nescience, he recited for the first time this confidential knowledge.

There is no point in arguing that a materialistic man can be happy. No materialistic creature—be he the great Brahmā or an insignificant ant—can be happy. Everyone tries to make a permanent plan for happiness, but everyone is baffled by the laws of material nature. Therefore the materialistic world is called the darkest region of God's creation. Yet the unhappy materialists can get out of it simply by desiring to get out. Unfortunately they are so foolish that they do not want to escape. Therefore they are compared to the camel who relishes thorny twigs because he likes the taste of the twigs mixed with blood. He does not realize that it is his own blood and that his tongue is being cut by the thorns. Similarly, to the materialist his own blood is as sweet as honey, and although he is always harassed by his own material creations, he does not wish to escape. Such materialists are called *karmīs.* Out of hundreds of thousands of *karmīs,* only a few may feel tired of material engagement and desire to get out of the labyrinth. Such intelligent persons are called *jñānīs*. The *Vedānta-sūtra* is directed to such *jñānīs*. But Śrīla Vyāsadeva, being the incarnation of the Supreme Lord, could foresee the misuse of the *Vedānta-sūtra* by unscrupulous men, and, therefore, he personally supplemented the *Vedānta-sūtra* with the *Bhāgavata Purāṇa*. It is clearly said that this *Bhāgavatam* is the original commentary on the *Brahma-sūtras*. Śrīla Vyāsadeva also instructed the *Bhāgavatam* to his own son, Śrīla Śukadeva Gosvāmī, who was already at the liberated stage of transcendence. Śrīla Śukadeva realized it personally and then explained it. By the mercy of Śrīla Śukadeva, the *Bhāgavata-vedānta-sūtra* is available for all those sincere souls who want to get out of material existence.

Śrīmad-Bhāgavatam is the one unrivaled commentary on *Vedānta-sūtra*. Śrīpāda Śaṅkarācārya intentionally did not touch it because he knew that the natural commentary would be difficult for him to surpass. He wrote his *Śārīraka-bhāṣya*, and his so-called followers deprecated the *Bhāgavatam* as some "new" presentation. One should not be misled by such propaganda directed against the *Bhāgavatam* by the Māyāvāda school. From this introductory *śloka*, the beginning student should know that *Śrīmad-Bhāgavatam* is the only transcendental literature meant for those who are *paramahaṁsas* and completely freed from the material disease called malice. The Māyāvādīs are envious of the Personality of Godhead despite Śrīpāda Śaṅkarācārya's admission that Nārāyaṇa, the Personality of Godhead, is above the material creation. The envious Māyāvādī cannot have access to the *Bhāgavatam*, but those who are really anxious to get out of this material existence may take shelter of this *Bhāgavatam* because it is uttered by the liberated Śrīla Śukadeva Gosvāmī. It is the transcendental torchlight by which one can see perfectly the transcendental Absolute Truth realized as Brahman, Paramātmā and Bhagavān.

TEXT 4

नारायणं नमस्कृत्य नरं चैव नरोत्तमम् ।
देवीं सरस्वतीं व्यासं ततो जयमुदीरयेत् ॥ ४ ॥

nārāyaṇaṁ namaskṛtya naraṁ caiva narottamam
devīṁ sarasvatīṁ vyāsaṁ tato jayam udīrayet

nārāyaṇam—the Personality of Godhead; *namaḥ-kṛtya*—after offering respectful obeisances; *naram ca eva*—and Nārāyaṇa Ṛṣi;

nara-uttamam—the supermost human being; *devīm*—the goddess; *sarasvatīm*—the mistress of learning; *vyāsam*—Vyāsadeva; *tataḥ*—thereafter; *jayam*—all that is meant for conquering; *udīrayet*—be announced.

Before reciting this Śrīmad-Bhāgavatam, which is the very means of conquest, one should offer respectful obeisances unto the Personality of Godhead, Nārāyaṇa, unto Nara-nārāyaṇa Ṛṣi, the supermost human being, unto mother Sarasvatī, the goddess of learning, and unto Śrīla Vyāsadeva, the author.

PURPORT All the Vedic literatures and the *Purāṇas* are meant for conquering the darkest region of material existence. The living being is in the state of forgetfulness of his relation with God due to his being overly attracted to material sense gratification from time immemorial. His struggle for existence in the material world is perpetual, and it is not possible for him to get out of it by making plans. If he at all wants to conquer this perpetual struggle for existence, he must reestablish his eternal relation with God. And one who wants to adopt such remedial measures must take shelter of literatures such as the *Vedas* and the *Purāṇas*. Foolish people say that the *Purāṇas* have no connection with the *Vedas*. However, the *Purāṇas* are supplementary explanations of the *Vedas* intended for different types of men. All men are not equal. There are men who are conducted by the mode of goodness, others who are under the mode of passion and others who are under the mode of ignorance. The *Purāṇas* are so divided that any class of men can take advantage of them and gradually regain their lost position and get out of the hard struggle for existence. Śrīla Sūta Gosvāmī shows the way of chanting the *Purāṇas*. This may be followed by persons who aspire to be preachers of the Vedic literatures and the *Purāṇas*. *Śrīmad-Bhāgavatam* is the spotless *Purāṇa*, and it is especially meant for those who desire to get out of the material entanglement permanently.

TEXT 5

मुनयः साधु पृष्टोऽहं भवद्भिर्लोकमङ्गलम् ।
यत्कृतः कृष्णसम्प्रश्नो येनात्मा सुप्रसीदति ॥ ५ ॥

munayaḥ sādhu pṛṣṭo 'haṁ bhavadbhir loka-maṅgalam
yat kṛtaḥ kṛṣṇa-sampraśno yenātmā suprasīdati

munayaḥ—O sages; *sādhu*—this is relevant; *pṛṣṭaḥ*—questioned; *aham*—myself; *bhavadbhiḥ*—by all of you; *loka*—the world; *maṅgalam*—welfare; *yat*—because; *kṛtaḥ*—made; *kṛṣṇa*—the Personality of Godhead; *sampraśnaḥ*—relevant question; *yena*—by which; *ātmā*—self; *suprasīdati*—completely pleased.

O sages, I have been justly questioned by you. Your questions are worthy because they relate to Lord Kṛṣṇa and so are of relevance to the world's welfare. Only questions of this sort are capable of completely satisfying the self.

PURPORT Since it has been stated hereinbefore that in the *Bhāgavatam* the Absolute Truth is to be known, the questions of the sages of Naimiṣāraṇya are proper and just, because they pertain to Kṛṣṇa, who is the Supreme Personality of Godhead, the Absolute Truth. In *Bhagavad-gītā* (15.15) the Personality of Godhead says that in all the *Vedas* there is nothing but the urge for searching after Him, Lord Kṛṣṇa. Thus the questions that pertain to Kṛṣṇa are the sum and substance of all the Vedic inquiries.

The whole world is full of questions and answers. The birds, beasts and men are all busy in the matter of perpetual questions and answers. In the morning the birds in the nest become busy with questions and answers, and in the evening also the same birds come back and again become busy with questions and answers. The human being, unless he is fast asleep at night, is busy with questions and answers. The businessmen in the market are busy with questions and answers, and so also the lawyers in the court and the students in the schools and colleges. The legislators in the parliament are also busy with questions and answers, and the politicians and the press representatives are all busy with questions and answers. Although they go on making such questions and answers for their whole lives, they are not at all satisfied. Satisfaction of the soul can only be obtained by questions and answers on the subject of Kṛṣṇa.

Kṛṣṇa is our most intimate master, friend, father or son and object of conjugal love. Forgetting Kṛṣṇa, we have created so many objects of questions and answers, but none of them are able to give us complete satisfaction. All things—but Kṛṣṇa—give temporary satisfaction only, so if we are to have complete satisfaction we must take to the questions and answers about Kṛṣṇa. We cannot live for a moment without being questioned or without giving answers. Because the *Śrīmad-Bhāgavatam* deals with questions and answers that are related to Kṛṣṇa, we can derive the highest satisfaction only by reading and hearing this transcendental literature. One should learn the *Śrīmad-Bhāgavatam* and make an all-around solution to all problems pertaining to social, political or religious matters. *Śrīmad-Bhāgavatam* and Kṛṣṇa are the sum total of all things.

TEXT 6

स वै पुंसां परो धर्मो यतो भक्तिरधोक्षजे ।
अहैतुक्यप्रतिहता ययात्मा सुप्रसीदति ॥ ६ ॥

sa vai puṁsāṁ paro dharmo yato bhaktir adhokṣaje
ahaituky apratihatā yayātmā suprasīdati

saḥ—that; *vai*—certainly; *puṁsām*—for mankind; *paraḥ*—sublime; *dharmaḥ*—occupation; *yataḥ*—by which; *bhaktiḥ*—devotional service; *adhokṣaje*—unto the Transcendence; *ahaitukī*—causeless; *apratihatā*—unbroken; *yayā*—by which; *ātmā*—the self; *suprasīdati*—completely satisfied.

The supreme occupation [dharma] for all humanity is that by which men can attain to loving devotional service unto the transcendent Lord. Such devotional service must be unmotivated and uninterrupted to completely satisfy the self.

PURPORT In this statement, Śrī Sūta Gosvāmī answers the first question of the sages of Naimiṣāraṇya. The sages asked him to summarize the whole range of revealed scriptures and present the most essential part so that fallen people or the people in general might easily take it up. The *Vedas* prescribe two different types of occupation for the human being. One is called the *pravṛtti-mārga,* or the path of sense enjoyment, and the other is called the *nivṛtti-mārga,* or the path of renunciation. The path of enjoyment is inferior, and the path of sacrifice for the supreme cause is superior. The material existence of the living being is a diseased condition of actual life. Actual life is spiritual existence, or *brahma-bhūta* existence, where life is eternal, blissful and full of knowledge. Material existence is temporary, illusory and full of miseries. There is no happiness at all. There is just the futile attempt to get rid of the miseries, and temporary cessation of misery is falsely called happiness. Therefore, the path of progressive material enjoyment, which is temporary, miserable and illusory, is inferior. But devotional service to the Supreme Lord, which leads one to eternal, blissful and all-cognizant life, is called the superior quality of occupation. This is sometimes polluted when mixed with the inferior quality. For example, adoption of devotional service for material gain is certainly an obstruction to the progressive path of renunciation. Renunciation or abnegation for ultimate good is certainly a better occupation than enjoyment in the diseased condition of life. Such enjoyment only aggravates the symptoms of disease and increases its duration. Therefore devotional service to the Lord must be pure in quality, i.e., without the least desire for material enjoyment. One should, therefore, accept the superior quality of occupation in the form of the devotional service of the Lord without any tinge of unnecessary desire, fruitive action and philosophical speculation. This alone can lead one to perpetual solace in His service.

We have purposely denoted *dharma* as occupation because the root meaning of the word *dharma* is "that which sustains one's existence." A living being's sustenance of existence is to coordinate his activities with his eternal relation with the Supreme Lord Kṛṣṇa. Kṛṣṇa is the central pivot of living beings, and He is the all-attractive living entity or eternal form amongst all other living beings or eternal forms. Each and every living being has his eternal form in the spiritual existence, and Kṛṣṇa is the eternal attraction for all of them. Kṛṣṇa is the complete whole, and everything else is His part and parcel. The relation is one of the servant and the served. It is transcendental and is completely distinct from our experience in material existence. This relation of servant and the served is the most congenial form of intimacy. One can realize it as devotional service progresses. Everyone should engage himself in that transcendental loving service of the Lord, even in the present conditional state of material existence. That will gradually give one the clue to actual life and please him to complete satisfaction.

TEXT 7

वासुदेवे भगवति भक्तियोगः प्रयोजितः ।
जनयत्याशु वैराग्यं ज्ञानं च यदहैतुकम् ॥ ७ ॥

vāsudeve bhagavati bhakti-yogaḥ prayojitaḥ
janayaty āśu vairāgyaṁ jñānaṁ ca yad ahaitukam

vāsudeve—unto Kṛṣṇa; *bhagavati*—unto the Personality of Godhead; *bhakti-yogaḥ*—contact of devotional service; *prayojitaḥ*—being applied; *janayati*—does produce; *āśu*—very soon; *vairāgyam*—detachment; *jñānam*—knowledge; *ca*—and; *yat*—that which; *ahaitukam*—causeless.

By rendering devotional service unto the Personality of Godhead, Śrī Kṛṣṇa, one immediately acquires causeless knowledge and detachment from the world.

PURPORT Those who consider devotional service to the Supreme Lord Śrī Kṛṣṇa to be something like material emotional affairs may argue that in the revealed scriptures, sacrifice, charity, austerity, knowledge, mystic powers and similar other processes of transcendental realization are recommended. According to them, *bhakti,* or the devotional service of the Lord, is meant for those who cannot perform the high-grade activities. Generally it is said that the *bhakti* cult is meant for the *śūdras, vaiśyas* and the less intelligent woman class. But that is not the actual fact. The *bhakti* cult is the topmost of all transcendental activities, and therefore it is simultaneously sublime and easy. It is sublime for the pure devotees who are serious about getting in contact with the Supreme Lord, and it is easy for the neophytes who are just on the threshold of the house of *bhakti.* To achieve the contact of the Supreme Personality of Godhead Śrī Kṛṣṇa is a great science, and it is open for all living beings, including the *śūdras, vaiśyas,* women and even those lower than the lowborn *śūdras,* so what to speak of the high-class men like the qualified *brāhmaṇas* and the great self-realized kings. The other high-grade activities designated as sacrifice, charity, austerity, etc., are all corollary factors following the pure and scientific *bhakti* cult.

The principles of knowledge and detachment are two important factors on the path of transcendental realization. The whole spiritual process leads to perfect knowledge of everything material and spiritual, and the results of such perfect knowledge are that one becomes detached from material affection and becomes attached to spiritual activities. Becoming detached from material things does not mean becoming inert altogether, as men with a poor fund of knowledge think. *Naiṣkarma* means not undertaking activities that will produce good or bad effects. Negation does not mean negation of the positive. Negation of the nonessentials does not mean negation of the essential. Similarly, detachment from material forms does not mean nullifying the positive form. The *bhakti* cult is meant for realization of the positive form. When the positive form is realized, the negative forms are automatically eliminated. Therefore, with the development of the *bhakti* cult, with the application of positive service to the positive form, one naturally becomes detached from inferior things, and he becomes attached to superior things. Similarly, the *bhakti* cult, being the supermost occupation of the living being, leads him out of material sense enjoyment. That is the sign of a pure devotee. He is not a fool, nor is he engaged in the inferior energies, nor does he have material values. This is not possible by dry reasoning. It actually happens by the grace of the Almighty. In conclusion, one who is a pure devotee has all other good qualities, namely knowledge, detachment, etc., but one who has only knowledge or detachment is not necessarily well acquainted with the principles of the *bhakti* cult. *Bhakti* is the supermost occupation of the human being.

TEXT 8

धर्मः स्वनुष्ठितः पुंसां विष्वक्सेनकथासु यः ।
नोत्पादयेद्यदि रतिं श्रम एव हि केवलम् ॥ ८ ॥

dharmaḥ svanuṣṭhitaḥ puṁsāṁ viṣvaksena-kathāsu yaḥ
notpādayed yadi ratiṁ śrama eva hi kevalam

dharmaḥ—occupation; *svanuṣṭhitaḥ*—executed in terms of one's own position; *puṁsām*—of humankind; *viṣvaksena*—the Personality of Godhead (plenary portion); *kathāsu*—in the message of; *yaḥ*—what is; *na*—not; *utpādayet*—does produce; *yadi*—if; *ratim*—attraction; *śramaḥ*—useless labor; *eva*—only; *hi*—certainly; *kevalam*—entirely.

The occupational activities a man performs according to his own position are only so much useless labor if they do not provoke attraction for the message of the Personality of Godhead.

PURPORT There are different occupational activities in terms of man's different conceptions of life. To the gross materialist who cannot see anything beyond the gross material body, there is nothing beyond the senses.

Therefore his occupational activities are limited to concentrated and extended selfishness. Concentrated selfishness centers around the personal body—this is generally seen amongst the lower animals. Extended selfishness is manifested in human society and centers around the family, society, community, nation and world with a view to gross bodily comfort. Above these gross materialists are the mental speculators who hover aloft in the mental spheres, and their occupational duties involve making poetry and philosophy or propagating some *ism* with the same aim of selfishness limited to the body and the mind. But above the body and mind is the dormant spirit soul whose absence from the body makes the whole range of bodily and mental selfishness completely null and void. But less intelligent people have no information of the needs of the spirit soul.

Because foolish people have no information of the soul and how it is beyond the purview of the body and mind, they are not satisfied in the performance of their occupational duties. The question of the satisfaction of the self is raised herein. The self is beyond the gross body and subtle mind. He is the potent active principle of the body and mind. Without knowing the need of the dormant soul, one cannot be happy simply with emolument of the body and mind. The body and the mind are but superfluous outer coverings of the spirit soul. The spirit soul's needs must be fulfilled. Simply by cleansing the cage of the bird, one does not satisfy the bird. One must actually know the needs of the bird himself.

The need of the spirit soul is that he wants to get out of the limited sphere of material bondage and fulfill his desire for complete freedom. He wants to get out of the covered walls of the greater universe. He wants to see the free light and the spirit. That complete freedom is achieved when he meets the complete spirit, the Personality of Godhead. There is a dormant affection for God within everyone; spiritual existence is manifested through the gross body and mind in the form of perverted affection for gross and subtle matter. Therefore we have to engage ourselves in occupational engagements that will evoke our divine consciousness. This is possible only by hearing and chanting the divine activities of the Supreme Lord, and any occupational activity which does not help one to achieve attachment for hearing and chanting the transcendental message of Godhead is said herein to be simply a waste of time. This is because other occupational duties (whatever *ism* they may belong to) cannot give liberation to the soul. Even the activities of the salvationists are considered to be useless because of their failure to pick up the fountainhead of all liberties. The gross materialist can practically see that his material gain is limited only to time and space, either in this world or in the other. Even if he goes up to the Svargaloka, he will find no permanent abode for his hankering soul. The hankering soul must be satisfied by the perfect scientific process of perfect devotional service.

TEXT 9

धर्मस्य ह्यापवर्ग्यस्य नार्थोऽर्थायोपकल्पते ।
नार्थस्य धर्मैकान्तस्य कामो लाभाय हि स्मृतः ॥ ९ ॥

dharmasya hy āpavargyasya nārtho 'rthāyopakalpate
nārthasya dharmaikāntasya kāmo lābhāya hi smṛtaḥ

dharmasya—occupational engagement; *hi*—certainly; *āpavargyasya*—ultimate liberation; *na*—not; *arthaḥ*—end; *arthāya*—for material gain; *upakalpate*—is meant for; *na*—neither; *arthasya*—of material gain; *dharma-eka-antasya*—for one who is engaged in the ultimate occupational service; *kāmaḥ*—sense gratification; *lābhāya*—attainment of; *hi*—exactly; *smṛtaḥ*—is described by the great sages.

All occupational engagements are certainly meant for ultimate liberation. They should never be performed for material gain. Furthermore, according to sages, one who is engaged in the ultimate occupational service should never use material gain to cultivate sense gratification.

PURPORT We have already discussed that pure devotional service to the Lord is automatically followed by perfect knowledge and detachment from material existence. But there are others who consider that all kinds of different occupational engagements, including those of religion, are meant for material gain. The general tendency of any ordinary man in any part of the world is to gain some material profit in exchange for religious or any other occupational service. Even in the Vedic literatures, for all sorts of religious performances an allurement of material gain is offered, and most people are attracted by such allurements or blessings of religiosity. Why are such so-called men of religion allured by material gain?

Because material gain can enable one to fulfill desires, which in turn satisfy sense gratification. This cycle of occupational engagements includes so-called religiosity followed by material gain and material gain followed by fulfillment of desires. Sense gratification is the general way for all sorts of fully occupied men. But in the statement of Sūta Gosvāmī, as per the verdict of the *Śrīmad-Bhāgavatam,* this is nullified by the present *śloka.*

One should not engage himself in any sort of occupational service for material gain only. Nor should material gain be utilized for sense gratification. How material gain should be utilized is described as follows.

TEXT 10

कामस्य नेन्द्रियप्रीतिर्लाभो जीवेत यावता ।
जीवस्य तत्त्वजिज्ञासा नार्थो यश्चेह कर्मभिः ॥ १० ॥

kāmasya nendriya-prītir lābho jīveta yāvatā
jīvasya tattva-jijñāsā nārtho yaś ceha karmabhiḥ

kāmasya—of desires; *na*—not; *indriya*—senses; *prītiḥ*—satisfaction; *lābhaḥ*—gain; *jīveta*—self-preservation; *yāvatā*—so much so; *jīvasya*—of the living being; *tattva*—the Absolute Truth; *jijñāsā*—inquiries; *na*—not; *arthaḥ*—end; *yaḥ ca iha*—whatsoever else; *karmabhiḥ*—by occupational activities.

Life's desires should never be directed toward sense gratification. One should desire only a healthy life, or self-preservation, since a human being is meant for inquiry about the Absolute Truth. Nothing else should be the goal of one's works.

PURPORT The completely bewildered material civilization is wrongly directed towards the fulfillment of desires in sense gratification. In such civilization, in all spheres of life, the ultimate end is sense gratification. In politics, social service, altruism, philanthropy and ultimately in religion or even in salvation, the very same tint of sense gratification is ever-increasingly predominant. In the political field the leaders of men fight with one another to fulfill their personal sense gratification. The voters adore the so-called leaders only when they promise sense gratification. As soon as the voters are dissatisfied in their own sense satisfaction, they dethrone the leaders. The leaders must always disappoint the voters by not satisfying their senses. The same is applicable in all other fields; no one is serious about the problems of life. Even those who are on the path of salvation desire to become one with the Absolute Truth and desire to commit spiritual suicide for sense gratification. But the *Bhāgavatam* says that one should not live for sense gratification. One should satisfy the senses only insomuch as required for self-preservation, and not for sense gratification. Because the body is made of senses, which also require a certain amount of satisfaction, there are regulative directions for satisfaction of such senses. But the senses are not meant for unrestricted enjoyment. For example, marriage or the combination of a man with a woman is necessary for progeny, but it is not meant for sense enjoyment. In the absence of voluntary restraint, there is propaganda for family planning, but foolish men do not know that family planning is automatically executed as soon as there is search after the Absolute Truth. Seekers of the Absolute Truth are never allured by unnecessary engagements in sense gratification because the serious students seeking the Absolute Truth are always overwhelmed with the work of researching the Truth. In every sphere of life, therefore, the ultimate end must be seeking after the Absolute Truth, and that sort of engagement will make one happy because he will be less engaged in varieties of sense gratification. And what that Absolute Truth is is explained as follows.

TEXT 11

वदन्ति तत्तत्त्वविदस्तत्त्वं यज्ज्ञानमद्वयम् ।
ब्रह्मेति परमात्मेति भगवानिति शब्द्यते ॥ ११ ॥

vadanti tat tattva-vidas tattvaṁ yaj jñānam advayam
brahmeti paramātmeti bhagavān iti śabdyate

vadanti—they say; *tat*—that; *tattva-vidaḥ*—the learned souls; *tattvam*—the Absolute Truth; *yat*—which; *jñānam*—knowledge; *advayam*—nondual; *brahma iti*—known as Brahman; *paramātmā iti*—known as Paramātmā; *bhagavān iti*—known as Bhagavān; *śabdyate*—it so sounded.

Learned transcendentalists who know the Absolute Truth call this nondual substance Brahman, Paramātmā or Bhagavān.

PURPORT The Absolute Truth is both subject and object, and there is no qualitative difference there. Therefore, Brahman, Paramātmā and Bhagavān are qualitatively one and the same. The same substance is realized as impersonal Brahman by the students of the *Upaniṣads,* as localized Paramātmā by the Hiraṇyagarbhas or the *yogīs,* and as Bhagavān by the devotees. In other words, Bhagavān, or the Personality of Godhead, is the last word of the Absolute Truth. Paramātmā is the partial representation of the Personality of Godhead, and impersonal Brahman is the glowing effulgence of the Personality of Godhead, as the sun rays are to the sun-god. Less intelligent students of either of the above schools sometimes argue in favor of their own respective realization, but those who are perfect seers of the Absolute Truth know well that the above three features of the one Absolute Truth are different perspective views seen from different angles of vision.

As it is explained in the first *śloka* of the First Chapter of the *Bhāgavatam,* the Supreme Truth is self-sufficient, cognizant and free from the illusion of relativity. In the relative world the knower is different from the known, but in the Absolute Truth both the knower and the known are one and the same thing. In the relative world the knower is the living spirit or superior energy, whereas the known is inert matter or inferior energy. Therefore, there is a duality of inferior and superior energy, whereas in the absolute realm both the knower and the known are of the same superior energy. There are three kinds of energies of the supreme energetic. There is no difference between the energy and energetic, but there is a difference of quality of energies. The absolute realm and the living entities are of the same superior energy, but the material world is inferior energy. The living being in contact with the inferior energy is illusioned, thinking he belongs to the inferior energy. Therefore there is the sense of relativity in the material world. In the Absolute there is no such sense of difference between the knower and the known, and therefore everything there is absolute.

TEXT 12

तच्छ्रद्दधाना मुनयो ज्ञानवैराग्ययुक्तया ।
पश्यन्त्यात्मनि चात्मानं भक्त्या श्रुतगृहीतया ॥ १२ ॥

tac chraddadhānā munayo jñāna-vairāgya-yuktayā
paśyanty ātmani cātmānaṁ bhaktyā śruta-gṛhītayā

tat—that; *śraddadhānāḥ*—seriously inquisitive; *munayaḥ*—sages; *jñāna*—knowledge; *vairāgya*—detachment; *yuktayā*—well equipped with; *paśyanti*—see; *ātmani*—within himself; *ca*—and; *ātmānam*—the Paramātmā; *bhaktyā*—in devotional service; *śruta*—the *Vedas; gṛhītayā*—well received.

The seriously inquisitive student or sage, well equipped with knowledge and detachment, realizes that Absolute Truth by rendering devotional service in terms of what he has heard from the Vedānta-śruti.

PURPORT The Absolute Truth is realized in full by the process of devotional service to the Lord, Vāsudeva, or the Personality of Godhead, who is the full-fledged Absolute Truth. Brahman is His transcendental bodily effulgence, and Paramātmā is His partial representation. As such, Brahman or Paramātmā realization of the Absolute Truth is but a partial realization. There are four different types of human beings—the *karmīs,* the *jñānīs,* the *yogīs* and the devotees. The *karmīs* are materialistic, whereas the other three are transcendental. The first-class transcendentalists are the devotees who have realized the Supreme Person. The second-class transcendentalists are those who have partially realized the plenary portion of the absolute person. And the third-class transcendentalists are those who have barely realized the spiritual focus of the absolute person. As stated in the *Bhagavad-gītā* and other Vedic literatures, the Supreme Person is realized by devotional service, which is backed by full knowledge and detachment from material association. We have already discussed the point that devotional service is followed by knowledge and detachment from material association. As Brahman and Paramātmā realization are imperfect realizations of the Absolute Truth, so the means of realizing Brahman and Paramātmā, i.e., the paths of *jñāna* and *yoga,* are also imperfect means of realizing the Absolute Truth. Devotional service, which is based on the foreground of full knowledge combined with detachment from material association and which is fixed by the aural reception of the *Vedānta-śruti,* is the only perfect method by which the seriously inquisitive student can realize the Absolute Truth. Devotional service is not, therefore, meant for the less intelligent class of transcendentalist. There are three classes of devotees, namely first, second, and third class. The third-class devotees, or the neophytes, who have no knowledge and are not detached from material association, but who are simply attracted by the preliminary process of worshiping the Deity in the temple, are called material devotees. Material devotees are more attached to material benefit than transcendental profit. Therefore, one has to make definite progress from the position of material devotional service to the second-class devotional position. In the second-class position, the devotee can see four principles in the devotional line, namely the Personality of Godhead, His devotees, the ignorant and the envious. One has to raise himself at least to the stage of a second-class devotee and thus become eligible to know the Absolute Truth.

A third-class devotee, therefore, has to receive the instructions of devotional service from the authoritative sources of *Bhāgavata*. The number one *Bhāgavata* is the established personality of devotee, and the other *Bhāgavata* is the message of Godhead. The third-class devotee therefore has to go to the personality of devotee in order to learn the instructions of devotional service. Such a personality of devotee is not a professional man who earns his livelihood by the business of *Bhāgavatam*. Such a devotee must be a representative of Śukadeva Gosvāmī, like Sūta Gosvāmī, and must preach the cult of devotional service for the all-around benefit of all people. A neophyte devotee has very little taste for hearing from the authorities. Such a neophyte devotee makes a show of hearing from the professional man to satisfy his senses. This sort of hearing and chanting has spoiled the whole thing, so one should be very careful about the faulty process. The holy messages of Godhead, as inculcated in the *Bhagavad-gītā* or in the *Śrīmad-Bhāgavatam*, are undoubtedly transcendental subjects, but even though they are so, such transcendental matters are not to be received from the professional man, who spoils them as the serpent spoils milk simply by the touch of his tongue.

A sincere devotee must, therefore, be prepared to hear the Vedic literature like the *Upaniṣads*, *Vedānta* and other literatures left by the previous authorities or Gosvāmīs, for the benefit of his progress. Without hearing such literatures, one cannot make actual progress. And without hearing and following the instructions, the show of devotional service becomes worthless and therefore a sort of disturbance in the path of devotional service. Unless, therefore, devotional service is established on the principles of *śruti, smṛti, purāṇa* or *pañcarātra* authorities, the make-show of devotional service should at once be rejected. An unauthorized devotee should never be recognized as a pure devotee. By assimilation of such messages from the Vedic literatures, one can see the all-pervading localized aspect of the Personality of Godhead within his own self constantly. This is called *samādhi.*

TEXT 13

अतः पुम्भिर्द्विजश्रेष्ठा वर्णाश्रमविभागशः ।
स्वनुष्ठितस्य धर्मस्य संसिद्धिर्हरितोषणम् ॥ १३ ॥

ataḥ pumbhir dvija-śreṣṭhā varṇāśrama-vibhāgaśaḥ
svanuṣṭhitasya dharmasya saṁsiddhir hari-toṣaṇam

ataḥ—so; *pumbhiḥ*—by the human being; *dvija-śreṣṭhāḥ*—O best among the twice-born; *varṇa-āśrama*—the institution of four castes and four orders of life; *vibhāgaśaḥ*—by the division of; *svanuṣṭhitasya*—of one's own prescribed duties; *dharmasya*—occupational; *saṁsiddhiḥ*—the highest perfection; *hari*—the Personality of Godhead; *toṣaṇam*—pleasing.

O best among the twice-born, it is therefore concluded that the highest perfection one can achieve by discharging the duties prescribed for one's own occupation according to caste divisions and orders of life is to please the Personality of Godhead.

PURPORT Human society all over the world is divided into four castes and four orders of life. The four castes are the intelligent caste, the martial caste, the productive caste and the laborer caste. These castes are classified in terms of one's work and qualification and not by birth. Then again there are four orders of life, namely the student life, the householder's life, the retired and the devotional life. In the best interest of human society there must be such divisions of life, otherwise no social institution can grow in a healthy state. And in each and every one of the abovementioned divisions of life, *the aim must be to please the supreme authority of the Personality of Godhead.* This institutional function of human society is known as the system of *varṇāśrama-dharma,* which is quite natural for the civilized life. The *varṇāśrama* institution is constructed to enable one to realize the Absolute Truth. It is not for artificial domination of one division over another. When the aim of life, i.e., realization of the Absolute Truth, is missed by too much attachment for *indriya-prīti,* or sense gratification, as already discussed hereinbefore, the institution of the *varṇāśrama* is utilized by selfish men to pose an artificial predominance over the weaker section. In the Kali-yuga, or in the age of quarrel, this artificial predominance is already current, but the saner section of the people know it well that the divisions of castes and orders of life are meant for smooth social intercourse and high-thinking self-realization and not for any other purpose.

Herein the statement of *Bhāgavatam* is that the highest aim of life or the highest perfection of the institution of the *varṇāśrama-dharma* is to cooperate jointly for the satisfaction of the Supreme Lord. This is also confirmed in the *Bhagavad-gītā* (4.13).

TEXT 14

तस्मादेकेन मनसा भगवान् सात्वतां पतिः ।
श्रोतव्यः कीर्तितव्यश्च ध्येयः पूज्यश्च नित्यदा ॥ १४ ॥

tasmād ekena manasā bhagavān sātvatāṁ patiḥ
śrotavyaḥ kīrtitavyaś ca dhyeyaḥ pūjyaś ca nityadā

tasmāt—therefore; *ekena*—by one; *manasā*—attention of the mind; *bhagavān*—the Personality of Godhead; *sātvatām*—of the devotees; *patiḥ*—protector; *śrotavyaḥ*—is to be heard; *kīrtitavyaḥ*—to be glorified; *ca*—and; *dhyeyaḥ*—to be remembered; *pūjyaḥ*—to be worshiped; *ca*—and; *nityadā*—constantly.

Therefore, with one-pointed attention, one should constantly hear about, glorify, remember and worship the Personality of Godhead, who is the protector of the devotees.

PURPORT If realization of the Absolute Truth is the ultimate aim of life, it must be carried out by all means. In any one of the above-mentioned castes and orders of life, the four processes, namely glorifying, hearing, remembering and worshiping, are general occupations. Without these principles of life, no one can exist. Activities of the living being involve engagements in these four different principles of life. Especially in modern society, all activities are more or less dependent on hearing and glorifying. Any man from any social status becomes a well-known man in human society within a very short time if he is simply glorified truly or falsely in the daily newspapers. Sometimes political leaders of a particular party are also advertised by newspaper propaganda, and by such a method of glorification an insignificant man becomes an important man—within no time. But such propaganda by false glorification of an unqualified person cannot bring about any good, either for the particular man or for the society. There may be some temporary reactions to such propaganda, but there are no permanent effects. Therefore such activities are a waste of time. The actual object of glorification is the Supreme Personality of Godhead, who has created everything manifested before us. We have broadly discussed this fact in our comments on the "*janmādy asya*" *śloka*, at the beginning of the *Bhāgavatam*. The tendency to glorify others or hear others must be turned to the real object of glorification—the Supreme Being. And that will bring happiness.

TEXT 15

यदनुध्यासिना युक्ताः कर्मग्रन्थिनिबन्धनम् ।
छिन्दन्ति कोविदास्तस्य को न कुर्यात्कथारतिम् ॥ १५ ॥

yad-anudhyāsinā yuktāḥ karma-granthi-nibandhanam
chindanti kovidās tasya ko na kuryāt kathā-ratim

yat—which; *anudhyā*—remembrance; *asinā*—sword; *yuktāḥ*—being equipped with; *karma*—reactionary work; *granthi*—knot; *nibandhanam*—interknit; *chindanti*—cut; *kovidāḥ*—intelligent; *tasya*—His; *kaḥ*—who; *na*—not; *kuryāt*—shall do; *kathā*—messages; *ratim*—attention.

With sword in hand, intelligent men cut through the binding knots of reactionary work [karma] by remembering the Personality of Godhead. Therefore, who will not pay attention to His message?

PURPORT The contact of the spiritual spark with material elements creates a knot which must be cut if one wants to be liberated from the actions and reactions of fruitive work. Liberation means freedom from the cycle of reactionary work. This liberation automatically follows for one who constantly remembers the transcendental pastimes of the Personality of Godhead. This is because all the activities of the Supreme Lord (His *līlā*) are transcendental to the modes of the material energy. They are all-attractive spiritual activities, and therefore constant association with the spiritual activities of the Supreme Lord gradually spiritualizes the conditioned soul and ultimately severs the knot of material bondage.

Liberation from material bondage is, therefore, a by-product of devotional service. Attainment of spiritual knowledge is not sufficient to insure liberation. Such knowledge must be overcoated with devotional service so that ultimately the devotional service alone predominates. Then liberation is made possible. Even the reactionary work of the fruitive workers can lead one to liberation when it is overcoated with devotional service. *Karma* overcoated with devotional service is called *karma-yoga.* Similarly, empirical knowledge overcoated with devotional service is called *jñāna-yoga.* But pure *bhakti-yoga* is independent of such *karma* and *jñāna* because it alone can not only endow one with liberation from conditional life but also award one the transcendental loving service of the Lord.

Therefore, any sensible man who is above the average man with a poor fund of knowledge must constantly remember the Personality of Godhead by hearing about Him, by glorifying Him, by remembering Him and by worshiping Him always, without cessation. That is the perfect way of devotional service. The Gosvāmīs of Vṛndāvana, who were authorized by Śrī Caitanya Mahāprabhu to preach the *bhakti* cult, rigidly followed this rule and made immense literatures of transcendental science for our benefit. They have chalked out ways for all classes of men in terms of the different castes and orders of life in pursuance of the teachings of *Śrīmad-Bhāgavatam* and similar other authoritative scriptures.

TEXT 16

शुश्रूषोः श्रद्दधानस्य वासुदेवकथारुचिः ।
स्यान्महत्सेवया विप्राः पुण्यतीर्थनिषेवणात् ॥ १६ ॥

śuśrūṣoḥ śraddadhānasya vāsudeva-kathā-ruciḥ
syān mahat-sevayā viprāḥ puṇya-tīrtha-niṣevaṇāt

śuśrūṣoḥ—one who is engaged in hearing; *śraddadhānasya*—with care and attention; *vāsudeva*—in respect to Vāsudeva; *kathā*—the message; *ruciḥ*—affinity; *syāt*—is made possible; *mahat-sevayā*—by service rendered to pure devotees; *viprāḥ*—O twice-born; *puṇya-tīrtha*—those who are cleansed of all vice; *niṣevaṇāt*—by service.

O twice-born sages, by serving those devotees who are completely freed from all vice, great service is done. By such service, one gains affinity for hearing the messages of Vāsudeva.

PURPORT The conditioned life of a living being is caused by his revolting against the Lord. There are men called *devas,* or godly living beings, and there are men called *asuras,* or demons, who are against the authority of the Supreme Lord. In the *Bhagavad-gītā* (Sixteenth Chapter) a vivid description of the *asuras* is given in which it is said that the *asuras* are put into lower and lower states of ignorance life after life and so sink to the lower animal forms and have no information of the Absolute Truth, the Personality of Godhead. These *asuras* are gradually rectified to God consciousness by the mercy of the Lord's liberated servitors in different countries according to the supreme will. Such devotees of God are very confidential associates of the Lord, and when they come to save human society from the dangers of godlessness, they are known as the powerful incarnations of the Lord, as sons of the Lord, as servants of the Lord or as associates of the Lord. But none of them falsely claim to be God themselves. This is a blasphemy declared by the *asuras,* and the demoniac followers of such *asuras* also accept pretenders as God or His incarnation. In the revealed scriptures there is definite information of the incarnation of God. No one should be accepted as God or an incarnation of God unless he is confirmed by the revealed scriptures.

The servants of God are to be respected as God by the devotees who actually want to go back to Godhead. Such servants of God are called *mahātmās,* or *tīrthas,* and they preach according to particular time and place. The servants of God urge people to become devotees of the Lord. They never tolerate being called God. Śrī Caitanya Mahāprabhu was God Himself according to the indication of the revealed scriptures, but He played the part of a devotee. People who knew Him to be God addressed Him as God, but He used to block His ears with His hands and chant the name of Lord Viṣṇu. He strongly protested against being called God, although undoubtedly He was God Himself. The Lord behaves so to warn us against unscrupulous men who take pleasure in being addressed as God.

The servants of God come to propagate God consciousness, and intelligent people should cooperate with them in every respect. By serving the servant of God, one can please God more than by directly serving the Lord. The Lord is more pleased when He sees that His servants are properly respected because such servants risk everything for the service of the Lord and so are very dear to the Lord. The Lord declares in the *Bhagavad-gītā* (18.69) that no one is dearer to Him than one who risks everything to preach His glory. By serving the servants of the Lord, one gradually gets the quality of such servants, and thus one becomes qualified to hear the glories of God. The eagerness to hear about God is the first qualification of a devotee eligible for entering the kingdom of God.

TEXT 17

शृण्वतां स्वकथाः कृष्णः पुण्यश्रवणकीर्तनः ।
हृद्यन्तः स्थो ह्यभद्राणि विधुनोति सुहृत्सताम् ॥ १७ ॥

śṛṇvatāṁ sva-kathāḥ kṛṣṇaḥ puṇya-śravaṇa-kīrtanaḥ
hṛdy antaḥ stho hy abhadrāṇi vidhunoti suhṛt satām

śṛṇvatām—those who have developed the urge to hear the message of; *sva-kathāḥ*—His own words; *kṛṣṇaḥ*—the Personality of Godhead; *puṇya*—virtues; *śravaṇa*—hearing; *kīrtanaḥ*—chanting; *hṛdi antaḥ sthaḥ*—within one's heart; *hi*—certainly; *abhadrāṇi*—desire to enjoy matter; *vidhunoti*—cleanses; *suhṛt*—benefactor; *satām*—of the truthful.

Śrī Kṛṣṇa, the Personality of Godhead, who is the Paramātmā [Supersoul] in everyone's heart and the benefactor of the truthful devotee, cleanses desire for material enjoyment from the heart of the devotee who has developed the urge to hear His messages, which are in themselves virtuous when properly heard and chanted.

PURPORT Messages of the Personality of Godhead Śrī Kṛṣṇa are nondifferent from Him. Whenever, therefore, offenseless hearing and glorification of God are undertaken, it is to be understood that Lord Kṛṣṇa is present there in the form of transcendental sound, which is as powerful as the Lord personally. Śrī Caitanya Mahāprabhu, in His *Śikṣāṣṭaka,* declares clearly that the holy name of the Lord has all the potencies of the Lord and that He has endowed His innumerable names with the same potency. There is no rigid fixture of time, and anyone can chant the holy name with attention and reverence at his convenience. The Lord is so kind to us that He can be present before us personally in the form of transcendental sound, but unfortunately we have no taste for hearing and glorifying the Lord's name and activities. We have already discussed developing a taste for hearing and chanting the holy sound. It is done through the medium of service to the pure devotee of the Lord.

The Lord is reciprocally respondent to His devotees. When He sees that a devotee is completely sincere in getting admittance to the transcendental service of the Lord and has thus become eager to hear about Him, the Lord acts from within the devotee in such a way that the devotee may easily go back to Him. The Lord is more anxious to take us back into His kingdom than we can desire. Most of us do not desire at all to go back to Godhead. Only a very few men want to go back to Godhead. But anyone who desires to go back to Godhead, Śrī Kṛṣṇa helps in all respects.

One cannot enter into the kingdom of God unless one is perfectly cleared of all sins. The material sins are products of our desires to lord it over material nature. It is very difficult to get rid of such desires. Women and wealth are very difficult problems for the devotee making progress on the path back to Godhead. Many stalwarts in the devotional line fell victim to these allurements and thus retreated from the path of liberation. But when one is helped by the Lord Himself, the whole process becomes as easy as anything by the divine grace of the Lord.

To become restless in the contact of women and wealth is not an astonishment, because every living being is associated with such things from remote time, practically immemorial, and it takes time to recover from this foreign nature. But if one is engaged in hearing the glories of the Lord, gradually he realizes his real position. By the grace of God such a devotee gets sufficient strength to defend himself from the state of disturbances, and gradually all disturbing elements are eliminated from his mind.

TEXT 18

नष्टप्रायेष्वभद्रेषु नित्यं भागवतसेवया ।
भगवत्युत्तमश्लोके भक्तिर्भवति नैष्ठिकी ॥ १८ ॥

naṣṭa-prāyeṣv abhadreṣu nityaṁ bhāgavata-sevayā
bhagavaty uttama-śloke bhaktir bhavati naiṣṭhikī

naṣṭa—destroyed; *prāyeṣu*—almost to nil; *abhadreṣu*—all that is inauspicious; *nityam*—regularly; *bhāgavata*—*Śrīmad-Bhāgavatam,* or the pure devotee; *sevayā*—by serving; *bhagavati*—unto the Personality of Godhead; *uttama*—transcendental; *śloke*—prayers; *bhaktiḥ*—loving service; *bhavati*—comes into being; *naiṣṭhikī*—irrevocable.

By regular attendance in classes on the Bhāgavatam and by rendering of service to the pure devotee, all that is troublesome to the heart is almost completely destroyed, and loving service unto the Personality of Godhead, who is praised with transcendental songs, is established as an irrevocable fact.

PURPORT Here is the remedy for eliminating all inauspicious things within the heart which are considered to be obstacles in the path of self-realization. The remedy is the association of the *Bhāgavatas.* There are two types of *Bhāgavatas,* namely the book *Bhāgavata* and the devotee *Bhāgavata.* Both the *Bhāgavatas* are competent remedies, and both of them or either of them can be good enough to eliminate the obstacles. A devotee *Bhāgavata* is as good as the book *Bhāgavata* because the devotee *Bhāgavata* leads his life in terms of the book *Bhāgavata* and the book *Bhāgavata* is full of information about the Personality of Godhead and His pure devotees, who are also *Bhāgavatas. Bhāgavata* book and person are identical.

The devotee *Bhāgavata* is a direct representative of Bhagavān, the Personality of Godhead. So by pleasing the devotee *Bhāgavata* one can receive the benefit of the book *Bhāgavata.* Human reason fails to understand how by serving the devotee *Bhāgavata* or the book *Bhāgavata* one gets gradual promotion on the path of devotion. But actually these are facts explained by Śrīla Nāradadeva, who happened to be a maidservant's son in his previous life. The maidservant was engaged in the menial service of the sages, and thus he also came into contact with them. And simply by associating with them and accepting the remnants of foodstuff left by the sages, the son of the maidservant got the chance to become the great devotee and personality Śrīla Nāradadeva. These are the miraculous effects of the association of *Bhāgavatas.* And to understand these effects practically, it should be noted that by such sincere association of the *Bhāgavatas* one is sure to receive transcendental knowledge very easily, with the result that he becomes fixed in the devotional service of the

Lord. The more progress is made in devotional service under the guidance of the *Bhāgavatas,* the more one becomes fixed in the transcendental loving service of the Lord. The messages of the book *Bhāgavata,* therefore, have to be received from the devotee *Bhāgavata,* and the combination of these two *Bhāgavatas* will help the neophyte devotee to make progress on and on.

TEXT 19

तदा रजस्तमोभावाः कामलोभादयश्च ये ।
चेत एतैरनाविद्धं स्थितं सत्त्वे प्रसीदति ॥ १९ ॥

tadā rajas-tamo-bhāvāḥ kāma-lobhādayaś ca ye
ceta etair anāviddhaṁ sthitaṁ sattve prasīdati

tadā—at that time; *rajaḥ*—in the mode of passion; *tamaḥ*—the mode of ignorance; *bhāvāḥ*—the situation; *kāma*—lust and desire; *lobha*—hankering; *ādayaḥ*—others; *ca*—and; *ye*—whatever they are; *cetaḥ*—the mind; *etaiḥ*—by these; *anāviddham*—without being affected; *sthitam*—being fixed; *sattve*—in the mode of goodness; *prasīdati*—thus becomes fully satisfied.

As soon as irrevocable loving service is established in the heart, the effects of nature's modes of passion and ignorance, such as lust, desire and hankering, disappear from the heart. Then the devotee is established in goodness, and he becomes completely happy.

PURPORT A living being in his normal constitutional position is fully satisfied in spiritual bliss. This state of existence is called *brahma-bhūta* or *ātmānanda,* or the state of self-satisfaction. This self-satisfaction is not like the satisfaction of the inactive fool. The inactive fool is in the state of foolish ignorance, whereas the self-satisfied *ātmānandī* is transcendental to the material state of existence. This stage of perfection is attained as soon as one is fixed in irrevocable devotional service. Devotional service is not inactivity, but the unalloyed activity of the soul.

The soul's activity becomes adulterated in contact with matter, and as such the diseased activities are expressed in the form of lust, desire, hankering, inactivity, foolishness and sleep. The effect of devotional service becomes manifest by complete elimination of these effects of passion and ignorance. The devotee is fixed at once in the mode of goodness, and he makes further progress to rise to the position of *vasudeva,* or the state of unmixed *sattva,* or *śuddha-sattva.* Only in this *śuddha-sattva* state can one always see Kṛṣṇa eye to eye by dint of pure affection for the Lord.

A devotee is always in the mode of unalloyed goodness; therefore he harms no one. But the nondevotee, however educated he may be, is always harmful. A devotee is neither foolish nor passionate. The harmful, foolish and passionate cannot be devotees of the Lord, however they may advertise themselves as devotees by outward dress. A devotee is always qualified with all the good qualities of God. Quantitatively such qualifications may be different, but qualitatively both the Lord and His devotee are one and the same.

TEXT 20

एवं प्रसन्नमनसो भगवद्भक्तियोगतः ।
भगवत्तत्त्वविज्ञानं मुक्तसङ्गस्य जायते ॥ २० ॥

evaṁ prasanna-manaso bhagavad-bhakti-yogataḥ
bhagavat-tattva-vijñānaṁ mukta-saṅgasya jāyate

evam—thus; *prasanna*—enlivened; *manasaḥ*—of the mind; *bhagavat-bhakti*—the devotional service of the Lord; *yogataḥ*—by contact of; *bhagavat*—regarding the Personality of Godhead; *tattva*—knowledge; *vijñānam*—scientific; *mukta*—liberated; *saṅgasya*—of the association; *jāyate*—becomes effective.

Thus established in the mode of unalloyed goodness, the man whose mind has been enlivened by contact with devotional service to the Lord gains positive scientific knowledge of the Personality of Godhead in the stage of liberation from all material association.

PURPORT In the *Bhagavad-gītā* (7.3) it is said that out of many thousands of ordinary men, one fortunate man endeavors for perfection in life. Mostly men are conducted by the modes of passion and ignorance, and thus they are engaged always in lust, desire, hankerings, ignorance and sleep. Out of many such manlike animals, there is actually a man who knows the responsibility of human life and thus tries to make life perfect by following the prescribed duties. And out of many thousands of such persons who have thus attained success in human life, one may know scientifically about the Personality of Godhead Śrī Kṛṣṇa. In the same *Bhagavad-gītā* (18.55) it is also said that scientific knowledge of Śrī Kṛṣṇa is understood only by the process of devotional service (*bhakti-yoga).*

The very same thing is confirmed herein in the above words. No ordinary man, or even one who has attained success in human life, can know scientifically or perfectly the Personality of Godhead. Perfection of human life is attained when one can understand that he is not the product of matter but is in fact spirit. And as soon as one understands that he has nothing to do with matter, he at once ceases his material hankerings and becomes enlivened as a spiritual being. This attainment of success is possible when one is above the modes of passion and ignorance, or, in other words, when one is actually a *brāhmaṇa* by qualification. A *brāhmaṇa* is the symbol of *sattva-guṇa,* or the mode of goodness. And others, who are not in the mode of goodness, are either *kṣatriyas, vaiśyas, śūdras* or less than the *śūdras*. The brahminical stage is the highest stage of human life because of its good qualities. So one cannot be a devotee unless one at least qualifies as a *brāhmaṇa*. The devotee is already a *brāhmaṇa* by action. But that is not the end of it. As referred to above, such a *brāhmaṇa* has to become a Vaiṣṇava in fact to be actually in the transcendental stage. A pure Vaiṣṇava is a liberated soul and is transcendental even to the position of a *brāhmaṇa*. In the material stage even a *brāhmaṇa* is also a conditioned soul because although in the brahminical stage the conception of Brahman or transcendence is realized, scientific knowledge of the Supreme Lord is lacking. One has to surpass the brahminical stage and reach the *vasudeva* stage to understand the Personality of Godhead Kṛṣṇa. The science of the Personality of Godhead is the subject matter for study by the postgraduate students in the spiritual line. Foolish men, or men with a poor fund of knowledge, do not understand the Supreme Lord, and they interpret Kṛṣṇa according to their respective whims. The fact is, however, that one cannot understand the science of the Personality of Godhead unless one is freed from the contamination of the material modes, even up to the stage of a *brāhmaṇa*. When a qualified *brāhmaṇa* factually becomes a Vaiṣṇava, in the enlivened state of liberation he can know what is actually the Personality of Godhead.

TEXT 21

भिद्यते हृदयग्रन्थिश्छिद्यन्ते सर्वसंशयाः ।
क्षीयन्ते चास्य कर्माणि दृष्ट एवात्मनीश्वरे ॥ २१ ॥

bhidyate hṛdaya-granthiś chidyante sarva-saṁśayāḥ
kṣīyante cāsya karmāṇi dṛṣṭa evātmanīśvare

bhidyate—pierced; *hṛdaya*—heart; *granthiḥ*—knots; *chidyante*—cut to pieces; *sarva*—all; *saṁśayāḥ*—misgivings; *kṣīyante*—terminated; *ca*—and; *asya*—his; *karmāṇi*—chain of fruitive actions; *dṛṣṭe*—having seen; *eva*—certainly; *ātmani*—unto the self; *īśvare*—dominating.

Thus the knot in the heart is pierced, and all misgivings are cut to pieces. The chain of fruitive actions is terminated when one sees the self as master.

PURPORT Attaining scientific knowledge of the Personality of Godhead means seeing one's own self simultaneously. As far as the identity of the living being as spirit self is concerned, there are a number of speculations and misgivings. The materialist does not believe in the existence of the spirit self, and empiric philosophers believe in the impersonal feature of the whole spirit without individuality of the living beings. But the transcendentalists affirm that the soul and the Supersoul are two different identities, qualitatively one but quantitatively different. There are many other theories, but all these different speculations are at once cleared off as soon as Śrī Kṛṣṇa is realized in truth by the process of *bhakti-yoga.* Śrī Kṛṣṇa is like the sun, and the materialistic speculations about the Absolute Truth are like the darkest midnight. As soon as the Kṛṣṇa sun is arisen within one's heart, the darkness of materialistic speculations about the Absolute Truth and the living beings is at once cleared off. In the presence of the sun, the darkness cannot stand, and the relative truths that were hidden within the dense darkness of ignorance become clearly manifested by the mercy of Kṛṣṇa, who is residing in everyone's heart as the Supersoul.

In the *Bhagavad-gītā* (10.11) the Lord says that in order to show special favor to His pure devotees, He personally eradicates the dense darkness of all misgivings by switching on the light of pure knowledge within the heart of a devotee. Therefore, because of the Personality of Godhead's taking charge of illuminating the heart of His devotee, certainly a devotee, engaged in His service in transcendental love, cannot remain in darkness. He comes to know everything of the absolute and the relative truths. The devotee cannot remain in darkness, and because a devotee is enlightened by the Personality of Godhead, his knowledge is certainly perfect. This is not the case for those who speculate on the Absolute Truth by dint of their own limited power of approach. Perfect knowledge is called *paramparā,* or deductive knowledge coming down from the authority to the submissive aural receiver who is bona fide by service and surrender. One cannot challenge the authority of the Supreme and know Him also at the same time. He reserves the right of not being exposed to such a challenging spirit of an insignificant spark of the whole, a spark subjected to the control of illusory energy. The devotees are submissive, and therefore the transcendental knowledge descends from the Personality of Godhead to Brahmā and from Brahmā to his sons and disciples in succession. This process is helped by the Supersoul within such devotees. That is the perfect way of learning transcendental knowledge.

This enlightenment perfectly enables the devotee to distinguish spirit from matter because the knot of spirit and matter is untied by the Lord. This knot is called *ahaṅkāra,* and it falsely obliges a living being to become identified with matter. As soon as this knot is loosened, therefore, all the clouds of doubt are at once cleared off. One sees his master and fully engages himself in the transcendental loving service of the Lord, making a full termination of the chain of fruitive action. In material existence, a living being creates his own chain of fruitive work and enjoys the good and bad effects of those actions life after life. But as soon as he engages himself in the loving service of the Lord, he at once becomes free from the chain of *karma*. His actions no longer create any reaction.

TEXT 22

अतो वै कवयो नित्यं भक्तिं परमया मुदा ।
वासुदेवे भगवति कुर्वन्त्यात्मप्रसादनीम् ॥ २२ ॥

ato vai kavayo nityaṁ bhaktiṁ paramayā mudā
vāsudeve bhagavati kurvanty ātma-prasādanīm

ataḥ—therefore; *vai*—certainly; *kavayaḥ*—all transcendentalists; *nityam*—from time immemorial; *bhaktim*—service unto the Lord; *paramayā*—supreme; *mudā*—with great delight; *vāsudeve*—Śrī Kṛṣṇa; *bhagavati*—the Personality of Godhead; *kurvanti*—do render; *ātma*—self; *prasādanīm*—that which enlivens.

Certainly, therefore, since time immemorial, all transcendentalists have been rendering devotional service to Lord Kṛṣṇa, the Personality of Godhead, with great delight, because such devotional service is enlivening to the self.

PURPORT The speciality of devotional service unto the Personality of Godhead Lord Śrī Kṛṣṇa is specifically mentioned herein. Lord Śrī Kṛṣṇa is the *svayaṁ-rūpa* Personality of Godhead, and all other forms of Godhead, beginning from Śrī Baladeva, Saṅkarṣaṇa, Vāsudeva, Aniruddha, Pradyumna and Nārāyaṇa and extending to the *puruṣa-avatāras, guṇa-avatāras, līlā-avatāras, yuga-avatāras* and many other thousands of manifestations of the Personality of Godhead, are Lord Śrī Kṛṣṇa's plenary portions and integrated parts. The living entities are separated parts and parcels of the Personality of Godhead. Therefore Lord Sri Kṛṣṇa is the original form of Godhead, and He is the last word in the Transcendence. Thus He is more attractive to the higher transcendentalists who participate in the eternal pastimes of the Lord. In forms of the Personality of Godhead other than Śrī Kṛṣṇa and Baladeva, there is no facility for intimate personal contact as in the transcendental pastimes of the Lord at Vrajabhūmi. The transcendental pastimes of Lord Śrī Kṛṣṇa are not newly accepted, as argued by some less intelligent persons; His pastimes are eternal and are manifested in due course once in a day of Brahmājī, as the sun rises on the eastern horizon at the end of every twenty-four hours.

TEXT 23

सत्त्वं रजस्तम इति प्रकृतेर्गुणास्तैर्
युक्तः परः पुरुष एक इहास्य धत्ते ।
स्थित्यादये हरिविरिञ्चिहरेति संज्ञाः
श्रेयांसि तत्र खलु सत्त्वतनोर्नृणां स्युः ॥ २३ ॥

sattvaṁ rajas tama iti prakṛter guṇās tair
yuktaḥ paraḥ puruṣa eka ihāsya dhatte
sthity-ādaye hari-viriñci-hareti saṁjñāḥ
śreyāṁsi tatra khalu sattva-tanor nṛṇāṁ syuḥ

sattvam—goodness; *rajaḥ*—passion; *tamaḥ*—the darkness of ignorance; *iti*—thus; *prakṛteḥ*—of the material nature; *guṇāḥ*—qualities; *taiḥ*—by them; *yuktaḥ*—associated with; *paraḥ*—transcendental; *puruṣaḥ*—the personality; *ekaḥ*—one; *iha asya*—of this material world; *dhatte*—accepts; *sthiti-ādaye*—for the matter of creation, maintenance and destruction, etc.; *hari*—Viṣṇu, the Personality of Godhead; *viriñci*—Brahmā; *hara*—Lord Śiva; *iti*—thus; *saṁjñāḥ*—different features; *śreyāṁsi*—ultimate benefit; *tatra*—therein; *khalu*—of course; *sattva*—goodness; *tanoḥ*—form; *nṛṇām*—of the human being; *syuḥ*—derived.

The transcendental Personality of Godhead is indirectly associated with the three modes of material nature, namely passion, goodness and ignorance, and just for the material world's creation, maintenance and destruction He accepts the three qualitative forms of Brahmā, Viṣṇu and Śiva. Of these three, all human beings can derive ultimate benefit from Viṣṇu, the form of the quality of goodness.

PURPORT That Lord Śrī Kṛṣṇa, by His plenary parts, should be rendered devotional service, as explained above, is confirmed by this statement. Lord Śrī Kṛṣṇa and all His plenary parts are *viṣṇu-tattva,* or the Lordship of Godhead. From Śrī Kṛṣṇa, the next manifestation is Baladeva. From Baladeva is Saṅkarṣaṇa, from Saṅkarṣaṇa is Nārāyaṇa, from Nārāyaṇa there is the second Saṅkarṣaṇa, and from this Saṅkarṣaṇa the Viṣṇu *puruṣa-avatāras.* The Viṣṇu or the Deity of the quality of goodness in the material world is the *puruṣa-avatāra* known as Kṣīrodakaśāyī Viṣṇu or Paramātmā. Brahmā is the deity of *rajas* (passion), and Śiva of ignorance. They are the three departmental heads of the three qualities of this material world. The creation is made possible by Brahmā's quality of passion and his endeavor, it is maintained by the goodness of Viṣṇu, and when it requires to be destroyed, Lord Śiva does it by the *tāṇḍava-nṛtya.* The materialists and the foolish human beings worship

Brahmā and Śiva respectively. But the pure transcendentalists worship the form of goodness, Viṣṇu, in His various forms. Viṣṇu is manifested by His millions and billions of integrated forms and separated forms. The integrated forms are called Godhead, and the separated forms are called the living entities or the *jīvas*. Both the *jīvas* and Godhead have their original spiritual forms. *Jīvas* are sometimes subjected to the control of material energy, but the Viṣṇu forms are always controllers of this energy. When Viṣṇu, the Personality of Godhead, appears in the material world, He comes to deliver the conditioned living beings who are under the material energy. Such living beings appear in the material world with intentions of being lords, and thus they become entrapped by the three modes of nature. As such, the living entities have to change their material coverings for undergoing different terms of imprisonment. The prison house of the material world is created by Brahmā under instruction of the Personality of Godhead, and at the conclusion of a *kalpa* the whole thing is destroyed by Śiva. But as far as maintenance of the prison house is concerned, it is done by Viṣṇu, as much as the state prison house is maintained by the state. Anyone, therefore, who wishes to get out of this prison house of material existence, which is full of miseries like repetition of birth, death, disease and old age, must please Lord Viṣṇu for such liberation. Lord Viṣṇu is worshiped by devotional service only, and if anyone has to continue prison life in the material world, he may ask for relative facilities for temporary relief from the different demigods like Śiva, Brahmā, Indra and Varuṇa. No demigod, however, can release the imprisoned living being from the conditioned life of material existence. This can be done only by Viṣṇu. Therefore, the ultimate benefit may be derived from Viṣṇu, the Personality of Godhead.

TEXT 24

पार्थिवाद्दारुणो धूमस्तस्मादग्निस्त्रयीमयः ।
तमसस्तु रजस्तस्मात्सत्त्वं यद्ब्रह्मदर्शनम् ॥ २४ ॥

pārthivād dāruṇo dhūmas tasmād agnis trayīmayaḥ
tamasas tu rajas tasmāt sattvaṁ yad brahma-darśanam

pārthivāt—from earth; *dāruṇaḥ*—firewood; *dhūmaḥ*—smoke; *tasmāt*—from that; *agniḥ*—fire; *trayī*—Vedic sacrifices; *mayaḥ*—made of; *tama-*

saḥ—in the mode of ignorance; *tu*—but; *rajaḥ*—the mode of passion; *tasmāt*—from that; *sattvam*—the mode of goodness; *yat*—which; *brahma*—the Absolute Truth; *darśanam*—realization.

Firewood is a transformation of earth, but smoke is better than the raw wood. And fire is still better, for by fire we can derive the benefits of superior knowledge [through Vedic sacrifices]. Similarly, passion [rajas] is better than ignorance [tamas], but goodness [sattva] is best because by goodness one can come to realize the Absolute Truth.

PURPORT As explained above, one can get release from the conditioned life of material existence by devotional service to the Personality of Godhead. It is further comprehended herein that one has to rise to the platform of the mode of goodness (*sattva*) so that one can be eligible for the devotional service of the Lord. But if there are impediments on the progressive path, anyone, even from the platform of *tamas,* can gradually rise to the *sattva* platform by the expert direction of the spiritual master. Sincere candidates must, therefore, approach an expert spiritual master for such a progressive march, and the bona fide, expert spiritual master is competent to direct a disciple from any stage of life: *tamas, rajas* or *sattva.*

It is a mistake, therefore, to consider that worship of any quality or any form of the Supreme Personality of Godhead is equally beneficial. Except Viṣṇu, all forms are separated, being manifested under the conditions of material energy, and therefore these forms of material energy cannot help anyone rise to the platform of *sattva*, which alone can liberate a person from material bondage.

The uncivilized state of life, or the life of the lower animals, is controlled by the mode of *tamas.* The civilized life of man, with a passion for various types of material benefits, is the stage of *rajas.* The *rajas* stage of life gives a slight clue to the realization of the Absolute Truth in the forms of fine sentiments in philosophy, art and culture with moral and ethical principles, but the mode of *sattva* is a still higher stage of material quality, which actually helps one in realizing the Absolute Truth. In other words, there is a qualitative difference between the different kinds of worshiping methods as well as the respective results derived from the predominating deities, namely Brahmā, Viṣṇu and Hara.

TEXT 25

भेजिरे मुनयोऽथाग्रे भगवन्तमधोक्षजम् ।
सत्त्वं विशुद्धं क्षेमाय कल्पन्ते येऽनु तानिह ॥ २५ ॥

bhejire munayo 'thāgre bhagavantam adhokṣajam
sattvaṁ viśuddhaṁ kṣemāya kalpante ye 'nu tān iha

bhejire—rendered service unto; *munayaḥ*—the sages; *atha*—thus; *agre*—previously; *bhagavantam*—unto the Personality of Godhead; *adhokṣajam*—the Transcendence; *sattvam*—existence; *viśuddham*—above the three modes of nature; *kṣemāya*—to derive the ultimate benefit; *kalpante*—deserve; *ye*—those; *anu*—follow; *tān*—those; *iha*—in this material world.

Previously all the great sages rendered service unto the Personality of Godhead due to His existence above the three modes of material nature. They worshiped Him to become free from material conditions and thus derive the ultimate benefit. Whoever follows such great authorities is also eligible for liberation from the material world.

PURPORT The purpose of performing religion is neither to profit by material gain nor to get the simple knowledge of discerning matter from spirit. The ultimate aim of religious performances is to release oneself from material bondage and regain the life of freedom in the transcendental world, where the Personality of Godhead is the Supreme Person. Laws of religion, therefore, are directly enacted by the Personality of Godhead, and except for the *mahājanas,* or the authorized agents of the Lord, no one knows the purpose of religion. There are twelve particular agents of the Lord who know the purpose of religion, and all of them render transcendental service unto Him. Persons who desire their own good may follow these *mahājanas* and thus attain the supreme benefit.

TEXT 26

मुमुक्षवो घोररूपान् हित्वा भूतपतीनथ ।
नारायणकलाः शान्ता भजन्ति ह्यनसूयवः ॥ २६ ॥

mumukṣavo ghora-rūpān hitvā bhūta-patīn atha
nārāyaṇa-kalāḥ śāntā bhajanti hy anasūyavaḥ

mumukṣavaḥ—persons desiring liberation; *ghora*—horrible, ghastly; *rūpān*—forms like that; *hitvā*—rejecting; *bhūta-patīn*—demigods; *atha*—for this reason; *nārāyaṇa*—the Personality of Godhead; *kalāḥ*—plenary portions; *śāntāḥ*—all-blissful; *bhajanti*—do worship; *hi*—certainly; *anasūyavaḥ*—nonenvious.

Those who are serious about liberation are certainly nonenvious, and they respect all. Yet they reject the horrible and ghastly forms of the demigods and worship only the all-blissful forms of Lord Viṣṇu and His plenary portions.

PURPORT The Supreme Personality of Godhead Śrī Kṛṣṇa, who is the original person of the Viṣṇu categories, expands Himself in two different categories, namely integrated plenary portions and separated parts and parcels. The separated parts and parcels are the servitors, and the integrated plenary portions of *viṣṇu-tattvas* are the worshipful objects of service.

All demigods who are empowered by the Supreme Lord are also separated parts and parcels. They do not belong to the categories of *viṣṇu-tattva*. The *viṣṇu-tattvas* are living beings equally as powerful as the original form of the Personality of Godhead, and They display different categories of power in consideration of different times and circumstances. The separated parts and parcels are powerful by limitation. They do not have unlimited power like the *viṣṇu-tattvas*. Therefore, one should never classify the *viṣṇu-tattvas*, or the plenary portions of Nārāyaṇa, the Personality of Godhead, in the same categories with the parts and parcels. If anyone does so he becomes at once an offender by the name *pāṣaṇḍī*. In the age of Kali many foolish persons commit such unlawful offenses and equalize the two categories.

The separated parts and parcels have different positions in the estimation of material powers, and some of them are like Kāla-bhairava, Śmaśāna-bhairava, Śani, Mahākālī and Caṇḍikā. These demigods are worshiped mostly by those who are in the lowest categories of the mode of darkness or ignorance. Other demigods, like Brahmā, Śiva, Sūrya, Gaṇeśa and many similar deities, are worshiped by men in the mode of passion, urged on by the desire for material enjoyment. But those who are actually situated in the mode of goodness (*sattva-guṇa*) of material nature worship only *viṣṇu-tattvas. Viṣṇu-tattvas* are represented by various names and forms, such as Nārāyaṇa, Dāmodara, Vāmana, Govinda and Adhokṣaja.

The qualified *brāhmaṇas* worship the *viṣṇu-tattvas* represented by the *śālagrāma-śilā,* and some of the higher castes like the *kṣatriyas* and *vaiśyas* also generally worship the *viṣṇu-tattvas.*

Highly qualified *brāhmaṇas* situated in the mode of goodness have no grudges against the mode of worship of others. They have all respect for other demigods, even though they may look ghastly, like Kāla-bhairava or Mahākālī. They know very well that those horrible features of the Supreme Lord are all different servitors of the Lord under different conditions, yet they reject the worship of both horrible and attractive features of the demigods, and they concentrate only on the forms of Viṣṇu because they are serious about liberation from the material conditions. The demigods, even to the stage of Brahmā, the supreme of all the demigods, cannot offer liberation to anyone. Hiraṇyakaśipu underwent a severe type of penance to become eternal in life, but his worshipful deity, Brahmā, could not satisfy him with such blessings. Therefore Viṣṇu, and none else, is called *mukti-pāda,* or the Personality of Godhead who can bestow upon us *mukti,* liberation. The demigods, being like other living entities in the material world, are all liquidated at the time of the annihilation of the material structure. They are themselves unable to get liberation, and what to speak of giving liberation to their devotees. The demigods can award the worshipers some temporary benefit only, and not the ultimate one.

It is for this reason only that candidates for liberation deliberately reject the worship of the demigods, although they have no disrespect for any one of them.

TEXT 27

रजस्तमःप्रकृतयः समशीला भजन्ति वै ।
पितृभूतप्रजेशादीन् श्रियैश्वर्यप्रजेप्सवः ॥ २७ ॥

rajas-tamaḥ-prakṛtayaḥ sama-śīlā bhajanti vai
pitṛ-bhūta-prajeśādīn śriyaiśvarya-prajepsavaḥ

rajaḥ—the mode of passion; *tamaḥ*—the mode of ignorance; *prakṛta-*

yaḥ—of that mentality; *sama-śīlāḥ*—of the same categories; *bhajanti*—do worship; *vai*—actually; *pitṛ*—the forefathers; *bhūta*—other living beings; *prajeśa-ādīn*—controllers of cosmic administration; *śriyā*—enrichment; *aiśvarya*—wealth and power; *prajā*—progeny; *īpsavaḥ*—so desiring.

Those who are in the modes of passion and ignorance worship those in the same category—namely the forefathers, other living beings and the demigods who are in charge of cosmic activities—for they are urged by a desire to be materially benefited with women, wealth, power and progeny.

PURPORT There is no need to worship demigods of whatsoever category if one is serious about going back to Godhead. In the *Bhagavad-gītā* (7.20, 23) it is clearly said that those who are mad after material enjoyment approach the different demigods for temporary benefits, which are meant for men with a poor fund of knowledge. We should never desire to increase the depth of material enjoyment. Material enjoyment should be accepted only up to the point of the bare necessities of life and not more or less than that. To accept more material enjoyment means to bind oneself more and more to the miseries of material existence. More wealth, more women and false aristocracy are some of the demands of the materially disposed man because he has no information of the benefit derived from Viṣṇu worship. By Viṣṇu worship one can derive benefit in this life as well as in life after death. Forgetting these principles, foolish people who are after more wealth, more wives and more children worship various demigods. The aim of life is to end the miseries of life and not to increase them.

For material enjoyment there is no need to approach the demigods. The demigods are but servants of the Lord. As such, they are duty-bound to supply necessities of life in the form of water, light, air, etc. *One should work hard and worship the Supreme Lord by the fruits of one's hard labor for existence, and that should be the motto of life.* One should be careful to execute occupational service with faith in God in the proper way, and that will lead one gradually on the progressive march back to Godhead.

Lord Śrī Kṛṣṇa, when He was personally present at Vrajadhāma, stopped the worship of the demigod Indra and advised the residents of Vraja to worship their business and to have faith in God. Worshiping the multi-demigods for material gain is practically a perversity of religion. This sort of religious activity has been condemned in the very beginning of the *Bhāgavatam* as *kaitava-dharma*. There is only one religion in the world to be followed by one and all, and that is the *Bhāgavata-dharma*, or the religion which teaches one to worship the Supreme Personality of Godhead and no one else.

TEXTS 28–29

वासुदेवपरा वेदा वासुदेवपरा मखाः ।
वासुदेवपरा योगा वासुदेवपराः क्रियाः ॥ २८ ॥
वासुदेवपरं ज्ञानं वासुदेवपरं तपः ।
वासुदेवपरो धर्मो वासुदेवपरा गतिः ॥ २९ ॥

vāsudeva-parā vedā vāsudeva-parā makhāḥ
vāsudeva-parā yogā vāsudeva-parāḥ kriyāḥ

vāsudeva-paraṁ jñānaṁ vāsudeva-paraṁ tapaḥ
vāsudeva-paro dharmo vāsudeva-parā gatiḥ

vāsudeva—the Personality of Godhead; *parāḥ*—the ultimate goal; *vedāḥ*—revealed scriptures; *vāsudeva*—the Personality of Godhead; *parāḥ*—for worshiping; *makhāḥ*—sacrifices; *vāsudeva*—the Personality of Godhead; *parāḥ*—the means of attaining; *yogāḥ*—mystic paraphernalia; *vāsudeva*—the Personality of Godhead; *parāḥ*—under His control; *kriyāḥ*—fruitive activities; *vāsudeva*—the Personality of Godhead; *param*—the supreme; *jñānam*—knowledge; *vāsudeva*—the Personality of Godhead; *param*—best; *tapaḥ*—austerity; *vāsudeva*—the Personality of Godhead; *paraḥ*—superior quality; *dharmaḥ*—religion; *vāsudeva*—the Personality of Godhead; *parāḥ*—ultimate; *gatiḥ*—goal of life.

In the revealed scriptures, the ultimate object of knowledge is Śrī Kṛṣṇa, the Personality of Godhead. The purpose of performing sacrifice is to please Him. Yoga is for realizing Him. All fruitive activities are ultimately rewarded by Him only. He is supreme knowledge, and all severe austerities are performed to know Him. Religion [dharma] is rendering loving service unto Him. He is the supreme goal of life.

PURPORT That Śrī Kṛṣṇa, the Personality of Godhead, is the only object of worship is confirmed in these two *ślokas*. In the Vedic literature there is the same objective: establishing our relationship with Vāsudeva, acting according to that relationship, and ultimately reviving our lost loving service unto Him. That is the sum and substance of the *Vedas*. In the *Bhagavad-gītā* the same theory is confirmed by the Lord in His own words: the ultimate purpose of the *Vedas* is to know Him only. All the revealed scriptures are prepared by the Lord through His incarnation in the body of Śrīla Vyāsadeva just to remind the fallen souls, conditioned by material nature, of Śrī Kṛṣṇa, the Personality of Godhead. No demigod can award freedom from material bondage. That is the verdict of all the Vedic literatures. Impersonalists who have no information of the Personality of Godhead minimize the omnipotency of the Supreme Lord and put Him on equal footing with all other living beings, and for this act such impersonalists get freedom from material bondage only with great difficulty. They can surrender unto Him only after many, many births in the culture of transcendental knowledge.

One may argue that the Vedic activities are based on sacrificial ceremonies. That is true. But all such sacrifices are also meant for realizing the truth about Vāsudeva. Another name of Vāsudeva is Yajña (sacrifice), and in the *Bhagavad-gītā* it is clearly stated that all sacrifices and all activities are to be conducted for the satisfaction of Yajña, or Viṣṇu, the Personality of Godhead. This is the case also with the *yoga* systems. *Yoga* means to get into touch with the Supreme Lord. The process, however, includes several bodily features such as *āsana, dhyāna, prāṇāyāma* and meditation, and all of them are meant for concentrating upon the localized aspect of Vāsudeva represented as Paramātmā. Paramātmā realization is but partial realization of Vāsudeva, and if one is successful in that attempt, one realizes Vāsudeva in full. But by ill luck most *yogīs* are stranded by the powers of mysticism achieved through the bodily process. Ill-fated *yogīs* are given a chance in the next birth by being placed in the families of good learned *brāhmaṇas* or in the families of rich merchants in order to execute the unfinished task of Vāsudeva realization. If such fortunate *brāhmaṇas* and sons of rich men properly utilize the chance, they can easily realize Vāsudeva by good association with saintly persons. Unfortunately, such preferred persons are captivated again by material wealth and honor, and thus they practically forget the aim of life.

This is also so for the culture of knowledge. According to *Bhagavad-gītā* there are eighteen items in culturing knowledge. By such culture of knowledge one becomes gradually prideless, devoid of vanity, nonviolent, forbearing, simple, devoted to the great spiritual master, and self-controlled. By culture of knowledge one becomes unattached to hearth and home and becomes conscious of the miseries due to death, birth, old age and disease. And all culture of knowledge culminates in devotional service to the Personality of Godhead, Vāsudeva. Therefore, Vāsudeva is the ultimate aim in culturing all different branches of knowledge. Culture of knowledge leading one to the transcendental plane of meeting Vāsudeva is real knowledge. Physical knowledge in its various branches is condemned in the *Bhagavad-gītā* as *ajñāna,* or the opposite of real knowledge. The ultimate aim of physical knowledge is to satisfy the senses, which means prolongation of the term of material existence and thereby continuance of the threefold miseries. So prolonging the miserable life of material existence is nescience. But the same physical knowledge leading to the way of spiritual understanding helps one to end the miserable life of physical existence and to begin the life of spiritual existence on the plane of Vāsudeva.

The same applies to all kinds of austerities. *Tapasya* means voluntary acceptance of bodily pains to achieve some higher end of life. Rāvaṇa and Hiraṇyakaśipu underwent a severe type of bodily torture to achieve the end of sense gratification. Sometimes modern politicians also undergo severe types of austerities to achieve some political end. This is not actually *tapasya.* One should accept voluntary bodily inconvenience for the sake of knowing Vāsudeva because that is the way of real austerities. Otherwise all forms of austerities are classified as modes of passion and ignorance. Passion and ignorance cannot end the miseries of life. Only the mode of goodness can mitigate the threefold miseries of life. Vasudeva and Devakī, the so-called father and mother of Lord Kṛṣṇa, underwent penances to get Vāsudeva as their son. Lord Śrī Kṛṣṇa is the father of all living beings (Bg. 14.4). Therefore He is the original living being of all other living beings. He is the original eternal enjoyer amongst all other enjoyers. Therefore no one can be His begetting father, as the ignorant may think. Lord Śrī Kṛṣṇa agreed to become the son of Vasudeva and Devakī upon being pleased with their severe austerities. Therefore if any austerities have to be done, they must be done to achieve the end of knowledge, Vāsudeva.

Vāsudeva is the original Personality of Godhead Lord Śrī Kṛṣṇa. As explained before, the original Personality of Godhead expands Himself by innumerable forms. Such expansion of forms is made possible by His various energies. His energies are also multifarious, and His internal energies are superior and external energies inferior in quality. They are explained in the *Bhagavad-gītā* (7.4–6) as the *parā* and the *aparā prakṛtis*. So His expansions of various forms which take place via the internal energies are superior forms, whereas the expansions which take place via the external energies are inferior forms. The living entities are also His expansions. The living entities who are expanded by His internal potency are eternally liberated persons, whereas those who are expanded in terms of the material energies are eternally conditioned souls. Therefore, all culture of knowledge, austerities, sacrifice and activities should be aimed at changing the quality of the influence that is acting upon us. For the present, we are all being controlled by the external energy of the Lord, and just to change the quality of the influence, we must endeavor to cultivate spiritual energy. In the *Bhagavad-gītā* it is said that those who are *mahātmās,* or those whose minds have been so broadened as to be engaged in the service of Lord Kṛṣṇa, are under the influence of the internal potency, and the effect is that such broadminded living beings are constantly engaged in the service of the Lord without deviation. That should be the aim of life. And that is the verdict of all the Vedic literatures. No one should bother himself with fruitive activities or dry speculation about transcendental knowledge. Everyone should at once engage himself in the transcendental loving service of the Lord. Nor should one worship different demigods who work as different hands of the Lord for creation, maintenance or destruction of the material world. There are innumerable powerful demigods who look over the external management of the material world. They are all different assisting hands of Lord Vāsudeva. Even Lord Śiva and Lord Brahmā are included in the list of demigods, but Lord Viṣṇu, or Vāsudeva, is always transcendentally situated. Even though He accepts the quality of goodness of the material world, He is still transcendental to all the material modes. The following example will clear that matter more explicitly. In the prison house there are the prisoners and the managers of the prison house. Both the managers and the prisoners are bound by the laws of the king. But even though the king sometimes comes in the prison, he is not bound by the laws of the prison house. The king is therefore always transcendental to the laws of the prison house, as the Lord is always transcendental to the laws of the material world.

TEXT 30

स एवेदं ससर्जाग्रे भगवानात्ममायया ।
सदसद्रूपया चासौ गुणमयागुणो विभुः ॥ ३० ॥

sa evedaṁ sasarjāgre bhagavān ātma-māyayā
sad-asad-rūpayā cāsau guṇamayāguṇo vibhuḥ

saḥ—that; *eva*—certainly; *idam*—this; *sasarja*—created; *agre*—before; *bhagavān*—the Personality of Godhead; *ātma-māyayā*—by His personal potency; *sat*—the cause; *asat*—the effect; *rūpayā*—by forms; *ca*—and; *asau*—the same Lord; *guṇa-maya*—in the modes of material nature; *aguṇaḥ*—transcendental; *vibhuḥ*—the Absolute.

In the beginning of the material creation, that Absolute Personality of Godhead [Vāsudeva], in His transcendental position, created the energies of cause and effect by His own internal energy.

PURPORT The position of the Lord is always transcendental because the causal and effectual energies required for the creation of the material world were also created by Him. He is unaffected, therefore, by the qualities of the material modes. His existence, form, activities and paraphernalia all existed before the material creation.* He is all-spiritual and has nothing to do with the qualities of the material world, which are qualitatively distinct from the spiritual qualities of the Lord.

TEXT 31

तया विलसितेष्वेषु गुणेषु गुणवानिव ।
अन्तःप्रविष्ट आभाति विज्ञानेन विजृम्भितः ॥ ३१ ॥

tayā vilasiteṣv eṣu guṇeṣu guṇavān iva
antaḥ-praviṣṭa ābhāti vijñānena vijṛmbhitaḥ

---

* *Śrīpāda Śaṅkarācārya,* the head of the Māyāvāda school, accepts this transcendental position of Lord Kṛṣṇa in his commentation on *Bhagavad-gītā.*

tayā—by them; *vilasiteṣu*—although in the function; *eṣu*—these; *guṇeṣu*—the modes of material nature; *guṇavān*—affected by the modes; *iva*—as if; *antaḥ*—within; *praviṣṭaḥ*—entered into; *ābhāti*—appears to be; *vijñānena*—by transcendental consciousness; *vijṛmbhitaḥ*—fully enlightened.

After creating the material substance, the Lord [Vāsudeva] expands Himself and enters into it. And although He is within the material modes of nature and appears to be one of the created beings, He is always fully enlightened in His transcendental position.

PURPORT The living entities are separated parts and parcels of the Lord, and the conditioned living entities, who are unfit for the spiritual kingdom, are strewn within the material world to enjoy matter to the fullest extent. As Paramātmā and eternal friend of the living entities, the Lord, by one of His plenary portions, accompanies the living entities to guide them in their material enjoyment and to become witness to all activities. While the living entities enjoy the material conditions, the Lord maintains His transcendental position without being affected by the material atmosphere. In the Vedic literatures (*śruti*) it is said that there are two birds in one tree.* One of them is eating the fruit of the tree, while the other is witnessing the actions. The witness is the Lord, and the fruit-eater is the living entity. The fruit-eater (living entity) has forgotten his real identity and is overwhelmed in the fruitive activities of the material conditions, but the Lord (Paramātmā) is always full in transcendental knowledge. That is the difference between the Supersoul and the conditioned soul. The conditioned soul, the living entity, is controlled by the laws of nature, while the Paramātmā, or the Supersoul, is the controller of the material energy.

TEXT 32

यथा ह्यवहितो वह्निर्दारुष्वेकः स्वयोनिषु ।
नानेव भाति विश्वात्मा भूतेषु च तथा पुमान् ॥ ३२ ॥

yathā hy avahito vahnir dāruṣv ekaḥ sva-yoniṣu
nāneva bhāti viśvātmā bhūteṣu ca tathā pumān

* *dvā suparṇā sayujā sakhāyā samānaṁ vṛkṣaṁ pariṣasvajāte*
tayor anyaḥ pippalaṁ svādv atty anaśnann anyo 'bhicākaśīti
(*Muṇḍaka Upaniṣad* 3.1.1)

yathā—as much as; *hi*—exactly like; *avahitaḥ*—surcharged with; *vahniḥ*—fire; *dāruṣu*—in wood; *ekaḥ*—one; *sva-yoniṣu*—the source of manifestation; *nānā iva*—like different entities; *bhāti*—illuminates; *viśva-ātmā*—the Lord as Paramātmā; *bhūteṣu*—in the living entities; *ca*—and; *tathā*—in the same way; *pumān*—the Absolute Person.

The Lord, as Supersoul, pervades all things, just as fire permeates wood, and so He appears to be of many varieties, though He is the absolute one without a second.

PURPORT Lord Vāsudeva, the Supreme Personality of Godhead, by one of His plenary parts expands Himself all over the material world, and His existence can be perceived even within the atomic energy. Matter, antimatter, proton, neutron—in all these one can perceive the manifestation of the Paramātmā feature of the Lord by proper spiritual culture. As from wood, fire can be manifested, or as butter can be churned out of milk, so also the presence of the Lord as Paramātmā can be felt by the process of legitimate hearing and chanting of the transcendental subjects which are especially treated in the Vedic literatures like the *Upaniṣads* and *Vedānta. Śrīmad-Bhāgavatam* is the bona fide explanation of these Vedic literatures. The Lord can be realized through the aural reception of the transcendental message, and that is the only way to experience the transcendental subject. As fire is kindled from wood by another fire, the divine consciousness of man can similarly be kindled by another divine grace. His Divine Grace the spiritual master can kindle the spiritual fire from the woodlike living entity by imparting proper spiritual messages injected through the receptive ear. Therefore one is required to approach the proper spiritual master with receptive ears only, and thus divine existence is gradually realized. The difference between animality and humanity lies in this process only. A human being can hear properly, whereas an animal cannot.

TEXT 33

असौ गुणमयैर्भावैर्भूतसूक्ष्मेन्द्रियात्मभिः ।
स्वनिर्मितेषु निर्विष्टो भुङ्क्ते भूतेषु तद्गुणान् ॥ ३३ ॥

asau guṇamayair bhāvair bhūta-sūkṣmendriyātmabhiḥ
sva-nirmiteṣu nirviṣṭo bhuṅkte bhūteṣu tad-guṇān

asau—that Paramātmā; *guṇa-mayaiḥ*—influenced by the modes of nature; *bhāvaiḥ*—naturally; *bhūta*—created; *sūkṣma*—subtle; *indriya*—senses; *ātmabhiḥ*—by the living beings; *sva-nirmiteṣu*—in His own creation; *nirviṣṭaḥ*—entering; *bhuṅkte*—causes to enjoy; *bhūteṣu*—in the living entities; *tat-guṇān*—those modes of nature.

The Supersoul enters into the bodies of the created beings who are influenced by the modes of material nature and causes them to enjoy the effects of these modes by the subtle mind.

PURPORT There are 8,400,000 species of living beings beginning from the highest intellectual being, Brahmā, down to the insignificant ant, and all of them are enjoying the material world according to the desires of the subtle mind and gross material body. The gross material body is based on the conditions of the subtle mind, and the senses are created according to the desire of the living being. The Lord as Paramātmā helps the living being to get material happiness because the living being is helpless in all respects in obtaining what he desires. He proposes, and the Lord disposes. In another sense, the living beings are parts and parcels of the Lord. They are therefore one with the Lord. In the *Bhagavad-gītā* the living beings in all varieties of bodies have been claimed by the Lord as His sons. The sufferings and enjoyments of the sons are indirectly the sufferings and enjoyments of the father. Still the father is not in any way affected directly by the suffering and enjoyment of the sons. He is so kind that He constantly remains with the living being as Paramātmā and always tries to convert the living being towards the real happiness.

TEXT 34

भावयत्येष सत्त्वेन लोकान् वै लोकभावनः ।
लीलावतारानुरतो देवतिर्यङ्नरादिषु ॥ ३४ ॥

bhāvayaty eṣa sattvena lokān vai loka-bhāvanaḥ
līlāvatārānurato deva-tiryaṅ-narādiṣu

bhāvayati—maintains; *eṣaḥ*—all these; *sattvena*—in the mode of goodness; *lokān*—all over the universe; *vai*—generally; *loka-bhāvanaḥ*—the master of all the universes; *līlā*—pastimes; *avatāra*—incarnation;

anurataḥ—assuming the role; *deva*—the demigods; *tiryak*—lower animals; *nara-ādiṣu*—in the midst of human beings.

Thus the Lord of the universes maintains all planets inhabited by demigods, men and lower animals. Assuming the roles of incarnations, He performs pastimes to reclaim those in the mode of pure goodness.

PURPORT There are innumerable material universes, and in each and every universe there are innumerable planets inhabited by different grades of living entities in different modes of nature. The Lord (Viṣṇu) incarnates Himself in each and every one of them and in each and every type of living society. He manifests His transcendental pastimes amongst them just to create the desire to go back to Godhead. The Lord does not change His original transcendental position, but He appears to be differently manifested according to the particular time, circumstances and society.

Sometimes He incarnates Himself or empowers a suitable living being to act for Him, but in either case the purpose is the same: the Lord wants the suffering living beings to go back home, back to Godhead. The happiness which the living beings are hankering for is not to be found within any corner of the innumerable universes and material planets. The eternal happiness which the living being wants is obtainable in the kingdom of God, but the forgetful living beings under the influence of the material modes have no information of the kingdom of God. The Lord, therefore, comes to propagate the message of the kingdom of God, either personally as an incarnation or through His bona fide representative as the good son of God. Such incarnations or sons of God are not making propaganda for going back to Godhead only within the human society. Their work is also going on in all types of societies, amongst demigods and those other than human beings.

Thus end the Bhaktivedanta purports of the First Canto, Second Chapter, of the Śrīmad-Bhāgavatam, *entitled "Divinity and Divine Service."*

CHAPTER 3

Kṛṣṇa Is the Source of All Incarnations

सूत उवाच
TEXT 1 जगृहे पौरुषं रूपं भगवान्महदादिभिः ।
सम्भूतं षोडशकलमादौ लोकसिसृक्षया ॥ १ ॥

sūta uvāca
jagṛhe pauruṣaṁ rūpaṁ bhagavān mahad-ādibhiḥ
sambhūtaṁ ṣoḍaśa-kalam ādau loka-sisṛkṣayā

sūtaḥ uvāca—Sūta said; *jagṛhe*—accepted; *pauruṣam*—plenary portion as the *puruṣa* incarnation; *rūpam*—form; *bhagavān*—the Personality of Godhead; *mahat-ādibhiḥ*—with the ingredients of the material world; *sambhūtam*—thus there was the creation of; *ṣoḍaśa-kalam*—sixteen primary principles; *ādau*—in the beginning; *loka*—the universes; *sisṛkṣayā*—on the intention of creating.

Sūta said: In the beginning of the creation, the Lord first expanded Himself in the universal form of the puruṣa incarnation and manifested all the ingredients for the material creation. And thus at first there was the creation of the sixteen principles of material action. This was for the purpose of creating the material universes.

PURPORT The *Bhagavad-gītā* states that the Personality of Godhead Śrī Kṛṣṇa maintains these material universes by extending His plenary expansions. So this *puruṣa* form is the confirmation of the same principle. The original Personality of Godhead Vāsudeva, or Lord Kṛṣṇa, who is famous as the son of King Vasudeva or King Nanda, is full with all opulences, all potencies, all fame, all beauty, all knowledge and all renunciation. A part of His opulence is manifested as impersonal Brahman, and a part of His opulence is manifested as Paramātmā. This *puruṣa* feature of the same Personality of

Godhead Śrī Kṛṣṇa is the original Paramātmā manifestation of the Lord. There are three *puruṣa* features who effect material creation, and this form, who is known as the Kāraṇodakaśāyī Viṣṇu, is the first of the three. The others are known as the Garbhodakaśāyī Viṣṇu and the Kṣīrodakaśāyī Viṣṇu, which we shall know one after another. The innumerable universes are generated from the skin holes of this Kāraṇodakaśāyī Viṣṇu, and in each one of the universes the Lord enters as Garbhodakaśāyī Viṣṇu.

In the *Bhagavad-gītā* it is also mentioned that the material world is created at certain intervals and then again destroyed. This creation and destruction is done by the supreme will because of the conditioned souls, or the *nitya-baddha* living beings. The *nitya-baddha,* or the eternally conditioned souls, have the sense of individuality or *ahaṅkāra,* which dictates them sense enjoyment, which they are unable to have constitutionally. The Lord is the only enjoyer, and all others are enjoyed. The living beings are predominated enjoyers. But the eternally conditioned souls, forgetful of this constitutional position, have strong aspirations to enjoy. The chance to enjoy matter is given to the conditioned souls in the material world, and side by side they are given the chance to understand their real constitutional position. Those fortunate living entities who catch the truth and surrender unto the lotus feet of Vāsudeva after many, many births in the material world join the eternally liberated souls and thus are allowed to enter into the kingdom of Godhead. After this, such fortunate living entities need not come again within the occasional material creation. But those who cannot catch the constitutional truth are again merged into the *mahat-tattva* at the time of the annihilation of the material creation. When the creation is again set up, this *mahat-tattva* is again let loose. This *mahat-tattva* contains all the ingredients of the material manifestations, including the conditioned souls. Primarily this *mahat-tattva* is divided into sixteen parts, namely the five gross material elements and the eleven working instruments or senses. It is like the cloud in the clear sky. In the spiritual sky, the effulgence of Brahman is spread all around, and the whole system is dazzling in spiritual light. The *mahat-tattva* is assembled in some corner of the vast, unlimited spiritual sky, and the part which is thus covered by the *mahat-tattva* is called the material sky. This part of the spiritual sky, called the *mahat-tattva,* is only an insignificant portion of the whole spiritual sky, and within this *mahat-tattva* there are innumerable universes. All these universes are collectively produced by the Kāraṇodakaśāyī Viṣṇu, called also the Mahā-Viṣṇu, who simply throws His glance to impregnate the material sky.

TEXT 2

यस्याम्भसि शयानस्य योगनिद्रां वितन्वतः ।
नाभिहृदाम्बुजादासीद्ब्रह्मा विश्वसृजां पतिः ॥ २ ॥

yasyāmbhasi śayānasya yoga-nidrāṁ vitanvataḥ
nābhi-hradāmbujād āsīd brahmā viśva-sṛjāṁ patiḥ

yasya—whose; *ambhasi*—in the water; *śayānasya*—lying down; *yoga-nidrām*—sleeping in meditation; *vitanvataḥ*—ministering; *nābhi*—navel; *hrada*—out of the lake; *ambujāt*—from the lotus; *āsīt*—was manifested; *brahmā*—the grandfather of the living beings; *viśva*—the universe; *sṛjām*—the engineers; *patiḥ*—master.

A part of the puruṣa lies down within the water of the universe, from the navel lake of His body sprouts a lotus stem, and from the lotus flower atop this stem, Brahmā, the master of all engineers in the universe, becomes manifest.

PURPORT The first *puruṣa* is the Kāraṇodakaśāyī Viṣṇu. From His skin holes innumerable universes have sprung up. In each and every universe, the *puruṣa* enters as the Garbhodakaśāyī Viṣṇu. He is lying within the half of the universe which is full with the water of His body. And from the navel of Garbhodakaśāyī Viṣṇu has sprung the stem of the lotus flower, the birthplace of Brahmā, who is the father of all living beings and the master of all the demigod engineers engaged in the perfect design and working of the universal order. Within the stem of the lotus there are fourteen divisions of planetary systems, and the earthly planets are situated in the middle. Upwards there are other, better planetary systems, and the topmost system is called Brahmaloka or Satyaloka. Downwards from the earthly planetary system there are seven lower planetary systems inhabited by the *asuras* and similar other materialistic living beings.

From Garbhodakaśāyī Viṣṇu there is expansion of the Kṣīrodakaśāyī Viṣṇu, who is the collective Paramātmā of all living beings. He is called Hari, and from Him all incarnations within the universe are expanded.

Therefore, the conclusion is that the *puruṣa-avatāra* is manifested in three features—first the Kāraṇodakaśāyī who creates aggregate material ingredients in the *mahat-tattva,* second the Garbhodakaśāyī who enters in each and every universe, and third the Kṣīrodakaśāyī Viṣṇu who is the Paramātmā of every material object, organic or inorganic. One who knows these plenary features of the Personality of Godhead knows Godhead properly, and thus the knower becomes freed from the material conditions of birth, death, old age and disease, as it is confirmed in *Bhagavad-gītā.*

In this *śloka* the subject matter of Mahā-Viṣṇu is summarized. The Mahā-Viṣṇu lies down in some part of the spiritual sky by His own free will. Thus He lies on the ocean of *kāraṇa,* from where He glances over His material nature, and the *mahat-tattva* is at once created. Thus electrified by the power of the Lord, the material nature at once creates innumerable universes, just as in due course a tree decorates itself with innumerable grown fruits. The seed of the tree is sown by the cultivator, and the tree or creeper in due course becomes manifested with so many fruits. Nothing can take place without a cause. The Kāraṇa Ocean is therefore called the Causal Ocean. *Kāraṇa* means "causal." We should not foolishly accept the atheistic theory of creation. The description of the atheists is given in the *Bhagavad-gītā.* The atheist does not believe in the creator, but he cannot give a good theory to explain the creation. Material nature has no power to create without the power of the *puruṣa,* just as a *prakṛti,* or woman, cannot produce a child without the connection of a *puruṣa,* or man. The *puruṣa* impregnates, and the *prakṛti* delivers. We should not expect milk from the fleshy bags on the neck of a goat, although they look like breastly nipples. Similarly, we should not expect any creative power from the material ingredients; we must believe in the power of the *puruṣa,* who impregnates *prakṛti,* or nature. Because the Lord wished to lie down in meditation, the material energy created innumerable universes at once, in each of them the Lord lay down, and thus all the planets and the different paraphernalia were created at once by the will of the Lord. The Lord has unlimited potencies, and thus He can act as He likes by perfect planning, although personally He has nothing to do. No one is greater than or equal to Him. That is the verdict of the *Vedas.*

TEXT 3

यस्यावयवसंस्थानैः कल्पितो लोकविस्तरः ।
तद्वै भगवतो रूपं विशुद्धं सत्त्वमूर्जितम् ॥ ३ ॥

yasyāvayava-saṁsthānaiḥ kalpito loka-vistaraḥ
tad vai bhagavato rūpaṁ viśuddhaṁ sattvam ūrjitam

yasya—whose; *avayava*—bodily expansion; *saṁsthānaiḥ*—situated in; *kalpitaḥ*—is imagined; *loka*—planets of inhabitants; *vistaraḥ*—various; *tat vai*—but that is; *bhagavataḥ*—of the Personality of Godhead; *rūpam*—form; *viśuddham*—purely; *sattvam*—existence; *ūrjitam*—excellence.

It is believed that all the universal planetary systems are situated on the extensive body of the puruṣa, but He has nothing to do with the created material ingredients. His body is eternally in spiritual existence par excellence.

PURPORT The conception of the *virāṭ-rūpa* or *viśva-rūpa* of the Supreme Absolute Truth is especially meant for the neophyte who can hardly think of the transcendental form of the Personality of Godhead. To him a form means something of this material world, and therefore an opposite conception of the Absolute is necessary in the beginning to concentrate the mind on the power extension of the Lord. As stated above, the Lord extends His potency in the form of the *mahat-tattva,* which includes all material ingredients. The extension of power by the Lord and the Lord Himself personally are one in one sense, but at the same time the *mahat-tattva* is different from the Lord. Therefore the potency of the Lord and the Lord are simultaneously different and nondifferent. The conception of the *virāṭ-rūpa,* especially for the impersonalist, is thus nondifferent from the eternal form of the Lord. This eternal form of the Lord exists prior to the creation of the *mahat-tattva,* and it is stressed here that the eternal form of the Lord is par excellence spiritual or transcendental to the modes of material nature. The very same transcendental form of the Lord is manifested by His internal potency, and the formation of His multifarious manifestations of incarnations is always of the same transcendental quality, without any touch of the *mahat-tattva.*

TEXT 4

पश्यन्त्यदो रूपमदभ्रचक्षुषा
सहस्रपादोरुभुजाननाद्भुतम् ।

सहस्रमूर्धश्रवणाक्षिनासिकं
सहस्रमौल्यम्बरकुण्डलोल्लसत् ॥ ४ ॥

paśyanty ado rūpam adabhra-cakṣuṣā
sahasra-pādoru-bhujānanādbhutam
sahasra-mūrdha-śravaṇākṣi-nāsikaṁ
sahasra-mauly-ambara-kuṇḍalollasat

paśyanti—see; *adaḥ*—the form of the *puruṣa; rūpam*—form; *adabhra*—perfect; *cakṣuṣā*—by the eyes; *sahasra-pāda*—thousands of legs; *ūru*—thighs; *bhuja-ānana*—hands and faces; *adbhutam*—wonderful; *sahasra*—thousands of; *mūrdha*—heads; *śravaṇa*—ears; *akṣi*—eyes; *nāsikam*—noses; *sahasra*—thousands; *mauli*—garlands; *ambara*—dresses; *kuṇḍala*—earrings; *ullasat*—all glowing.

The devotees, with their perfect eyes, see the transcendental form of the puruṣa who has thousands of legs, thighs, arms and faces—all extraordinary. In that body there are thousands of heads, ears, eyes and noses. They are decorated with thousands of helmets and glowing earrings and are adorned with garlands.

PURPORT With our present materialized senses we cannot perceive anything of the transcendental Lord. Our present senses are to be rectified by the process of devotional service, and then the Lord Himself becomes revealed to us. In the *Bhagavad-gītā* it is confirmed that the transcendental Lord can be perceived only by pure devotional service. So it is confirmed in the *Vedas* that only devotional service can lead one to the side of the Lord and that only devotional service can reveal Him. In the *Brahma-saṁhitā* also it is said that the Lord is always visible to the devotees whose eyes have been anointed with the tinge of devotional service. So we have to take information of the transcendental form of the Lord from persons who have actually seen Him with perfect eyes smeared with devotional service. In the material world also we do not always see things with our own eyes; we sometimes see through the experience of those who have actually seen or done things. If that is the process for experiencing a mundane object, it is more perfectly applicable in matters transcendental. So only with patience and perseverance can we realize the transcendental subject matter regarding the Absolute Truth and His different forms. He is formless to the neophytes, but He is in transcendental form to the expert servitor.

TEXT 5

एतन्नानावताराणां निधानं बीजमव्ययम् ।
यस्यांशांशेन सृज्यन्ते देवतिर्यङ्नरादयः ॥ ५ ॥

etan nānāvatārāṇāṁ nidhānaṁ bījam avyayam
yasyāṁśāṁśena sṛjyante deva-tiryaṅ-narādayaḥ

etat—this (form); *nānā*—multifarious; *avatārāṇām*—of the incarnations; *nidhānam*—source; *bījam*—seed; *avyayam*—indestructible; *yasya*—whose; *aṁśa*—plenary portion; *aṁśena*—part of the plenary portion; *sṛjyante*—create; *deva*—demigods; *tiryak*—animals; *nara-ādayaḥ*—human beings and others.

This form [the second manifestation of the puruṣa] is the source and indestructible seed of multifarious incarnations within the universe. From the particles and portions of this form, different living entities, like demigods, men and others, are created.

PURPORT The *puruṣa,* after creating innumerable universes in the *mahat-tattva,* entered in each of them as the second *puruṣa,* Garbhodakaśāyī Viṣṇu. When He saw that within the universe there was only darkness and space, without a resting place, He filled half of the universe with water from His own perspiration and laid Himself down on the same water. This water is called Garbhodaka. Then from His navel the stem of the lotus flower sprouted, and on the flower petals the birth of Brahmā, or the master engineer of the universal plan, took place. Brahmā became the engineer of the universe, and the Lord Himself took charge of the maintenance of the universe as Viṣṇu. Brahmā was generated from *rajo-guṇa* of *prakṛti,* or the mode of passion in nature, and Viṣṇu became the Lord of the mode of goodness. Viṣṇu, being transcendental to all the modes, is always aloof from materialistic affection. This has already been explained. From Brahmā there is Rudra (Śiva), who is in charge of the mode of ignorance or darkness. He destroys the whole creation by the will of the Lord.

Therefore all three, namely Brahmā, Viṣṇu and Śiva, are incarnations of the Garbhodakaśāyī Viṣṇu. From Brahmā the other demigods like Dakṣa, Marīci, Manu and many others become incarnated to generate living entities within the universe. This Garbhodakaśāyī Viṣṇu is glorified in the *Vedas* in the hymns of *Garbha-stuti*, which begin with the description of the Lord as having thousands of heads, etc. The Garbhodakaśāyī Viṣṇu is the Lord of the universe, and although He appears to be lying within the universe, He is always transcendental. This also has already been explained. The Viṣṇu who is the plenary portion of the Garbhodakaśāyī Viṣṇu is the Supersoul of the universal life, and He is known as the maintainer of the universe or Kṣīrodakaśāyī Viṣṇu. So the three features of the original *puruṣa* are thus understood. And all the incarnations within the universe are emanations from this Kṣīrodakaśāyī Viṣṇu.

In different millennia there are different incarnations, and they are innumerable, although some of them are very prominent, such as Matsya, Kūrma, Varāha, Rāma, Nṛsiṁha, Vāmana and many others. These incarnations are called *līlā* incarnations. Then there are qualitative incarnations such as Brahmā, Viṣṇu, and Śiva (or Rudra) who take charge of the different modes of material nature.

Lord Viṣṇu is nondifferent from the Personality of Godhead. Lord Śiva is in the marginal position between the Personality of Godhead and the living entities, or *jīvas*. Brahmā is always a *jīva-tattva*. The highest pious living being, or the greatest devotee of the Lord, is empowered with the potency of the Lord for creation, and he is called Brahmā. His power is like the power of the sun reflected in valuable stones and jewels. When there is no such living being to take charge of the post of Brahmā, the Lord Himself becomes a Brahmā and takes charge of the post.

Lord Śiva is not an ordinary living being. He is the plenary portion of the Lord, but because Lord Śiva is in direct touch with material nature, he is not exactly in the same transcendental position as Lord Viṣṇu. The difference is like that between milk and yogurt. Yogurt is nothing but milk, and yet it cannot be used in place of milk.

The next incarnations are the Manus. Within one day's duration of the life of Brahmā (which is calculated by our solar year as 4,300,000 x 1,000 years) there are fourteen Manus. Therefore there are 420 Manus in one month of Brahmā and 5,040 Manus in one year of Brahmā. Brahmā lives for one hundred years of his age, and therefore there are 5,040 x 100 or

504,000 Manus in the duration of Brahmā's life. There are innumerable universes, with one Brahmā in each of them, and all of them are created and annihilated during the breathing time of the *puruṣa*. Therefore one can simply imagine how many millions of Manus there are during one breath of the *puruṣa*.

The Manus who are prominent within this universe are as follows: Yajña as Svāyambhuva Manu, Vibhu as Svārociṣa Manu, Satyasena as Uttama Manu, Hari as Tāmasa Manu, Vaikuṇṭha as Raivata Manu, Ajita as Cākṣuṣa Manu, Vāmana as Vaivasvata Manu (the present age is under the Vaivasvata Manu), Sārvabhauma as Sāvarṇi Manu, Ṛṣabha as Dakṣasāvarṇi Manu, Viṣvaksena as Brahma-sāvarṇi Manu, Dharmasetu as Dharma-sāvarṇi Manu, Sudhāmā as Rudra-sāvarṇi Manu, Yogeśvara as Deva-sāvarṇi Manu, and Bṛhadbhānu as Indra-sāvarṇi Manu. These are the names of one set of fourteen Manus covering 4,300,000,000 solar years as described above.

Then there are the *yugāvatāras,* or the incarnations of the millennia. The *yugas* are known as Satya-yuga, Tretā-yuga, Dvāpara-yuga and Kali-yuga. The incarnations of each *yuga* are of different color. The colors are white, red, black and yellow. In the Dvāpara-yuga, Lord Kṛṣṇa in black color appeared, and in the Kali-yuga Lord Caitanya in yellow color appeared.

So all the incarnations of the Lord are mentioned in the revealed scriptures. There is no scope for an imposter to become an incarnation, for an incarnation must be mentioned in the *śāstras*. An incarnation does not declare Himself to be an incarnation of the Lord, but great sages agree by the symptoms mentioned in the revealed scriptures. The features of the incarnation and the particular type of mission which He has to execute are mentioned in the revealed scriptures.

Apart from the direct incarnations, there are innumerable empowered incarnations. They are also mentioned in the revealed scriptures. Such incarnations are directly as well as indirectly empowered. When they are directly empowered they are called incarnations, but when they are indirectly empowered they are called *vibhūtis*. Directly empowered incarnations are the Kumāras, Nārada, Pṛthu, Śeṣa, Ananta, etc. As far as *vibhūtis* are concerned, they are very explicitly described in the *Bhagavad-gītā* in the *Vibhūti-yoga* chapter. And for all these different types of incarnations, the fountainhead is the Garbhodakaśāyī Viṣṇu.

TEXT 6

स एव प्रथमं देवः कौमारं सर्गमाश्रितः ।
चचार दुश्चरं ब्रह्मा ब्रह्मचर्यमखण्डितम् ॥ ६ ॥

sa eva prathamaṁ devaḥ kaumāraṁ sargam āśritaḥ
cacāra duścaraṁ brahmā brahmacaryam akhaṇḍitam

saḥ—that; *eva*—certainly; *prathamam*—first; *devaḥ*—Supreme Lord; *kaumāram*—named the Kumāras (unmarried); *sargam*—creation; *āśritaḥ*—under; *cacāra*—performed; *duścaram*—very difficult to do; *brahmā*—in the order of Brahman; *brahmacaryam*—under discipline to realize the Absolute (Brahman); *akhaṇḍitam*—unbroken.

First of all, in the beginning of creation, there were the four unmarried sons of Brahmā [the Kumāras], who, being situated in a vow of celibacy, underwent severe austerities for realization of the Absolute Truth.

PURPORT The creation of the material world is effected, maintained and then again annihilated at certain intervals. So there are different names of the creations in terms of the particular types of Brahmā, the father of the living beings in the creation. The Kumāras, as above mentioned, appeared in the Kaumāra creation of the material world, and to teach us the process of Brahman realization, they underwent a severe type of disciplinary action as bachelors. These Kumāras are empowered incarnations. And before executing the severe type of disciplinary actions, all of them became qualified *brāhmaṇas*. This example suggests that one must first acquire the qualifications of a *brāhmaṇa,* not simply by birth but also by quality, and then one can undergo the process of Brahman realization.

TEXT 7

द्वितीयं तु भवायास्य रसातलगतां महीम् ।
उद्धरिष्यन्नुपादत्त यज्ञेशः सौकरं वपुः ॥ ७ ॥

dvitīyaṁ tu bhavāyāsya rasātala-gatāṁ mahīm
uddhariṣyann upādatta yajñeśaḥ saukaraṁ vapuḥ

dvitīyam—the second; *tu*—but; *bhavāya*—for the welfare; *asya*—of this earth; *rasātala*—of the lowest region; *gatām*—having gone; *mahīm*—the earth; *uddhariṣyan*—lifting; *upādatta*—established; *yajñeśaḥ*—the proprietor or the supreme enjoyer; *saukaram*—hoggish; *vapuḥ*—incarnation.

The supreme enjoyer of all sacrifices accepted the incarnation of a boar [the second incarnation], and for the welfare of the earth He lifted the earth from the nether regions of the universe.

PURPORT The indication is that for each and every incarnation of the Personality of Godhead, the particular function executed is also mentioned. There cannot be any incarnation without a particular function, and such functions are always extraordinary. They are impossible for any living being to perform. The incarnation of the boar was to take the earth out of Pluto's region of filthy matter. Picking up something from a filthy place is done by a boar, and the all-powerful Personality of Godhead displayed this wonder to the *asuras,* who had hidden the earth in such a filthy place. There is nothing impossible for the Personality of Godhead, and although He played the part of a boar, by the devotees He is worshiped, staying always in transcendence.

TEXT 8

तृतीयमृषिसर्गं वै देवर्षित्वमुपेत्य सः ।
तन्त्रं सात्वतमाचष्ट नैष्कर्म्यं कर्मणां यतः ॥ ८ ॥

tṛtīyam ṛṣi-sargaṁ vai devarṣitvam upetya saḥ
tantraṁ sātvatam ācaṣṭa naiṣkarmyaṁ karmaṇāṁ yataḥ

tṛtīyam—the third one; *ṛṣi-sargam*—the millennium of the *ṛṣis; vai*—certainly; *devarṣitvam*—incarnation of the *ṛṣi* amongst the demigods; *upetya*—having accepted; *saḥ*—he; *tantram*—exposition of the *Vedas; sātvatam*—which is especially meant for devotional service; *ācaṣṭa*—collected; *naiṣkarmyam*—nonfruitive; *karmaṇām*—of work; *yataḥ*—from which.

In the millennium of the ṛṣis, the Personality of Godhead accepted the third empowered incarnation in the form of Devarṣi Nārada, who is a great sage among the demigods. He collected expositions of the

Vedas which deal with devotional service and which inspire nonfruitive action.

PURPORT The great Ṛṣi Nārada, who is an empowered incarnation of the Personality of Godhead, propagates devotional service all over the universe. All great devotees of the Lord all over the universe and in different planets and species of life are his disciples. Śrīla Vyāsadeva, the compiler of the *Śrīmad-Bhāgavatam,* is also one of his disciples. Nārada is the author of *Nārada Pañcarātra,* which is the exposition of the *Vedas* particularly for the devotional service of the Lord. This *Nārada Pañcarātra* trains the *karmīs,* or the fruitive workers, to achieve liberation from the bondage of fruitive work. The conditioned souls are mostly attracted by fruitive work because they want to enjoy life by the sweat of their own brows. The whole universe is full of fruitive workers in all species of life. The fruitive works include all kinds of economic development plans. But the law of nature provides that every action has its resultant reaction, and the performer of the work is bound up by such reactions, good or bad. The reaction of good work is comparative material prosperity, whereas the reaction of bad work is comparative material distress. But material conditions, either in so-called happiness or in so-called distress, are all meant ultimately for distress only. Foolish materialists have no information of how to obtain eternal happiness in the unconditional state. Śrī Nārada informs these foolish fruitive workers how to realize the reality of happiness. He gives direction to the diseased men of the world how one's present engagement can lead one to the path of spiritual emancipation. The physician directs the patient to take treated milk in the form of yogurt for his sufferings from indigestion due to his taking another milk preparation. So the cause of the disease and the remedy of the disease may be the same, but it must be treated by an expert physician like Nārada. The *Bhagavad-gītā* also gives the same solution of serving the Lord by the fruits of one's labor. That will lead one to the path of *naiṣkarmya,* or liberation.

TEXT 9

तुर्ये धर्मकलासर्गे नरनारायणावृषी ।
भूत्वात्मोपशमोपेतमकरोद् दुश्चरं तपः ॥ ९ ॥

turye dharma-kalā-sarge nara-nārāyaṇāv ṛṣī
bhūtvātmopaśamopetam akarod duścaraṁ tapaḥ

turye—in the fourth of the line; *dharma-kalā*—wife of Dharmarāja; *sarge*—being born of; *nara-nārāyaṇau*—named Nara and Nārāyaṇa; *ṛṣī*—sages; *bhūtvā*—becoming; *ātma-upaśama*—controlling the senses; *upetam*—for achievement of; *akarot*—undertook; *duścaram*—very strenuous; *tapaḥ*—penance.

In the fourth incarnation, the Lord became Nara and Nārāyaṇa, the twin sons of the wife of King Dharma. Thus He undertook severe and exemplary penances to control the senses.

PURPORT As King Ṛṣabha advised His sons, *tapasya*, or voluntary acceptance of penance for realization of the Transcendence, is the only duty of the human being; it was so done by the Lord Himself in an exemplary manner to teach us. The Lord is very kind to the forgetful souls. He therefore comes Himself and leaves behind necessary instructions and also sends His good sons as representatives to call all the conditioned souls back to Godhead. Recently, within the memory of everyone, Lord Caitanya also appeared for the same purpose: to show special favor to fallen souls of this age of iron industry. The incarnation of Nārāyaṇa is worshiped still at Badarī-nārāyaṇa, on the range of the Himalayas.

TEXT 10

पञ्चमः कपिलो नाम सिद्धेशः कालविप्लुतम् ।
प्रोवाचासुरये सांख्यं तत्त्वग्रामविनिर्णयम् ॥ १० ॥

pañcamaḥ kapilo nāma siddheśaḥ kāla-viplutam
provācāsuraye sāṅkhyaṁ tattva-grāma-vinirṇayam

pañcamaḥ—the fifth one; *kapilaḥ*—Kapila; *nāma*—of the name; *siddheśaḥ*—the foremost amongst the perfect; *kāla*—time; *viplutam*—lost; *provāca*—said; *āsuraye*—unto the *brāhmaṇa* named Āsuri; *sāṅkhyam*—metaphysics; *tattva-grāma*—the sum total of the creative elements; *vinirṇayam*—exposition.

The fifth incarnation, named Lord Kapila, is foremost among perfected beings. He gave an exposition of the creative elements and metaphysics to Āsuri Brāhmaṇa, for in course of time this knowledge had been lost.

PURPORT The sum total of the creative elements is twenty-four in all. Each and every one of them is explicitly explained in the system of Sāṅkhya philosophy. Sāṅkhya philosophy is generally called metaphysics by the European scholars. The etymological meaning of *sāṅkhya* is "that which explains very lucidly by analysis of the material elements." This was done for the first time by Lord Kapila, who is said herein to be the fifth in the line of incarnations.

TEXT 11

षष्ठम् अत्रेरपत्यत्वं वृतः प्राप्तोऽनसूयया ।
आन्वीक्षिकीमलर्काय प्रह्लादादिभ्य ऊचिवान् ॥ ११ ॥

ṣaṣṭham atrer apatyatvaṁ vṛtaḥ prāpto 'nasūyayā
ānvīkṣikīm alarkāya prahlādādibhya ūcivān

ṣaṣṭham—the sixth one; *atreḥ*—of Atri; *apatyatvam*—sonship; *vṛtaḥ*—being prayed for; *prāptaḥ*—obtained; *anasūyayā*—by Anasūyā; *ānvīkṣikīm*—on the subject of transcendence; *alarkāya*—unto Alarka; *prahlāda-ādibhyaḥ*—unto Prahlāda and others; *ūcivān*—spoke.

The sixth incarnation of the puruṣa was the son of the sage Atri. He was born from the womb of Anasūyā, who prayed for an incarnation. He spoke on the subject of transcendence to Alarka, Prahlāda and others [Yadu, Haihaya, etc.].

PURPORT The Lord incarnated Himself as Dattātreya, the son of Ṛṣi Atri and Anasūyā. The history of the birth of Dattātreya as an incarnation of the Lord is mentioned in the *Brahmāṇḍa Purāṇa* in connection with the story of the devoted wife. It is said there that Anasūyā, the wife of Ṛṣi Atri, prayed before the Lords Brahmā, Viṣṇu and Śiva as follows: "My lords, if [illegible]re pleased with me, and if you desire me to ask from you some sort [illegible]ngs, then I pray that you combine together to become my son."

This was accepted by the lords, and as Dattātreya the Lord expounded the philosophy of the spirit soul and especially instructed Alarka, Prahlāda, Yadu, Haihaya, etc.

TEXT 12

ततः सप्तम आकूत्यां रुचेर्यज्ञोऽभ्यजायत ।
स यामाद्यैः सुरगणैरपात्स्वायम्भुवान्तरम् ॥ १२ ॥

tataḥ saptama ākūtyāṁ rucer yajño 'bhyajāyata
sa yāmādyaiḥ sura-gaṇair apāt svāyambhuvāntaram

tataḥ—after that; *saptame*—the seventh in the line; *ākūtyām*—in the womb of Ākūti; *ruceḥ*—by Prajāpati Ruci; *yajñaḥ*—the Lord's incarnation as Yajña; *abhyajāyata*—advented; *saḥ*—He; *yāma-ādyaiḥ*—with Yāma and others; *sura-gaṇaiḥ*—with demigods; *apāt*—ruled; *svāyambhuva-antaram*—the reign of Svāyambhuva Manu.

The seventh incarnation was Yajña, the son of Prajāpati Ruci and his wife Ākūti. He controlled the period during the reign of Svāyambhuva Manu and was assisted by demigods such as His son Yāma.

PURPORT The administrative posts occupied by the demigods for maintaining the regulations of the material world are offered to the highly elevated pious living beings. When there is a scarcity of such pious living beings, the Lord incarnates Himself as Brahmā, Prajāpati, Indra, etc., and takes up the charge. During the period of Svāyambhuva Manu (the present period is of Vaivasvata Manu) there was no suitable living being who could occupy the post of Indra, the King of the Indraloka (heaven) planet. The Lord Himself at that time became Indra. Assisted by His own sons like Yāma and other demigods, Lord Yajña ruled the administration of the universal affairs.

TEXT 13

अष्टमे मेरुदेव्यां तु नाभेर्जात उरुक्रमः ।
दर्शयन् वर्त्म धीराणां सर्वाश्रमनमस्कृतम् ॥ १३ ॥

aṣṭame merudevyāṁ tu nābher jāta urukramaḥ
darśayan vartma dhīrāṇāṁ sarvāśrama-namaskṛtam

aṣṭame—the eighth of the incarnations; *merudevyām tu*—in the womb of Merudevī, the wife of; *nābheḥ*—King Nābhi; *jātaḥ*—took birth; *urukramaḥ*—the all-powerful Lord; *darśayan*—by showing; *vartma*—the way; *dhīrāṇām*—of the perfect beings; *sarva*—all; *āśrama*—orders of life; *namaskṛtam*—honored by.

The eighth incarnation was King Ṛṣabha, son of King Nābhi and his wife Merudevī. In this incarnation the Lord showed the path of perfection, which is followed by those who have fully controlled their senses and who are honored by all orders of life.

PURPORT The society of human beings is naturally divided into eight by orders and statuses of life—the four divisions of occupation and four divisions of cultural advancement. The intelligent class, the administrative class, the productive class and the laborer class are the four divisions of occupation. And the student life, the householder's life, retired life and renounced life are the four statuses of cultural advancement towards the path of spiritual realization. Out of these, the renounced order of life, or the order of *sannyāsa,* is considered the highest of all, and a *sannyāsī* is constitutionally the spiritual master for all the orders and divisions. In the *sannyāsa* order also there are four stages of upliftment toward perfection. These stages are called *kuṭīcaka, bahūdaka, parivrājakācārya,* and *paramahaṁsa.* The *paramahaṁsa* stage of life is the highest stage of perfection. This order of life is respected by all others. Mahārāja Ṛṣabha, the son of King Nābhi and Merudevī, was an incarnation of the Lord, and He instructed His sons to follow the path of perfection by *tapasya,* which sanctifies one's existence and enables one to attain the stage of spiritual happiness which is eternal and ever increasing. Every living being is searching after happiness, but no one knows where eternal and unlimited happiness is obtainable. Foolish men seek after material sense pleasure as a substitute for real happiness, but such foolish men forget that temporary so-called happiness derived from sense pleasures is also enjoyed by the dogs and hogs. No animal, bird or beast is bereft of this sense pleasure. In every species of life, including the human form of life, such happiness is immensely obtainable. The human form of life, however, is not meant for such cheap happiness. The human life is meant for attaining eternal and unlimited happiness by spiritual realization. This spiritual realization is obtained by *tapasya,* or undergoing voluntarily the path of penance and abstinence from material pleasure. Those who have been trained for abstinence in material pleasures are called *dhīra,* or men undisturbed by the senses. Only these *dhīras* can accept the orders of *sannyāsa,* and they can gradually rise to the status of the *paramahaṁsa,* which is adored by all members of society. King Ṛṣabha propagated this mission, and at the last stage He became completely aloof from the material bodily needs, which is a rare stage not to be imitated by foolish men, but to be worshiped by all.

TEXT 14

ऋषिभिर्याचितो भेजे नवमं पार्थिवं वपुः ।
दुग्धेमामोषधीर्विप्रास्तेनायं स उशत्तमः ॥ १४ ॥

ṛṣibhir yācito bheje navamaṁ pārthivaṁ vapuḥ
dugdhemām oṣadhīr viprās tenāyaṁ sa uśattamaḥ

ṛṣibhiḥ—by the sages; *yācitaḥ*—being prayed for; *bheje*—accepted; *navamam*—the ninth one; *pārthivam*—the ruler of the earth; *vapuḥ*—body; *dugdha*—milking; *imām*—all these; *oṣadhīḥ*—products of the earth; *viprāḥ*—O *brāhmaṇas; tena*—by; *ayam*—this; *saḥ*—he; *uśattamaḥ*—beautifully attractive.

O brāhmaṇas, in the ninth incarnation, the Lord, prayed for by sages, accepted the body of a king [Pṛthu] who cultivated the land to yield various products, and for that reason the earth was beautiful and attractive.

PURPORT Before the advent of King Pṛthu, there was great havoc of maladministration due to the vicious life of the previous king, the father of Mahārāja Pṛthu. The intelligent class of men (namely the sages and the *brāhmaṇas*) not only prayed for the Lord to come down, but also dethroned the previous king. It is the duty of the king to be pious and thus look after the all-around welfare of the citizens. Whenever there is some negligence on the part of the king in discharging his duty, the intelligent class of men must dethrone him. The intelligent class of men, however, do not occupy the royal throne, because they have much more important duties for the welfare of the public. Instead of occupying the royal throne, they prayed for the incarnation of the Lord, and the Lord came as Mahārāja Pṛthu. Real intelligent men, or qualified *brāhmaṇas,* never aspire for political posts. Mahārāja Pṛthu excavated many produces from the earth, and thus not only did the citizens become happy to have such a good king, but the complete sight of the earth also became beautiful and attractive.

TEXT 15

रूपं स जगृहे मात्स्यं चाक्षुषोदधिसम्प्लवे ।
नाव्यारोप्य महीमय्यामपाद्वैवस्वतं मनुम् ॥ १५ ॥

rūpaṁ sa jagṛhe mātsyaṁ cākṣuṣodadhi-samplave
nāvy āropya mahī-mayyām apād vaivasvataṁ manum

rūpam—form; *saḥ*—He; *jagṛhe*—accepted; *mātsyam*—of a fish; *cākṣuṣa*—Cākṣuṣa; *udadhi*—water; *samplave*—inundation; *nāvi*—on the boat; *āropya*—keeping on; *mahī*—the earth; *mayyām*—drowned in; *apāt*—protected; *vaivasvatam*—Vaivasvata; *manum*—Manu, the father of man.

When there was a complete inundation after the period of the Cākṣuṣa Manu and the whole world was deep within water, the Lord accepted the form of a fish and protected Vaivasvata Manu, keeping him up on a boat.

PURPORT According to Śrīpāda Śrīdhara Svāmī, the original commentator on the *Bhāgavatam,* there is not always a devastation after the change of every Manu. And yet this inundation after the period of Cākṣuṣa Manu took place in order to show some wonders to Satyavrata. But Śrī Jīva Gosvāmī has given definite proofs from authoritative scriptures (like *Viṣṇu-dharmottara, Mārkaṇḍeya Purāṇa, Harivaṁśa,* etc.) that there is always a devastation after the end of each and every Manu. Śrīla Viśvanātha Cakravartī has also supported Śrīla Jīva Gosvāmī, and he (Śrī Cakravartī) has also quoted from *Bhāgavatāmṛta* about this inundation after each Manu. Apart from this, the Lord, in order to show special favor to Satyavrata, a devotee of the Lord, in this particular period, incarnated Himself.

TEXT 16

सुरासुराणामुदधिं मथ्नतां मन्दराचलम् ।
दध्रे कमठरूपेण पृष्ठ एकादशे विभुः ॥ १६ ॥

surāsurāṇām udadhiṁ mathnatāṁ mandarācalam
dadhre kamaṭha-rūpeṇa pṛṣṭha ekādaśe vibhuḥ

sura—the theists; *asurāṇām*—of the atheists; *udadhim*—in the ocean; *mathnatām*—churning; *mandarācalam*—the Mandarācala Hill; *dadhre*—sustained; *kamaṭha*—tortoise; *rūpeṇa*—in the form of; *pṛṣṭhe*—shell; *ekādaśe*—the eleventh in the line; *vibhuḥ*—the great.

The eleventh incarnation of the Lord took the form of a tortoise whose shell served as a pivot for the Mandarācala Hill, which was being used as a churning rod by the theists and atheists of the universe.

PURPORT Once both the atheists and the theists were engaged in producing nectar from the sea so that all of them could become deathless by drinking it. At that time the Mandarācala Hill was used as the churning rod, and the shell of Lord Tortoise, the incarnation of Godhead, became the resting place (pivot) of the hill in the seawater.

TEXT 17

धान्वन्तरं द्वादशमं त्रयोदशममेव च ।
अपाययत्सुरानन्यान्मोहिन्या मोहयन् स्त्रिया ॥ १७ ॥

dhānvantaraṁ dvādaśamaṁ trayodaśamam eva ca
apāyayat surān anyān mohinyā mohayan striyā

dhānvantaram—the incarnation of Godhead named Dhanvantari; *dvādaśamam*—the twelfth in the line; *trayodaśamam*—the thirteenth in the line; *eva*—certainly; *ca*—and; *apāyayat*—gave to drink; *surān*—the demigods; *anyān*—others; *mohinyā*—by charming beauty; *mohayan*—alluring; *striyā*—in the form of a woman.

In the twelfth incarnation, the Lord appeared as Dhanvantari, and in the thirteenth He allured the atheists by the charming beauty of a woman and gave nectar to the demigods to drink.

TEXT 18

चतुर्दशं नारसिंहं बिभ्रद्दैत्येन्द्रमूर्जितम् ।
ददार करजैरूरावेरकां कटकृद्यथा ॥ १८ ॥

caturdaśaṁ nārasiṁhaṁ bibhrad daityendram ūrjitam
dadāra karajair ūrāv erakāṁ kaṭa-kṛd yathā

caturdaśam—the fourteenth in the line; *nāra-siṁham*—the incarnation of the Lord as half-man and half-lion; *bibhrat*—advented; *daitya-indram*—the king of the atheists; *ūrjitam*—strongly built; *dadāra*—bifurcated; *karajaiḥ*—by the nails; *ūrau*—on the lap; *erakām*—canes; *kaṭa-kṛt*—carpenter; *yathā*—just like.

In the fourteenth incarnation, the Lord appeared as Nṛsiṁha and bifurcated the strong body of the atheist Hiraṇyakaśipu with His nails, just as a carpenter pierces cane.

TEXT 19

पञ्चदशं वामनकं कृत्वागादध्वरं बलेः ।
पदत्रयं याचमानः प्रत्यादित्सुस्त्रिपिष्टपम् ॥ १९ ॥

pañcadaśaṁ vāmanakaṁ kṛtvāgād adhvaraṁ baleḥ
pada-trayaṁ yācamānaḥ pratyāditsus tri-piṣṭapam

pañcadaśam—the fifteenth in the line; *vāmanakam*—the dwarf *brāhmaṇa; kṛtvā*—by assumption of; *agāt*—went; *adhvaram*—arena of sacrifice; *baleḥ*—of King Bali; *pada-trayam*—three steps only; *yācamānaḥ*—begging; *pratyāditsuḥ*—willing at heart to return; *tri-piṣṭapam*—the kingdom of the three planetary systems.

In the fifteenth incarnation, the Lord assumed the form of a dwarf brāhmaṇa [Vāmana] and visited the arena of sacrifice arranged by Mahārāja Bali. Although at heart He was willing to regain the kingdom of the three planetary systems, He simply asked for a donation of three steps of land.

PURPORT The Almighty God can bestow upon anyone the kingdom of the universe from a very small beginning, and similarly, He can take away the kingdom of the universe on the plea of begging a small piece of land.

TEXT 20

अवतारे षोडशमे पश्यन् ब्रह्मद्रुहो नृपान् ।
त्रिःसप्तकृत्वः कुपितो निःक्षत्रामकरोन्महीम् ॥ २० ॥

avatāre ṣoḍaśame paśyan brahma-druho nṛpān
triḥ-sapta-kṛtvaḥ kupito niḥ-kṣatrām akaron mahīm

avatāre—in the incarnation of the Lord; *ṣoḍaśame*—the sixteenth; *paśyan*—seeing; *brahma-druhaḥ*—disobedient to the orders of the *brāhmaṇas; nṛpān*—the kingly order; *triḥ-sapta*—thrice seven times; *kṛtvaḥ*—had done; *kupitaḥ*—being enraged; *niḥ*—negation; *kṣatrām*—the administrative class; *akarot*—did perform; *mahīm*—the earth.

In the sixteenth incarnation of the Godhead, the Lord [as Bhṛgupati] annihilated the administrative class [kṣatriyas] twenty-one times, being angry with them because of their rebellion against the brāhmaṇas [the intelligent class].

PURPORT The *kṣatriyas,* or the administrative class of men, are expected to rule the planet by the direction of the intelligent class of men, who give direction to the rulers in terms of the standard *śāstras,* or the books of revealed knowledge. The rulers carry on the administration according to that direction. Whenever there is disobedience on the part of the *kṣatriyas,* or the administrative class, against the orders of the learned and intelligent *brāhmaṇas,* the administrators are removed by force from the posts, and arrangement is made for better administration.

TEXT 21

ततः सप्तदशे जातः सत्यवत्यां पराशरात् ।
चक्रे वेदतरोः शाखा दृष्ट्वा पुंसोऽल्पमेधसः ॥ २१ ॥

tataḥ saptadaśe jātaḥ satyavatyāṁ parāśarāt
cakre veda-taroḥ śākhā dṛṣṭvā puṁso 'lpa-medhasaḥ

tataḥ—thereafter; *saptadaśe*—in the seventeenth incarnation; *jātaḥ*—advented; *satyavatyām*—in the womb of Satyavatī; *parāśarāt*—by Parāśara

Muni; *cakre*—prepared; *veda-taroḥ*—of the desire tree of the *Vedas; śākhāḥ*—branches; *dṛṣṭvā*—be seeing; *puṁsaḥ*—the people in general; *alpa-medhasaḥ*—less intelligent.

Thereafter, in the seventeenth incarnation of Godhead, Śrī Vyāsadeva appeared in the womb of Satyavatī through Parāśara Muni, and he divided the one Veda into several branches and subbranches, seeing that the people in general were less intelligent.

PURPORT Originally the *Veda* is one. But Śrīla Vyāsadeva divided the original *Veda* into four, namely *Sāma, Yajur, Ṛg, Atharva,* and then again they were explained in different branches like the *Purāṇas* and the *Mahābhārata.* Vedic language and the subject matter are very difficult for ordinary men. They are understood by the highly intelligent and self-realized *brāhmaṇas.* But the present age of Kali is full of ignorant men. Even those who are born by a *brāhmaṇa* father are, in the present age, no better than the *śūdras* or the women. The twice-born men, namely the *brāhmaṇas, kṣatriyas* and *vaiśyas,* are expected to undergo a cultural purificatory process known as *saṁskāras,* but because of the bad influence of the present age the so-called members of the *brāhmaṇa* and other high-order families are no longer highly cultured. They are called the *dvija-bandhus,* or the friends and family members of the twice-born. But these *dvija-bandhus* are classified amongst the *śūdras* and the women. Śrīla Vyāsadeva divided the *Vedas* into various branches and subbranches for the sake of the less intelligent classes like the *dvija-bandhus, śūdras* and women.

TEXT 22

नरदेवत्वमापन्नः सुरकार्यचिकीर्षया ।
समुद्रनिग्रहादीनि चक्रे वीर्याण्यतः परम् ॥ २२ ॥

nara-devatvam āpannaḥ sura-kārya-cikīrṣayā
samudra-nigrahādīni cakre vīryāṇy ataḥ param

nara—human being; *devatvam*—divinity; *āpannaḥ*—having assumed the form of; *sura*—the demigods; *kārya*—activities; *cikīrṣayā*—for the purpose of performing; *samudra*—the Indian Ocean; *nigraha-ādīni*—controlling, etc.; *cakre*—did perform; *vīryāṇi*—superhuman prowess; *ataḥ param*—thereafter.

In the eighteenth incarnation, the Lord appeared as King Rāma. In order to perform some pleasing work for the demigods, He exhibited superhuman powers by controlling the Indian Ocean and then killing the atheist King Rāvaṇa, who was on the other side of the sea.

PURPORT The Personality of Godhead Śrī Rāma assumed the form of a human being and appeared on the earth for the purpose of doing some pleasing work for the demigods or the administrative personalities to maintain the order of the universe. Sometimes great demons and atheists like Rāvaṇa and Hiraṇyakaśipu and many others become very famous due to advancing material civilization by the help of material science and other activities with a spirit of challenging the established order of the Lord. For example, the attempt to fly to other planets by material means is a challenge to the established order. The conditions of each and every planet are different, and different classes of human beings are accommodated there for particular purposes mentioned in the codes of the Lord. But, puffed up by tiny success in material advancement, sometimes the godless materialists challenge the existence of God. Rāvaṇa was one of them, and he wanted to deport ordinary men to the planet of Indra (heaven) by material means without consideration of the necessary qualifications. He wanted a staircase to be built up directly reaching the heavenly planet so that people might not be required to undergo the routine of pious work necessary to enter that planet. He also wanted to perform other acts against the established rule of the Lord. He even challenged the authority of Śrī Rāma, the Personality of Godhead, and kidnapped His wife, Sītā. Of course, Lord Rāma had come to chastise such atheists, answering the prayer and desire of the demigods. He therefore took up the challenge of Rāvaṇa, and the complete activity is the subject matter of the *Rāmāyaṇa*. Because Lord Rāmacandra was the Personality of Godhead, He exhibited superhuman activities which no human being, including the materially advanced Rāvaṇa, could perform. Lord Rāmacandra prepared a royal road on the Indian Ocean with stones that floated on the water. The modern scientists have done research in the area of weightlessness, but it is not possible to bring in weightlessness anywhere and everywhere. But because weightlessness is the creation of the Lord by which He can make the gigantic planets fly and float in the air, He made the stones even within this earth to be weightless and prepared a stone bridge on the sea without any supporting pillar. That is the display of the power of God.

TEXT 23

एकोनविंशे विंशतिमे वृष्णिषु प्राप्य जन्मनी ।
रामकृष्णाविति भुवो भगवानहरद्भरम् ॥ २३ ॥

ekonaviṁśe viṁśatime vṛṣṇiṣu prāpya janmanī
rāma-kṛṣṇāv iti bhuvo bhagavān aharad bharam

ekonaviṁśe—in the nineteenth; *viṁśatime*—in the twentieth also; *vṛṣṇiṣu*—in the Vṛṣṇi dynasty; *prāpya*—having obtained; *janmanī*—births; *rāma*—Balarāma; *kṛṣṇau*—Śrī Kṛṣṇa; *iti*—thus; *bhuvaḥ*—of the world; *bhagavān*—the Personality of Godhead; *aharat*—removed; *bharam*—burden.

In the nineteenth and twentieth incarnations, the Lord advented Himself as Lord Balarāma and Lord Kṛṣṇa in the family of Vṛṣṇi [the Yadu dynasty], and by so doing He removed the burden of the world.

PURPORT The specific mention of the word *bhagavān* in this text indicates that Balarāma and Kṛṣṇa are original forms of the Lord. This will be further explained later. Lord Kṛṣṇa is not an incarnation of the *puruṣa,* as we learned from the beginning of this chapter. He is directly the original Personality of Godhead, and Balarāma is the first plenary manifestation of the Lord. From Baladeva the first phalanx of plenary expansions, Vāsudeva, Saṅkarṣaṇa, Aniruddha and Pradyumna, expands. Lord Śrī Kṛṣṇa is Vāsudeva, and Baladeva is Saṅkarṣaṇa.

TEXT 24

ततः कलौ सम्प्रवृत्ते सम्मोहाय सुरद्विषाम् ।
बुद्धो नाम्नाञ्जनसुतः कीकटेषु भविष्यति ॥ २४ ॥

tataḥ kalau sampravṛtte sammohāya sura-dviṣām
buddho nāmnāñjana-sutaḥ kīkaṭeṣu bhaviṣyati

tataḥ—thereafter; *kalau*—the age of Kali; *sampravṛtte*—having ensued;

sammohāya—for the purpose of deluding; *sura*—the theists; *dviṣām*—those who are envious; *buddhaḥ*—Lord Buddha; *nāmnā*—of the name; *añjana-sutaḥ*—whose mother was Añjanā; *kīkaṭeṣu*—in the province of Gayā (Bihar); *bhaviṣyati*—will take place.

Then, in the beginning of Kali-yuga, the Lord will appear as Lord Buddha, the son of Añjanā, in the province of Gayā, just for the purpose of deluding those who are envious of the faithful theist.

PURPORT Lord Buddha, a powerful incarnation of the Personality of Godhead, appeared in the province of Gayā (Bihar) as the son of Añjanā, and he preached his own conception of nonviolence and deprecated even the animal sacrifices sanctioned in the *Vedas.* At the time when Lord Buddha appeared, the people in general were atheistic and preferred animal flesh to anything else. On the plea of Vedic sacrifice, every place was practically turned into a slaughterhouse, and animal-killing was indulged in unrestrictedly. Lord Buddha preached nonviolence, taking pity on the poor animals. He preached that he did not believe in the tenets of the *Vedas* and stressed the adverse psychological effects incurred by animal-killing. Less intelligent men of the age of Kali, who had no faith in God, followed his principle, and for the time being they were trained in moral discipline and nonviolence, the preliminary steps for proceeding further on the path of God realization. He deluded the atheists because such atheists who followed his principles did not believe in God, but they kept their absolute faith in Lord Buddha, who himself was the incarnation of God. Thus the faithless people were made to believe in God in the form of Lord Buddha. That was the mercy of Lord Buddha: he made the faithless faithful to him.

Killing of animals before the advent of Lord Buddha was the most prominent feature of the society. People claimed that these were Vedic sacrifices. When the *Vedas* are not accepted through the authoritative disciplic succession, the casual readers of the *Vedas* are misled by the flowery language of that system of knowledge. In the *Bhagavad-gītā* a comment has been made on such foolish scholars (*avipaścitaḥ*). The foolish scholars of Vedic literature who do not care to receive the transcendental message through the transcendental realized sources of disciplic succession are sure to be bewildered. To them, the ritualistic ceremonies are considered to be all in all. They have no depth of knowledge. According to the *Bhagavad-gītā* (15.15), *vedaiś ca sarvair aham eva vedyaḥ:* the whole system of the *Vedas* is to lead one gradually to the path of the Supreme Lord. The whole theme of Vedic literature is to know the Supreme Lord, the individual soul, the cosmic situation and the relation between all these items. When the relation is known, the relative function begins, and as a result of such a function the ultimate goal of life or going back to Godhead takes place in the easiest manner. Unfortunately, unauthorized scholars of the *Vedas* become captivated by the purificatory ceremonies only, and natural progress is thereby checked.

To such bewildered persons of atheistic propensity, Lord Buddha is the emblem of theism. He therefore first of all wanted to check the habit of animal-killing. The animal-killers are dangerous elements on the path going back to Godhead. There are two types of animal-killers. The soul is also sometimes called the "animal" or the living being. Therefore, both the slaughterer of animals and those who have lost their identity of soul are animal-killers.

Mahārāja Parīkṣit said that only the animal-killer cannot relish the transcendental message of the Supreme Lord. Therefore if people are to be educated to the path of Godhead, they must be taught first and foremost to *stop the process of animal-killing* as above mentioned. *It is nonsensical to say that animal-killing has nothing to do with spiritual realization.* By this dangerous theory many so-called *sannyāsīs* have sprung up by the grace of Kali-yuga who preach animal-killing under the garb of the *Vedas.* The subject matter has already been discussed in the conversation between Lord Caitanya and Maulana Chand Kazi Shaheb. The animal sacrifice as stated in the *Vedas* is different from the unrestricted animal-killing in the slaughterhouse. Because the *asuras* or the so-called scholars of Vedic literatures put forward the evidence of animal-killing in the *Vedas,* Lord Buddha superficially denied the authority of the *Vedas.* This rejection of the *Vedas* by Lord Buddha was adopted in order to save people from the vice of animal-killing as well as to save the poor animals from the slaughtering process of their big brothers who clamor for universal brotherhood, peace, justice and equity. There is no justice when there is animal-killing. Lord Buddha wanted to stop it completely, and therefore his cult of *ahiṁsā* was propagated not only in India but also outside the country.

Technically Lord Buddha's philosophy is called atheistic because there is no acceptance of the Supreme Lord and because that system of philosophy denied the authority of the *Vedas.* But that is an act of camouflage by the Lord. Lord Buddha is the incarnation of Godhead. As such, he is the original propounder of Vedic knowledge. He therefore cannot reject Vedic philosophy. But he rejected it outwardly because the *sura-dviṣa,* or the demons who are always envious of the devotees of Godhead, try to support cow-killing or animal-killing from the pages of the *Vedas,* and this is now being done by the modernized *sannyāsīs.* Lord Buddha had to reject the authority of the *Vedas* altogether. This is simply technical, and had it not been so he would not have been so accepted as the incarnation of Godhead. Nor would he have been worshiped in the transcendental songs of the poet Jayadeva, who is a Vaiṣṇava *ācārya.* Lord Buddha preached the preliminary principles of the *Vedas* in a manner suitable for the time being, and so also did Śaṅkarācārya to establish the authority of the *Vedas.* Therefore both Lord Buddha and Ācārya Śaṅkara paved the path of theism, and Vaiṣṇava *ācāryas,* specifically Lord Śrī Caitanya Mahāprabhu, led the people on the path towards a realization of going back to Godhead.

We are glad that people are taking interest in the nonviolent movement of Lord Buddha. But will they take the matter very seriously and close the animal slaughterhouses altogether? If not, there is no meaning to the *ahiṁsā* cult.

Śrīmad-Bhāgavatam was composed just prior to the beginning of the age of Kali (about five thousand years ago), and Lord Buddha appeared about twenty-six hundred years ago. Therefore in the *Śrīmad-Bhāgavatam* Lord Buddha is foretold. Such is the authority of this clear scripture. There are many such prophecies, and they are being fulfilled one after another. They will indicate the positive standing of *Śrīmad-Bhāgavatam,* which is *without trace of mistake, illusion, cheating and imperfection,* which are the four flaws of all conditioned souls. The liberated souls are above these flaws; therefore they can see and foretell things which are to take place on distant future dates.

TEXT 25

अथासौ युगसन्ध्यायां दस्युप्रायेषु राजसु ।
जनिता विष्णुयशसो नाम्ना कल्किर्जगत्पतिः ॥ २५ ॥

athāsau yuga-sandhyāyāṁ dasyu-prāyeṣu rājasu
janitā viṣṇu-yaśaso nāmnā kalkir jagat-patiḥ

atha—thereafter; *asau*—the same Lord; *yuga-sandhyāyām*—at the conjunction of the *yugas; dasyu*—plunderers; *prāyeṣu*—almost all; *rājasu*—the governing personalities; *janitā*—will take His birth; *viṣṇu*—named Viṣṇu; *yaśasaḥ*—surnamed Yaśā; *nāmnā*—in the name of; *kalkiḥ*—the incarnation of the Lord; *jagat-patiḥ*—the Lord of the creation.

Thereafter, at the conjunction of two yugas, the Lord of the creation will take His birth as the Kalki incarnation and become the son of Viṣṇu Yaśā. At this time almost all the rulers of the earth will have degenerated into plunderers.

PURPORT Here is another foretelling of the advent of Lord Kalki, the incarnation of Godhead. He is to appear at the conjunction of the two *yugas,* namely at the end of Kali-yuga and the beginning of Satya-yuga. The cycle of the four *yugas,* namely Satya, Tretā, Dvāpara and Kali, rotates like the calendar months. The present Kali-yuga lasts 432,000 years, out of which we have passed only 5,000 years after the Battle of Kurukṣetra and the end of the regime of King Parīkṣit. So there are 427,000 years balance yet to be finished. Therefore at the end of this period, the incarnation of Kalki will take place, as foretold in the *Śrīmad-Bhāgavatam.* The name of His father, Viṣṇu Yaśā, a learned *brāhmaṇa,* and the village Śambhala are also mentioned. As above mentioned, all these foretellings will prove to be factual in chronological order. That is the authority of *Śrīmad-Bhāgavatam.*

TEXT 26

अवतारा ह्यसंख्येया हरेः सत्त्वनिधेर्द्विजाः ।
यथाविदासिनः कुल्याः सरसः स्युः सहस्रशः ॥ २६ ॥

avatārā hy asaṅkhyeyā hareḥ sattva-nidher dvijāḥ
yathāvidāsinaḥ kulyāḥ sarasaḥ syuḥ sahasraśaḥ

avatārāḥ—incarnations; *hi*—certainly; *asaṅkhyeyāḥ*—innumerable; *hareḥ*—of Hari, the Lord; *sattva-nidheḥ*—of the ocean of goodness; *dvi-*

jāḥ—the *brāhmaṇas; yathā*—as it is; *avidāsinaḥ*—inexhaustible; *kulyāḥ*—rivulets; *sarasaḥ*—of vast lakes; *syuḥ*—are; *sahasraśaḥ*—thousands of.

O brāhmaṇas, the incarnations of the Lord are innumerable, like rivulets flowing from inexhaustible sources of water.

PURPORT The list of incarnations of the Personality of Godhead given herein is not complete. It is only a partial view of all the incarnations. There are many others, such as Śrī Hayagrīva, Hari, Haṁsa, Pṛśnigarbha, Vibhu, Satyasena, Vaikuṇṭha, Sārvabhauma, Viṣvaksena, Dharmasetu, Sudhāmā, Yogeśvara, Bṛhadbhānu and others of the bygone ages. Śrī Prahlāda Mahārāja said in his prayer, "My Lord, You manifest as many incarnations as there are species of life, namely the aquatics, the vegetables, the reptiles, the birds, the beasts, the men, the demigods, etc., just for the maintenance of the faithful and the annihilation of the unfaithful. You advent Yourself in this way in accordance with the necessity of the different *yugas*. In the Kali-yuga You have incarnated garbed as a devotee." This incarnation of the Lord in the Kali-yuga is Lord Caitanya Mahāprabhu. There are many other places, both in the *Bhāgavatam* and in other scriptures, in which the incarnation of the Lord as Śrī Caitanya Mahāprabhu is explicitly mentioned. In the *Brahma-saṁhitā* also it is said indirectly that although there are many incarnations of the Lord, such as Rāma, Nṛsiṁha, Varāha, Matsya, Kūrma and many others, the Lord Himself sometimes incarnates in person. Lord Kṛṣṇa and Lord Śrī Caitanya Mahāprabhu are not, therefore, incarnations but the original source of all incarnations. This will be clearly explained in the next *ślokas*. So the Lord is the inexhaustible source for innumerable incarnations which are not always mentioned. But such incarnations are distinguished by specific extraordinary feats which are impossible to be performed by any living being. That is the general test to identify an incarnation of the Lord, directly and indirectly empowered. Some incarnations mentioned above are almost plenary portions. For instance, the Kumāras are empowered with transcendental knowledge. Śrī Nārada is empowered with devotional service. Mahārāja Pṛthu is an empowered incarnation with executive function. The Matsya incarnation is directly a plenary portion. So the innumerable incarnations of the Lord are manifested all over the universes constantly, without cessation, as water flows constantly from waterfalls.

TEXT 27

ऋषयो मनवो देवा मनुपुत्रा महौजसः ।
कलाः सर्वे हरेरेव सप्रजापतयः स्मृताः ॥ २७ ॥

ṛṣayo manavo devā manu-putrā mahaujasaḥ
kalāḥ sarve harer eva saprajāpatayaḥ smṛtāḥ

ṛṣayaḥ—all the sages; *manavaḥ*—all the Manus; *devāḥ*—all the demigods; *manu-putrāḥ*—all the descendants of Manu; *mahā-ojasaḥ*—very powerful; *kalāḥ*—portion of the plenary portion; *sarve*—all collectively; *hareḥ*—of the Lord; *eva*—certainly; *sa-prajāpatayaḥ*—along with the Prajāpatis; *smṛtāḥ*—are known.

All the ṛṣis, Manus, demigods and descendants of Manu, who are especially powerful, are plenary portions or portions of the plenary portions of the Lord. This also includes the Prajāpatis.

PURPORT Those who are comparatively less powerful are called *vibhūti,* and those who are comparatively more powerful are called *āveśa* incarnations.

TEXT 28

एते चांशकलाः पुंसः कृष्णस्तु भगवान् स्वयम् ।
इन्द्रारिव्याकुलं लोकं मृडयन्ति युगे युगे ॥ २८ ॥

ete cāṁśa-kalāḥ puṁsaḥ kṛṣṇas tu bhagavān svayam
indrāri-vyākulaṁ lokaṁ mṛḍayanti yuge yuge

ete—all these; *ca*—and; *aṁśa*—plenary portions; *kalāḥ*—portions of the plenary portions; *puṁsaḥ*—of the Supreme; *kṛṣṇaḥ*—Lord Kṛṣṇa; *tu*—but; *bhagavān*—the Personality of Godhead; *svayam*—in person; *indra-ari*—the enemies of Indra; *vyākulam*—disturbed; *lokam*—all the planets; *mṛḍayanti*—gives protection; *yuge yuge*—in different ages.

All of the above-mentioned incarnations are either plenary portions or portions of the plenary portions of the Lord, but Lord Śrī Kṛṣṇa is the original Personality of Godhead. All of them appear on planets whenever there is a disturbance created by the atheists. The Lord incarnates to protect the theists.

PURPORT In this particular stanza Lord Śrī Kṛṣṇa, the Personality of Godhead, is distinguished from other incarnations. He is counted amongst the *avatāras* (incarnations) because out of His causeless mercy the Lord descends from His transcendental abode. *Avatāra* means "one who descends." All the incarnations of the Lord, including the Lord Himself, descend on the different planets of the material world as also in different species of life to fulfill particular missions. Sometimes He comes Himself, and sometimes His different plenary portions or parts of the plenary portions, or His differentiated portions directly or indirectly empowered by Him, descend on this material world to execute certain specific functions. Originally the Lord is full of all opulences, all prowess, all fame, all beauty, all knowledge and all renunciation. When they are partly manifested through the plenary portions or parts of the plenary portions, it should be noted that certain manifestations of His different powers are required for those particular functions. When in the room small electric bulbs are displayed, it does not mean that the electric powerhouse is limited by the small bulbs. The same powerhouse can supply power to operate large-scale industrial dynamos with greater volts. Similarly, the incarnations of the Lord display limited powers because so much power is needed at that particular time.

For example, Lord Paraśurāma and Lord Nṛsiṁha displayed unusual opulence by killing the disobedient *kṣatriyas* twenty-one times and killing the greatly powerful atheist Hiraṇyakaśipu. Hiraṇyakaśipu was so powerful that even the demigods in other planets would tremble simply by the unfavorable raising of his eyebrow. The demigods in the higher level of material existence many, many times excel the most well-to-do human beings, in duration of life, beauty, wealth, paraphernalia, and in all other respects. Still they were afraid of Hiraṇyakaśipu. Thus we can simply imagine how powerful Hiraṇyakaśipu was in this material world. But even Hiraṇyakaśipu was cut into small pieces by the nails of Lord Nṛsiṁha. This means that anyone materially powerful cannot stand the strength of the Lord's nails. Similarly, Jāmadagnya displayed the Lord's power to kill all the disobedient kings powerfully situated in their respective states. The Lord's empowered incarnation Nārada and plenary incarnation Varāha, as well as indirectly empowered Lord Buddha, created faith in the mass of people. The incarnations of Rāma and Dhanvantari displayed His fame, and Balarāma, Mohinī and Vāmana exhibited His beauty. Dattātreya, Matsya,

Kumāra and Kapila exhibited His transcendental knowledge. Nara and Nārāyaṇa Ṛṣis exhibited His renunciation. So all the different indirectly or directly empowered incarnations of the Lord manifested different features, but Lord Kṛṣṇa, the primeval Lord, exhibited the complete features of Godhead, and thus it is confirmed that He is the source of all other incarnations. And the most extraordinary feature exhibited by Lord Śrī Kṛṣṇa was His internal energetic manifestation of His pastimes with the cowherd girls. His pastimes with the *gopīs* are all displays of transcendental existence, bliss and knowledge, although these are manifested apparently as sex love. The specific attraction of His pastimes with the *gopīs* should never be misunderstood. The *Bhāgavatam* relates these transcendental pastimes in the Tenth Canto. And in order to reach the position to understand the transcendental nature of Lord Kṛṣṇa's pastimes with the *gopīs,* the *Bhāgavatam* promotes the student gradually in nine other cantos.

According to Śrīla Jīva Gosvāmī's statement, in accordance with authoritative sources, Lord Kṛṣṇa is the source of all other incarnations. It is not that Lord Kṛṣṇa has any source of incarnation. All the symptoms of the Supreme Truth in full are present in the person of Lord Śrī Kṛṣṇa, and in the *Bhagavad-gītā* the Lord emphatically declares that there is no truth greater than or equal to Himself. In this stanza the word *svayam* is particularly mentioned to confirm that Lord Kṛṣṇa has no other source than Himself. Although in other places the incarnations are described as *bhagavān* because of their specific functions, nowhere are they declared to be the Supreme Personality. In this stanza the word *svayam* signifies the supremacy as the *summum bonum.*

The *summum bonum* Kṛṣṇa is one without a second. He Himself has expanded Himself in various parts, portions and particles as *svayaṁ-rūpa, svayam-prakāśa, tad-ekātmā, prābhava, vaibhava, vilāsa, avatāra, āveśa,* and *jīvas,* all provided with innumerable energies just suitable to the respective persons and personalities. Learned scholars in transcendental subjects have carefully analyzed the *summum bonum* Kṛṣṇa to have sixty-four principal attributes. All the expansions or categories of the Lord possess only some percentages of these attributes. But Śrī Kṛṣṇa is the possessor of the attributes cent percent. And His personal expansions such as *svayam-prakāśa, tad-ekātmā* up to the categories of the *avatāras* who are all *viṣṇu-tattva,* possess up to ninety-three percent of these transcendental attributes. Lord Śiva, who is neither *avatāra* nor *āveśa* nor in between them, possesses almost eighty-four percent of the attributes. But the *jīvas*, or the individual living beings in different statuses of life, possess up to the limit of seventy-eight percent of the attributes. In the conditioned state of material existence, the living being possesses these attributes in very minute quantity, varying in terms of the pious life of the living being. The most perfect of living beings is Brahmā, the supreme administrator of one universe. He possesses seventy-eight percent of the attributes in full. All other demigods have the same attributes in less quantity, whereas human beings possess the attributes in very minute quantity. The standard of perfection for a human being is to develop the attributes up to seventy-eight percent in full. The living being can never possess attributes like Śiva, Viṣṇu or Lord Kṛṣṇa. A living being can become godly by developing the seventy-eight-percent transcendental attributes in fullness, but he can never become a God like Śiva, Viṣṇu or Kṛṣṇa. He can become a Brahmā in due course. The godly living beings who are all residents of the planets in the spiritual sky are eternal associates of God in different spiritual planets called Hari-dhāma and Maheśa-dhāma. The abode of Lord Kṛṣṇa above all spiritual planets is called Kṛṣṇaloka or Goloka Vṛndāvana, and the perfected living being, by developing seventy-eight percent of the above attributes in fullness, can enter the planet of Kṛṣṇaloka after leaving the present material body.

TEXT 29

जन्म गुह्यं भगवतो य एतत्प्रयतो नरः ।
सायं प्रातर्गृणन् भक्त्या दुःखग्रामाद्विमुच्यते ॥ २९ ॥

janma guhyaṁ bhagavato ya etat prayato naraḥ
sāyaṁ prātar gṛṇan bhaktyā duḥkha-grāmād vimucyate

janma—birth; *guhyam*—mysterious; *bhagavataḥ*—of the Lord; *yaḥ*—one; *etat*—all these; *prayataḥ*—carefully; *naraḥ*—man; *sāyam*—evening; *prātaḥ*—morning; *gṛṇan*—recites; *bhaktyā*—with devotion; *duḥkha-grāmāt*—from all miseries; *vimucyate*—gets relief from.

Whoever carefully recites the mysterious appearances of the Lord, with devotion in the morning and in the evening, gets relief from all miseries of life.

PURPORT In the *Bhagavad-gītā* the Personality of Godhead has declared that anyone who knows the principles of the transcendental birth and activities of the Lord will go back to Godhead after being relieved from this material tabernacle. So simply knowing factually the mysterious way of the Lord's incarnation in this material world can liberate one from material bondage. Therefore the birth and activities of the Lord, as manifested by Him for the welfare of the people in general, are not ordinary. They are mysterious, and only by one who carefully tries to go deep into the matter by spiritual devotion is the mystery discovered. Thus the knower is relieved of all miseries. In other words, one gets liberation from material bondage. It is advised therefore that one who simply recites this chapter of *Bhāgavatam*, describing the appearance of the Lord in different incarnations, in sincerity and devotion, can have insight into the birth and activities of the Lord. The very word *vimukti,* or liberation, indicates that the Lord's birth and activities are all transcendental; otherwise simply by reciting them one could not attain liberation. They are therefore mysterious, and those who do not follow the prescribed regulations of devotional service are not entitled to enter into the mysteries of His births and activities.

TEXT 30

एतद्रूपं भगवतो ह्यरूपस्य चिदात्मनः ।
मायागुणैर्विरचितं महदादिभिरात्मनि ॥ ३० ॥

etad rūpaṁ bhagavato hy arūpasya cid-ātmanaḥ
māyā-guṇair viracitaṁ mahadādibhir ātmani

etat—all these; *rūpam*—forms; *bhagavataḥ*—of the Lord; *hi*—certainly; *arūpasya*—of one who has no material form; *cit-ātmanaḥ*—of the Transcendence; *māyā*—material energy; *guṇaiḥ*—by the qualities; *viracitam*—manufactured; *mahat-ādibhiḥ*—with the ingredients of matter; *ātmani*—in the self.

The conception of the virāṭ universal form of the Lord, as appearing in the material world, is imaginary. It is to enable the less intelligent [and neophytes] to adjust to the idea of the Lord's having form. But factually the Lord has no material form.

PURPORT The conception of the Lord known as the *viśva-rūpa* or the *virāṭ-rūpa* is particularly not mentioned along with the various incarnations of the Lord because all the incarnations of the Lord mentioned above are transcendental and there is not a tinge of materialism in their bodies. There is no difference between the body and self as there is in the conditioned soul. The *virāṭ-rūpa* is conceived for those who are just neophyte worshipers. For them the material *virāṭ-rūpa* is presented, and it will be explained in the Second Canto. In the *virāṭ-rūpa* the material manifestations of different planets have been conceived as His legs, hands, etc. Actually all such descriptions are for the neophytes. The neophytes cannot conceive of anything beyond matter. The material conception of the Lord is not counted in the list of His factual forms. As Paramātmā, or Supersoul, the Lord is within each and every material form, even within the atoms, but the outward material form is but an imagination, both for the Lord and for the living being. The present forms of the conditioned souls are also not factual. The conclusion is that the material conception of the body of the Lord as *virāṭ* is imaginary. Both the Lord and the living beings are living spirits and have original spiritual bodies.

TEXT 31

यथा नभसि मेघौघो रेणुर्वा पार्थिवोऽनिले ।
एवं द्रष्टरि दृश्यत्वमारोपितमबुद्धिभिः ॥ ३१ ॥

yathā nabhasi meghaugho reṇur vā pārthivo 'nile
evaṁ draṣṭari dṛśyatvam āropitam abuddhibhiḥ

yathā—as it is; *nabhasi*—in the sky; *megha-oghaḥ*—a mass of clouds; *reṇuḥ*—dust; *vā*—as well as; *pārthivaḥ*—muddiness; *anile*—in the air; *evam*—thus; *draṣṭari*—to the seer; *dṛśyatvam*—for the purpose of seeing; *āropitam*—is implied; *abuddhibhiḥ*—by the less intelligent persons.

Clouds and dust are carried by the air, but less intelligent persons say that the sky is cloudy and the air is dirty. Similarly, they also implant material bodily conceptions on the spirit self.

PURPORT It is further confirmed herein that with our material eyes and senses we cannot see the Lord, who is all spirit. We cannot even detect the spiritual spark which exists within the material body of the living being.

We look to the outward covering of the body or subtle mind of the living being, but we cannot see the spiritual spark within the body. So we have to accept the living being's presence by the presence of his gross body. Similarly, those who want to see the Lord with their present material eyes or with the material senses are advised to meditate on the gigantic external feature called the *virāṭ-rūpa*. For instance, when a particular gentleman goes in his car, which can be seen very easily, we identify the car with the man within the car. When the President goes out in his particular car, we say, "There is the President." For the time being we identify the car with the President. Similarly, less intelligent men who want to see God immediately without necessary qualification are shown first the gigantic material cosmos as the form of the Lord, although the Lord is within and without. The clouds in the sky and the blue of the sky are better appreciated in this connection. Although the bluish tint of the sky and the sky itself are different, we conceive of the color of the sky as blue. But that is a general conception for the laymen only.

TEXT 32

अतः परं यदव्यक्तमव्यूढगुणबृंहितम् ।
अदृष्टाश्रुतवस्तुत्वात्स जीवो यत्पुनर्भवः ॥ ३२ ॥

ataḥ paraṁ yad avyaktam avyūḍha-guṇa-bṛṁhitam
adṛṣṭāśruta-vastutvāt sa jīvo yat punar-bhavaḥ

ataḥ—this; *param*—beyond; *yat*—which; *avyaktam*—unmanifested; *avyūḍha*—without formal shape; *guṇa-bṛṁhitam*—affected by the qualities; *adṛṣṭa*—unseen; *aśruta*—unheard; *vastutvāt*—being like that; *saḥ*—that; *jīvaḥ*—living being; *yat*—that which; *punaḥ-bhavaḥ*—takes birth repeatedly.

Beyond this gross conception of form is another, subtle conception of form which is without formal shape and is unseen, unheard and unmanifest. The living being has his form beyond this subtlety, otherwise he could not have repeated births.

PURPORT As the gross cosmic manifestation is conceived as the gigantic body of the Lord, so also there is the conception of His subtle form, which is simply realized without being seen, heard or manifested. But in fact all these gross or subtle conceptions of the body are in relation with the living beings. The living being has his spiritual form beyond this gross material or subtle psychic existence. The gross body and psychic functions cease to act as soon as the living being leaves the visible gross body. In fact, we say that the living being has gone away because he is unseen and unheard. Even when the gross body is not acting when the living being is in sound sleep, we know that he is within the body by his breathing. So the living being's passing away from the body does not mean that there is no existence of the living soul. It is there, otherwise how can he repeat his births again and again?

The conclusion is that the Lord is eternally existent in His transcendental form, which is neither gross nor subtle like that of the living being; His body is never to be compared to the gross and subtle bodies of the living being. All such conceptions of God's body are imaginary. The living being has his eternal spiritual form, which is conditioned only by his material contamination.

TEXT 33

यत्रेमे सदसद्रूपे प्रतिषिद्धे स्वसंविदा ।
अविद्ययात्मनि कृते इति तद्ब्रह्मदर्शनम् ॥ ३३ ॥

yatreme sad-asad-rūpe pratiṣiddhe sva-saṁvidā
avidyayātmani kṛte iti tad brahma-darśanam

yatra—whenever; *ime*—in all these; *sat-asat*—gross and subtle; *rūpe*—in the forms of; *pratiṣiddhe*—on being nullified; *sva-saṁvidā*—by self-realization; *avidyayā*—by ignorance; *ātmani*—in the self; *kṛte*—having been imposed; *iti*—thus; *tat*—that is; *brahma-darśanam*—the process of seeing the Absolute.

Whenever a person experiences, by self-realization, that both the gross and subtle bodies have nothing to do with the pure self, at that time he sees himself as well as the Lord.

PURPORT The difference between self-realization and material illusion is to know that the temporary or illusory impositions of material energy in the shape of gross and subtle bodies are superficial coverings of the self. The coverings take place due to ignorance. Such coverings are never effective in the person of the Personality of Godhead. Knowing this convincingly is called liberation, or seeing the Absolute. This means that perfect self-realization is made possible by adoption of godly or spiritual life. Self-realization means becoming indifferent to the needs of the gross and subtle bodies and becoming serious about the activities of the self. The impetus for activities is generated from the self, but such activities become illusory due to ignorance of the real position of the self. By ignorance, self-interest is calculated in terms of the gross and subtle bodies, and therefore a whole set of activities is spoiled, life after life. When, however, one meets the self by proper culture, the activities of the self begin. Therefore a man who is engaged in the activities of the self is called *jīvan-mukta,* or a liberated person even in the conditional existence.

This perfect stage of self-realization is attained not by artificial means, but under the lotus feet of the Lord, who is always transcendental. In the *Bhagavad-gītā* the Lord says that He is present in everyone's heart, and from Him only all knowledge, remembrance or forgetfulness take place. When the living being desires to be an enjoyer of material energy (illusory phenomena), the Lord covers the living being in the mystery of forgetfulness, and thus the living being misinterprets the gross body and subtle mind to be his own self. And by culture of transcendental knowledge, when the living being prays to the Lord for deliverance from the clutches of forgetfulness, the Lord, by His causeless mercy, removes the living being's illusory curtain, and thus he realizes his own self. He then engages himself in the service of the Lord in his eternal constitutional position, becoming liberated from the conditioned life. All this is executed by the Lord either through His external potency or directly by the internal potency.

TEXT 34

यद्येषोपरता देवी माया वैशारदी मतिः ।
सम्पन्न एवेति विदुर्महिम्नि स्वे महीयते ॥ ३४ ॥

yady eṣoparatā devī māyā vaiśāradī matiḥ
sampanna eveti vidur mahimni sve mahīyate

yadi—if, however; *eṣā*—they; *uparatā*—subsided; *devī māyā*—illusory energy; *vaiśāradī*—full of knowledge; *matiḥ*—enlightenment; *sampannaḥ*—enriched with; *eva*—certainly; *iti*—thus; *viduḥ*—being cognizant of; *mahimni*—in the glories; *sve*—of the self; *mahīyate*—being situated in.

If the illusory energy subsides and the living entity becomes fully enriched with knowledge by the grace of the Lord, then he becomes at once enlightened with self-realization and thus becomes situated in his own glory.

PURPORT Because the Lord is the absolute Transcendence, all of His forms, names, pastimes, attributes, associates and energies are identical with Him. His transcendental energy acts according to His omnipotency. The same energy acts as His external, internal and marginal energies, and by His omnipotency He can perform anything and everything through the agency of any of the above energies. He can turn the external energy into internal by His will. Therefore by His grace the external energy, which is employed in illusioning those living beings who want to have it, subsides by the will of the Lord in terms of repentance and penance for the conditioned soul. And the very same energy then acts to help the purified living being make progress on the path of self-realization. The example of electrical energy is very appropriate in this connection. The expert electrician can utilize the electrical energy for both heating and cooling by adjustment only. Similarly, the external energy, which now bewilders the living being into continuation of birth and death, is turned into internal potency by the will of the Lord to lead the living being to eternal life. When a living being is thus graced by the Lord, he is placed in his proper constitutional position to enjoy eternal spiritual life.

TEXT 35

एवं जन्मानि कर्माणि ह्यकर्तुरजनस्य च ।
वर्णयन्ति स्म कवयो वेदगुह्यानि हृत्पतेः ॥ ३५ ॥

evaṁ janmāni karmāṇi hy akartur ajanasya ca
varṇayanti sma kavayo veda-guhyāni hṛt-pateḥ

evam—thus; *janmāni*—birth; *karmāṇi*—activities; *hi*—certainly; *akartuḥ*—of the inactive; *ajanasya*—of the unborn; *ca*—and; *varṇayanti*—describe; *sma*—in the past; *kavayaḥ*—the learned; *veda-guhyāni*—undiscoverable by the *Vedas; hṛt-pateḥ*—of the Lord of the heart.

Thus learned men describe the births and activities of the unborn and inactive, which are undiscoverable even in the Vedic literatures. He is the Lord of the heart.

PURPORT Both the Lord and the living entities are essentially all spiritual. Therefore both of them are eternal, and neither of them has birth and death. The difference is that the so-called births and disappearances of the Lord are unlike those of the living beings. The living beings who take birth and then again accept death are bound by the laws of material nature. But the so-called appearance and disappearance of the Lord are not actions of material nature, but are demonstrations of the internal potency of the Lord. They are described by the great sages for the purpose of self-realization. It is stated in the *Bhagavad-gītā* by the Lord that His so-called birth in the material world and His activities are all transcendental. And simply by meditation on such activities one can attain realization of Brahman and thus become liberated from material bondage. In the *śrutis* it is said that the birthless appears to take birth. The Supreme has nothing to do, but because He is omnipotent, everything is performed by Him naturally, as if done automatically. As a matter of fact, the appearance and disappearance of the Supreme Personality of Godhead and His different activities are all confidential, even to the Vedic literatures. Yet they are displayed by the Lord to bestow mercy upon the conditioned souls. We should always take advantage of the narrations of the activities of the Lord, which are meditations on Brahman in the most convenient and palatable form.

TEXT 36

स वा इदं विश्वममोघलीलः
सृजत्यवत्यत्ति न सज्जतेऽस्मिन् ।
भूतेषु चान्तर्हित आत्मतन्त्रः
षाड्वर्गिकं जिघ्रति षड्गुणेशः ॥ ३६ ॥

sa vā idaṁ viśvam amogha-līlaḥ
sṛjaty avaty atti na sajjate 'smin
bhūteṣu cāntarhita ātma-tantraḥ
ṣāḍ-vargikaṁ jighrati ṣaḍ-guṇeśaḥ

saḥ—the Supreme Lord; *vā*—alternately; *idam*—this; *viśvam*—manifested universes; *amogha-līlaḥ*—one whose activities are spotless; *sṛjati*—creates; *avati atti*—maintains and annihilates; *na*—not; *sajjate*—is affected by; *asmin*—in them; *bhūteṣu*—in all living beings; *ca*—also; *antarhitaḥ*—living within; *ātma-tantraḥ*—self-independent; *ṣāṭ-vargikam*—endowed with all the potencies of His opulences; *jighrati*—superficially attached, like smelling the fragrance; *ṣaṭ-guṇa-īśaḥ*—master of the six senses.

The Lord, whose activities are always spotless, is the master of the six senses and is fully omnipotent with six opulences. He creates the manifested universes, maintains them and annihilates them without being in the least affected. He is within every living being and is always independent.

PURPORT The prime difference between the Lord and the living entities is that the Lord is the creator and the living entities are the created. Here He is called the *amogha-līlaḥ,* which indicates that there is nothing lamentable in His creation. Those who create disturbance in His creation are themselves disturbed. He is transcendental to all material afflictions because He is full with all six opulences, namely wealth, power, fame, beauty, knowledge and renunciation, and thus He is the master of the senses. He creates these manifested universes in order to reclaim the living beings who are within them suffering threefold miseries, maintains them, and in due course annihilates them without being the least affected by such actions. He is connected with this material creation very superficially, as one smells odor without being connected with the odorous article. Nongodly elements, therefore, can never approach Him, despite all endeavors.

TEXT 37

न चास्य कश्चिन्निपुणेन धातुर्
अवैति जन्तुः कुमनीष ऊतीः ।

नामानि रूपाणि मनोवचोभिः
सन्तन्वतो नटचर्यामिवाज्ञः ॥ ३७ ॥

na cāsya kaścin nipuṇena dhātur
avaiti jantuḥ kumanīṣa ūtīḥ
nāmāni rūpāṇi mano-vacobhiḥ
santanvato naṭa-caryām ivājñaḥ

na—not; *ca*—and; *asya*—of Him; *kaścit*—anyone; *nipuṇena*—by dexterity; *dhātuḥ*—of the creator; *avaiti*—can know; *jantuḥ*—the living being; *kumanīṣaḥ*—with a poor fund of knowledge; *ūtīḥ*—activities of the Lord; *nāmāni*—His names; *rūpāṇi*—His forms; *manaḥ-vacobhiḥ*—by dint of mental speculation or deliverance of speeches; *santanvataḥ*—displaying; *naṭa-caryām*—a dramatic action; *iva*—like; *ajñaḥ*—the foolish.

The foolish with a poor fund of knowledge cannot know the transcendental nature of the forms, names and activities of the Lord, who is playing like an actor in a drama. Nor can they express such things, neither in their speculations nor in their words.

PURPORT No one can properly describe the transcendental nature of the Absolute Truth. Therefore it is said that He is beyond the expression of mind and speech. And yet there are some men, with a poor fund of knowledge, who desire to understand the Absolute Truth by imperfect mental speculation and faulty description of His activities. To the layman His activities, appearance and disappearance, His names, His forms, His paraphernalia, His personalities and all things in relation with Him are mysterious. There are two classes of materialists, namely the fruitive workers and the empiric philosophers. The fruitive workers have practically no information of the Absolute Truth, and the mental speculators, after being frustrated in fruitive activities, turn their faces towards the Absolute Truth and try to know Him by mental speculation. And for all these men, the Absolute Truth is a mystery, as the jugglery of the magician is a mystery to children. Being deceived by the jugglery of the Supreme Being, the nondevotees, who may be very dexterous in fruitive work and mental speculation, are always in ignorance. With such limited knowledge, they are unable to penetrate into the mysterious region of transcendence. The mental speculators are a little more progressive than the gross materialists or the fruitive workers, but because they are also within the grip of illusion, they take it for granted that anything which has form, a name and activities is but a product of material energy. For them the Supreme Spirit is formless, nameless and inactive. And because such mental speculators equalize the transcendental name and form of the Lord with mundane names and form, they are in fact in ignorance. With such a poor fund of knowledge, there is no access to the real nature of the Supreme Being. As stated in *Bhagavad-gītā,* the Lord is always in a transcendental position, even when He is within the material world. But ignorant men consider the Lord one of the great personalities of the world, and thus they are misled by the illusory energy.

TEXT 38

स वेद धातुः पदवीं परस्य
दुरन्तवीर्यस्य रथाङ्गपाणेः ।
योऽमायया सन्ततयानुवृत्त्या
भजेत तत्पादसरोजगन्धम् ॥ ३८ ॥

sa veda dhātuḥ padavīṁ parasya
duranta-vīryasya rathāṅga-pāṇeḥ
yo 'māyayā santatayānuvṛttyā
bhajeta tat-pāda-saroja-gandham

saḥ—He alone; *veda*—can know; *dhātuḥ*—of the creator; *padavīm*—glories; *parasya*—of the transcendence; *duranta-vīryasya*—of the greatly powerful; *ratha-aṅga-pāṇeḥ*—of Lord Kṛṣṇa, who bears in His hand the wheel of a chariot; *yaḥ*—one who; *amāyayā*—without reservation; *santatayā*—without any gap; *anuvṛttyā*—favorably; *bhajeta*—renders service; *tat-pāda*—of His feet; *saroja-gandham*—fragrance of the lotus.

Only those who render unreserved, uninterrupted, favorable service unto the lotus feet of Lord Kṛṣṇa, who carries the wheel of the chariot in His hand, can know the creator of the universe in His full glory, power and transcendence.

PURPORT Only the pure devotees can know the transcendental name, form and activities of Lord Kṛṣṇa due to their being completely freed from the reactions of fruitive work and mental speculation. The pure devotees have nothing to derive as personal profit from their unalloyed service to the Lord. They render favorable service to the Lord incessantly and spontaneously, without any reservation. Everyone within the creation of the Lord is rendering service to the Lord indirectly or directly. No one is an exception to this law of the Lord. Those who are rendering service indirectly, being forced by the illusory agent of the Lord, are rendering service unto Him unfavorably. But those who are rendering service unto Him directly under the direction of His beloved agent are rendering service unto Him favorably. Such favorable servitors are devotees of the Lord, and by the grace of the Lord they can enter into the mysterious region of transcendence by the mercy of the Lord. But the mental speculators remain in darkness all the time. As stated in *Bhagavad-gītā,* the Lord Himself guides the pure devotees toward the path of realization due to their constant engagement in the loving service of the Lord in spontaneous affection. That is the secret of entering into the kingdom of God. Fruitive activities and speculation are no qualifications for entering.

TEXT 39

अथेह धन्या भगवन्त इत्थं
यद्वासुदेवेऽखिललोकनाथे ।
कुर्वन्ति सर्वात्मकमात्मभावं
न यत्र भूयः परिवर्त उग्रः ॥ ३९ ॥

atheha dhanyā bhagavanta itthaṁ
yad vāsudeve 'khila-loka-nāthe
kurvanti sarvātmakam ātma-bhāvaṁ
na yatra bhūyaḥ parivarta ugraḥ

atha—thus; *iha*—in this world; *dhanyāḥ*—successful; *bhagavantaḥ*—perfectly cognizant; *ittham*—such; *yat*—what; *vāsudeve*—unto the Personality of Godhead; *akhila*—all-embracing; *loka-nāthe*—unto the proprietor of all the universes; *kurvanti*—inspires; *sarva-ātmakam*—one hundred percent; *ātma*—spirit; *bhāvam*—ecstasy; *na*—never; *yatra*—wherein; *bhūyaḥ*—again; *parivartaḥ*—repetition; *ugraḥ*—dreadful.

Only by making such inquiries in this world can one be successful and perfectly cognizant, for such inquiries invoke transcendental ecstatic love unto the Personality of Godhead, who is the proprietor of all the universes, and guarantee cent-percent immunity from the dreadful repetition of birth and death.

PURPORT The inquiries of the sages headed by Śaunaka are herewith praised by Sūta Gosvāmī on the merit of their transcendental nature. As already concluded, only the devotees of the Lord can know Him to a considerable extent, and no one else can know Him at all, so the devotees are perfectly cognizant of all spiritual knowledge. The Personality of Godhead is the last word in Absolute Truth. Impersonal Brahman and localized Paramātmā (Supersoul) are included in the knowledge of the Personality of Godhead. So one who knows the Personality of Godhead can automatically know all about Him, His multipotencies and His expansions. So the devotees are congratulated as being all-successful. A cent-percent devotee of the Lord is immune to the dreadful material miseries of repeated birth and death.

TEXT 40

इदं भागवतं नाम पुराणं ब्रह्मसम्मितम् ।
उत्तमश्लोकचरितं चकार भगवानृषिः ।
निःश्रेयसाय लोकस्य धन्यं स्वस्त्ययनं महत् ॥ ४० ॥

idaṁ bhāgavataṁ nāma purāṇaṁ brahma-sammitam
uttama-śloka-caritaṁ cakāra bhagavān ṛṣiḥ
niḥśreyasāya lokasya dhanyaṁ svasty-ayanaṁ mahat

idam—this; *bhāgavatam*—book containing the narration of the Supreme Personality of Godhead and His pure devotees; *nāma*—of the name; *purā-ṇam*—supplementary to the *Vedas; brahma-sammitam*—incarnation of Lord Śrī Kṛṣṇa; *uttama-śloka*—of the Personality of Godhead; *caritam*—activities; *cakāra*—compiled; *bhagavān*—incarnation of the Personality of Godhead; *ṛṣiḥ*—Śrī Vyāsadeva; *niḥśreyasāya*—for the ultimate good; *lokasya*—of all people; *dhanyam*—fully successful; *svasti-ayanam*—all-blissful; *mahat*—all-perfect.

This scripture named Śrīmad-Bhāgavatam is the literary incarnation of God, and it is compiled by Śrīla Vyāsadeva, the incarnation of God. It is meant for the ultimate good of all people, and it is all-successful, all-blissful and all-perfect.

PURPORT Lord Śrī Caitanya Mahāprabhu declared that *Śrīmad-Bhāgavatam* is the spotless sound representation of all Vedic knowledge and history. There are selected histories of great devotees who are in direct contact with the Personality of Godhead. *Śrīmad-Bhāgavatam* is the literary incarnation of Lord Śrī Kṛṣṇa and is therefore nondifferent from Him. *Śrīmad-Bhāgavatam* should be worshiped as respectfully as we worship the Lord. Thereby we can derive the ultimate blessings of the Lord through its careful and patient study. As God is all light, all bliss and all perfection, so also is *Śrīmad-Bhāgavatam.* We can have all the transcendental light of the Supreme Brahman, Śrī Kṛṣṇa, from the recitation of *Śrīmad-Bhāgavatam,* provided it is received through the medium of the transparent spiritual master. Lord Caitanya's private secretary Śrīla Svarūpa Dāmodara Gosvāmī advised all intending visitors who came to see the Lord at Purī to make a study of the *Bhāgavatam* from the person *Bhāgavatam.* Person *Bhāgavatam* is the self-realized bona fide spiritual master, and through him only can one understand the lessons of *Bhāgavatam* in order to receive the desired result. One can derive from the study of the *Bhāgavatam* all benefits that are possible to be derived from the personal presence of the Lord. It carries with it all the transcendental blessings of Lord Śrī Kṛṣṇa that we can expect from His personal contact.

TEXT 41

तदिदं ग्राहयामास सुतमात्मवतां वरम् ।
सर्ववेदेतिहासानां सारं सारं समुद्धृतम् ॥ ४१ ॥

tad idaṁ grāhayām āsa sutam ātmavatāṁ varam
sarva-vedetihāsānāṁ sāraṁ sāraṁ samuddhṛtam

tat—that; *idam*—this; *grāhayām āsa*—made to accept; *sutam*—unto his son; *ātmavatām*—of the self-realized; *varam*—most respectful; *sarva*—all; *veda*—Vedic literatures (books of knowledge); *itihāsānām*—of all the histories; *sāram*—cream; *sāram*—cream; *samuddhṛtam*—taken out.

Śrī Vyāsadeva delivered it to his son, who is the most respected among the self-realized, after extracting the cream of all Vedic literatures and histories of the universe.

PURPORT Men with a poor fund of knowledge only accept the history of the world from the time of Buddha, or since 600 B.C., and prior to this period all histories mentioned in the scriptures are calculated by them to be only imaginary stories. That is not a fact. All the stories mentioned in the *Purāṇas* and *Mahābhārata,* etc., are actual histories, not only of this planet but also of millions of other planets within the universe. Sometimes the history of planets beyond this world appear to such men to be unbelievable. But they do not know that different planets are not equal in all respects and that therefore some of the historical facts derived from other planets do not correspond with the experience of this planet. Considering the different situation of different planets and also time and circumstances, there is nothing wonderful in the stories of the *Purāṇas,* nor are they imaginary. We should always remember the maxim that one man's food is another man's poison. We should not, therefore, reject the stories and histories of the *Purāṇas* as imaginary. The great *ṛṣis* like Vyāsa had no business putting some imaginary stories in their literatures.

In the *Śrīmad-Bhāgavatam* historical facts selected from the histories of different planets have been depicted. It is therefore accepted by all the spiritual authorities as the *Mahā-Purāṇa.* The special significance of these histories is that they are all connected with activities of the Lord in a different time and atmosphere. Śrīla Śukadeva Gosvāmī is the topmost personality of all the self-realized souls, and he accepted this as the subject of studies from his father, Vyāsadeva. Śrīla Vyāsadeva is the great authority, and the subject matter of *Śrīmad-Bhāgavatam* being so important, he delivered the message first to his great son Śrīla Śukadeva Gosvāmī. It is compared to the cream of the milk. Vedic literature is like the milk ocean of knowledge. Cream or butter is the most palatable essence of milk, and so also is *Śrīmad-Bhāgavatam,* for it contains all palatable, instructive and authentic versions of different activities of the Lord and His devotees. There is no gain, however, in accepting the message of *Bhāgavatam* from the unbelievers, atheists and professional reciters who make a trade of *Bhāgavatam* for the laymen. It was delivered to Śrīla Śukadeva Gosvāmī, and he had nothing to do with the *Bhāgavata* business. He did not have to maintain family expenses by such trade. *Śrīmad-Bhāgavatam* should therefore be received from the representative of Śukadeva, who must be in the renounced order of life without family encumbrance. Milk is undoubtedly very good and nourishing, but when it is touched by the mouth of a snake it is no longer nourishing; rather, it becomes a source of death. Similarly, those who are not strictly in the Vaiṣṇava discipline should not make a business of this *Bhāgavatam* and become a cause of spiritual death for so many hearers. In the *Bhagavad-gītā* the Lord says that the purpose of all the *Vedas* is to know Him (Lord Kṛṣṇa), and *Śrīmad-Bhāgavatam* is Lord Śrī Kṛṣṇa Himself in the form of recorded knowledge. Therefore, it is the cream of all the *Vedas,* and it contains all historical facts of all times in relation with Śrī Kṛṣṇa. It is factually the essence of all histories.

TEXT 42

स तु संश्रावयामास महाराजं परीक्षितम् ।
प्रायोपविष्टं गङ्गायां परीतं परमर्षिभिः ॥ ४२ ॥

sa tu saṁśrāvayām āsa mahārājaṁ parīkṣitam
prāyopaviṣṭaṁ gaṅgāyāṁ parītaṁ paramarṣibhiḥ

saḥ—the son of Vyāsadeva; *tu*—again; *saṁśrāvayām āsa*—make them audible; *mahā-rājam*—unto the emperor; *parīkṣitam*—of the name Parīkṣit; *prāya-upaviṣṭam*—who sat until death without food or drink; *gaṅgāyām*—on the bank of the Ganges; *parītam*—being surrounded; *parama-ṛṣibhiḥ*—by great sages.

Śukadeva Gosvāmī, the son of Vyāsadeva, in his turn delivered the Bhāgavatam to the great Emperor Parīkṣit, who sat surrounded by sages on the bank of the Ganges, awaiting death without taking food or drink.

PURPORT All transcendental messages are received properly in the chain of disciplic succession. This disciplic succession is called *paramparā.* Unless therefore *Bhāgavatam* or any other Vedic literatures are received through the *paramparā* system, the reception of knowledge is not bona fide. Vyāsadeva delivered the message to Śukadeva Gosvāmī, and from Śukadeva Gosvāmī, Sūta Gosvāmī received the message. One should therefore receive the message of *Bhāgavatam* from Sūta Gosvāmī or from his representative and not from any irrelevant interpreter.

Emperor Parīkṣit received the information of his death in time, and he at once left his kingdom and family and sat down on the bank of the Ganges to fast till death. All great sages, *ṛṣis,* philosophers, mystics, etc., went there due to his imperial position. They offered many suggestions about his immediate duty, and at last it was settled that he would hear from Śukadeva Gosvāmī about Lord Kṛṣṇa. Thus the *Bhāgavatam* was spoken to him.

Śrīpāda Śaṅkarācārya, who preached Māyāvāda philosophy and stressed the impersonal feature of the Absolute, also at last recommended that one must take shelter at the lotus feet of Lord Śrī Kṛṣṇa, for there is no hope of gain from debating. Indirectly Śrīpāda Śaṅkarācārya admitted that what he had preached in the flowery grammatical interpretations of the *Vedānta-sūtra* cannot help one at the time of death. At the critical hour of death one must recite the name of Govinda. This is the recommendation of all great transcendentalists. Śukadeva Gosvāmī had long ago stated the same truth, that at the end one must remember Nārāyaṇa. That is the essence of all spiritual activities. In pursuance of this eternal truth, *Śrīmad-Bhāgavatam* was heard by Emperor Parīkṣit, and it was recited by the able Śukadeva Gosvāmī. And both the speaker and the receiver of the messages of *Bhāgavatam* were duly delivered by the same medium.

TEXT 43

कृष्णे स्वधामोपगते धर्मज्ञानादिभिः सह ।
कलौ नष्टदृशामेष पुराणार्कोऽधुनोदितः ॥ ४३ ॥

kṛṣṇe sva-dhāmopagate dharma-jñānādibhiḥ saha
kalau naṣṭa-dṛśām eṣa purāṇārko 'dhunoditaḥ

kṛṣṇe—in Kṛṣṇa's; *sva-dhāma*—own abode; *upagate*—having returned; *dharma*—religion; *jñāna*—knowledge; *ādibhiḥ*—combined together; *saha*—along with; *kalau*—in the Kali-yuga; *naṣṭa-dṛśām*—of persons who have lost their sight; *eṣaḥ*—all these; *purāṇa-arkaḥ*—the *Purāṇa* which is brilliant like the sun; *adhunā*—just now; *uditaḥ*—has arisen.

This Bhāgavata Purāṇa is as brilliant as the sun, and it has arisen just after the departure of Lord Kṛṣṇa to His own abode, accompanied by

religion, knowledge, etc. Persons who have lost their vision due to the dense darkness of ignorance in the age of Kali shall get light from this Purāṇa.

PURPORT Lord Śrī Kṛṣṇa has His eternal *dhāma*, or abode, where He eternally enjoys Himself with His eternal associates and paraphernalia. And His eternal abode is a manifestation of His internal energy, whereas the material world is a manifestation of His external energy. When He descends on the material world, He displays Himself with all paraphernalia in His internal potency, which is called *ātma-māyā*. In the *Bhagavad-gītā* the Lord says that He descends by His own potency (*ātma-māyā*). His form, name, fame, paraphernalia, abode, etc., are not, therefore, creations of matter. He descends to reclaim the fallen souls and to reestablish codes of religion, which are directly enacted by Him. Except for God, no one can establish the principles of religion. Either He or a suitable person empowered by Him can dictate the codes of religion. Real religion means to know God, our relation with Him and our duties in relation with Him and to know ultimately our destination after leaving this material body. The conditioned souls, who are entrapped by the material energy, hardly know all these principles of life. Most of them are like animals engaged in eating, sleeping, fearing and mating. They are mostly engaged in sense enjoyment under the pretension of religiosity, knowledge or salvation. They are still more blind in the present age of quarrel, or Kali-yuga. In the Kali-yuga the population is just a royal edition of the animals. They have nothing to do with spiritual knowledge or godly religious life. They are so blind that they cannot see anything beyond the needs of the body. They have no information of the spirit soul beyond the jurisdiction of the subtle mind, intelligence or ego, but they are very much proud of their advancement in knowledge, science and material prosperity. They can risk their lives to become a dog or hog just after leaving the present body, for they have completely lost sight of the ultimate aim of life. The Personality of Godhead Śrī Kṛṣṇa appeared before us just a little prior to the beginning of Kali-yuga, and He returned to His eternal home practically at the commencement of Kali-yuga. While He was present, He exhibited everything by His different activities. He spoke the *Bhagavad-gītā* specifically and eradicated all pretentious principles of religiosity. And prior to His departure from this material world, He empowered Śrī Vyāsadeva through Nārada to compile the messages of the *Śrīmad-Bhāgavatam,* and thus both the *Bhagavad-gītā* and the *Śrīmad-Bhāgavatam* are like torchbearers for the blind people of this age. In other words, if men in this age of Kali want to see the real light of life, they must take to these two books only, and their aim of life will be fulfilled. *Bhagavad-gītā* is the preliminary study of the *Bhāgavatam.* And *Śrīmad-Bhāgavatam* is the *summum bonum* of life, Lord Śrī Kṛṣṇa personified. We must therefore accept *Śrīmad-Bhāgavatam* as the direct representation of Lord Kṛṣṇa. One who can see *Śrīmad-Bhāgavatam* can see also Lord Śrī Kṛṣṇa in person. They are identical.

TEXT 44

तत्र कीर्तयतो विप्रा विप्रर्षेर्भूरितेजसः ।
अहं चाध्यगमं तत्र निविष्टस्तदनुग्रहात् ।
सोऽहं वः श्रावयिष्यामि यथाधीतं यथामति ॥ ४४ ॥

tatra kīrtayato viprā viprarṣer bhūri-tejasaḥ
ahaṁ cādhyagamaṁ tatra niviṣṭas tad-anugrahāt
so 'haṁ vaḥ śrāvayiṣyāmi yathādhītaṁ yathā-mati

tatra—there; *kīrtayataḥ*—while reciting; *viprāḥ*—O *brāhmaṇas; viprarṣeḥ*—from the great *brāhmaṇa-ṛṣi; bhūri*—greatly; *tejasaḥ*—powerful; *aham*—I; *ca*—also; *adhyagamam*—could understand; *tatra*—in that meeting; *niviṣṭaḥ*—being perfectly attentive; *tat-anugrahāt*—by his mercy; *saḥ*—that very thing; *aham*—I; *vaḥ*—unto you; *śrāvayiṣyāmi*—shall let you hear; *yathā-adhītam yathā-mati*—as far as my realization.

O learned brāhmaṇas, when Śukadeva Gosvāmī recited Bhāgavatam there [in the presence of Emperor Parīkṣit], I heard him with rapt attention, and thus, by his mercy, I learned the Bhāgavatam from that great and powerful sage. Now I shall try to make you hear the very same thing as I learned it from him and as I have realized it.

PURPORT One can certainly see directly the presence of Lord Śrī Kṛṣṇa in the pages of *Bhāgavatam* if one has heard it from a self-realized great soul like Śukadeva Gosvāmī. One cannot, however, learn *Bhāgavatam* from a bogus hired reciter whose aim of life is to earn some money out of such recitation and employ the earning in sex indulgence. No one can learn

Śrīmad-Bhāgavatam who is associated with persons engaged in sex life. That is the secret of learning *Bhāgavatam.* Nor can one learn *Bhāgavatam* from one who interprets the text by his mundane scholarship. One has to learn *Bhāgavatam* from the representative of Śukadeva Gosvāmī, and no one else, if one at all wants to see Lord Śrī Kṛṣṇa in the pages. That is the process, and there is no alternative. Sūta Gosvāmī is a bona fide representative of Śukadeva Gosvāmī because he wants to present the message which he received from the great learned *brāhmaṇa.* Śukadeva Gosvāmī presented *Bhāgavatam* as he heard it from his great father, and so also Sūta Gosvāmī is presenting *Bhāgavatam* as he had heard it from Śukadeva Gosvāmī. Simple hearing is not all; one must realize the text with proper attention. The word *niviṣṭa* means that Sūta Gosvāmī drank the juice of *Bhāgavatam* through his ears. That is the real process of receiving *Bhāgavatam.* One should hear with rapt attention from the real person, and then he can at once realize the presence of Lord Kṛṣṇa in every page. The secret of knowing *Bhāgavatam* is mentioned here. No one can give rapt attention who is not pure in mind. No one can be pure in mind who is not pure in action. No one can be pure in action who is not pure in eating, sleeping, fearing and mating. But somehow or other if someone hears with rapt attention from the right person, at the very beginning one can assuredly see Lord Śrī Kṛṣṇa in person in the pages of *Bhāgavatam.*

Thus end the Bhaktivedanta purports of the First Canto, Third Chapter, of the Śrīmad-Bhāgavatam, *entitled "Kṛṣṇa Is the Source of All Incarnations."*

CHAPTER FOUR

The Appearance of Śrī Nārada

व्यास उवाच

TEXT 1

इति ब्रुवाणं संस्तूय मुनीनां दीर्घसत्रिणाम् ।
वृद्धः कुलपतिः सूतं बह्वृचः शौनकोऽब्रवीत् ॥ १ ॥

vyāsa uvāca
iti bruvāṇaṁ saṁstūya munīnāṁ dīrgha-satriṇām
vṛddhaḥ kula-patiḥ sūtaṁ bahvṛcaḥ śaunako 'bravīt

vyāsaḥ—Vyāsadeva; *uvāca*—said; *iti*—thus; *bruvāṇam*—speaking; *saṁstūya*—congratulating; *munīnām*—of the great sages; *dīrgha*—prolonged; *satriṇām*—of those engaged in the performance of sacrifice; *vṛddhaḥ*—elderly; *kula-patiḥ*—head of the assembly; *sūtam*—unto Sūta Gosvāmī; *bahu-ṛcaḥ*—learned; *śaunakaḥ*—of the name Śaunaka; *abravīt*—addressed.

On hearing Sūta Gosvāmī speak thus, Śaunaka Muni, who was the elderly, learned leader of all the ṛṣis engaged in that prolonged sacrificial ceremony, congratulated Sūta Gosvāmī by addressing him as follows.

PURPORT In a meeting of learned men, when there are congratulations or addresses for the speaker, the qualifications of the congratulator should be as follows. He must be the leader of the house and an elderly man. He must be vastly learned also. Śrī Śaunaka Ṛṣi had all these qualifications, and thus he stood up to congratulate Śrī Sūta Gosvāmī when he expressed his desire to present *Śrīmad-Bhāgavatam* exactly as he heard it from Śukadeva Gosvāmī and also realized it personally. Personal realization does not mean that one should, out of vanity, attempt to show one's own learning by trying to surpass the previous *ācārya*. He must have full confidence in the previous *ācārya,* and at the same time he must realize the subject matter so nicely that he can present the matter for the particular circumstances in a suitable manner. *The original purpose of the text must be maintained.* No obscure meaning should be screwed out of it, yet it should be presented in an interesting manner for the understanding of the audience. This is called realization. The leader of the assembly, Śaunaka, could estimate the value of the speaker, Śrī Sūta Gosvāmī, simply by his uttering *yathādhītam* and *yathā-mati,* and therefore he was very glad to congratulate him in ecstasy. No learned man should be willing to hear a person who does not represent the original *ācārya.* So the speaker and the audience were bona fide in this meeting where *Bhāgavatam* was being recited for the second time. That should be the standard of recitation of *Bhāgavatam,* so that its real purpose can be served and Lord Kṛṣṇa can be realized without difficulty. Unless this situation is created, *Bhāgavatam* recitation will be for ulterior purposes, and such recitation is useless labor both for the speaker and for the audience.

शौनक उवाच

TEXT 2

सूत सूत महाभाग वद नो वदतां वर ।
कथां भागवतीं पुण्यां यदाह भगवाञ्छुकः ॥ २ ॥

śaunaka uvāca

sūta sūta mahā-bhāga vada no vadatāṁ vara
kathāṁ bhāgavatīṁ puṇyāṁ yad āha bhagavāñ chukaḥ

śaunakaḥ—Śaunaka; *uvāca*—said; *sūta sūta*—O Sūta Gosvāmī; *mahā-bhāga*—the most fortunate; *vada*—please speak; *naḥ*—unto us; *vadatām*—of those who can speak; *vara*—respected; *kathām*—message; *bhāgavatīm*—of the *Bhāgavatam; puṇyām*—pious; *yat*—which; *āha*—said; *bhagavān*—greatly powerful; *śukaḥ*—Śrī Śukadeva Gosvāmī.

Śaunaka said: O Sūta Gosvāmī, you are the most fortunate and respected of all those who can speak and recite. Please relate the pious message of Śrīmad-Bhāgavatam, which was spoken by the great and powerful sage Śukadeva Gosvāmī.

PURPORT Sūta Gosvāmī is twice addressed herein by Śaunaka Gosvāmī out of great joy because he and the members of the assembly were eager to hear the text of *Bhāgavatam* uttered by Śukadeva Gosvāmī. They were not interested in hearing it from a bogus person who would interpret in his own way to suit his own purpose. Generally the so-called *Bhāgavatam* reciters are either professional readers or so-called learned impersonalists who cannot enter into the transcendental personal activities of the Supreme Person. Such impersonalists twist some meanings out of *Bhāgavatam* to suit and support impersonalist views, and the professional readers at once go to the Tenth Canto to misexplain the most confidential part of the Lord's pastimes. Neither of these reciters are bona fide persons to recite *Bhāgavatam*. Only one who is prepared to present *Bhāgavatam* in the light of Śukadeva Gosvāmī and only those who are prepared to hear Śukadeva Gosvāmī and his representative are bona fide participants in the transcendental discussion of *Śrīmad-Bhāgavatam*.

TEXT 3

कस्मिन् युगे प्रवृत्तेयं स्थाने वा केन हेतुना ।
कुतः सञ्चोदितः कृष्णः कृतवान् संहितां मुनिः ॥ ३ ॥

kasmin yuge pravṛtteyaṁ sthāne vā kena hetunā
kutaḥ sañcoditaḥ kṛṣṇaḥ kṛtavān saṁhitāṁ muniḥ

kasmin—in which; *yuge*—period; *pravṛttā*—was begun; *iyam*—this; *sthāne*—in the place; *vā*—or; *kena*—on what; *hetunā*—ground; *kutaḥ*—wherefrom; *sañcoditaḥ*—inspired by; *kṛṣṇaḥ*—Kṛṣṇa-dvaipāyana Vyāsa; *kṛtavān*—compiled; *saṁhitām*—Vedic literature; *muniḥ*—the learned.

In what period and at what place was this first begun, and why was this taken up? From where did Kṛṣṇa-dvaipāyana Vyāsa, the great sage, get the inspiration to compile this literature?

PURPORT Because *Śrīmad-Bhāgavatam* is the special contribution of Śrīla Vyāsadeva, there are so many inquiries by the learned Śaunaka Muni. It was known to him that Śrīla Vyāsadeva had already explained the text of the *Vedas* in various ways up to the *Mahābhārata* for the understanding of less intelligent women, *śūdras* and fallen members of the family of twice-born men. *Śrīmad-Bhāgavatam* is transcendental to all of them because it has nothing to do with anything mundane. So the inquiries are very intelligent and relevant.

TEXT 4

तस्य पुत्रो महायोगी समदृङ् निर्विकल्पकः ।
एकान्तमतिरुन्निद्रो गूढो मूढ इवेयते ॥ ४ ॥

tasya putro mahā-yogī sama-dṛṅ nirvikalpakaḥ
ekānta-matir unnidro gūḍho mūḍha iveyate

tasya—his; *putraḥ*—son; *mahā-yogī*—a great devotee; *sama-dṛk*—equibalanced; *nirvikalpakaḥ*—absolute monist; *ekānta-matiḥ*—fixed in monism or oneness of mind; *unnidraḥ*—surpassed nescience; *gūḍhaḥ*—not exposed; *mūḍhaḥ*—stunted; *iva*—like; *īyate*—appears like.

His [Vyāsadeva's] son was a great devotee, an equibalanced monist, whose mind was always concentrated in monism. He was transcendental to mundane activities, but being unexposed, he appeared like an ignorant person.

PURPORT Śrīla Śukadeva Gosvāmī was a liberated soul, and thus he remained always alert not to be trapped by the illusory energy. In the *Bhagavad-gītā* this alertness is very lucidly explained. The liberated soul and the conditioned soul have different engagements. The liberated soul is always engaged in the progressive path of spiritual attainment, which is something like a dream for the conditioned soul. The conditioned soul cannot imagine the actual engagements of the liberated soul. While the conditioned soul thus dreams about spiritual engagements, the liberated soul is awake. Similarly, the engagement of a conditioned soul appears to be a dream for the liberated soul. A conditioned soul and a liberated soul may apparently be on the same platform, but factually they are differently engaged, and their attention is always alert, either in sense enjoyment or in self-realization, respectively. The conditioned soul is absorbed in matter, whereas the liberated soul is completely indifferent to matter. This indifference is explained as follows.

TEXT 5

दृष्ट्वानुयान्तमृषिमात्मजमप्यनग्नं
देव्यो ह्रिया परिदधुर्न सुतस्य चित्रम् ।
तद्वीक्ष्य पृच्छति मुनौ जगदुस्तवास्ति
स्त्रीपुम्भिदा न तु सुतस्य विविक्तदृष्टेः ॥ ५ ॥

dṛṣṭvānuyāntam ṛṣim ātmajam apy anagnaṁ
devyo hriyā paridadhur na sutasya citram
tad vīkṣya pṛcchati munau jagadus tavāsti
strī-pum-bhidā na tu sutasya vivikta-dṛṣṭeḥ

dṛṣṭvā—by seeing; *anuyāntam*—following; *ṛṣim*—the sage; *ātmajam*—his son; *api*—in spite of; *anagnam*—not naked; *devyaḥ*—beautiful damsels; *hriyā*—out of shyness; *paridadhuḥ*—covered the body; *na*—not; *sutasya*—of the son; *citram*—astonishing; *tat vīkṣya*—by seeing that; *pṛcchati*—asking; *munau*—unto the *muni* (Vyāsa); *jagaduḥ*—replied; *tava*—your; *asti*—there are; *strī-pum*—male and female; *bhidā*—differences; *na*—not; *tu*—but; *sutasya*—of the son; *vivikta*—purified; *dṛṣṭeḥ*—of one who looks.

While Śrī Vyāsadeva was following his son, beautiful young damsels who were bathing naked covered their bodies with cloth, although Śrī Vyāsadeva himself was not naked. But they had not done so when his son had passed. The sage inquired about this, and the young ladies replied that his son was purified and when looking at them made no distinction between male and female but the sage made such distinctions.

PURPORT In the *Bhagavad-gītā* (5.18) it is said that a learned sage looks equally on a learned and gentle *brāhmaṇa,* a *caṇḍāla* (dog-eater), a dog or a cow due to his spiritual vision. Śrīla Śukadeva Gosvāmī attained that stage. Thus he did not see a male or female; he saw all living entities in different dress. The ladies who were bathing could understand the mind of a man simply by studying his demeanor, just as by looking at a child one can understand how innocent he is. Śukadeva Gosvāmī was a young boy sixteen years old, and therefore all the parts of his body were developed. He was naked also, and so were the ladies. But because Śukadeva Gosvāmī was transcendental to sex relations, the way he looked at them was very innocent and had nothing to do with worldly affairs. The ladies, by their special qualifications, could sense this at once, and therefore they were not very concerned about him. But when his father passed, the ladies quickly dressed. Śrīla Vyāsadeva was an old man and was fully dressed, and the ladies were exactly like his children or grandchildren, yet they reacted to his presence according to the social custom because he played the part of a householder. A householder has to distinguish between a male and female, otherwise he cannot be a householder. One should therefore attempt to know the distinction between body and soul without any attachment for male and female. As long as such attachment is there, one should not try to become a *sannyāsī* like Śukadeva Gosvāmī. At least theoretically one must be convinced that a living entity is neither male nor female. The outward dress is made of matter by material nature to attract the opposite sex and thus keep one entangled in material existence. A liberated soul is above this perverted distinction. He does not distinguish between one living being and another. For him they are all one and the same spirit. The perfection of this spiritual vision is the liberated stage, and Śrīla Śukadeva Gosvāmī attained that stage. Śrīla Vyāsadeva was also in the transcendental stage, but because he was in the householder's life, he did not pretend to be a liberated soul, as a matter of custom.

TEXT 6

कथमालक्षितः पौरैः सम्प्राप्तः कुरुजाङ्गलान् ।
उन्मत्तमूकजडवद्विचरन् गजसाह्वये ॥ ६ ॥

katham ālakṣitaḥ pauraiḥ samprāptaḥ kuru-jāṅgalān
unmatta-mūka-jaḍavad vicaran gaja-sāhvaye

katham—how; *ālakṣitaḥ*—recognized; *pauraiḥ*—by the citizens; *samprāptaḥ*—reaching; *kuru-jāṅgalān*—the Kuru-jāṅgala provinces; *unmatta*—mad; *mūka*—dumb; *jaḍavat*—stunted; *vicaran*—wandering; *gaja-sāhvaye*—Hastināpura.

How was he [Śrīla Śukadeva, the son of Vyāsa] recognized by the citizens when he entered the city of Hastināpura [now Delhi], after wandering in the provinces of Kuru and Jāṅgala, appearing like a madman, dumb and retarded?

PURPORT The present city of Delhi was formerly known as Hastināpura because it was first established by King Hastī. Gosvāmī Śukadeva, after leaving his paternal home, was roaming like a madman, and therefore it was very difficult for the citizens to recognize him in his exalted position. A sage is not, therefore, recognized by sight, but by hearing. One should approach a *sādhu* or great sage not to see but to hear him. If one is not prepared to hear the words of a *sādhu,* there is no profit. Śukadeva Gosvāmī was a *sādhu* who could speak on the transcendental activities of the Lord. He did not satisfy the whims of ordinary citizens. He was recognized when he spoke on the subject of *Bhāgavatam,* and he never attempted jugglery like a magician. Outwardly he appeared to be a retarded, dumb madman, but in fact he was the most elevated transcendental personality.

TEXT 7

कथं वा पाण्डवेयस्य राजर्षेर्मुनिना सह ।
संवादः समभूत्तात यत्रैषा सात्वती श्रुतिः ॥ ७ ॥

katham vā pāṇḍaveyasya rājarṣer muninā saha
saṁvādaḥ samabhūt tāta yatraiṣā sātvatī śrutiḥ

katham—how is it; *vā*—also; *pāṇḍaveyasya*—of the descendant of Pāṇḍu (Parīkṣit); *rājarṣeḥ*—of the king who was a sage; *muninā*—with the *muni; saha*—with; *saṁvādaḥ*—discussion; *samabhūt*—took place; *tāta*—O darling; *yatra*—whereupon; *eṣā*—like this; *sātvatī*—transcendental; *śrutiḥ*—essence of the *Vedas.*

How did it so happen that King Parīkṣit met this great sage, making it possible for this great transcendental essence of the Vedas [Bhāgavatam] to be sung to him?

PURPORT *Śrīmad-Bhāgavatam* is stated here as the essence of the *Vedas.* It is not an imaginary story as it is sometimes considered by unauthorized men. It is also called *Śuka-saṁhitā,* or the Vedic hymn spoken by Śrī Śukadeva Gosvāmī, the great liberated sage.

TEXT 8

स गोदोहनमात्रं हि गृहेषु गृहमेधिनाम् ।
अवेक्षते महाभागस्तीर्थीकुर्वंस्तदाश्रमम् ॥ ८ ॥

sa go-dohana-mātraṁ hi gṛheṣu gṛha-medhinām
avekṣate mahā-bhāgas tīrthī-kurvaṁs tad āśramam

saḥ—he (Śukadeva Gosvāmī); *go-dohana-mātram*—only for the time of milking the cow; *hi*—certainly; *gṛheṣu*—in the house; *gṛha-medhinām*—of the householders; *avekṣate*—waits; *mahā-bhāgaḥ*—the most fortunate; *tīrthī*—pilgrimage; *kurvan*—transforming; *tat āśramam*—the residence.

He [Śukadeva Gosvāmī] is accustomed to stay at the door of a householder only long enough for a cow to be milked. And he does this just to sanctify the residence.

PURPORT Śukadeva Gosvāmī met Emperor Parīkṣit and explained the text of *Śrīmad-Bhāgavatam*. He was not accustomed to stay at any householder's residence for more than half an hour (at the time of milking the cow), and he would just take alms from the fortunate householder. That was to sanctify the residence by his auspicious presence. Therefore Śukadeva Gosvāmī is an ideal preacher established in the transcendental position. From his activities, those who are in the renounced order of life and dedicated to the mission of preaching the message of Godhead should learn that they have no business with householders save and except to enlighten them in transcendental knowledge. Such asking for alms from the householder should be for the purpose of sanctifying his home. One who is in the renounced order of life should not be allured by the glamor of the householder's worldly possessions and thus become subservient to worldly men. For one who is in the renounced order of life, this is much more dangerous than drinking poison and committing suicide.

TEXT 9

अभिमन्युसुतं सूत प्राहुर्भागवतोत्तमम् ।
तस्य जन्म महाश्चर्यं कर्माणि च गृणीहि नः ॥ ९ ॥

abhimanyu-sutaṁ sūta prāhur bhāgavatottamam
tasya janma mahāścaryaṁ karmāṇi ca gṛṇīhi naḥ

abhimanyu-sutam—the son of Abhimanyu; *sūta*—O Sūta; *prāhuḥ*—is said to be; *bhāgavata-uttamam*—the first-class devotee of the Lord; *tasya*—his; *janma*—birth; *mahā-āścaryam*—very wonderful; *karmāṇi*—activities; *ca*—and; *gṛṇīhi*—please speak to; *naḥ*—us.

It is said that Mahārāja Parīkṣit is a great first-class devotee of the

Lord and that his birth and activities are all wonderful. Please tell us about him.

PURPORT The birth of Mahārāja Parīkṣit is wonderful because in the womb of his mother he was protected by the Personality of Godhead Śrī Kṛṣṇa. His activities are also wonderful because he chastised Kali, who was attempting to kill a cow. To kill cows means to end human civilization. He wanted to protect the cow from being killed by the great representative of sin. His death is also wonderful because he got previous notice of his death, which is wonderful for any mortal being, and thus he prepared himself for passing away by sitting down on the bank of the Ganges and hearing the transcendental activities of the Lord. During all the days he heard *Bhāgavatam,* he did not take food or drink, nor did he sleep a moment. So everything about him is wonderful, and his activities are worth hearing attentively. The desire is expressed herein to hear about him in detail.

TEXT 10

स सम्राट् कस्य वा हेतोः पाण्डूनां मानवर्धनः ।
प्रायोपविष्टो गङ्गायामनादृत्याधिराट्श्रियम् ॥ १० ॥

sa samrāṭ kasya vā hetoḥ pāṇḍūnāṁ māna-vardhanaḥ
prāyopaviṣṭo gaṅgāyām anādṛtyādhirāṭ-śriyam

saḥ—he; *samrāṭ*—the Emperor; *kasya*—for what; *vā*—or; *hetoḥ*—reason; *pāṇḍūnām*—of the sons of Pāṇḍu; *māna-vardhanaḥ*—one who enriches the family; *prāya-upaviṣṭaḥ*—sitting and fasting; *gaṅgāyām*—on the bank of the Ganges; *anādṛtya*—neglecting; *adhirāṭ*—acquired kingdom; *śriyam*—opulences.

He was a great emperor and possessed all the opulences of his acquired kingdom. He was so exalted that he was increasing the prestige of the Pāṇḍu dynasty. Why did he give up everything to sit down on the bank of the Ganges and fast until death?

PURPORT Mahārāja Parīkṣit was the Emperor of the world and all the seas and oceans, and he did not have to take the trouble to acquire such a kingdom by his own effort. He inherited it from his grandfathers Mahārāja Yudhiṣṭhira and brothers. Besides that, he was doing well in the administration and was worthy of the good names of his forefathers. Consequently there was nothing undesirable in his opulence and administration. Then why should he give up all these favorable circumstances and sit down on the bank of the Ganges, fasting till death? This is astonishing, and therefore all were eager to know the cause.

TEXT 11

नमन्ति यत्पादनिकेतमात्मनः
शिवाय हानीय धनानि शत्रवः ।
कथं स वीरः श्रियमङ्ग दुस्त्यजां
युवैषतोत्स्रष्टुमहो सहासुभिः ॥ ११ ॥

namanti yat-pāda-niketam ātmanaḥ
śivāya hānīya dhanāni śatravaḥ
kathaṁ sa vīraḥ śriyam aṅga dustyajāṁ
yuvaiṣatotsraṣṭum aho sahāsubhiḥ

namanti—bow down; *yat-pāda*—whose feet; *niketam*—under; *ātmanaḥ*—own; *śivāya*—welfare; *hānīya*—used to bring about; *dhanāni*—wealth; *śatravaḥ*—enemies; *katham*—for what reason; *saḥ*—he; *vīraḥ*—the chivalrous; *śriyam*—opulences; *aṅga*—O Sūta Gosvāmī; *dustyajām*—inseparable; *yuvā*—in full youth; *aiṣata*—desired; *utsraṣṭum*—to give up; *aho*—exclamation; *saha*—with; *asubhiḥ*—life.

He was such a great emperor that all his enemies would come and bow down at his feet and surrender all their wealth for their own benefit. He was full of youth and strength, and he possessed kingly opulences that were difficult to give up. Why did he want to give up everything, including his life?

PURPORT There was nothing undesirable in his life. He was quite a young man and could enjoy life with power and opulence. So there was no question of retiring from active life. There was no difficulty in collecting the state taxes because he was so powerful and chivalrous that even his enemies would come to him and bow down at his feet and surrender all wealth for their own benefit. Mahārāja Parīkṣit was a pious king. He conquered his enemies, and therefore the kingdom was full of prosperity. There was enough milk, grains and metals, and all the rivers and mountains were full of potency. So materially everything was satisfactory. Therefore, there was no question of untimely giving up his kingdom and life. The sages were eager to hear about all this.

TEXT 12

शिवाय लोकस्य भवाय भूतये
य उत्तमश्लोकपरायणा जनाः ।
जीवन्ति नात्मार्थमसौ पराश्रयं
मुमोच निर्विद्य कुतः कलेवरम् ॥ १२ ॥

śivāya lokasya bhavāya bhūtaye
ya uttama-śloka-parāyaṇā janāḥ
jīvanti nātmārtham asau parāśrayaṁ
mumoca nirvidya kutaḥ kalevaram

śivāya—welfare; *lokasya*—of all living beings; *bhavāya*—for flourishing; *bhūtaye*—for economic development; *ye*—one who is; *uttama-śloka-parāyaṇāḥ*—devoted to the cause of the Personality of Godhead; *janāḥ*—men; *jīvanti*—do live; *na*—but not; *ātma-artham*—selfish interest; *asau*—that; *para-āśrayam*—shelter for others; *mumoca*—gave up; *nirvidya*—being freed from all attachment; *kutaḥ*—for what reason; *kalevaram*—mortal body.

Those who are devoted to the cause of the Personality of Godhead live only for the welfare, development and happiness of others. They do not live for any selfish interest. So even though the Emperor [Parīkṣit] was free from all attachment to worldly possessions, how could he give up his mortal body, which was the shelter for others?

PURPORT Parīkṣit Mahārāja was an ideal king and householder because he was a devotee of the Personality of Godhead. A devotee of the Lord automatically has all good qualifications. And the Emperor was a typical example of this. Personally he had no attachment for all the worldly opulences in his possession. But since he was king for the all-around welfare of his citizens, he was always busy in the welfare work of the public, not only for this life, but also for the next. He would not allow slaughterhouses or killing of cows. He was not a foolish and partial administrator who would arrange for the protection of one living being and allow another to be killed. Because he was a devotee of the Lord, he knew perfectly well how to conduct his administration for everyone's happiness—men, animals, plants and all living creatures. He was not selfishly interested. Selfishness is either self-centered or self-extended. He was neither. His interest was to please the Supreme Truth, the Personality of Godhead. The king is the representative of the Supreme Lord, and therefore the king's interest must be identical with that of the Supreme Lord. The Supreme Lord wants all living beings to be obedient to Him and thereby become happy. Therefore the king's interest is to guide all subjects back to the kingdom of God. Hence the activities of the citizens should be so coordinated that they can at the end go back home, back to Godhead. Under the administration of a representative king, the kingdom is full of opulence. At that time, human beings need not eat animals. There are ample food grains, milk, fruit and vegetables so that the human beings as well as the animals can eat sumptuously and to their heart's content. If all living beings are satisfied with food and shelter and obey the prescribed rules, there cannot be any disturbance between one living being and another. Emperor Parīkṣit was a worthy king, and therefore all were happy during his reign.

TEXT 13

तत्सर्वं नः समाचक्ष्व पृष्टो यदिह किञ्चन ।
मन्ये त्वां विषये वाचां स्नातमन्यत्र छान्दसात् ॥ १३ ॥

tat sarvaṁ naḥ samācakṣva pṛṣṭo yad iha kiñcana
manye tvāṁ viṣaye vācāṁ snātam anyatra chāndasāt

tat—that; *sarvam*—all; *naḥ*—unto us; *samācakṣva*—clearly explain; *pṛṣṭaḥ*—questioned; *yat iha*—herein; *kiñcana*—all that; *manye*—we think; *tvām*—you; *viṣaye*—in all subjects; *vācām*—meanings of words; *snātam*—fully acquainted; *anyatra*—except; *chāndasāt*—portion of the *Vedas.*

We know that you are expert in the meaning of all subjects, except

some portions of the Vedas, and thus you can clearly explain the answers to all the questions we have just put to you.

PURPORT The difference between the *Vedas* and the *Purāṇas* is like that between the *brāhmaṇas* and the *parivrājakas.* The *brāhmaṇas* are meant to administer some fruitive sacrifices mentioned in the *Vedas,* but the *parivrājakācāryas,* or learned preachers, are meant to disseminate transcendental knowledge to one and all. As such, the *parivrājakācāryas* are not always expert in pronouncing the Vedic *mantras,* which are practiced systematically by accent and meter by the *brāhmaṇas* who are meant for administering Vedic rites. Yet it should not be considered that the *brāhmaṇas* are more important than the itinerant preachers. They are one and different simultaneously because they are meant for the same end, in different ways.

There is no difference also between the Vedic *mantras* and what is explained in the *Purāṇas* and *Itihāsas.* According to Śrīla Jīva Gosvāmī, it is mentioned in the *Mādhyandina-śruti* that all the *Vedas,* namely the *Sāma, Atharva, Ṛg, Yajur, Purāṇas, Itihāsas, Upaniṣads,* etc., are emanations from the breathing of the Supreme Being. The only differences are that the Vedic *mantras* mostly begin with *praṇava oṁkāra* and that it requires some training to pronounce the metrical accent, without which the *mantras* cannot be successfully chanted. Although Śrīla Sūta Gosvāmī was a preacher of the first order, he did not bother much about the metrical pronunciation of the Vedic *mantras.* But that does not mean *Śrīmad-Bhāgavatam* is of less importance than the Vedic *mantras.* On the contrary, it is the ripened fruit of all the *Vedas,* as stated before. Besides that, the most perfectly liberated soul, Śrīla Śukadeva Gosvāmī, is absorbed in the studies of the *Bhāgavatam,* although he is already self-realized. Śrīla Sūta Gosvāmī is following his footsteps, and therefore his position is not the least less important because he was not expert in chanting Vedic *mantras* with metric pronunciation, which depends more on practice than actual realization. Realization is more important than parrotlike chanting.

सूत उवाच

TEXT 14

द्वापरे समनुप्राप्ते तृतीये युगपर्यये ।
जातः पराशराद्योगी वासव्यां कलया हरेः ॥ १४ ॥

sūta uvāca
dvāpare samanuprāpte tṛtīye yuga-paryaye
jātaḥ parāśarād yogī vāsavyāṁ kalayā hareḥ

sūtaḥ—Sūta Gosvāmī; *uvāca*—said; *dvāpare*—in the second millennium; *samanuprāpte*—on the advent of; *tṛtīye*—third; *yuga*—millennium; *paryaye*—in the place of; *jātaḥ*—was begotten; *parāśarāt*—by Parāśara; *yogī*—the great sage; *vāsavyām*—in the womb of the daughter of Vasu; *kalayā*—in the plenary portion; *hareḥ*—of the Personality of Godhead.

Sūta Gosvāmī said: When the second millennium overlapped the third, the great sage [Vyāsadeva] was born to Parāśara in the womb of Satyavatī, the daughter of Vasu.

PURPORT There is a chronological order of the four millenniums, namely Satya, Dvāpara, Tretā and Kali. But sometimes there is overlapping. During the regime of Vaivasvata Manu, there was an overlapping of the twenty-eighth round of the four millenniums, and the third millennium appeared prior to the second. In that particular millennium, Lord Śrī Kṛṣṇa also descends, and because of this there was some particular alteration. The mother of the great sage was Satyavatī, the daughter of the Vasu (fisherman), and the father was the great Parāśara Muni. That is the history of Vyāsadeva's birth. Every millennium is divided into three periods, and each period is called a *sandhyā*. Vyāsadeva appeared in the third *sandhyā* of that particular age.

TEXT 15

स कदाचित्सरस्वत्या उपस्पृश्य जलं शुचिः ।
विविक्त एक आसीन उदिते रविमण्डले ॥ १५ ॥

sa kadācit sarasvatyā upaspṛśya jalaṁ śuciḥ
vivikta eka āsīna udite ravi-maṇḍale

saḥ—he; *kadācit*—once; *sarasvatyāḥ*—on the bank of the Sarasvatī; *upaspṛśya*—after finishing morning ablutions; *jalam*—water; *śuciḥ*—being purified; *vivikte*—concentration; *ekaḥ*—alone; *āsīnaḥ*—being thus seated; *udite*—on the rise; *ravi-maṇḍale*—of the sun disc.

Once upon a time he [Vyāsadeva], as the sun rose, took his morning ablution in the waters of the Sarasvatī and sat alone to concentrate.

PURPORT The river Sarasvatī is flowing in the Badarikāśrama area of the Himalayas. So the place indicated here is Śamyāprāsa in Badarikāśrama, where Śrī Vyāsadeva is residing.

TEXT 16

परावरज्ञः स ऋषिः कालेनाव्यक्तरंहसा ।
युगधर्मव्यतिकरं प्राप्तं भुवि युगे युगे ॥ १६ ॥

parāvara-jñaḥ sa ṛṣiḥ kālenāvyakta-raṁhasā
yuga-dharma-vyatikaraṁ prāptaṁ bhuvi yuge yuge

para-avara—past and future; *jñaḥ*—one who knows; *saḥ*—he; *ṛṣiḥ*—Vyāsadeva; *kālena*—by time; *avyakta*—unmanifested; *raṁhasā*—whose great force; *yuga-dharma*—acts in terms of the millennium; *vyati-karam*—anomalies; *prāptam*—having accrued; *bhuvi*—on the earth; *yuge yuge*—different ages.

The great sage Vyāsadeva saw anomalies in the duties of the millennium. This happens on the earth in different ages, due to the unseen force of time.

PURPORT The great sages like Vyāsadeva are liberated souls, and therefore they can see clearly past and future. Thus he could see the future anomalies in the Kali age, and accordingly he made arrangement for the people in general so that they can execute a progressive life in this age, which is full of darkness. The people in general in this age of Kali are too much interested in matter, which is temporary. Because of ignorance they are unable to evaluate the assets of life and be enlightened in spiritual knowledge.

TEXTS 17–18

भौतिकानां च भावानां शक्तिह्रासं च तत्कृतम् ।
अश्रद्दधानान्निःसत्त्वान्दुर्मेधान् ह्रसितायुषः ॥ १७ ॥
दुर्भगांश्च जनान् वीक्ष्य मुनिर्दिव्येन चक्षुषा ।
सर्ववर्णाश्रमाणां यद्दध्यौ हितममोघदृक् ॥ १८ ॥

bhautikānāṁ ca bhāvānāṁ śakti-hrāsaṁ ca tat-kṛtam
aśraddadhānān niḥsattvān durmedhān hrasitāyuṣaḥ

durbhagāṁś ca janān vīkṣya munir divyena cakṣuṣā
sarva-varṇāśramāṇāṁ yad dadhyau hitam amogha-dṛk

bhautikānām ca—also of everything that is made of matter; *bhāvānām*—actions; *śakti-hrāsam ca*—and deterioration of natural power; *tat-kṛtam*—rendered by that; *aśraddadhānān*—of the faithless; *niḥsattvān*—impatient due to want of the mode of goodness; *durmedhān*—dull-witted; *hrasita*—reduced; *āyuṣaḥ*—of duration of life; *durbhagān ca*—also the unlucky; *janān*—people in general; *vīkṣya*—by seeing; *muniḥ*—the *muni; divyena*—by transcendental; *cakṣuṣā*—vision; *sarva*—all; *varṇa-āśramāṇām*—of all the statuses and orders of life; *yat*—what; *dadhyau*—contemplated; *hitam*—welfare; *amogha-dṛk*—one who is fully equipped in knowledge.

The great sage, who was fully equipped in knowledge, could see through his transcendental vision the deterioration of everything material due to the influence of the age. He could also see that the faithless people in general would be reduced in duration of life and would be impatient due to lack of goodness. Thus he contemplated for the welfare of men in all statuses and orders of life.

PURPORT The unmanifested forces of time are so powerful that they decay all matter in due course. In Kali-yuga, the last millennium of a round of four millenniums, the power of all material objects deteriorates by the influence of time. In this age the duration of the material body of the people in general is much reduced, and so is the memory. The action of matter has also not so much incentive. The land does not produce food grains in the same proportions as it did in other ages. The cow does not give as much milk as it used to give formerly. The production of vegetables and fruits is less than before. As such, all living beings, both men and animals, do not have sumptuous, nourishing food. Due to want of so many necessities of life, naturally the duration of life is reduced, the memory is short, intelligence is meager, mutual dealings are full of hypocrisy and so on.

Being a liberated soul, the great sage Vyāsadeva could see this by his transcendental vision. As an astrologer can see the future fate of a man, or an astronomer can foretell the solar and lunar eclipses, liberated souls can foretell the future of all mankind by seeing through the scriptures. They can see this due to their sharp vision of spiritual attainment.

And all such transcendentalists, who are naturally devotees of the Lord, are always eager to render welfare service to the people in general. They are the real friends of the people in general, not the so-called public leaders who are unable to see what is going to happen five minutes ahead. In this age the people in general as well as their so-called leaders are all unlucky fellows, faithless in spiritual knowledge and influenced by the age of Kali. They are always disturbed by various diseases. For example, in the present age there are so many TB patients and TB hospitals, but formerly this was not so because the time was not so unfavorable. The unfortunate men of this age are always reluctant to give a reception to the transcendentalists who are representatives of Śrīla Vyāsadeva, and yet these selfless workers are always busy in planning something which may help everyone in all statuses and orders of life. The greatest philanthropists are those transcendentalists who represent the mission of Vyāsa, Nārada, Madhva, Caitanya, Rūpa, Sarasvatī, etc. They are all one and the same. The personalities may be different, but the aim of the mission is one and the same, namely, to deliver the fallen souls back home, back to Godhead.

TEXT 19

चातुर्होत्रं कर्म शुद्धं प्रजानां वीक्ष्य वैदिकम् ।
व्यदधाद्यज्ञसन्तत्यै वेदमेकं चतुर्विधम् ॥ १९ ॥

cātur-hotraṁ karma śuddhaṁ prajānāṁ vīkṣya vaidikam
vyadadhād yajña-santatyai vedam ekaṁ catur-vidham

cātuḥ—four; *hotram*—sacrificial fires; *karma śuddham*—purification of work; *prajānām*—of the people in general; *vīkṣya*—after seeing; *vaidikam*—according to Vedic rites; *vyadadhāt*—made into; *yajña*—sacrifice; *santatyai*—to expand; *vedam ekam*—only one *Veda; catuḥ-vidham*—in four divisions.

He saw that the sacrifices mentioned in the Vedas were means by which the people's occupations could be purified. And to simplify the

process he divided the one Veda into four, in order to expand them among men.

PURPORT Formerly there was only the *Veda* of the name *Yajur,* and the four divisions of sacrifices were there specifically mentioned. But to make them more easily performable, the *Veda* was divided into four divisions of sacrifice, just to purify the occupational service of the four orders. Above the four *Vedas,* namely *Ṛg, Yajur, Sāma,* and *Atharva,* there are the *Purāṇas,* the *Mahābhārata, Saṁhitās,* etc., which are known as the fifth *Veda.* Śrī Vyāsadeva and his many disciples were all historical personalities, and they were very kind and sympathetic toward the fallen souls of this age of Kali. As such, the *Purāṇas* and *Mahābhārata* were made from related historical facts which explained the teaching of the four *Vedas.* There is no point in doubting the authority of the *Purāṇas* and *Mahābhārata* as parts and parcels of the *Vedas.* In the *Chāndogya Upaniṣad* (7.1.4), the *Purāṇas* and *Mahābhārata,* generally known as histories, are mentioned as the fifth *Veda.* According to Śrīla Jīva Gosvāmī, that is the way of ascertaining the respective values of the revealed scriptures.

TEXT 20

ऋग्यजुःसामाथर्वाख्या वेदाश्चत्वार उद्धृताः ।
इतिहासपुराणं च पञ्चमो वेद उच्यते ॥ २० ॥

ṛg-yajuḥ-sāmātharvākhyā vedāś catvāra uddhṛtāḥ
itihāsa-purāṇaṁ ca pañcamo veda ucyate

ṛg-yajuḥ-sāma-atharva-ākhyāḥ—the names of the four *Vedas; vedāḥ*—the *Vedas; catvāraḥ*—four; *uddhṛtāḥ*—made into separate parts; *itihāsa*—historical records (*Mahābhārata*); *purāṇam ca*—and the *Purāṇas; pañcamaḥ*—the fifth; *vedaḥ*—the original source of knowledge; *ucyate*—is said to be.

The four divisions of the original sources of knowledge [the Vedas] were made separately. But the historical facts and authentic stories mentioned in the Purāṇas are called the fifth Veda.

TEXT 21

तत्रर्ग्वेदधरः पैलः सामगो जैमिनिः कविः ।
वैशम्पायन एवैको निष्णातो यजुषामुत ॥ २१ ॥

tatrarg-veda-dharaḥ pailaḥ sāmago jaiminiḥ kaviḥ
vaiśampāyana evaiko niṣṇāto yajuṣām uta

tatra—thereupon; *ṛg-veda-dharaḥ*—the professor of the *Ṛg Veda; pailaḥ*—the *ṛṣi* named Paila; *sāma-gaḥ*—that of the *Sāma Veda; jaiminiḥ*—the *ṛṣi* named Jaimini; *kaviḥ*—highly qualified; *vaiśampāyanaḥ*—the *ṛṣi* named Vaiśampāyana; *eva*—only; *ekaḥ*—alone; *niṣṇātaḥ*—well versed; *yajuṣām*—of the *Yajur Veda; uta*—glorified.

After the Vedas were divided into four divisions, Paila Ṛṣi became the professor of the Ṛg Veda, Jaimini the professor of the Sāma Veda, and Vaiśampāyana alone became glorified by the Yajur Veda.

PURPORT The different *Vedas* were entrusted to different learned scholars for development in various ways.

TEXT 22

अथर्वाङ्गिरसामासीत्सुमन्तुर्दारुणो मुनिः ।
इतिहासपुराणानां पिता मे रोमहर्षणः ॥ २२ ॥

atharvāṅgirasām āsīt sumantur dāruṇo muniḥ
itihāsa-purāṇānāṁ pitā me romaharṣaṇaḥ

atharva—the *Atharva Veda; aṅgirasām*—unto the *ṛṣi* Aṅgirā; *āsīt*—was entrusted; *sumantuḥ*—also known as Sumantu Muni; *dāruṇaḥ*—seriously devoted to the *Atharva Veda; muniḥ*—the sage; *itihāsa-purāṇānām*—of the historical records and the *Purāṇas; pitā*—father; *me*—mine; *romaharṣaṇaḥ*—the *ṛṣi* Romaharṣaṇa.

The Sumantu Muni Aṅgirā, who was very devotedly engaged, was entrusted with the Atharva Veda. And my father, Romaharṣaṇa, was entrusted with the Purāṇas and historical records.

PURPORT In the *śruti-mantras* also it is stated that Aṅgirā Muni, who strictly followed the rigid principles of the *Atharva Vedas,* was the leader of the followers of the *Atharva Vedas.*

TEXT 23

त एत ऋषयो वेदं स्वं स्वं व्यस्यन्ननेकधा ।
शिष्यैः प्रशिष्यैस्तच्छिष्यैर्वेदास्ते शाखिनोऽभवन् ॥ २३ ॥

ta eta ṛṣayo vedaṁ svaṁ svaṁ vyasyann anekadhā
śiṣyaiḥ praśiṣyais tac-chiṣyair vedās te śākhino 'bhavan

te—they; *ete*—all these; *ṛṣayaḥ*—learned scholars; *vedam*—the respective *Vedas; svam svam*—in their own entrusted matters; *vyasyan*—rendered; *anekadhā*—many; *śiṣyaiḥ*—disciples; *praśiṣyaiḥ*—granddisciples; *tat-śiṣyaiḥ*—great-granddisciples; *vedāḥ te*—followers of the respective *Vedas; śākhinaḥ*—different branches; *abhavan*—thus became.

All these learned scholars, in their turn, rendered their entrusted Vedas unto their many disciples, granddisciples and great-granddisciples, and thus the respective branches of the followers of the Vedas came into being.

PURPORT The original source of knowledge is the *Vedas.* There are no branches of knowledge, either mundane or transcendental, which do not belong to the original text of the *Vedas.* They have simply been developed into different branches. They were originally rendered by great, respectable and learned professors. In other words, the Vedic knowledge, divided into different branches, has been distributed all over the world by different disciplic successions. No one, therefore, can claim independent knowledge beyond the *Vedas.*

TEXT 24

त एव वेदा दुर्मेधैर्धार्यन्ते पुरुषैर्यथा ।
एवं चकार भगवान् व्यासः कृपणवत्सलः ॥ २४ ॥

ta eva vedā durmedhair dhāryante puruṣair yathā
evaṁ cakāra bhagavān vyāsaḥ kṛpaṇa-vatsalaḥ

te—that; *eva*—certainly; *vedāḥ*—the book of knowledge; *durmedhaiḥ*—by the less intellectual; *dhāryante*—can assimilate; *puruṣaiḥ*—by the man; *yathā*—as much as; *evam*—thus; *cakāra*—edited; *bhagavān*—the powerful; *vyāsaḥ*—the great sage Vyāsa; *kṛpaṇa-vatsalaḥ*—very kind to the ignorant mass.

Thus the great sage Vyāsadeva, who is very kind to the ignorant masses, edited the Vedas so they might be assimilated by less intellectual men.

PURPORT The *Veda* is one, and the reasons for its divisions in many parts are explained herewith. The seed of all knowledge, or the *Veda,* is not a subject matter which can easily be understood by any ordinary man. There is a stricture that no one should try to learn the *Vedas* who is not a qualified *brāhmaṇa.* This stricture has been wrongly interpreted in so many ways. A class of men, who claim brahminical qualification simply by their birthright in the family of a *brāhmaṇa,* claim that the study of the *Vedas* is a monopoly of the *brāhmaṇa* caste only. Another section of the people take this as an injustice to members of other castes, who do not happen to take birth in a *brāhmaṇa* family. But both of them are misguided. The *Vedas* are subjects which had to be explained even to Brahmājī by the Supreme Lord. Therefore the subject matter is understood by persons with exceptional qualities of goodness. Persons who are in the modes of passion and ignorance are unable to understand the subject matter of the *Vedas.* The ultimate goal of Vedic knowledge is Śrī Kṛṣṇa, the Personality of Godhead. This Personality is very rarely understood by those who are in the modes of passion and ignorance. In the Satya-yuga everyone was situated in the mode of goodness. Gradually the mode of goodness declined during the Tretā and Dvāpara-yugas, and the general mass of people became corrupt. In the present age the mode of goodness is almost nil, and so for the general mass of people, the kind-hearted, powerful sage Śrīla Vyāsadeva divided the *Vedas* in various ways so that they may be practically followed by less intelligent persons in the modes of passion and ignorance. It is explained in the next *śloka* as follows.

TEXT 25

स्त्रीशूद्रद्विजबन्धूनां त्रयी न श्रुतिगोचरा ।
कर्मश्रेयसि मूढानां श्रेय एवं भवेदिह ।
इति भारतमाख्यानं कृपया मुनिना कृतम् ॥ २५ ॥

strī-śūdra-dvijabandhūnāṁ trayī na śruti-gocarā
karma-śreyasi mūḍhānāṁ śreya evaṁ bhaved iha
iti bhāratam ākhyānaṁ kṛpayā muninā kṛtam

strī—the woman class; *śūdra*—the laboring class; *dvija-bandhūnām*—of the friends of the twice-born; *trayī*—three; *na*—not; *śruti-gocarā*—for understanding; *karma*—in activities; *śreyasi*—in welfare; *mūḍhānām*—of the fools; *śreyaḥ*—supreme benefit; *evam*—thus; *bhavet*—achieved; *iha*—by this; *iti*—thus thinking; *bhāratam*—the great *Mahābhārata; ākhyānam*—historical facts; *kṛpayā*—out of great mercy; *muninā*—by the *muni; kṛtam*—is completed.

Out of compassion, the great sage thought it wise that this would enable men to achieve the ultimate goal of life. Thus he compiled the great historical narration called the Mahābhārata for women, laborers and friends of the twice-born.

PURPORT The friends of the twice-born families are those who are born in the families of *brāhmaṇas, kṣatriyas* and *vaiśyas,* or the spiritually cultured families, but who themselves are not equal to their forefathers. Such descendants are not recognized as such, for want of purificatory achievements. The purificatory activities begin even before the birth of a child, and the seed-giving reformatory process is called *garbhādhāna-saṁskāra.* One who has not undergone such *garbhādhāna-saṁskāra,* or spiritual family planning, is not accepted as being of an actual twice-born family. The *garbhādhāna-saṁskāra* is followed by other purificatory processes, out of which the sacred thread ceremony is one. This is performed at the time of spiritual initiation. After this particular *saṁskāra,* one is rightly called twice-born. One birth is calculated during the seed-giving *saṁskāra,* and the second birth is calculated at the time of spiritual initiation. One who has been able to undergo such important *saṁskāras* can be called a bona fide twice-born.

If the father and the mother do not undertake the process of spiritual family planning and simply beget children out of passion only, their children are called *dvija-bandhus.* These *dvija-bandhus* are certainly not as intelligent as the children of the regular twice-born families. The *dvija-bandhus* are classified with the *śūdras* and the woman class, who are by nature less intelligent. The *śūdras* and the woman class do not have to undergo any *saṁskāra* save and except the ceremony of marriage.

The less intelligent classes of men, namely women, *śūdras* and unqualified sons of the higher castes, are devoid of necessary qualifications to understand the purpose of the transcendental *Vedas.* For them the *Mahābhārata* was prepared. The purpose of the *Mahābhārata* is to administer the purpose of the *Vedas,* and therefore within the *Mahābhārata* is placed the *Bhagavad-gītā,* the summary *Veda.* The less intelligent are more interested in stories than in philosophy, and therefore the philosophy of the *Vedas* is included within the *Mahābhārata* in the form of the *Bhagavad-gītā,* spoken by Lord Śrī Kṛṣṇa. Vyāsadeva and Lord Kṛṣṇa are both on the transcendental plane, and therefore they collaborated in doing good to the fallen souls of this age. The *Bhagavad-gītā* is the essence of all Vedic knowledge. It is the first book of spiritual values, as the *Upaniṣads* are. The Vedānta philosophy is the subject matter for study by the spiritual graduates. Only the post-graduate spiritual student can enter into the spiritual or devotional service of the Lord. It is a great science, and the great professor is the Lord Himself in the form of Lord Śrī Caitanya Mahāprabhu. And persons who are empowered by Him can initiate others in the transcendental loving service of the Lord.

TEXT 26

एवं प्रवृत्तस्य सदा भूतानां श्रेयसि द्विजाः ।
सर्वात्मकेनापि यदा नातुष्यद्धृदयं ततः ॥ २६ ॥

evaṁ pravṛttasya sadā bhūtānāṁ śreyasi dvijāḥ
sarvātmakenāpi yadā nātuṣyad dhṛdayaṁ tataḥ

evam—thus; *pravṛttasya*—one who is engaged in; *sadā*—always; *bhūtānām*—of the living beings; *śreyasi*—in the ultimate good; *dvijāḥ*—O twice-born; *sarvātmakena api*—by all means; *yadā*—when; *na*—not; *atuṣ-yat*—become satisfied; *hṛdayam*—mind; *tataḥ*—at that.

O twice-born brāhmaṇas, still his mind was not satisfied, although he engaged himself in working for the total welfare of all people.

PURPORT Śrī Vyāsadeva was not satisfied with himself, although he had prepared literatures of Vedic value for the all-around welfare of the general mass of people. It was expected that he would be satisfied by all such activities, but ultimately he was not satisfied.

TEXT 27

नातिप्रसीदद्धृदयः सरस्वत्यास्तटे शुचौ ।
वितर्कयन् विविक्तस्थ इदं चोवाच धर्मवित् ॥ २७ ॥

nātiprasīdad-dhṛdayaḥ sarasvatyās taṭe śucau
vitarkayan vivikta-stha idaṁ covāca dharma-vit

na—not; *atiprasīdat*—very much satisfied; *hṛdayaḥ*—at heart; *sarasvatyāḥ*—of the river Sarasvatī; *taṭe*—on the bank of; *śucau*—being purified; *vitarkayan*—having considered; *vivikta-sthaḥ*—situated in a lonely place; *idam ca*—also this; *uvāca*—said; *dharma-vit*—one who knows what religion is.

Thus the sage, being dissatisfied at heart, at once began to reflect, because he knew the essence of religion, and he said within himself:

PURPORT The sage began to search out the cause of not being satisfied at heart. Perfection is never attained until one is satisfied at heart. This satisfaction of heart has to be searched out beyond matter.

TEXTS 28–29

धृतव्रतेन हि मया छन्दांसि गुरवोऽग्नयः ।
मानिता निर्व्यलीकेन गृहीतं चानुशासनम् ॥ २८ ॥
भारतव्यपदेशेन ह्याम्नायार्थश्च दर्शितः ।
दृश्यते यत्र धर्मादि स्त्रीशूद्रादिभिरप्युत ॥ २९ ॥

dhṛta-vratena hi mayā chandāṁsi guravo 'gnayaḥ
mānitā nirvyalīkena gṛhītaṁ cānuśāsanam

bhārata-vyapadeśena hy āmnāyārthaś ca darśitaḥ
dṛśyate yatra dharmādi strī-śūdrādibhir apy uta

dhṛta-vratena—under a strict disciplinary vow; *hi*—certainly; *mayā*—by me; *chandāṁsi*—the Vedic hymns; *guravaḥ*—the spiritual masters; *ag-*

nayaḥ—the sacrificial fire; *mānitāḥ*—properly worshiped; *nirvyalīkena*—without pretense; *gṛhītam ca*—also accepted; *anuśāsanam*—traditional discipline; *bhārata*—the *Mahābhārata; vyapadeśena*—by compilation of; *hi*—certainly; *āmnāya-arthaḥ*—import of disciplic succession; *ca*—and; *darśitaḥ*—properly explained; *dṛśyate*—by what is necessary; *yatra*—where; *dharma-ādiḥ*—the path of religion; *strī-śūdra-ādibhiḥ api*—even by women, *śūdras*, etc.; *uta*—spoken.

I have, under strict disciplinary vows, unpretentiously worshiped the Vedas, the spiritual masters and the altar of sacrifice. I have also abided by the rulings and have shown the import of disciplic succession through the explanation of the Mahābhārata, by which even women, śūdras and others [friends of the twice-born] can see the path of religion.

PURPORT No one can understand the import of the *Vedas* without having undergone a strict disciplinary vow and disciplic succession. The *Vedas*, spiritual masters and sacrificial fire must be worshiped by the desiring candidate. All these intricacies of Vedic knowledge are systematically presented in the *Mahābhārata* for the understanding of the woman class, the laborer class and the unqualified members of *brāhmaṇa, kṣatriya* or *vaiśya* families. In this age, the *Mahābhārata* is more essential than the original *Vedas*.

TEXT 30

तथापि बत मे दैह्यो ह्यात्मा चैवात्मना विभुः ।
असम्पन्न इवाभाति ब्रह्मवर्चस्य सत्तमः ॥ ३० ॥

tathāpi bata me daihyo hy ātmā caivātmanā vibhuḥ
asampanna ivābhāti brahma-varcasya sattamaḥ

tathāpi—although; *bata*—defect; *me*—mine; *daihyaḥ*—situated in the body; *hi*—certainly; *ātmā*—living being; *ca*—and; *eva*—even; *ātmanā*—myself; *vibhuḥ*—sufficient; *asampannaḥ*—wanting in; *iva ābhāti*—it appears to be; *brahma-varcasya*—of the Vedāntists; *sattamaḥ*—the supreme.

I am feeling incomplete, though I myself am fully equipped with everything required by the Vedas.

PURPORT Undoubtedly Śrīla Vyāsadeva was complete in all the details of Vedic achievements. Purification of the living being submerged in matter is made possible by the prescribed activities in the *Vedas,* but the ultimate achievement is different. Unless it is attained, the living being, even though fully equipped, cannot be situated in the transcendentally normal stage. Śrīla Vyāsadeva appeared to have lost the clue and therefore felt dissatisfaction.

TEXT 31

किं वा भागवता धर्मा न प्रायेण निरूपिताः ।
प्रियाः परमहंसानां त एव ह्यच्युतप्रियाः ॥ ३१ ॥

kiṁ vā bhāgavatā dharmā na prāyeṇa nirūpitāḥ
priyāḥ paramahaṁsānāṁ ta eva hy acyuta-priyāḥ

kim vā—or; *bhāgavatāḥ dharmāḥ*—devotional activities of the living beings; *na*—not; *prāyeṇa*—almost; *nirūpitāḥ*—directed; *priyāḥ*—dear; *paramahaṁsānām*—of the perfect beings; *te eva*—that also; *hi*—certainly; *acyuta*—the infallible; *priyāḥ*—attractive.

This may be because I did not specifically point out the devotional service of the Lord, which is dear both to perfect beings and to the infallible Lord.

PURPORT The cause of the dissatisfaction which was being felt by Śrīla Vyāsadeva is expressed herein in his own words. This was felt for the normal condition of the living being in the devotional service of the Lord. Unless one is fixed in the normal condition of service, neither the Lord nor the living being can become fully satisfied. This defect was felt by him when Nārada Muni, his spiritual master, reached him. It is described as follows.

TEXT 32

तस्यैवं खिलमात्मानं मन्यमानस्य खिद्यतः ।
कृष्णस्य नारदोऽभ्यागादाश्रमं प्रागुदाहृतम् ॥ ३२ ॥

tasyaivaṁ khilam ātmānaṁ manyamānasya khidyataḥ
kṛṣṇasya nārado 'bhyāgād āśramaṁ prāg udāhṛtam

tasya—his; *evam*—thus; *khilam*—inferior; *ātmānam*—soul; *manya-mānasya*—thinking within the mind; *khidyataḥ*—regretting; *kṛṣṇasya*—of Kṛṣṇa-dvaipāyana Vyāsa; *nāradaḥ abhyāgāt*—Nārada came there; *āśramam*—the cottage; *prāk*—before; *udāhṛtam*—said.

As mentioned before, Nārada reached the cottage of Kṛṣṇa-dvaipāyana Vyāsa on the banks of the Sarasvatī just as Vyāsadeva was regretting his defects.

PURPORT The vacuum felt by Vyāsadeva was not due to his lack of knowledge. *Bhāgavata-dharma* is purely devotional service of the Lord to which the monist has no access. The monist is not counted amongst the *paramahaṁsas* (the most perfect of the renounced order of life). *Śrīmad-Bhāgavatam* is full of narrations of the transcendental activities of the Personality of Godhead. Although Vyāsadeva was an empowered divinity, he still felt dissatisfaction because in none of his works were the transcendental activities of the Lord properly explained. The inspiration was infused by Śrī Kṛṣṇa directly in the heart of Vyāsadeva, and thus he felt the vacuum as explained above. It is definitely expressed herewith that without the transcendental loving service of the Lord, everything is void; but in the transcendental service of the Lord, everything is tangible without any separate attempt at fruitive work or empiric philosophical speculation.

TEXT 33

तमभिज्ञाय सहसा प्रत्युत्थायागतं मुनिः ।
पूजयामास विधिवन्नारदं सुरपूजितम् ॥ ३३ ॥

tam abhijñāya sahasā pratyutthāyāgataṁ muniḥ
pūjayām āsa vidhivan nāradaṁ sura-pūjitam

tam abhijñāya—seeing the good fortune of his (Nārada's) arrival; *sahasā*—all of a sudden; *pratyutthāya*—getting up; *āgatam*—arrived at; *muniḥ*—Vyāsadeva; *pūjayām āsa*—worship; *vidhi-vat*—with the same respect as offered to Vidhi (Brahmā); *nāradam*—to Nārada; *sura-pūjitam*—worshiped by the demigods.

At the auspicious arrival of Śrī Nārada, Śrī Vyāsadeva got up respectfully and worshiped him, giving him veneration equal to that given to Brahmājī, the creator.

PURPORT *Vidhi* means Brahmā, the first created living being. He is the original student as well as professor of the *Vedas.* He learned it from Śrī Kṛṣṇa and taught Nārada first. So Nārada is the second *ācārya* in the line of spiritual disciplic succession. He is the representative of Brahmā, and therefore he is respected exactly like Brahmā, the father of all *vidhis* (regulations); similarly all other successive disciples in the chain are also equally respected as representatives of the original spiritual master.

Thus end the Bhaktivedanta purports of the First Canto, Fourth Chapter, of the Śrīmad-Bhāgavatam, *entitled "The Appearance of Śrī Nārada."*

CHAPTER FIVE

Nārada's Instructions on Śrīmad-Bhāgavatam for Vyāsadeva

सूत उवाच

TEXT 1

अथ तं सुखमासीन उपासीनं बृहच्छ्रवाः ।
देवर्षिः प्राह विप्रर्षिं वीणापाणिः स्मयन्निव ॥ १ ॥

sūta uvāca

atha taṁ sukham āsīna upāsīnaṁ bṛhac-chravāḥ
devarṣiḥ prāha viprarṣiṁ vīṇā-pāṇiḥ smayann iva

sūtaḥ—Sūta; *uvāca*—said; *atha*—therefore; *tam*—him; *sukham āsīnaḥ*—comfortably seated; *upāsīnam*—unto one sitting nearby; *bṛhat-śravāḥ*—greatly respected; *devarṣiḥ*—the great *ṛṣi* among the gods; *prāha*—said; *viprarṣim*—unto the *ṛṣi* among the *brāhmaṇas; vīṇā-pāṇiḥ*—one who carries a *vīṇā* in his hand; *smayan iva*—apparently smiling.

Sūta Gosvāmī said: Thus the sage amongst the gods [Nārada], comfortably seated and apparently smiling, addressed the ṛṣi amongst the brāhmaṇas [Vedavyāsa].

PURPORT Nārada was smiling because he well knew the great sage Vedavyāsa and the cause of his disappointment. As he will explain gradually, Vyāsadeva's disappointment was due to insufficiency in presenting the science of devotional service. Nārada knew the defect, and it was confirmed by the position of Vyāsa.

नारद उवाच

TEXT 2

पाराशर्य महाभाग भवतः कच्चिदात्मना ।
परितुष्यति शारीर आत्मा मानस एव वा ॥ २ ॥

nārada uvāca
pārāśarya mahā-bhāga bhavataḥ kaccid ātmanā
parituṣyati śārīra ātmā mānasa eva vā

nāradaḥ—Nārada; *uvāca*—said; *pārāśarya*—O son of Parāśara; *mahā-bhāga*—the greatly fortunate; *bhavataḥ*—your; *kaccit*—if it is; *ātmanā*—by the self-realization of; *parituṣyati*—does it satisfy; *śārīraḥ*—identifying the body; *ātmā*—self; *mānasaḥ*—identifying the mind; *eva*—certainly; *vā*—and.

Addressing Vyāsadeva, the son of Parāśara, Nārada inquired: Are you satisfied by identifying with the body or the mind as objects of self-realization?

PURPORT This was a hint by Nārada to Vyāsadeva regarding the cause of his despondency. Vyāsadeva, as the descendant of Parāśara, a greatly powerful sage, had the privilege of having a great parentage which should not have given Vyāsadeva cause for despondency. Being a great son of a great father, he should not have identified the self with the body or the mind. Ordinary men with a poor fund of knowledge can identify the body as self or the mind as self, but Vyāsadeva should not have done so. One cannot be cheerful by nature unless one is factually seated in self-realization, which is transcendental to the material body and mind.

TEXT 3

जिज्ञासितं सुसम्पन्नमपि ते महदद्भुतम् ।
कृतवान् भारतं यस्त्वं सर्वार्थपरिबृंहितम् ॥ ३ ॥

jijñāsitaṁ susampannam api te mahad-adbhutam
kṛtavān bhārataṁ yas tvaṁ sarvārtha-paribṛṁhitam

jijñāsitam—fully inquired; *susampannam*—well versed; *api*—in spite of; *te*—your; *mahat-adbhutam*—great and wonderful; *kṛtavān*—prepared; *bhāratam*—the *Mahābhārata; yaḥ tvam*—what you have done; *sarva-artha*—including all sequences; *paribṛṁhitam*—elaborately explained.

No doubt your inquiries were full and your studies also well fulfilled,

since you have prepared a great and wonderful work, the Mahābhārata, which is full of all kinds of Vedic sequences elaborately explained.

PURPORT The despondency of Vyāsadeva was certainly not due to his lack of sufficient knowledge because as a student he had fully inquired about the Vedic literatures, as a result of which the *Mahābhārata* is compiled with full explanation of the *Vedas*.

TEXT 4

जिज्ञासितमधीतं च ब्रह्म यत्तत्सनातनम् ।
तथापि शोचस्यात्मानमकृतार्थ इव प्रभो ॥ ४ ॥

jijñāsitam adhītaṁ ca brahma yat tat sanātanam
tathāpi śocasy ātmānam akṛtārtha iva prabho

jijñāsitam—deliberated fully well; *adhītam*—the knowledge obtained; *ca*—and; *brahma*—the Absolute; *yat*—what; *tat*—that; *sanātanam*—eternal; *tathāpi*—in spite of that; *śocasi*—lamenting; *ātmānam*—unto the self; *akṛta-arthaḥ*—undone; *iva*—like; *prabho*—my dear sir.

You have fully delineated the subject of impersonal Brahman as well as the knowledge derived therefrom. Why should you be despondent in spite of all this, thinking that you are undone, my dear prabhu?

PURPORT The *Vedānta-sūtra*, or *Brahma-sūtra*, compiled by Śrī Vyāsadeva is the full deliberation of the impersonal absolute feature, and it is accepted as the most exalted philosophical exposition in the world. It covers the subject of eternity, and the methods are scholarly. So there cannot be any doubt about the transcendental scholarship of Vyāsadeva. So why should he lament?

व्यास उवाच

TEXT 5

अस्त्येव मे सर्वमिदं त्वयोक्तं
तथापि नात्मा परितुष्यते मे ।
तन्मूलमव्यक्तमगाधबोधं
पृच्छामहे त्वात्मभवात्मभूतम् ॥ ५ ॥

vyāsa uvāca
asty eva me sarvam idaṁ tvayoktaṁ
tathāpi nātmā paritusyate me
tan-mūlam avyaktam agādha-bodhaṁ
pṛcchāmahe tvātma-bhavātma-bhūtam

vyāsaḥ—Vyāsa; *uvāca*—said; *asti*—there is; *eva*—certainly; *me*—mine; *sarvam*—all; *idam*—this; *tvayā*—by you; *uktam*—uttered; *tathāpi*—and yet; *na*—not; *ātmā*—self; *paritusyate*—does pacify; *me*—unto me; *tat*—of which; *mūlam*—root; *avyaktam*—undetected; *agādha-bodham*—the man of unlimited knowledge; *pṛcchāmahe*—do inquire; *tvā*—unto you; *ātma-bhava*—self-born; *ātma-bhūtam*—offspring.

Śrī Vyāsadeva said: All you have said about me is perfectly correct. Despite all this, I am not pacified. I therefore question you about the root cause of my dissatisfaction, for you are a man of unlimited knowledge due to your being the offspring of one [Brahmā] who is self-born [without mundane father and mother].

PURPORT In the material world everyone is engrossed with the idea of identifying the body or the mind with the self. As such, all knowledge disseminated in the material world is related either with the body or with the mind, and that is the root cause of all despondencies. This is not always detected, even though one may be the greatest erudite scholar in materialistic knowledge. It is good, therefore, to approach a personality like Nārada to solve the root cause of all despondencies. Why Nārada should be approached is explained below.

TEXT 6

स वै भवान् वेद समस्तगुह्यम्
उपासितो यत्पुरुषः पुराणः ।
परावरेशो मनसैव विश्वं
सृजत्यवत्यत्ति गुणैरसङ्गः ॥ ६ ॥

sa vai bhavān veda samasta-guhyam
upāsito yat puruṣaḥ purāṇaḥ

parāvareśo manasaiva viśvaṁ
sṛjaty avaty atti guṇair asaṅgaḥ

saḥ—thus; *vai*—certainly; *bhavān*—yourself; *veda*—know; *samasta*—all-inclusive; *guhyam*—confidential; *upāsitaḥ*—devotee of; *yat*—because; *puruṣaḥ*—the Personality of Godhead; *purāṇaḥ*—the oldest; *parāvareśaḥ*—the controller of the material and spiritual worlds; *manasā*—mind; *eva*—only; *viśvam*—the universe; *sṛjati*—creates; *avati atti*—annihilates; *guṇaiḥ*—by the qualitative matter; *asaṅgaḥ*—unattached.

My lord! Everything that is mysterious is known to you because you worship the creator and destroyer of the material world and the maintainer of the spiritual world, the original Personality of Godhead, who is transcendental to the three modes of material nature.

PURPORT A person who is cent-percent engaged in the service of the Lord is the emblem of all knowledge. Such a devotee of the Lord in full perfection of devotional service is also perfect by the qualification of the Personality of Godhead. As such, the eightfold perfections of mystic power (*aṣṭa-siddhi*) constitute very little of his godly opulence. A devotee like Nārada can act wonderfully by his spiritual perfection, which every individual is trying to attain. Śrīla Nārada is a cent-percent perfect living being, although not equal to the Personality of Godhead.

TEXT 7

त्वं पर्यटन्नर्क इव त्रिलोकीम्
अन्तश्चरो वायुरिवात्मसाक्षी ।
परावरे ब्रह्मणि धर्मतो व्रतैः
स्नातस्य मे न्यूनमलं विचक्ष्व ॥ ७ ॥

tvaṁ paryaṭann arka iva tri-lokīm
antaś-caro vāyur ivātma-sākṣī
parāvare brahmaṇi dharmato vrataiḥ
snātasya me nyūnam alaṁ vicakṣva

tvam—Your Goodness; *paryaṭan*—traveling; *arkaḥ*—the sun; *iva*—like; *tri-lokīm*—the three worlds; *antaḥ-carah*—can penetrate into everyone's heart; *vāyuḥ iva*—as good as the all-pervading air; *ātma*—self-realized; *sākṣī*—witness; *parāvare*—in the matter of cause and effect; *brahmaṇi*—in the Absolute; *dharmataḥ*—under disciplinary regulations; *vrataiḥ*—in vow; *snātasya*—having been absorbed in; *me*—mine; *nyūnam*—deficiency; *alam*—clearly; *vicakṣva*—search out.

Like the sun, Your Goodness can travel everywhere in the three worlds, and like the air you can penetrate the internal region of everyone. As such, you are as good as the all-pervasive Supersoul. Please, therefore, find out the deficiency in me, despite my being absorbed in transcendence under disciplinary regulations and vows.

PURPORT Transcendental realization, pious activities, worshiping the Deities, charity, mercifulness, nonviolence and studying the scriptures under strict disciplinary regulations are always helpful.

श्रीनारद उवाच

TEXT 8

भवतानुदितप्रायं यशो भगवतोऽमलम् ।
येनैवासौ न तुष्येत मन्ये तद्दर्शनं खिलम् ॥ ८ ॥

śrī-nārada uvāca
bhavatānudita-prāyaṁ yaśo bhagavato 'malam
yenaivāsau na tuṣyeta manye tad darśanaṁ khilam

śrī-nāradaḥ—Śrī Nārada; *uvāca*—said; *bhavatā*—by you; *anudita-prāyam*—almost not praised; *yaśaḥ*—glories; *bhagavataḥ*—of the Personality of Godhead; *amalam*—spotless; *yena*—by which; *eva*—certainly; *asau*—He (the Personality of Godhead); *na*—does not; *tuṣyeta*—be pleased; *manye*—I think; *tat*—that; *darśanam*—philosophy; *khilam*—inferior.

Śrī Nārada said: You have not actually broadcast the sublime and spotless glories of the Personality of Godhead. That philosophy which does not satisfy the transcendental senses of the Lord is considered worthless.

PURPORT The eternal relation of an individual soul with the Supreme Soul Personality of Godhead is constitutionally one of being the eternal servitor of the eternal master. The Lord has expanded Himself as living beings in order to accept loving service from them, and this alone can satisfy both the Lord and the living beings. Such a scholar as Vyāsadeva has completed many expansions of the Vedic literatures, ending with the Vedānta philosophy, but none of them have been written directly glorifying the Personality of Godhead. Dry philosophical speculations even on the transcendental subject of the Absolute have very little attraction without directly dealing with the glorification of the Lord. The Personality of Godhead is the last word in transcendental realization. The Absolute realized as impersonal Brahman or localized Supersoul, Paramātmā, is less productive of transcendental bliss than the supreme personal realization of His glories.

The compiler of the *Vedānta-darśana* is Vyāsadeva himself. Yet he is troubled, although he is the author. So what sort of transcendental bliss can be derived by the readers and listeners of Vedānta which is not explained directly by Vyāsadeva, the author? Herein arises the necessity of explaining *Vedānta-sūtra* in the form of *Śrīmad-Bhāgavatam* by the self-same author.

TEXT 9

यथा धर्मादयश्चार्था मुनिवर्यानुकीर्तिताः ।
न तथा वासुदेवस्य महिमा ह्यनुवर्णितः ॥ ९ ॥

yathā dharmādayaś cārthā muni-varyānukīrtitāḥ
na tathā vāsudevasya mahimā hy anuvarṇitaḥ

yathā—as much as; *dharma-ādayaḥ*—all four principles of religious behavior; *ca*—and; *arthāḥ*—purposes; *muni-varya*—by yourself, the great sage; *anukīrtitāḥ*—repeatedly described; *na*—not; *tathā*—in that way; *vāsudevasya*—of the Personality of Godhead Śrī Kṛṣṇa; *mahimā*—glories; *hi*—certainly; *anuvarṇitaḥ*—so constantly described.

Although, great sage, you have very broadly described the four principles beginning with religious performances, you have not described to such an extent the glories of the Supreme Personality, Vāsudeva.

PURPORT The prompt diagnosis of Śrī Nārada is at once declared. The root cause of the despondency of Vyāsadeva was his deliberate avoidance of glorifying the Lord in his various editions of the *Purāṇas.* He has certainly, as a matter of course, given descriptions of the glories of the Lord (Śrī Kṛṣṇa) but not as many as given to religiosity, economic development, sense gratification and salvation. These four items are by far inferior to engagement in the devotional service of the Lord. Śrī Vyāsadeva, as the authorized scholar, knew very well this difference. And still instead of giving more importance to the better type of engagement, namely, devotional service to the Lord, he had more or less improperly used his valuable time, and thus he was despondent. From this it is clearly indicated that no one can be pleased substantially without being engaged in the devotional service of the Lord. In the *Bhagavad-gītā* this fact is clearly mentioned.

After liberation, which is the last item in the line of performing religiosity, etc., one is engaged in pure devotional service. This is called the stage of self-realization, or the *brahma-bhūta* stage. After attainment of this *brahma-bhūta* stage, one is satisfied. But satisfaction is the beginning of transcendental bliss. One should progress by attaining neutrality and equality in the relative world. And passing this stage of equanimity, one is fixed in the transcendental loving service of the Lord. This is the instruction of the Personality of Godhead in the *Bhagavad-gītā*. The conclusion is that in order to maintain the status quo of the *brahma-bhūta* stage, as also to increase the degree of transcendental realization, Nārada recommended to Vyāsadeva that he (Vyāsadeva) should now eagerly and repeatedly describe the path of devotional service. This would cure him from gross despondency.

TEXT 10

न यद्वचश्चित्रपदं हरेर्यशो
जगत्पवित्रं प्रगृणीत कर्हिचित् ।
तद्वायसं तीर्थमुशन्ति मानसा
न यत्र हंसा निरमन्त्युशिक्क्षयाः ॥ १० ॥

na yad vacaś citra-padaṁ harer yaśo
jagat-pavitraṁ pragṛṇīta karhicit
tad vāyasaṁ tīrtham uśanti mānasā
na yatra haṁsā niramanty uśik-kṣayāḥ

na—not; *yat*—that; *vacaḥ*—vocabulary; *citra-padam*—decorative; *hareḥ*—of the Lord; *yaśaḥ*—glories; *jagat*—universe; *pavitram*—sanctified; *pragṛṇīta*—described; *karhicit*—hardly; *tat*—that; *vāyasam*—crows; *tīrtham*—place of pilgrimage; *uśanti*—think; *mānasāḥ*—saintly persons; *na*—not; *yatra*—where; *haṁsāḥ*—all-perfect beings; *niramanti*—take pleasure; *uśik-kṣayāḥ*—those who reside in the transcendental abode.

Those words which do not describe the glories of the Lord, who alone can sanctify the atmosphere of the whole universe, are considered by saintly persons to be like unto a place of pilgrimage for crows. Since the all-perfect persons are inhabitants of the transcendental abode, they do not derive any pleasure there.

PURPORT Crows and swans are not birds of the same feather, because of their different mental attitudes. The fruitive workers or passionate men are compared to the crows, whereas the all-perfect saintly persons are compared to the swans. The crows take pleasure in a place where garbage is thrown out, just as the passionate fruitive workers take pleasure in wine and woman and places for gross sense pleasure. The swans do not take pleasure in the places where crows are assembled for conferences and meetings. They are instead seen in the atmosphere of natural scenic beauty where there are transparent reservoirs of water nicely decorated with stems of lotus flowers in variegated colors of natural beauty. That is the difference between the two classes of birds.

Nature has influenced different species of life with different mentalities, and it is not possible to bring them up into the same rank and file.

Similarly, there are different kinds of literature for different types of men of different mentality. Mostly the market literatures which attract men of the crow's categories are literatures containing refused remnants of sensuous topics. They are generally known as mundane talks in relation with the gross body and subtle mind. They are full of subject matter described in decorative language full of mundane similes and metaphorical arrangements. Yet with all that, they do not glorify the Lord. Such poetry and prose, on any subject matter, is considered decoration of a dead body. Spiritually advanced men who are compared to the swans do not take pleasure in such dead literatures, which are sources of pleasure for men who are spiritually dead. These literatures in the modes of passion and ignorance are distributed under different labels, but they can hardly help the spiritual urge of the human being, and thus the swanlike spiritually advanced men have nothing to do with them. Such spiritually advanced men are also called *mānasa* because they always keep up the standard of transcendental voluntary service to the Lord on the spiritual plane. This completely forbids fruitive activities for gross bodily sense satisfaction or subtle speculation of the material egoistic mind.

Social literary men, scientists, mundane poets, theoretical philosophers and politicians who are completely absorbed in the material advancement of sense pleasure are all dolls of the material energy. They take pleasure in a place where rejected subject matters are thrown. According to Svāmī Śrīdhara, this is the pleasure of the prostitute-hunters.

But literatures which describe the glories of the Lord are enjoyed by the *paramahaṁsas* who have grasped the essence of human activities.

TEXT 11

तद्वाग्विसर्गो जनताघविप्लवो
यस्मिन् प्रतिश्लोकमबद्धवत्यपि ।
नामान्यनन्तस्य यशोऽङ्कितानि यत्
शृण्वन्ति गायन्ति गृणन्ति साधवः ॥ ११ ॥

tad-vāg-visargo janatāgha-viplavo
yasmin prati-ślokam abaddhavaty api
nāmāny anantasya yaśo 'ṅkitāni yat
śṛṇvanti gāyanti gṛṇanti sādhavaḥ

tat—that; *vāk*—vocabulary; *visargaḥ*—creation; *janatā*—the people in general; *agha*—sins; *viplavaḥ*—revolutionary; *yasmin*—in which; *prati-ślokam*—each and every stanza; *abaddhavati*—irregularly composed; *api*—in spite of; *nāmāni*—transcendental names, etc.; *anantasya*—of the unlimited Lord; *yaśaḥ*—glories; *aṅkitāni*—depicted; *yat*—what; *śṛṇvanti*—do hear; *gāyanti*—do sing; *gṛṇanti*—do accept; *sādhavaḥ*—the purified men who are honest.

On the other hand, that literature which is full of descriptions of the transcendental glories of the name, fame, forms, pastimes, etc., of the

unlimited Supreme Lord is a different creation, full of transcendental words directed toward bringing about a revolution in the impious lives of this world's misdirected civilization. Such transcendental literatures, even though imperfectly composed, are heard, sung and accepted by purified men who are thoroughly honest.

PURPORT It is a qualification of the great thinkers to pick up the best even from the worst. It is said that the intelligent man should pick up nectar from a stock of poison, should accept gold even from a filthy place, should accept a good and qualified wife even from an obscure family and should accept a good lesson even from a man or from a teacher who comes from the untouchables. These are some of the ethical instructions for everyone in every place without exception. But a saint is far above the level of an ordinary man. He is always absorbed in glorifying the Supreme Lord because by broadcasting the holy name and fame of the Supreme Lord, the polluted atmosphere of the world will change, and as a result of propagating the transcendental literatures like *Śrīmad-Bhāgavatam,* people will become sane in their transactions. While preparing this commentation on this particular stanza of *Śrīmad-Bhāgavatam* we have a crisis before us. Our neighboring friend China has attacked the border of India with a militaristic spirit. We have practically no business in the political field, yet we see that previously there were both China and India, and they both lived peacefully for centuries without ill feeling. The reason is that they lived those days in an atmosphere of God consciousness, and every country, over the surface of the world, was God-fearing, pure-hearted and simple, and there was no question of political diplomacy. There is no cause of quarrel between the two countries China and India over land which is not very suitable for habitation, and certainly there is no cause for fighting on this issue. But due to the age of quarrel, Kali, which we have discussed, there is always a chance of quarrel on slight provocation. This is due not to the issue in question but to the polluted atmosphere of this age: systematically there is propaganda by a section of people *to stop glorification of the name and fame of the Supreme Lord.* Therefore, there is a great need for disseminating the message of *Śrīmad-Bhāgavatam* all over the world. It is the duty of every responsible Indian to broadcast the transcendental message of *Śrīmad-Bhāgavatam* throughout the world to do all the supermost good as well as to bring about the desired peace in the world. Because India has failed in her duty by neglecting this responsible work, there is so much quarrel and trouble all over the world. We are confident that if the transcendental message of *Śrīmad-Bhāgavatam* is received only by the leading men of the world, certainly there will be a change of heart, and naturally the people in general will follow them. The mass of people in general are tools in the hands of the modern politicians and leaders of the people. If there is a change of heart of the leaders only, certainly there will be a radical change in the atmosphere of the world. We know that our honest attempt to present this great literature conveying transcendental messages for reviving the God consciousness of the people in general and respiritualizing the world atmosphere is fraught with many difficulties. Our presenting this matter in adequate language, especially a foreign language, will certainly fail, and there will be so many literary discrepancies despite our honest attempt to present it in the proper way. But we are sure that with all our faults in this connection the seriousness of the subject matter will be taken into consideration, and the leaders of society will still accept this due to its being an honest attempt to glorify the Almighty God. When there is fire in a house, the inmates of the house go out to get help from the neighbors who may be foreigners, and yet without knowing the language the victims of the fire express themselves, and the neighbors understand the need, even though not expressed in the same language. The same spirit of cooperation is needed to broadcast this transcendental message of the *Śrīmad-Bhāgavatam* throughout the polluted atmosphere of the world. After all, it is a technical science of spiritual values, and thus we are concerned with the techniques and not with the language. If the techniques of this great literature are understood by the people of the world, there will be success.

When there are too many materialistic activities by the people in general all over the world, there is no wonder that a person or a nation attacks another person or nation on slight provocation. That is the rule of this age of Kali or quarrel. The atmosphere is already polluted with corruption of all description, and everyone knows it well. There are so many unwanted literatures full of materialistic ideas of sense gratification. In many countries there are bodies appointed by the state to detect and censor obscene literature. This means that neither the government nor the responsible leaders of the public want such literature, yet it is in the marketplace because the people want it for sense gratification. The people in general want to read (that is a natural instinct), but because their minds are polluted they want such literatures. Under the circumstances, transcendental literature like *Śrīmad-Bhāgavatam* will not only diminish the activities of the corrupt mind of the people in general, but also it will supply food for their hankering after reading some interesting literature. In the beginning they may not like it because one suffering from jaundice is reluctant to take sugar candy, but we should know that sugar candy is the only remedy for jaundice. Similarly, let there be systematic propaganda for popularizing reading of the *Bhagavad-gītā* and the *Śrīmad-Bhāgavatam,* which will act like sugar candy for the jaundicelike condition of sense gratification. When men have a taste for this literature, the other literatures, which are catering poison to society, will then automatically cease.

We are sure, therefore, that everyone in human society will welcome *Śrīmad-Bhāgavatam,* even though it is now presented with so many faults, for it is recommended by such an authority as Śrī Nārada, who has very kindly appeared in this chapter.

TEXT 12

नैष्कर्म्यमप्यच्युतभाववर्जितं
न शोभते ज्ञानमलं निरञ्जनम् ।
कुतः पुनः शश्वदभद्रमीश्वरे
न चार्पितं कर्म यदप्यकारणम् ॥ १२ ॥

naiṣkarmyam apy acyuta-bhāva-varjitaṁ
na śobhate jñānam alaṁ nirañjanam
kutaḥ punaḥ śaśvad abhadram īśvare
na cārpitaṁ karma yad apy akāraṇam

naiṣkarmyam—self-realization, being freed from the reactions of fruitive work; *api*—in spite of; *acyuta*—the infallible Lord; *bhāva*—conception; *varjitam*—devoid of; *na*—does not; *śobhate*—look well; *jñānam*—transcendental knowledge; *alam*—by and by; *nirañjanam*—free from designations; *kutaḥ*—where is; *punaḥ*—again; *śaśvat*—always; *abhadram*—uncongenial; *īśvare*—unto the Lord; *na*—not; *ca*—and; *arpitam*—offered; *karma*—fruitive work; *yat api*—what is; *akāraṇam*—not fruitive.

Knowledge of self-realization, even though free from all material affinity, does not look well if devoid of a conception of the Infallible [God]. What, then, is the use of fruitive activities, which are naturally painful from the very beginning and transient by nature, if they are not utilized for the devotional service of the Lord?

PURPORT As referred to above, not only ordinary literatures devoid of the transcendental glorification of the Lord are condemned, but also Vedic literatures and speculation on the subject of impersonal Brahman when they are devoid of devotional service. When speculation on the impersonal Brahman is condemned on the above ground, then what to speak of ordinary fruitive work which is not meant to fulfill the aim of devotional service. Such speculative knowledge and fruitive work cannot lead one to the goal of perfection. Fruitive work, in which almost all people in general are engaged, is always painful either in the beginning or at the end. It can be fruitful only when made subservient to the devotional service of the Lord. In the *Bhagavad-gītā* also it is confirmed that the result of such fruitive work may be offered for the service of the Lord, otherwise it leads to material bondage. The bona fide enjoyer of the fruitive work is the Personality of Godhead, and thus when the results of such work are engaged for the sense gratification of the living beings, those results become acute sources of trouble for such false enjoyers.

TEXT 13

अथो महाभाग भवानमोघदृक्
शुचिश्रवाः सत्यरतो धृतव्रतः ।
उरुक्रमस्याखिलबन्धमुक्तये
समाधिनानुस्मर तद्विचेष्टितम् ॥ १३ ॥

atho mahā-bhāga bhavān amogha-dṛk
śuci-śravāḥ satya-rato dhṛta-vrataḥ
urukramasyākhila-bandha-muktaye
samādhinānusmara tad-viceṣṭitam

atho—therefore; *mahā-bhāga*—highly fortunate; *bhavān*—yourself; *amogha-dṛk*—the perfect seer; *śuci*—spotless; *śravāḥ*—famous; *satya-rataḥ*—having taken the vow of truthfulness; *dhṛta-vrataḥ*—fixed in spiritual qualities; *urukramasya*—of the one who performs supernatural activities (God); *akhila*—universal; *bandha*—bondage; *muktaye*—for liberation from; *samādhinā*—by trance; *anusmara*—think repeatedly and then describe them; *tat-viceṣṭitam*—various pastimes of the Lord.

O Vyāsadeva, your vision is completely perfect. Your good fame is spotless. You are firm in vow and situated in truthfulness. And thus you can think of the pastimes of the Lord in trance for the liberation of the people in general from all material bondage.

PURPORT People in general have a taste for literatures by instinct. They want to hear and read from the authorities something about the unknown, but their taste is exploited by unfortunate literatures which are full of subject matter for satisfaction of the material senses. Such literatures contain different kinds of mundane poems and philosophical speculations, more or less under the influence of *māyā,* ending in sense gratification. These literatures, although worthless in the true sense of the term, are variously decorated to attract the attention of the less intelligent men. Thus the attracted living entities are more and more entangled in material bondage without hope of liberation for thousands and thousands of generations. Śrī Nārada Ṛṣi, being the best amongst the Vaiṣṇavas, is compassionate toward such unfortunate victims of worthless literatures, and thus he advises Śrī Vyāsadeva to compose transcendental literature which is not only attractive but which can also actually bring liberation from all kinds of bondage. Śrīla Vyāsadeva or his representatives are qualified because they are rightly trained to see things in true perspective. Śrīla Vyāsadeva and his representatives are pure in thought due to their spiritual enlightenment, fixed in their vows due to their devotional service, and determined to deliver the fallen souls rotting in material activities. The fallen souls are very eager to receive novel informations every day, and the transcendentalists like Vyāsadeva or Nārada can supply such eager people in general with unlimited news from the spiritual world. In the *Bhagavad-gītā* it is said that the material world is only a part of the whole creation and that this earth is only a fragment of the whole material world.

There are thousands and thousands of literary men all over the world, and they have created many, many thousands of literary works for the information of the people in general for thousands and thousands of years. Unfortunately none of them have brought peace and tranquillity on the earth. This is due to a spiritual vacuum in those literatures; therefore the Vedic literatures, especially the *Bhagavad-gītā* and the *Śrīmad-Bhāgavatam,* are specifically recommended to suffering humanity to bring about the desired effect of liberation from the pangs of material civilization, which is eating the vital part of human energy. The *Bhagavad-gītā* is the spoken message of the Lord Himself recorded by Vyāsadeva, and the *Śrīmad-Bhāgavatam* is the transcendental narration of the activities of the same Lord Kṛṣṇa, which alone can satisfy the hankering desires of the living being for eternal peace and liberation from miseries. *Śrīmad-Bhāgavatam,* therefore, is meant for all the living beings all over the universe for total liberation from all kinds of material bondage. Such transcendental narrations of the pastimes of the Lord can be described only by liberated souls like Vyāsadeva and his bona fide representatives who are completely merged in the transcendental loving service of the Lord. Only to such devotees do the pastimes of the Lord and their transcendental nature become automatically manifest by dint of devotional service. No one else can either know or describe the acts of the Lord, even if they speculate on the subject for many, many years. The descriptions of the *Bhāgavatam* are so precise and accurate that whatever has been predicted in this great literature about five thousand years ago is now exactly happening. Therefore, the vision of the author comprehends past, present and future. Such liberated persons as Vyāsadeva are perfect not only by the power of vision and wisdom, but also in aural reception, in thinking, feeling and all other sense activities. A liberated person possesses perfect senses, and with perfect senses only can one serve the sense proprietor, Hṛṣīkeśa, Śrī Kṛṣṇa the Personality of Godhead. *Śrīmad-Bhāgavatam,* therefore, is the perfect description of the all-perfect Personality of Godhead by the all-perfect personality Śrīla Vyāsadeva, the compiler of the *Vedas.*

TEXT 14

ततोऽन्यथा किञ्चन यद्विवक्षतः
पृथग्दृशस्तत्कृतरूपनामभिः ।
न कर्हिचित्क्वापि च दुःस्थिता मतिर्
लभेत वाताहतनौरिवास्पदम् ॥ १४ ॥

tato 'nyathā kiñcana yad vivakṣataḥ
pṛthag dṛśas tat-kṛta-rūpa-nāmabhiḥ
na karhicit kvāpi ca duḥsthitā matir
labheta vātāhata-naur ivāspadam

tataḥ—from that; *anyathā*—apart; *kiñcana*—something; *yat*—whatsoever; *vivakṣataḥ*—desiring to describe; *pṛthak*—separately; *dṛśaḥ*—vision; *tat-kṛta*—reactionary to that; *rūpa*—form; *nāmabhiḥ*—by names; *na karhicit*—never; *kvāpi*—any; *ca*—and; *duḥsthitā matiḥ*—oscillating mind; *labheta*—gains; *vāta-āhata*—troubled by the wind; *nauḥ*—boat; *iva*—like; *āspadam*—place.

Whatever you desire to describe that is separate in vision from the Lord simply reacts with different forms and names to agitate the mind, as the wind agitates a boat which has no resting place.

PURPORT Śrī Vyāsadeva is the editor of all descriptions of the Vedic literatures, and thus he has described transcendental realization in different ways, namely by fruitive activities, speculative knowledge, mystic power and devotional service. Besides that, in his various *Purāṇas* he has recommended the worship of so many demigods in different forms and names. The result is that people in general are puzzled how to fix their minds in the service of the Lord; they are always disturbed about finding the real path of self-realization. Śrīla Nāradadeva is stressing this particular defect in the Vedic literatures compiled by Vyāsadeva, and thus he is trying to emphasize describing everything in relation with the Supreme Lord, and no one else. In fact, there is nothing existent except the Lord. The Lord is manifested in different expansions. He is the root of the complete tree. He is the stomach of the complete body. Pouring water on the root is the right process to water the tree, as much as feeding the stomach supplies energy to all parts of the body. Therefore, Śrīla Vyāsadeva should not have compiled any *Purāṇas* other than the *Bhāgavata Purāṇa* because a slight deviation from that may create havoc for self-realization. If a slight deviation can create such havoc, then what to speak of deliberate expansion of the ideas separate from the Absolute Truth Personality of Godhead. The most defective part of worshiping demigods is that it creates a definite conception of pantheism, ending disastrously in many religious sects detrimental to the progress of the principles of the *Bhāgavatam,* which alone can give the accurate direction for self-realization in eternal relation with the Personality of Godhead by devotional service in transcendental love. The example of the boat disturbed by whirling wind is suitable in this respect. The diverted mind of the pantheist can never reach the perfection of self-realization, due to the disturbed condition of the selection of object.

TEXT 15

जुगुप्सितं धर्मकृतेऽनुशासतः
स्वभावरक्तस्य महान् व्यतिक्रमः ।
यद्वाक्यतो धर्म इतीतरः स्थितो
न मन्यते तस्य निवारणं जनः ॥ १५ ॥

jugupsitaṁ dharma-kṛte 'nuśāsataḥ
svabhāva-raktasya mahān vyatikramaḥ
yad-vākyato dharma itītaraḥ sthito
na manyate tasya nivāraṇaṁ janaḥ

jugupsitam—verily condemned; *dharma-kṛte*—for the matter of religion; *anuśāsataḥ*—instruction; *svabhāva-raktasya*—naturally inclined; *mahān*—great; *vyatikramaḥ*—unreasonable; *yat-vākyataḥ*—under whose instruction; *dharmaḥ*—religion; *iti*—it is thus; *itaraḥ*—the people in general; *sthitaḥ*—fixed; *na*—do not; *manyate*—think; *tasya*—of that; *nivāraṇam*—prohibition; *janaḥ*—they.

The people in general are naturally inclined to enjoy, and you have encouraged them in that way in the name of religion. This is verily condemned and is quite unreasonable. Because they are guided under your instructions, they will accept such activities in the name of religion and will hardly care for prohibitions.

PURPORT Śrīla Vyāsadeva's compilation of different Vedic literatures on the basis of regulated performances of fruitive activities as depicted in the *Mahābhārata* and other literature is condemned herewith by Śrīla Nārada. The human beings, by long material association, life after life, have a natural inclination, by practice, to endeavor to lord it over material energy. They have no sense of the responsibility of human life. This human form of life is a chance to get out of the clutches of illusory matter. The *Vedas* are meant for going back to Godhead, going back home. To revolve in the cycle of transmigration in a series of lives numbering 8,400,000 is an imprisoned life for the condemned conditioned souls. The human form of life is a chance to get out of this imprisoned life, and as such the only occupation of the human being is to reestablish his lost relationship with God. Under the circumstances, one should never be encouraged in making a plan for sense enjoyment in the name of religious functions. Such diversion of the human energy results in a misguided civilization. Śrīla Vyāsadeva is the authority in Vedic explanations in the *Mahābhārata,* etc., and his encouragement in sense enjoyment in some form or other is a great barrier for spiritual advancement because the people in general will not agree to renounce material activities which hold them in material bondage. At a certain stage of human civilization when such material activities in the name of religion (as sacrificing animals in the name of *yajña*) were too much rampant, the Lord incarnated Himself as Buddha and decried the authority of the *Vedas* in order to stop animal sacrifice in the name of religion. This was foreseen by Nārada, and therefore he condemned such literatures. The flesh-eaters still continue to perform animal sacrifice before some demigod or goddess in the name of religion because in some of the Vedic literatures such regulated sacrifices are recommended. They are so recommended to discourage flesh-eating, but gradually the purpose of such religious activities is forgotten, and the slaughterhouse becomes prominent. This is because foolish materialistic men do not care to listen to others who are actually in a position to explain the Vedic rites.

In the *Vedas* it is distinctly said that the perfection of life is never to be attained either by voluminous work, or by accumulation of wealth or even by increasing the population. But it is so attained only by renunciation. The materialistic men do not care to listen to such injunctions. According to them, the so-called renounced order of life is meant for those who are unable to earn their livelihood because of some corporeal defects, or for persons who have failed to achieve prosperity in family life.

In histories like the *Mahābhārata,* of course, there are topics on transcendental subjects along with material topics. The *Bhagavad-gītā* is there in the *Mahābhārata.* The whole idea of the *Mahābhārata* culminates in the ultimate instructions of the *Bhagavad-gītā,* that one should relinquish all other engagements and should engage oneself solely and fully in surrendering unto the lotus feet of Lord Śrī Kṛṣṇa. But men with materialistic tendencies are more attracted to the politics, economics and philanthropic activities mentioned in the *Mahābhārata* than to the principal topic, namely the *Bhagavad-gītā*. This compromising spirit of Vyāsadeva is directly condemned by Nārada, who advises him to directly proclaim that the prime necessity of human life is to realize one's eternal relation with the Lord and thus surrender unto Him without delay.

A patient suffering from a particular type of malady is almost always inclined to accept eatables which are forbidden for him. The expert physician does not make any compromise with the patient by allowing him to take partially what he should not at all take. In the *Bhagavad-gītā* it is also said that a man attached to fruitive work should not be discouraged from his occupation, for gradually he may be elevated to the position of self-realization. This is sometimes applicable for those who are only dry empiric philosophers without spiritual realization. But those who are in the devotional line should never be so advised.

TEXT 16

विचक्षणोऽस्यार्हति वेदितुं विभोर्
अनन्तपारस्य निवृत्तितः सुखम् ।
प्रवर्तमानस्य गुणैरनात्मनस्
ततो भवान्दर्शय चेष्टितं विभोः ॥ १६ ॥

vicakṣaṇo 'syārhati veditum vibhor
ananta-pārasya nivṛttitaḥ sukham
pravartamānasya guṇair anātmanas
tato bhavān darśaya ceṣṭitam vibhoḥ

vicakṣaṇaḥ—very expert; *asya*—of him; *arhati*—deserves; *veditum*—to understand; *vibhoḥ*—of the Lord; *ananta-pārasya*—of the unlimited; *nivṛttitaḥ*—retired from; *sukham*—mterial happiness; *pravartamānasya*—those who are attached to; *guṇaiḥ*—by the material qualities; *anātmanaḥ*—devoid of knowledge in spiritual value; *tataḥ*—therefore; *bhavān*—Your Goodness; *darśaya*—show the ways; *ceṣṭitam*—activities; *vibhoḥ*—of the Lord.

The Supreme Lord is unlimited. Only a very expert personality, retired from the activities of material happiness, deserves to understand this knowledge of spiritual values. Therefore those who are not so well situated, due to material attachment, should be shown the ways of transcendental realization, by Your Goodness, through descriptions of the transcendental activities of the Supreme Lord.

PURPORT Theological science is a difficult subject, especially when it deals with the transcendental nature of God. It is not a subject matter to be understood by persons who are too much attached to material activities. Only the very expert, who have almost retired from materialistic activities by culture of spiritual knowledge, can be admitted to the study of this great science. In the *Bhagavad-gītā* it is clearly stated that out of many hundreds and thousands of men only one person deserves to enter into transcendental realization. And out of many thousands of such transcendentally realized persons, only a few can understand the theological science specifically dealing with God as a person. Śrī Vyāsadeva is therefore advised by Nārada to describe the science of God directly by relating His transcendental activities. Vyāsadeva is himself a personality expert in this science, and he is unattached to material enjoyment. Therefore he is the right person to describe it, and Śukadeva Gosvāmī, the son of Vyāsadeva, is the right person to receive it.

Śrīmad-Bhāgavatam is the topmost theological science, and therefore it can react on the laymen as medicinal doses. Because it contains the transcendental activities of the Lord, there is no difference between the Lord and the literature. The literature is the factual literary incarnation of the Lord. So the laymen can hear the narration of the activities of the Lord. Thereby they are able to associate with the Lord and thus gradually become purified from material diseases. The expert devotees also can discover novel ways and means to convert the nondevotees in terms of particular time and circumstance. Devotional service is dynamic activity, and the expert devotees can find out competent means to inject it into the dull brains of the materialistic population. Such transcendental activities of the devotees for the service of the Lord can bring a new order of life to the foolish society of materialistic men. Lord Śrī Caitanya Mahāprabhu and His subsequent followers exhibited expert dexterity in this connection. By following the same method, one can bring the materialistic men of this age of quarrel into order for peaceful life and transcendental realization.

TEXT 17

त्यक्त्वा स्वधर्मं चरणाम्बुजं हरेर्
भजन्नपक्वोऽथ पतेत्ततो यदि ।
यत्र क्व वाभद्रमभूदमुष्य किं
को वार्थ आप्तोऽभजतां स्वधर्मतः ॥ १७ ॥

tyaktvā sva-dharmaṁ caraṇāmbujaṁ harer
bhajann apakvo 'tha patet tato yadi
yatra kva vābhadram abhūd amuṣya kiṁ
ko vārtha āpto 'bhajatāṁ sva-dharmataḥ

tyaktvā—having forsaken; *sva-dharmam*—one's own occupational engagement; *caraṇa-ambujam*—the lotus feet; *hareḥ*—of Hari (the Lord); *bhajan*—in the course of devotional service; *apakvaḥ*—immature; *atha*—for the matter of; *patet*—falls down; *tataḥ*—from that place; *yadi*—if; *yatra*—whereupon; *kva*—what sort of; *vā*—or (used sarcastically); *abhadram*—unfavorable; *abhūt*—shall happen; *amuṣya*—of him; *kim*—nothing; *kaḥ vā arthaḥ*—what interest; *āptaḥ*—obtained; *abhajatām*—of the nondevotee; *sva-dharmataḥ*—being engaged in occupational service.

One who has forsaken his material occupations to engage in the devotional service of the Lord may sometimes fall down while in an immature stage, yet there is no danger of his being unsuccessful. On the other hand, a nondevotee, though fully engaged in occupational duties, does not gain anything.

PURPORT As far as the duties of mankind are concerned, there are innumerable duties. Every man is duty-bound not only to his parents, family members, society, country, humanity, other living beings, the demigods, etc., but also to the great philosophers, poets, scientists, etc. It is enjoined in the scriptures that one can relinquish all such duties and surrender unto the service of the Lord. So if one does so and becomes successful in the discharge of his devotional service unto the Lord, it is well and good. But it so happens sometimes that one surrenders himself unto the service of the Lord by some temporary sentiment, and in the long run, due to so many other reasons, he falls down from the path of service by undesirable association. There are so many instances of this in the histories. Bharata Mahārāja was obliged to take his birth as a stag due to his intimate attachment to a stag. He thought of this stag when he died. As such, in the next birth he became a stag, although he did not forget the incident of his previous birth. Similarly, Citraketu also fell down due to his offenses at the feet of Śiva. But in spite of all this, the stress is given here to surrendering unto the lotus feet of the Lord, even if there is a chance of falling down, because even though one falls down from the prescribed duties of devotional service, he will never forget the lotus feet of the Lord. Once engaged in the devotional service of the Lord, one will continue the service in all circumstances. In the *Bhagavad-gītā* it is said that even a small quantity of devotional service can save one from the most dangerous position. There are many instances of such examples in history. Ajāmila is one of them. Ajāmila in his early life was a devotee, but in his youth he fell down. Still he was saved by the Lord at the end.

TEXT 18

तस्यैव हेतोः प्रयतेत कोविदो
न लभ्यते यद्भ्रमतामुपर्यधः ।
तल्लभ्यते दुःखवदन्यतः सुखं
कालेन सर्वत्र गभीररंहसा ॥ १८ ॥

tasyaiva hetoḥ prayateta kovido
na labhyate yad bhramatām upary adhaḥ
tal labhyate duḥkhavad anyataḥ sukhaṁ
kālena sarvatra gabhīra-raṁhasā

tasya—for that purpose; *eva*—only; *hetoḥ*—reason; *prayateta*—should endeavor; *kovidaḥ*—one who is philosophically inclined; *na labhyate*—is not obtained; *yat*—what; *bhramatām*—wandering; *upari adhaḥ*—from top to bottom; *tat*—that; *labhyate*—can be obtained; *duḥkhavat*—like the miseries; *anyataḥ*—as a result of previous work; *sukham*—sense enjoyment; *kālena*—in course of time; *sarvatra*—everywhere; *gabhīra*—subtle; *raṁhasā*—progress.

Persons who are actually intelligent and philosophically inclined should endeavor only for that purposeful end which is not obtainable even by wandering from the topmost planet [Brahmaloka] down to the lowest planet [Pātāla]. As far as happiness derived from sense enjoyment is concerned, it can be obtained automatically in course of time, just as in course of time we obtain miseries even though we do not desire them.

PURPORT Every man everywhere is trying to obtain the greatest amount of sense enjoyment by various endeavors. Some men are busy engaged in trade, industry, economic development, political supremacy, etc., and some of them are engaged in fruitive work to become happy in the next life by attaining higher planets. It is said that on the moon the inhabitants are fit for greater sense enjoyment by drinking *soma-rasa,* and the Pitṛloka is obtained by good charitable work. So there are various programs for sense enjoyment, either during this life or in the life after death. Some are trying to reach the moon or other planets by some mechanical arrangement, for they are very anxious to get into such planets without doing good work. But it is not to happen. By the law of the Supreme, different places are meant for different grades of living beings according to the work they have performed. By good work only, as prescribed in the scriptures, can one obtain birth in a good family, opulence, good education and good bodily features. We see also that even in this life one obtains a good education or money by good work. Similarly, in our next birth we get such desirable positions only by good work. Otherwise, it would not so happen that two persons born in the same place at the same time are seen differently placed according to previous work. But all such material positions are impermanent. The positions in the topmost Brahmaloka and in the lowest Pātāla are also changeable according to our own work. The philosophically inclined person must not be tempted by such changeable positions. He should try to get into the permanent life of bliss and knowledge where he will not be forced to come back again to the miserable material world, either in this or that planet. Miseries and mixed happiness are two features of material life, and they are obtained in Brahmaloka and in other *lokas* also. They are obtained in the life of the demigods and also in the life of the dogs and hogs. The miseries and mixed happiness of all living beings are only of different degree and quality, but no one is free from the miseries of birth, death, old age and disease. Similarly, everyone has his destined happiness also. No one can get more or less of these things simply by personal endeavors. Even if they are obtained, they can be lost again. One should not, therefore, waste time with these flimsy things; one should only endeavor to go back to Godhead. That should be the mission of everyone's life.

TEXT 19

न वै जनो जातु कथञ्चनाव्रजेन्
मुकुन्दसेव्यन्यवदङ्ग संसृतिम् ।
स्मरन्मुकुन्दाङ्घ्र्युपगूहनं पुनर्
विहातुमिच्छेन्न रसग्रहो जनः ॥ १९ ॥

na vai jano jātu kathañcanāvrajen
mukunda-sevy anyavad aṅga saṁsṛtim
smaran mukundāṅghry-upagūhanaṁ punar
vihātum icchen na rasa-graho janaḥ

na—never; *vai*—certainly; *janaḥ*—a person; *jātu*—at any time; *kathañcana*—somehow or other; *āvrajet*—does not undergo; *mukunda-sevī*—the devotee of the Lord; *anyavat*—like others; *aṅga*—O my dear; *saṁsṛtim*—material existence; *smaran*—remembering; *mukunda-aṅghri*—the lotus feet of the Lord; *upagūhanam*—embracing; *punaḥ*—again; *vihātum*—willing to give up; *icchet*—desire; *na*—never; *rasa-grahaḥ*—one who has relished the mellow; *janaḥ*—person.

My dear Vyāsa, even though a devotee of Lord Kṛṣṇa sometimes falls down somehow or other, he certainly does not undergo material existence like others [fruitive workers, etc.] because a person who has once relished the taste of the lotus feet of the Lord can do nothing but remember that ecstasy again and again.

PURPORT A devotee of the Lord automatically becomes uninterested in the enchantment of material existence because he is *rasa-graha,* or one who has tasted the sweetness of the lotus feet of Lord Kṛṣṇa. There are certainly many instances where devotees of the Lord have fallen down due to uncongenial association, just like fruitive workers, who are always prone to degradation. But even though he falls down, a devotee is never to be considered the same as a fallen *karmī*. A *karmī* suffers the result of his own fruitive reactions, whereas a devotee is reformed by chastisement directed by the Lord Himself. The sufferings of an orphan and the sufferings of a beloved child of a king are not one and the same. An orphan is really poor because he has no one to take care of him, but a beloved son of a rich man, although he appears to be on the same level as the orphan, is always under the vigilance of his capable father. A devotee of the Lord, due to wrong association, sometimes imitates the fruitive workers. The fruitive workers want to lord it over the material world. Similarly, a neophyte devotee foolishly thinks of accumulating some material power in exchange for devotional service. Such foolish devotees are sometimes put into difficulty by the Lord Himself. As a special favor, He may remove all material paraphernalia. By such action, the bewildered devotee is forsaken by all friends and relatives, and so he comes to his senses again by the mercy of the Lord and is set right to execute his devotional service.

In the *Bhagavad-gītā* it is also said that such fallen devotees are given a chance to take birth in a family of highly qualified *brāhmaṇas* or in a rich mercantile family. A devotee in such a position is not as fortunate as one who is chastised by the Lord and put into a position seemingly of helplessness. The devotee who becomes helpless by the will of the Lord is more fortunate than those who are born in good families. The fallen devotees born in a good family may forget the lotus feet of the Lord because they are less fortunate, but the devotee who is put into a forlorn condition is more fortunate because he swiftly returns to the lotus feet of the Lord, thinking himself helpless all around.

Pure devotional service is so spiritually relishable that a devotee becomes automatically uninterested in material enjoyment. That is the sign of perfection in progressive devotional service. A pure devotee continuously remembers the lotus feet of Lord Śrī Kṛṣṇa and does not forget Him even for a moment, not even in exchange for all the opulence of the three worlds.

TEXT 20

इदं हि विश्वं भगवानिवेतरो
यतो जगत्स्थाननिरोधसम्भवाः ।
तद्धि स्वयं वेद भवांस्तथापि ते
प्रादेशमात्रं भवतः प्रदर्शितम् ॥ २० ॥

idaṁ hi viśvaṁ bhagavān ivetaro
yato jagat-sthāna-nirodha-sambhavāḥ
tad dhi svayaṁ veda bhavāṁs tathāpi te
prādeśa-mātraṁ bhavataḥ pradarśitam

idam—this; *hi*—all; *viśvam*—cosmos; *bhagavān*—the Supreme Lord; *iva*—almost the same; *itaraḥ*—different from; *yataḥ*—from whom; *jagat*—the worlds; *sthāna*—exist; *nirodha*—annihilation; *sambhavāḥ*—creation; *tat hi*—all about; *svayam*—personally; *veda*—know; *bhavān*—your good self; *tathā api*—still; *te*—unto you; *prādeśa-mātram*—a synopsis only; *bhavataḥ*—unto you; *pradarśitam*—explained.

The Supreme Lord Personality of Godhead is Himself this cosmos, and still He is aloof from it. From Him only has this cosmic manifestation emanated, in Him it rests, and unto Him it enters after annihilation. Your good self knows all about this. I have given only a synopsis.

PURPORT For a pure devotee, the conception of Mukunda, Lord Śrī Kṛṣṇa, is both personal and impersonal. The impersonal cosmic situation is also Mukunda because it is the emanation of the energy of Mukunda. For example, a tree is a complete unit, whereas the leaves and the branches of the tree are emanated parts and parcels of the tree. The leaves and branches of the tree are also the tree, but the tree itself is neither the leaves nor the branches. The Vedic version that the whole cosmic creation is nothing but Brahman means that since everything is emanating from the Supreme Brahman, nothing is apart from Him. Similarly, the part-and-parcel hands and legs are called the body, but the body as the whole unit is neither the hands nor the legs. The Lord is the transcendental form of eternity, cognition and beauty. And thus the creation of the energy of the Lord appears to be partially eternal, full of knowledge and beautiful also. The captivated conditioned souls under the influence of the external energy, *māyā,* are therefore entrapped in the network of the material nature. They accept this as all in all, for they have no information of the Lord who is the primeval cause. Nor have they information that the parts and parcels of the body, being detached from the whole body, are no longer the same hand or leg as when attached to the body.

Similarly, a godless civilization detached from the transcendental loving service of the Supreme Personality of Godhead is just like a detached hand or leg. Such parts and parcels may appear like hands and legs, but they have no efficiency. The devotee of the Lord, Śrīla Vyāsadeva, knows this very well. He is further advised by Śrīla Nārada to expand the idea so that the entrapped conditioned souls may take lessons from him to understand the Supreme Lord as the primeval cause.

According to the Vedic version, the Lord is naturally fully powerful, and thus His supreme energies are always perfect and identical with Him. Both the spiritual and the material skies and their paraphernalia are emanations of the internal and external energies of the Lord. The external energy is comparatively inferior, whereas the internal potency is superior. The superior energy is living force, and therefore she is completely identical, but the external energy, being inert, is partially identical. But both the energies are neither equal to nor greater than the Lord, who is the generator of all energies; such energies are always under His control, exactly as electrical energy, however powerful it may be, is always under the control of the engineer.

The human being and all other living beings are products of His internal energies. Thus the living being is also identical with the Lord. But he is never equal or superior to the Personality of Godhead. The Lord and living beings are all individual persons. With the help of the material energies the living beings are also creating something, but none of their creations are equal or superior to the creations of the Lord. The human being may create a small playful sputnik and may throw it into outer space, but that does not mean that he can create a planet like the earth or moon and float it in the air as the Lord does. Men with a poor fund of knowledge claim to be equal to the Lord. They are never equal to the Lord. This is never to be. The human being, after attaining complete perfection, may achieve a large percentage of the qualities of the Lord (say up to seventy-eight percent), but it is never possible to surpass the Lord or to become equal with Him. In a diseased condition only, the foolish being claims to be one with the Lord and thus becomes misled by the illusory energy. The misguided living beings, therefore, must accept the supremacy of the Lord and agree to render loving service to Him. For this they have been created. Without this, there cannot be any peace or tranquillity in the world. Śrīla Vyāsadeva is advised by Śrīla Nārada to expand this idea in the *Bhāgavatam*. In the *Bhagavad-gītā* also the same idea is explained: surrender fully unto the lotus feet of the Lord. That is the only business of the perfect human being.

TEXT 21

त्वमात्मनात्मानमवेह्यमोघदृक्
परस्य पुंसः परमात्मनः कलाम् ।
अजं प्रजातं जगतः शिवाय तन्
महानुभावाभ्युदयोऽधिगण्यताम् ॥ २१ ॥

tvam ātmanātmānam avehy amogha-dṛk
parasya puṁsaḥ paramātmanaḥ kalām
ajaṁ prajātaṁ jagataḥ śivāya tan
mahānubhāvābhyudayo 'dhigaṇyatām

tvam—yourself; *ātmanā*—by your own self; *ātmānam*—the Supersoul; *avehi*—search out; *amogha-dṛk*—one who has perfect vision; *parasya*—of the Transcendence; *puṁsaḥ*—the Personality of Godhead; *param-ātmanaḥ*—of the Supreme Lord; *kalām*—plenary part; *ajam*—birthless; *prajātam*—have taken birth; *jagataḥ*—of the world; *śivāya*—for the well-being; *tat*—that; *mahā-anubhāva*—of the Supreme Personality of Godhead Śrī Kṛṣṇa; *abhyudayaḥ*—pastimes; *adhigaṇya-tām*—describe most vividly.

Your Goodness has perfect vision. You yourself can know the Supersoul Personality of Godhead because you are present as the plenary portion of the Lord. Although you are birthless, you have appeared on this earth for the well-being of all people. Please, therefore, describe the transcendental pastimes of the Supreme Personality of Godhead Śrī Kṛṣṇa more vividly.

PURPORT Śrīla Vyāsadeva is the empowered plenary portion incarnation of the Personality of Godhead Śrī Kṛṣṇa. He descended by his causeless mercy to deliver the fallen souls in the material world. The fallen and forgotten souls are detached from the transcendental loving service of the Lord. The living entities are parts and parcels of the Lord, and they are eternally servitors of the Lord. All the Vedic literatures, therefore, are put into systematic order for the benefit of the fallen souls, and it is the duty of the fallen souls to take advantage of such literatures and be freed from the bondage of material existence. Although formally Śrīla Nārada Ṛṣi is his spiritual master, Śrīla Vyāsadeva is not at all dependent on a spiritual master because in essence he is the spiritual master of everyone else. But because he is doing the work of an *ācārya,* he has taught us by his own conduct that one must have a spiritual master, even though he be God Himself. Lord Śrī Kṛṣṇa, Lord Śrī Rāma and Lord Śrī Caitanya Mahāprabhu, all incarnations of Godhead, accepted formal spiritual masters, although by Their transcendental nature They were cognizant of all knowledge. In order to direct people in general to the lotus feet of Lord Śrī Kṛṣṇa, He Himself in the incarnation of Vyāsadeva is delineating the transcendental pastimes of the Lord.

TEXT 22

इदं हि पुंसस्तपसः श्रुतस्य वा
स्विष्टस्य सूक्तस्य च बुद्धिदत्तयोः ।
अविच्युतोऽर्थः कविभिर्निरूपितो
यदुत्तमश्लोकगुणानुवर्णनम् ॥ २२ ॥

idaṁ hi puṁsas tapasaḥ śrutasya vā
sviṣṭasya sūktasya ca buddhi-dattayoḥ
avicyuto 'rthaḥ kavibhir nirūpito
yad-uttamaśloka-guṇānuvarṇanam

idam—this; *hi*—certainly; *puṁsaḥ*—of everyone; *tapasaḥ*—by dint of austerities; *śrutasya*—by dint of study of the *Vedas; vā*—or; *sviṣṭasya*—sacrifice; *sūktasya*—spiritual education; *ca*—and; *buddhi*—culture of knowledge; *dattayoḥ*—charity; *avicyutaḥ*—infallible; *arthaḥ*—interest; *kavibhiḥ*—by the recognized learned person; *nirūpitaḥ*—concluded; *yat*—what; *uttamaśloka*—the Lord, who is described by choice poetry; *guṇa-anuvarṇanam*—description of the transcendental qualities of.

Learned circles have positively concluded that the infallible purpose of the advancement of knowledge, namely austerities, study of the Vedas, sacrifice, chanting of hymns and charity, culminates in the transcendental descriptions of the Lord, who is defined in choice poetry.

PURPORT Human intellect is developed for advancement of learning in art, science, philosophy, physics, chemistry, psychology, economics, politics, etc. By culture of such knowledge the human society can attain perfection of life. This perfection of life culminates in the realization of the Supreme Being, Viṣṇu. The *śruti* therefore directs that those who are actually advanced in learning should aspire for the service of Lord Viṣṇu. Unfortunately persons who are enamored by the external beauty of *viṣṇu-māyā* do not understand that culmination of perfection or self-realization depends on Viṣṇu. *Viṣṇu-māyā* means sense enjoyment, which is transient and miserable. Those who are entrapped by *viṣṇu-māyā* utilize advancement of knowledge for sense enjoyment. Śrī Nārada Muni has explained that all paraphernalia of the cosmic universe is but an emanation from the Lord out of His different energies because the Lord has set in motion, by His inconceivable energy, the actions and reactions of the created manifestation. They have come to be out of His energy, they rest on His energy, and after annihilation they merge into Him. Nothing is, therefore, different from Him, but at the same time the Lord is always different from them.

When advancement of knowledge is applied in the service of the Lord, the whole process becomes absolute. The Personality of Godhead and His transcendental name, fame, glory, etc., are all nondifferent from Him. Therefore, all the sages and devotees of the Lord have recommended that the subject matter of art, science, philosophy, physics, chemistry, psychology and all other branches of knowledge should be wholly and solely applied in the service of the Lord. Art, literature, poetry, painting, etc., may be used in glorifying the Lord. The fiction writers, poets and celebrated litterateurs are generally engaged in writing of sensuous subjects, but if they turn towards the service of the Lord they can describe the transcendental pastimes of the Lord. Vālmīki was a great poet, and similarly Vyāsadeva is a great writer, and both of them have absolutely engaged themselves in delineating the transcendental activities of the Lord and by doing so have become immortal. Similarly, science and philosophy also should be applied in the service of the Lord. There is no use presenting dry speculative theories for sense gratification. Philosophy and science should be engaged to establish the glory of the Lord. Advanced people are eager to understand the Absolute Truth through the medium of science, and therefore a great scientist should endeavor to prove the existence of the Lord on a scientific basis. Similarly, philosophical speculations should be utilized to establish the Supreme Truth as sentient and all-powerful. Similarly, all other branches of knowledge should always be engaged in the service of the Lord. In the *Bhagavad-gītā* also the same is affirmed. All "knowledge" not engaged in the service of the Lord is but nescience. Real utilization of advanced knowledge is to establish the glories of the Lord, and that is the real import. Scientific knowledge engaged in the service of the Lord and all similar activities are all factually *hari-kīrtana,* or glorification of the Lord.

TEXT 23

अहं पुरातीतभवेऽभवं मुने
दास्यास्तु कस्याश्चन वेदवादिनाम् ।
निरूपितो बालक एव योगिनां
शुश्रूषणे प्रावृषि निर्विविक्षताम् ॥ २३ ॥

ahaṁ purātīta-bhave 'bhavaṁ mune
dāsyās tu kasyāścana veda-vādinām
nirūpito bālaka eva yogināṁ
śuśrūṣaṇe prāvṛṣi nirvivikṣatām

aham—I; *purā*—formerly; *atīta-bhave*—in the previous millennium; *abhavam*—became; *mune*—O *muni; dāsyāḥ*—of the maidservant; *tu*—but; *kasyāścana*—certain; *veda-vādinām*—of the followers of Vedānta; *nirūpitaḥ*—engaged; *bālakaḥ*—boy servant; *eva*—only; *yoginām*—of the devotees; *śuśrūṣaṇe*—in the service of; *prāvṛṣi*—during the four months of the rainy season; *nirvivikṣatām*—living together.

O muni, in my past life, in the last millennium, I was born as the son of a certain maidservant engaged in the service of brāhmaṇas who were following the principles of Vedānta. When they were living together during the four months of the rainy season, I was engaged in their personal service.

PURPORT The wonder of an atmosphere surcharged with devotional service to the Lord is briefly described herein by Śrī Nārada Muni. He was the son of the most insignificant parentage. He was not properly educated. Still, because his complete energy was engaged in the service of the Lord, he became an immortal sage. Such is the powerful action of devotional service. The living entities are the marginal energy of the Lord, and therefore they are meant for being properly utilized in the transcendental loving service of the Lord. When this is not done, one's situation is called *māyā*. Therefore the illusion of *māyā* is at once dissipated as soon as one's full energy is converted in the service of the Lord instead of in sense enjoyment. From the personal example of Śrī Nārada Muni in his previous birth, it is clear that the service of the Lord begins with the service of the Lord's bona fide servants. The Lord says that the service of His servants is greater than His personal service. Service of the devotee is more valuable than the service of the Lord. One should therefore choose a bona fide servant of the Lord constantly engaged in His service, accept such a servant as the spiritual master and engage himself in his (the spiritual master's) service. Such a spiritual master is the transparent medium by which to visualize the Lord, who is beyond the conception of the material senses. By service of the bona fide spiritual master, the Lord consents to reveal Himself in proportion to the service rendered. Utilization of the human energy in the service of the Lord is the progressive path of salvation. The whole cosmic creation becomes at once identical with the Lord as soon as service in relation with the Lord is rendered under the guidance of a bona fide spiritual master. The expert spiritual master knows the art of utilizing everything to glorify the Lord, and therefore under his guidance the whole world can be turned into the spiritual abode by the divine grace of the Lord's servant.

TEXT 24

ते मय्यपेताखिलचापलेऽर्भके
दान्तेऽधृतक्रीडनकेऽनुवर्तिनि ।
चक्रुः कृपां यद्यपि तुल्यदर्शनाः
शुश्रूषमाणे मुनयोऽल्पभाषिणि ॥ २४ ॥

te mayy apetākhila-cāpale 'rbhake
dānte 'dhṛta-krīḍanake 'nuvartini
cakruḥ kṛpāṁ yadyapi tulya-darśanāḥ
śuśrūṣamāṇe munayo 'lpa-bhāṣiṇi

te—they; *mayi*—unto me; *apeta*—not having undergone; *akhila*—all kinds of; *cāpale*—proclivities; *arbhake*—unto a boy; *dānte*—having controlled the senses; *adhṛta-krīḍanake*—without being accustomed to sporting habits; *anuvartini*—obedient; *cakruḥ*—did bestow; *kṛpām*—causeless mercy; *yadyapi*—although; *tulya-darśanāḥ*—impartial by nature; *śuśrūṣamāṇe*—unto the faithful; *munayaḥ*—the *muni* followers of the Vedānta; *alpa-bhāṣiṇi*—one who does not speak more than required.

Although they were impartial by nature, those followers of the Vedānta blessed me with their causeless mercy. As far as I was concerned, I was self-controlled and had no attachment for sports, even though I was a boy. In addition, I was not naughty, and I did not speak more than required.

PURPORT In the *Bhagavad-gītā* the Lord says, "All the *Vedas* are searching after Me." Lord Śrī Caitanya says that in the *Vedas* the subject matters are only three, namely to establish the relation of the living entities with the Personality of Godhead, perform the relative duties in devotional service and thus achieve the ultimate goal, back to Godhead. As such, *vedānta-vādīs,* or the followers of the Vedānta, indicate the pure devotees of the Personality of Godhead. Such *vedānta-vādīs,* or the *bhakti-vedāntas,* are impartial in distributing the transcendental knowledge of devotional service. To them no one is enemy or friend; no one is educated or uneducated. No one is especially favorable, and no one is unfavorable. The *bhakti-vedāntas* see that the people in general are wasting time in false sensuous things. Their business is to get the ignorant mass of people to reestablish their lost relationship with the Personality of Godhead. By such endeavor, even the most forgotten soul is roused up to the sense of spiritual life, and thus being initiated by the *bhakti-vedāntas,* the people in general gradually progress on the path of transcendental realization. So the *vedānta-vādīs* initiated the boy even before he became self-controlled and was detached from childish sporting, etc. But before the initiation, he (the boy) became more and more advanced in discipline, which is very essential for one who wishes to make progress in the line. In the system of *varṇāśrama-dharma,* which is the beginning of actual human life, small boys after five years of age are sent to become *brahmacārīs* at the *guru's āśrama,* where these things are systematically taught to every boy, be he a king's son or the son of an ordinary citizen. The training was compulsory not only to create good citizens of the state but also to prepare the boy's future life for spiritual realization. The irresponsible life of sense enjoyment was unknown to the children of the followers of the *varṇāśrama* system. A boy was even injected with spiritual acumen before being placed by the father in the womb of the mother. Both the father and the mother were responsible for the boy's success in being liberated from the material bondage. That is the process of successful family planning. It is to beget children for complete perfection. Without being self-controlled, without being disciplined and without being fully obedient, no one can become successful in following the instructions of the spiritual master, and without doing so, no one is able to go back to Godhead.

TEXT 25

उच्छिष्टलेपाननुमोदितो द्विजैः
सकृत्स्म भुञ्जे तदपास्तकिल्बिषः ।
एवं प्रवृत्तस्य विशुद्धचेतसस्
तद्धर्म एवात्मरुचिः प्रजायते ॥ २५ ॥

ucchiṣṭa-lepān anumodito dvijaiḥ
sakṛt sma bhuñje tad-apāsta-kilbiṣaḥ
evaṁ pravṛttasya viśuddha-cetasas
tad-dharma evātma-ruciḥ prajāyate

ucchiṣṭa-lepān—the remnants of foodstuff; *anumoditaḥ*—being permitted; *dvijaiḥ*—by the Vedāntist *brāhmaṇas; sakṛt*—once upon a time; *sma*—in the past; *bhuñje*—took; *tat*—by that action; *apāsta*—eliminated; *kilbiṣaḥ*—all sins; *evam*—thus; *pravṛttasya*—being engaged; *viśuddha-cetasaḥ*—of one whose mind is purified; *tat*—that particular; *dharmaḥ*—nature; *eva*—certainly; *ātma-ruciḥ*—transcendental attraction; *prajāyate*—was manifested.

Once only, by their permission, I took the remnants of their food, and by so doing all my sins were at once eradicated. Thus being engaged, I became purified in heart, and at that time the very nature of the transcendentalist became attractive to me.

PURPORT Pure devotion is as much infectious, in a good sense, as infectious diseases. A pure devotee is cleared from all kinds of sins. The Personality of Godhead is the purest entity, and unless one is equally pure from the infection of material qualities, one cannot become a pure devotee of the Lord. The *bhakti-vedāntas* as above mentioned were pure devotees, and the boy became infected with their qualities of purity by their association and by eating once the remnants of the foodstuff taken by them. Such remnants may be taken even without permission of the pure devotees. There are sometimes pseudodevotees, and one should be very much cautious about them. There are many things which hinder one from entering devotional service. But by the association of pure devotees all these obstacles are removed. The neophyte devotee becomes practically enriched with the transcendental qualities of the pure devotee, which means attraction for the Personality of Godhead's name, fame, quality, pastimes, etc. Infection of the qualities of the pure devotee means to imbibe the taste of pure devotion always in the transcendental activities of the Personality of Godhead. This transcendental taste at once makes all material things distasteful. Therefore a pure devotee is not at all attracted by material activities. After the elimination of all sins or obstacles on the path of devotional service, one can become attracted, one can have steadiness, one can have perfect taste, one can have transcendental emotions, and at last one can be situated on the plane of loving service of the Lord. All these stages develop by the association of pure devotees, and that is the purport of this stanza.

TEXT 26

तत्रान्वहं कृष्णकथाः प्रगायताम्
अनुग्रहेणाशृणवं मनोहराः ।
ताः श्रद्धया मेऽनुपदं विशृण्वतः
प्रियश्रवस्यङ्ग ममाभवद्रुचिः ॥ २६ ॥

tatrānvahaṁ kṛṣṇa-kathāḥ pragāyatām
anugraheṇāśṛṇavaṁ manoharāḥ
tāḥ śraddhayā me 'nupadaṁ viśṛṇvataḥ
priya-śravasy aṅga mamābhavad ruciḥ

tatra—thereupon; *anu*—every day; *aham*—I; *kṛṣṇa-kathāḥ*—narration of Lord Kṛṣṇa's activities; *pragāyatām*—describing; *anugraheṇa*—by causeless mercy; *aśṛṇavam*—giving aural reception; *manaḥ-harāḥ*—attractive; *tāḥ*—those; *śraddhayā*—respectfully; *me*—unto me; *anupadam*—every step; *viśṛṇvataḥ*—hearing attentively; *priya-śravasi*—of the Personality of Godhead; *aṅga*—O Vyāsadeva; *mama*—mine; *abhavat*—it so became; *ruciḥ*—taste.

O Vyāsadeva, in that association and by the mercy of those great Vedāntists, I could hear them describe the attractive activities of Lord Kṛṣṇa And thus listening attentively, my taste for hearing of the Personality of Godhead increased at every step.

PURPORT Lord Śrī Kṛṣṇa, the Absolute Personality of Godhead, is attractive not only in His personal features, but also in His transcendental activities. It is so because the Absolute is absolute by His name, fame, form, pastimes, entourage, paraphernalia, etc. The Lord descends on this material world out of His causeless mercy and displays His various transcendental pastimes as a human being so that human beings attracted towards Him become able to go back to Godhead. Men are naturally apt to hear histories and narrations of various personalities performing mundane activities, without knowing that by such association one simply wastes valuable time and also becomes addicted to the three qualities of mundane nature. Instead of wasting time, one can get spiritual success by turning his attention to the transcendental pastimes of the Lord. By hearing the narration of the pastimes of the Lord, one contacts directly the Personality of Godhead, and, as explained before, by hearing about the Personality of Godhead, from within, all accumulated sins of the mundane creature are cleared. Thus being cleared of all sins, the hearer gradually becomes liberated from mundane association and becomes attracted to the features of the Lord. Nārada Muni has just explained this by his personal experience. The whole idea is that simply by hearing about the Lord's pastimes one can become one of the associates of the Lord. Nārada Muni has eternal life, unlimited knowledge and unfathomed bliss, and he can travel all over the material and spiritual worlds without restriction. One can attain to the highest perfection of life simply by attentive hearing of the transcendental pastimes of the Lord from the right sources, as Śrī Nārada heard them from the pure devotees (*bhakti-vedāntas*) in his previous life. This process of hearing in the association of the devotees is especially recommended in this age of quarrel (Kali).

TEXT 27

तस्मिंस्तदा लब्धरुचेर्महामते
प्रियश्रवस्यस्खलिता मतिर्मम ।
ययाहमेतत्सदसत्स्वमायया
पश्ये मयि ब्रह्मणि कल्पितं परे ॥ २७ ॥

tasmiṁs tadā labdha-rucer mahā-mate
priya-śravasy askhalitā matir mama
yayāham etat sad-asat sva-māyayā
paśye mayi brahmaṇi kalpitaṁ pare

tasmin—it being so; *tadā*—at that time; *labdha*—achieved; *ruceḥ*—taste; *mahā-mate*—O great sage; *priya-śravasi*—upon the Lord; *askhalitā matiḥ*—uninterrupted attention; *mama*—mine; *yayā*—by which; *aham*—I; *etat*—all these; *sat-asat*—gross and subtle; *sva-māyayā*—one's own ignorance; *paśye*—see; *mayi*—in me; *brahmaṇi*—the Supreme; *kalpitam*—is accepted; *pare*—in the Transcendence.

O great sage, as soon as I got a taste for the Personality of Godhead, my attention to hear of the Lord was unflinching. And as my taste developed, I could realize that it was only in my ignorance that I had accepted gross and subtle coverings, for both the Lord and I are transcendental.

PURPORT Ignorance in material existence is compared to darkness, and in all Vedic literatures the Personality of Godhead is compared to the sun. Wherever there is light there cannot be darkness. Hearing of the Lord's pastimes is itself transcendental association with the Lord because there is no difference between the Lord and His transcendental pastimes. To become associated with the supreme light is to dissipate all ignorance. By ignorance only, the conditioned soul wrongly thinks that both he and the Lord are products of material nature. But in fact the

Personality of Godhead and the living beings are transcendental, and they have nothing to do with the material nature. When ignorance is removed and it is perfectly realized that there is nothing existing without the Personality of Godhead, then nescience is removed. Since the gross and subtle bodies are emanations from the Personality of Godhead, the knowledge of light permits one to engage both of them in the service of the Lord. The gross body should be engaged in acts of rendering service to the Lord (as in bringing water, cleansing the temple or making obeisances, etc.). The path of *arcanā,* or worshiping the Lord in the temple, involves engaging one's gross body in the service of the Lord. Similarly, the subtle mind should be engaged in hearing the transcendental pastimes of the Lord, thinking about them, chanting His name, etc. All such activities are transcendental. None of the gross or subtle senses should otherwise be engaged. Such realization of transcendental activities is made possible by many, many years of apprenticeship in the devotional service, but simply attraction of love for the Personality of Godhead, as it was developed in Nārada Muni, by hearing, is highly effective.

TEXT 28

इत्थं शरत्प्रावृषिकावृतू हरेर्
विशृण्वतो मेऽनुसवं यशोऽमलम् ।
सङ्कीर्त्यमानं मुनिभिर्महात्मभिर्
भक्तिः प्रवृत्तात्मरजस्तमोपहा ॥ २८ ॥

ittham śarat-prāvṛṣikāv ṛtū harer
viśṛṇvato me 'nusavaṁ yaśo 'malam
saṅkīrtyamānaṁ munibhir mahātmabhir
bhaktiḥ pravṛttātma-rajas-tamopahā

ittham—thus; *śarat*—autumn; *prāvṛṣikau*—rainy season; *ṛtū*—two seasons; *hareḥ*—of the Lord; *viśṛṇvataḥ*—continuously hearing; *me*—myself; *anusavam*—constantly; *yaśaḥ amalam*—unadulterated glories; *saṅkīrtya-mānam*—chanted by; *munibhiḥ*—the great sages; *mahā-ātmabhiḥ*—great souls; *bhaktiḥ*—devotional service; *pravṛttā*—began to flow; *ātma*—living being; *rajaḥ*—mode of passion; *tama*—mode of ignorance; *upahā*—vanishing.

Thus during two seasons—the rainy season and autumn—I had the opportunity to hear these great-souled sages constantly chant the unadulterated glories of the Lord Hari. As the flow of my devotional service began, the coverings of the modes of passion and ignorance vanished.

PURPORT Transcendental loving service for the Supreme Lord is the natural inclination of every living being. The instinct is dormant in everyone, but due to the association of material nature the modes of passion and ignorance cover this from time immemorial. If, by the grace of the Lord and the great-souled devotees of the Lord, a living being becomes fortunate enough to associate with the unadulterated devotees of the Lord and gets a chance to hear the unadulterated glories of the Lord, certainly the dormant instinct of devotional service is at once awakened and the flow of devotional service takes place like the flow of a river. As the river flows on till she reaches the sea, similarly pure devotional service flows by the association of pure devotees till it reaches the ultimate goal, namely, transcendental love of God. Such a flow of devotional service cannot stop. On the contrary, it increases more and more without limitation. The flow of devotional service is so potent that any onlooker also becomes liberated from the influence of the modes of passion and ignorance. These two qualities of nature are thus removed, and the living being is liberated, being situated in his original position.

TEXT 29

तस्यैवं मेऽनुरक्तस्य प्रश्रितस्य हतैनसः ।
श्रद्दधानस्य बालस्य दान्तस्यानुचरस्य च ॥ २९ ॥

tasyaivaṁ me 'nuraktasya praśritasya hatainasaḥ
śraddadhānasya bālasya dāntasyānucarasya ca

tasya—his; *evam*—thus; *me*—mine; *anuraktasya*—attached to them; *praśritasya*—obediently; *hata*—freed from; *enasaḥ*—sins; *śraddadhānasya*—of the faithful; *bālasya*—of the boy; *dāntasya*—subjugated; *anucarasya*—strictly following the instructions; *ca*—and.

I was very much attached to those sages. I was gentle in behavior, and all my sins were eradicated in their service. In my heart I had strong

faith in them. I had subjugated the senses, and I was strictly following them with body and mind.

PURPORT These are the necessary qualifications of a prospective candidate who can expect to be elevated to the position of a pure unadulterated devotee. Such a candidate must always seek the association of pure devotees. One should not be misled by a pseudodevotee. He himself must be plain and gentle to receive the instructions of such a pure devotee. A pure devotee is a completely surrendered soul unto the Personality of Godhead. He knows the Personality of Godhead as the supreme proprietor and all others as His servitors. And by the association of pure devotees only, one can get rid of all sins accumulated by mundane association. A neophyte devotee must faithfully serve the pure devotee, and he should be very much obedient and strictly follow the instructions. These are the signs of a devotee who is determined to achieve success even in the existing duration of life.

TEXT 30

ज्ञानं गुह्यतमं यत्तत्साक्षाद्भगवतोदितम् ।
अन्ववोचन् गमिष्यन्तः कृपया दीनवत्सलाः ॥ ३० ॥

jñānaṁ guhyatamaṁ yat tat sākṣād bhagavatoditam
anvavocan gamiṣyantaḥ kṛpayā dīna-vatsalāḥ

jñānam—knowledge; *guhyatamam*—most confidential; *yat*—what is; *tat*—that; *sākṣāt*—directly; *bhagavatā uditam*—propounded by the Lord Himself; *anvavocan*—gave instruction; *gamiṣyantaḥ*—while departing from; *kṛpayā*—by causeless mercy; *dīna-vatsalāḥ*—those who are very kind to the poor and meek.

As they were leaving, those bhakti-vedāntas, who are very kind to poor-hearted souls, instructed me in that most confidential subject which is instructed by the Personality of Godhead Himself.

PURPORT A pure Vedāntist, or a *bhakti-vedānta*, instructs followers exactly according to the instructions of the Lord Himself. The Personality of Godhead, both in the *Bhagavad-gītā* and in all other scriptures, has definitely instructed men to follow the Lord only. The Lord is the creator, maintainer and annihilator of everything. The whole manifested creation is existing by His will, and by His will when the whole show is finished He will remain in His eternal abode with all His paraphernalia. Before the creation He was there in the eternal abode, and after the annihilation He will continue to remain. He is not, therefore, one of the created beings. He is transcendental. In the *Bhagavad-gītā* the Lord says that long, long before the instruction was imparted to Arjuna, the same was instructed to the sun-god, and in course of time, the same instruction, being wrongly handled and being broken, was again instructed to Arjuna because he was His perfect devotee and friend. Therefore, the instruction of the Lord can be understood by the devotees only and no one else. The impersonalist, who has no idea of the transcendental form of the Lord, cannot understand this most confidential message of the Lord. The expression "most confidential" is significant here because knowledge of devotional service is far, far above knowledge of impersonal Brahman. *Jñānam* means ordinary knowledge or any branch of knowledge. This knowledge develops up to the knowledge of impersonal Brahman. Above this, when it is partially mixed with devotion, such knowledge develops to knowledge of Paramātmā, or the all-pervading Godhead. This is more confidential. But when such knowledge is turned into pure devotional service and the confidential part of transcendental knowledge is attained, it is called the most confidential knowledge. This most confidential knowledge was imparted by the Lord to Brahmā, Arjuna, Uddhava, etc.

TEXT 31

येनैवाहं भगवतो वासुदेवस्य वेधसः ।
मायानुभावमविदं येन गच्छन्ति तत्पदम् ॥ ३१ ॥

yenaivāhaṁ bhagavato vāsudevasya vedhasaḥ
māyānubhāvam avidaṁ yena gacchanti tat-padam

yena—by which; *eva*—certainly; *aham*—I; *bhagavataḥ*—of the Personality of Godhead; *vāsudevasya*—of Lord Śrī Kṛṣṇa; *vedhasaḥ*—of the supreme creator; *māyā*—energy; *anubhāvam*—influence; *avidam*—easily understood; *yena*—by which; *gacchanti*—they go; *tat-padam*—at the lotus feet of the Lord.

By that confidential knowledge, I could understand clearly the influence of the energy of Lord Śrī Kṛṣṇa, the creator, maintainer and annihilator of everything. By knowing that, one can return to Him and personally meet Him.

PURPORT By devotional service or by the most confidential knowledge, one can understand very easily how the different energies of the Lord are working. One part of His energy is manifesting the material world; the other (superior) part of His energy is manifesting the spiritual world. And His intermediate energy is manifesting the living entities who are serving either of the above-mentioned energies. The living entities serving material energy are struggling hard for existence, and the happiness which is presented to them is illusory. But those in the spiritual energy are placed under the direct service of the Lord in eternal life, complete knowledge and perpetual bliss. The Lord desires, as He has directly said in the *Bhagavad-gītā,* that all conditioned souls, rotting in the kingdom of material energy, come back to Him by giving up all engagements in the material world. This is the most confidential part of knowledge. But this can be understood only by the pure devotees, and only such devotees enter the kingdom of God to see Him personally and serve Him personally. The concrete example is Nārada himself, who attained this stage of eternal knowledge and eternal bliss. And the ways and means are open to all, provided one agrees to follow in the footsteps of Śrī Nārada Muni. According to *śruti,* the Supreme Lord has unlimited energies (without effort by Him), and these are described under three principal headings, as above mentioned.

TEXT 32

एतत्संसूचितं ब्रह्मंस्तापत्रयचिकित्सितम् ।
यदीश्वरे भगवति कर्म ब्रह्मणि भावितम् ॥ ३२ ॥

etat saṁsūcitaṁ brahmaṁs tāpa-traya-cikitsitam
yad īśvare bhagavati karma brahmaṇi bhāvitam

etat—this much; *saṁsūcitam*—decided by the learned; *brahman*—O *brāhmaṇa* Vyāsa; *tāpa-traya*—three kinds of miseries; *cikitsitam*—remedial measures; *yat*—what; *īśvare*—the supreme controller;

bhagavati—unto the Personality of Godhead; *karma*—one's prescribed activities; *brahmaṇi*—unto the great; *bhāvitam*—dedicated.

O Brāhmaṇa Vyāsadeva, it is decided by the learned that the best remedial measure for removing all troubles and miseries is to dedicate one's activities to the service of the Supreme Lord Personality of Godhead [Śrī Kṛṣṇa].

PURPORT Śrī Nārada Muni personally experienced that the most feasible and practical way to open the path of salvation or get relief from all miseries of life is to hear submissively the transcendental activities of the Lord from the right and bona fide sources. This is the only remedial process. The entire material existence is full of miseries. Foolish people have manufactured, out of their tiny brains, many remedial measures for removing the threefold miseries pertaining to the body and mind, pertaining to the natural disturbances and in relation with other living beings. The whole world is struggling very hard to exist out of these miseries, but men do not know that without the sanction of the Lord no plan or no remedial measure can actually bring about the desired peace and tranquillity. The remedial measure to cure a patient by medical treatment is useless if it is not sanctioned by the Lord, the attempt to cross a river or the ocean by a suitable boat will fail if it is not sanctioned by the Lord, and parents' attempt to protect their children cannot succeed if it is not sanctioned by the Lord. We should know for certain that the Lord is the ultimate sanctioning officer, and we must therefore dedicate our attempts to the mercy of the Lord for ultimate success or to get rid of the obstacles on the path of success. The Lord is all-pervading, all-powerful, omniscient and omnipresent. He is the ultimate sanctioning agent of all good or bad effects. We should, therefore, learn to dedicate our activities unto the mercy of the Lord and accept Him either as impersonal Brahman, localized Paramātmā or the Supreme Personality of Godhead. It does not matter what one is. One must dedicate everything in the service of the Lord. If one is a learned scholar, scientist, philosopher, poet, etc., then he should employ his learning to establish the supremacy of the Lord. Try to study the energy of the Lord in every sphere of life. Do not decry Him and try to become like Him or take His position simply by fragmental accumulation of knowledge. If one is an administrator, statesman, warrior, politician, etc., then one should try to establish the Lord's supremacy in statesmanship. Fight for the cause of the Lord as Śrī Arjuna did. In the beginning, Śrī Arjuna, the great fighter, declined to fight, but when he was convinced by the Lord that the fighting was necessary, Śrī Arjuna changed his decision and fought for His cause. Similarly, if one is a businessman, an industrialist, an agriculturist, etc., then one should spend his hard-earned money for the cause of the Lord. Think always that the money which is accumulated is the wealth of the Lord. Wealth is considered to be the goddess of fortune (Lakṣmī), and the Lord is Nārāyaṇa, or the husband of Lakṣmī. Try to engage Lakṣmī in the service of Lord Nārāyaṇa and be happy. That is the way to realize the Lord in every sphere of life. The best thing is, after all, to get relief from all material activities and engage oneself completely in hearing the transcendental pastimes of the Lord. But in case of the absence of such an opportunity, one should try to engage in the service of the Lord everything for which one has specific attraction. That is the way of peace and prosperity, and that is the remedial measure for all the miseries of material existence. The word *saṁsūcitam* in this stanza is also significant. One should not think for a moment that the realization of Nārada was childish imagination only. It is not like that. It is so realized by the expert and erudite scholars, and that is the real import of the word *saṁsūcitam.*

TEXT 33

आमयो यश्च भूतानां जायते येन सुव्रत ।
तदेव ह्यामयं द्रव्यं न पुनाति चिकित्सितम् ॥ ३३ ॥

āmayo yaś ca bhūtānāṁ jāyate yena suvrata
tad eva hy āmayaṁ dravyaṁ na punāti cikitsitam

āmayaḥ—diseases; *yaḥ ca*—whatever; *bhūtānām*—of the living being; *jāyate*—become possible; *yena*—by the agency; *suvrata*—O good soul; *tat*—that; *eva*—very; *hi*—certainly; *āmayam*—disease; *dravyam*—thing; *na*—does it not; *punāti*—cure; *cikitsitam*—treated with.

O good soul, does not a thing, applied therapeutically, cure a disease which was caused by that very same thing?

PURPORT An expert physician treats his patient with a therapeutic diet.

For example, milk preparations sometimes cause disorder of the bowels, but the very same milk converted into yogurt and mixed with some other remedial ingredients cures such disorders. Similarly, the threefold miseries of material existence cannot be mitigated simply by material activities. Such activities have to be spiritualized, just as by fire iron is made red-hot, and thereby the action of fire begins. Similarly, the material conception of a thing is at once changed as soon as it is put into the service of the Lord. That is the secret of spiritual success. We should not try to lord it over the material nature, nor should we reject material things. The best way to make the best use of a bad bargain is to use everything in relation with the supreme spiritual being. Everything is an emanation from the Supreme Spirit, and by His inconceivable power He can convert spirit into matter and matter into spirit. Therefore a material thing (so-called) is at once turned into a spiritual force by the great will of the Lord. The necessary condition for such a change is to employ so-called matter in the service of the spirit. That is the way to treat our material diseases and elevate ourselves to the spiritual plane where there is no misery, no lamentation and no fear. When everything is thus employed in the service of the Lord, we can experience that there is nothing except the Supreme Brahman. The Vedic *mantra* that "everything is Brahman" is thus realized by us.

TEXT 34

एवं नृणां क्रियायोगाः सर्वे संसृतिहेतवः ।
त एवात्मविनाशाय कल्पन्ते कल्पिताः परे ॥ ३४ ॥

evaṁ nṛṇāṁ kriyā-yogāḥ sarve saṁsṛti-hetavaḥ
ta evātma-vināśāya kalpante kalpitāḥ pare

evam—thus; *nṛṇām*—of the human being; *kriyā-yogāḥ*—all activities; *sarve*—everything; *saṁsṛti*—material existence; *hetavaḥ*—causes; *te*—that; *eva*—certainly; *ātma*—the tree of work; *vināśāya*—killing; *kalpante*—become competent; *kalpitāḥ*—dedicated; *pare*—unto the Transcendence.

Thus when all a man's activities are dedicated to the service of the Lord, those very activities which caused his perpetual bondage become the destroyer of the tree of work.

PURPORT Fruitive work which has perpetually engaged the living being is compared to the banyan tree in the *Bhagavad-gītā,* for it is certainly very deeply rooted. As long as the propensity for enjoying the fruit of work is there, one has to continue the transmigration of the soul from one body or place to another, according to one's nature of work. The propensity for enjoyment may be turned into the desire for serving the mission of the Lord. By doing so, one's activity is changed into *karma-yoga,* or the way by which one can attain spiritual perfection while engaging in the work for which he has a natural tendency. Here the word *ātmā* indicates the categories of all fruitive work. The conclusion is that when the result of all fruitive and other work is dovetailed with the service of the Lord, it will cease to generate further *karma* and will gradually develop into transcendental devotional service, which will not only cut off completely the root of the banyan tree of work but will also carry the performer to the lotus feet of the Lord.

The summary is that one has to, first of all, seek the association of pure devotees who not only are learned in the Vedānta but are self-realized souls and unalloyed devotees of Lord Śrī Kṛṣṇa, the Personality of Godhead. In that association, the neophyte devotees must render loving service physically and mentally without reservation. This service attitude will induce the great souls to be more favorable in bestowing their mercy, which injects the neophyte with all the transcendental qualities of the pure devotees. Gradually this is developed into a strong attachment to hearing the transcendental pastimes of the Lord, which makes him able to catch up the constitutional position of the gross and subtle bodies and beyond them the knowledge of the pure soul and his eternal relation with the Supreme Soul, the Personality of Godhead. After the relation is ascertained by establishment of the eternal relation, pure devotional service to the Lord begins gradually developing into perfect knowledge of the Personality of Godhead beyond the purview of impersonal Brahman and localized Paramātmā. By such *puruṣottama-yoga,* as it is stated in the *Bhagavad-gītā,* one is made perfect even during the present corporeal existence, and one exhibits all the good qualities of the Lord to the highest percentage. Such is the gradual development by association of pure devotees.

TEXT 35

यदत्र क्रियते कर्म भगवत्परितोषणम् ।
ज्ञानं यत्तदधीनं हि भक्तियोगसमन्वितम् ॥ ३५ ॥

yad atra kriyate karma bhagavat-paritoṣaṇam
jñānaṁ yat tad adhīnaṁ hi bhakti-yoga-samanvitam

yat—whatever; *atra*—in this life or world; *kriyate*—does perform; *karma*—work; *bhagavat*—unto the Personality of Godhead; *paritoṣaṇam*—satisfaction of; *jñānam*—knowledge; *yat tat*—what is so called; *adhīnam*—dependent; *hi*—certainly; *bhakti-yoga*—with devotional service; *samanvitam*—dovetailed.

Whatever work is done here in this life for the satisfaction of the mission of the Lord is called bhakti-yoga, or transcendental loving service to the Lord, and what is called knowledge becomes a concomitant factor.

PURPORT The general and popular notion is that by discharging fruitive work in terms of the direction of the scriptures one becomes perfectly able to acquire transcendental knowledge for spiritual realization. *Bhakti-yoga* is considered by some to be another form of *karma*. But factually *bhakti-yoga* is above both *karma* and *jñāna*. *Bhakti-yoga* is independent of *jñāna* or *karma;* on the other hand, *jñāna* and *karma* are dependent on *bhakti-yoga*. This *kriyā-yoga* or *karma-yoga,* as recommended by Śrī Nārada to Vyāsa, is specifically recommended because the principle is to satisfy the Lord. The Lord does not want His sons, the living beings, to suffer the threefold miseries of life. He desires that all of them come to Him and live with Him, but going back to Godhead means that one must purify himself from material infections. When work is performed, therefore, to satisfy the Lord, the performer becomes gradually purified from the material affection. This purification means attainment of spiritual knowledge. Therefore knowledge is dependent on *karma,* or work, done on behalf of the Lord. Other knowledge, being devoid of *bhakti-yoga* or satisfaction of the Lord, cannot lead one back to the kingdom of God, which means that it cannot even offer salvation, as already explained in connection with the stanza *naiṣkarmyam apy acyuta-bhāva-varjitam* (*Śrīmad-Bhāgavatam* 1.5.12). The conclusion is that a devotee engaged in the unalloyed service of the Lord, specifically in hearing and chanting of His transcendental glories, becomes simultaneously spiritually enlightened by the divine grace, as confirmed in the *Bhagavad-gītā*.

TEXT 36

कुर्वाणा यत्र कर्माणि भगवच्छिक्षयासकृत् ।
गृणन्ति गुणनामानि कृष्णस्यानुस्मरन्ति च ॥ ३६ ॥

kurvāṇā yatra karmāṇi bhagavac-chikṣayāsakṛt
gṛṇanti guṇa-nāmāni kṛṣṇasyānusmaranti ca

kurvāṇāḥ—while performing; *yatra*—thereupon; *karmāṇi*—duties; *bhagavat*—the Personality of Godhead; *śikṣayā*—by the will of; *asakṛt*—constantly; *gṛṇanti*—takes on; *guṇa*—qualities; *nāmāni*—names; *kṛṣṇasya*—of Kṛṣṇa; *anusmaranti*—constantly remembers; *ca*—and.

While performing duties according to the order of Śrī Kṛṣṇa, the Supreme Personality of Godhead, one constantly remembers Him, His names and His qualities.

PURPORT An expert devotee of the Lord can mold his life in such a way that while performing all kinds of duties either for this or the next life, he can constantly remember the Lord's name, fame, qualities, etc. The order of the Lord is distinctly there in the *Bhagavad-gītā:* one should work only for the Lord in all spheres of life. In every sphere of life the Lord should be situated as the proprietor. According to the Vedic rites, even in the worship of some demigods like Indra, Brahmā, Sarasvatī and Gaṇeśa, the system is that in all circumstances the representation of Viṣṇu must be there as *yajñeśvara,* or the controlling power of such sacrifices. It is recommended that a particular demigod be worshiped for a particular purpose, but still the presence of Viṣṇu is compulsory in order to make the function proper.

Apart from such Vedic duties, even in our ordinary dealings (for example, in our household affairs or in our business or profession) we must consider that the result of all activities must be given over to the supreme enjoyer, Lord Kṛṣṇa. In the *Bhagavad-gītā* the Lord has declared Himself to be the supreme enjoyer of everything, the supreme proprietor of every planet and the supreme friend of all beings. No one else but Lord Śrī Kṛṣṇa can claim to be the proprietor of everything within His creation. A pure devotee remembers this constantly, and in doing so he repeats the transcendental name, fame and qualities of the Lord, which means that he is constantly in touch with the Lord. The Lord is identical with His name, fame, etc., and therefore to be associated with His name, fame, etc., constantly, means actually to associate with the Lord.

The major portion of our monetary income, not less than fifty percent, must be spent to carry out the order of Lord Kṛṣṇa. Not only should we give the profit of our earning to this cause, but we must also arrange to preach this cult of devotion to others because that is also one of the orders of the Lord. The Lord definitely says that no one is more dear to Him than one who is always engaged in the preaching work of the Lord's name and fame all over the world. The scientific discoveries of the material world can also be equally engaged in carrying out His order. He wants the message of the *Bhagavad-gītā* to be preached amongst His devotees. It may not be so done amongst those who have no credit of austerities, charity, education, etc. Therefore, the attempt must go on to convert unwilling men to become His devotees. Lord Caitanya has taught a very simple method in this connection. He has taught the lesson for preaching the transcendental message through singing, dancing and refreshment. As such, fifty percent of our income may be spent for this purpose. In this fallen age of quarrel and dissension, if only the leading and wealthy persons of society agree to spend fifty percent of their income in the service of the Lord, as it is taught by Lord Śrī Caitanya Mahāprabhu, there is absolute certainty of converting this hell of pandemonium to the transcendental abode of the Lord. No one will disagree to partake in a function where good singing, dancing and refreshment are administered. Everyone will attend such a function, and everyone is sure to feel individually the transcendental presence of the Lord. This alone will help the attendants associate with the Lord and thereby purify themselves in spiritual realization. The only condition for successfully executing such spiritual activities is that they must be conducted under the guidance of a pure devotee who is completely free from all mundane desires, fruitive activities and dry speculations about the nature of the Lord. No one has to discover the nature of the Lord. It is already spoken by the Lord Himself in the *Bhagavad-gītā* especially and in all other Vedic literatures generally. We have simply to accept them *in toto* and abide by the orders of the Lord. That will guide us to the path of perfection. One can remain in his own position. No one has to change his position, especially in this age of variegated difficulties. The only condition is that one must give up the habit of dry speculation aimed at becoming one with the Lord. And after giving up such lofty puffed-up vanities, one may very submissively receive the orders of the Lord in the *Bhagavad-gītā* or *Bhāgavatam* from the lips of a bona fide devotee whose qualification is mentioned above. That will make everything successful, without a doubt.

TEXT 37

ॐ नमो भगवते तुभ्यं वासुदेवाय धीमहि ।
प्रद्युम्नायानिरुद्धाय नमः सङ्कर्षणाय च ॥ ३७ ॥

oṁ namo bhagavate tubhyaṁ vāsudevāya dhīmahi
pradyumnāyāniruddhāya namaḥ saṅkarṣaṇāya ca

oṁ—the sign of chanting the transcendental glory of the Lord; *namaḥ*—offering obeisances unto the Lord; *bhagavate*—unto the Personality of Godhead; *tubhyam*—unto You; *vāsudevāya*—unto the Lord, the son of Vasudeva; *dhīmahi*—let us chant; *pradyumnāya, aniruddhāya* and *saṅkarṣaṇāya*—all plenary expansions of Vāsudeva; *namaḥ*—respectful obeisances; *ca*—and.

Let us all chant the glories of Vāsudeva along with His plenary expansions Pradyumna, Aniruddha and Saṅkarṣaṇa.

PURPORT According to *Pañcarātra,* Nārāyaṇa is the primeval cause of all expansions of Godhead. These are Vāsudeva, Saṅkarṣaṇa, Pradyumna and Aniruddha. Vāsudeva and Saṅkarṣaṇa are on the middle left and right, Pradyumna is on the right of Saṅkarṣaṇa, and Aniruddha is on the left of Vāsudeva, and thus the four Deities are situated. They are known as the four aides-de-camp of Lord Śrī Kṛṣṇa.

This is a Vedic hymn or *mantra* beginning with *oṁkāra praṇava,* and thus the *mantra* is established by the transcendental chanting process, namely, *oṁ namo dhīmahi,* etc.

The purport is that any transaction, either in the field of fruitive work or in empiric philosophy, which is not ultimately aimed at transcendental realization of the Supreme Lord is considered to be useless. Nāradajī has therefore explained the nature of unalloyed devotional service by his personal experience in the development of intimacy between the Lord and the living entity by a gradual process of progressive devotional activities. Such a progressive march of transcendental devotion for the Lord culminates in the attainment of loving service of the Lord, which is called *prema* in different transcendental variegatedness called *rasas* (tastes). Such devotional service is also executed in mixed forms, namely mixed with fruitive work or empiric philosophical speculations.

Now the question which was raised by the great *ṛṣis* headed by Śaunaka regarding the confidential part of Sūta's achievement through the spiritual masters is explained herein by the chanting of this hymn consisting of thirty-three letters. And this *mantra* is addressed to the four Deities, or the Lord with His plenary expansions. The central figure is Lord Śrī Kṛṣṇa because the plenary portions are His aides-de-camp. The most confidential part of the instruction is that one should always chant and remember the glories of the Lord Śrī Kṛṣṇa, the Supreme Personality of Godhead, along with His different plenary portions expanded as Vāsudeva, Saṅkarṣaṇa, Pradyumna and Aniruddha. Those expansions are the original Deities for all other truths, namely either *viṣṇu-tattva* or *śakti-tattvas*.

TEXT 38

इति मूर्त्यभिधानेन मन्त्रमूर्तिममूर्तिकम् ।
यजते यज्ञपुरुषं स सम्यग्दर्शनः पुमान् ॥ ३८ ॥

iti mūrty-abhidhānena mantra-mūrtim amūrtikam
yajate yajña-puruṣaṁ sa samyag darśanaḥ pumān

iti—thus; *mūrti*—representation; *abhidhānena*—in sound; *mantra-mūrtim*—form representation of transcendental sound; *amūrtikam*—the Lord, who has no material form; *yajate*—worship; *yajña*—Viṣṇu; *puruṣam*—the Personality of Godhead; *saḥ*—he alone; *samyak*—perfectly; *darśanaḥ*—one who has seen; *pumān*—person.

Thus he is the actual seer who worships, in the form of transcendental sound representation, the Supreme Personality of Godhead, Viṣṇu, who has no material form.

PURPORT Our present senses are all made of material elements, and therefore they are imperfect in realizing the transcendental form of Lord Viṣṇu. He is therefore worshiped by sound representation via the transcendental method of chanting. Anything which is beyond the scope of experience by our imperfect senses can be realized fully by the sound representation. A person transmitting sound from a far distant place can be factually experienced. If this is materially possible, why not spiritually? This experience is not a vague impersonal experience. It is actually an experience of the transcendental Personality of Godhead, who possesses the pure form of eternity, bliss and knowledge.

In the *Amarakośa* Sanskrit dictionary the word *mūrti* carries import in twofold meanings, namely, form and difficulty. Therefore *amūrtikam* is explained by Ācārya Śrī Viśvanātha Cakravartī Ṭhākura as meaning "without difficulty." The transcendental form of eternal bliss and knowledge can be experienced by our original spiritual senses, which can be revived by chanting of the holy *mantras,* or transcendental sound representations. Such sound should be received from the transparent agency of the bona fide spiritual master, and the chanting may be practiced by the direction of the spiritual master. That will gradually lead us nearer to the Lord. This method of worship is recommended in the *pāñcarātrika* system, which is both recognized and authorized. The *pāñcarātrika* system has the most authorized codes for transcendental devotional service. Without the help of such codes, one cannot approach the Lord, certainly not by dry philosophical speculation. The *pāñcarātrika* system is both practical and suitable for this age of quarrel. The *Pañcarātra* is more important than the *Vedānta* for this modern age.

TEXT 39

इमं स्वनिगमं ब्रह्मन्नवेत्य मदनुष्ठितम् ।
अदान्मे ज्ञानमैश्वर्यं स्वस्मिन् भावं च केशवः ॥ ३९ ॥

imaṁ sva-nigamaṁ brahmann avetya mad-anuṣṭhitam
adān me jñānam aiśvaryaṁ svasmin bhāvaṁ ca keśavaḥ

imam—thus; *sva-nigamam*—confidential knowledge of the *Vedas* in respect to the Supreme Personality of Godhead; *brahman*—O *brāhmaṇa* (Vyāsadeva); *avetya*—knowing it well; *mat*—by me; *anuṣṭhitam*—executed; *adāt*—bestowed upon me; *me*—me; *jñānam*—transcendental knowledge; *aiśvaryam*—opulence; *svasmin*—personal; *bhāvam*—intimate affection and love; *ca*—and; *keśavaḥ*—Lord Kṛṣṇa.

O brāhmaṇa, thus by the Supreme Lord Kṛṣṇa I was endowed first with the transcendental knowledge of the Lord as inculcated in the confidential parts of the Vedas, then with the spiritual opulences, and then with His intimate loving service.

PURPORT Communion with the Lord by transmission of the transcendental sound is nondifferent from the whole spirit Lord Śrī Kṛṣṇa. It is a completely perfect method for approaching the Lord. By such pure contact with the Lord, without offense of material conceptions (numbering ten), the devotee can rise above the material plane to understand the inner meaning of the Vedic literatures, including the Lord's existence in the transcendental realm. The Lord reveals His identity gradually to one who has unflinching faith, both in the spiritual master and in the Lord. After this, the devotee is endowed with mystic opulences, which are eight in number. And above all, the devotee is accepted in the confidential entourage of the Lord and is entrusted with specific service of the Lord through the agency of the spiritual master. A pure devotee is more interested in serving the Lord than in showing an exhibition of the mystic powers dormant in him. Śrī Nārada has explained all these from his personal experience, and one can obtain all the facilities which Śrī Nārada obtained by perfecting the chanting process of the sound representation of the Lord. There is no bar for chanting this transcendental sound by anyone, provided it is received through Nārada's representative, coming down by the chain of disciplic succession, or the *paramparā* system.

TEXT 40

त्वमप्यदभ्रश्रुत विश्रुतं विभोः
समाप्यते येन विदां बुभुत्सितम् ।
प्राख्याहि दुःखैर्मुहुरर्दितात्मनां
संक्लेशनिर्वाणमुशन्ति नान्यथा ॥ ४० ॥

tvam apy adabhra-śruta viśrutaṁ vibhoḥ
samāpyate yena vidāṁ bubhutsitam
prākhyāhi duḥkhair muhur arditātmanāṁ
saṅkleśa-nirvāṇam uśanti nānyathā

tvam—your good soul; *api*—also; *adabhra*—vast; *śruta*—Vedic literatures; *viśrutam*—have heard also; *vibhoḥ*—of the Almighty; *samāpyate*—satisfied; *yena*—by which; *vidām*—of the learned; *bubhutsitam*—who always desire to learn transcendental knowledge; *prākhyāhi*—describe; *duḥkhaiḥ*—by miseries; *muhuḥ*—always; *ardita-ātmanām*—suffering mass of people; *saṅkleśa*—sufferings; *nirvāṇam*—mitigation; *uśanti na*—do not get out of; *anyathā*—by other means.

Please, therefore, describe the Almighty Lord's activities which you have learned by your vast knowledge of the Vedas, for that will satisfy the hankerings of great learned men and at the same time mitigate the miseries of the masses of common people who are always suffering from material pangs. Indeed, there is no other way to get out of such miseries.

PURPORT Śrī Nārada Muni from practical experience definitely asserts that the prime solution of all problems of material work is to broadcast very widely the transcendental glories of the Supreme Lord. There are four classes of good men, and there are four classes of bad men also. The four classes of good men acknowledge the authority of the Almighty God, and therefore such good men (1) when they are in difficulty, (2) when they are in need of money, (3) when they are advanced in knowledge and (4) when they are inquisitive to know more and more about God, intuitively take shelter of the Lord. As such, Nāradajī advises Vyāsadeva to broadcast the transcendental knowledge of God in terms of the vast Vedic knowledge which he had already attained.

As far as the bad men are concerned, they are also four in number: (1) those who are simply addicted to the mode of progressive fruitive work and thus are subjected to the accompanying miseries, (2) those who are simply addicted to vicious work for sense satisfaction and so suffer the consequence, (3) those who are materially very much advanced in knowledge, but who suffer because they do not have the sense to acknowledge the authority of the Almighty Lord, and (4) the class of men who are known as atheists and who therefore purposely hate the very name of God, although they are always in difficulty.

Śrī Nāradajī advised Vyāsadeva to describe the glories of the Lord just to do good to all eight classes of men, both good and bad. *Śrīmad-Bhāgavatam* is therefore not meant for any particular class of men or sect. It is for the sincere soul who actually wants his own welfare and peace of mind.

Thus end the Bhaktivedanta purports of the First Canto, Fifth Chapter, of the Śrīmad-Bhāgavatam, *entitled "Nārada's Instructions on* Śrīmad-Bhāgavatam *for Vyāsadeva."*

CHAPTER SIX

Conversation Between Nārada and Vyāsadeva

सूत उवाच

TEXT 1

एवं निशम्य भगवान्देवर्षेर्जन्म कर्म च ।
भूयः पप्रच्छ तं ब्रह्मन् व्यासः सत्यवतीसुतः ॥ १ ॥

sūta uvāca
evaṁ niśamya bhagavān devarṣer janma karma ca
bhūyaḥ papraccha taṁ brahman vyāsaḥ satyavatī-sutaḥ

sūtaḥ uvāca—Sūta said; *evam*—thus; *niśamya*—hearing; *bhagavān*—the powerful incarnation of God; *devarṣeḥ*—of the great sage among the gods; *janma*—birth; *karma*—work; *ca*—and; *bhūyaḥ*—again; *papraccha*—asked; *tam*—him; *brahman*—O *brāhmaṇas; vyāsaḥ*—Vyāsadeva; *satyavatī-sutaḥ*—the son of Satyavatī.

Sūta said: O brāhmaṇas, thus hearing all about Śri Nārada's birth and activities, Vyāsadeva, the incarnation of God and son of Satyavatī, inquired as follows.

PURPORT Vyāsadeva was further inquisitive to know about the perfection of Nāradajī, and therefore he wanted to know about him more and more. In this chapter Nāradajī will describe how he was able to have a brief audience with the Lord while he was absorbed in the transcendental thought of separation from the Lord and when it was very painful for him.

व्यास उवाच

TEXT 2

भिक्षुभिर्विप्रवसिते विज्ञानादेष्टृभिस्तव ।
वर्तमानो वयस्याद्ये ततः किमकरोद्भवान् ॥ २ ॥

vyāsa uvāca
bhikṣubhir vipravasite vijñānādeṣṭṛbhis tava
vartamāno vayasy ādye tataḥ kim akarod bhavān

vyāsaḥ uvāca—Śrī Vyāsadeva said; *bhikṣubhiḥ*—by the great mendicants; *vipravasite*—having departed for other places; *vijñāna*—scientific knowledge in transcendence; *ādeṣṭṛbhiḥ*—those who had instructed; *tava*—of your; *vartamānaḥ*—present; *vayasi*—of the duration of life; *ādye*—before the beginning of; *tataḥ*—after that; *kim*—what; *akarot*—did; *bhavān*—your good self.

Śrī Vyāsadeva said: What did you [Nārada] do after the departure of the great sages who had instructed you in scientific transcendental knowledge before the beginning of your present birth?

PURPORT Vyāsadeva himself was the disciple of Nāradajī, and therefore it was natural to be anxious to hear what Nārada did after initiation from the spiritual masters. He wanted to follow in Nārada's footsteps in order to attain to the same perfect stage of life. This desire to inquire from the spiritual master is an essential factor to the progressive path. This process is technically known as *sad-dharma-pṛcchā*.

TEXT 3

स्वायम्भुव कया वृत्त्या वर्तितं ते परं वयः ।
कथं चेदमुदस्राक्षीः काले प्राप्ते कलेवरम् ॥ ३ ॥

svāyambhuva kayā vṛttyā vartitaṁ te paraṁ vayaḥ
kathaṁ cedam udasrākṣīḥ kāle prāpte kalevaram

svāyambhuva—O son of Brahmā; *kayā*—under what condition; *vṛttyā*—occupation; *vartitam*—was spent; *te*—you; *param*—after the initiation; *vayaḥ*—duration of life; *katham*—how; *ca*—and; *idam*—this; *udasrākṣīḥ*—did you quit; *kāle*—in due course; *prāpte*—having attained; *kalevaram*—body.

O son of Brahmā, how did you pass your life after initiation, and how did you attain this body, having quit your old one in due course?

PURPORT Śrī Nārada Muni in his previous life was just an ordinary maidservant's son, so how he became so perfectly transformed into the spiritual body of eternal life, bliss and knowledge is certainly important. Śrī Vyāsadeva desired him to disclose the facts for everyone's satisfaction.

TEXT 4

प्राक्कल्पविषयामेतां स्मृतिं ते मुनिसत्तम ।
न ह्येष व्यवधात्काल एष सर्वनिराकृतिः ॥ ४ ॥

prāk-kalpa-viṣayām etāṁ smṛtiṁ te muni-sattama
na hy eṣa vyavadhāt kāla eṣa sarva-nirākṛtiḥ

prāk—prior; *kalpa*—the duration of Brahmā's day; *viṣayām*—subject matter; *etām*—all these; *smṛtim*—remembrance; *te*—your; *muni-sattama*—O great sage; *na*—not; *hi*—certainly; *eṣaḥ*—all these; *vyavadhāt*—made any difference; *kālaḥ*—course of time; *eṣaḥ*—all these; *sarva*—all; *nirākṛtiḥ*—annihilation.

O great sage, time annihilates everything in due course, so how is it that this subject matter, which happened prior to this day of Brahmā, is still fresh in your memory, undisturbed by time?

PURPORT As spirit is not annihilated even after the annihilation of the material body, so also spiritual consciousness is not annihilated. Śrī Nārada developed this spiritual consciousness even when he had his material body in the previous *kalpa.* Consciousness of the material body means spiritual consciousness expressed through the medium of a material body. This consciousness is inferior, destructible and perverted. But superconsciousness of the supramind in the spiritual plane is as good as the spirit soul and is never annihilated.

नारद उवाच

TEXT 5

भिक्षुभिर्विप्रवसिते विज्ञानादेष्टृभिर्मम ।
वर्तमानो वयस्याद्ये तत एतदकारषम् ॥ ५ ॥

nārada uvāca
bhikṣubhir vipravasite vijñānādeṣṭṛbhir mama
vartamāno vayasy ādye tata etad akāraṣam

nāradaḥ uvāca—Śrī Nārada said; *bhikṣubhiḥ*—by the great sages; *vipravasite*—having departed for other places; *vijñāna*—scientific spiritual knowledge; *ādeṣṭṛbhiḥ*—those who imparted unto me; *mama*—mine; *vartamānaḥ*—present; *vayasi ādye*—before this life; *tataḥ*—thereafter; *etat*—this much; *akāraṣam*—performed.

Śrī Nārada said: The great sages, who had imparted scientific knowledge of transcendence to me, departed for other places, and I had to pass my life in this way.

PURPORT In his previous life, when Nāradajī was impregnated with spiritual knowledge by the grace of the great sages, there was a tangible change in his life, although he was only a boy of five years. That is an important symptom visible after initiation by the bona fide spiritual master. Actual association of devotees brings about a quick change in life for spiritual realization. How it so acted upon the previous life of Śrī Nārada Muni is described by and by in this chapter.

TEXT 6

एकात्मजा मे जननी योषिन्मूढा च किङ्करी ।
मय्यात्मजेऽनन्यगतौ चक्रे स्नेहानुबन्धनम् ॥ ६ ॥

ekātmajā me jananī yoṣin mūḍhā ca kiṅkarī
mayy ātmaje 'nanya-gatau cakre snehānubandhanam

eka-ātmajā—having only one son; *me*—my; *jananī*—mother; *yoṣit*—woman by class; *mūḍhā*—foolish; *ca*—and; *kiṅkarī*—maidservant; *mayi*—unto me; *ātmaje*—being her offspring; *ananya-gatau*—one who has no alternative for protection; *cakre*—did it; *sneha-anubandhanam*—tied by affectionate bondage.

I was the only son of my mother, who was not only a simple woman but a maidservant as well. Since I was her only offspring, she had no other

alternative for protection: she bound me with the tie of affection.

TEXT 7

सास्वतन्त्रा न कल्पासीद्योगक्षेमं ममेच्छती ।
ईशस्य हि वशे लोको योषा दारुमयी यथा ॥ ७ ॥

sāsvatantrā na kalpāsīd yoga-kṣemaṁ mamecchatī
īśasya hi vaśe loko yoṣā dārumayī yathā

sā—she; *asvatantrā*—was dependent; *na*—not; *kalpā*—able; *āsīt*—was; *yoga-kṣemam*—maintenance; *mama*—my; *icchatī*—although desirous; *īśasya*—of providence; *hi*—for; *vaśe*—under the control of; *lokaḥ*—everyone; *yoṣā*—doll; *dāru-mayī*—made of wood; *yathā*—as much as.

She wanted to look after my maintenance properly, but because she was not independent, she was not able to do anything for me. The world is under the full control of the Supreme Lord; therefore everyone is like a wooden doll in the hands of a puppet master.

TEXT 8

अहं च तद्ब्रह्मकुले ऊषिवांस्तदुपेक्षया ।
दिग्देशकालाव्युत्पन्नो बालकः पञ्चहायनः ॥ ८ ॥

ahaṁ ca tad-brahma-kule ūṣivāṁs tad-upekṣayā
dig-deśa-kālāvyutpanno bālakaḥ pañca-hāyanaḥ

aham—I; *ca*—also; *tat*—that; *brahma-kule*—in the school of the *brāhmaṇas; ūṣivān*—lived; *tat*—her; *upekṣayā*—being dependent on; *dik-deśa*—direction and country; *kāla*—time; *avyutpannaḥ*—having no experience; *bālakaḥ*—a mere child; *pañca*—five; *hāyanaḥ*—years old.

When I was a mere child of five years, I lived in a brāhmaṇa school. I was dependent on my mother's affection and had no experience of different lands.

TEXT 9

एकदा निर्गतां गेहाद्दुहन्तीं निशि गां पथि ।
सर्पोऽदशत्पदा स्पृष्टः कृपणां कालचोदितः ॥ ९ ॥

ekadā nirgatāṁ gehād duhantīṁ niśi gāṁ pathi
sarpo 'daśat padā spṛṣṭaḥ kṛpaṇāṁ kāla-coditaḥ

ekadā—once upon a time; *nirgatām*—having gone away; *gehāt*—from home; *duhantīm*—for milking; *niśi*—at night; *gām*—the cow; *pathi*—on the path; *sarpaḥ*—snake; *adaśat*—bitten; *padā*—on the leg; *spṛṣṭaḥ*—thus struck; *kṛpaṇām*—the poor woman; *kāla-coditaḥ*—influenced by supreme time.

Once upon a time, my poor mother, when going out one night to milk a cow, was bitten on the leg by a serpent, influenced by supreme time.

PURPORT That is the way of dragging a sincere soul nearer to God. The poor boy was being looked after only by his affectionate mother, and yet the mother was taken from the world by the supreme will in order to put him completely at the mercy of the Lord.

TEXT 10

तदा तदहमीशस्य भक्तानां शमभीप्सतः ।
अनुग्रहं मन्यमानः प्रातिष्ठं दिशमुत्तराम् ॥ १० ॥

tadā tad aham īśasya bhaktānāṁ śam abhīpsataḥ
anugrahaṁ manyamānaḥ prātiṣṭhaṁ diśam uttarām

tadā—at that time; *tat*—that; *aham*—I; *īśasya*—of the Lord; *bhaktānām*—of the devotees; *śam*—mercy; *abhīpsataḥ*—desiring; *anugraham*—special benediction; *manyamānaḥ*—thinking in that way; *prātiṣṭham*—departed; *diśam uttarām*—in the northern direction.

I took this as the special mercy of the Lord, who always desires benediction for His devotees, and so thinking, I started for the north.

PURPORT Confidential devotees of the Lord see in every step a benedictory direction of the Lord. What is considered to be an odd or difficult moment in the mundane sense is accepted as special mercy of the Lord. Mundane prosperity is a kind of material fever, and by the grace of the Lord the temperature of this material fever is gradually diminished, and spiritual health is obtained step by step. Mundane people misunderstand it.

TEXT 11

स्फीताञ्जनपदांस्तत्र पुरग्रामव्रजाकरान् ।
खेटखर्वटवाटीश्च वनान्युपवनानि च ॥ ११ ॥

sphītāñ janapadāṁs tatra pura-grāma-vrajākarān
kheṭa-kharvaṭa-vāṭīś ca vanāny upavanāni ca

sphītān—very flourishing; *jana-padān*—metropolises; *tatra*—there; *pura*—towns; *grāma*—villages; *vraja*—big farms; *ākarān*—mineral fields (mines); *kheṭa*—agricultural lands; *kharvaṭa*—valleys; *vāṭīḥ*—flower gardens; *ca*—and; *vanāni*—forests; *upavanāni*—nursery gardens; *ca*—and.

After my departure, I passed through many flourishing metropolises, towns, villages, animal farms, mines, agricultural lands, valleys, flower gardens, nursery gardens and natural forests.

PURPORT Man's activities in agriculture, mining, farming, industries, gardening, etc., were all on the same scale as they are now, even previous to the present creation, and the same activities will remain as they are, even in the next creation. After many hundreds of millions of years, one creation is started by the law of nature, and the history of the universe repeats itself practically in the same way. The mundane wranglers waste time with archaeological excavations without searching into the vital necessities of life. After getting an impetus in spiritual life, Śrī Nārada Muni, even though a mere child, did not waste time for a single moment with economic development, although he passed towns and villages, mines and industries. He continually went on to progressive spiritual emancipation. *Śrīmad-Bhāgavatam* is the repetition of history which happened some hundreds of millions of years ago. As it was said hereinbefore, only the most important factors of history are picked up to be recorded in this transcendental literature.

TEXT 12

चित्रधातुविचित्राद्रीनिभभग्नभुजद्रुमान् ।
जलाशयाञ्छिवजलान्नलिनीः सुरसेविताः ।
चित्रस्वनैः पत्ररथैर्विभ्रमद्भ्रमरश्रियः ॥ १२ ॥

citra-dhātu-vicitrādrīn ibha-bhagna-bhuja-drumān
jalāśayāñ chiva-jalān nalinīḥ sura-sevitāḥ
citra-svanaiḥ patra-rathair vibhramad bhramara-śriyaḥ

citra-dhātu—valuable minerals like gold, silver and copper; *vicitra*—full of variegatedness; *adrīn*—hills and mountains; *ibha-bhagna*—broken by the giant elephants; *bhuja*—branches; *drumān*—trees; *jalāśayān śiva*—health-giving; *jalān*—reservoirs of water; *nalinīḥ*—lotus flowers; *sura-sevitāḥ*—aspired to by the denizens of heaven; *citra-svanaiḥ*—pleasing to the heart; *patra-rathaiḥ*—by the birds; *vibhramat*—bewildering; *bhramara-śriyaḥ*—decorated by drones.

I passed through hills and mountains full of reservoirs of various minerals like gold, silver and copper, and through tracts of land with reservoirs of water filled with beautiful lotus flowers, fit for the denizens of heaven, decorated with bewildered bees and singing birds.

TEXT 13

नलवेणुशरस्तन्बकुशकीचकगह्वरम् ।
एक एवातियातोऽहमद्राक्षं विपिनं महत् ।
घोरं प्रतिभयाकारं व्यालोलूकशिवाजिरम् ॥ १३ ॥

nala-veṇu-śaras-tanba- kuśa-kīcaka-gahvaram
eka evātiyāto 'ham adrākṣaṁ vipinaṁ mahat
ghoraṁ pratibhayākāraṁ vyālolūka-śivājiram

nala—pipes; *veṇu*—bamboo; *śaraḥ*—pens; *tanba*—full of; *kuśa*—sharp grass; *kīcaka*—weeds; *gahvaram*—caves; *ekaḥ*—alone; *eva*—only; *atiyātaḥ*—difficult to go through; *aham*—I; *adrākṣam*—visited; *vipinam*—deep forests; *mahat*—great; *ghoram*—fearful; *pratibhaya-ākāram*—dangerously; *vyāla*—snakes; *ulūka*—owls; *śiva*—jackals; *ajiram*—playgrounds.

I then passed alone through many forests of rushes, bamboo, reeds, sharp grass, weeds and caves, which were very difficult to go through alone. I visited deep, dark and dangerously fearful forests, which were the play yards of snakes, owls and jackals.

His Divine Grace A. C. Bhaktivedanta Swami Prabhupāda

The Founder-Ācārya of ISKCON and greatest exponent of Kṛṣṇa consciousness in the Western world.

The scripture named *Śrīmad-Bhāgavatam* is the literary incarnation of God. Compiled by Śrīla Vyāsadeva, the incarnation of God, it is meant for the ultimate good of all people. It is all-successful, all-blissful and all-perfect. (p. 174)

The beautiful *Bhāgavatam* is sufficient in itself for God realization. As soon as one attentively and submissively hears the message of the *Bhāgavatam*, by this culture of knowledge the Supreme Lord is established within one's heart. (p. 50)

Śrīmad-Bhāgavatam was composed about five thousand years ago, and Lord Buddha appeared about twenty-six hundred years ago. Therefore in the *Śrīmad-Bhāgavatam* Lord Buddha is foretold. Such is the authority of this clear scripture. (p. 155)

The present age, Kali-yuga, lasts 432,000 years, out of which we have passed only 5,000. So there are 427,000 years left. The *Śrīmad-Bhāgavatam* predicts that at the end of this period Lord Kṛṣṇa will appear as the incarnation known as Kalki. (p. 156)

The *Śrīmad-Bhāgavatam* is as brilliant as the sun, and it has arisen just after the departure of Lord Kṛṣṇa to His own abode, accompanied by religion, knowledge, etc. Persons who have lost their vision due to the dense darkness of ignorance in the Age of Kali shall get light from this *Purāṇa*. (pp. 177–78)

To revolve in the cycle of transmigration is an imprisoned life for the condemned conditioned souls. The human form of life is a chance to get out of this imprisoned life, and as such the only occupation of the human being is to reestablish his lost relationship with God. (p. 227)

Lord Śrī Kṛṣṇa, the Personality of Godhead, along with Balarāma, played like a human being, and so masked He performed many superhuman acts. These pastimes are elaborately described in the Tenth Canto of *Śrīmad-Bhāgavatam*. (pp. 75–76)

PURPORT It is the duty of a mendicant (*parivrājakācārya*) to experience all varieties of God's creation by traveling alone through all forests, hills, towns, villages, etc., to gain faith in God and strength of mind as well as to enlighten the inhabitants with the message of God. A *sannyāsī* is duty-bound to take all these risks without fear, and the most typical *sannyāsī* of the present age is Lord Caitanya, who traveled in the same manner through the central Indian jungles, enlightening even the tigers, bears, snakes, deer, elephants and many other jungle animals. In this age of Kali, *sannyāsa* is forbidden for ordinary men. One who changes his dress to make propaganda is a different man from the original ideal *sannyāsī*. One should, however, take the vow to stop social intercourse completely and devote life exclusively to the service of the Lord. The change of dress is only a formality. Lord Caitanya did not accept the name of a *sannyāsī*, and in this age of Kali the so-called *sannyāsīs* should not change their former names, following in the footsteps of Lord Caitanya. In this age, devotional service of hearing and repeating the holy glories of the Lord is strongly recommended, and one who takes the vow of renunciation of family life need not imitate the *parivrājakācārya* like Nārada or Lord Caitanya, but may sit down at some holy place and devote his whole time and energy to hear and repeatedly chant the holy scriptures left by the great *ācāryas* like the Six Gosvāmīs of Vṛndāvana.

TEXT 14

परिश्रान्तेन्द्रियात्माहं तृट्परीतो बुभुक्षितः ।
स्नात्वा पीत्वा ह्रदे नद्या उपस्पृष्टो गतश्रमः ॥ १४ ॥

pariśrāntendriyātmāhaṁ tṛṭ-parīto bubhukṣitaḥ
snātvā pītvā hrade nadyā upaspṛṣṭo gata-śramaḥ

pariśrānta—being tired; *indriya*—bodily; *ātmā*—mentally; *aham*—I; *tṛṭ-parītaḥ*—being thirsty; *bubhukṣitaḥ*—and hungry; *snātvā*—taking a bath; *pītvā*—and drinking water also; *hrade*—in the lake; *nadyāḥ*—of a river; *upaspṛṣṭaḥ*—being in contact with; *gata*—got relief from; *śramaḥ*—tiredness.

Thus traveling, I felt tired, both bodily and mentally, and I was both thirsty and hungry. So I took a bath in a river lake and also drank water. By contacting water, I got relief from my exhaustion.

PURPORT A traveling mendicant can meet the needs of body, namely thirst and hunger, by the gifts of nature without being a beggar at the doors of the householders. The mendicant therefore does not go to the house of a householder to beg but to enlighten him spiritually.

TEXT 15

तस्मिन्निर्मनुजेऽरण्ये पिप्पलोपस्थ आश्रितः ।
आत्मनात्मानमात्मस्थं यथाश्रुतमचिन्तयम् ॥ १५ ॥

tasmin nirmanuje 'raṇye pippalopastha āśritaḥ
ātmanātmānam ātmasthaṁ yathā-śrutam acintayam

tasmin—in that; *nirmanuje*—without human habitation; *araṇye*—in the forest; *pippala*—banyan tree; *upasthe*—sitting under it; *āśritaḥ*—taking shelter of; *ātmanā*—by intelligence; *ātmānam*—the Supersoul; *ātmastham*—situated within myself; *yathā-śrutam*—as I had heard it from the liberated souls; *acintayam*—thought over.

After that, under the shadow of a banyan tree in an uninhabited forest I began to meditate upon the Supersoul situated within, using my intelligence, as I had learned from liberated souls.

PURPORT One should not meditate according to one's personal whims. One should know perfectly well from the authoritative sources of scriptures through the transparent medium of a bona fide spiritual master and by proper use of one's trained intelligence for meditating upon the Supersoul dwelling within every living being. This consciousness is firmly developed by a devotee who has rendered loving service unto the Lord by carrying out the orders of the spiritual master. Śrī Nāradajī contacted bona fide spiritual masters, served them sincerely and got enlightenment rightly. Thus he began to meditate.

TEXT 16

ध्यायतश्चरणाम्भोजं भावनिर्जितचेतसा ।
औत्कण्ठ्याश्रुकलाक्षस्य हृद्यासीन्मे शनैर्हरिः ॥ १६ ॥

dhyāyataś caraṇāmbhojaṁ bhāva-nirjita-cetasā
autkaṇṭhyāśru-kalākṣasya hṛdy āsīn me śanair hariḥ

dhyāyataḥ—thus meditating upon; *caraṇa-ambhojam*—the lotus feet of the localized Personality of Godhead; *bhāva-nirjita*—mind transformed in transcendental love for the Lord; *cetasā*—all mental activities (thinking, feeling and willing); *autkaṇṭhya*—eagerness; *aśru-kala*—tears rolled down; *akṣasya*—of the eyes; *hṛdi*—within my heart; *āsīt*—appeared; *me*—my; *śanaiḥ*—without delay; *hariḥ*—the Personality of Godhead.

As soon as I began to meditate upon the lotus feet of the Personality of Godhead with my mind transformed in transcendental love, tears rolled down my eyes, and without delay the Personality of Godhead Śrī Kṛṣṇa appeared on the lotus of my heart.

PURPORT The word *bhāva* is significant here. This *bhāva* stage is attained after one has transcendental affection for the Lord. The first initial stage is called *śraddhā,* or a liking for the Supreme Lord, and in order to increase that liking one has to associate with pure devotees of the Lord. The third stage is to practice the prescribed rules and regulations of devotional service. This will dissipate all sorts of misgivings and remove all personal deficiencies that hamper progress in devotional service.

When all misgivings and personal deficiencies are removed, there is a standard faith in transcendental matter, and the taste for it increases in greater proportion. This stage leads to attraction, and after this there is *bhāva,* or the prior stage of unalloyed love for God. All the above different stages are but different stages of development of transcendental love. Being so surcharged with transcendental love, there comes a strong feeling of separation which leads to eight different kinds of ecstasies. Tears from the eyes of a devotee are an automatic reaction, and because Śrī Nārada Muni in his previous birth attained that stage very quickly after his departure from home, it was quite possible for him to perceive the actual presence of the Lord, which he tangibly experienced by his developed spiritual senses without material tinge.

TEXT 17

प्रेमातिभरनिर्भिन्नपुलकाङ्गोऽतिनिर्वृतः ।
आनन्दसम्प्लवे लीनो नापश्यमुभयं मुने ॥ १७ ॥

premātibhara-nirbhinna- pulakāṅgo 'tinirvṛtaḥ
ānanda-samplave līno nāpaśyam ubhayaṁ mune

premā—love; *atibhara*—excessive; *nirbhinna*—especially distinguished; *pulaka*—feelings of happiness; *aṅgaḥ*—different bodily parts; *ati-nirvṛtaḥ*—being fully overwhelmed; *ānanda*—ecstasy; *samplave*—in the ocean of; *līnaḥ*—absorbed in; *na*—not; *apaśyam*—could see; *ubhayam*—both; *mune*—O Vyāsadeva.

O Vyāsadeva, at that time, being exceedingly overpowered by feelings of happiness, every part of my body became separately enlivened. Being absorbed in an ocean of ecstasy, I could see neither myself nor the Lord.

PURPORT Spiritual feelings of happiness and intense ecstasies have no mundane comparison. Therefore it is very difficult to give expression to such feelings. We can just have a glimpse of such ecstasy in the words of Śrī Nārada Muni. Each and every part of the body or senses has its particular function. After seeing the Lord, all the senses become fully awakened to render service unto the Lord because in the liberated state the senses are fully efficient in serving the Lord. As such, in that transcendental ecstasy it so happened that the senses became separately enlivened to serve the Lord. This being so, Nārada Muni lost sight of both himself and the Lord simultaneously.

TEXT 18

रूपं भगवतो यत्तन्मनःकान्तं शुचापहम् ।
अपश्यन् सहसोत्तस्थे वैक्लव्याद्दुर्मना इव ॥ १८ ॥

rūpaṁ bhagavato yat tan manaḥ-kāntaṁ śucāpaham
apaśyan sahasottasthe vaiklavyād durmanā iva

rūpam—form; *bhagavataḥ*—of the Personality of Godhead; *yat*—as it is; *tat*—that; *manaḥ*—of the mind; *kāntam*—as it desires; *śuca-apaham*—vanishing all disparity; *apaśyan*—without seeing; *sahasā*—all of a sudden; *uttasthe*—got up; *vaiklavyāt*—being perturbed; *durmanāḥ*—having lost the desirable; *iva*—as it were.

The transcendental form of the Lord, as it is, satisfies the mind's desire and at once erases all mental incongruities. Upon losing sight of that

form, I suddenly got up, being perturbed, as is usual when one loses that which is desirable.

PURPORT That the Lord is not formless is experienced by Nārada Muni. But His form is completely different from all forms of our material experience. For the whole duration of our life we go on seeing different forms in the material world, but none of them is just apt to satisfy the mind, nor can any one of them vanish all perturbance of the mind. These are the special features of the transcendental form of the Lord, and one who has once seen that form is not satisfied with anything else; no form in the material world can any longer satisfy the seer. That the Lord is formless or impersonal means that He has nothing like a material form and is not like any material personality.

As spiritual beings, having eternal relations with that transcendental form of the Lord, we are, life after life, searching after that form of the Lord, and we are not satisfied by any other form of material appeasement. Nārada Muni got a glimpse of this, but having not seen it again he became perturbed and stood up all of a sudden to search it out. What we desire life after life was obtained by Nārada Muni, and losing sight of Him again was certainly a great shock for him.

TEXT 19

दिदृक्षुस्तदहं भूयः प्रणिधाय मनो हृदि ।
वीक्षमाणोऽपि नापश्यमवितृप्त इवातुरः ॥ १९ ॥

didṛkṣus tad ahaṁ bhūyaḥ praṇidhāya mano hṛdi
vīkṣamāṇo 'pi nāpaśyam avitṛpta ivāturaḥ

didṛkṣuḥ—desiring to see; *tat*—that; *aham*—I; *bhūyaḥ*—again; *praṇidhāya*—having concentrated the mind; *manaḥ*—mind; *hṛdi*—upon the heart; *vīkṣamāṇaḥ*—waiting to see; *api*—in spite of; *na*—never; *apaśyam*—saw Him; *avitṛptaḥ*—without being satisfied; *iva*—like; *āturaḥ*—aggrieved.

I desired to see again that transcendental form of the Lord, but despite my attempts to concentrate upon the heart with eagerness to view the form again, I could not see Him any more, and thus dissatisfied, I was very much aggrieved.

PURPORT There is no mechanical process to see the form of the Lord. It completely depends on the causeless mercy of the Lord. We cannot demand the Lord to be present before our vision, just as we cannot demand the sun to rise whenever we like. The sun rises out of his own accord; so also the Lord is pleased to be present out of His causeless mercy. One should simply await the opportune moment and go on discharging his prescribed duty in devotional service of the Lord. Nārada Muni thought that the Lord could be seen again by the same mechanical process which was successful in the first attempt, but in spite of his utmost endeavor he could not make the second attempt successful. The Lord is completely independent of all obligations. He can simply be bound up by the tie of unalloyed devotion. Nor is He visible or perceivable by our material senses. When He pleases, being satisfied with the sincere attempt of devotional service depending completely on the mercy of the Lord, then He may be seen out of His own accord.

TEXT 20

एवं यतन्तं विजने मामाहागोचरो गिराम् ।
गम्भीरश्लक्ष्णया वाचा शुचः प्रशमयन्निव ॥ २० ॥

evaṁ yatantaṁ vijane mām āhāgocaro girām
gambhīra-ślakṣṇayā vācā śucaḥ praśamayann iva

evam—thus; *yatantam*—one who is engaged in attempting; *vijane*—in that lonely place; *mām*—unto me; *āha*—said; *agocaraḥ*—beyond the range of physical sound; *girām*—utterances; *gambhīra*—grave; *ślakṣṇayā*—pleasing to hear; *vācā*—words; *śucaḥ*—grief; *praśamayan*—mitigating; *iva*—like.

Seeing my attempts in that lonely place, the Personality of Godhead, who is transcendental to all mundane description, spoke to me with gravity and pleasing words, just to mitigate my grief.

PURPORT In the *Vedas* it is said that God is beyond the approach of mundane words and intelligence. And yet by His causeless mercy one can have suitable senses to hear Him or to speak to Him. This is the Lord's inconceivable energy. One upon whom His mercy is bestowed can hear Him.

The Lord was much pleased with Nārada Muni, and therefore the necessary strength was invested in him so that he could hear the Lord. It is not, however, possible for others to perceive directly the touch of the Lord during the probationary stage of regulative devotional service. It was a special gift for Nārada. When he heard the pleasing words of the Lord, the feelings of separation were to some extent mitigated. A devotee in love with God feels always the pangs of separation and is therefore always enwrapped in transcendental ecstasy.

TEXT 21

हन्तास्मिञ्जन्मनि भवान्मा मां द्रष्टुमिहार्हति ।
अविपक्वकषायाणां दुर्दर्शोऽहं कुयोगिनाम् ॥ २१ ॥

hantāsmiñ janmani bhavān mā māṁ draṣṭum ihārhati
avipakva-kaṣāyāṇāṁ durdarśo 'haṁ kuyoginām

hanta—O Nārada; *asmin*—this; *janmani*—duration of life; *bhavān*—yourself; *mā*—not; *mām*—Me; *draṣṭum*—to see; *iha*—here; *arhati*—deserve; *avipakva*—immature; *kaṣāyāṇām*—material dirt; *durdarśaḥ*—difficult to be seen; *aham*—I; *kuyoginām*—incomplete in service.

O Nārada [the Lord spoke], I regret that during this lifetime you will not be able to see Me anymore. Those who are incomplete in service and who are not completely free from all material taints can hardly see Me.

PURPORT The Personality of Godhead is described in the *Bhagavad-gītā* as the most pure, the Supreme and the Absolute Truth. There is no trace of a tinge of materiality in His person, and thus one who has the slightest tinge of material affection cannot approach Him. The beginning of devotional service starts from the point when one is freed from at least two forms of material modes, namely the mode of passion and the mode of ignorance. The result is exhibited by the signs of being freed from *kāma* (lust) and *lobha* (covetousness). That is to say, one must be freed from the desires for sense satisfaction and avarice for sense gratification. The balanced mode of nature is goodness. And to be completely freed from all material tinges is to become free from the mode of goodness also. To search the audience of God in a lonely forest is considered to be in the mode of goodness. One can go out into the forest to attain spiritual perfection, but that does not mean that one can see the Lord personally there. One must be completely freed from all material attachment and be situated on the plane of transcendence, which alone will help the devotee get in personal touch with the Personality of Godhead. The best method is that one should live at a place where the transcendental form of the Lord is worshiped. The temple of the Lord is a transcendental place, whereas the forest is a materially good habitation. A neophyte devotee is always recommended to worship the Deity of the Lord (*arcanā*) rather than go into the forest to search out the Lord. Devotional service begins from the process of *arcanā*, which is better than going out in the forest. In his present life, which is completely freed from all material hankerings, Śrī Nārada Muni does not go into the forest, although he can turn every place into Vaikuṇṭha by his presence only. He travels from one planet to another to convert men, gods, Kinnaras, Gandharvas, *ṛṣis*, *munis* and all others to become devotees of the Lord. By his activities he has engaged many devotees like Prahlāda Mahārāja, Dhruva Mahārāja and many others in the transcendental service of the Lord. A pure devotee of the Lord, therefore, follows in the footsteps of the great devotees like Nārada and Prahlāda and engages his whole time in glorifying the Lord by the process of *kīrtana*. Such a preaching process is transcendental to all material qualities.

TEXT 22

सकृद्यद् दर्शितं रूपमेतत्कामाय तेऽनघ ।
मत्कामः शनकैः साधु सर्वान्मुञ्चति हृच्छयान् ॥ २२ ॥

sakṛd yad darśitaṁ rūpam etat kāmāya te 'nagha
mat-kāmaḥ śanakaiḥ sādhu sarvān muñcati hṛc-chayān

sakṛt—once only; *yat*—that; *darśitam*—shown; *rūpam*—form; *etat*—this is; *kāmāya*—for hankerings; *te*—your; *anagha*—O virtuous one; *mat*—Mine; *kāmaḥ*—desire; *śanakaiḥ*—by increasing; *sādhuḥ*—devotee; *sarvān*—all; *muñcati*—gives away; *hṛt-śayān*—material desires.

O virtuous one, you have only once seen My person, and this is just to

increase your desire for Me, because the more you hanker for Me, the more you will be freed from all material desires.

PURPORT A living being cannot be vacant of desires. He is not a dead stone. He must be working, thinking, feeling and willing. But when he thinks, feels and wills materially, he becomes entangled, and conversely when he thinks, feels and wills for the service of the Lord, he becomes gradually freed from all entanglement. The more a person is engaged in the transcendental loving service of the Lord, the more he acquires a hankering for it. That is the transcendental nature of godly service. Material service has satiation, whereas spiritual service of the Lord has neither satiation nor end. One can go on increasing his hankerings for the loving transcendental service of the Lord, and yet he will not find satiation or end. By intense service of the Lord, one can experience the presence of the Lord transcendentally. Therefore seeing the Lord means being engaged in His service because His service and His person are identical. The sincere devotee should go on with sincere service of the Lord. The Lord will give proper direction as to how and where it has to be done. There was no material desire in Nārada, and yet just to increase his intense desire for the Lord, he was so advised.

TEXT 23

सत्सेवयादीर्घयापि जाता मयि दृढा मतिः ।
हित्वावद्यमिमं लोकं गन्ता मज्जनतामसि ॥ २३ ॥

sat-sevayādīrghayāpi jātā mayi dṛḍhā matiḥ
hitvāvadyam imaṁ lokaṁ gantā maj-janatām asi

sat-sevayā—by service of the Absolute Truth; *adīrghayā*—for some days; *api*—even; *jātā*—having attained; *mayi*—unto Me; *dṛḍhā*—firm; *matiḥ*—intelligence; *hitvā*—having given up; *avadyam*—deplorable; *imam*—this; *lokam*—material worlds; *gantā*—going to; *mat-janatām*—My associates; *asi*—become.

By service of the Absolute Truth, even for a few days, a devotee attains firm and fixed intelligence in Me. Consequently he goes on to become My associate in the transcendental world after giving up the present deplorable material worlds.

PURPORT Serving the Absolute Truth means rendering service unto the Absolute Personality of Godhead under the direction of the bona fide spiritual master, who is a transparent medium between the Lord and the neophyte devotee. The neophyte devotee has no ability to approach the Absolute Personality of Godhead by the strength of his present imperfect material senses, and therefore under the direction of the spiritual master he is trained in transcendental service of the Lord. And by such training, even for some days, the neophyte devotee gets intelligence in such transcendental service, which leads him ultimately to get free from perpetual inhabitation in the material worlds and to be promoted to the transcendental world to become one of the liberated associates of the Lord in the kingdom of God.

TEXT 24

मतिर्मयि निबद्धेयं न विपद्येत कर्हिचित् ।
प्रजासर्गनिरोधेऽपि स्मृतिश्च मदनुग्रहात् ॥ २४ ॥

matir mayi nibaddheyaṁ na vipadyeta karhicit
prajā-sarga-nirodhe 'pi smṛtiś ca mad-anugrahāt

matiḥ—intelligence; *mayi*—devoted to Me; *nibaddhā*—engaged; *iyam*—this; *na*—never; *vipadyeta*—separate; *karhicit*—at any time; *prajā*—living beings; *sarga*—at the time of creation; *nirodhe*—also at the time of annihilation; *api*—even; *smṛtiḥ*—remembrance; *ca*—and; *mat*—Mine; *anugrahāt*—by the mercy of.

Intelligence engaged in My devotion cannot be thwarted at any time. Even at the time of creation, as well as at the time of annihilation, your remembrance will continue by My mercy.

PURPORT Devotional service rendered to the Personality of Godhead never goes in vain. Since the Personality of Godhead is eternal, intelligence applied in His service or anything done in His relation is also permanent. In the *Bhagavad-gītā* it is said that such transcendental service rendered unto the Personality of Godhead accumulates birth after birth, and when the devotee is fully matured, the total service counted together makes him eligible to enter into the association of the Personality of Godhead. Such accumulation of God's service is never vanquished, but increases till fully matured.

TEXT 25

एतावदुक्त्वोपरराम तन्महद्
भूतं नभोलिङ्गमलिङ्गमीश्वरम् ।
अहं च तस्मै महतां महीयसे
शीर्ष्णावनामं विदधेऽनुकम्पितः ॥ २५ ॥

etāvad uktvopararāma tan mahad
bhūtaṁ nabho-liṅgam aliṅgam īśvaram
ahaṁ ca tasmai mahatāṁ mahīyase
śīrṣṇāvanāmaṁ vidadhe 'nukampitaḥ

etāvat—thus; *uktvā*—spoken; *upararāma*—stopped; *tat*—that; *mahat*—great; *bhūtam*—wonderful; *nabhaḥ-liṅgam*—personified by sound; *aliṅgam*—unseen by the eyes; *īśvaram*—the supreme authority; *aham*—I; *ca*—also; *tasmai*—unto Him; *mahatām*—the great; *mahīyase*—unto the glorified; *śīrṣṇā*—by the head; *avanāmam*—obeisances; *vidadhe*—executed; *anukampitaḥ*—being favored by Him.

Then that supreme authority, personified by sound and unseen by eyes, but most wonderful, stopped speaking. Feeling a sense of gratitude, I offered my obeisances unto Him, bowing my head.

PURPORT That the Personality of Godhead was not seen but only heard does not make any difference. The Personality of Godhead produced the four *Vedas* by His breathing, and He is seen and realized through the transcendental sound of the *Vedas*. Similarly, the *Bhagavad-gītā* is the sound representation of the Lord, and there is no difference in identity. The conclusion is that the Lord can be seen and heard by persistent chanting of the transcendental sound.

TEXT 26

नामान्यनन्तस्य हतत्रपः पठन्
गुह्यानि भद्राणि कृतानि च स्मरन् ।
गां पर्यटंस्तुष्टमना गतस्पृहः
कालं प्रतीक्षन् विमदो विमत्सरः ॥ २६ ॥

nāmāny anantasya hata-trapaḥ paṭhan
guhyāni bhadrāṇi kṛtāni ca smaran
gāṁ paryaṭaṁs tuṣṭa-manā gata-spṛhaḥ
kālaṁ pratīkṣan vimado vimatsaraḥ

nāmāni—the holy name, fame, etc.; *anantasya*—of the unlimited; *hata-trapaḥ*—being freed from all formalities of the material world; *paṭhan*—by recitation, repeated reading, etc.; *guhyāni*—mysterious; *bhadrāṇi*—all-benedictory; *kṛtāni*—activities; *ca*—and; *smaran*—constantly remembering; *gām*—on the earth; *paryaṭan*—traveling all through; *tuṣṭa-manāḥ*—fully satisfied; *gata-spṛhaḥ*—completely freed from all material desires; *kālam*—time; *pratīkṣan*—awaiting; *vimadaḥ*—without being proud; *vimatsaraḥ*—without being envious.

Thus I began chanting the holy name and fame of the Lord by repeated recitation, ignoring all the formalities of the material world. Such chanting and remembering of the transcendental pastimes of the Lord are benedictory. So doing, I traveled all over the earth, fully satisfied, humble and unenvious.

PURPORT The life of a sincere devotee of the Lord is thus explained in a nutshell by Nārada Muni by his personal example. Such a devotee, after his initiation by the Lord or His bona fide representative, takes very seriously chanting of the glories of the Lord and traveling all over the world so that others may also hear the glories of the Lord. Such devotees have no desire for material gain. They are conducted by one single desire: to go back to Godhead. This awaits them in due course on quitting the material body. Because they have the highest aim of life, going back to Godhead, they are never envious of anyone, nor are they proud of being eligible to go back to Godhead. Their only business is to chant and remember the holy name, fame and pastimes of the Lord and, according to personal capacity, to distribute the message for others' welfare without motive of material gain.

TEXT 27

एवं कृष्णमतेर्ब्रह्मन्नासक्तस्यामलात्मनः ।
कालः प्रादुरभूत्काले तडित्सौदामनी यथा ॥ २७ ॥

evaṁ kṛṣṇa-mater brahman nāsaktasyāmalātmanaḥ
kālaḥ prādurabhūt kāle taḍit saudāmanī yathā

evam—thus; *kṛṣṇa-mateḥ*—one who is fully absorbed in thinking of Kṛṣṇa; *brahman*—O Vyāsadeva; *na*—not; *āsaktasya*—of one who is attached; *amala-ātmanaḥ*—of one who is completely free from all material dirt; *kālaḥ*—death; *prādurabhūt*—become visible; *kāle*—in the course of time; *taḍit*—lightning; *saudāmanī*—illuminating; *yathā*—as it is.

And so, O Brāhmaṇa Vyāsadeva, in due course of time I, who was fully absorbed in thinking of Kṛṣṇa and who therefore had no attachments, being completely freed from all material taints, met with death, as lightning and illumination occur simultaneously.

PURPORT To be fully absorbed in the thought of Kṛṣṇa means clearance of material dirts or hankerings. As a very rich man has no hankerings for small petty things, so also a devotee of Lord Kṛṣṇa, who is guaranteed to pass on to the kingdom of God, where life is eternal, fully cognizant and blissful, naturally has no hankerings for petty material things, which are like dolls or shadows of the reality and are without permanent value. That is the sign of spiritually enriched persons. And in due course of time, when a pure devotee is completely prepared, all of a sudden the change of body occurs which is commonly called death. And for the pure devotee such a change takes place exactly like lightning, and illumination follows simultaneously. That is to say a devotee simultaneously changes his material body and develops a spiritual body by the will of the Supreme. Even before death, a pure devotee has no material affection, due to his body's being spiritualized like a red-hot iron in contact with fire.

TEXT 28

प्रयुज्यमाने मयि तां शुद्धां भागवतीं तनुम् ।
आरब्धकर्मनिर्वाणो न्यपतत् पाञ्चभौतिकः ॥ २८ ॥

prayujyamāne mayi tāṁ śuddhāṁ bhāgavatīṁ tanum
ārabdha-karma-nirvāṇo nyapatat pāñca-bhautikaḥ

prayujyamāne—having been awarded; *mayi*—on me; *tām*—that;

śuddhām—transcendental; *bhāgavatīm*—fit for associating with the Personality of Godhead; *tanum*—body; *ārabdha*—acquired; *karma*—fruitive work; *nirvāṇaḥ*—prohibitive; *nyapatat*—quit; *pāñca-bhautikaḥ*—body made of five material elements.

Having been awarded a transcendental body befitting an associate of the Personality of Godhead, I quit the body made of five material elements, and thus all acquired fruitive results of work [karma] stopped.

PURPORT Informed by the Personality of Godhead that he would be awarded a transcendental body befitting the Lord's association, Nārada got his spiritual body as soon as he quitted his material body. This transcendental body is free from material affinity and invested with three primary transcendental qualities, namely eternity, freedom from material modes, and freedom from reactions of fruitive activities. The material body is always afflicted with the lack of these three qualities. A devotee's body becomes at once surcharged with the transcendental qualities as soon as he is engaged in the devotional service of the Lord. It acts like the magnetic influence of a touchstone upon iron. The influence of transcendental devotional service is like that. Therefore change of the body means stoppage of the reaction of three qualitative modes of material nature upon the pure devotee. There are many instances of this in the revealed scriptures. Dhruva Mahārāja and Prahlāda Mahārāja and many other devotees were able to see the Personality of Godhead face to face apparently in the same body. This means that the quality of a devotee's body changes from material to transcendence. That is the opinion of the authorized Gosvāmīs via the authentic scriptures. In the *Brahma-saṁhitā* it is said that beginning from the *indra-gopa* germ up to the great Indra, King of heaven, all living beings are subjected to the law of *karma* and are bound to suffer and enjoy the fruitive results of their own work. Only the devotee is exempt from such reactions, by the causeless mercy of the supreme authority, the Personality of Godhead.

TEXT 29

कल्पान्त इदमादाय शयानेऽम्भस्युदन्वतः ।
शिशयिषोरनुप्राणं विविशेऽन्तरहं विभोः ॥ २९ ॥

kalpānta idam ādāya śayāne 'mbhasy udanvataḥ
śiśayiṣor anuprāṇaṁ viviśe 'ntar ahaṁ vibhoḥ

kalpa-ante—at the end of Brahmā's day; *idam*—this; *ādāya*—taking together; *śayāne*—having gone to lie down; *ambhasi*—in the causal water; *udanvataḥ*—devastation; *śiśayiṣoḥ*—lying of the Personality of Godhead (Nārāyaṇa); *anuprāṇam*—breathing; *viviśe*—entered into; *antaḥ*—within; *aham*—I; *vibhoḥ*—of Lord Brahmā.

At the end of the millennium, when the Personality of Godhead Lord Nārāyaṇa lay down within the water of devastation, Brahmā began to enter into Him along with all creative elements, and I also entered through His breathing.

PURPORT Nārada is known as the son of Brahmā, as Lord Kṛṣṇa is known as the son of Vasudeva. The Personality of Godhead and His liberated devotees like Nārada appear in the material world by the same process. As it is said in the *Bhagavad-gītā,* the birth and activities of the Lord are all transcendental. Therefore, according to authorized opinion, the birth of Nārada as the son of Brahmā is also a transcendental pastime. His appearance and disappearance are practically on the same level as that of the Lord. The Lord and His devotees are therefore simultaneously one and different as spiritual entities. They belong to the same category of transcendence.

TEXT 30

सहस्रयुगपर्यन्ते उत्थायेदं सिसृक्षतः ।
मरीचिमिश्रा ऋषयः प्राणेभ्योऽहं च जज्ञिरे ॥ ३० ॥

sahasra-yuga-paryante utthāyedaṁ sisṛkṣataḥ
marīci-miśrā ṛṣayaḥ prāṇebhyo 'haṁ ca jajñire

sahasra—one thousand; *yuga*—4,300,000 years; *paryante*—at the end of the duration; *utthāya*—having expired; *idam*—this; *sisṛkṣataḥ*—desired to create again; *marīci-miśrāḥ*—*ṛṣis* like Marīci; *ṛṣayaḥ*—all the *ṛṣis; prāṇebhyaḥ*—out of His senses; *aham*—I; *ca*—also; *jajñire*—appeared.

After 4,300,000,000 solar years, when Brahmā awoke to create again by the will of the Lord, all the ṛṣis like Marīci, Aṅgirā, Atri and so on were created from the transcendental body of the Lord, and I also appeared along with them.

PURPORT The duration of a day in the life of Brahmā is 4,320,000,000 solar years. This is stated also in the *Bhagavad-gītā*. And for this same period Brahmājī rests at night in *yoga-nidrā* within the body of the Garbhodakaśāyī Viṣṇu, the generator of Brahmā. Thus after the sleeping period of Brahmā, when there is again creation by the will of the Lord through the agency of Brahmā, all the great *ṛṣis* again appear from different parts of the transcendental body, and Nārada also appears. This means that Nārada appears in the same transcendental body, just as a man awakes from sleep in the same body. Śrī Nārada is eternally free to move in all parts of the transcendental and material creations of the Almighty. He appears and disappears in his own transcendental body, which is without distinction of body and soul, unlike conditioned beings.

TEXT 31

अन्तर्बहिश्च लोकांस्त्रीन् पर्येम्यस्कन्दितव्रतः ।
अनुग्रहान्महाविष्णोरविघातगतिः क्वचित् ॥ ३१ ॥

antar bahiś ca lokāṁs trīn paryemy askandita-vrataḥ
anugrahān mahā-viṣṇor avighāta-gatiḥ kvacit

antaḥ—in the transcendental world; *bahiḥ*—in the material world; *ca*—and; *lokān*—planets; *trīn*—three (divisions); *paryemi*—travel; *askandita*—unbroken; *vrataḥ*—vow; *anugrahāt*—by the causeless mercy; *mahā-viṣṇoḥ*—of the Mahā-Viṣṇu (Kāraṇodakaśāyī Viṣṇu); *avighāta*—without restriction; *gatiḥ*—entrance; *kvacit*—at any time.

Since then, by the grace of the almighty Viṣṇu, I travel everywhere without restriction both in the transcendental world and in the three divisions of the material world. This is because I am fixed in unbroken devotional service of the Lord.

PURPORT As stated in the *Bhagavad-gītā*, there are three divisions of the material spheres, namely the *ūrdhva-loka* (topmost planets), *madhya-loka* (midway planets) and *adho-loka* (downward planets). Beyond the *ūrdhva-loka* planets, that is to say above the Brahmaloka, are the material coverings of the universes, and above that is the spiritual sky, which is unlimited in expansion, containing unlimited self-illuminated Vaikuṇṭha planets inhabited by God Himself along with His associates, who are all eternally liberated living entities. Śrī Nārada Muni could enter all these planets in both the material and spiritual spheres without restriction, as much as the almighty Lord is free to move personally in any part of His creation. In the material world the living beings are influenced by the three material modes of nature, namely goodness, passion and ignorance. But Śrī Nārada Muni is transcendental to all these material modes, and thus he can travel everywhere unrestricted. He is a liberated spaceman. The causeless mercy of Lord Viṣṇu is unparalleled, and such mercy is perceived by the devotees only by the grace of the Lord. Therefore, the devotees never fall down, but the materialists, i.e., the fruitive workers and the speculative philosophers, do fall down, being forced by their respective modes of nature. The *ṛṣis,* as above mentioned, cannot enter into the transcendental world like Nārada. This fact is disclosed in the *Narasiṁha Purāṇa*. *Ṛṣis* like Marīci are authorities in fruitive work, and *ṛṣis* like Sanaka and Sanātana are authorities in philosophical speculations. But Śrī Nārada Muni is the prime authority for transcendental devotional service of the Lord. All the great authorities in the devotional service of the Lord follow in the footsteps of Nārada Muni in the order of the *Nārada-bhakti-sūtra,* and therefore all the devotees of the Lord are unhesitatingly qualified to enter into the kingdom of God, Vaikuṇṭha.

TEXT 32

देवदत्तामिमां वीणां स्वरब्रह्मविभूषिताम् ।
मूर्च्छयित्वा हरिकथां गायमानश्चराम्यहम् ॥ ३२ ॥

deva-dattām imāṁ vīṇāṁ svara-brahma-vibhūṣitām
mūrcchayitvā hari-kathāṁ gāyamānaś carāmy aham

deva—the Supreme Personality of Godhead (Śrī Kṛṣṇa); *dattām*—gifted by; *imām*—this; *vīṇām*—a musical stringed instrument; *svara*—singing meter; *brahma*—transcendental; *vibhūṣitām*—decorated with;

mūrcchayitvā—vibrating; *hari-kathām*—transcendental message; *gāyamānaḥ*—singing constantly; *carāmi*—do move; *aham*—I.

And thus I travel, constantly singing the transcendental message of the glories of the Lord, vibrating this instrument called a viṇā, which is charged with transcendental sound and which was given to me by Lord Kṛṣṇa.

PURPORT The musical stringed instrument called the *viṇā*, which was handed to Nārada by Lord Śrī Kṛṣṇa, is described in the *Liṅga Purāṇa*, and this is confirmed by Śrīla Jīva Gosvāmī. This transcendental instrument is identical with Lord Śrī Kṛṣṇa and Nārada because all of them are of the same transcendental category. Sound vibrated by the instrument cannot be material, and therefore the glories and pastimes which are broadcast by the instrument of Nārada are also transcendental, without a tinge of material inebriety. The seven singing meters, namely *ṣa* (*ṣaḍja*), *ṛ* (*ṛṣabha*), *gā* (*gāndhāra*), *ma* (*madhyama*), *pa* (*pañcama*), *dha* (*dhaivata*) and *ni* (*niṣāda*), are also transcendental and specifically meant for transcendental songs. As a pure devotee of the Lord, Śrī Nāradadeva is always fulfilling his obligation to the Lord for His gift of the instrument, and thus he is always engaged in singing His transcendental glories and is therefore infallible in his exalted position. Following in the footsteps of Śrīla Nārada Muni, a self-realized soul in the material world also properly uses the sound meters, namely *ṣa, ṛ, gā, mā,* etc., in the service of the Lord by constantly singing His glories. As confirmed in the *Bhagavad-gītā* (9.14), the *mahātmās,* or great souls, have no business in life except singing the transcendental glories of the Lord, following in the footsteps of Śrīla Nāradadeva.

TEXT 33

प्रगायतः स्ववीर्याणि तीर्थपादः प्रियश्रवाः ।
आहूत इव मे शीघ्रं दर्शनं याति चेतसि ॥ ३३ ॥

pragāyataḥ sva-vīryāṇi tīrtha-pādaḥ priya-śravāḥ
āhūta iva me śīghraṁ darśanaṁ yāti cetasi

pragāyataḥ—thus singing; *sva-vīryāṇi*—own activities; *tīrtha-pādaḥ*—

the Lord, whose lotus feet are the source of all virtues or holiness; *priya-śravāḥ*—pleasing to hear; *āhūtaḥ*—called for; *iva*—just like; *me*—to me; *śīghram*—very soon; *darśanam*—sight; *yāti*—appears; *cetasi*—on the seat of the heart.

The Supreme Lord Śrī Kṛṣṇa, whose glories and activities are pleasing to hear, at once appears on the seat of my heart, as if called for, as soon as I begin to chant His holy activities.

PURPORT The Absolute Personality of Godhead is not different from His transcendental name, form, pastimes and the sound vibrations thereof. As soon as a pure devotee engages himself in the pure devotional service of hearing, chanting and remembering the name, fame and activities of the Lord, at once He becomes visible to the transcendental eyes of the pure devotee by reflecting Himself on the mirror of the heart by spiritual television. Therefore a pure devotee who is related with the Lord in loving transcendental service can experience the presence of the Lord at every moment. It is a natural psychology in every individual case that a person likes to hear and enjoy his personal glories enumerated by others. That is a natural instinct, and the Lord, being also an individual personality like others, is not an exception to this psychology because psychological characteristics visible in the individual souls are but reflections of the same psychology in the Absolute Lord. The only difference is that the Lord is the greatest personality of all and absolute in all His affairs. If, therefore, the Lord is attracted by the pure devotee's chanting of His glories, there is nothing astonishing. Since He is absolute, He can appear Himself in the picture of His glorification, the two things being identical. Śrīla Nārada chants the glorification of the Lord not for his personal benefit but because the glorifications are identical with the Lord. Nārada Muni penetrates into the presence of the Lord by the transcendental chanting.

TEXT 34

एतद्ध्यातुरचित्तानां मात्रास्पर्शेच्छया मुहुः ।
भवसिन्धुप्लवो दृष्टो हरिचर्यानुवर्णनम् ॥ ३४ ॥

etad dhy ātura-cittānāṁ mātrā-sparśecchayā muhuḥ
bhava-sindhu-plavo dṛṣṭo hari-caryānuvarṇanam

etat—this; *hi*—certainly; *ātura-cittānām*—of those whose minds are always full of cares and anxieties; *mātrā*—objects of sense enjoyment; *sparśa*—senses; *icchayā*—by desires; *muhuḥ*—always; *bhava-sindhu*—the ocean of nescience; *plavaḥ*—boat; *dṛṣṭaḥ*—experienced; *hari-carya*—activities of Hari, the Personality of Godhead; *anuvarṇanam*—constant recitation.

It is personally experienced by me that those who are always full of cares and anxieties due to desiring contact of the senses with their objects can cross the ocean of nescience on a most suitable boat—the constant chanting of the transcendental activities of the Personality of Godhead.

PURPORT The symptom of a living being is that he cannot remain silent even for some time. He must be doing something, thinking of something or talking about something. Generally the materialistic men think and discuss about subjects which satisfy their senses. But as these things are exercised under the influence of the external, illusory energy, such sensual activities do not actually give them any satisfaction. On the contrary, they become full with cares and anxieties. This is called *māyā,* or what is not. That which cannot give them satisfaction is accepted as an object for satisfaction. So Nārada Muni, by his personal experience, says that satisfaction for such frustrated beings engaged in sense gratification is to chant always the activities of the Lord. The point is that the subject matter only should be changed. No one can check the thinking activities of a living being, nor the feeling, willing or working processes. But if one wants actual happiness, one must change the subject matter only. Instead of talking of the politics of a dying man, one might discuss the politics administered by the Lord Himself. Instead of relishing activities of the cinema artists, one can turn his attention to the activities of the Lord with His eternal associates like the *gopīs* and Lakṣmīs. The almighty Personality of Godhead, by His causeless mercy, descends on the earth and manifests activities almost on the line of the worldly men, but at the same time extraordinarily, because He is almighty. He does so for the benefit of all conditioned souls so that they can turn their attention to transcendence. By doing so, the conditioned soul will gradually be promoted to the transcendental position and easily cross the ocean of nescience, the source of all miseries. This is stated from personal experience by such an authority as Śrī Nārada Muni. And we can have the same experience also if we begin to follow in the footsteps of the great sage, the dearmost devotee of the Lord.

TEXT 35

यमादिभिर्योगपथैः कामलोभहतो मुहुः ।
मुकुन्दसेवया यद्वत्तथात्माद्धा न शाम्यति ॥ ३५ ॥

yamādibhir yoga-pathaiḥ kāma-lobha-hato muhuḥ
mukunda-sevayā yadvat tathātmāddhā na śāmyati

yama-ādibhiḥ—by the process of practicing self-restraint; *yoga-pathaiḥ*—by the system of *yoga* (mystic bodily power to attain the godly stage); *kāma*—desires for sense satisfaction; *lobha*—lust for satisfaction of the senses; *hataḥ*—curbed; *muhuḥ*—always; *mukunda*—the Personality of Godhead; *sevayā*—by the service of; *yadvat*—as it is; *tathā*—like that; *ātmā*—the soul; *addhā*—for all practical purposes; *na*—does not; *śāmyati*—be satisfied.

It is true that by practicing restraint of the senses by the yoga system one can get relief from the disturbances of desire and lust, but this is not sufficient to give satisfaction to the soul, for this [satisfaction] is derived from devotional service to the Personality of Godhead.

PURPORT *Yoga* aims at controlling the senses. By practice of the mystic process of bodily exercise in sitting, thinking, feeling, willing, concentrating, meditating and at last being merged into transcendence, one can control the senses. The senses are considered like venomous serpents, and the *yoga* system is just to control them. On the other hand, Nārada Muni recommends another method for controlling the senses in the transcendental loving service of Mukunda, the Personality of Godhead. By his experience he says that devotional service to the Lord is more effective and practical than the system of artificially controlling the senses. In the service of the Lord Mukunda, the senses are transcendentally engaged. Thus there is no chance of their being engaged in sense satisfaction. The senses want some engagement. To check them artificially is no check at all because as soon as there is some opportunity for enjoyment, the serpentlike senses will certainly take advantage of it. There are many such instances in history, just like Viśvāmitra Muni's falling a victim to the beauty of Menakā. But Ṭhākura Haridāsa was allured at midnight by the well-dressed Māyā, and still she could not induce that great devotee into her trap.

The whole idea is that without devotional service of the Lord, neither the *yoga* system nor dry philosophical speculation can ever become successful. Pure devotional service of the Lord, without being tinged with fruitive work, mystic *yoga* or speculative philosophy, is the foremost procedure to attain self-realization. Such pure devotional service is transcendental in nature, and the systems of *yoga* and *jñāna* are subordinate to such a process. When the transcendental devotional service is mixed with a subordinate process, it is no longer transcendental but is called mixed devotional service. Śrīla Vyāsadeva, the author of *Śrīmad-Bhāgavatam,* will gradually develop all these different systems of transcendental realization in the text.

TEXT 36

सर्वं तदिदमाख्यातं यत्पृष्टोऽहं त्वयानघ ।
जन्मकर्मरहस्यं मे भवतश्चात्मतोषणम् ॥ ३६ ॥

sarvaṁ tad idam ākhyātaṁ yat pṛṣṭo 'haṁ tvayānagha
janma-karma-rahasyaṁ me bhavataś cātma-toṣaṇam

sarvam—all; *tat*—that; *idam*—this; *ākhyātam*—described; *yat*—whatever; *pṛṣṭaḥ*—asked by; *aham*—me; *tvayā*—by you; *anagha*—without any sins; *janma*—birth; *karma*—activities; *rahasyam*—mysteries; *me*—mine; *bhavataḥ*—your; *ca*—and; *ātma*—self; *toṣaṇam*—satisfaction.

O Vyāsadeva, you are freed from all sins. Thus I have explained my birth and activities for self-realization, as you asked. All this will be conducive for your personal satisfaction also.

PURPORT The process of devotional activities from the beginning to the stage of transcendence has all been duly explained to satisfy the inquiries of Vyāsadeva. Nārada has explained how the seeds of devotional service were sown by transcendental association and how they gradually developed by hearing the sages. The result of such hearing is detachment from worldliness, so much so that even a small boy could receive the death news of his mother, who was his only caretaker, as the blessing of God. And at once he took the opportunity to search out the Lord. A sincere urge for having an interview with the Lord was also granted to him, although it is not possible for anyone to see the Lord with mundane eyes. He also explained how by execution of pure transcendental service one can get rid of the fruitive action of accumulated work and how he transformed his material body into a spiritual one. The spiritual body is alone able to enter into the spiritual realm of the Lord, and no one but a pure devotee is eligible to enter into the kingdom of God. All the mysteries of transcendental realization are duly experienced by Nārada Muni himself, and therefore by hearing such an authority one can have some idea of the results of devotional life, which are hardly delineated even in the original texts of the *Vedas*. In the *Vedas* and *Upaniṣads* there are only indirect hints to all this. Nothing is directly explained there, and therefore *Śrīmad-Bhāgavatam* is the mature fruit of all the Vedic trees of literatures.

सूत उवाच

TEXT 37

एवं सम्भाष्य भगवान्नारदो वासवीसुतम् ।
आमन्त्र्य वीणां रणयन् ययौ यादृच्छिको मुनिः ॥ ३७ ॥

sūta uvāca
evaṁ sambhāṣya bhagavān nārado vāsavī-sutam
āmantrya vīṇāṁ raṇayan yayau yādṛcchiko muniḥ

sūtaḥ—Sūta Gosvāmī; *uvāca*—said; *evam*—thus; *sambhāṣya*—addressing; *bhagavān*—transcendentally powerful; *nāradaḥ*—Nārada Muni; *vāsavī*—named Vāsavī (Satyavatī); *sutam*—son; *āmantrya*—inviting; *vīṇām*—instrument; *raṇayan*—vibrating; *yayau*—went; *yādṛcchikaḥ*—wherever willing; *muniḥ*—the sage.

Sūta Gosvāmī said: Thus addressing Vyāsadeva, Śrīla Nārada Muni took leave of him, and vibrating on his vīṇā instrument, he left to wander at his free will.

PURPORT Every living being is anxious for full freedom because that is his transcendental nature. And this freedom is obtained only through the transcendental service of the Lord. Illusioned by the external energy, everyone thinks that he is free, but actually he is bound up by the laws of nature. A conditioned soul cannot freely move from one place to another even on this earth, and what to speak of one planet to another. But a full-fledged free soul like Nārada, always engaged in chanting the Lord's glory, is free to move not only on earth but also in any part of the universe, as well as in any part of the spiritual sky. We can just imagine the extent and unlimitedness of his freedom, which is as good as that of the Supreme Lord. There is no reason or obligation for his traveling, and no one can stop him from his free movement. Similarly, the transcendental system of devotional service is also free. It may or may not develop in a particular person even after he undergoes all the detailed formulas. Similarly, the association of the devotee is also free. One may be fortunate to have it, or one may not have it even after thousands of endeavors. Therefore, in all spheres of devotional service, freedom is the main pivot. Without freedom there is no execution of devotional service. The freedom surrendered to the Lord does not mean that the devotee becomes dependent in every respect. To surrender unto the Lord through the transparent medium of the spiritual master is to attain complete freedom of life.

TEXT 38

अहो देवर्षिर्धन्योऽयं यत्कीर्तिं शार्ङ्गधन्वनः ।
गायन्माद्यन्निदं तन्त्र्या रमयत्यातुरं जगत् ॥ ३८ ॥

aho devarṣir dhanyo 'yaṁ yat-kīrtiṁ śārṅgadhanvanaḥ
gāyan mādyann idaṁ tantryā ramayaty āturaṁ jagat

aho—all glory to; *devarṣiḥ*—the sage of the gods; *dhanyaḥ*—all success; *ayam yat*—one who; *kīrtim*—glories; *śārṅga-dhanvanaḥ*—of the Personality of Godhead; *gāyan*—singing; *mādyan*—taking pleasure in; *idam*—this; *tantryā*—by means of the instrument; *ramayati*—enlivens; *āturam*—distressed; *jagat*—world.

All glory and success to Śrīla Nārada Muni because he glorifies the activities of the Personality of Godhead, and so doing he himself takes pleasure and also enlivens all the distressed souls of the universe.

PURPORT Śrī Nārada Muni plays on his instrument to glorify the transcendental activities of the Lord and to give relief to all miserable living entities of the universe. No one is happy here within the universe, and what is felt as happiness is *māyā's* illusion. The illusory energy of the Lord is so strong that even the hog who lives on filthy stool feels happy. No one can be truly happy within the material world. Śrīla Nārada Muni, in order to enlighten the miserable inhabitants, wanders everywhere. His mission is to get them back home, back to Godhead. That is the mission of all genuine devotees of the Lord following the footsteps of that great sage.

Thus end the Bhaktivedanta purports of the First Canto, Sixth Chapter, of the Śrīmad-Bhāgavatam, *entitled "Conversation Between Nārada and Vyāsa."*

CHAPTER SEVEN

The Son of Droṇa Punished

शौनक उवाच

TEXT 1

निर्गते नारदे सूत भगवान् बादरायणः ।
श्रुतवांस्तदभिप्रेतं ततः किमकरोद्विभुः ॥ १ ॥

śaunaka uvāca
nirgate nārade sūta bhagavān bādarāyaṇaḥ
śrutavāṁs tad-abhipretaṁ tataḥ kim akarod vibhuḥ

śaunakaḥ—Śrī Śaunaka; *uvāca*—said; *nirgate*—having gone; *nārade*—Nārada Muni; *sūta*—O Sūta; *bhagavān*—the transcendentally powerful; *bādarāyaṇaḥ*—Vedavyāsa; *śrutavān*—who heard; *tat*—his; *abhipretam*—desire of the mind; *tataḥ*—thereafter; *kim*—what; *akarot*—did he do; *vibhuḥ*—the great.

Ṛṣi Śaunaka asked: O Sūta, the great and transcendentally powerful Vyāsadeva heard everything from Śrī Nārada Muni. So after Nārada's departure, what did Vyāsadeva do?

PURPORT In this chapter the clue for describing *Śrīmad-Bhāgavatam* is picked up as Mahārāja Parīkṣit is miraculously saved in the womb of his mother. This was caused by Drauṇi (Aśvatthāmā), Ācārya Droṇa's son, who killed the five sons of Draupadī while they were asleep, for which he was punished by Arjuna. Before commencing the great epic *Śrīmad-Bhāgavatam,* Śrī Vyāsadeva realized the whole truth by trance in devotion.

सूत उवाच

TEXT 2

ब्रह्मनद्यां सरस्वत्यामाश्रमः पश्चिमे तटे ।
शम्याप्रास इति प्रोक्त ऋषीणां सत्रवर्धनः ॥ २ ॥

sūta uvāca
brahma-nadyāṁ sarasvatyām āśramaḥ paścime taṭe
śamyāprāsa iti prokta ṛṣīṇāṁ satra-vardhanaḥ

sūtaḥ—Śrī Sūta; *uvāca*—said; *brahma-nadyām*—on the bank of the river intimately related with *Vedas, brāhmaṇas,* saints, and the Lord; *sarasvatyām*—Sarasvatī; *āśramaḥ*—cottage for meditation; *paścime*—on the west; *taṭe*—bank; *śamyāprāsaḥ*—the place named Śamyāprāsa; *iti*—thus; *proktaḥ*—said to be; *ṛṣīṇām*—of the sages; *satra-vardhanaḥ*—that which enlivens activities.

Śrī Sūta said: On the western bank of the river Sarasvatī, which is intimately related with the Vedas, there is a cottage for meditation at Śamyāprāsa which enlivens the transcendental activities of the sages.

PURPORT For spiritual advancement of knowledge a suitable place and atmosphere are definitely required. The place on the western bank of the Sarasvatī is especially suitable for this purpose. And there is the *āśrama* of Vyāsadeva at Śamyāprāsa. Śrīla Vyāsadeva was a householder, yet his residential place is called an *āśrama.* An *āśrama* is a place where spiritual culture is always foremost. It does not matter whether the place belongs to a householder or a mendicant. The whole *varṇāśrama* system is so designed that each and every status of life is called an *āśrama.* This means that spiritual culture is the common factor for all. The *brahmacārīs,* the *gṛhasthas,* the *vāna-prasthas* and the *sannyāsīs* all belong to the same mission of life, namely, realization of the Supreme. Therefore none of them are less important as far as spiritual culture is concerned. The difference is a matter of formality on the strength of renunciation. The *sannyāsīs* are held in high estimation on the strength of practical renunciation.

TEXT 3

तस्मिन् स्व आश्रमे व्यासो बदरीषण्डमण्डिते ।
आसीनोऽप उपस्पृश्य प्रणिदध्यौ मनः स्वयम् ॥ ३ ॥

tasmin sva āśrame vyāso badarī-ṣaṇḍa-maṇḍite
āsīno 'pa upaspṛśya praṇidadhyau manaḥ svayam

tasmin—in that (*āśrama*); *sve*—own; *āśrame*—in the cottage; *vyāsaḥ*—Vyāsadeva; *badarī*—berry; *ṣaṇḍa*—trees; *maṇḍite*—surrounded by; *āsīnaḥ*—sitting; *apaḥ upaspṛśya*—touching water; *praṇidadhyau*—concentrated; *manaḥ*—the mind; *svayam*—himself.

In that place, Śrīla Vyāsadeva, in his own āśrama, which was surrounded by berry trees, sat down to meditate after touching water for purification.

PURPORT Under instructions of his spiritual master Śrīla Nārada Muni, Vyāsadeva concentrated his mind in that transcendental place of meditation.

TEXT 4

भक्तियोगेन मनसि सम्यक् प्रणिहितेऽमले ।
अपश्यत्पुरुषं पूर्णं मायां च तदपाश्रयम् ॥ ४ ॥

bhakti-yogena manasi samyak praṇihite 'male
apaśyat puruṣaṁ pūrṇaṁ māyāṁ ca tad-apāśrayām

bhakti—devotional service; *yogena*—by the process of linking up; *manasi*—upon the mind; *samyak*—perfectly; *praṇihite*—engaged in and fixed upon; *amale*—without any matter; *apaśyat*—saw; *puruṣam*—the Personality of Godhead; *pūrṇam*—absolute; *māyām*—energy; *ca*—also; *tat*—His; *apāśrayām*—under full control.

Thus he fixed his mind, perfectly engaging it by linking it in devotional service [bhakti-yoga] without any tinge of materialism, and thus he saw the Absolute Personality of Godhead along with His external energy, which was under full control.

PURPORT Perfect vision of the Absolute Truth is possible only by the linking process of devotional service. This is also confirmed in the *Bhagavad-gītā*. One can perfectly realize the Absolute Truth Personality of Godhead only by the process of devotional service, and one can enter into the kingdom of God by such perfect knowledge. Imperfect realization of the Absolute by the partial approach of the impersonal Brahman or localized Paramātmā does not permit anyone to enter into the kingdom of God. Śrī Nārada advised Śrīla Vyāsadeva to become absorbed in transcendental meditation on the Personality of Godhead and His activities. Śrīla Vyāsadeva did not take notice of the effulgence of Brahman because that is not absolute vision. The absolute vision is the Personality of Godhead, as it is confirmed in the *Bhagavad-gītā* (7.19): *vāsudevaḥ sarvam iti.* In the *Upaniṣads* also it is confirmed that Vāsudeva, the Personality of Godhead, is covered by the golden glowing *hiraṇmayena pātreṇa* veil of impersonal Brahman, and when that curtain is removed by the mercy of the Lord the real face of the Absolute is seen. The Absolute is mentioned here as the *puruṣa,* or person. The Absolute Personality of Godhead is mentioned in so many Vedic literatures, and in the *Bhagavad-gītā,* the *puruṣa* is confirmed as the eternal and original person. The Absolute Personality of Godhead is the perfect person. The Supreme Person has manifold energies, out of which the internal, external and marginal energies are specifically important. The energy mentioned here is the external energy, as will be clear from the statements of her activities. The internal energy is there along with the Absolute Person as the moonlight is there with the moon. The external energy is compared to darkness because it keeps the living entities in the darkness of ignorance. The word *apāśrayam* suggests that this energy of the Lord is under full control. The internal potency or superior energy is also called *māyā,* but it is spiritual *māyā,* or energy exhibited in the absolute realm. When one is under the shelter of this internal potency, the darkness of material ignorance is at once dissipated. And even those who are *ātmārāma,* or fixed in trance, take shelter of this *māyā,* or internal energy. Devotional service, or *bhakti-yoga,* is the function of the internal energy; thus there is no place for the inferior energy, or material energy, just as there is no place for darkness in the effulgence of spiritual light. Such internal energy is even superior to the spiritual bliss attainable in the conception of impersonal Brahman. It is stated in the *Bhagavad-gītā* that the impersonal Brahman effulgence is also an emanation from the Absolute Personality of Godhead Śrī Kṛṣṇa. The *parama-puruṣa* cannot be anyone except Śrī Kṛṣṇa Himself, as will be explained in the later *ślokas.*

TEXT 5

यया सम्मोहितो जीव आत्मानं त्रिगुणात्मकम् ।
परोऽपि मनुतेऽनर्थं तत्कृतं चाभिपद्यते ॥ ५ ॥

yayā sammohito jīva ātmānaṁ tri-guṇātmakam
paro 'pi manute 'narthaṁ tat-kṛtaṁ cābhipadyate

yayā—by whom; *sammohitaḥ*—illusioned; *jīvaḥ*—the living entities; *ātmānam*—self; *tri-guṇa-ātmakam*—conditioned by the three modes of nature, or a product of matter; *paraḥ*—transcendental; *api*—in spite of; *manute*—takes it for granted; *anartham*—things not wanted; *tat*—by that; *kṛtam ca*—reaction; *abhipadyate*—undergoes thereof.

Due to this external energy, the living entity, although transcendental to the three modes of material nature, thinks of himself as a material product and thus undergoes the reactions of material miseries.

PURPORT The root cause of suffering by the materialistic living beings is pointed out with remedial measures which are to be undertaken and also the ultimate perfection to be gained. All this is mentioned in this particular verse. The living being is by constitution transcendental to material encagement, but he is now imprisoned by the external energy, and therefore he thinks himself one of the material products. And due to this unholy contact, the pure spiritual entity suffers material miseries under the modes of material nature. The living entity misunderstands himself to be a material product. This means that the present perverted way of thinking, feeling and willing, under material conditions, is not natural for him. But he has his normal way of thinking, feeling and willing. The living being in his original state is not without thinking, willing and feeling power. It is also confirmed in the *Bhagavad-gītā* that the actual knowledge of the conditioned soul is now covered by nescience. Thus the theory that a living being is absolute impersonal Brahman is refuted herein. This cannot be, because the living entity has his own way of thinking in his original unconditional state also. The present conditional state is due to the influence of the external energy, which means that the illusory energy takes the initiative while the Supreme Lord is aloof. The Lord does not desire that a living being be illusioned by external energy. The external energy is aware of this fact, but still she accepts a thankless task of keeping the forgotten soul under illusion by her bewildering influence. The Lord does not interfere with the task of the illusory energy because such performances of the illusory energy are also necessary for reformation of the conditioned soul. An affectionate father does not like his children to be chastised by another agent, yet he puts his disobedient children under the custody of a severe man just to bring them to order. But the all-affectionate Almighty Father at the same time desires relief for the conditioned soul, relief from the clutches of the illusory energy. The king puts the disobedient citizens within the walls of the jail, but sometimes the king, desiring the prisoners' relief, personally goes there and pleads for reformation, and on his doing so the prisoners are set free. Similarly, the Supreme Lord descends from His kingdom upon the kingdom of the illusory energy and personally gives relief in the form of the *Bhagavad-gītā,* wherein He personally suggests that although the ways of the illusory energy are very stiff to overcome, one who surrenders unto the lotus feet of the Lord is set free by the order of the Supreme. This surrendering process is the remedial measure for getting relief from the bewildering ways of the illusory energy. The surrendering process is completed by the influence of association. The Lord has suggested, therefore, that by the influence of the speeches of saintly persons who have actually realized the Supreme, men are engaged in His transcendental loving service. The conditioned soul gets a taste for hearing about the Lord, and by such hearing only he is gradually elevated to the platform of respect, devotion and attachment for the Lord. The whole thing is completed by the surrendering process. Herein also the same suggestion is made by the Lord in His incarnation of Vyāsadeva. This means that the conditioned souls are being reclaimed by the Lord both ways, namely by the process of punishment by the external energy of the Lord, and by Himself as the spiritual master within and without. Within the heart of every living being the Lord Himself as the Supersoul (Paramātmā) becomes the spiritual master, and from without He becomes the spiritual master in the shape of scriptures, saints and the initiator spiritual master. This is still more explicitly explained in the next *śloka.*

Personal superintendence of the illusory energy is confirmed in the *Vedas* (the *Kena Upaniṣad*) in relation to the demigods' controlling power. Herein also it is clearly stated that the living entity is controlled by the external energy in a personal capacity. The living being thus subject to the control of the external energy is differently situated. It is clear, however, from the present statement of the *Bhāgavatam* that the same external energy is situated in the inferior position before the Personality of

Godhead, or the perfect being. The perfect being, or the Lord, cannot be approached even by the illusory energy, who can only work on the living entities. Therefore it is sheer imagination that the Supreme Lord is illusioned by the illusory energy and thus becomes a living being. If the living being and the Lord were in the same category, then it would have been quite possible for Vyāsadeva to see it, and there would have been no question of material distress on the part of the illusioned being, for the Supreme Being is fully cognizant. So there are so many unscrupulous imaginations on the part of the monists to endeavor to put both the Lord and the living being in the same category. Had the Lord and the living beings been the same, then Śrīla Śukadeva Gosvāmī would not have taken the trouble to describe the transcendental pastimes of the Lord, for they would all be manifestations of the illusory energy.

Śrīmad-Bhāgavatam is the *summum bonum* remedy for suffering humanity in the clutches of *māyā*. Śrīla Vyāsadeva therefore first of all diagnosed the actual disease of the conditioned souls, i.e., their being illusioned by the external energy. He also saw the perfect Supreme Being, from whom the illusory energy is far removed, though He saw both the diseased conditioned souls and also the cause of the disease. And the remedial measures are suggested in the next verse. Both the Supreme Personality of Godhead and the living beings are undoubtedly qualitatively one, but the Lord is the controller of the illusory energy, whereas the living entity is controlled by the illusory energy. Thus the Lord and the living beings are simultaneously one and different. Another point is distinct herein: that eternal relation between the Lord and the living being is transcendental, otherwise the Lord would not have taken the trouble to reclaim the conditioned souls from the clutches of *māyā*. In the same way, the living entity is also required to revive his natural love and affection for the Lord, and that is the highest perfection of the living entity. *Śrīmad-Bhāgavatam* treats the conditioned soul with an aim to that goal of life.

TEXT 6

अनर्थोपशमं साक्षाद्भक्तियोगमधोक्षजे ।
लोकस्याजानतो विद्वांश्चक्रे सात्वतसंहिताम् ॥ ६ ॥

anarthopaśamaṁ sākṣād bhakti-yogam adhokṣaje
lokasyājānato vidvāṁś cakre sātvata-saṁhitām

anartha—things which are superfluous; *upaśamam*—mitigation; *sākṣāt*—directly; *bhakti-yogam*—the linking process of devotional service; *adhokṣaje*—unto the Transcendence; *lokasya*—of the general mass of men; *ajānataḥ*—those who are unaware of; *vidvān*—the supremely learned; *cakre*—compiled; *sātvata*—in relation with the Supreme Truth; *saṁhitām*—Vedic literature.

The material miseries of the living entity, which are superfluous to him, can be directly mitigated by the linking process of devotional service. But the mass of people do not know this, and therefore the learned Vyāsadeva compiled this Vedic literature, which is in relation to the Supreme Truth.

PURPORT Śrīla Vyāsadeva saw the all-perfect Personality of Godhead. This statement suggests that the complete unit of the Personality of Godhead includes His parts and parcels also. He saw, therefore, His different energies, namely the internal energy, the marginal energy and the external energy. He also saw His different plenary portions and parts of the plenary portions, namely His different incarnations also, and he specifically observed the unwanted miseries of the conditioned souls, who are bewildered by the external energy. And at last he saw the remedial measure for the conditioned souls, namely, the process of devotional service. It is a great transcendental science and begins with the process of hearing and chanting the name, fame, glory, etc., of the Supreme Personality of Godhead. Revival of the dormant affection or love of Godhead does not depend on the mechanical system of hearing and chanting, but it solely and wholly depends on the causeless mercy of the Lord. When the Lord is fully satisfied with the sincere efforts of the devotee, He may endow him with His loving transcendental service. But even with the prescribed forms of hearing and chanting, there is at once mitigation of the superfluous and unwanted miseries of material existence. Such mitigation of material affection does not wait for development of transcendental knowledge. Rather, knowledge is dependent on devotional service for the ultimate realization of the Supreme Truth.

TEXT 7

यस्यां वै श्रूयमाणायां कृष्णे परमपूरुषे ।
भक्तिरुत्पद्यते पुंसः शोकमोहभयापहा ॥ ७ ॥

yasyāṁ vai śrūyamāṇāyāṁ kṛṣṇe parama-pūruṣe
bhaktir utpadyate puṁsaḥ śoka-moha-bhayāpahā

yasyām—this Vedic literature; *vai*—certainly; *śrūyamāṇāyām*—simply by giving aural reception; *kṛṣṇe*—unto Lord Kṛṣṇa; *parama*—supreme; *pūruṣe*—unto the Personality of Godhead; *bhaktiḥ*—feelings of devotional service; *utpadyate*—sprout up; *puṁsaḥ*—of the living being; *śoka*—lamentation; *moha*—illusion; *bhaya*—fearfulness; *apahā*—that which extinguishes.

Simply by giving aural reception to this Vedic literature, the feeling for loving devotional service to Lord Kṛṣṇa, the Supreme Personality of Godhead, sprouts up at once to extinguish the fire of lamentation, illusion and fearfulness.

PURPORT There are various senses, of which the ear is the most effective. This sense works even when a man is deep asleep. One can protect himself from the hands of an enemy while awake, but while asleep one is protected by the ear only. The importance of hearing is mentioned here in connection with attaining the highest perfection of life, namely, getting free from three material pangs. Everyone is full of lamentation at every moment, he is after the mirage of illusory things, and he is always afraid of his supposed enemy. These are the primary symptoms of the material disease. And it is definitely suggested herein that simply by hearing the message of *Śrīmad-Bhāgavatam* one gets attachment for the Supreme Personality of Godhead Śrī Kṛṣṇa, and as soon as this is effected the symptoms of the material disease disappear. Śrīla Vyāsadeva saw the all-perfect Personality of Godhead, and in this statement it is clearly confirmed that the all-perfect Personality of Godhead is Śrī Kṛṣṇa.

The ultimate result of devotional service is to develop genuine love for the Supreme Personality. Love is a word which is often used in relation with man and woman. And love is the only word that can be properly used to indicate the relation between Lord Kṛṣṇa and the living entities. The living entities are mentioned as *prakṛti* in the *Bhagavad-gītā,* and in Sanskrit *prakṛti* is a feminine object. The Lord is always described as the *parama-puruṣa,* or the supreme male personality. Thus the affection between the Lord and the living entities is something like that between the male and the female. Therefore the term love of Godhead is quite appropriate.

Loving devotional service to the Lord begins with hearing about the Lord. There is no difference between the Lord and the subject matter heard about Him. The Lord is absolute in all respects, and thus there is no difference between Him and the subject matter heard about Him. Therefore, hearing about Him means immediate contact with Him by the process of vibration of the transcendental sound. And the transcendental sound is so effective that it acts at once by removing all material affections mentioned above. As mentioned before, a living entity develops a sort of complexity by material association, and the illusory encagement of the material body is accepted as an actual fact. Under such false complexity, the living beings under different categories of life become illusioned in different ways. Even in the most developed stage of human life, the same illusion prevails in the form of many *isms* and divides the loving relation with the Lord and thereby divides the loving relation between man and man. By hearing the subject matter of *Śrīmad-Bhāgavatam* this false complexity of materialism is removed, and real peace in society begins, which politicians aspire for so eagerly in so many political situations. The politicians want a peaceful situation between man and man, and nation and nation, but at the same time, because of too much attachment for material domination, there is illusion and fearfulness. Therefore the politicians' peace conferences cannot bring about peace in society. It can only be done by hearing the subject matter described in the *Śrīmad-Bhāgavatam* about the Supreme Personality of Godhead Śrī Kṛṣṇa. The foolish politicians may go on holding peace and summit conferences for hundreds of years, but they will fail to achieve success. Until we reach the stage of reestablishing our lost relation with Kṛṣṇa, the illusion of accepting the body as the self will prevail, and thus fearfulness will also prevail. As for the validity of Śrī Kṛṣṇa as the Supreme Personality of Godhead, there are hundreds and thousands of evidences from revealed scriptures, and there are hundreds and thousands of evidences from personal experiences of devotees in various places like Vṛndāvana, Navadvīpa and Purī. Even in the *Kaumudī* dictionary the synonyms of Kṛṣṇa are given as the son of Yaśodā and the Supreme Personality of Godhead Parabrahman. The conclusion is that simply by hearing the Vedic literature *Śrīmad-Bhāgavatam*, one can have direct connection with the Supreme

Personality of Godhead Śrī Kṛṣṇa, and thereby one can attain the highest perfection of life by transcending worldly miseries, illusion and fearfulness. These are practical tests for one who has actually given a submissive hearing to the readings of the *Śrīmad-Bhāgavatam.*

TEXT 8

स संहितां भागवतीं कृत्वानुक्रम्य चात्मजम् ।
शुकमध्यापयामास निवृत्तिनिरतं मुनिः ॥ ८ ॥

sa saṁhitāṁ bhāgavatīṁ kṛtvānukramya cātma-jam
śukam adhyāpayām āsa nivṛtti-nirataṁ muniḥ

saḥ—that; *saṁhitām*—Vedic literature; *bhāgavatīm*—in relation with the Personality of Godhead; *kṛtvā*—having done; *anukramya*—by correction and repetition; *ca*—and; *ātma-jam*—his own son; *śukam*—Śukadeva Gosvāmī; *adhyāpayām āsa*—taught; *nivṛtti*—path of self-realization; *niratam*—engaged; *muniḥ*—the sage.

The great sage Vyāsadeva, after compiling the Śrīmad-Bhāgavatam and revising it, taught it to his own son, Śrī Śukadeva Gosvāmī, who was already engaged in self-realization.

PURPORT *Śrīmad-Bhāgavatam* is the natural commentation on the *Brahma-sūtras* compiled by the same author. This *Brahma-sūtra,* or *Vedānta-sūtra,* is meant for those who are already engaged in self-realization. *Śrīmad-Bhāgavatam* is so made that one becomes at once engaged in the path of self-realization simply by hearing the topics. Although it is especially meant for the *paramahaṁsas,* or those who are totally engaged in self-realization, it works into the depths of the hearts of those who may be worldly men. Worldly men are all engaged in sense gratification. But even such men will find in this Vedic literature a remedial measure for their material diseases. Śukadeva Gosvāmī was a liberated soul from the very beginning of his birth, and his father taught him *Śrīmad-Bhāgavatam.* Amongst mundane scholars, there is some diversity of opinion as to the date of compilation of *Śrīmad-Bhāgavatam.* It is, however, certain from the text of the *Bhāgavatam* that it was compiled before the disappearance of King Parīkṣit and after the departure of Lord Kṛṣṇa. When Mahārāja Parīkṣit was ruling the world as the King of Bhārata-varṣa, he chastised the personality of Kali. According to revealed scriptures and astrological calculation, the age of Kali is in its five thousandth year. Therefore, *Śrīmad-Bhāgavatam* was compiled not less than five thousand years ago. *Mahābhārata* was compiled before *Śrīmad-Bhāgavatam,* and the *Purāṇas* were compiled before *Mahābhārata.* That is an estimation of the date of compilation of the different Vedic literatures. The synopsis of *Śrīmad-Bhāgavatam* was given before the detailed description under instruction of Nārada. *Śrīmad-Bhāgavatam* is the science for following the path of *nivṛtti-mārga.* The path of *pravṛtti-mārga* was condemned by Nārada. That path is the natural inclination for all conditioned souls. The theme of *Śrīmad-Bhāgavatam* is the cure of the materialistic disease of the human being, or stopping completely the pangs of material existence.

शौनक उवाच

TEXT 9

स वै निवृत्तिनिरतः सर्वत्रोपेक्षको मुनिः ।
कस्य वा बृहतीमेतामात्मारामः समभ्यसत् ॥ ९ ॥

śaunaka uvāca
sa vai nivṛtti-nirataḥ sarvatropekṣako muniḥ
kasya vā bṛhatīm etām ātmārāmaḥ samabhyasat

śaunakaḥ uvāca—Śrī Śaunaka asked; *saḥ*—he; *vai*—of course; *nivṛtti*—on the path of self-realization; *nirataḥ*—always engaged; *sarvatra*—in every respect; *upekṣakaḥ*—indifferent; *muniḥ*—sage; *kasya*—for what reason; *vā*—or; *bṛhatīm*—vast; *etām*—this; *ātma-ārāmaḥ*—one who is pleased in himself; *samabhyasat*—undergo the studies.

Śrī Śaunaka asked Sūta Gosvāmī: Śrī Śukadeva Gosvāmī was already on the path of self-realization, and thus he was pleased with his own self. So why did he take the trouble to undergo the study of such a vast literature?

PURPORT For the people in general the highest perfection of life is to cease from material activities and be fixed on the path of self-realization. Those who take pleasure in sense enjoyment, or those who are fixed in material bodily welfare work, are called *karmīs.* Out of thousands and millions of such *karmīs,* one may become an *ātmārāma* by self-realization. *Ātmā* means self, and *ārāma* means to take pleasure. Everyone is searching after the highest pleasure, but the standard of pleasure of one may be different from the standard of another. Therefore, the standard of pleasure enjoyed by the *karmīs* is different from that of the *ātmārāmas.* The *ātmārāmas* are completely indifferent to material enjoyment in every respect. Śrīla Śukadeva Gosvāmī had already attained that stage, and still he was attracted to undergo the trouble of studying the great *Bhāgavatam* literature. This means that *Śrīmad-Bhāgavatam* is a postgraduate study even for the *ātmārāmas,* who have surpassed all the studies of Vedic knowledge.

सूत उवाच

TEXT 10

आत्मारामाश्च मुनयो निर्ग्रन्था अप्युरुक्रमे ।
कुर्वन्त्यहैतुकीं भक्तिमित्थम्भूतगुणो हरिः ॥ १० ॥

sūta uvāca
ātmārāmāś ca munayo nirgranthā apy urukrame
kurvanty ahaitukīṁ bhaktim ittham-bhūta-guṇo hariḥ

sūtaḥ uvāca—Sūta Gosvāmī said; *ātmārāmāḥ*—those who take pleasure in the *ātmā* (generally, spirit self); *ca*—also; *munayaḥ*—sages; *nirgranthāḥ*—freed from all bondage; *api*—in spite of; *urukrame*—unto the great adventurer; *kurvanti*—do; *ahaitukīm*—unalloyed; *bhaktim*—devotional service; *ittham-bhūta*—such wonderful; *guṇaḥ*—qualities; *hariḥ*—of the Lord.

Sūta Gosvāmī said: All different varieties of ātmārāmas [those who take pleasure in the ātmā, or spirit self], especially those established on the path of self-realization, though freed from all kinds of material bondage, desire to render unalloyed devotional service unto the Personality of Godhead. This means that the Lord possesses transcendental qualities and therefore can attract everyone, including liberated souls.

PURPORT Lord Śrī Caitanya Mahāprabhu explained this *ātmārāma śloka* very vividly before His chief devotee Śrīla Sanātana Gosvāmī. He points out eleven factors in the *śloka,* namely (1) *ātmārāma,* (2) *munayaḥ,* (3) *nirgrantha,* (4) *api,* (5) *ca,* (6) *urukrama,* (7) *kurvanti,* (8) *ahaitukīm,* (9) *bhaktim,* (10) *ittham-bhūta-guṇaḥ* and (11) *hariḥ.* According to the *Viśva-prakāśa* Sanskrit dictionary, there are seven synonyms for the word *ātmā,* which are as follows: (1) Brahman (the Absolute Truth), (2) body, (3) mind, (4) endeavor, (5) endurance, (6) intelligence and (7) personal habits.

The word *munayaḥ* refers to (1) those who are thoughtful, (2) those who are grave and silent, (3) ascetics, (4) the persistent, (5) mendicants, (6) sages and (7) saints.

The word *nirgrantha* conveys these ideas: (1) one who is liberated from nescience, (2) one who has no connection with scriptural injunction, i.e., who is freed from the obligation of the rules and regulations mentioned in the revealed scriptures like ethics, *Vedas,* philosophy, psychology and metaphysics (in other words the fools, illiterate, urchins, etc., who have no connection with regulative principles), (3) a capitalist, and also (4) one who is penniless.

According to the *Śabda-kośa* dictionary, the affix *ni* is used in the sense of (1) certainty, (2) counting, (3) building, and (4) forbiddance, and the word *grantha* is used in the sense of wealth, thesis, vocabulary, etc.

The word *urukrama* means "the one whose activities are glorious." *Krama* means "step." This word *urukrama* specifically indicates the Lord's incarnation as Vāmana, who covered the whole universe by immeasurable steps. Lord Viṣṇu is powerful, and His activities are so glorious that He has created the spiritual world by His internal potency and the material world by His external potency. By His all-pervading features He is everywhere present as the Supreme Truth, and in His personal feature He is always present in His transcendental abode of Goloka Vṛndāvana, where He displays His transcendental pastimes in all variegatedness. His activities cannot be compared to anyone else's, and therefore the word *urukrama* is just applicable to Him only.

According to Sanskrit verbal arrangement, *kurvanti* refers to doing things for someone else. Therefore, it means that the *ātmārāmas* render devotional service unto the Lord not for personal interest but for the pleasure of the Lord, Urukrama.

Hetu means "causal." There are many causes for one's sense satisfaction, and they can be chiefly classified as material enjoyment, mystic powers and liberation, which are generally desired by progressive persons. As far as material enjoyments are concerned, they are innumerable, and the materialists are eager to increase them more and more because they are under the illusory energy. There is no end to the list of material enjoyments, nor can anyone in the material universe have all of them. As far as the mystic powers are concerned, they are eight in all (such as to become the minutest in form, to become weightless, to have anything one desires, to lord it over the material nature, to control other living beings, to throw earthly globes in outer space, etc.). These mystic powers are mentioned in the *Bhāgavatam.* The forms of liberation are five in number.

Therefore, unalloyed devotion means service to the Lord without desire for the above-mentioned personal benefits. And the powerful Personality of Godhead Śrī Kṛṣṇa can be fully satisfied by such unalloyed devotees free from all sorts of desires for personal benefit.

Unalloyed devotional service of the Lord progresses in different stages. Practice of devotional service in the material field is of eighty-one different qualities, and above such activities is the transcendental practice of devotional service, which is one and is called *sādhana-bhakti.* When unalloyed practice of *sādhana-bhakti* is matured into transcendental love for the Lord, the transcendental loving service of the Lord begins gradually developing into nine progressive stages of loving service under the headings of attachment, love, affection, feelings, affinity, adherence, following, ecstasy, and intense feelings of separation.

The attachment of an inactive devotee develops up to the stage of transcendental love of God. Attachment of an active servitor develops up to the stage of adherence, and that of a friendly devotee develops up to the stage of following, and the same is also the case for the parental devotees. Devotees in conjugal love develop ecstasy up to the stage of intense feelings of separation. These are some of the features of unalloyed devotional service of the Lord.

According to *Hari-bhakti-sudhodaya,* the import of the word *itthambhūta* is "complete bliss." Transcendental bliss in the realization of impersonal Brahman becomes comparable to the scanty water contained in the pit made by a cow's hoof. It is nothing compared with the ocean of bliss of the vision of the Personality of Godhead. The personal form of Lord Śrī Kṛṣṇa is so attractive that it comprehends all attraction, all bliss and all tastes (*rasas*). These attractions are so strong that *no one wants to exchange them for material enjoyment, mystic powers and liberation.* There is no need of logical arguments in support of this statement, but out of one's own nature one becomes attracted by the qualities of Lord Śrī Kṛṣṇa. We must know for certain that the qualities of the Lord have nothing to do with mundane qualities. All of them are full of bliss, knowledge and eternity. There are innumerable qualities of the Lord, and one is attracted by one quality while another is attracted by another.

Great sages, such as the four bachelor-devotees Sanaka, Sanātana, Sananda and Sanat-kumāra, were attracted by the fragrance of flowers and *tulasī* leaves anointed with the pulp of sandalwood offered at the lotus feet of the Lord. Similarly, Śukadeva Gosvāmī was attracted by the transcendental pastimes of the Lord. Śukadeva Gosvāmī was already situated in the liberated stage, yet he was attracted by the pastimes of the Lord. This proves that the quality of His pastimes has nothing to do with material affinity. Similarly, the young cowherd damsels were attracted by the bodily features of the Lord, and Rukmiṇī was attracted by hearing about the glories of the Lord. Lord Kṛṣṇa attracts even the mind of the goddess of fortune. He attracts, in special cases, the minds of all young girls. He attracts the minds of the elderly ladies by parental affection. He attracts the mind of the male in the humors of servitude and friendship.

The word *hari* conveys various meanings, but the chief import of the word is that He (the Lord) vanquishes everything inauspicious and takes away the mind of the devotee by awarding pure transcendental love. By remembering the Lord in acute distress one can be free from all varieties of miseries and anxieties. Gradually the Lord vanquishes all obstacles on the path of devotional service of a pure devotee, and the result of nine devotional activities, such as hearing and chanting, becomes manifested.

By His personal features and transcendental attributes, the Lord attracts all psychological activities of a pure devotee. Such is the attractive power of Lord Kṛṣṇa. The attraction is so powerful that a pure devotee never hankers for any one of the four principles of religion. These are the attractive features of the transcendental attributes of the Lord. And adding to this the words *api* and *ca,* one can increase the imports unlimitedly. According to Sanskrit grammar there are seven synonyms for the word *api.*

So by interpreting each and every word of this *śloka,* one can see unlimited numbers of transcendental qualities of Lord Kṛṣṇa that attract the mind of a pure devotee.

TEXT 11

हरेर्गुणाक्षिप्तमतिर्भगवान् बादरायणिः ।
अध्यगान्महदाख्यानं नित्यं विष्णुजनप्रियः ॥ ११ ॥

harer guṇākṣipta-matir bhagavān bādarāyaṇiḥ
adhyagān mahad ākhyānaṁ nityaṁ viṣṇu-jana-priyaḥ

hareḥ—of Hari, the Personality of Godhead; *guṇa*—transcendental attributes; *ākṣipta*—being absorbed in; *matiḥ*—mind; *bhagavān*—powerful; *bādarāyaṇiḥ*—the son of Vyāsadeva; *adhyagāt*—underwent studies; *mahat*—great; *ākhyānam*—narration; *nityam*—regularly; *viṣṇu-jana*—devotees of the Lord; *priyaḥ*—beloved.

Śrīla Śukadeva Gosvāmī, son of Śrīla Vyāsadeva, was not only transcendentally powerful. He was also very dear to the devotees of the Lord. Thus he underwent the study of this great narration [Śrīmad-Bhāgavatam].

PURPORT According to *Brahma-vaivarta Purāṇa,* Śrīla Śukadeva Gosvāmī was a liberated soul even within the womb of his mother. Śrīla Vyāsadeva knew that the child, after his birth, would not stay at home. Therefore he (Vyāsadeva) impressed upon him the synopsis of the *Bhāgavatam* so that the child could be made attached to the transcendental activities of the Lord. After his birth, the child was still more educated in the subject of the *Bhāgavatam* by recitation of the actual poems.

The idea is that generally the liberated souls are attached to the feature of impersonal Brahman with a monistic view of becoming one with the supreme whole. But by the association of pure devotees like Vyāsadeva, even the liberated soul becomes attracted to the transcendental qualities of the Lord. By the mercy of Śrī Nārada, Śrīla Vyāsadeva was able to narrate the great epic of *Śrīmad-Bhāgavatam,* and by the mercy of Vyāsadeva, Śrīla Śukadeva Gosvāmī was able to grasp the import. The transcendental qualities of the Lord are so attractive that Śrīla Śukadeva Gosvāmī became detached from being completely absorbed in impersonal Brahman and positively took up the personal activity of the Lord.

Practically he was thrown from the impersonal conception of the Absolute, thinking within himself that he had simply wasted so much time in devoting himself to the impersonal feature of the Supreme, or in other words, he realized more transcendental bliss with the personal feature than the impersonal. And from that time, not only did he himself become very dear to the *viṣṇu-janas,* or the devotees of the Lord, but also the *viṣṇu-janas* became very dear to him. The devotees of the Lord, who do not wish to kill the individuality of the living entities and who desire to become personal servitors of the Lord, do not very much like the impersonalists, and similarly the impersonalists, who desire to become one with the Supreme, are unable to evaluate the devotees of the Lord. Thus from time immemorial these two transcendental pilgrims have sometimes been competitors. In other words, each of them likes to keep separate from the other because of the ultimate personal and impersonal realizations. Therefore it appears that Śrīla Śukadeva Gosvāmī also had no liking for the devotees. But since he himself became a saturated devotee, he desired always the transcendental association of the *viṣṇu-janas,* and the *viṣṇu-janas* also liked his association, since he became a personal *Bhāgavata.* Thus both the son and the father were completely cognizant of transcendental knowledge in Brahman, and afterwards both of them became absorbed in the personal features of the Supreme Lord. The question as to how Śukadeva Gosvāmī was attracted by the narration of the *Bhāgavatam* is thus completely answered by this *śloka.*

TEXT 12

परीक्षितोऽथ राजर्षेर्जन्मकर्मविलापनम् ।
संस्थां च पाण्डुपुत्राणां वक्ष्ये कृष्णकथोदयम् ॥ १२ ॥

parīkṣito 'tha rājarṣer janma-karma-vilāpanam
saṁsthāṁ ca pāṇḍu-putrāṇāṁ vakṣye kṛṣṇa-kathodayam

parīkṣitaḥ—of King Parīkṣit; *atha*—thus; *rājarṣeḥ*—of the King who was the *ṛṣi* among the kings; *janma*—birth; *karma*—activities; *vilāpanam*—deliverance; *saṁsthām*—renunciation of the world; *ca*—and; *pāṇḍu-putrāṇām*—of the sons of Pāṇḍu; *vakṣye*—I shall speak; *kṛṣṇa-kathā-udayam*—that which gives rise to the transcendental narration of Kṛṣṇa, the Supreme Personality of Godhead.

Sūta Gosvāmī thus addressed the ṛṣis headed by Śaunaka: Now I shall

begin the transcendental narration of the Lord Śrī Kṛṣṇa and topics of the birth, activities and deliverance of King Parīkṣit, the sage amongst kings, as well as topics of the renunciation of the worldly order by the sons of Pāṇḍu.

PURPORT Lord Kṛṣṇa is so kind to the fallen souls that He personally incarnates Himself amongst the different kinds of living entities and takes part with them in daily activities. Any historical fact old or new which has a connection with the activities of the Lord is to be understood as a transcendental narration of the Lord. Without Kṛṣṇa, all the supplementary literatures like the *Purāṇas* and *Mahābhārata* are simply stories or historical facts. But with Kṛṣṇa they become transcendental, and when we hear of them we at once become transcendentally related with the Lord. *Śrīmad-Bhāgavatam* is also a *Purāṇa,* but the special significance of this *Purāṇa* is that the activities of the Lord are central and not just supplementary historical facts. *Śrīmad-Bhāgavatam* is thus recommended by Lord Śrī Caitanya Mahāprabhu as the spotless *Purāṇa.* There is a class of less intelligent devotees of the *Bhāgavata Purāṇa* who desire to relish at once the activities of the Lord narrated in the Tenth Canto without first understanding the primary cantos. They are under the false impression that the other cantos are not concerned with Kṛṣṇa, and thus more foolishly than intelligently they take to the reading of the Tenth Canto. These readers are specifically told herein that the other cantos of the *Bhāgavatam* are as important as the Tenth Canto. No one should try to go into the matters of the Tenth Canto without having thoroughly understood the purport of the other nine cantos. Kṛṣṇa and His pure devotees like the Pāṇḍavas are on the same plane. Kṛṣṇa is not without His devotees of all the *rasas,* and the pure devotees like the Pāṇḍavas are not without Kṛṣṇa. The devotees and the Lord are interlinked, and they cannot be separated. Therefore talks about them are all *kṛṣṇa-kathā,* or topics of the Lord.

TEXTS 13–14

यदा मृधे कौरवसृञ्जयानां
वीरेष्वथो वीरगतिं गतेषु ।
वृकोदराविद्धगदाभिमर्श-
भग्नोरुदण्डे धृतराष्ट्रपुत्रे ॥ १३ ॥

भर्तुः प्रियं द्रौणिरिति स्म पश्यन्
कृष्णासुतानां स्वपतां शिरांसि ।
उपाहरद्विप्रियमेव तस्य
जुगुप्सितं कर्म विगर्हयन्ति ॥ १४ ॥

yadā mṛdhe kaurava-sṛñjayānāṁ
vīreṣv atho vīra-gatiṁ gateṣu
vṛkodarāviddha-gadābhimarśa-
bhagnoru-daṇḍe dhṛtarāṣṭra-putre

bhartuḥ priyaṁ drauṇir iti sma paśyan
kṛṣṇā-sutānāṁ svapatāṁ śirāṁsi
upāharad vipriyam eva tasya
jugupsitaṁ karma vigarhayanti

yadā—when; *mṛdhe*—in the battlefield; *kaurava*—the party of Dhṛtarāṣṭra; *sṛñjayānām*—of the party of the Pāṇḍavas; *vīreṣu*—of the warriors; *atho*—thus; *vīra-gatim*—the destination deserved by the warriors; *gateṣu*—being obtained; *vṛkodara*—Bhīma (the second Pāṇḍava); *āviddha*—beaten; *gadā*—by the club; *abhimarśa*—lamenting; *bhagna*—broken; *uru-daṇḍe*—spinal cord; *dhṛtarāṣṭra-putre*—the son of King Dhṛtarāṣṭra; *bhartuḥ*—of the master; *priyam*—pleasing; *drauṇiḥ*—the son of Droṇācārya; *iti*—thus; *sma*—shall be; *paśyan*—seeing; *kṛṣṇā*—Draupadī; *sutānām*—of the sons; *svapatām*—while sleeping; *śirāṁsi*—heads; *upāharat*—delivered as a prize; *vipriyam*—displeasing; *eva*—like; *tasya*—his; *jugupsitam*—most heinous; *karma*—act; *vigarhayanti*—disapproving.

When the respective warriors of both camps, namely the Kauravas and the Pāṇḍavas, were killed on the Battlefield of Kurukṣetra and the dead warriors obtained their deserved destinations, and when the son of Dhṛtarāṣṭra fell down lamenting, his spine broken, being beaten by the club of Bhīmasena, the son of Droṇācārya [Aśvatthāmā] beheaded the five sleeping sons of Draupadī and delivered the heads as a prize to his master, foolishly thinking that he would be pleased. Duryodhana, however, disapproved of the heinous act, and he was not pleased in the least.

PURPORT Transcendental topics of the activities of Lord Śrī Kṛṣṇa in the *Śrīmad-Bhāgavatam* begin from the end of the battle at Kurukṣetra, where the Lord Himself spoke about Himself in the *Bhagavad-gītā*. Therefore, both the *Bhagavad-gītā* and *Śrīmad-Bhāgavatam* are transcendental topics of Lord Kṛṣṇa. The *Gītā* is *kṛṣṇa-kathā,* or topics of Kṛṣṇa, because it is spoken by the Lord, and the *Bhāgavatam* is also *kṛṣṇa-kathā* because it is spoken about the Lord. Lord Śrī Caitanya Mahāprabhu wanted everyone to be informed of both *kṛṣṇa-kathās* by His order. Lord Kṛṣṇa Caitanya is Kṛṣṇa Himself in the garb of a devotee of Kṛṣṇa, and therefore the versions of both Lord Kṛṣṇa and Śrī Kṛṣṇa Caitanya Mahāprabhu are identical. *Lord Caitanya desired that all who are born in India seriously understand such kṛṣṇa-kathās* and then after full realization preach the transcendental message to everyone in all parts of the world. That will bring about the desired peace and prosperity of the stricken world.

TEXT 15

माता शिशूनां निधनं सुतानां
निशम्य घोरं परितप्यमाना ।
तदारुदद्वाष्पकलाकुलाक्षी
तां सान्त्वयन्नाह किरीटमाली ॥ १५ ॥

mātā śiśūnāṁ nidhanaṁ sutānāṁ
niśamya ghoraṁ paritapyamānā
tadārudad vāṣpa-kalākulākṣī
tāṁ sāntvayann āha kirīṭamālī

mātā—the mother; *śiśūnām*—of the children; *nidhanam*—massacre; *sutānām*—of the sons; *niśamya*—after hearing; *ghoram*—ghastly; *paritapyamānā*—lamenting; *tadā*—at that time; *arudat*—began to cry; *vāṣpa-kala-ākula-akṣī*—with tears in the eyes; *tām*—her; *sāntvayan*—pacifying; *āha*—said; *kirīṭamālī*—Arjuna.

Draupadī, the mother of the five children of the Pāṇḍavas, after hearing of the massacre of her sons, began to cry in distress with eyes full of tears. Trying to pacify her in her great loss, Arjuna spoke to her thus:

TEXT 16

तदा शुचस्ते प्रमृजामि भद्रे
यद्ब्रह्मबन्धोः शिर आततायिनः ।
गाण्डीवमुक्तैर्विशिखैरुपाहरे
त्वाक्रम्य यत्स्नास्यसि दग्धपुत्रा ॥ १६ ॥

tadā śucas te pramṛjāmi bhadre
yad brahma-bandhoḥ śira ātatāyinaḥ
gāṇḍīva-muktair viśikhair upāhare
tvākramya yat snāsyasi dagdha-putrā

tadā—at that time only; *śucaḥ*—tears in grief; *te*—your; *pramṛjāmi*—shall wipe away; *bhadre*—O gentle lady; *yat*—when; *brahma-bandhoḥ*—of a degraded *brāhmaṇa; śiraḥ*—head; *ātatāyinaḥ*—of the aggressor; *gāṇḍīva-muktaiḥ*—shot by the bow named Gāṇḍīva; *viśikhaiḥ*—by the arrows; *upāhare*—shall present to you; *tvā*—yourself; *ākramya*—riding on it; *yat*—which; *snāsyasi*—take your bath; *dagdha-putrā*—after burning the sons.

O gentle lady, when I present you with the head of that brāhmaṇa, after beheading him with arrows from my Gāṇḍīva bow, I shall then wipe the tears from your eyes and pacify you. Then, after burning your sons' bodies, you can take your bath standing on his head.

PURPORT An enemy who sets fire to the house, administers poison, attacks all of a sudden with deadly weapons, plunders wealth or usurps agricultural fields, or entices one's wife is called an aggressor. Such an aggressor, though he be a *brāhmaṇa* or a so-called son of a *brāhmaṇa,* has to be punished in all circumstances. When Arjuna promised to behead the aggressor named Aśvatthāmā, he knew well that Aśvatthāmā was the son of a *brāhmaṇa,* but because the so-called *brāhmaṇa* acted like a butcher, he was taken as such, and there was no question of sin in killing such a *brāhmaṇa's* son who proved to be a villain.

TEXT 17

इति प्रियां वल्गुविचित्रजल्पैः
स सान्त्वयित्वाच्युतमित्रसूतः ।

अन्वाद्रवद्दंशित उग्रधन्वा
कपिध्वजो गुरुपुत्रं रथेन ॥ १७ ॥

iti priyāṁ valgu-vicitra-jalpaiḥ
sa sāntvayitvācyuta-mitra-sūtaḥ
anvādravad daṁśita ugra-dhanvā
kapi-dhvajo guru-putraṁ rathena

iti—thus; *priyām*—unto the dear; *valgu*—sweet; *vicitra*—variegated; *jalpaiḥ*—by statements; *saḥ*—he; *sāntvayitvā*—satisfying; *acyuta-mitra-sūtaḥ*—Arjuna, who is guided by the infallible Lord as a friend and driver; *anvādravat*—followed; *daṁśitaḥ*—being protected by *kavaca; ugra-dhanvā*—equipped with furious weapons; *kapi-dhvajaḥ*—Arjuna; *guru-putram*—the son of the martial teacher; *rathena*—getting on the chariot.

Arjuna, who is guided by the infallible Lord as friend and driver, thus satisfied the dear lady by such statements. Then he dressed in armor and armed himself with furious weapons, and getting into his chariot, he set out to follow Aśvatthāmā, the son of his martial teacher.

TEXT 18

तमापतन्तं स विलक्ष्य दूरात्
कुमारहोद्विग्नमना रथेन ।
पराद्रवत्प्राणपरीप्सुरुर्व्यां
यावद्गमं रुद्रभयाद्यथाकः ॥ १८ ॥

tam āpatantaṁ sa vilakṣya dūrāt
kumāra-hodvigna-manā rathena
parādravat prāṇa-parīpsur urvyāṁ
yāvad-gamaṁ rudra-bhayād yathā kaḥ

tam—him; *āpatantam*—coming over furiously; *saḥ*—he; *vilakṣya*—seeing; *dūrāt*—from a distance; *kumāra-hā*—the murderer of the princes; *udvigna-manāḥ*—disturbed in mind; *rathena*—on the chariot; *parādravat*—fled; *prāṇa*—life; *parīpsuḥ*—for protecting; *urvyām*—with great speed; *yāvat-gamam*—as he fled; *rudra-bhayāt*—by fear of Śiva; *yathā*—as; *kaḥ*—Brahmā (or *arkaḥ*—Sūrya).

Aśvatthāmā, the murderer of the princes, seeing from a great distance Arjuna coming at him with great speed, fled in his chariot, panic-stricken, just to save his life, as Brahmā fled in fear from Śiva.

PURPORT According to the reading matter, either *kaḥ* or *arkaḥ*, there are two references in the *Purāṇas*. *Kaḥ* means Brahmā, who once became allured by his daughter and began to follow her, which infuriated Śiva, who attacked Brahmā with his trident. Brahmājī fled in fear of his life. As far as *arkaḥ* is concerned, there is a reference in the *Vāmana Purāṇa*. There was a demon by the name Vidyunmālī who was gifted with a glowing golden airplane which traveled to the back of the sun, and night disappeared because of the glowing effulgence of this plane. Thus the sun-god became angry, and with his virulent rays he melted the plane. This enraged Lord Śiva. Lord Śiva then attacked the sun-god, who fled away and at last fell down at Kāśī (Vārāṇasī), and the place became famous as Lolārka.

TEXT 19

यदाशरणमात्मानमैक्षत श्रान्तवाजिनम् ।
अस्त्रं ब्रह्मशिरो मेने आत्मत्राणं द्विजात्मजः ॥ १९ ॥

yadāśaraṇam ātmānam aikṣata śrānta-vājinam
astraṁ brahma-śiro mene ātma-trāṇaṁ dvijātmajaḥ

yadā—when; *aśaraṇam*—without being alternatively protected; *ātmānam*—his own self; *aikṣata*—saw; *śrānta-vājinam*—the horses being tired; *astram*—weapon; *brahma-śiraḥ*—the topmost or ultimate (nuclear); *mene*—applied; *ātma-trāṇam*—just to save himself; *dvija-ātmajaḥ*—the son of a *brāhmaṇa*.

When the son of the brāhmaṇa [Aśvatthāmā] saw that his horses were tired, he considered that there was no alternative for protection outside of his using the ultimate weapon, the brahmāstra [nuclear weapon].

PURPORT In the ultimate issue only, when there is no alternative, the nuclear weapon called the *brahmāstra* is applied. The word *dvijātmajaḥ* is significant here because Aśvatthāmā, although the son of Droṇācārya, was not exactly a qualified *brāhmaṇa*. The most intelligent man is called a *brāhmaṇa*, and it is not a hereditary title. Aśvatthāmā was also formerly called the *brahma-bandhu*, or the friend of a *brāhmaṇa*. Being a friend of a *brāhmaṇa* does not mean that one is a *brāhmaṇa* by qualification. A friend or son of a *brāhmaṇa*, when fully qualified, can be called a *brāhmaṇa* and not otherwise. Since Aśvatthāmā's decision is immature, he is purposely called herein the son of a *brāhmaṇa*.

TEXT 20

अथोपस्पृश्य सलिलं सन्दधे तत्समाहितः ।
अजानन्नपिसंहारं प्राणकृच्छ्र उपस्थिते ॥ २० ॥

athopaspṛśya salilaṁ sandadhe tat samāhitaḥ
ajānann api saṁhāraṁ prāṇa-kṛcchra upasthite

atha—thus; *upaspṛśya*—touching in sanctity; *salilam*—water; *sandadhe*—chanted the hymns; *tat*—that; *samāhitaḥ*—being in concentration; *ajānan*—without knowing; *api*—although; *saṁhāram*—withdrawal; *prāṇa-kṛcchre*—life being put in danger; *upasthite*—being placed in such a position.

Since his life was in danger, he touched water in sanctity and concentrated upon the chanting of the hymns for throwing nuclear weapons, although he did not know how to withdraw such weapons.

PURPORT The subtle forms of material activities are finer than grosser methods of material manipulation. Such subtle forms of material activities are effected through purification of sound. The same method is adopted here by chanting hymns to act as nuclear weapons.

TEXT 21

ततः प्रादुष्कृतं तेजः प्रचण्डं सर्वतोदिशम् ।
प्राणापदमभिप्रेक्ष्य विष्णुं जिष्णुरुवाच ह ॥ २१ ॥

tataḥ prāduṣkṛtaṁ tejaḥ pracaṇḍaṁ sarvato diśam
prāṇāpadam abhiprekṣya viṣṇuṁ jiṣṇur uvāca ha

tataḥ—thereafter; *prāduṣkṛtam*—disseminated; *tejaḥ*—glare; *pracaṇḍam*—fierce; *sarvataḥ*—all around; *diśam*—directions; *prāṇa-āpadam*—affecting life; *abhiprekṣya*—having observed it; *viṣṇum*—unto the Lord; *jiṣṇuḥ*—Arjuna; *uvāca*—said; *ha*—in the past.

Thereupon a glaring light spread in all directions. It was so fierce that Arjuna thought his own life in danger, and so he began to address Lord Śrī Kṛṣṇa.

TEXT 22

अर्जुन उवाच
कृष्ण कृष्ण महाबाहो भक्तानामभयङ्कर ।
त्वमेको दह्यमानानामपवर्गोऽसि संसृतेः ॥ २२ ॥

arjuna uvāca
kṛṣṇa kṛṣṇa mahā-bāho bhaktānām abhayaṅkara
tvam eko dahyamānānām apavargo 'si saṁsṛteḥ

arjunaḥ uvāca—Arjuna said; *kṛṣṇa*—O Lord Kṛṣṇa; *kṛṣṇa*—O Lord Kṛṣṇa; *mahā-bāho*—He who is the Almighty; *bhaktānām*—of the devotees; *abhayaṅkara*—eradicating the fears of; *tvam*—You; *ekaḥ*—alone; *dahyamānānām*—those who are suffering from; *apavargaḥ*—the path of liberation; *asi*—are; *saṁsṛteḥ*—in the midst of material miseries.

Arjuna said: O my Lord Śrī Kṛṣṇa, You are the almighty Personality of Godhead. There is no limit to Your different energies. Therefore only You are competent to instill fearlessness in the hearts of Your devotees. Everyone in the flames of material miseries can find the path of liberation in You only.

PURPORT Arjuna was aware of the transcendental qualities of Lord Śrī Kṛṣṇa, as he had already experienced them during the Kurukṣetra War, in which both of them were present. Therefore, Arjuna's version of Lord Kṛṣṇa is authoritative. Kṛṣṇa is almighty and is especially the cause of fearlessness for the devotees. A devotee of the Lord is always fearless because of the protection given by the Lord. Material existence is something like a blazing fire in the forest, which can be extinguished by the mercy of the Lord Śrī Kṛṣṇa. The spiritual master is the mercy representative of the Lord. Therefore, a person burning in the flames of material existence may receive the rains of mercy of the Lord through the transparent medium of the self-realized spiritual master. The spiritual master, by his words, can penetrate into the heart of the suffering person and inject knowledge transcendental, which alone can extinguish the fire of material existence.

TEXT 23

त्वमाद्यः पुरुषः साक्षादीश्वरः प्रकृतेः परः ।
मायां व्युदस्य चिच्छक्त्या कैवल्ये स्थित आत्मनि ॥ २३ ॥

tvam ādyaḥ puruṣaḥ sākṣād īśvaraḥ prakṛteḥ paraḥ
māyāṁ vyudasya cic-chaktyā kaivalye sthita ātmani

tvam ādyaḥ—You are the original; *puruṣaḥ*—the enjoying personality; *sākṣāt*—directly; *īśvaraḥ*—the controller; *prakṛteḥ*—of material nature; *paraḥ*—transcendental; *māyām*—the material energy; *vyudasya*—one who has thrown aside; *cit-śaktyā*—by dint of internal potency; *kaivalye*—in pure eternal knowledge and bliss; *sthitaḥ*—placed; *ātmani*—own self.

You are the original Personality of Godhead who expands Himself all over the creations and is transcendental to material energy. You have cast away the effects of the material energy by dint of Your spiritual potency. You are always situated in eternal bliss and transcendental knowledge.

PURPORT The Lord states in the *Bhagavad-gītā* that one who surrenders unto the lotus feet of the Lord can get release from the clutches of nescience. Kṛṣṇa is just like the sun, and *māyā* or material existence is just like darkness. Wherever there is the light of the sun, darkness or ignorance at once vanishes. The best means to get out of the world of ignorance is suggested here. The Lord is addressed herein as the original Personality of Godhead. From Him all other Personalities of Godhead expand. The all-pervasive Lord Viṣṇu is Lord Kṛṣṇa's plenary portion or expansion. The Lord expands Himself in innumerable forms of Godhead and living beings, along with His different energies. But Śrī Kṛṣṇa is the original primeval Lord from whom everything emanates. The all-pervasive feature of the Lord experienced within the manifested world is also a partial representation of the Lord. Paramātmā, therefore, is included within Him. He is the Absolute Personality of Godhead. He has nothing to do with the actions and reactions of the material manifestation because He is far above the material creation. Darkness is a perverse representation of the sun, and therefore the existence of darkness depends on the existence of the sun, but in the sun proper there is no trace of darkness. As the sun is full of light only, similarly the Absolute Personality of Godhead, beyond the material existence, is full of bliss. He is not only full of bliss, but also full of transcendental variegatedness. Transcendence is not at all static, but full of dynamic variegatedness. He is distinct from the material nature, which is complicated by the three modes of material nature. He is *parama,* or the chief. Therefore He is absolute. He has manifold energies, and through His diverse energies He creates, manifests, maintains and destroys the material world. In His own abode, however, everything is eternal and absolute. The world is not conducted by the energies or powerful agents by themselves, but by the potent all-powerful with all energies.

TEXT 24

स एव जीवलोकस्य मायामोहितचेतसः ।
विधत्से स्वेन वीर्येण श्रेयो धर्मादिलक्षणम् ॥ २४ ॥

sa eva jīva-lokasya māyā-mohita-cetasaḥ
vidhatse svena vīryeṇa śreyo dharmādi-lakṣaṇam

saḥ—that Transcendence; *eva*—certainly; *jīva-lokasya*—of the conditioned living beings; *māyā-mohita*—captivated by the illusory energy; *cetasaḥ*—by the heart; *vidhatse*—execute; *svena*—by Your own; *vīryeṇa*—influence; *śreyaḥ*—ultimate good; *dharma-ādi*—four principles of liberation; *lakṣaṇam*—characterized by.

And yet, though You are beyond the purview of the material energy, You execute the four principles of liberation characterized by religion and so on for the ultimate good of the conditioned souls.

PURPORT The Personality of Godhead Śrī Kṛṣṇa, out of His causeless mercy, descends on the manifested world without being influenced by the material modes of nature. He is eternally beyond the material manifestations. He descends out of His causeless mercy only to reclaim the fallen souls who are captivated by the illusory energy. They are attacked by the material energy, and they want to enjoy her under false pretexts, although in essence the living entity is unable to enjoy. One is eternally the servitor of the Lord, and when he forgets this position he thinks of enjoying the material world, but factually he is in illusion. The Lord descends to eradicate this false sense of enjoyment and thus reclaim conditioned souls back to Godhead. That is the all-merciful nature of the Lord for the fallen souls.

TEXT 25

तथायं चावतारस्ते भुवो भारजिहीर्षया ।
स्वानां चानन्यभावानामनुध्यानाय चासकृत् ॥ २५ ॥

tathāyaṁ cāvatāras te bhuvo bhāra-jihīrṣayā
svānāṁ cānanya-bhāvānām anudhyānāya cāsakṛt

tathā—thus; *ayam*—this; *ca*—and; *avatāraḥ*—incarnation; *te*—Your; *bhuvaḥ*—of the material world; *bhāra*—burden; *jihīrṣayā*—for removing; *svānām*—of the friends; *ca ananya-bhāvānām*—and of the exclusive devotees; *anudhyānāya*—for remembering repeatedly; *ca*—and; *asakṛt*—fully satisfied.

Thus You descend as an incarnation to remove the burden of the world and to benefit Your friends, especially those who are Your exclusive devotees and are constantly rapt in meditation upon You.

PURPORT It appears that the Lord is partial to His devotees. Everyone is related with the Lord. He is equal to everyone, and yet He is more inclined to His own men and devotees. The Lord is everyone's father. No one can be His father, and yet no one can be His son. His devotees are His kinsmen, and His devotees are His relations. This is His transcendental pastime. It has nothing to do with mundane ideas of relations, fatherhood or anything like that. As mentioned above, the Lord is above the modes of material nature, and thus there is nothing mundane about His kinsmen and relations in devotional service.

TEXT 26

किमिदं स्वित्कुतो वेति देवदेव न वेद्म्यहम् ।
सर्वतोमुखमायाति तेजः परमदारुणम् ॥ २६ ॥

kim idaṁ svit kuto veti deva-deva na vedmy aham
sarvato mukham āyāti tejaḥ parama-dāruṇam

kim—what is; *idam*—this; *svit*—does it come; *kutaḥ*—wherefrom; *vā iti*—be either; *deva-deva*—O Lord of lords; *na*—not; *vedmi*—do I know; *aham*—I; *sarvataḥ*—all around; *mukham*—directions; *āyāti*—coming from; *tejaḥ*—effulgence; *parama*—very much; *dāruṇam*—dangerous.

O Lord of lords, how is it that this dangerous effulgence is spreading all around? Where does it come from? I do not understand it.

PURPORT Anything that is presented before the Personality of Godhead should be so done after due presentation of respectful prayers. That is the standard procedure, and Śrī Arjuna, although an intimate friend of the Lord, is observing this method for general information.

TEXT 27

श्रीभगवानुवाच
वेत्थेदं द्रोणपुत्रस्य ब्राह्ममस्त्रं प्रदर्शितम् ।
नैवासौ वेद संहारं प्राणबाध उपस्थिते ॥ २७ ॥

śrī-bhagavān uvāca
vetthedaṁ droṇa-putrasya brāhmam astraṁ pradarśitam
naivāsau veda saṁhāraṁ prāṇa-bādha upasthite

śrī-bhagavān—the Supreme Personality of Godhead; *uvāca*—said; *vettha*—just know from Me; *idam*—this; *droṇa-putrasya*—of the son of Droṇa; *brāhmam astram*—hymns of the *brāhma* (nuclear) weapon; *pradarśitam*—exhibited; *na*—not; *eva*—even; *asau*—he; *veda*—know it; *saṁhāram*—retraction; *prāṇa-bādhe*—extinction of life; *upasthite*—being imminent.

The Supreme Personality of Godhead said: Know from Me that this is the act of the son of Droṇa. He has thrown the hymns of nuclear energy [brahmāstra], and he does not know how to retract the glare.

He has helplessly done this, being afraid of imminent death.

PURPORT The *brahmāstra* is similar to the modern nuclear weapon manipulated by atomic energy. The atomic energy works wholly on total combustibility, and so the *brahmāstra* also acts. It creates an intolerable heat similar to atomic radiation, but the difference is that the atomic bomb is a gross type of nuclear weapon, whereas the *brahmāstra* is a subtle type of weapon produced by chanting hymns. It is a different science, and in the days gone by such science was cultivated in the land of Bhārata-varṣa. The subtle *science of chanting hymns* is also *material,* but it has yet to be known by the modern material scientists. Subtle material science *is not spiritual,* but it has a direct relationship with the spiritual method, which is still subtler. A chanter of hymns knew how to apply the weapon as well as how to retract it. That was perfect knowledge. But the son of Droṇācārya, who made use of this subtle science, did not know how to retract. He applied it, being afraid of his imminent death, and thus the practice was not only improper but also irreligious. As the son of a *brāhmaṇa,* he should not have made so many mistakes, and for such gross negligence of duty he was to be punished by the Lord Himself.

TEXT 28

न ह्यस्यान्यतमं किञ्चिदस्त्रं प्रत्यवकर्शनम् ।
जह्यस्त्रतेज उन्नद्धमस्त्रज्ञो ह्यस्त्रतेजसा ॥ २८ ॥

na hy asyānyatamaṁ kiñcid astraṁ pratyavakarśanam
jahy astra-teja unnaddham astra-jño hy astra-tejasā

na—not; *hi*—certainly; *asya*—of it; *anyatamam*—other; *kiñcit*—anything; *astram*—weapon; *prati*—counter; *avakarśanam*—reactionary; *jahi*—subdue it; *astra-tejaḥ*—the glare of this weapon; *unnaddham*—very powerful; *astra-jñaḥ*—expert in military science; *hi*—as a matter of fact; *astra-tejasā*—by the influence of your weapon.

O Arjuna, only another brahmāstra can counteract this weapon. Since you are expert in the military science, subdue this weapon's glare with the power of your own weapon.

PURPORT For the atomic bombs there is no counterweapon to neutralize the effects. But by subtle science the action of a *brahmāstra* can be counteracted, and those who were expert in the military science in those days could counteract the *brahmāstra*. The son of Droṇācārya did not know the art of counteracting the weapon, and therefore Arjuna was asked to counteract it by the power of his own weapon.

सूत उवाच

TEXT 29

श्रुत्वा भगवता प्रोक्तं फाल्गुनः परवीरहा ।
स्पृष्ट्वापस्तं परिक्रम्य ब्राह्मं ब्राह्मास्त्रं सन्दधे ॥ २९ ॥

sūta uvāca
śrutvā bhagavatā proktaṁ phālgunaḥ para-vīra-hā
spṛṣṭvāpas taṁ parikramya brāhmaṁ brāhmāstraṁ sandadhe

sūtaḥ—Sūta Gosvāmī; *uvāca*—said; *śrutvā*—after hearing; *bhagavatā*—by the Personality of Godhead; *proktam*—what was said; *phālgunaḥ*—another name of Śrī Arjuna; *para-vīra-hā*—the killer of the opposing warrior; *spṛṣṭvā*—after touching; *āpaḥ*—water; *tam*—Him; *parikramya*—circumambulating; *brāhmam*—the Supreme Lord; *brāhma-astram*—the supreme weapon; *sandadhe*—acted on.

Śrī Sūta Gosvāmī said: Hearing this from the Personality of Godhead, Arjuna touched water for purification, and after circumambulating Lord Śrī Kṛṣṇa, he cast his brahmāstra weapon to counteract the other one.

TEXT 30

संहत्यान्योन्यमुभयोस्तेजसी शरसंवृते ।
आवृत्य रोदसी खं च ववृधातेऽर्कवह्निवत् ॥ ३० ॥

saṁhatyānyonyam ubhayos tejasī śara-saṁvṛte
āvṛtya rodasī khaṁ ca vavṛdhāte 'rka-vahnivat

saṁhatya—by combination of; *anyonyam*—one another; *ubhayoḥ*—of both; *tejasī*—the glares; *śara*—weapons; *saṁvṛte*—covering; *āvṛtya*—

covering; *rodasī*—the complete firmament; *kham ca*—outer space also; *vavṛdhāte*—increasing; *arka*—the sun globe; *vahni-vat*—like fire.

When the rays of the two brahmāstras combined, a great circle of fire, like the disc of the sun, covered all outer space and the whole firmament of planets.

PURPORT The heat created by the flash of a *brahmāstra* resembles the fire exhibited in the sun globe at the time of cosmic annihilation. The radiation of atomic energy is very insignificant in comparison to the heat produced by a *brahmāstra*. The atomic bomb explosion can at utmost blow up one globe, but the heat produced by the *brahmāstra* can destroy the whole cosmic situation. The comparison is therefore made to the heat at the time of annihilation.

TEXT 31

दृष्ट्वास्त्रतेजस्तु तयोस्त्रींल्लोकान् प्रदहन्महत् ।
दह्यमानाः प्रजाः सर्वाः सांवर्तकममंसत ॥ ३१ ॥

dṛṣṭvāstra-tejas tu tayos tril lokān pradahan mahat
dahyamānāḥ prajāḥ sarvāḥ sāṁvartakam amaṁsata

dṛṣṭvā—thus seeing; *astra*—weapon; *tejaḥ*—heat; *tu*—but; *tayoḥ*—of both; *trīn*—three; *lokān*—planets; *pradahat*—blazing; *mahat*—severely; *dahyamānāḥ*—burning; *prajāḥ*—population; *sarvāḥ*—all over; *sāṁvartakam*—the name of the fire which devastates during the annihilation of the universe; *amaṁsata*—began to think.

All the population of the three worlds was scorched by the combined heat of the weapons. Everyone was reminded of the sāṁvartaka fire which takes place at the time of annihilation.

PURPORT The three worlds are the upper, lower and intermediate planets of the universe. Although the *brahmāstra* was released on this earth, the heat produced by the combination of both weapons covered all the universe, and all the populations on all the different planets began to feel the heat excessively and compared it to that of the *sāṁvartaka* fire. No planet, therefore, is without living beings, as less intelligent materialistic men think.

TEXT 32

प्रजोपद्रवमालक्ष्य लोकव्यतिकरं च तम् ।
मतं च वासुदेवस्य सञ्जहारार्जुनो द्वयम् ॥ ३२ ॥

prajopadravam ālakṣya loka-vyatikaraṁ ca tam
mataṁ ca vāsudevasya sañjahārārjuno dvayam

prajā—the people in general; *upadravam*—disturbance; *ālakṣya*—having seen it; *loka*—the planets; *vyatikaram*—destruction; *ca*—also; *tam*—that; *matam ca*—and the opinion; *vāsudevasya*—of Vāsudeva, Śrī Kṛṣṇa; *sañjahāra*—retracted; *arjunaḥ*—Arjuna; *dvayam*—both the weapons.

Thus seeing the disturbance of the general populace and the imminent destruction of the planets, Arjuna at once retracted both brahmāstra weapons, as Lord Śrī Kṛṣṇa desired.

PURPORT The theory that the modern atomic bomb explosions can annihilate the world is childish imagination. First of all, the atomic energy is not powerful enough to destroy the world. And secondly, ultimately it all rests on the supreme will of the Supreme Lord because without His will or sanction nothing can be built up or destroyed. It is foolish also to think that natural laws are ultimately powerful. Material nature's law works under the direction of the Lord, as confirmed in the *Bhagavad-gītā*. The Lord says there that natural laws work under His supervision. The world can be destroyed only by the will of the Lord and not by the whims of tiny politicians. Lord Śrī Kṛṣṇa desired that the weapons released by both Drauṇi and Arjuna be withdrawn, and it was carried out by Arjuna at once. Similarly, there are many agents of the all-powerful Lord, and by His will only can one execute what He desires.

TEXT 33

तत आसाद्य तरसा दारुणं गौतमीसुतम् ।
बबन्धामर्षताम्राक्षः पशुं रशनया यथा ॥ ३३ ॥

tata āsādya tarasā dāruṇaṁ gautamī-sutam
babandhāmarṣa-tāmrākṣaḥ paśuṁ raśanayā yathā

tataḥ—thereupon; *āsādya*—arrested; *tarasā*—dexterously; *dāruṇam*—dangerous; *gautamī-sutam*—the son of Gautamī; *babandha*—bound up; *amarṣa*—angry; *tāmra-akṣaḥ*—with copper-red eyes; *paśum*—animal; *raśanayā*—by ropes; *yathā*—as it were.

Arjuna, his eyes blazing in anger like two red balls of copper, dexterously arrested the son of Gautamī and bound him with ropes like an animal.

PURPORT Aśvatthāmā's mother, Kṛpī, was born in the family of Gautama. The significant point in this *śloka* is that Aśvatthāmā was caught and bound up with ropes like an animal. According to Śrīdhara Svāmī, Arjuna was obliged to catch this son of a *brāhmaṇa* like an animal as a part of his duty (*dharma*). This suggestion by Śrīdhara Svāmī is also confirmed in the later statement of Śrī Kṛṣṇa. Aśvatthāmā was a bona fide son of Droṇācārya and Kṛpī, but because he had degraded himself to a lower status of life, it was proper to treat him as an animal and not as a *brāhmaṇa*.

TEXT 34

शिबिराय निनीषन्तं रज्ज्वाबद्ध्वारिपुं बलात् ।
प्राहार्जुनं प्रकुपितो भगवानम्बुजेक्षणः ॥ ३४ ॥

śibirāya ninīṣantaṁ rajjvā baddhvā ripuṁ balāt
prāhārjunaṁ prakupito bhagavān ambujekṣaṇaḥ

śibirāya—on the way to the military camp; *ninīṣantam*—while bringing him; *rajjvā*—by the ropes; *baddhvā*—bound up; *ripum*—the enemy; *balāt*—by force; *prāha*—said; *arjunam*—unto Arjuna; *prakupitaḥ*—in an angry mood; *bhagavān*—the Personality of Godhead; *ambuja-īkṣaṇaḥ*—who looks with His lotus eyes.

After binding Aśvatthāmā, Arjuna wanted to take him to the military camp. The Personality of Godhead Śrī Kṛṣṇa, looking on with His lotus eyes, spoke to Arjuna in an angry mood.

PURPORT Both Arjuna and Lord Śrī Kṛṣṇa are described here in an angry mood, but Arjuna's eyes were like balls of red copper whereas the eyes of the Lord were like lotuses. This means that the angry mood of Arjuna and that of the Lord are not on the same level. The Lord is Transcendence, and thus He is absolute in any stage. His anger is not like the anger of a conditioned living being within the modes of qualitative material nature. Because He is absolute, both His anger and pleasure are the same. His anger is not exhibited in the three modes of material nature. It is only a sign of His bent of mind towards the cause of His devotee because that is His transcendental nature. Therefore, even if He is angry, the object of anger is blessed. He is unchanged in all circumstances.

TEXT 35

मैनं पार्थार्हसि त्रातुं ब्रह्मबन्धुमिमं जहि ।
योऽसावनागसः सुप्तानवधीन्निशि बालकान् ॥ ३५ ॥

mainaṁ pārthārhasi trātuṁ brahma-bandhum imaṁ jahi
yo 'sāv anāgasaḥ suptān avadhīn niśi bālakān

mā enam—never unto him; *pārtha*—O Arjuna; *arhasi*—ought to; *trātum*—give release; *brahma-bandhum*—a relative of a *brāhmaṇa; imam*—him; *jahi*—kill; *yaḥ*—he (who has); *asau*—those; *anāgasaḥ*—faultless; *suptān*—while sleeping; *avadhīt*—killed; *niśi*—at night; *bālakān*—the boys.

Lord Śrī Kṛṣṇa said: O Arjuna, you should not show mercy by releasing this relative of a brāhmaṇa [brahma-bandhu], for he has killed innocent boys in their sleep.

PURPORT The word *brahma-bandhu* is significant. A person who happens to take birth in the family of a *brāhmaṇa* but is not qualified to be called a *brāhmaṇa* is addressed as the relative of a *brāhmaṇa,* and not as a *brāhmaṇa.* The son of a high-court judge is not virtually a high-court judge, but there is no harm in addressing a high-court judge's son as a relative of the Honorable Justice. Therefore, as by birth only one does not become a high-court judge, so also one does not become a *brāhmaṇa* simply by birthright but by acquiring the necessary qualifications of a *brāhmaṇa.*

As the high-court judgeship is a post for the qualified man, so also the post of a *brāhmaṇa* is attainable by qualification only. The *śāstra* enjoins that if good qualifications are seen in a person born in a family other than that of a *brāhmaṇa,* the qualified man has to be accepted as a *brāhmaṇa,* and similarly if a person born in the family of a *brāhmaṇa* is void of brahminical qualification, then he must be treated as a non-*brāhmaṇa* or, in better terms, a relative of a *brāhmaṇa*. Lord Śrī Kṛṣṇa, the supreme authority of all religious principles, the *Vedas,* has personally pointed out these differences, and He is about to explain the reason for this in the following *ślokas*.

TEXT 36

मत्तं प्रमत्तमुन्मत्तं सुप्तं बालं स्त्रियं जडम् ।
प्रपन्नं विरथं भीतं न रिपुं हन्ति धर्मवित् ॥ ३६ ॥

mattaṁ pramattam unmattaṁ suptaṁ bālaṁ striyaṁ jaḍam
prapannaṁ virathaṁ bhītaṁ na ripuṁ hanti dharma-vit

mattam—careless; *pramattam*—intoxicated; *unmattam*—insane; *suptam*—asleep; *bālam*—boy; *striyam*—woman; *jaḍam*—foolish; *prapannam*—surrendered; *viratham*—one who has lost his chariot; *bhītam*—afraid; *na*—not; *ripum*—enemy; *hanti*—kill; *dharma-vit*—one who knows the principles of religion.

A person who knows the principles of religion does not kill an enemy who is careless, intoxicated, insane, asleep, afraid or devoid of his chariot. Nor does he kill a boy, a woman, a foolish creature or a surrendered soul.

PURPORT An enemy who does not resist is never killed by a warrior who knows the principles of religion. Formerly battles were fought on the *principles of religion* and not for the sake of sense gratification. If the enemy happened to be intoxicated, asleep, etc., as above mentioned, he was never to be killed. These are some of the codes of religious war. Formerly war was never declared by the whims of selfish political leaders; it was carried out on religious principles free from all vices. Violence carried out on religious principles is far superior to so-called nonviolence.

TEXT 37

स्वप्राणान् यः परप्राणैः प्रपुष्णात्यघृणः खलः ।
तद्वधस्तस्य हि श्रेयो यद्दोषाद्यात्यधः पुमान् ॥ ३७ ॥

sva-prāṇān yaḥ para-prāṇaiḥ prapuṣṇāty aghṛṇaḥ khalaḥ
tad-vadhas tasya hi śreyo yad-doṣād yāty adhaḥ pumān

sva-prāṇān—one's own life; *yaḥ*—one who; *para-prāṇaiḥ*—at the cost of others' lives; *prapuṣṇāti*—maintains properly; *aghṛṇaḥ*—shameless; *khalaḥ*—wretched; *tat-vadhaḥ*—killing of him; *tasya*—his; *hi*—certainly; *śreyaḥ*—well-being; *yat*—by which; *doṣāt*—by the fault; *yāti*—goes; *adhaḥ*—downwards; *pumān*—a person.

A cruel and wretched person who maintains his existence at the cost of others' lives deserves to be killed for his own well-being, otherwise he will go down by his own actions.

PURPORT A life for a life is just punishment for a person who cruelly and shamelessly lives at the cost of another's life. Political morality is to punish a person by a death sentence in order to save a cruel person from going to hell. That a murderer is condemned to a death sentence by the state is good for the culprit because in his next life he will not have to suffer for his act of murder. Such a death sentence for the murderer is the lowest possible punishment offered to him, and it is said in the *smṛti-śāstras* that men who are punished by the king on the principle of a life for a life are purified of all their sins, so much so that they may be eligible for being promoted to the planets of heaven. According to Manu, the great author of civic codes and religious principles, even the killer of an animal is to be considered a murderer because animal food is never meant for the civilized man, whose prime duty is to prepare himself for going back to Godhead. He says that in the act of killing an animal, there is a regular conspiracy by the party of sinners, and all of them are liable to be punished as murderers exactly like a party of conspirators who kill a human being combinedly. *He who gives permission, he who kills the animal, he who sells the slaughtered animal, he who cooks the animal, he who administers distribution of the foodstuff, and at last he who eats such cooked animal food are all murderers, and all of them are liable to be punished by the laws of nature.* No one can create a living being despite all advancement of material science, and therefore no one has the right to kill a living being by one's independent whims. For the animal-eaters, the scriptures have sanctioned restricted animal sacrifices only, and such sanctions are there just to restrict the opening of slaughterhouses and not to encourage animal-killing. The procedure under which animal sacrifice is allowed in the scriptures is good both for the animal sacrificed and the animal-eaters. It is good for the animal in the sense that the sacrificed animal is at once promoted to the human form of life after being sacrificed at the altar, and the animal-eater is saved from grosser types of sins (eating meats supplied by organized slaughterhouses which are ghastly places for breeding all kinds of material afflictions to society, country and the people in general). The material world is itself a place always full of anxieties, and by encouraging animal slaughter the whole atmosphere becomes polluted more and more by war, pestilence, famine and many other unwanted calamities.

TEXT 38

प्रतिश्रुतं च भवता पाञ्चाल्यै शृण्वतो मम ।
आहरिष्ये शिरस्तस्य यस्ते मानिनि पुत्रहा ॥ ३८ ॥

pratiśrutaṁ ca bhavatā pāñcālyai śṛṇvato mama
āhariṣye śiras tasya yas te mānini putra-hā

pratiśrutam—it is promised; *ca*—and; *bhavatā*—by you; *pāñcālyai*—unto the daughter of the King of Pāñcāla (Draupadī); *śṛṇvataḥ*—which was heard; *mama*—by Me personally; *āhariṣye*—must I bring; *śiraḥ*—the head; *tasya*—of him; *yaḥ*—whom; *te*—your; *mānini*—consider; *putra-hā*—the killer of your sons.

Furthermore, I have personally heard you promise Draupadī that you would bring forth the head of the killer of her sons.

TEXT 39

तदसौ वध्यतां पाप आतताय्यात्मबन्धुहा ।
भर्तुश्च विप्रियं वीर कृतवान् कुलपांसनः ॥ ३९ ॥

tad asau vadhyatāṁ pāpa ātatāyy ātma-bandhu-hā
bhartuś ca vipriyaṁ vīra kṛtavān kula-pāṁsanaḥ

tat—therefore; *asau*—this man; *vadhyatām*—will be killed; *pāpaḥ*—the sinner; *ātatāyī*—assaulter; *ātma*—own; *bandhu-hā*—killer of sons; *bhartuḥ*—of the master; *ca*—also; *vipriyam*—having not satisfied; *vīra*—O warrior; *kṛtavān*—one who has done it; *kula-pāṁsanaḥ*—the burnt remnants of the family.

This man is an assassin and murderer of your own family members. Not only that, but he has also dissatisfied his master. He is but the burnt remnants of his family. Kill him immediately.

PURPORT The son of Droṇācārya is condemned here as the burnt remnants of his family. The good name of Droṇācārya was very much respected. Although he joined the enemy camp, the Pāṇḍavas held him always in respect, and Arjuna saluted him before beginning the fight. There was nothing wrong in that way. But the son of Droṇācārya degraded himself by committing acts which are never done by the *dvijas,* or the twice-born higher castes. Aśvatthāmā, the son of Droṇācārya, committed murder by killing the five sleeping sons of Draupadī, by which he dissatisfied his master Duryodhana, who never approved of the heinous act of killing the five sleeping sons of the Pāṇḍavas. This means that Aśvatthāmā became an assaulter of Arjuna's own family members, and thus he was liable to be punished by him. In the *śāstras,* he who attacks without notice or kills from behind or sets fire to another's house or kidnaps one's wife is condemned to death. Kṛṣṇa reminded Arjuna of these facts so that he might take notice of them and do the needful.

सूत उवाच

TEXT 40

एवं परीक्षता धर्मं पार्थः कृष्णेन चोदितः ।
नैच्छद्धन्तुं गुरुसुतं यद्यप्यात्महनं महान् ॥ ४० ॥

sūta uvāca

evaṁ parīkṣatā dharmaṁ pārthaḥ kṛṣṇena coditaḥ
naicchad dhantuṁ guru-sutaṁ yadyapy ātma-hanaṁ mahān

sūtaḥ—Sūta Gosvāmī; *uvāca*—said; *evam*—this; *parīkṣatā*—being examined; *dharmam*—in the matter of duty; *pārthaḥ*—Śrī Arjuna; *kṛṣṇena*—by Lord Kṛṣṇa; *coditaḥ*—being encouraged; *na aicchat*—did not like; *hantum*—to kill; *guru-sutam*—the son of his teacher; *yadyapi*—although; *ātma-hanam*—murderer of sons; *mahān*—very great.

Sūta Gosvāmī said: Although Kṛṣṇa, who was examining Arjuna in religion, encouraged Arjuna to kill the son of Droṇācārya, Arjuna, a great soul, did not like the idea of killing him, although Aśvatthāmā was a heinous murderer of Arjuna's family members.

PURPORT Arjuna was a great soul undoubtedly, which is proved here also. He is encouraged herein personally by the Lord to kill the son of Droṇa, but Arjuna considers that the son of his great teacher should be spared, for he happens to be the son of Droṇācārya, even though he is an unworthy son, having done all sorts of heinous acts whimsically for no one's benefit.

Lord Śrī Kṛṣṇa encouraged Arjuna outwardly just to test Arjuna's sense of duty. It is not that Arjuna was incomplete in the sense of his duty, nor was Lord Śrī Kṛṣṇa unaware of Arjuna's sense of duty. But Lord Śrī Kṛṣṇa puts many of His pure devotees to the test just to magnify their sense of duty. The *gopīs* were put to such tests as well. Prahlāda Mahārāja also was put to such a test. All pure devotees come out successful in the respective tests by the Lord.

TEXT 41

अथोपेत्य स्वशिबिरं गोविन्दप्रियसारथिः ।
न्यवेदयत्तं प्रियायै शोचन्त्या आत्मजान् हतान् ॥ ४१ ॥

athopetya sva-śibiraṁ govinda-priya-sārathiḥ
nyavedayat taṁ priyāyai śocantyā ātma-jān hatān

atha—thereafter; *upetya*—having reached; *sva*—own; *śibiram*—camp; *govinda*—one who enlivens the senses (Lord Śrī Kṛṣṇa); *priya*—dear; *sārathiḥ*—the charioteer; *nyavedayat*—entrusted to; *tam*—him; *priyāyai*—unto the dear; *śocantyai*—lamenting for; *ātma-jān*—own sons; *hatān*—murdered.

After reaching his own camp, Arjuna, along with his dear friend and charioteer [Śrī Kṛṣṇa], entrusted the murderer unto his dear wife, who was lamenting for her murdered sons.

PURPORT The transcendental relation of Arjuna with Kṛṣṇa is of the dearmost friendship. In the *Bhagavad-gītā* the Lord Himself has claimed Arjuna as His dearmost friend. Every living being is thus related with the Supreme Lord by some sort of affectionate relation, either as servant or as friend or as parent or as an object of conjugal love. Everyone thus can enjoy the company of the Lord in the spiritual realm if he at all desires and sincerely tries for it by the process of *bhakti-yoga.*

TEXT 42

तथाहृतं पशुवत् पाशबद्धम्
अवाङ्मुखं कर्मजुगुप्सितेन ।
निरीक्ष्य कृष्णापकृतं गुरोः सुतं
वामस्वभावा कृपया ननाम च ॥ ४२ ॥

tathāhṛtaṁ paśuvat pāśa-baddham
avāṅ-mukhaṁ karma-jugupsitena
nirīkṣya kṛṣṇāpakṛtaṁ guroḥ sutaṁ
vāma-svabhāvā kṛpayā nanāma ca

tathā—thus; *āhṛtam*—brought in; *paśu-vat*—like an animal; *pāśa-baddham*—tied with ropes; *avāk-mukham*—without a word in his mouth; *karma*—activities; *jugupsitena*—being heinous; *nirīkṣya*—by seeing; *kṛṣṇā*—Draupadī; *apakṛtam*—the doer of the degrading; *guroḥ*—the teacher; *sutam*—son; *vāma*—beautiful; *svabhāvā*—nature; *kṛpayā*—out of compassion; *nanāma*—offered obeisances; *ca*—and.

Śrī Sūta Gosvāmī said: Draupadī then saw Aśvatthāmā, who was bound with ropes like an animal and silent for having enacted the most inglorious murder. Due to her female nature, and due to her being naturally good and well-behaved, she showed him due respects as a brāhmaṇa.

PURPORT Aśvatthāmā was condemned by the Lord Himself, and he was treated by Arjuna just like a culprit, not like the son of a *brāhmaṇa* or teacher. But when he was brought before Śrīmatī Draupadī, she, although begrieved for the murder of her sons, and although the murderer was present before her, could not withdraw the due respect generally offered to a *brāhmaṇa* or to the son of a *brāhmaṇa*. This is due to her mild nature as a woman. Women as a class are no better than boys, and therefore they have no discriminatory power like that of a man. Aśvatthāmā proved himself to be an unworthy son of Droṇācārya or of a *brāhmaṇa*, and for this reason he was condemned by the greatest authority, Lord Śrī Kṛṣṇa, and yet a mild woman could not withdraw her natural courtesy for a *brāhmaṇa*.

Even to date, in a Hindu family a woman shows proper respect to the *brāhmaṇa* caste, however fallen and heinous a *brahma-bandhu* may be. But the men have begun to protest against *brahma-bandhus* who are born in families of good *brāhmaṇas* but by action are less than *śūdras*.

The specific word used in this *śloka* is *vāma-svabhāvā*, "mild and gentle by nature." A good man or woman accepts anything very easily, but a man of average intelligence does not do so. But, anyway, we should not give up our reason and discriminatory power just to be gentle. One must have good discriminatory power to judge a thing on its merit. We should not follow the mild nature of a woman and thereby accept that which is not genuine. Aśvatthāmā may be respected by a good-natured woman, but that does not mean that he is as good as a genuine *brāhmaṇa*.

TEXT 43

उवाच चासहन्त्यस्य बन्धनानयनं सती ।
मुच्यतां मुच्यतामेष ब्राह्मणो नितरां गुरुः ॥ ४३ ॥

uvāca cāsahanty asya bandhanānayanaṁ satī
mucyatāṁ mucyatām eṣa brāhmaṇo nitarāṁ guruḥ

uvāca—said; *ca*—and; *asahantī*—being unbearable for her; *asya*—his; *bandhana*—being bound; *ānayanam*—bringing him; *satī*—the devoted; *mucyatām mucyatām*—just get him released; *eṣaḥ*—this; *brāhmaṇaḥ*—a *brāhmaṇa; nitarām*—our; *guruḥ*—teacher.

She could not tolerate Aśvatthāmā's being bound by ropes, and being a devoted lady, she said: Release him, release him, for he is a brāhmaṇa, our spiritual master.

PURPORT As soon as Aśvatthāmā was brought before Draupadī, she thought it intolerable that a *brāhmaṇa* should be arrested like a culprit and brought before her in that condition, especially when the *brāhmaṇa* happened to be a teacher's son.

Arjuna arrested Aśvatthāmā knowing perfectly well that he was the son of Droṇācārya. Kṛṣṇa also knew him to be so, but both of them condemned the murderer without consideration of his being the son of a *brāhmaṇa.* According to revealed scriptures, a teacher or spiritual master is liable to be rejected if he proves himself unworthy of the position of a *guru* or spiritual master. A *guru* is called also an *ācārya,* or a person who has personally assimilated all the essence of *śāstras* and has helped his disciples to adopt the ways. Aśvatthāmā failed to discharge the duties of a *brāhmaṇa* or teacher, and therefore he was liable to be rejected from the exalted position of a *brāhmaṇa.* On this consideration, both Lord Śrī Kṛṣṇa and Arjuna were right in condemning Aśvatthāmā. But to a good lady like Draupadī, the matter was considered not from the angle of *śāstric* vision, but as a matter of custom. By custom, Aśvatthāmā was offered the same respect as offered to his father. It was so because generally the people accept the son of a *brāhmaṇa* as a real *brāhmaṇa,* by sentiment only. Factually the matter is different. A *brāhmaṇa* is accepted on the merit of qualification and not on the merit of simply being the son of a *brāhmaṇa.*

But in spite of all this, Draupadī desired that Aśvatthāmā be at once released, and it was all the same a good sentiment for her. This means that a devotee of the Lord can tolerate all sorts of tribulation personally, but still such devotees are never unkind to others, even to the enemy. These are the characteristics of one who is a pure devotee of the Lord.

TEXT 44

सरहस्यो धनुर्वेदः सविसर्गोपसंयमः ।
अस्त्रग्रामश्च भवता शिक्षितो यदनुग्रहात् ॥ ४४ ॥

sarahasyo dhanur-vedaḥ savisargopasaṁyamaḥ
astra-grāmaś ca bhavatā śikṣito yad-anugrahāt

sa-rahasyaḥ—confidential; *dhanuḥ-vedaḥ*—knowledge in the art of manipulating bows and arrows; *sa-visarga*—releasing; *upasaṁyamaḥ*—controlling; *astra*—weapons; *grāmaḥ*—all kinds of; *ca*—and; *bhavatā*—by yourself; *śikṣitaḥ*—learned; *yat*—by whose; *anugrahāt*—mercy of.

It was by Droṇācārya's mercy that you learned the military art of throwing arrows and the confidential art of controlling weapons.

PURPORT *Dhanur-veda,* or military science, was taught by Droṇācārya with all its confidential secrets of throwing and controlling by Vedic hymns. Gross military science is dependent on material weapons, but finer than that is the art of throwing the arrows saturated with Vedic hymns, which act more effectively than gross material weapons like machine guns or atomic bombs. The control is by Vedic *mantras,* or the transcendental science of sound. It is said in the *Rāmāyaṇa* that Mahārāja Daśaratha, the father of Lord Śrī Rāma, used to control arrows by sound only. He could pierce his target with his arrow by only hearing the sound, without seeing the object. So this is a finer military science than that of the gross material military weapons used nowadays. Arjuna was taught all this, and therefore Draupadī wished that Arjuna feel obliged to Ācārya Droṇa for all these benefits. And in the absence of Droṇācārya, his son was his representative. That was the opinion of the good lady Draupadī. It may be argued why Droṇācārya, a rigid *brāhmaṇa,* should be a teacher in military science. But the reply is that a *brāhmaṇa* should become a teacher, regardless of what his department of knowledge is. A learned *brāhmaṇa* should become a teacher, a priest and a recipient of charity. A bona fide *brāhmaṇa* is authorized to accept such professions.

TEXT 45

स एष भगवान् द्रोणः प्रजारूपेण वर्तते ।
तस्यात्मनोऽर्धं पत्न्यास्ते नान्वगाद्वीरसूः कृपी ॥ ४५ ॥

sa eṣa bhagavān droṇaḥ prajā-rūpeṇa vartate
tasyātmano 'rdhaṁ patny āste nānvagād vīrasūḥ kṛpī

saḥ—he; *eṣaḥ*—certainly; *bhagavān*—lord; *droṇaḥ*—Droṇācārya; *prajā-rūpeṇa*—in the form of his son Aśvatthāmā; *vartate*—is existing; *tasya*—his; *ātmanaḥ*—of the body; *ardham*—half; *patnī*—wife; *āste*—living; *na*—not; *anvagāt*—undertook; *vīrasūḥ*—having the son present; *kṛpī*—the sister of Kṛpācārya.

He [Droṇācārya] is certainly still existing, being represented by his son. His wife Kṛpī did not undergo a satī with him because she had a son.

PURPORT The wife of Droṇācārya, Kṛpī, is the sister of Kṛpācārya. A devoted wife, who is according to revealed scripture the better half of her husband, is justified in embracing voluntary death along with her husband if she is without issue. But in the case of the wife of Droṇācārya, she did not undergo such a trial because she had her son, the representative of her husband. A widow is a widow only in name if there is a son of her husband existing. So in either case Aśvatthāmā was the representative of Droṇācārya, and therefore killing Aśvatthāmā would be like killing Droṇācārya. That was the argument of Draupadī against the killing of Aśvatthāmā.

TEXT 46

तद् धर्मज्ञ महाभाग भवद्भिर्गौरवं कुलम् ।
वृजिनं नार्हति प्राप्तुं पूज्यं वन्द्यमभीक्ष्णशः ॥ ४६ ॥

tad dharmajña mahā-bhāga bhavadbhir gauravaṁ kulam
vṛjinaṁ nārhati prāptuṁ pūjyaṁ vandyam abhīkṣṇaśaḥ

tat—therefore; *dharma-jña*—one who is aware of the principles of religion; *mahā-bhāga*—the most fortunate; *bhavadbhiḥ*—by your good self; *gauravam*—glorified; *kulam*—the family; *vṛjinam*—that which is painful; *na*—not; *arhati*—does deserve; *prāptum*—for obtaining; *pūjyam*—the worshipable; *vandyam*—respectable; *abhīkṣṇaśaḥ*—constantly.

O most fortunate one who know the principles of religion, it is not good for you to cause grief to glorious family members who are always respectable and worshipful.

PURPORT A slight insult for a respectable family is sufficient to invoke grief. Therefore, a cultured man should always be careful in dealing with worshipful family members.

TEXT 47

मा रोदीदस्य जननी गौतमी पतिदेवता ।
यथाहं मृतवत्सार्ता रोदिम्यश्रुमुखी मुहुः ॥ ४७ ॥

mā rodīd asya jananī gautamī pati-devatā
yathāhaṁ mṛta-vatsārtā rodimy aśru-mukhī muhuḥ

mā—do not; *rodīt*—make cry; *asya*—his; *jananī*—mother; *gautamī*—the wife of Droṇa; *pati-devatā*—chaste; *yathā*—as has; *aham*—myself; *mṛta-vatsā*—one whose child is dead; *ārtā*—distressed; *rodimi*—crying; *aśru-mukhī*—tears in the eyes; *muhuḥ*—constantly.

My lord, do not make the wife of Droṇācārya cry like me. I am aggrieved for the death of my sons. She need not cry constantly like me.

PURPORT Sympathetic good lady as she was, Śrīmatī Draupadī did not want to put the wife of Droṇācārya in the same position of childlessness, both from the point of motherly feelings and from the respectable position held by the wife of Droṇācārya.

TEXT 48

यैः कोपितं ब्रह्मकुलं राजन्यैरजितात्मभिः ।
तत् कुलं प्रदहत्याशु सानुबन्धं शुचार्पितम् ॥ ४८ ॥

yaiḥ kopitaṁ brahma-kulaṁ rājanyair ajitātmabhiḥ
tat kulaṁ pradahaty āśu sānubandhaṁ śucārpitam

yaiḥ—by those; *kopitam*—enraged; *brahma-kulam*—the order of the *brāhmaṇas; rājanyaiḥ*—by the administrative order; *ajita*—unrestricted; *ātmabhiḥ*—by oneself; *tat*—that; *kulam*—family; *pradahati*—is burnt up; *āśu*—within no time; *sa-anubandham*—together with family members; *śucā-arpitam*—being put into grief.

If the kingly administrative order, being unrestricted in sense control, offends the brāhmaṇa order and enrages them, then the fire of that rage burns up the whole body of the royal family and brings grief upon them all.

PURPORT The *brāhmaṇa* order of society, or the spiritually advanced caste or community, and the members of such highly elevated families, were always held in great esteem by the other, subordinate castes, namely the administrative kingly order, the mercantile order and the laborers.

TEXT 49

सूत उवाच
धर्म्यं न्याय्यं सकरुणं निर्व्यलीकं समं महत् ।
राजा धर्मसुतो राज्ञयाः प्रत्यनन्दद्वचो द्विजाः ॥ ४९ ॥

sūta uvāca
dharmyaṁ nyāyyaṁ sakaruṇaṁ nirvyalīkaṁ samaṁ mahat
rājā dharma-suto rājñyāḥ pratyanandad vaco dvijāḥ

sūtaḥ uvāca—Sūta Gosvāmī said; *dharmyam*—in accordance with the principles of religion; *nyāyyam*—justice; *sa-karuṇam*—full of mercy; *nirvyalīkam*—without duplicity in *dharma; samam*—equity; *mahat*—glorious; *rājā*—the King; *dharma-sutaḥ*—son; *rājñyāḥ*—by the Queen; *pratyanandat*—supported; *vacaḥ*—statements; *dvijāḥ*—O *brāhmaṇas.*

Sūta Gosvāmī said: O brāhmaṇas, King Yudhiṣṭhira fully supported the statements of the Queen, which were in accordance with the principles of religion and were justified, glorious, full of mercy and equity, and without duplicity.

PURPORT Mahārāja Yudhiṣṭhira, who was the son of Dharmarāja, or Yamarāja, fully supported the words of Queen Draupadī in asking Arjuna to release Aśvatthāmā. One should not tolerate the humiliation of a member of a great family. Arjuna and his family were indebted to the family of Droṇācārya because of Arjuna's learning the military science from him. If ingratitude were shown to such a benevolent family, it would not be at all justified from the moral standpoint. The wife of Droṇācārya, who was the half body of the great soul, must be treated with compassion, and she should not be put into grief because of her son's death. That is compassion. Such statements by Draupadī are without duplicity because actions should be taken with full knowledge. The feeling of equality was there because Draupadī spoke out of her personal experience. A barren woman cannot understand the grief of a mother. Draupadī was herself a mother, and therefore her calculation of the depth of Kṛpī's grief was quite to the point. And it was glorious because she wanted to show proper respect to a great family.

TEXT 50

नकुलः सहदेवश्च युयुधानो धनञ्जयः ।
भगवान् देवकीपुत्रो ये चान्ये याश्च योषितः ॥ ५० ॥

nakulaḥ sahadevaś ca yuyudhāno dhanañjayaḥ
bhagavān devakī-putro ye cānye yāś ca yoṣitaḥ

nakulaḥ—Nakula; *sahadevaḥ*—Sahadeva; *ca*—and; *yuyudhānaḥ*—Sātyaki; *dhanañjayaḥ*—Arjuna; *bhagavān*—the Personality of Godhead; *devakī-putraḥ*—the son of Devakī, Lord Śrī Kṛṣṇa; *ye*—those; *ca*—and; *anye*—others; *yāḥ*—those; *ca*—and; *yoṣitaḥ*—ladies.

Nakula and Sahadeva [the younger brothers of the King] and also Sātyaki, Arjuna, the Personality of Godhead Lord Sri Kṛṣṇa, son of Devakī, and the ladies and others all unanimously agreed with the King.

TEXT 51

तत्राहामर्षितो भीमस्तस्य श्रेयान् वधः स्मृतः ।
न भर्तुर्नात्मनश्चार्थे योऽहन् सुप्तान् शिशून् वृथा ॥ ५१ ॥

tatrāhāmarṣito bhīmas tasya śreyān vadhaḥ smṛtaḥ
na bhartur nātmanaś cārthe yo 'han suptān śiśūn vṛthā

tatra—thereupon; *āha*—said; *amarṣitaḥ*—in an angry mood; *bhīmaḥ*—Bhīma; *tasya*—his; *śreyān*—ultimate good; *vadhaḥ*—killing; *smṛtaḥ*—recorded; *na*—not; *bhartuḥ*—of the master; *na*—nor; *ātmanaḥ*—of his own self; *ca*—and; *arthe*—for the sake of; *yaḥ*—one who; *ahan*—killed; *suptān*—sleeping; *śiśūn*—children; *vṛthā*—without purpose.

Bhīma, however, angrily disagreed with them and recommended killing this culprit, who had murdered sleeping children for no purpose and for neither his nor his master's interest.

TEXT 52

निशम्य भीमगदितं द्रौपद्याश्च चतुर्भुजः ।
आलोक्य वदनं सख्युरिदमाह हसन्निव ॥ ५२ ॥

niśamya bhīma-gaditaṁ draupadyāś ca catur-bhujaḥ
ālokya vadanaṁ sakhyur idam āha hasann iva

niśamya—just after hearing; *bhīma*—Bhīma; *gaditam*—spoken by; *draupadyāḥ*—of Draupadī; *ca*—and; *catuḥ-bhujaḥ*—the four-handed (Personality of Godhead); *ālokya*—having seen; *vadanam*—the face; *sakhyuḥ*—of His friend; *idam*—this; *āha*—said; *hasan*—smiling; *iva*—as if.

Caturbhuja [the four-armed one], or the Personality of Godhead, after hearing the words of Bhīma, Draupadī and others, saw the face of His dear friend Arjuna, and He began to speak as if smiling.

PURPORT Lord Śrī Kṛṣṇa had two arms, and why He is designated as four-armed is explained by Śrīdhara Svāmī. Both Bhīma and Draupadī held opposite views about killing Aśvatthāmā. Bhīma wanted him to be immediately killed, whereas Draupadī wanted to save him. We can imagine Bhīma ready to kill while Draupadī is obstructing him. And in order to prevent both of them, the Lord discovered another two arms. Originally, the primeval Lord Śrī Kṛṣṇa displays only two arms, but in His Nārāyaṇa feature He exhibits four. In His Nārāyaṇa feature He resides with His devotees in the Vaikuṇṭha planets, while in His original Śrī Kṛṣṇa feature He resides in the Kṛṣṇaloka planet far, far above the Vaikuṇṭha planets in the spiritual sky. Therefore, if Śrī Kṛṣṇa is called *catur-bhujaḥ,* there is no contradiction. If need be He can display hundreds of arms, as He exhibited in His *viśva-rūpa* shown to Arjuna. Therefore, one who can display hundreds and thousands of arms can also manifest four whenever needed.

When Arjuna was perplexed about what to do with Aśvatthāmā, Lord Śrī Kṛṣṇa, as the very dear friend of Arjuna, voluntarily took up the matter just to make a solution. And He was smiling also.

श्रीभगवानुवाच

TEXTS 53–54

ब्रह्मबन्धुर्न हन्तव्य आततायी वधार्हणः ।
मयैवोभयमाम्नातं परिपाह्यनुशासनम् ॥ ५३ ॥

कुरु प्रतिश्रुतं सत्यं यत्तत्सान्त्वयता प्रियाम् ।
प्रियं च भीमसेनस्य पाञ्चाल्या मह्यमेव च ॥ ५४ ॥

śrī-bhagavān uvāca
brahma-bandhur na hantavya ātatāyī vadhārhaṇaḥ
mayaivobhayam āmnātaṁ paripāhy anuśāsanam

kuru pratiśrutaṁ satyaṁ yat tat sāntvayatā priyām
priyaṁ ca bhīmasenasya pāñcālyā mahyam eva ca

śrī-bhagavān—the Personality of Godhead; *uvāca*—said; *brahma-bandhuḥ*—the relative of a *brāhmaṇa; na*—not; *hantavyaḥ*—to be killed; *ātatāyī*—the aggressor; *vadha-arhaṇaḥ*—is due to be killed; *mayā*—by Me; *eva*—certainly; *ubhayam*—both; *āmnātam*—described according to rulings of the authority; *paripāhi*—carry out; *anuśāsanam*—rulings; *kuru*—abide by; *pratiśrutam*—as promised by; *satyam*—truth; *yat tat*—that which; *sāntvayatā*—while pacifying; *priyām*—dear wife; *priyam*—satisfaction; *ca*—also; *bhīmasenasya*—of Śrī Bhīmasena; *pāñcālyāḥ*—of Draupadī; *mahyam*—unto Me also; *eva*—certainly; *ca*—and.

The Personality of Godhead Śrī Kṛṣṇa said: A friend of a brāhmaṇa is not to be killed, but if he is an aggressor he must be killed. All these rulings are in the scriptures, and you should act accordingly. You have to fulfill your promise to your wife, and you must also act to the satisfaction of Bhīmasena and Me.

PURPORT Arjuna was perplexed because Aśvatthāmā was to be killed as well as spared according to different scriptures cited by different persons. As a *brahma-bandhu,* or a worthless son of a *brāhmaṇa,* Aśvatthāmā was not to be killed, but he was at the same time an aggressor also. And according to the rulings of Manu, an aggressor, even though he be a *brāhmaṇa* (and what to speak of an unworthy son of a *brāhmaṇa*), is to be killed. Droṇācārya was certainly a *brāhmaṇa* in the true sense of the term, but because he stood in the battlefield he was killed. But although Aśvatthāmā was an aggressor, he stood without any fighting weapons. The ruling is that an aggressor, when he is without weapon or chariot, cannot be killed. All these were certainly perplexities. Besides that, Arjuna had to keep the promise he had made before Draupadī just to pacify her. And he also had to satisfy both Bhīma and Kṛṣṇa, who advised killing him. This dilemma was present before Arjuna, and the solution was awarded by Kṛṣṇa.

सूत उवाच

TEXT 55

अर्जुनः सहसाज्ञाय हरेर्हार्दमथासिना ।
मणिं जहार मूर्धन्यं द्विजस्य सहमूर्धजम् ॥ ५५ ॥

sūta uvāca
arjunaḥ sahasājñāya harer hārdam athāsinā
maṇiṁ jahāra mūrdhanyaṁ dvijasya saha-mūrdhajam

sūtaḥ—Sūta Gosvāmī; *uvāca*—said; *arjunaḥ*—Arjuna; *sahasā*—just at that time; *ājñāya*—knowing it; *hareḥ*—of the Lord; *hārdam*—motive; *atha*—thus; *asinā*—by the sword; *maṇim*—the jewel; *jahāra*—separated; *mūrdhanyam*—on the head; *dvijasya*—of the twice-born; *saha*—with; *mūrdhajam*—hairs.

Sūta Gosvāmī said: Just then Arjuna could understand the motive of the Lord by His equivocal orders, and thus with his sword he severed both hair and jewel from the head of Aśvatthāmā.

PURPORT Contradictory orders of different persons are impossible to carry out. Therefore a compromise was selected by Arjuna by his sharp intelligence, and he separated the jewel from the head of Aśvatthāmā. This was as good as cutting off his head, and yet his life was saved for all practical purposes. Here Aśvatthāmā is indicated as twice-born. Certainly he was twice-born, but he fell down from his position, and therefore he was properly punished.

TEXT 56

विमुच्य रशनाबद्धं बालहत्याहतप्रभम् ।
तेजसा मणिना हीनं शिबिरान्निरयापयत् ॥ ५६ ॥

vimucya raśanā-baddhaṁ bāla-hatyā-hata-prabham
tejasā maṇinā hīnaṁ śibirān nirayāpayat

vimucya—after releasing him; *raśanā-baddham*—from the bondage of ropes; *bāla-hatyā*—infanticide; *hata-prabham*—loss of bodily luster; *tejasā*—of the strength of; *maṇinā*—by the jewel; *hīnam*—being deprived of; *śibirāt*—from the camp; *nirayāpayat*—drove him out.

He [Aśvatthāmā] had already lost his bodily luster due to infanticide, and now, moreover, having lost the jewel from his head, he lost even more strength. Thus he was unbound and driven out of the camp.

PURPORT Thus being insulted, the humiliated Aśvatthāmā was simultaneously killed and not killed by the intelligence of Lord Kṛṣṇa and Arjuna.

TEXT 57

वपनं द्रविणादानं स्थानान्निर्यापणं तथा ।
एष हि ब्रह्मबन्धूनां वधो नान्योऽस्ति दैहिकः ॥ ५७ ॥

vapanaṁ draviṇādānaṁ sthānān niryāpaṇaṁ tathā
eṣa hi brahma-bandhūnāṁ vadho nānyo 'sti daihikaḥ

vapanam—cleaving the hairs from the head; *draviṇa*—wealth; *adānam*—forfeiting; *sthānāt*—from the residence; *niryāpaṇam*—driving away; *tathā*—also; *eṣaḥ*—all these; *hi*—certainly; *brahma-bandhūnām*—of the relatives of a *brāhmaṇa; vadhaḥ*—killing; *na*—not; *anyaḥ*—any other method; *asti*—there is; *daihikaḥ*—in the matter of the body.

Cutting the hair from his head, depriving him of his wealth and driving him from his residence are the prescribed punishments for the relative of a brāhmaṇa. There is no injunction for killing the body.

TEXT 58

पुत्रशोकातुराः सर्वे पाण्डवाः सह कृष्णया ।
स्वानां मृतानां यत्कृत्यं चक्रुर्निर्हरणादिकम् ॥ ५८ ॥

putra-śokāturāḥ sarve pāṇḍavāḥ saha kṛṣṇayā
svānāṁ mṛtānāṁ yat kṛtyaṁ cakrur nirharaṇādikam

putra—son; *śoka*—bereavement; *āturāḥ*—overwhelmed with; *sarve*—all of them; *pāṇḍavāḥ*—the sons of Pāṇḍu; *saha*—along with;

kṛṣṇayā—with Draupadī; *svānām*—of the kinsmen; *mṛtānām*—of the dead; *yat*—what; *kṛtyam*—ought to be done; *cakruḥ*—did perform; *nirharaṇa-ādikam*—undertakable.

Thereafter, the sons of Pāṇḍu and Draupadī, overwhelmed with grief, performed the proper rituals for the dead bodies of their relatives.

Thus end the Bhaktivedanta purports of the First Canto, Seventh Chapter, of the Śrīmad-Bhāgavatam, *entitled "The Son of Droṇa Punished."*

CHAPTER EIGHT

Prayers by Queen Kuntī, and Parīkṣit Saved

TEXT 1

सूत उवाच
अथ ते सम्परेतानां स्वानामुदकमिच्छताम् ।
दातुं सकृष्णा गङ्गायां पुरस्कृत्य ययुः स्त्रियः ॥ १ ॥

sūta uvāca
atha te samparetānāṁ svānām udakam icchatām
dātuṁ sakṛṣṇā gaṅgāyāṁ puraskṛtya yayuḥ striyaḥ

sūtaḥ uvāca—Sūta said; *atha*—thus; *te*—the Pāṇḍavas; *samparetānām*—of the dead; *svānām*—of the relatives; *udakam*—water; *icchatām*—willing to have; *dātum*—to deliver; *sa-kṛṣṇāḥ*—along with Draupadī; *gaṅgāyām*—on the Ganges; *puraskṛtya*—putting in the front; *yayuḥ*—went; *striyaḥ*—the women.

Sūta Gosvāmī said: Thereafter the Pāṇḍavas, desiring to deliver water to the dead relatives who had desired it, went to the Ganges with Draupadī. The ladies walked in front.

PURPORT To date it is the custom in Hindu society to go to the Ganges or any other sacred river to take bath when death occurs in the family. Each of the family members pours out a potful of the Ganges water for the departed soul and walks in a procession, with the ladies in the front. The Pāṇḍavas also followed the rules more than five thousand years ago. Lord Kṛṣṇa, being a cousin of the Pāṇḍavas, was also amongst the family members.

TEXT 2

ते निनीयोदकं सर्वे विलप्य च भृशं पुनः ।
आप्लुता हरिपादाब्जरजःपूतसरिज्जले ॥ २ ॥

te ninīyodakaṁ sarve vilapya ca bhṛśaṁ punaḥ
āplutā hari-pādābja- rajaḥ-pūta-sarij-jale

te—all of them; *ninīya*—having offered; *udakam*—water; *sarve*—every one of them; *vilapya*—having lamented; *ca*—and; *bhṛśam*—sufficiently; *punaḥ*—again; *āplutāḥ*—took bath; *hari-pādābja*—the lotus feet of the Lord; *rajaḥ*—dust; *pūta*—purified; *sarit*—of the Ganges; *jale*—in the water.

Having lamented over them and sufficiently offered Ganges water, they bathed in the Ganges, whose water is sanctified due to being mixed with the dust of the lotus feet of the Lord.

TEXT 3

तत्रासीनं कुरुपतिं धृतराष्ट्रं सहानुजम् ।
गान्धारीं पुत्रशोकार्तां पृथां कृष्णां च माधवः ॥ ३ ॥

tatrāsīnaṁ kuru-patiṁ dhṛtarāṣṭraṁ sahānujam
gāndhārīṁ putra-śokārtāṁ pṛthāṁ kṛṣṇāṁ ca mādhavaḥ

tatra—there; *āsīnam*—sitting; *kuru-patim*—the King of the Kurus; *dhṛtarāṣṭram*—Dhṛtarāṣṭra; *saha-anujam*—with his younger brothers; *gāndhārīm*—Gāndhārī; *putra*—son; *śoka-artām*—overtaken by bereavement; *pṛthām*—Kuntī; *kṛṣṇām*—Draupadī; *ca*—also; *mādhavaḥ*—Lord Śrī Kṛṣṇa.

There sat the King of the Kurus, Mahārāja Yudhiṣṭhira, along with his younger brothers and Dhṛtarāṣṭra, Gāndhārī, Kuntī and Draupadī, all overwhelmed with grief. Lord Kṛṣṇa was also there.

PURPORT The Battle of Kurukṣetra was fought between family members, and thus all affected persons were also family members like Mahārāja Yudhiṣṭhira and brothers, Kuntī, Draupadī, Subhadrā, Dhṛtarāṣṭra, Gāndhārī and her daughters-in-law, etc. All the principal dead bodies were in some way or other related with each other, and therefore the family grief was combined. Lord Kṛṣṇa was also one of them as a cousin of the Pāṇḍavas and nephew of Kuntī, as well as brother of Subhadrā, etc. The Lord, therefore, was equally sympathetic toward all of them, and therefore he began to pacify them befittingly.

TEXT 4

सान्त्वयामास मुनिभिर्हतबन्धूञ् शुचार्पितान् ।
भूतेषु कालस्य गतिं दर्शयन्नप्रतिक्रियाम् ॥ ४ ॥

sāntvayām āsa munibhir hata-bandhūñ śucārpitān
bhūteṣu kālasya gatiṁ darśayan na pratikriyām

sāntvayām āsa—pacified; *munibhiḥ*—along with the *munis* present there; *hata-bandhūn*—those who lost their friends and relatives; *śucārpitān*—all shocked and affected; *bhūteṣu*—unto the living beings; *kālasya*—of the supreme law of the Almighty; *gatim*—reactions; *darśayan*—demonstrated; *na*—no; *pratikriyām*—remedial measures.

Citing the stringent laws of the Almighty and their reactions upon living beings, Lord Śrī Kṛṣṇa and the munis began to pacify those who were shocked and affected.

PURPORT The stringent laws of nature, under the order of the Supreme Personality of Godhead, cannot be altered by any living entity. The living entities are eternally under the subjugation of the almighty Lord. The Lord makes all the laws and orders, and these laws and orders are generally called *dharma* or religion. No one can create any religious formula. Bona fide religion is to abide by the orders of the Lord. The Lord's orders are clearly declared in the *Bhagavad-gītā*. Everyone should follow Him only or His orders, and that will make all happy, both materially and spiritually. As long as we are in the material world, our duty is to follow the orders of the Lord, and if by the grace of the Lord we are liberated from the clutches of the material world, then in our liberated stage also we can render transcendental loving service unto the Lord. In our material stage we can see neither ourselves nor the Lord for want of spiritual vision. But when we are liberated from material affection and are situated in our original spiritual form we can see both ourselves and the Lord face to face. *Mukti* means to be reinstated in one's original spiritual status after giving up the material conception of life. Therefore, human life is specifically meant for qualifying ourselves for this spiritual liberty. Unfortunately, under the influence of illusory material energy, we accept this spot-life of only a few years as our permanent existence and thus become illusioned by possessing so-called country, home, land, children, wife, community, wealth, etc., which are false representations created by *māyā* (illusion). And under the dictation of *māyā,* we fight with one another to protect these false possessions. By cultivating spiritual knowledge, we can realize that we have nothing to do with all this material paraphernalia. Then at once we become free from material attachment. This clearance of the misgivings of material existence at once takes place by association with the Lord's devotees, who are able to inject the transcendental sound into the depths of the bewildered heart and thus make one practically liberated from all lamentation and illusion. That is a summary of the pacifying measures for those affected by the reaction of stringent material laws, exhibited in the forms of birth, death, old age and disease, which are insoluble factors of material existence. The victims of war, namely, the family members of the Kurus, were lamenting the problems of death, and the Lord pacified them on the basis of knowledge.

TEXT 5

साधयित्वाजातशत्रोः स्वं राज्यं कितवैर्हृतम् ।
घातयित्वासतो राज्ञः कचस्पर्शक्षतायुषः ॥ ५ ॥

sādhayitvājāta-śatroḥ svaṁ rājyaṁ kitavair hṛtam
ghātayitvāsato rājñaḥ kaca-sparśa-kṣatāyuṣaḥ

sādhayitvā—having executed; *ajāta-śatroḥ*—of one who has no enemy; *svam rājyam*—own kingdom; *kitavaiḥ*—by the clever (Duryodhana and party); *hṛtam*—usurped; *ghātayitvā*—having killed; *asataḥ*—the unscrupulous; *rājñaḥ*—of the queen's; *kaca*—bunch of hair; *sparśa*—roughly handled; *kṣata*—decreased; *āyuṣaḥ*—by the duration of life.

The clever Duryodhana and his party cunningly usurped the kingdom of Yudhiṣṭhira, who had no enemy. By the grace of the Lord, the recovery was executed, and the unscrupulous kings who joined with Duryodhana were killed by Him. Others also died, their duration of life having decreased for their rough handling of the hair of Queen Draupadī.

PURPORT In the glorious days, or before the advent of the age of Kali, the *brāhmaṇas,* the cows, the women, the children and the old men were properly given protection.

1. The protection of the *brāhmaṇas* maintains the institution of *varṇa* and

āśrama, the most scientific culture for attainment of spiritual life.

2. The protection of cows maintains the most miraculous form of food, i.e., milk for maintaining the finer tissues of the brain for understanding higher aims of life.

3. The protection of women maintains the chastity of society, by which we can get a good generation for peace, tranquillity and progress of life.

4. The protection of children gives the human form of life its best chance to prepare the way of liberty from material bondage. Such protection of children begins from the very day of begetting a child by the purificatory process of *garbhādhāna-saṁskāra,* the beginning of pure life.

5. The protection of the old men gives them a chance to prepare themselves for better life after death.

This complete outlook is based on factors leading to successful humanity as against the civilization of polished cats and dogs. The killing of the above-mentioned innocent creatures is totally forbidden because even by insulting them one loses one's duration of life. In the age of Kali they are not properly protected, and therefore the duration of life of the present generation has shortened considerably. In the *Bhagavad-gītā* it is stated that when the women become unchaste for want of proper protection, there are unwanted children called *varṇa-saṅkara.* To insult a chaste woman means to bring about disaster in the duration of life. Duḥśāsana, a brother of Duryodhana, insulted Draupadī, an ideal chaste lady, and therefore the miscreants died untimely. These are some of the stringent laws of the Lord mentioned above.

TEXT 6

याजयित्वाश्वमेधैस्तं त्रिभिरुत्तमकल्पकैः ।
तद्यशः पावनं दिक्षु शतमन्योरिवातनोत् ॥ ६ ॥

yājayitvāśvamedhais taṁ tribhir uttama-kalpakaiḥ
tad-yaśaḥ pāvanaṁ dikṣu śata-manyor ivātanot

yājayitvā—by performing; *aśvamedhaiḥ*—*yajña* in which a horse is sacrificed; *tam*—him (King Yudhiṣṭhira); *tribhiḥ*—three; *uttama*—best; *kalpakaiḥ*—supplied with proper ingredients and performed by able priests; *tat*—that; *yaśaḥ*—fame; *pāvanam*—virtuous; *dikṣu*—all directions; *śata-manyoḥ*—Indra, who performed one hundred such sacrifices; *iva*—like; *atanot*—spread.

Lord Śrī Kṛṣṇa caused three well-performed Aśvamedha-yajñas [horse sacrifices] to be conducted by Mahārāja Yudhiṣṭhira and thus caused his virtuous fame to be glorified in all directions, like that of Indra, who had performed one hundred such sacrifices.

PURPORT This is something like the preface to the performances of Aśvamedha-yajña by Mahārāja Yudhiṣṭhira. The comparison of Mahārāja Yudhiṣṭhira to the King of heaven is significant. The King of heaven is thousands and thousands of times greater than Mahārāja Yudhiṣṭhira in opulence, yet the fame of Mahārāja Yudhiṣṭhira was not less. The reason is that Mahārāja Yudhiṣṭhira was a pure devotee of the Lord, and by His grace only was King Yudhiṣṭhira on the level of the King of heaven, even though he performed only three *yajñas* whereas the King of heaven performed hundreds. That is the prerogative of the devotee of the Lord. The Lord is equal to everyone, but a devotee of the Lord is more glorified because he is always in touch with the all-great. The sun rays are equally distributed, but still there are some places which are always dark. This is not due to the sun but to the receptive power. Similarly, those who are cent percent devotees of the Lord get the full-fledged mercy of the Lord, which is always equally distributed everywhere.

TEXT 7

आमन्त्र्य पाण्डुपुत्रांश्च शैनेयोद्धवसंयुतः ।
द्वैपायनादिभिर्विप्रैः पूजितैः प्रतिपूजितः ॥ ७ ॥

āmantrya pāṇḍu-putrāṁś ca śaineyoddhava-saṁyutaḥ
dvaipāyanādibhir vipraiḥ pūjitaiḥ pratipūjitaḥ

āmantrya—inviting; *pāṇḍu-putrān*—all the sons of Pāṇḍu; *ca*—also; *śaineya*—Sātyaki; *uddhava*—Uddhava; *saṁyutaḥ*—accompanied; *dvaipāyana-ādibhiḥ*—by the *ṛṣis* like Vedavyāsa; *vipraiḥ*—by the *brāhmaṇas; pūjitaiḥ*—being worshiped; *pratipūjitaḥ*—the Lord also reciprocated equally.

Lord Śrī Kṛṣṇa then prepared for His departure. He invited the sons of Pāṇḍu, after having been worshiped by the brāhmaṇas, headed by Śrīla Vyāsadeva. The Lord also reciprocated greetings.

PURPORT Apparently Lord Śrī Kṛṣṇa was a *kṣatriya* and was not worshipable by the *brāhmaṇas*. But the *brāhmaṇas* present there, headed by Śrīla Vyāsadeva, all knew Him to be the Personality of Godhead, and therefore they worshiped Him. The Lord reciprocated the greetings just to honor the social order that a *kṣatriya* is obedient to the orders of the *brāhmaṇas*. Although Lord Śrī Kṛṣṇa was always offered the respects due the Supreme Lord from all responsible quarters, the Lord never deviated from the customary usages between the four orders of society. The Lord purposely observed all these social customs so that others would follow Him in the future.

TEXT 8

गन्तुं कृतमतिर्ब्रह्मन् द्वारकां रथमास्थितः ।
उपलेभेऽभिधावन्तीमुत्तरां भयविह्वलाम् ॥ ८ ॥

gantuṁ kṛtamatir brahman dvārakāṁ ratham āsthitaḥ
upalebhe 'bhidhāvantīm uttarāṁ bhaya-vihvalām

gantum—just desiring to start; *kṛtamatiḥ*—having decided; *brahman*—O *brāhmaṇa; dvārakām*—towards Dvārakā; *ratham*—on the chariot; *āsthitaḥ*—seated; *upalebhe*—saw; *abhidhāvantīm*—coming hurriedly; *uttarām*—Uttarā; *bhaya-vihvalām*—being afraid.

As soon as He seated Himself on the chariot to start for Dvārakā, He saw Uttarā hurrying toward Him in fear.

PURPORT All the members of the family of the Pāṇḍavas were completely dependent on the protection of the Lord, and therefore the Lord protected all of them in all circumstances. The Lord protects everyone, but one who depends completely upon Him is especially looked after by the Lord. The father is more attentive to the little son who is exclusively dependent on the father.

उत्तरोवाच

TEXT 9

पाहि पाहि महायोगिन्देवदेव जगत्पते ।
नान्यं त्वदभयं पश्ये यत्र मृत्युः परस्परम् ॥ ९ ॥

uttarovāca
pāhi pāhi mahā-yogin deva-deva jagat-pate
nānyaṁ tvad abhayaṁ paśye yatra mṛtyuḥ parasparam

uttarā uvāca—Uttarā said; *pāhi pāhi*—protect, protect; *mahā-yogin*—the greatest mystic; *deva-deva*—the worshipable of the worshiped; *jagat-pate*—O Lord of the universe; *na*—not; *anyam*—anyone else; *tvat*—than You; *abhayam*—fearlessness; *paśye*—do I see; *yatra*—where there is; *mṛtyuḥ*—death; *parasparam*—in the world of duality.

Uttarā said: O Lord of lords, Lord of the universe! You are the greatest of mystics. Please protect me, protect me, for there is no one else who can save me from the clutches of death in this world of duality.

PURPORT This material world is the world of duality, in contrast with the oneness of the absolute realm. The world of duality is composed of matter and spirit, whereas the absolute world is complete spirit without any tinge of the material qualities. In the dual world everyone is falsely trying to become the master of the world, whereas in the absolute world the Lord is the absolute Lord, and all others are His absolute servitors. In the world of duality everyone is *envious* of all others, and death is inevitable due to the dual existence of matter and spirit. The Lord is the only shelter of fearlessness for the surrendered soul. One cannot save himself from the cruel hands of death in the material world without having surrendered himself at the lotus feet of the Lord.

TEXT 10

अभिद्रवति मामीश शरस्तप्तायसो विभो ।
कामं दहतु मां नाथ मा मे गर्भो निपात्यताम् ॥ १० ॥

abhidravati māṁ īśa śaras taptāyaso vibho
kāmaṁ dahatu māṁ nātha mā me garbho nipātyatām

abhidravati—coming towards; *mām*—me; *īśa*—O Lord; *śaraḥ*—the arrow; *tapta*—fiery; *ayasaḥ*—iron; *vibho*—O great one; *kāmam*—desire; *dahatu*—let it burn; *mām*—me; *nātha*—O protector; *mā*—not; *me*—my; *garbhaḥ*—embryo; *nipātyatām*—be aborted.

O my Lord, You are all-powerful. A fiery iron arrow is coming towards me fast. My Lord, let it burn me personally, if You so desire, but please do not let it burn and abort my embryo. Please do me this favor, my Lord.

PURPORT This incident took place after the death of Abhimanyu, the husband of Uttarā. Abhimanyu's widow, Uttarā, should have followed the path of her husband, but because she was pregnant, and Mahārāja Parīkṣit, a great devotee of the Lord, was lying in embryo, she was responsible for his protection. The mother of a child has a great responsibility in giving all protection to the child, and therefore Uttarā was not ashamed to express this frankly before Lord Kṛṣṇa. Uttarā was the daughter of a great king, the wife of a great hero, and student of a great devotee, and later she was the mother of a good king also. She was fortunate in every respect.

TEXT 11

सूत उवाच
उपधार्य वचस्तस्या भगवान् भक्तवत्सलः ।
अपाण्डवमिदं कर्तुं द्रौणेरस्त्रमबुध्यत ॥ ११ ॥

sūta uvāca
upadhārya vacas tasyā bhagavān bhakta-vatsalaḥ
apāṇḍavam idaṁ kartuṁ drauṇer astram abudhyata

sūtaḥ uvāca—Sūta Gosvāmī said; *upadhārya*—by hearing her patiently; *vacaḥ*—words; *tasyāḥ*—her; *bhagavān*—the Personality of Godhead; *bhakta-vatsalaḥ*—He who is very much affectionate towards His devotees; *apāṇḍavam*—without the existence of the Pāṇḍavas' descendants; *idam*—this; *kartum*—to do it; *drauṇeḥ*—of the son of Droṇācārya; *astram*—weapon; *abudhyata*—understood.

Sūta Gosvāmī said: Having patiently heard her words, Lord Śrī Kṛṣṇa, who is always very affectionate to His devotees, could at once understand that Aśvatthāmā, the son of Droṇācārya, had thrown the brahmāstra to finish the last life in the Pāṇḍava family.

PURPORT The Lord is impartial in every respect, but still He is inclined towards His devotees because there is a great necessity of this for everyone's wellbeing. The Pāṇḍava family was a family of devotees, and therefore the Lord wanted them to rule the world. That was the reason He vanquished the rule of the company of Duryodhana and established the rule of Mahārāja Yudhiṣṭhira. Therefore, He also wanted to protect Mahārāja Parīkṣit, who was lying in embryo. He did not like the idea that the world should be without the Pāṇḍavas, the ideal family of devotees.

TEXT 12

तर्ह्येवाथ मुनिश्रेष्ठ पाण्डवाः पञ्च सायकान् ।
आत्मनोऽभिमुखान्दीप्तानालक्ष्यास्त्राण्युपाददुः ॥ १२ ॥

tarhy evātha muni-śreṣṭha pāṇḍavāḥ pañca sāyakān
ātmano 'bhimukhān dīptān ālakṣyāstrāṇy upādaduḥ

tarhi—then; *eva*—also; *atha*—therefore; *muni-śreṣṭha*—O chief amongst the *munis; pāṇḍavāḥ*—all the sons of Pāṇḍu; *pañca*—five; *sāyakān*—weapons; *ātmanaḥ*—own selves; *abhimukhān*—towards; *dīptān*—glaring; *ālakṣya*—seeing it; *astrāṇi*—weapons; *upādaduḥ*—took up.

O foremost among the great thinkers [munis] [Śaunaka], seeing the glaring brahmāstra proceeding towards them, the Pāṇḍavas took up their five respective weapons.

PURPORT The *brahmāstras* are finer than the nuclear weapons. Aśvatthāmā discharged the *brahmāstra* simply to kill the Pāṇḍavas, namely the five brothers headed by Mahārāja Yudhiṣṭhira and their only grandson, who was lying within the womb of Uttarā. Therefore the *brahmāstra,* more effective and finer than the atomic weapons, was not as blind as the atomic bombs. When the atomic bombs are discharged they do not discriminate between the target and others. Mainly the atomic bombs do harm to the innocent because there is no control. The *brahmāstra* is not like that. It marks out the target and proceeds accordingly without harming the innocent.

TEXT 13

व्यसनं वीक्ष्य तत्तेषामनन्यविषयात्मनाम् ।
सुदर्शनेन स्वास्त्रेण स्वानां रक्षां व्यधाद्विभुः ॥ १३ ॥

vyasanaṁ vīkṣya tat teṣām ananya-viṣayātmanām
sudarśanena svāstreṇa svānāṁ rakṣāṁ vyadhād vibhuḥ

vyasanam—great danger; *vīkṣya*—having observed; *tat*—that; *teṣām*—their; *ananya*—no other; *viṣaya*—means; *ātmanām*—thus inclined; *sudarśanena*—by the wheel of Śrī Kṛṣṇa; *sva-astreṇa*—by the weapon; *svānām*—of His own devotees; *rakṣām*—protection; *vyadhāt*—did it; *vibhuḥ*—the Almighty.

The almighty Personality of Godhead, Śrī Kṛṣṇa, having observed that a great danger was befalling His unalloyed devotees, who were fully surrendered souls, at once took up His Sudarśana disc to protect them.

PURPORT The *brahmāstra,* the supreme weapon released by Aśvatthāmā, was something similar to the nuclear weapon but with more radiation and heat. This *brahmāstra* is the product of a more subtle science, being the product of a finer sound, a *mantra* recorded in the *Vedas.* Another advantage of this weapon is that it is not blind like the nuclear weapon because it can be directed only to the target and nothing else. Aśvatthāmā released the weapon just to finish all the male members of Pāṇḍu's family; therefore in one sense it was more dangerous than the atomic bombs because it could penetrate even the most protected place and would never miss the target. Knowing all this, Lord Śrī Kṛṣṇa at once took up His personal weapon to protect His devotees, who did not know anyone other than Kṛṣṇa. In the *Bhagavad-gītā* the Lord has clearly promised that His devotees are never to be vanquished. And He behaves according to the quality or degree of the devotional service rendered by the devotees. Here the word *ananya-viṣayātmanām* is significant. The Pāṇḍavas were cent percent dependent on the protection of the Lord, although they were all great warriors themselves. But the Lord neglects even the greatest warriors and also vanquishes them in no time. When the Lord saw that there was no time for the Pāṇḍavas to counteract the *brahmāstra* of Aśvatthāmā, He took up His weapon even at the risk of breaking His own vow. Although the Battle of Kurukṣetra was almost finished, still, according to His vow, He should not have taken up His own weapon. But the emergency was more important than the vow. He is better known as the *bhakta-vatsala,* or the lover of His devotee, and thus He preferred to continue as *bhakta-vatsala* than to be a worldly moralist who never breaks his solemn vow.

TEXT 14

अन्तःस्थः सर्वभूतानामात्मा योगेश्वरो हरिः ।
स्वमाययावृणोद्गर्भं वैराट्याः कुरुतन्तवे ॥ १४ ॥

antaḥsthaḥ sarva-bhūtānām ātmā yogeśvaro hariḥ
sva-māyayāvṛṇod garbhaṁ vairāṭyāḥ kuru-tantave

antaḥsthaḥ—being within; *sarva*—all; *bhūtānām*—of the living beings; *ātmā*—soul; *yoga-īśvaraḥ*—the Lord of all mysticism; *hariḥ*—the Supreme Lord; *sva-māyayā*—by the personal energy; *āvṛṇot*—covered; *garbham*—embryo; *vairāṭyāḥ*—of Uttarā; *kuru-tantave*—for the progeny of Mahārāja Kuru.

The Lord of supreme mysticism, Śrī Kṛṣṇa, resides within everyone's heart as the Paramātmā. As such, just to protect the progeny of the Kuru dynasty, He covered the embryo of Uttarā by His personal energy.

PURPORT The Lord of supreme mysticism can simultaneously reside within everyone's heart, or even within the atoms, by His Paramātmā feature, His plenary portion. Therefore, from within the body of Uttarā He covered the embryo to save Mahārāja Parīkṣit and protect the progeny of Mahārāja Kuru, of whom King Pāṇḍu was also a descendant. Both the sons of Dhṛtarāṣṭra and those of Pāṇḍu belonged to the same dynasty of Mahārāja Kuru; therefore both of them were generally known as Kurus. But when there were differences between the two families, the sons of Dhṛtarāṣṭra were known as Kurus whereas the sons of Pāṇḍu were known as Pāṇḍavas. Since the sons and grandsons of Dhṛtarāṣṭra were all killed in the Battle of Kurukṣetra, the last son of the dynasty is designated as the son of the Kurus.

TEXT 15

यद्यप्यस्त्रं ब्रह्मशिरस्त्वमोघं चाप्रतिक्रियम् ।
वैष्णवं तेज आसाद्य समशाम्यद् भृगूद्वह ॥ १५ ॥

yadyapy astraṁ brahma-śiras tv amoghaṁ cāpratikriyam
vaiṣṇavaṁ teja āsādya samaśāmyad bhṛgūdvaha

yadyapi—although; *astram*—weapon; *brahma-śiraḥ*—supreme; *tu*—but; *amogham*—without check; *ca*—and; *apratikriyam*—not to be counteracted; *vaiṣṇavam*—in relation with Viṣṇu; *tejaḥ*—strength; *āsādya*—being confronted with; *samaśāmyat*—was neutralized; *bhṛgu-udvaha*—O glory of the family of Bhṛgu.

O Śaunaka, glory of Bhṛgu's family, although the supreme brahmāstra weapon released by Aśvatthāmā was irresistible and without check or counteraction, it was neutralized and foiled when confronted by the strength of Viṣṇu [Lord Kṛṣṇa].

PURPORT In the *Bhagavad-gītā* it is said that the *brahma-jyoti,* or the glowing transcendental effulgence, is resting on Lord Śrī Kṛṣṇa. In other words, the glowing effulgence known as *brahma-tejas* is nothing but the rays of the Lord, just as the sun rays are rays of the sun disc. So this Brahma weapon also, although materially irresistible, could not surpass the supreme strength of the Lord. The weapon called *brahmāstra,* released by Aśvatthāmā, was neutralized and foiled by Lord Śrī Kṛṣṇa by His own energy; that is to say, He did not wait for any other's help because He is absolute.

TEXT 16

मा मंस्था ह्येतदाश्चर्यं सर्वाश्चर्यमयेऽच्युते ।
य इदं मायया देव्या सृजत्यवति हन्त्यजः ॥ १६ ॥

mā maṁsthā hy etad āścaryaṁ sarvāścaryamaye 'cyute
ya idaṁ māyayā devyā sṛjaty avati hanty ajaḥ

mā—do not; *maṁsthāḥ*—think; *hi*—certainly; *etat*—all these; *āścaryam*—wonderful; *sarva*—all; *āścarya-maye*—in the all-mysterious; *acyute*—the infallible; *yaḥ*—one who; *idam*—this (creation); *māyayā*—by His energy; *devyā*—transcendental; *sṛjati*—creates; *avati*—maintains; *hanti*—annihilates; *ajaḥ*—unborn.

O brāhmaṇas, do not think this to be especially wonderful in the activities of the mysterious and infallible Personality of Godhead. By His own transcendental energy He creates, maintains and annihilates all material things, although He Himself is unborn.

PURPORT The activities of the Lord are always inconceivable to the tiny brain of the living entities. Nothing is impossible for the Supreme Lord, but all His actions are wonderful for us, and thus He is always beyond the range of our conceivable limits. The Lord is the all-powerful, all-perfect Personality of Godhead. The Lord is cent percent perfect, whereas others, namely Nārāyaṇa, Brahmā, Śiva, the demigods and all other living beings, possess only different percentages of such perfection. No one is equal to or greater than Him. He is unrivaled.

TEXT 17

ब्रह्मतेजोविनिर्मुक्तैरात्मजैः सह कृष्णया ।
प्रयाणाभिमुखं कृष्णमिदमाह पृथा सती ॥ १७ ॥

brahma-tejo-vinirmuktair ātmajaiḥ saha kṛṣṇayā
prayāṇābhimukhaṁ kṛṣṇam idam āha pṛthā sate

brahma-tejaḥ—the radiation of the *brahmāstra; vinirmuktaiḥ*—being saved from; *ātma-jaiḥ*—along with her sons; *saha*—with; *kṛṣṇayā*—Draupadī; *prayāṇa*—outgoing; *abhimukham*—towards; *kṛṣṇam*—unto Lord Kṛṣṇa; *idam*—this; *āha*—said; *pṛthā*—Kuntī; *satī*—chaste, devoted to the Lord.

Thus saved from the radiation of the brahmāstra, Kuntī, the chaste devotee of the Lord, and her five sons and Draupadī addressed Lord Kṛṣṇa as He started for home.

PURPORT Kuntī is described herein as *satī*, or chaste, due to her unalloyed devotion to Lord Śrī Kṛṣṇa. Her mind will now be expressed in the following prayers for Lord Kṛṣṇa. A chaste devotee of the Lord does not look to others, namely any other living being or demigod, even for deliverance from danger. That was all along the characteristic of the whole family of the Pāṇḍavas. They knew nothing except Kṛṣṇa, and therefore the Lord was also always ready to help them in all respects and in all circumstances. That is the transcendental nature of the Lord. He reciprocates the dependence of the devotee. One should not, therefore, look for help from imperfect living beings or demigods, but one should look for all help from Lord Kṛṣṇa, who is competent to save His devotees. Such a chaste devotee also never asks the Lord for help, but the Lord, out of His own accord, is always anxious to render it.

TEXT 18

कुन्त्युवाच
नमस्ये पुरुषं त्वाद्यमीश्वरं प्रकृतेः परम् ।
अलक्ष्यं सर्वभूतानामन्तर्बहिरवस्थितम् ॥ १८ ॥

kunty uvāca
namasye puruṣaṁ tvādyam īśvaraṁ prakṛteḥ param
alakṣyaṁ sarva-bhūtānām antar bahir avasthitam

kuntī uvāca—Śrīmatī Kuntī said; *namasye*—let me bow down; *puruṣam*—the Supreme Person; *tvā*—You; *ādyam*—the original; *īśvaram*—the controller; *prakṛteḥ*—of the material cosmos; *param*—beyond; *alakṣyam*—the invisible; *sarva*—all; *bhūtānām*—of living beings; *antaḥ*—within; *bahiḥ*—without; *avasthitam*—existing.

Śrīmatī Kuntī said: O Kṛṣṇa, I offer my obeisances unto You because You are the original personality and are unaffected by the qualities of the material world. You are existing both within and without everything, yet You are invisible to all.

PURPORT Śrīmatī Kuntīdevī was quite aware that Kṛṣṇa is the original Personality of Godhead, although He was playing the part of her nephew. Such an enlightened lady could not commit a mistake by offering obeisances unto her nephew. Therefore, she addressed Him as the original *puruṣa* beyond the material cosmos. Although all living entities are also transcendental, they are neither original nor infallible. The living entities are apt to fall down under the clutches of material nature, but the Lord is never like that. In the *Vedas,* therefore, He is described as the chief among all living entities (*nityo nityānāṁ cetanaś cetanānām* (*Kaṭha Upaniṣad* 2.2.13)). Then again He is addressed as *īśvara,* or the controller. The living entities or the demigods like Indra, Candra and Sūrya are also to some extent *īśvara,* but none of them is the supreme *īśvara,* or the ultimate controller. He is the *parameśvara,* or the Supersoul. He is both within and without. Although He was present before Śrīmatī Kuntī as her nephew, He was also within her and everyone else. In the *Bhagavad-gītā* (15.15) the Lord says, "I am situated in everyone's heart, and only due to Me one remembers, forgets and is cognizant, etc. Through all the *Vedas* I am to be known because I am the compiler of the *Vedas,* and I am the teacher of the *Vedānta*." Queen Kuntī affirms that the Lord, although both within and without all living beings, is still invisible. The Lord is, so to speak, a puzzle for the common man. Queen Kuntī experienced personally that Lord Kṛṣṇa was present before her, yet He entered within the womb of Uttarā to save her embryo from the attack of Aśvatthāmā's *brahmāstra*. Kuntī herself was puzzled about whether Śrī Kṛṣṇa is all-pervasive or localized. In fact, He is both, but He reserves the right of not being exposed to persons who are not surrendered souls. This checking curtain is called the *māyā* energy of the Supreme Lord, and it controls the limited vision of the rebellious soul. It is explained as follows.

TEXT 19

मायाजवनिकाच्छन्नमज्ञाधोक्षजमव्ययम् ।
न लक्ष्यसे मूढदृशा नटो नाट्यधरो यथा ॥ १९ ॥

māyā-javanikācchannam ajñādhokṣajam avyayam
na lakṣyase mūḍha-dṛśā naṭo nāṭyadharo yathā

māyā—deluding; *javanikā*—curtain; *ācchannam*—covered by; *ajñā*—ignorant; *adhokṣajam*—beyond the range of material conception (transcendental); *avyayam*—irreproachable; *na*—not; *lakṣyase*—observed; *mūḍha-dṛśā*—by the foolish observer; *naṭaḥ*—artist; *nāṭya-dharaḥ*—dressed as a player; *yathā*—as.

Being beyond the range of limited sense perception, You are the eternally irreproachable factor covered by the curtain of deluding energy. You are invisible to the foolish observer, exactly as an actor dressed as a player is not recognized.

PURPORT In the *Bhagavad-gītā* Lord Śrī Kṛṣṇa affirms that less intelligent persons mistake Him to be an ordinary man like us, and thus they deride Him. The same is confirmed herein by Queen Kuntī. The less intelligent persons are those who rebel against the authority of the Lord. Such persons are known as *asuras*. The *asuras* cannot recognize the Lord's authority. When the Lord Himself appears amongst us, as Rāma, Nṛsiṁha, Varāha or in His original form as Kṛṣṇa, He performs many wonderful acts which are humanly impossible. As we shall find in the Tenth Canto of this great literature, Lord Śrī Kṛṣṇa exhibited His humanly impossible activities even from the days of His lying on the lap of His mother. He killed the Pūtanā witch, although she smeared her breast with poison just to kill the Lord. The Lord sucked her breast like a natural baby, and He sucked out her very life also. Similarly, He lifted the Govardhana Hill, just as a boy picks up a frog's umbrella, and stood several days continuously just to give protection to the residents of Vṛndāvana. These are some of the superhuman activities of the Lord described in the authoritative Vedic literatures like the *Purāṇas, Itihāsas* (histories) and *Upaniṣads.* He has delivered wonderful instructions in the shape of the *Bhagavad-gītā.* He has shown marvelous capacities as a hero, as a householder, as a teacher and as a renouncer. He is accepted as the Supreme Personality of Godhead by such authoritative personalities as Vyāsa, Devala, Asita, Nārada, Madhva, Śaṅkara, Rāmānuja, Śrī Caitanya Mahāprabhu, Jīva Gosvāmī, Viśvanātha Cakravartī, Bhaktisiddhānta Sarasvatī and all other authorities of the line. He Himself has declared as much in many places of the authentic literatures. And yet there is a class of men with demoniac mentality who are always reluctant to accept the Lord as the Supreme Absolute Truth. This is partially due to their poor fund of knowledge and partially due to their stubborn obstinacy, which results from various misdeeds in the past and present. Such persons could not recognize Lord Śrī Kṛṣṇa even when He was present before them. Another difficulty is that those who depend more on their imperfect senses cannot realize Him as the Supreme Lord. Such persons are like the modern scientist. They want to know everything by their experimental knowledge. But it is not possible to know the Supreme Person by imperfect experimental knowledge. He is described herein as *adhokṣaja,* or beyond the range of experimental knowledge. All our senses are imperfect. We claim to observe everything and anything, but we must admit that we can observe things under certain material conditions only, which are also beyond our control. The Lord is beyond the observation of sense perception. Queen Kuntī accepts this deficiency of the conditioned soul, especially of the woman class, who are less intelligent. For less intelligent men there must be such things as temples, mosques or churches so that they may begin to recognize the authority of the Lord and hear about Him from authorities in such holy places. For less intelligent men, this beginning of spiritual life is essential, and only foolish men decry the establishment of such places of worship, which are required to raise the standard of spiritual attributes for the mass of people. For less intelligent persons, bowing down before the authority of the Lord, as generally done in the temples, mosques or churches, is as beneficial as it is for the advanced devotees to meditate upon Him by active service.

TEXT 20

तथा परमहंसानां मुनीनाममलात्मनाम् ।
भक्तियोगविधानार्थं कथं पश्येम हि स्त्रियः ॥ २० ॥

tathā paramahaṁsānāṁ munīnām amalātmanām
bhakti-yoga-vidhānārthaṁ kathaṁ paśyema hi striyaḥ

tathā—besides that; *paramahaṁsānām*—of the advanced transcendentalists; *munīnām*—of the great philosophers or mental speculators; *amala-ātmanām*—those whose minds are competent to discern between spirit and matter; *bhakti-yoga*—the science of devotional service; *vidhāna-artham*—for executing; *katham*—how; *paśyema*—can observe; *hi*—certainly; *striyaḥ*—women.

You Yourself descend to propagate the transcendental science of devotional service unto the hearts of the advanced transcendentalists and mental speculators, who are purified by being able to discriminate between matter and spirit. How, then, can we women know You perfectly?

PURPORT Even the greatest philosophical speculators cannot have access to the region of the Lord. It is said in the *Upaniṣads* that the Supreme Truth, the Absolute Personality of Godhead, is beyond the range of the thinking power of the greatest philosopher. He is unknowable by great learning or by the greatest brain. He is knowable only by one who has His mercy. Others may go on thinking about Him for years together, yet He is unknowable. This very fact is corroborated by the Queen, who is playing the part of an innocent woman. Women in general are unable to speculate like philosophers, but they are blessed by the Lord because they believe at once in the superiority and almightiness of the Lord and thus offer obeisances without reservation. The Lord is so kind that He does not show special favor only to one who is a great philosopher. He knows the sincerity of purpose. For this reason only, women generally assemble in great number in any sort of religious function. In every country and in every sect of religion it appears that the women are more interested than the men. This simplicity of acceptance of the Lord's authority is more effective than showy insincere religious fervor.

TEXT 21

कृष्णाय वासुदेवाय देवकीनन्दनाय च ।
नन्दगोपकुमाराय गोविन्दाय नमो नमः ॥ २१ ॥

kṛṣṇāya vāsudevāya devakī-nandanāya ca
nanda-gopa-kumārāya govindāya namo namaḥ

kṛṣṇāya—the Supreme Lord; *vāsudevāya*—unto the son of Vasudeva; *devakī-nandanāya*—unto the son of Devakī; *ca*—and; *nanda-gopa*—Nanda and the cowherd men; *kumārāya*—unto their son; *govindāya*—unto the Personality of Godhead, who enlivens the cows and the senses; *namaḥ*—respectful obeisances; *namaḥ*—obeisances.

Let me therefore offer my respectful obeisances unto the Lord, who has become the son of Vasudeva, the pleasure of Devakī, the boy of Nanda and the other cowherd men of Vṛndāvana, and the enlivener of the cows and the senses.

PURPORT The Lord, being thus unapproachable by any material assets, out of unbounded and causeless mercy descends on the earth as He is in order to show His special mercy upon His unalloyed devotees and to diminish the upsurges of the demoniac persons. Queen Kuntī specifically adores the incarnation or descent of Lord Kṛṣṇa above all other incarnations because in this particular incarnation He is more approachable. In the Rāma incarnation He remained a king's son from His very childhood, but in the incarnation of Kṛṣṇa, although He was the son of a king, He at once left the shelter of His real father and mother (King Vasudeva and Queen Devakī) just after His appearance and went to the lap of Yaśodāmāyī to play the part of an ordinary cowherd boy in the blessed Vrajabhūmi, which is very sanctified because of His childhood pastimes. Therefore Lord Kṛṣṇa is more merciful than Lord Rāma. He was undoubtedly very kind to Kuntī's brother Vasudeva and the family. Had He not become the son of Vasudeva and Devakī, Queen Kuntī could not claim Him to be her nephew and thus address Kṛṣṇa in parental affection. But Nanda and Yaśodā are more fortunate because they could relish the Lord's childhood pastimes, which are more attractive than all other pastimes. There is no parallel to His childhood pastimes as exhibited at Vrajabhūmi, which are replicas of His eternal affairs in the original Kṛṣṇaloka, described as the *cintāmaṇi-dhāma* in the *Brahma-saṁhitā*. Lord Śrī Kṛṣṇa descended Himself at Vrajabhūmi with all His transcendental entourage and paraphernalia. Śrī Caitanya Mahāprabhu therefore confirmed that no one is as fortunate as the residents of Vrajabhūmi, and specifically the cowherd girls, who dedicated their everything for the satisfaction of the Lord. His pastimes with Nanda and Yaśodā and His pastimes with the cowherd men and especially with the cowherd boys and the cows have caused Him to be known as Govinda. Lord Kṛṣṇa as Govinda is more inclined to the *brāhmaṇas* and the cows, indicating thereby that human prosperity depends more on these two items, namely brahminical culture and cow protection. Lord Kṛṣṇa is never satisfied where these are lacking.

TEXT 22

नमः पङ्कजनाभाय नमः पङ्कजमालिने ।
नमः पङ्कजनेत्राय नमस्ते पङ्कजाङ्घ्रये ॥ २२ ॥

namaḥ paṅkaja-nābhāya namaḥ paṅkaja-māline
namaḥ paṅkaja-netrāya namas te paṅkajāṅghraye

namaḥ—all respectful obeisances; *paṅkaja-nābhāya*—unto the Lord who has a specific depression resembling a lotus flower in the center of His abdomen; *namaḥ*—obeisances; *paṅkaja-māline*—one who is always decorated with a garland of lotus flowers; *namaḥ*—obeisances; *paṅkaja-netrāya*—one whose glance is as cooling as a lotus flower; *namaḥ te*—respectful obeisances unto You; *paṅkaja-aṅghraye*—unto You, the soles of whose feet are engraved with lotus flowers (and who are therefore said to possess lotus feet).

My respectful obeisances are unto You, O Lord, whose abdomen is marked with a depression like a lotus flower, who are always decorated with garlands of lotus flowers, whose glance is as cool as the lotus and whose feet are engraved with lotuses.

PURPORT Here are some of the specific symbolical marks on the spiritual body of the Personality of Godhead which distinguish His body from the bodies of all others. They are all special features of the body of the Lord. The Lord may appear as one of us, but He is always distinct by His specific bodily features. Śrīmatī Kuntī claims herself unfit to see the Lord because of her being a woman. This is claimed because women, śūdras (the laborer class) and the *dvija-bandhus,* or the wretched descendants of the higher three classes, are unfit by intelligence to understand transcendental subject matter concerning the spiritual name, fame, attributes, forms, etc., of the Supreme Absolute Truth. Such persons, although they are unfit to enter into the spiritual affairs of the Lord, can see Him as the *arcā-vigraha,* who descends on the material world just to distribute favors to the fallen souls, including the above-mentioned women, śūdras and *dvija-bandhus*. Because such fallen souls cannot see anything beyond matter, the Lord condescends to enter into each and every one of the innumerable universes as the Garbhodakaśāyī Viṣṇu, who grows a lotus stem from the lotuslike depression in the center of His transcendental abdomen, and thus Brahmā, the first living being in the universe, is born. Therefore, the Lord is known as the Paṅkajanābhi. The Paṅkajanābhi Lord accepts the *arcā-vigraha* (His transcendental form) in different elements, namely a form within the mind, a form made of wood, a form made of earth, a form made of metal, a form made of jewel, a form made of paint, a form drawn on sand, etc. All such forms of the Lord are always decorated with garlands of lotus flowers, and there should be a soothing atmosphere in the temple of worship to attract the burning attention of the nondevotees always engaged in material wranglings. The meditators worship a form within the mind. Therefore, the Lord is merciful even to the women, *śūdras* and *dvija-bandhus,* provided they agree to visit the temple of worship in different forms made for them. Such temple visitors are not idolaters, as alleged by some men with a poor fund of knowledge. All the great *ācāryas* established such temples of worship in all places just to favor the less intelligent, and one should not pose himself as transcending the stage of temple worship while one is actually in the category of the *śūdras* and the women or less. One should begin to see the Lord from His lotus feet, gradually rising to the thighs, waist, chest and face. One should not try to look at the face of the Lord without being accustomed to seeing the lotus feet of the Lord. Śrīmatī Kuntī, because of her being the aunt of the Lord, did not begin to see the Lord from the lotus feet because the Lord might feel ashamed, and thus Kuntīdevī, just to save a painful situation for the Lord, began to see the Lord just above

His lotus feet, i.e., from the waist of the Lord, gradually rising to the face, and then down to the lotus feet. In the round, everything there is in order.

TEXT 23

यथा हृषीकेश खलेन देवकी
कंसेन रुद्धातिचिरं शुचार्पिता ।
विमोचिताहं च सहात्मजा विभो
त्वयैव नाथेन मुहुर्विपद्गणात् ॥ २३ ॥

yathā hṛṣīkeśa khalena devakī
kaṁsena ruddhāticiraṁ śucārpitā
vimocitāhaṁ ca sahātmajā vibho
tvayaiva nāthena muhur vipad-gaṇāt

yathā—as it were; *hṛṣīkeśa*—the master of the senses; *khalena*—by the envious; *devakī*—Devakī (the mother of Śrī Kṛṣṇa); *kaṁsena*—by King Kaṁsa; *ruddhā*—imprisoned; *ati-ciram*—for a long time; *śuca-arpitā*—distressed; *vimocitā*—released; *aham ca*—also myself; *saha-ātma-jā*—along with my children; *vibho*—O great one; *tvayā eva*—by Your Lordship; *nāthena*—as the protector; *muhuḥ*—constantly; *vipat-gaṇāt*—from a series of dangers.

O Hṛṣīkeśa, master of the senses and Lord of lords, You have released Your mother, Devakī, who was long imprisoned and distressed by the envious King Kaṁsa, and me and my children from a series of constant dangers.

PURPORT Devakī, the mother of Kṛṣṇa and sister of King Kaṁsa, was put into prison along with her husband, Vasudeva, because the envious King was afraid of being killed by Devakī's eighth son (Kṛṣṇa). He killed all the sons of Devakī who were born before Kṛṣṇa, but Kṛṣṇa escaped the danger of child-slaughter because He was transferred to the house of Nanda Mahārāja, Lord Kṛṣṇa's foster father. Kuntīdevī, along with her children, was also saved from a series of dangers. But Kuntīdevī was shown far more favor because Lord Kṛṣṇa did not save the other children of Devakī, whereas He saved the children of Kuntīdevī. This was done because Devakī's husband, Vasudeva, was living, whereas Kuntīdevī was a widow, and there was none to help her except Kṛṣṇa. The conclusion is that Kṛṣṇa endows more favor to a devotee who is in greater dangers. Sometimes He puts His pure devotees in such dangers because in that condition of helplessness the devotee becomes more attached to the Lord. The more the attachment is there for the Lord, the more success is there for the devotee.

TEXT 24

विषान्महाग्नेः पुरुषाददर्शना-
दसत्सभाया वनवासकृच्छ्रतः ।
मृधे मृधेऽनेकमहारथास्त्रतो
द्रौण्यस्त्रतश्चास्म हरेऽभिरक्षिताः ॥ २४ ॥

viṣān mahāgneḥ puruṣāda-darśanād
asat-sabhāyā vana-vāsa-kṛcchrataḥ
mṛdhe mṛdhe 'neka-mahārathāstrato
drauṇy-astrataś cāsma hare 'bhirakṣitāḥ

viṣāt—from poison; *mahā-agneḥ*—from the great fire; *puruṣa-ada*—the man-eaters; *darśanāt*—by combating; *asat*—vicious; *sabhāyāḥ*—assembly; *vana-vāsa*—exiled to the forest; *kṛcchrataḥ*—sufferings; *mṛdhe mṛdhe*—again and again in battle; *aneka*—many; *mahā-ratha*—great generals; *astrataḥ*—weapons; *drauṇi*—the son of Droṇācārya; *astrataḥ*—from the weapon of; *ca*—and; *āsma*—indicating past tense; *hare*—O my Lord; *abhirakṣitāḥ*—protected completely.

My dear Kṛṣṇa, Your Lordship has protected us from a poisoned cake, from a great fire, from cannibals, from the vicious assembly, from sufferings during our exile in the forest and from the battle where great generals fought. And now You have saved us from the weapon of Aśvatthāmā.

PURPORT The list of dangerous encounters is submitted herein. Devakī was once put into difficulty by her envious brother, otherwise she was well. But Kuntīdevī and her sons were put into one difficulty after another for years and years together. They were put into trouble by Duryodhana and his party due to the kingdom, and each and every time the sons of Kuntī were saved by the Lord. Once Bhīma was administered poison in a cake, once they were put into the house made of shellac and set afire, and once Draupadī was dragged out, and attempts were made to insult her by stripping her naked in the vicious assembly of the Kurus. The Lord saved Draupadī by supplying an immeasurable length of cloth, and Duryodhana's party failed to see her naked. Similarly, when they were exiled in the forest, Bhīma had to fight with the man-eater demon Hiḍimbā Rākṣasa, but the Lord saved him. So it was not finished there. After all these tribulations, there was the great Battle of Kurukṣetra, and Arjuna had to meet such great generals as Droṇa, Bhīṣma and Karṇa, all powerful fighters. And at last, even when everything was done away with, there was the *brahmāstra* released by the son of Droṇācārya to kill the child within the womb of Uttarā, and so the Lord saved the only surviving descendant of the Kurus, Mahārāja Parīkṣit.

TEXT 25

विपदः सन्तु ताः शश्वत्तत्र तत्र जगद्गुरो ।
भवतो दर्शनं यत्स्यादपुनर्भवदर्शनम् ॥ २५ ॥

vipadaḥ santu tāḥ śaśvat tatra tatra jagad-guro
bhavato darśanaṁ yat syād apunar bhava-darśanam

vipadaḥ—calamities; *santu*—let there be; *tāḥ*—all; *śaśvat*—again and again; *tatra*—there; *tatra*—and there; *jagat-guro*—O Lord of the universe; *bhavataḥ*—Your; *darśanam*—meeting; *yat*—that which; *syāt*—is; *apunaḥ*—not again; *bhava-darśanam*—seeing repetition of birth and death.

I wish that all those calamities would happen again and again so that we could see You again and again, for seeing You means that we will no longer see repeated births and deaths.

PURPORT Generally the distressed, the needy, the intelligent and the inquisitive who have performed some pious activities worship or begin to worship the Lord. Others, who are thriving on misdeeds only, regardless of status, cannot approach the Supreme due to being misled by the illusory energy. Therefore, for a pious person, if there is some calamity there is no other alternative than to take shelter of the lotus feet of the Lord. Constantly remembering the lotus feet of the Lord means preparing for liberation from birth and death. Therefore, even though there are so-called calamities, they are welcome because they give us an opportunity to remember the Lord, which means liberation.

One who has taken shelter of the lotus feet of the Lord, which are accepted as the most suitable boat for crossing the ocean of nescience, can achieve liberation as easily as one leaps over the holes made by the hoofs of a calf. Such persons are meant to reside in the abode of the Lord, and they have nothing to do with a place where there is danger in every step.

This material world is certified by the Lord in the *Bhagavad-gītā* as a dangerous place full of calamities. Less intelligent persons prepare plans to adjust to those calamities without knowing that the nature of this place is itself full of calamities. They have no information of the abode of the Lord, which is full of bliss and without trace of calamity. The duty of the sane person, therefore, is to be undisturbed by worldly calamities, which are sure to happen in all circumstances. Suffering all sorts of unavoidable misfortunes, one should make progress in spiritual realization because that is the mission of human life. The spirit soul is transcendental to all material calamities; therefore, the so-called calamities are called false. A man may see a tiger swallowing him in a dream, and he may cry for this calamity. Actually there is no tiger and there is no suffering; it is simply a case of dreams. In the same way, all calamities of life are said to be dreams. If someone is lucky enough to get in contact with the Lord by devotional service, it is all gain. Contact with the Lord by any one of the nine devotional services is always a forward step on the path going back to Godhead.

TEXT 26

जन्मैश्वर्यश्रुतश्रीभिरेधमानमदः पुमान् ।
नैवार्हत्यभिधातुं वै त्वामकिञ्चनगोचरम् ॥ २६ ॥

janmaiśvarya-śruta-śrībhir edhamāna-madaḥ pumān
naivārhaty abhidhātuṁ vai tvām akiñcana-gocaram

janma—birth; *aiśvarya*—opulence; *śruta*—education; *śrībhiḥ*—by the possession of beauty; *edhamāna*—progressively increasing; *madaḥ*—intoxication; *pumān*—the human being; *na*—never; *eva*—ever; *arhati*—deserves; *abhidhātum*—to address in feeling; *vai*—certainly; *tvām*—You; *akiñcana-gocaram*—one who is approached easily by the materially exhausted man.

My Lord, Your Lordship can easily be approached, but only by those who are materially exhausted. One who is on the path of [material] progress, trying to improve himself with respectable parentage, great opulence, high education and bodily beauty, cannot approach You with sincere feeling.

PURPORT Being materially advanced means taking birth in an aristocratic family and possessing great wealth, an education and attractive personal beauty. All materialistic men are mad after possessing all these material opulences, and this is known as the advancement of material civilization. But the result is that by possessing all these material assets one becomes artificially puffed up, intoxicated by such temporary possessions. Consequently, such materially puffed up persons are incapable of uttering the holy name of the Lord by addressing Him feelingly, "O Govinda, O Kṛṣṇa." It is said in the *śāstras* that by once uttering the holy name of the Lord, the sinner gets rid of a quantity of sins that he is unable to commit. Such is the power of uttering the holy name of the Lord. There is not the least exaggeration in this statement. Actually the Lord's holy name has such powerful potency. But there is a quality to such utterances also. It depends on the quality of feeling. A helpless man can feelingly utter the holy name of the Lord, whereas a man who utters the same holy name in great material satisfaction cannot be so sincere. A materially puffed up person may utter the holy name of the Lord occasionally, but he is incapable of uttering the name in quality. Therefore, the four principles of material advancement, namely (1) high parentage, (2) good wealth, (3) high education and (4) attractive beauty, are, so to speak, disqualifications for progress on the path of spiritual advancement. The material covering of the pure spirit soul is an external feature, as much as fever is an external feature of the unhealthy body. The general process is to decrease the degree of the fever and not to aggravate it by maltreatment. Sometimes it is seen that spiritually advanced persons become materially impoverished. This is no discouragement. On the other hand, such impoverishment is a good sign as much as the falling of temperature is a good sign. The principle of life should be to decrease the degree of material intoxication which leads one to be more and more illusioned about the aim of life. Grossly illusioned persons are quite unfit for entrance into the kingdom of God.

TEXT 27

नमोऽकिञ्चनवित्ताय निवृत्तगुणवृत्तये ।
आत्मारामाय शान्ताय कैवल्यपतये नमः ॥ २७ ॥

namo 'kiñcana-vittāya nivṛtta-guṇa-vṛttaye
ātmārāmāya śāntāya kaivalya-pataye namaḥ

namaḥ—all obeisances unto You; *akiñcana-vittāya*—unto the property of the materially impoverished; *nivṛtta*—completely transcendental to the actions of the material modes; *guṇa*—material modes; *vṛttaye*—affection; *ātma-ārāmāya*—one who is self-satisfied; *śāntāya*—the most gentle; *kaivalya-pataye*—unto the master of the monists; *namaḥ*—bowing down.

My obeisances are unto You, who are the property of the materially impoverished. You have nothing to do with the actions and reactions of the material modes of nature. You are self-satisfied, and therefore You are the most gentle and are master of the monists.

PURPORT A living being is finished as soon as there is nothing to possess. Therefore a living being cannot be, in the real sense of the term, a renouncer. A living being renounces something for gaining something more valuable. A student sacrifices his childish proclivities to gain better education. A servant gives up his job for a better job. Similarly, a devotee renounces the material world not for nothing but for something tangible in spiritual value. Śrīla Rūpa Gosvāmī, Sanātana Gosvāmī and Śrīla Raghunātha dāsa Gosvāmī and others gave up their worldly pomp and prosperity for the sake of the service of the Lord. They were big men in the worldly sense. The Gosvāmīs were ministers in the government service of Bengal, and Śrīla Raghunātha dāsa Gosvāmī was the son of a big *zamindar* of his time. But they left everything to gain something superior to what they previously possessed. The devotees are generally without material prosperity, but they have a very secret treasure-house in the lotus feet of the Lord. There is a nice story about Śrīla Sanātana Gosvāmī. He had a touchstone with him, and this stone was left in a pile of refuse. A needy man took it, but later on wondered why the valuable stone was kept in such a neglected place. He therefore asked him for the most valuable thing, and then he was given the holy name of the Lord. *Akiñcana* means one who has nothing to give materially. A factual devotee, or *mahātmā,* does not give anything material to anyone because he has already left all material assets. He can, however, deliver the supreme asset, namely the Personality of Godhead, because He is the only property of a factual devotee. The touchstone of Sanātana Gosvāmī, which was thrown in the rubbish, was not the property of the Gosvāmī, otherwise it would not have been kept in such a place. This specific example is given for the neophyte devotees just to convince them that material hankerings and spiritual advancement go ill together. Unless one is able to see everything as spiritual in relation with the Supreme Lord, one must always distinguish between spirit and matter. A spiritual master like Śrīla Sanātana Gosvāmī, although personally able to see everything as spiritual, set this example for us only because we have no such spiritual vision.

Advancement of material vision or material civilization is a great stumbling block for spiritual advancement. Such material advancement entangles the living being in the bondage of a material body followed by all sorts of material miseries. Such material advancement is called *anartha,* or things not wanted. Actually this is so. In the present context of material advancement one uses lipstick at a cost of fifty cents, and there are so many unwanted things which are all products of the material conception of life. By diverting attention to so many unwanted things, human energy is spoiled without achievement of spiritual realization, the prime necessity of human life. The attempt to reach the moon is another example of spoiling energy because even if the moon is reached, the problems of life will not be solved. The devotees of the Lord are called *akiñcanas* because they have practically no material assets. Such material assets are all products of the three modes of material nature. They foil spiritual energy, and thus the less we possess such products of material nature, the more we have a good chance for spiritual progress.

The Supreme Personality of Godhead has no direct connection with material activities. All His acts and deeds, which are exhibited even in this material world, are spiritual and unaffected by the modes of material nature. In the *Bhagavad-gītā* the Lord says that all His acts, even His appearance and disappearance in and out of the material world, are transcendental, and one who knows this perfectly shall not take his birth again in this material world, but will go back to Godhead.

The material disease is due to hankering after and lording it over material nature. This hankering is due to an interaction of the three modes of nature, and neither the Lord nor the devotees have attachment for such false enjoyment. Therefore, the Lord and the devotees are called *nivṛtta-guṇa-vṛtti.* The perfect *nivṛtta-guṇa-vṛtti* is the Supreme Lord because He never becomes attracted by the modes of material nature, whereas the living beings have such a tendency. Some of them are entrapped by the illusory attraction of material nature.

Because the Lord is the property of the devotees, and the devotees are the property of the Lord reciprocally, the devotees are certainly transcendental to the modes of material nature. That is a natural conclusion. Such unalloyed devotees are distinct from the mixed devotees who approach the Lord for mitigation of miseries and poverty or because of inquisitiveness and speculation. The unalloyed devotees and the Lord are transcendentally attached to one another. For others, the Lord has nothing to reciprocate, and therefore He is called *ātmārāma,* self-satisfied. Self-satisfied as He is, He is the master of all monists who seek to merge into the existence of the Lord. Such monists merge within the personal effulgence of the Lord called the *brahma-jyoti,* but the devotees enter into the transcendental pastimes of the Lord, which are never to be misunderstood as material.

TEXT 28

मन्ये त्वां कालमीशानमनादिनिधनं विभुम् ।
समं चरन्तं सर्वत्र भूतानां यन्मिथः कलिः ॥ २८ ॥

manye tvāṁ kālam īśānam anādi-nidhanaṁ vibhum
samaṁ carantaṁ sarvatra bhūtānāṁ yan mithaḥ kaliḥ

manye—I consider; *tvām*—Your Lordship; *kālam*—the eternal time; *īśānam*—the Supreme Lord; *anādi-nidhanam*—without beginning and end; *vibhum*—all-pervading; *samam*—equally merciful; *carantam*—distributing; *sarvatra*—everywhere; *bhūtānām*—of the living beings; *yat mithaḥ*—by intercourse; *kaliḥ*—dissension.

My Lord, I consider Your Lordship to be eternal time, the supreme controller, without beginning and end, the all-pervasive one. In distributing Your mercy, You are equal to everyone. The dissensions between living beings are due to social intercourse.

PURPORT Kuntīdevī knew that Kṛṣṇa was neither her nephew nor an ordinary family member of her paternal house. She knew perfectly well that Kṛṣṇa is the primeval Lord who lives in everyone's heart as the Supersoul, Paramātmā. Another name of the Paramātmā feature of the Lord is *kāla,* or eternal time. Eternal time is the witness of all our actions, good and bad, and thus resultant reactions are destined by Him. It is no use saying that we do not know why and for what we are suffering. We may forget the misdeed for which we may suffer at this present moment, but we must remember that Paramātmā is our constant companion, and therefore He knows everything, past, present and future. And because the Paramātmā feature of Lord Kṛṣṇa destines all actions and reactions, He is the supreme controller also. Without His sanction not a blade of grass can move. The living beings are given as much freedom as they deserve, and misuse of that freedom is the cause of suffering. The devotees of the Lord do not misuse their freedom, and therefore they are the good sons of the Lord. Others, who misuse freedom, are put into miseries destined by the eternal *kāla*. The *kāla* offers the conditioned souls both happiness and miseries. It is all predestined by eternal time. As we have miseries uncalled-for, so we may have happiness also without being asked, for they are all predestined by *kāla*. No one is therefore either an enemy or friend of the Lord. Everyone is suffering and enjoying the result of his own destiny. This destiny is made by the living beings in course of social intercourse. Everyone here wants to lord it over the material nature, and thus everyone creates his own destiny under the supervision of the Supreme Lord. He is all-pervading and therefore He can see everyone's activities. And because the Lord has no beginning or end, He is known also as the eternal time, *kāla*.

TEXT 29

न वेद कश्चिद्भगवंश्चिकीर्षितं
तवेहमानस्य नृणां विडम्बनम् ।
न यस्य कश्चिद्दयितोऽस्ति कर्हिचिद्
द्वेष्यश्च यस्मिन् विषमा मतिर्नृणाम् ॥ २९ ॥

na veda kaścid bhagavaṁś cikīrṣitaṁ
tavehamānasya nṛṇāṁ viḍambanam
na yasya kaścid dayito 'sti karhicid
dveṣyaś ca yasmin viṣamā matir nṛṇām

na—does not; *veda*—know; *kaścit*—anyone; *bhagavan*—O Lord; *cikīrṣitam*—pastimes; *tava*—Your; *īhamānasya*—like the worldly men; *nṛṇām*—of the people in general; *viḍambanam*—misleading; *na*—never; *yasya*—His; *kaścit*—anyone; *dayitaḥ*—object of specific favor; *asti*—there is; *karhicit*—anywhere; *dveṣyaḥ*—object of envy; *ca*—and; *yasmin*—unto Him; *viṣamā*—partiality; *matiḥ*—conception; *nṛṇām*—of the people.

O Lord, no one can understand Your transcendental pastimes, which appear to be human and are so misleading. You have no specific object of favor, nor do You have any object of envy. People only imagine that You are partial.

PURPORT The Lord's mercy upon the fallen souls is equally distributed. He has no one as the specific object of hostility. The very conception of the Personality of Godhead as a human being is misleading. His pastimes *appear* to be exactly like a human being's, but actually they are transcendental and without any tinge of material contamination. He is undoubtedly known as partial to His pure devotees, but in fact He is never partial, as much as the sun is never partial to anyone. By utilizing the sun rays, sometimes even the stones become valuable, whereas a blind man cannot see the sun, although there are enough sun rays before him. Darkness and light are two opposite conceptions, but this does not mean that the sun is partial in distributing its rays. The sun rays are open to everyone, but the capacities of the receptacles differ. Foolish people think that devotional service is flattering the Lord to get special mercy. Factually the pure devotees who are engaged in the transcendental loving service of the Lord are not a mercantile community. A mercantile house renders service to someone in exchange for values. The pure devotee does not render service unto the Lord for such exchange, and therefore the full mercy of the Lord is open for him. Suffering and needy men, inquisitive persons or philosophers make temporary connections with the Lord to serve a particular purpose. When the purpose is served, there is no more relation with the Lord. A suffering man, if he is pious at all, prays to the Lord for his recovery. But as soon as the recovery is over, in most cases the suffering man no longer cares to keep any connection with the Lord. The mercy of the Lord is open for him, but he is reluctant to receive it. That is the difference between a pure devotee and a mixed devotee. Those who are completely against the service of the Lord are considered to be in abject darkness, those who ask for the Lord's favor only at the time of necessity are partial recipients of the mercy of the Lord, and those who are cent percent engaged in the service of the Lord are full recipients of the mercy of the Lord. Such partiality in receiving the Lord's mercy is relative to the recipient, and it is not due to the partiality of the all-merciful Lord.

When the Lord descends on this material world by His all-merciful energy, He plays like a human being, and therefore it appears that the Lord is partial to His devotees only, but that is not a fact. Despite such apparent manifestation of partiality, His mercy is equally distributed. In the Battlefield of Kurukṣetra all persons who died in the fight before the presence of the Lord got salvation without the necessary qualifications because death before the presence of the Lord purifies the passing soul from the effects of all sins, and therefore the dying man gets a place somewhere in the transcendental abode. Somehow or other if someone puts himself open in the sun rays, he is sure to get the requisite benefit both by heat and by ultraviolet rays. Therefore, the conclusion is that the Lord is never partial. It is wrong for the people in general to think of Him as partial.

TEXT 30

जन्म कर्म च विश्वात्मन्नजस्याकर्तुरात्मनः ।
तिर्यङ्नृषिषु यादःसु तदत्यन्तविडम्बनम् ॥ ३० ॥

janma karma ca viśvātmann ajasyākartur ātmanaḥ
tiryaṅ-nṝṣiṣu yādaḥsu tad atyanta-viḍambanam

janma—birth; *karma*—activity; *ca*—and; *viśva-ātman*—O soul of the universe; *ajasya*—of the unborn; *akartuḥ*—of the inactive; *ātmanaḥ*—of the vital energy; *tiryak*—animal; *nṛ*—human being; *ṛṣiṣu*—in the sages; *yādaḥsu*—in the water; *tat*—that; *atyanta*—veritable; *viḍambanam*—bewildering.

Of course it is bewildering, O soul of the universe, that You work, though You are inactive, and that You take birth, though You are the vital force and the unborn. You Yourself descend amongst animals, men, sages and aquatics. Verily, this is bewildering.

PURPORT The transcendental pastimes of the Lord are not only bewildering but also apparently contradictory. In other words, they are all inconceivable to the limited thinking power of the human being. The Lord is the all-prevailing Supersoul of all existence, and yet He appears in the form of a boar amongst the animals, in the form of a human being as Rāma, Kṛṣṇa, etc., in the form of a *ṛṣi* like Nārāyaṇa, and in the form of an aquatic like a fish. Yet it is said that He is unborn, and He has nothing to do. In the *śruti mantra* it is said that the Supreme Brahman has nothing to do. No one is equal to or greater than Him. He has manifold energies, and everything is performed by Him perfectly by automatic knowledge, strength and activity. All these statements prove without any question that the Lord's activities, forms and deeds are all inconceivable to our limited thinking power, and because He is inconceivably powerful, everything is possible in Him. Therefore no one can calculate Him exactly; every action of the Lord is bewildering to the common man. He cannot be understood by the Vedic knowledge, but He can be easily understood by the pure devotees because they are intimately related with Him. The devotees therefore know that although He appears amongst the animals, He is not an animal, nor a man, nor a *ṛṣi,* nor a fish. He is eternally the Supreme Lord, in all circumstances.

TEXT 31

गोप्याददे त्वयि कृतागसि दाम तावद्
या ते दशाश्रुकलिलाञ्जनसम्भ्रमाक्षम् ।
वक्त्रं निनीय भयभावनया स्थितस्य
सा मां विमोहयति भीरपि यद्बिभेति ॥ ३१ ॥

gopy ādade tvayi kṛtāgasi dāma tāvad
yā te daśāśru-kalilāñjana-sambhramākṣam
vaktraṁ ninīya bhaya-bhāvanayā sthitasya
sā māṁ vimohayati bhīr api yad bibheti

gopī—the cowherd lady (Yaśodā); *ādade*—took up; *tvayi*—on Your; *kṛtāgasi*—creating disturbances (by breaking the butter pot); *dāma*—rope; *tāvat*—at that time; *yā*—that which; *te*—Your; *daśā*—situation; *aśru-kalila*—overflooded with tears; *añjana*—ointment; *sambhrama*—perturbed; *akṣam*—eyes; *vaktram*—face; *ninīya*—downwards; *bhaya-bhāvanayā*—by thoughts of fear; *sthitasya*—of the situation; *sā*—that; *mām*—me; *vimohayati*—bewilders; *bhīḥ api*—even fear personified; *yat*—whom; *bibheti*—is afraid.

My dear Kṛṣṇa, Yaśodā took up a rope to bind You when You committed an offense, and Your perturbed eyes overflooded with tears, which washed the mascara from Your eyes. And You were afraid, though fear personified is afraid of You. This sight is bewildering to me.

PURPORT Here is another example of the bewilderment created by the pastimes of the Supreme Lord. The Supreme Lord is the Supreme in all circumstances, as already explained. Here is a specific example of the Lord's being the Supreme and at the same time a plaything in the presence of His pure devotee. The Lord's pure devotee renders service unto the Lord out of unalloyed love only, and while discharging such devotional service the pure devotee forgets the position of the Supreme Lord. The Supreme Lord also accepts the loving service of His devotees more relishably when the service is rendered spontaneously out of pure affection, without anything of reverential admiration. Generally the Lord is worshiped by the devotees in a reverential attitude, but the Lord is meticulously pleased when the devotee, out of pure affection and love, considers the Lord to be less important than himself. The Lord's pastimes in the original abode of Goloka Vṛndāvana are exchanged in that spirit. The friends of Kṛṣṇa consider Him one of them. They do not consider Him to be of reverential importance. The parents of the Lord (who are all pure devotees) consider Him a child only. The Lord accepts the chastisements of the parents more cheerfully than the prayers of the Vedic hymns. Similarly, He accepts the reproaches of His fiancees more palatably than the Vedic hymns. When Lord Kṛṣṇa was present in this material world to manifest His eternal pastimes of the transcendental realm of Goloka Vṛndāvana as an attraction for the people in general, He displayed a unique picture of subordination before His foster mother, Yaśodā. The Lord, in His naturally childish playful activities, used to spoil the stocked butter of Mother Yaśodā by breaking the pots and distributing the contents to His friends and playmates, including the celebrated monkeys of Vṛndāvana, who took advantage of the Lord's munificence. Mother Yaśodā saw this, and out of her pure love she wanted to make a show of punishment for her transcendental child. She took a rope and threatened the Lord that she would tie Him up, as is generally done in the ordinary household. Seeing the rope in the hands of Mother Yaśodā, the Lord bowed down His head and began to weep just like a child, and tears rolled down His cheeks, washing off the black ointment smeared about His beautiful eyes. This picture of the Lord is adored by Kuntīdevī because she is conscious of the Lord's supreme position. He is feared often by fear personified, yet He is afraid of His mother, who wanted to punish Him just in an ordinary manner. Kuntī was conscious of the exalted position of Kṛṣṇa, whereas Yaśodā was not. Therefore Yaśodā's position was more exalted than Kuntī's. Mother Yaśodā got the Lord as her child, and the Lord made her forget altogether that her child was the Lord Himself. If Mother Yaśodā had been conscious of the exalted position of the Lord, she would certainly have hesitated to punish the Lord. But she was made to forget this situation because the Lord wanted to make a complete gesture of childishness before the affectionate Yaśodā. This exchange of love between the mother and the son was performed in a natural way, and Kuntī, remembering the scene, was bewildered, and she could do nothing but praise the transcendental filial love. Indirectly Mother Yaśodā is praised for her unique position of love, for she could control even the all-powerful Lord as her beloved child.

TEXT 32

केचिदाहुरजं जातं पुण्यश्लोकस्य कीर्तये ।
यदोः प्रियस्यान्ववाये मलयस्येव चन्दनम् ॥ ३२ ॥

kecid āhur ajaṁ jātaṁ puṇya-ślokasya kīrtaye
yadoḥ priyasyānvavāye malayasyeva candanam

kecit—someone; *āhuḥ*—says; *ajam*—the unborn; *jātam*—being born; *puṇya-ślokasya*—of the great pious king; *kīrtaye*—for glorifying; *yadoḥ*—of King Yadu; *priyasya*—of the dear; *anvavāye*—in the family of; *malayasya*—Malaya hills; *iva*—as; *candanam*—sandalwood.

Some say that the Unborn is born for the glorification of pious kings, and others say that He is born to please King Yadu, one of Your dearest devotees. You appear in his family as sandalwood appears in the Malaya hills.

PURPORT Because the Lord's appearance in this material world is bewildering, there are different opinions about the birth of the Unborn. In the *Bhagavad-gītā* the Lord says that He takes His birth in the material world, although He is the Lord of all creations and He is unborn. So there cannot be any denial of the birth of the Unborn because He Himself establishes the truth. But still there are different opinions as to why He takes His birth. That is also declared in the *Bhagavad-gītā*. He appears by His own internal potency to reestablish the principles of religion and to protect the pious and to annihilate the impious. That is the mission of the appearance of the Unborn. Still, it is said that the Lord is there to glorify the pious King Yudhiṣṭhira. Lord Śrī Kṛṣṇa certainly wanted to establish the kingdom of the Pāṇḍavas for the good of all in the world. When there is a pious king ruling over the world, the people are happy. When the ruler is impious, the people are unhappy. In the age of Kali in most cases the rulers are impious, and therefore the citizens are also continuously unhappy. But in the case of democracy, the impious citizens themselves elect their representative to rule over them, and therefore they cannot blame anyone for their unhappiness. Mahārāja Nala was also celebrated as a great pious king, but he had no connection with Lord Kṛṣṇa. Therefore Mahārāja Yudhiṣṭhira is meant here to be glorified by Lord Kṛṣṇa. He had also glorified King Yadu, having taken His birth in the family. He is known as Yādava, Yaduvīra, Yadunandana, etc., although the Lord is always independent of such obligation. He is just like the sandalwood that grows in the Malaya hills. Trees can grow anywhere and everywhere, yet because the sandalwood trees grow mostly in the area of the Malaya hills, the name sandalwood and the Malaya hills are interrelated. Therefore, the conclusion is that the Lord is ever unborn like the sun, and yet He appears as the sun rises on the eastern horizon. As the sun is never the son of the eastern horizon, so the Lord is no one's son, but He is the father of everything that be.

TEXT 33

अपरे वसुदेवस्य देवक्यां याचितोऽभ्यगात् ।
अजस्त्वमस्य क्षेमाय वधाय च सुरद्विषाम् ॥ ३३ ॥

apare vasudevasya devakyāṁ yācito 'bhyagāt
ajas tvam asya kṣemāya vadhāya ca sura-dviṣām

apare—others; *vasudevasya*—of Vasudeva; *devakyām*—of Devakī; *yācitaḥ*—being prayed for; *abhyagāt*—took birth; *ajaḥ*—unborn; *tvam*—You are; *asya*—of him; *kṣemāya*—for the good; *vadhāya*—for the purpose of killing; *ca*—and; *sura-dviṣām*—of those who are envious of the demigods.

Others say that since both Vasudeva and Devakī prayed for You, You have taken Your birth as their son. Undoubtedly You are unborn, yet You take Your birth for their welfare and to kill those who are envious of the demigods.

PURPORT It is also said that Vasudeva and Devakī, in their previous birth as Sutapā and Pṛśni, underwent a severe type of penance to get the Lord as their son, and as a result of such austerities the Lord appeared as their son. It is already declared in the *Bhagavad-gītā* that the Lord appears for the welfare of all people of the world and to vanquish the *asuras,* or the materialistic atheists.

TEXT 34

भारावतारणायान्ये भुवो नाव इवोदधौ ।
सीदन्त्या भूरिभारेण जातो ह्यात्मभुवार्थितः ॥ ३४ ॥

bhārāvatāraṇāyānye bhuvo nāva ivodadhau
sīdantyā bhūri-bhāreṇa jāto hy ātma-bhuvārthitaḥ

bhāra-avatāraṇāya—just to reduce the burden to the world; *anye*—others; *bhuvaḥ*—of the world; *nāvaḥ*—boat; *iva*—like; *udadhau*—on the sea; *sīdantyāḥ*—aggrieved; *bhūri*—extremely; *bhāreṇa*—by the burden; *jātaḥ*—You were born; *hi*—certainly; *ātma-bhuvā*—by Brahmā; *arthitaḥ*—being prayed for.

Others say that the world, being overburdened like a boat at sea, is much aggrieved, and that Brahmā, who is Your son, prayed for You, and so You have appeared to diminish the trouble.

PURPORT Brahmā, or the first living being born just after the creation, is the direct son of Nārāyaṇa. Nārāyaṇa, as Garbhodakaśāyī Viṣṇu, first of all entered the material universe. Without spiritual contact, matter cannot create. This principle was followed from the very beginning of the creation. The Supreme Spirit entered the universe, and the first living being, Brahmā, was born on a lotus flower grown out of the transcendental abdomen of Viṣṇu. Viṣṇu is therefore known as Padmanābha. Brahmā is known as *ātma-bhū* because he was begotten directly from the father without any contact of mother Lakṣmījī. Lakṣmījī was present near Nārāyaṇa, engaged in the service of the Lord, and still, without contact with Lakṣmījī, Nārāyaṇa begot Brahmā. That is the omnipotency of the Lord. One who foolishly considers Nārāyaṇa like other living beings should take a lesson from this. Nārāyaṇa is not an ordinary living being. He is the Personality of Godhead Himself, and

He has all the potencies of all the senses in all parts of His transcendental body. An ordinary living being begets a child by sexual intercourse, and he has no other means to beget a child other than the one designed for him. But Nārāyaṇa, being omnipotent, is not bound to any condition of energy. He is complete and independent to do anything and everything by His various potencies, very easily and perfectly. Brahmā is therefore directly the son of the father and was not put into the womb of a mother. Therefore he is known as *ātma-bhū*. This Brahmā is in charge of further creations in the universe, secondarily reflected by the potency of the Omnipotent. Within the halo of the universe there is a transcendental planet known as Śvetadvīpa, which is the abode of the Kṣīrodakaśāyī Viṣṇu, the Paramātmā feature of the Supreme Lord. Whenever there is trouble in the universe that cannot be solved by the administrative demigods, they approach Brahmājī for a solution, and if it is not to be solved even by Brahmājī, then Brahmājī consults and prays to the Kṣīrodakaśāyī Viṣṇu for an incarnation and solution to the problems. Such a problem arose when Kaṁsa and others were ruling over the earth and the earth became too much overburdened by the misdeeds of the *asuras*. Brahmājī, along with other demigods, prayed at the shore of the Kṣīrodaka Ocean, and they were advised of the descent of Kṛṣṇa as the son of Vasudeva and Devakī. So some people say that the Lord appeared because of the prayers of Brahmājī.

TEXT 35

भवेऽस्मिन् क्लिश्यमानानामविद्याकामकर्मभिः ।
श्रवणस्मरणार्हाणि करिष्यन्निति केचन ॥ ३५ ॥

bhave 'smin kliśyamānānām avidyā-kāma-karmabhiḥ
śravaṇa-smaraṇārhāṇi kariṣyann iti kecana

bhave—in the material creation; *asmin*—this; *kliśyamānānām*—of those who are suffering from; *avidyā*—nescience; *kāma*—desire; *karmabhiḥ*—by execution of fruitive work; *śravaṇa*—hearing; *smaraṇa*—remembering; *arhāṇi*—worshiping; *kariṣyan*—may perform; *iti*—thus; *kecana*—others.

And yet others say that You appeared for the sake of rejuvenating the devotional service of hearing, remembering, worshiping and so on in

order that the conditioned souls suffering from material pangs might take advantage and gain liberation.

PURPORT In the *Śrīmad Bhagavad-gītā* the Lord asserts that He appears in every millennium just to reestablish the way of religion. The way of religion is made by the Supreme Lord. No one can manufacture a new path of religion, as is the fashion for certain ambitious persons. The factual way of religion is to accept the Lord as the supreme authority and thus render service unto Him in spontaneous love. A living being cannot help but render service because he is constitutionally made for that purpose. The only function of the living being is to render service to the Lord. The Lord is great, and living beings are subordinate to Him. Therefore, the duty of the living being is just to serve Him only. Unfortunately the illusioned living beings, out of misunderstanding only, become servants of the senses by material desire. This desire is called *avidyā,* or nescience. And out of such illegitimate desire the living being makes different plans for material enjoyment centered about a perverted sex life. He therefore becomes entangled in the chain of birth and death by transmigrating into different bodies on different planets under the direction of the Supreme Lord. Unless, therefore, one is beyond the boundary of this nescience, one cannot get free from the threefold miseries of material life. That is the law of nature.

The Lord, however, out of His causeless mercy, because He is more merciful to the suffering living beings than they can expect, appears before them and renovates the principles of devotional service comprised of hearing, chanting, remembering, serving, worshiping, praying, cooperating and surrendering unto Him. Adoption of all the above-mentioned items, or any one of them, can help a conditioned soul get out of the tangle of nescience and thus become liberated from all material sufferings created by the living being illusioned by the external energy. This particular type of mercy is bestowed upon the living being by the Lord in the form of Lord Śrī Caitanya Mahāprabhu.

TEXT 36

शृण्वन्ति गायन्ति गृणन्त्यभीक्ष्णशः
स्मरन्ति नन्दन्ति तवेहितं जनाः ।
त एव पश्यन्त्यचिरेण तावकं
भवप्रवाहोपरमं पदाम्बुजम् ॥ ३६ ॥

śṛṇvanti gāyanti gṛṇanty abhīkṣṇaśaḥ
smaranti nandanti tavehitaṁ janāḥ
ta eva paśyanty acireṇa tāvakaṁ
bhava-pravāhoparamaṁ padāmbujam

śṛṇvanti—hear; *gāyanti*—chant; *gṛṇanti*—take; *abhīkṣṇaśaḥ*—continuously; *smaranti*—remember; *nandanti*—take pleasure; *tava*—Your; *īhitam*—activities; *janāḥ*—people in general; *te*—they; *eva*—certainly; *paśyanti*—can see; *acireṇa*—very soon; *tāvakam*—Your; *bhava-pravāha*—the current of rebirth; *uparamam*—cessation; *pada-ambujam*—lotus feet.

O Kṛṣṇa, those who continuously hear, chant and repeat Your transcendental activities, or take pleasure in others' doing so, certainly see Your lotus feet, which alone can stop the repetition of birth and death.

PURPORT The Supreme Lord Śrī Kṛṣṇa cannot be seen by our present conditional vision. In order to see Him, one has to change his present vision by developing a different condition of life full of spontaneous love of Godhead. When Śrī Kṛṣṇa was personally present on the face of the globe, not everyone could see Him as the Supreme Personality of Godhead. Materialists like Rāvaṇa, Hiraṇyakaśipu, Kaṁsa, Jarāsandha and Śiśupāla, were highly qualified personalities by acquisition of material assets, but they were unable to appreciate the presence of the Lord. Therefore, even though the Lord may be present before our eyes, it is not possible to see Him unless we have the necessary vision. This necessary qualification is developed by the process of devotional service only, beginning with hearing about the Lord from the right sources. The *Bhagavad-gītā* is one of the popular literatures which are generally heard, chanted, repeated, etc., by the people in general, but in spite of such hearing, etc., sometimes it is experienced that the performer of such devotional service does not see the Lord eye to eye. The reason is that the first item, *śravaṇa,* is very important. If hearing is from the right sources, it acts very quickly. Generally people hear from unauthorized persons. Such unauthorized persons may be very learned by academic qualifications, but because they do not follow the principles of devotional service, hearing from them becomes a sheer waste of time. Sometimes the texts are interpreted fashionably to suit their own purposes. Therefore, first one should select a competent and bona fide speaker and then hear from him. When the hearing process is perfect and complete, the other processes become automatically perfect in their own way.

There are different transcendental activities of the Lord, and each and every one of them is competent to bestow the desired result, provided the hearing process is perfect. In the *Bhāgavatam* the activities of the Lord begin from His dealings with the Pāṇḍavas. There are many other pastimes of the Lord in connection with His dealings with the *asuras* and others. And in the Tenth Canto the sublime dealings with His conjugal associates, the *gopīs,* as well as with His married wives at Dvārakā are mentioned. Since the Lord is absolute, there is no difference in the transcendental nature of each and every dealing of the Lord. But sometimes people, in an unauthorized hearing process, take more interest in hearing about His dealings with the *gopīs.* Such an inclination indicates the lusty feelings of the hearer, so a bona fide speaker of the dealings of the Lord never indulges in such hearings. One must hear about the Lord from the very beginning, as in the *Śrīmad-Bhāgavatam* or any other scriptures, and that will help the hearer attain perfection by progressive development. One should not, therefore, consider that His dealings with the Pāṇḍavas are less important than His dealings with the *gopīs.* We must always remember that the Lord is always transcendental to all mundane attachment. In all the above-mentioned dealings of the Lord, He is the hero in all circumstances, and hearing about Him or about His devotees or combatants is conducive to spiritual life. It is said that the *Vedas* and *Purāṇas,* etc., are all made to revive our lost relation with Him. Hearing of all these scriptures is essential.

TEXT 37

अप्यद्य नस्त्वं स्वकृतेहित प्रभो
जिहाससि स्वित्सुहृदोऽनुजीविनः ।
येषां न चान्यद्भवतः पदाम्बुजात्
परायणं राजसु योजितांहसाम् ॥ ३७ ॥

apy adya nas tvaṁ sva-kṛtehita prabho
jihāsasi svit suhṛdo 'nujīvinaḥ
yeṣāṁ na cānyad bhavataḥ padāmbujāt
parāyaṇaṁ rājasu yojitāṁhasām

api—if; *adya*—today; *naḥ*—us; *tvam*—You; *sva-kṛta*—self-executed;

īhita—all duties; *prabho*—O my Lord; *jihāsasi*—giving up; *svit*—possibly; *suhṛdaḥ*—intimate friends; *anujīvinaḥ*—living at the mercy of; *yeṣām*—of whom; *na*—nor; *ca*—and; *anyat*—anyone else; *bhavataḥ*—Your; *pada-ambujāt*—from the lotus feet; *parāyaṇam*—dependent; *rājasu*—unto the kings; *yojita*—engaged in; *aṁhasām*—enmity.

O my Lord, You have executed all duties Yourself. Are you leaving us today, though we are completely dependent on Your mercy and have no one else to protect us, now when all kings are at enmity with us?

PURPORT The Pāṇḍavas are most fortunate because with all good luck they were entirely dependent on the mercy of the Lord. In the material world, to be dependent on the mercy of someone else is the utmost sign of misfortune, but in the case of our transcendental relation with the Lord, it is the most fortunate case when we can live completely dependent on Him. The material disease is due to thinking of becoming independent of everything. But the cruel material nature does not allow us to become independent. The false attempt to become independent of the stringent laws of nature is known as material advancement of experimental knowledge. The whole material world is moving on this false attempt of becoming independent of the laws of nature. Beginning from Rāvaṇa, who wanted to prepare a direct staircase to the planets of heaven, down to the present age, they are trying to overcome the laws of nature. They are trying now to approach distant planetary systems by electronic mechanical power. But the highest goal of human civilization is to work hard under the guidance of the Lord and become completely dependent on Him. The highest achievement of perfect civilization is to work with valor but at the same time depend completely on the Lord. The Pāṇḍavas were the ideal executors of this standard of civilization. Undoubtedly they were completely dependent on the good will of Lord Śrī Kṛṣṇa, but they were not idle parasites of the Lord. They were all highly qualified both by personal character and by physical activities. Still they always looked for the mercy of the Lord because they knew that every living being is dependent by constitutional position. The perfection of life is, therefore, to become dependent on the will of the Lord, instead of becoming falsely independent in the material world. Those who try to become falsely independent of the Lord are called *anātha*, or without any guardian, whereas those who are completely dependent on the will of the Lord are called *sanātha*, or those having someone to protect them. Therefore we must try to be *sanātha* so that we can always be protected from the unfavorable condition of material existence. By the deluding power of the external material nature we forget that the material condition of life is the most undesirable perplexity. The *Bhagavad-gītā* therefore directs us (7.19) that after many, many births one fortunate person becomes aware of the fact that Vāsudeva is all in all and that the best way of leading one's life is to surrender unto Him completely. That is the sign of a *mahātmā*. All the members of the Pāṇḍava family were *mahātmās* in household life. Mahārāja Yudhiṣṭhira was the head of these *mahātmās,* and Queen Kuntīdevī was the mother. The lessons of the *Bhagavad-gītā* and all the *Purāṇas,* specifically the *Bhāgavata Purāṇa,* are therefore inevitably connected with the history of the Pāṇḍava *mahātmās*. For them, separation from the Lord was just like the separation of a fish from water. Śrīmatī Kuntīdevī, therefore, felt such separation like a thunderbolt, and the whole prayer of the Queen is to try to persuade the Lord to stay with them. After the Battle of Kurukṣetra, although the inimical kings were killed, their sons and grandsons were still there to deal with the Pāṇḍavas. It is not only the Pāṇḍavas who were put into the condition of enmity, but all of us are always in such a condition, and the best way of living is to become completely dependent on the will of the Lord and thereby overcome all difficulties of material existence.

TEXT 38

के वयं नामरूपाभ्यां यदुभिः सह पाण्डवाः ।
भवतोऽदर्शनं यर्हि हृषीकाणामिवेशितुः ॥ ३८ ॥

ke vayaṁ nāma-rūpābhyāṁ yadubhiḥ saha pāṇḍavāḥ
bhavato 'darśanaṁ yarhi hṛṣīkāṇām iveśituḥ

ke—who are; *vayam*—we; *nāma-rūpābhyām*—without fame and ability; *yadubhiḥ*—with the Yadus; *saha*—along with; *pāṇḍavāḥ*—and the Pāṇḍavas; *bhavataḥ*—Your; *adarśanam*—absence; *yarhi*—as if; *hṛṣīkāṇām*—of the senses; *iva*—like; *īśituḥ*—of the living being.

As the name and fame of a particular body is finished with the disappearance of the living spirit, similarly if You do not look upon us, all our fame and activities, along with the Pāṇḍavas and Yadus, will end at once.

PURPORT Kuntīdevī is quite aware that the existence of the Pāṇḍavas is due to Śrī Kṛṣṇa only. The Pāṇḍavas are undoubtedly well established in name and fame and are guided by the great King Yudhiṣṭhira, who is morality personified, and the Yadus are undoubtedly great allies, but without the guidance of Lord Kṛṣṇa all of them are nonentities, as much as the senses of the body are useless without the guidance of consciousness. No one should be proud of his prestige, power and fame without being guided by the favor of the Supreme Lord. The living beings are always dependent, and the ultimate dependable object is the Lord Himself. We may, therefore, invent by our advancement of material knowledge all sorts of counteracting material resources, but without being guided by the Lord all such inventions end in fiasco, however strong and stout the reactionary elements may be.

TEXT 39

नेयं शोभिष्यते तत्र यथेदानीं गदाधर ।
त्वत्पदैरङ्किता भाति स्वलक्षणविलक्षितैः ॥ ३९ ॥

neyaṁ śobhiṣyate tatra yathedānīṁ gadādhara
tvat-padair aṅkitā bhāti sva-lakṣaṇa-vilakṣitaiḥ

na—not; *iyam*—this land of our kingdom; *śobhiṣyate*—will appear beautiful; *tatra*—then; *yathā*—as it is; *idānīm*—now; *gadādhara*—O Kṛṣṇa; *tvat*—Your; *padaiḥ*—by the feet; *aṅkitā*—marked; *bhāti*—is dazzling; *sva-lakṣaṇa*—Your own marks; *vilakṣitaiḥ*—by the impressions.

O Gadādhara [Kṛṣṇa], our kingdom is now being marked by the impressions of Your feet, and therefore it appears beautiful. But when You leave, it will no longer be so.

PURPORT There are certain particular marks on the feet of the Lord which distinguish the Lord from others. The marks of a flag, thunderbolt, and instrument to drive an elephant, umbrella, lotus, disc, etc., are on the bottom of the Lord's feet. These marks are impressed upon the soft dust of the land where the Lord traverses. The land of Hastināpura was thus marked while Lord Śrī Kṛṣṇa was there with the Pāṇḍavas, and the kingdom of the Pāṇḍavas thus flourished by such auspicious signs. Kuntīdevī pointed out these distinguished features and was afraid of ill luck in the absence of the Lord.

TEXT 40

इमे जनपदाः स्वृद्धाः सुपक्वौषधिवीरुधः ।
वनाद्रिनद्युदन्वन्तो ह्येधन्ते तव वीक्षितैः ॥ ४० ॥

ime jana-padāḥ svṛddhāḥ supakvauṣadhi-vīrudhaḥ
vanādri-nady-udanvanto hy edhante tava vīkṣitaiḥ

ime—all these; *jana-padāḥ*—cities and towns; *svṛddhāḥ*—flourished; *supakva*—nature; *auṣadhi*—herbs; *vīrudhaḥ*—vegetables; *vana*—forests; *adri*—hills; *nadī*—rivers; *udanvantaḥ*—seas; *hi*—certainly; *edhante*—increasing; *tava*—by You; *vīkṣitaiḥ*—seen.

All these cities and villages are flourishing in all respects because the herbs and grains are in abundance, the trees are full of fruits, the rivers are flowing, the hills are full of minerals and the oceans full of wealth. And this is all due to Your glancing over them.

PURPORT Human prosperity flourishes by natural gifts and not by gigantic industrial enterprises. The gigantic industrial enterprises are products of a godless civilization, and they cause the destruction of the noble aims of human life. The more we go on increasing such troublesome industries to squeeze out the vital energy of the human being, the more there will be unrest and dissatisfaction of the people in general, although a few only can live lavishly by exploitation. The natural gifts such as grains and vegetables, fruits, rivers, the hills of jewels and minerals, and the seas full of pearls are supplied by the order of the Supreme, and as He desires, material nature produces them in abundance or restricts them at times. The natural law is that the human being may take advantage of these godly gifts by nature and satisfactorily flourish on them without being captivated by the exploitative motive of lording it over material nature. The more we attempt to exploit material nature according to our whims of enjoyment, the more we shall become entrapped by the reaction of such exploitative attempts. If we have sufficient grains, fruits, vegetables and herbs, then what is the necessity of running a slaughterhouse and killing poor animals? A man need not kill an animal if he has sufficient grains and vegetables to eat. The flow of river waters fertilizes the fields, and there is more than what we need. Minerals are produced in the hills, and the jewels in the ocean. If the human civilization has sufficient grains, minerals, jewels, water, milk, etc., then why should it hanker after terrible industrial enterprises at the cost of the labor of some unfortunate men? But all these natural gifts are dependent on the mercy of the Lord. What we need, therefore, is to be obedient to the laws of the Lord and achieve the perfection of human life by devotional service. The indications by Kuntīdevī are just to the point. She desires that God's mercy be bestowed upon them so that natural prosperity be maintained by His grace.

TEXT 41

अथ विश्वेश विश्वात्मन् विश्वमूर्ते स्वकेषु मे ।
स्नेहपाशमिमं छिन्धि दृढं पाण्डुषु वृष्णिषु ॥ ४१ ॥

atha viśveśa viśvātman viśva-mūrte svakeṣu me
sneha-pāśam imaṁ chindhi dṛḍhaṁ pāṇḍuṣu vṛṣṇiṣu

atha—therefore; *viśva-īśa*—O Lord of the universe; *viśva-ātman*—O soul of the universe; *viśva-mūrte*—O personality of the universal form; *svakeṣu*—unto my own kinsmen; *me*—my; *sneha-pāśam*—tie of affection; *imam*—this; *chindhi*—cut off; *dṛḍham*—deep; *pāṇḍuṣu*—for the Pāṇḍavas; *vṛṣṇiṣu*—for the Vṛṣṇis also.

O Lord of the universe, soul of the universe, O personality of the form of the universe, please, therefore, sever my tie of affection for my kinsmen, the Pāṇḍavas and the Vṛṣṇis.

PURPORT A pure devotee of the Lord is ashamed to ask anything in self-interest from the Lord. But the householders are sometimes obliged to ask favors from the Lord, being bound by the tie of family affection. Śrīmatī Kuntīdevī was conscious of this fact, and therefore she prayed to the Lord to cut off the affectionate tie from her own kinsmen, the Pāṇḍavas and the Vṛṣṇis. The Pāṇḍavas are her own sons, and the Vṛṣṇis are the members of her paternal family. Kṛṣṇa was equally related to both the families. Both the families required the Lord's help because both were dependent devotees of the Lord. Śrīmatī Kuntīdevī wished Śrī Kṛṣṇa to remain with her sons the Pāṇḍavas, but by His doing so her paternal house would be bereft of the benefit. All these partialities troubled the mind of Kuntī, and therefore she desired to cut off the affectionate tie.

A pure devotee cuts off the limited ties of affection for his family and widens his activities of devotional service for all forgotten souls. The typical example is the band of Six Gosvāmīs, who followed the path of Lord Caitanya. All of them belonged to the most enlightened and cultured rich families of the higher castes, but for the benefit of the mass of population they left their comfortable homes and became mendicants. To cut off all family affection means to broaden the field of activities. Without doing this, no one can be qualified as a *brāhmaṇa,* a king, a public leader or a devotee of the Lord. The Personality of Godhead, as an ideal king, showed this by example. Śrī Rāmacandra cut off the tie of affection for His beloved wife to manifest the qualities of an ideal king.

Such personalities as a *brāhmaṇa,* a devotee, a king or a public leader must be very broadminded in discharging their respective duties. Śrīmatī Kuntīdevī was conscious of this fact, and being weak she prayed to be free from such bondage of family affection. The Lord is addressed as the Lord of the universe, or the Lord of the universal mind, indicating His all-powerful ability to cut the hard knot of family affection. Therefore, it is sometimes experienced that the Lord, out of His special affinity toward a weak devotee, breaks the family affection by force of circumstances arranged by His all-powerful energy. By doing so He causes the devotee to become completely dependent on Him and thus clears the path for his going back to Godhead.

TEXT 42

त्वयि मेऽनन्यविषया मतिर्मधुपतेऽसकृत् ।
रतिमुद्वहतादद्धा गङ्गेवौघमुदन्वति ॥ ४२ ॥

tvayi me 'nanya-viṣayā matir madhu-pate 'sakṛt
ratim udvahatād addhā gaṅgevaugham udanvati

tvayi—unto You; *me*—my; *ananya-viṣayā*—unalloyed; *matiḥ*—attention; *madhu-pate*—O Lord of Madhu; *asakṛt*—continuously; *ratim*—attraction; *udvahatāt*—may overflow; *addhā*—directly; *gaṅgā*—the Ganges; *iva*—like; *ogham*—flows; *udanvati*—down to the sea.

O Lord of Madhu, as the Ganges forever flows to the sea without hindrance, let my attraction be constantly drawn unto You without being diverted to anyone else.

PURPORT Perfection of pure devotional service is attained when all attention is diverted towards the transcendental loving service of the Lord. To cut off the tie of all other affections does not mean complete negation of the finer elements, like affection for someone else. This is not possible. A living being, whoever he may be, must have this feeling of affection for others because this is a symptom of life. The symptoms of life, such as desire, anger, hankerings, feelings of attraction, etc., cannot be annihilated. Only the objective has to be changed. Desire cannot be negated, but in devotional service the desire is changed only for the service of the Lord in place of desire for sense gratification. The so-called affection for family, society, country, etc., consists of different phases of sense gratification. When this desire is changed for the satisfaction of the Lord, it is called devotional service.

In the *Bhagavad-gītā* we can see that it was just to satisfy his own personal desires that Arjuna refused to fight with his brothers and relations. But when he heard the message of the Lord, *Śrīmad Bhagavad-gītā,* he changed his decision and served the Lord. And for his doing so, he became a famous devotee of the Lord, for it is declared in all the scriptures that Arjuna attained spiritual perfection by devotional service to the Lord in friendship. The fighting was there, the friendship was there, Arjuna was there, and Kṛṣṇa was there, but Arjuna became a different person by devotional service. Therefore, the prayers of Kuntī also indicate the same categorical changes in activities. Śrīmatī Kuntī wanted to serve the Lord without diversion, and that was her prayer. This unalloyed devotion is the ultimate goal of life. Our attention is usually diverted to the service of something which is nongodly or not in the program of the Lord. When the program is changed into the service of the Lord, that is to say when the senses are purified in relation with the service of the Lord, it is called pure unalloyed devotional service. Śrīmatī Kuntīdevī wanted that perfection and prayed for it from the Lord.

Her affection for the Pāṇḍavas and the Vṛṣṇis is not out of the range of devotional service because the service of the Lord and the service of the devotees are identical. Sometimes service to the devotee is more valuable than service to the Lord. But here the affection of Kuntīdevī for the Pāṇḍavas and the Vṛṣṇis was due to family relation. This tie of affection in terms of material relation is the relation of *māyā* because the relations of the body or the mind are due to the influence of the external energy. Relations of the soul, established in relation with the Supreme Soul, are factual relations. When Kuntīdevī wanted to cut off the family relation, she meant to cut off the relation of the skin. The skin relation is the cause of material bondage, but the relation of the soul is the cause of freedom. This relation of the soul to the soul can be established by the via medium of the relation with the Supersoul. Seeing in the darkness is not seeing. But seeing by the light of the sun means to see the sun and everything else which was unseen in the darkness. That is the way of devotional service.

TEXT 43

श्रीकृष्ण कृष्णसख वृष्ण्यृषभावनिध्रुग्
राजन्यवंशदहनानपवर्गवीर्य ।
गोविन्द गोद्विजसुरार्तिहरावतार
योगेश्वराखिलगुरो भगवन्नमस्ते ॥ ४३ ॥

śrī-kṛṣṇa kṛṣṇa-sakha vṛṣṇy-ṛṣabhāvani-dhrug-
rājanya-vaṁśa-dahanānapavarga-vīrya
govinda go-dvija-surārti-harāvatāra
yogeśvarākhila-guro bhagavan namas te

śrī-kṛṣṇa—O Śrī Kṛṣṇa; *kṛṣṇa-sakha*—O friend of Arjuna; *vṛṣṇi*—of descendants of Vṛṣṇi; *ṛṣabha*—O chief; *avani*—the earth; *dhruk*—rebellious; *rājanya-vaṁśa*—dynasties of the kings; *dahana*—O annihilator; *anapavarga*—without deterioration of; *vīrya*—prowess; *govinda*—O proprietor of Golokadhāma; *go*—of the cows; *dvija*—the *brāhmaṇas; sura*—the demigods; *arti-hara*—to relieve distress; *avatāra*—O Lord who descend; *yoga-īśvara*—O master of all mystic powers; *akhila*—universal; *guro*—O preceptor; *bhagavan*—O possessor of all opulences; *namaḥ te*—respectful obeisances unto You.

O Kṛṣṇa, O friend of Arjuna, O chief amongst the descendants of Vṛṣṇi, You are the destroyer of those political parties which are disturbing elements on this earth. Your prowess never deteriorates. You are the proprietor of the transcendental abode, and You descend to relieve the distresses of the cows, the brāhmaṇas and the devotees. You possess all mystic powers, and You are the preceptor of the entire universe. You are the almighty God, and I offer You my respectful obeisances.

PURPORT A summary of the Supreme Lord Śrī Kṛṣṇa is made herein by Śrīmatī Kuntīdevī. The almighty Lord has His eternal transcendental abode where He is engaged in keeping *surabhi* cows. He is served by hundreds and thousands of goddesses of fortune. He descends on the material world to reclaim His devotees and to annihilate the disturbing elements in groups of political parties and kings who are supposed to be in charge of administration work. He creates, maintains and annihilates by His unlimited energies, and still He is always full with prowess and does not deteriorate in potency. The cows, the *brāhmaṇas* and the devotees of the Lord are all objects of His special attention because they are very important factors for the general welfare of living beings.

सूत उवाच

TEXT 44

पृथयेत्थं कलपदः परिणूताखिलोदयः ।
मन्दं जहास वैकुण्ठो मोहयन्निव मायया ॥ ४४ ॥

sūta uvāca
pṛthayetthaṁ kala-padaiḥ pariṇūtākhilodayaḥ
mandaṁ jahāsa vaikuṇṭho mohayann iva māyayā

sūtaḥ uvāca—Sūta said; *pṛthayā*—by Pṛthā (Kuntī); *ittham*—this; *kala-padaiḥ*—by chosen words; *pariṇūta*—being worshiped; *akhila*—universal; *udayaḥ*—glories; *mandam*—mildly; *jahāsa*—smiled; *vaikuṇṭhaḥ*—the Lord; *mohayan*—captivating; *iva*—like; *māyayā*—His mystic power.

Sūta Gosvāmī said: The Lord, thus hearing the prayers of Kuntīdevī, composed in choice words for His glorification, mildly smiled. That smile was as enchanting as His mystic power.

PURPORT Anything that is enchanting in the world is said to be a representation of the Lord. The conditioned souls, who are engaged in trying to lord it over the material world, are also enchanted by His mystic powers, but His devotees are enchanted in a different way by the glories of the Lord, and His merciful blessings are upon them. His energy is displayed in different ways, as electrical energy works in manifold capacities. Śrīmatī Kuntīdevī has prayed to the Lord just to enunciate a fragment of His glories. All His devotees worship Him in that way, by chosen words, and therefore the Lord is known as Uttamaśloka. No amount of chosen words is sufficient to enumerate the Lord's glory, and yet He is satisfied by such prayers as the father is satisfied even by the broken linguistic attempts of the growing child. The word *māyā* is used both in the sense of delusion and mercy. Herein the word *māyā* is used in the sense of the Lord's mercy upon Kuntīdevī.

TEXT 45

तां बाढमित्युपामन्त्र्य प्रविश्य गजसाह्वयम् ।
स्त्रियश्च स्वपुरं यास्यन् प्रेम्णा राज्ञा निवारितः ॥ ४५ ॥

tāṁ bāḍham ity upāmantrya praviśya gajasāhvayam
striyaś ca sva-puraṁ yāsyan premṇā rājñā nivāritaḥ

tām—all those; *bāḍham*—accepted; *iti*—thus; *upāmantrya*—subsequently informed; *praviśya*—entering; *gajasāhvayam*—the palace of Hastināpura; *striyaḥ ca*—other ladies; *sva-puram*—own residence; *yāsyan*—while starting for; *premṇā*—with love; *rājñā*—by the King; *nivāritaḥ*—stopped.

Thus accepting the prayers of Śrīmatī Kuntīdevī, the Lord subsequently informed other ladies of His departure by entering the palace of Hastināpura. But upon preparing to leave, He was stopped by King Yudhiṣṭhira, who implored Him lovingly.

PURPORT No one could make Lord Kṛṣṇa stay at Hastināpura when He decided to start for Dvārakā, but the simple request of King Yudhiṣṭhira that the Lord remain there for a few days more was immediately effective. This signifies that the power of King Yudhiṣṭhira was loving affection, which the Lord could not deny. The almighty God is thus conquered only by loving service and nothing else. He is fully independent in all His dealings, but He voluntarily accepts obligations by the loving affection of His pure devotees.

TEXT 46

व्यासाद्यैरीश्वरेहाज्ञैः कृष्णेनाद्भुतकर्मणा ।
प्रबोधितोऽपीतिहासैर्नाबुध्यत शुचार्पितः ॥ ४६ ॥

vyāsādyair īśvarehājñaiḥ kṛṣṇenādbhuta-karmaṇā
prabodhito 'pītihāsair nābudhyata śucārpitaḥ

vyāsa-ādyaiḥ—by great sages headed by Vyāsa; *īśvara*—the almighty God; *īhā*—by the will of; *jñaiḥ*—by the learned; *kṛṣṇena*—by Kṛṣṇa Himself; *adbhuta-karmaṇā*—by one who performs all superhuman work; *prabodhitaḥ*—being solaced; *api*—although; *itihāsaiḥ*—by evidences from the histories; *na*—not; *abudhyata*—satisfied; *śucā arpitaḥ*—distressed.

King Yudhiṣṭhira, who was much aggrieved, could not be convinced, despite instructions by great sages headed by Vyāsa and the Lord Kṛṣṇa Himself, the performer of superhuman feats, and despite all historical evidence.

PURPORT The pious King Yudhiṣṭhira was mortified because of the mass massacre of human beings in the Battle of Kurukṣetra, especially on his account. Duryodhana was there on the throne, and he was doing well in his administration, and in one sense there was no need of fighting. But on the principle of justice Yudhiṣṭhira was to replace him. The whole clique of politics centered around this point, and all the kings and residents of the whole world became involved in this fight between the rival brothers. Lord Kṛṣṇa was also there on the side of King Yudhiṣṭhira. It is said in the *Mahābhārata* (*Ādi-parva* 2.25) that 640,000,000 men were killed in the eighteen days of the Battle of Kurukṣetra, and millions were missing. Practically this was the greatest battle in the world within five thousand years.

This mass killing simply to enthrone Mahārāja Yudhiṣṭhira was too mortifying, so he tried to be convinced with evidences from histories by great sages like Vyāsa and the Lord Himself that the fight was just because the cause was just. But Mahārāja Yudhiṣṭhira would not be satisfied, even though he was instructed by the greatest personalities of the time. Kṛṣṇa is designated herein as the performer of superhuman actions, but in this particular instance neither He nor Vyāsa could convince King Yudhiṣṭhira. Does it mean that He failed to be a superhuman actor? No, certainly not. The interpretation is that the Lord as *īśvara,* or the Supersoul in the hearts of both King Yudhiṣṭhira and Vyāsa, performed still more superhuman action because the Lord desired it. As Supersoul of King Yudhiṣṭhira, He did not allow the King to be convinced by the words of Vyāsa and others, including Himself, because

He desired that the King hear instructions from the dying Bhīṣmadeva, who was another great devotee of the Lord. The Lord wanted that at the last stage of his material existence the great warrior Bhīṣmadeva see Him personally and see his beloved grandchildren, King Yudhiṣṭhira, etc., now situated on the throne, and thus pass away very peacefully. Bhīṣmadeva was not at all satisfied to fight against the Pāṇḍavas, who were his beloved fatherless grandchildren. But the *kṣatriyas* are also very stern people, and therefore he was obliged to take the side of Duryodhana because he was maintained at the expense of Duryodhana. Besides this, the Lord also desired that King Yudhiṣṭhira be pacified by the words of Bhīṣmadeva so that the world could see that Bhīṣmadeva excelled all in knowledge, including the Lord Himself.

TEXT 47

आह राजा धर्मसुतश्चिन्तयन् सुहृदां वधम् ।
प्राकृतेनात्मना विप्राः स्नेहमोहवशं गतः ॥ ४७ ॥

āha rājā dharma-sutaś cintayan suhṛdāṁ vadham
prākṛtenātmanā viprāḥ sneha-moha-vaśaṁ gataḥ

āha—said; *rājā*—King Yudhiṣṭhira; *dharma-sutaḥ*—the son of Dharma (Yamarāja); *cintayan*—thinking of; *suhṛdām*—of the friends; *vadham*—killing; *prākṛtena*—by material conception only; *ātmanā*—by the self; *viprāḥ*—O *brāhmaṇa; sneha*—affection; *moha*—delusion; *vaśam*—being carried away by; *gataḥ*—having gone.

King Yudhiṣṭhira, son of Dharma, overwhelmed by the death of his friends, was aggrieved just like a common, materialistic man. O sages, thus deluded by affection, he began to speak.

PURPORT King Yudhiṣṭhira, though he was not expected to become aggrieved like a common man, became deluded by worldly affection by the will of the Lord (just as Arjuna was apparently deluded). A man who sees knows well that the living entity is neither the body nor the mind, but is transcendental to the material conception of life. The common man thinks of violence and nonviolence in terms of the body, but that is a kind of delusion. Everyone is duty-bound according to one's occupational duties. A *kṣatriya* is bound to fight for the right cause, regardless of the opposite party. In such discharge of duty, one should not be disturbed by annihilation of the material body, which is only an external dress of the living soul. All this was perfectly known to Mahārāja Yudhiṣṭhira, but by the will of the Lord he became just like a common man because there was another great idea behind this delusion: the King would be instructed by Bhīṣma as Arjuna was instructed by the Lord Himself.

TEXT 48

अहो मे पश्यताज्ञानं हृदि रूढं दुरात्मनः ।
पारक्यस्यैव देहस्य बह्व्यो मेऽक्षौहिणीर्हताः ॥ ४८ ॥

aho me paśyatājñānaṁ hṛdi rūḍhaṁ durātmanaḥ
pārakyasyaiva dehasya bahvyo me 'kṣauhiṇīr hatāḥ

aho—O; *me*—my; *paśyata*—just see; *ajñānam*—ignorance; *hṛdi*—in the heart; *rūḍham*—situated in; *durātmanaḥ*—of the sinful; *pārakyasya*—meant for others; *eva*—certainly; *dehasya*—of the body; *bahvyaḥ*—many, many; *me*—by me; *akṣauhiṇīḥ*—combination of military phalanxes; *hatāḥ*—killed.

King Yudhiṣṭhira said: O my lot! I am the most sinful man! Just see my heart, which is full of ignorance! This body, which is ultimately meant for others, has killed many, many phalanxes of men.

PURPORT A solid phalanx of 21,870 chariots, 21,870 elephants, 109,650 infantry and 65,600 cavalry is called an *akṣauhiṇī*. And many *akṣauhiṇīs* were killed on the Battlefield of Kurukṣetra. Mahārāja Yudhiṣṭhira, as the most pious king of the world, takes for himself the responsibility for killing such a huge number of living beings because the battle was fought to reinstate him on the throne. This body is, after all, meant for others. While there is life in the body, it is meant for the service of others, and when it is dead it is meant to be eaten by dogs and jackals or maggots. He is sorry because for such a temporary body such a huge massacre was committed.

TEXT 49

बालद्विजसुहृन्मित्रपितृभ्रातृगुरुद्रुहः ।
न मे स्यान्निरयान्मोक्षो ह्यपि वर्षायुतायुतैः ॥ ४९ ॥

bāla-dvija-suhṛn-mitra- pitṛ-bhrātṛ-guru-druhaḥ
na me syān nirayān mokṣo hy api varṣāyutāyutaiḥ

bāla—boys; *dvi-ja*—the twice-born; *suhṛt*—well-wishers; *mitra*—friends; *pitṛ*—parents; *bhrātṛ*—brothers; *guru*—preceptors; *druhaḥ*—one who has killed; *na*—never; *me*—my; *syāt*—there shall be; *nirayāt*—from hell; *mokṣaḥ*—liberation; *hi*—certainly; *api*—although; *varṣa*—years; *ayuta*—millions; *āyutaiḥ*—being added.

I have killed many boys, brāhmaṇas, well-wishers, friends, parents, preceptors and brothers. I will not be relieved from the hell that awaits me for all these sins, though I live there for millions of years.

PURPORT Whenever there is a war, there is certainly a massacre of many innocent living beings, such as boys, *brāhmaṇas* and women, whose killing is considered to be the greatest of sins. They are all innocent creatures, and in all circumstances killing of them is forbidden in the scriptures. Mahārāja Yudhiṣṭhira was aware of these mass killings. Similarly, there were friends, parents and preceptors also on both sides, and all of them were killed. It was simply horrible for him to think of such killing, and therefore he was thinking of residing in hell for millions and billions of years.

TEXT 50

नैनो राज्ञः प्रजाभर्तुर्धर्मयुद्धे वधो द्विषाम् ।
इति मे न तु बोधाय कल्पते शासनं वचः ॥ ५० ॥

naino rājñaḥ prajā-bhartur dharma-yuddhe vadho dviṣām
iti me na tu bodhāya kalpate śāsanaṁ vacaḥ

na—never; *enaḥ*—sins; *rājñaḥ*—of the king; *prajā-bhartuḥ*—of one who is engaged in the maintenance of the citizens; *dharma*—for the right cause; *yuddhe*—in the fight; *vadhaḥ*—killing; *dviṣām*—of the enemies; *iti*—all these; *me*—for me; *na*—never; *tu*—but; *bodhāya*—for satisfaction; *kalpate*—they are meant for administration; *śāsanam*—injunction; *vacaḥ*—words of.

There is no sin for a king who kills for the right cause, who is engaged in maintaining his citizens. But this injunction is not applicable to me.

PURPORT Mahārāja Yudhiṣṭhira thought that although he was not actually involved in the administration of the kingdom, which was being carried on well by Duryodhana without harm to the citizens, he caused the killing of so many living beings only for his personal gain of the kingdom from the hands of Duryodhana. The killing was committed not in the course of administration but for the sake of self-aggrandizement, and as such he thought himself responsible for all the sins.

TEXT 51

स्त्रीणां मद्धतबन्धूनां द्रोहो योऽसाविहोत्थितः ।
कर्मभिर्गृहमेधीयैर्नाहं कल्पो व्यपोहितुम् ॥ ५१ ॥

strīṇāṁ mad-dhata-bandhūnāṁ droho yo 'sāv ihotthitaḥ
karmabhir gṛhamedhīyair nāhaṁ kalpo vyapohitum

strīṇām—of the women; *mat*—by me; *hata-bandhūnām*—of the friends who are killed; *drohaḥ*—enmity; *yaḥ*—that; *asau*—all those; *iha*—herewith; *utthitaḥ*—has accrued; *karmabhiḥ*—by dint of work; *gṛhamedhīyaiḥ*—by persons engaged in material welfare; *na*—never; *aham*—I; *kalpaḥ*—can expect; *vyapohitum*—undoing the same.

I have killed many friends of women, and I have thus caused enmity to such an extent that it is not possible to undo it by material welfare work.

PURPORT The *gṛhamedhīs* are those whose only business is to perform welfare work for the sake of material prosperity. Such material prosperity is sometimes hampered by sinful activities, for the materialist is sure to commit sins, even unintentionally, in the course of discharging material duties. To get relief from such sinful reactions, the *Vedas* prescribe several kinds of sacrifices. It is said in the *Vedas* that by performing the Aśvamedha-yajña (horse sacrifice) one can get relief from even *brahma-hatyā* (killing of a *brāhmaṇa*).

Yudhiṣṭhira Mahārāja performed this Aśvamedha-yajña, but he thinks that even by performing such *yajñas* it is not possible to get relief from the great sins he committed by killing the friends and relatives of innocent women. In war either a woman's husband or brother or even father or sons go to fight. And when they are killed, a fresh enmity is created, and thus a chain of actions and reactions increases which is not possible to be counteracted even by thousands of Aśvamedha-yajñas.

The way of work (*karma*) is like that. It creates one action and another reaction simultaneously and thus increases the chain of material activities, binding the performer in material bondage. In the *Bhagavad-gītā* (Bg. 9.27–28) the remedy is suggested that such actions and reactions of the path of work can be checked only when work is done on behalf of the Supreme Lord. The Battle of Kurukṣetra was actually fought by the will of the Supreme Lord Śrī Kṛṣṇa, as it is evident from His version, and only by His will was Yudhiṣṭhira placed on the throne of Hastināpura. Therefore, factually no sin whatsoever touched the Pāṇḍavas, who were only the order carriers of the Lord. For others, who declare war out of personal interest, the whole responsibility lies on them.

TEXT 52

यथा पङ्केन पङ्काम्भः सुरया वा सुराकृतम् ।
भूतहत्यां तथैवैकां न यज्ञैर्मार्ष्टुमर्हति ॥ ५२ ॥

yathā paṅkena paṅkāmbhaḥ surayā vā surākṛtam
bhūta-hatyāṁ tathaivaikāṁ na yajñair mārṣṭum arhati

yathā—as much as; *paṅkena*—by the mud; *paṅka-ambhaḥ*—water mixed with mud; *surayā*—by wine; *vā*—either; *surākṛtam*—impurity caused by the slight touch of wine; *bhūta-hatyām*—killing of animals; *tathā*—like that; *eva*—certainly; *ekām*—one; *na*—never; *yajñaiḥ*—by the prescribed sacrifices; *mārṣṭum*—to counteract; *arhati*—is worthwhile.

As it is not possible to filter muddy water through mud, or purify a wine-stained pot with wine, it is not possible to counteract the killing of men by sacrificing animals.

PURPORT *Aśvamedha-yajñas* or *gomedha-yajñas,* sacrifices in which a horse or a bull is sacrificed, were not, of course, for the purpose of killing the animals. Lord Caitanya said that such animals sacrificed on the altar of *yajña* were rejuvenated and a new life was given to them. It was just to prove the efficacy of the hymns of the *Vedas.* By recitation of the hymns of the *Vedas* in the proper way, certainly the performer gets relief from the reactions of sins, but in case of such sacrifices improperly done under inexpert management, surely one has to become responsible for animal sacrifice. In this age of quarrel and hypocrisy there is no possibility of performing the *yajñas* perfectly for want of expert *brāhmaṇas* who are able to conduct such *yajñas*. Mahārāja Yudhiṣṭhira therefore gives a hint to performing sacrifices in the age of Kali. In the Kali-yuga the only sacrifice recommended is the performance of *harināma-yajña* inaugurated by Lord Śrī Caitanya Mahāprabhu. But one should not indulge in animal killing and counteract it by performing the *harināma-yajña*. Those who are devotees of the Lord never kill an animal for self-interest, and (as the Lord ordered Arjuna) they do not refrain from performing the duty of a *kṣatriya*. The whole purpose, therefore, is served when everything is done for the will of the Lord. This is possible only for the devotees.

Thus end the Bhaktivedanta purports of the First Canto, Eighth Chapter, of the Śrīmad-Bhāgavatam, *entitled "Prayers by Queen Kuntī, and Parīkṣit Saved."*

APPENDIXES

THE AUTHOR

His Divine Grace A. C. Bhaktivedanta Swami Prabhupāda appeared in this world in 1896 in Calcutta, India. He first met his spiritual master, Śrīla Bhaktisiddhānta Sarasvatī Gosvāmī, in Calcutta in 1922. Bhaktisiddhānta Sarasvatī, a prominent religious scholar and the founder of sixty-four Gauḍīya Maṭhas (Vedic institutes), liked this educated young man and convinced him to dedicate his life to teaching Vedic knowledge. Śrīla Prabhupāda became his student and, in 1933, his formally initiated disciple.

At their first meeting, in 1922, Śrīla Bhaktisiddhānta Sarasvatī requested Śrīla Prabhupāda to broadcast Vedic knowledge in English. In the years that followed, Śrīla Prabhupāda wrote a commentary on the *Bhagavad-gītā,* assisted the Gauḍīya Maṭha in its work, and, in 1944, started *Back to Godhead,* an English fortnightly magazine. Single-handedly, Śrīla Prabhupāda edited it, typed the manuscripts, checked the galley proofs, and even distributed the individual copies. The magazine is now being continued by his followers.

In 1950 Śrīla Prabhupāda retired from married life, adopting the *vānaprastha* (retired) order to devote more time to his studies and writing. He traveled to the holy city of Vṛndāvana, where he lived in humble circumstances in the historic temple of Rādhā-Dāmodara. There he engaged for several years in deep study and writing. He accepted the renounced order of life (*sannyāsa*) in 1959. At Rādhā-Dāmodara, Śrīla Prabhupāda began work on his life's masterpiece: a multivolume commentated translation of the eighteen-thousand-verse *Śrīmad-Bhāgavatam* (*Bhāgavata Purāṇa*). He also wrote *Easy Journey to Other Planets.*

After publishing three volumes of the *Śrīmad-Bhāgavatam,* Śrīla Prabhupāda came to the United States, in September 1965, to fulfill the mission of his spiritual master. Subsequently, His Divine Grace wrote more than fifty volumes of authoritative commentated translations and summary studies of the philosophical and religious classics of India.

When he first arrived by freighter in New York City, Śrīla Prabhupāda was practically penniless. Only after almost a year of great difficulty did he establish the International Society for Krishna Consciousness, in July of 1966. Before he passed away on November 14, 1977, he had guided the Society and seen it grow to a worldwide confederation of more than one hundred *āśramas,* schools, temples, institutes, and farm communities.

In 1972 His Divine Grace introduced the Vedic system of primary and secondary education in the West by founding the *gurukula* school in Dallas, Texas. Since then his disciples have established similar schools throughout the United States and the rest of the world.

Śrīla Prabhupāda also inspired the construction of several large international cultural centers in India. At Śrīdhāma Māyāpur, in West Bengal, devotees are building a spiritual city centered on a magnificent temple—an ambitious project for which construction will extend over many years to come. In Vṛndāvana are the Kṛṣṇa-Balarāma Temple and International Guesthouse, *gurukula* school, and Śrīla Prabhupāda Memorial and Museum. There are also major temples and cultural centers in Mumbai, New Delhi, Ahmedabad, Siliguri, and Ujjain. Other centers are planned in many important locations on the Indian subcontinent.

Śrīla Prabhupāda's most significant contribution, however, is his books. Highly respected by scholars for their authority, depth, and clarity, they are used as textbooks in numerous college courses. His writings have been translated into over fifty languages. The Bhaktivedanta Book Trust, established in 1972 to publish the works of His Divine Grace, has thus become the world's largest publisher of books in the field of Indian religion and philosophy.

In just twelve years, despite his advanced age, Śrīla Prabhupāda circled the globe fourteen times on lecture tours that took him to six continents. In spite of such a vigorous schedule, Śrīla Prabhupāda continued to write prolifically. His writings constitute a veritable library of Vedic philosophy, religion, literature, and culture.

REFERENCES

The purports of the *Śrīmad-Bhāgavatam* are all confirmed by standard Vedic authorities. The following authentic scriptures are cited in this volume. For specific page references, consult the general index.

Amarakośa dictionary
Bhagavad-gītā
Brahmāṇḍa Purāṇa
Brahma-saṁhitā
Brahma-sūtra (Vedānta-sūtra)
Brahma-vaivarta Purāṇa
Bṛhan-nāradīya Purāṇa
Chāndogya Upaniṣad
Hari-nāmāmṛta-vyākaraṇa
Hari-bhakti-sudhodaya
Kaṭha Upaniṣad
Kaumudī dictionary
Mādhyandina-śruti
Mahābhārata
Matsya Purāṇa
Narasiṁha Purāṇa
Padma Purāṇa
Rāmāyaṇa
Sāma-veda
Śabda-kośa dictionary
Śrīmad-Bhāgavatam (Bhāgavata Purāṇa)
Vāmana Purāṇa
Varāha Purāṇa
Vāyavīya Tantra
Viṣṇu Purāṇa

GLOSSARY

A

Ācārya—a spiritual master who teaches by example.
Anna-prāśana—the ceremony of offering a child his first solid food; one of the ten purificatory *saṁskāras*.
Ārati—a ceremony for greeting the Lord with offerings of food, lamps, fans, flowers and incense.
Arcanā—the devotional process of Deity worship.
Āsana—a sitting posture in *yoga*.
Āśrama—the four spiritual orders of life: celibate student, householder, retired life and renounced life.
Asuras—atheistic demons.
Avatāra—a descent of the Supreme Lord.

B

Bhagavad-gītā—the basic directions for spiritual life spoken by the Lord Himself.
Bhāgavata—anything related to Bhagavān, the Supreme Lord, especially the devotee of the Lord and the scripture *Śrīmad-Bhāgavatam*.
Bhāgavata-dharma—the science of devotional service.
Bhakta—a devotee.
Bhakti-vedāntas—advanced transcendentalists who have realized the conclusion of the *Vedas* through devotional service.
Bhakti-yoga—linking with the Supreme Lord by devotional service.
Brahmacarya—celibate student life; the first order of Vedic spiritual life.
Brahman—the Absolute Truth; especially the impersonal aspect of the Absolute.
Brāhmaṇa—one wise in the *Vedas* who can guide society; the first Vedic social order.

C

Caṇḍālas—lowborn persons accustomed to filthy habits such as dog-eating.

D

Dharma—eternal occupational duty; religious principles.
Dhyāna—meditational *yoga*.

E

Ekādaśī—a special fast day for increased remembrance of Kṛṣṇa, which comes on the eleventh day of both the waxing and waning moon.

G

Gandharvas—demigod singers and musicians.
Goloka (Kṛṣṇaloka)—the highest spiritual planet, containing Kṛṣṇa's personal abodes, namely Dvārakā, Mathurā and Vṛndāvana.
Gopīs—Kṛṣṇa's cowherd girlfriends, His most confidential servitors.
Gosvāmīs—*See: Svāmī*
Gṛhastha—regulated householder life; the second order of Vedic spiritual life.
Guṇa-avatāras—Viṣṇu, Brahmā and Śiva, the presiding deities of the three modes of nature.

H

Hare Kṛṣṇa mantra—*See: Mahā-mantra*
Haṭha-yoga—the system of practicing sitting postures for sense control.

I

Itihāsa—a historical account.

J

Jīva-tattva—the living entities, atomic parts of the Lord.
Jñāna—theoretical knowledge.
Jñāna-kāṇḍa—the *Upaniṣad* portion of the *Vedas,* containing knowledge of Brahman, spirit.

K

Kali-yuga (the Age of Kali)—the present age, characterized by quarrel; it is last in the cycle of four ages and began five thousand years ago.

Kalpa—Brahmā's daytime, 4,320,000,000 years.
Karatālas—hand cymbals used in *kīrtana.*
Karma—fruitive action, for which there is always reaction, good or bad.
Karmī—a person satisfied with working hard for flickering sense gratification.
Kīrtana—chanting the glories of the Supreme Lord.
Kṛṣṇaloka—*See: Goloka*
Kṣatriya—a warrior or administrator; the second Vedic social order.

L

Lakṣmīs—goddesses of fortune, the consorts of Lord Nārāyaṇa.
Līlā-avatāras—innumerable incarnations who descend to display the spiritual pastimes of the Lord.

M

Mahā-mantra—the great chant for deliverance: Hare Kṛṣṇa, Hare Kṛṣṇa, Kṛṣṇa Kṛṣṇa, Hare Hare/ Hare Rāma, Hare Rāma, Rāma Rāma, Hare Hare
Mantra—a sound vibration that can deliver the mind from illusion.
Mathurā—Lord Kṛṣṇa's abode, surrounding Vṛndāvana, where He took birth and later returned to after performing His Vṛndāvana pastimes.
Māyā—illusion; forgetfulness of one's relationship with Kṛṣṇa.
Māyāvādīs—impersonal philosophers who say that the Lord cannot have a transcendental body.
Mṛdaṅga—a clay drum used for congregational chanting.

N

Nivṛtti-mārga—the path of liberation.

P

Pañcarātra—Vedic supplementary literatures describing the process of Deity worship for devotees in the present age.
Paṇḍita—a scholar.

Paramahaṁsa—the highest stage of the *sannyāsa* order; a topmost devotee of the Lord.
Paramparā—the chain of spiritual masters in disciplic succession.
Prāṇāyāma—control of the breathing process; part of *aṣṭāṅga-yoga*.
Pravṛtti-mārga—the path of sense enjoyment in accordance with Vedic regulations.
Purāṇas—Vedic histories of the universe in relation to the Supreme Lord and His devotees.
Puruṣas—the expansions of Viṣṇu as creators of the universe.

R

Ṛṣis—sages.

S

Sac-cid-ānanda-vigraha—the Lord's transcendental form, which is eternal and full of knowledge and bliss.
Śālagrāma-śilā—the Lord's stone Deity worshiped by Vedic *brāhmaṇas*.
Sampradāya—a disciplic succession of spiritual masters.
Saṅkīrtana—public chanting of the names of God, the approved *yoga* process for this age.
Sannyāsa—renounced life; the fourth order of Vedic spiritual life.
Śāstras—revealed scriptures.
Smṛti—supplementary explanations of the *Vedas*.
Soma-rasa—a heavenly elixir available on the moon.
Śravaṇaṁ kīrtanaṁ viṣṇoḥ—the devotional processes of hearing and chanting about Lord Viṣṇu, or Kṛṣṇa.
Śruti—the original Vedic literatures; the four Vedas and the *Upaniṣads*.
Śūdra—a laborer; the fourth of the Vedic social orders.
Svāmī—one who controls his mind and senses; title of one in the renounced order of life.
Svargaloka—the heavenly planets.

T

Tapasya—austerity; accepting some voluntary inconvenience for a higher purpose.

Tilaka—auspicious clay marks that sanctify a devotee's body as a temple of the Lord.

Tulasī—a tree sacred to worshipers of Lord Viṣṇu.

V

Vaikuṇṭha—the spiritual world.

Vaiṣṇava—a devotee of Lord Viṣṇu, Kṛṣṇa.

Vaiśyas—farmers and merchants; the third Vedic social order.

Vānaprastha—one who has retired from family life; the third order of Vedic spiritual life.

Varṇas—the four occupational divisions of society: the intellectual class, the administrative class, the mercantile class, and the laborer class.

Varṇāśrama—the Vedic social system of four social and four spiritual orders.

Vedas—the original revealed scriptures, first spoken by the Lord Himself.

Viṣṇu, Lord—Kṛṣṇa's first expansion for the creation and maintenance of the material universes.

Viṣṇu-tattva—the original Personality of Godhead's primary expansions, each of whom is equally God.

Vṛndāvana—Kṛṣṇa's personal abode, where He fully manifests His quality of sweetness.

Vyāsadeva—Kṛṣṇa's incarnation, at the end of Dvāpara-yuga, for compiling the *Vedas*.

Y

Yajña—sacrifice; work done for the satisfaction of Lord Viṣṇu.

Yogī—a transcendentalist who, in one way or another, is striving for union with the Supreme.

Yuga-avatāra—an incarnation of the Lord who appears in a particular millennium to prescribe the appropriate method of spiritual realization.

Yugas—ages in the life of a universe, recurring in cycles of four.

SANSKRIT PRONUNCIATION GUIDE

Throughout the centuries, the Sanskrit language has been written in a variety of alphabets. The mode of writing most widely used throughout India, however, is called *devanāgarī,* which means, literally, the writing used in "the cities of the demigods." The *devanāgarī* alphabet consists of forty-eight characters: thirteen vowels and thirty-five consonants. Ancient Sanskrit grammarians arranged this alphabet according to practical linguistic principles, and this order has been accepted by all Western scholars. The system of transliteration used in this book conforms to a system that scholars have accepted to indicate the pronunciation of each Sanskrit sound.

Vowels

अ **a** आ **ā** इ **i** ई **ī** उ **u** ऊ **ū** ऋ **ṛ**

ॠ **ṝ** ऌ **ḷ** ए **e** ऐ **ai** ओ **o** औ **au**

Consonants

Gutturals:	क **ka**	ख **kha**	ग **ga**	घ **gha**	ङ **ṅa**
Palatals:	च **ca**	छ **cha**	ज **ja**	झ **jha**	ञ **ña**
Cerebrals:	ट **ṭa**	ठ **ṭha**	ड **ḍa**	ढ **ḍha**	ण **ṇa**
Dentals:	त **ta**	थ **tha**	द **da**	ध **dha**	न **na**
Labials:	प **pa**	फ **pha**	ब **ba**	भ **bha**	म **ma**
Semivowels:	य **ya**	र **ra**	ल **la**	व **va**	
Sibilants:	श **śa**	ष **ṣa**	स **sa**		
Aspirate:	ह **ha**	Anusvāra: ं **ṁ**		Visarga: ः **ḥ**	

Numerals

० – 0 १ – 1 २ – 2 ३ – 3 ४ – 4 ५ – 5 ६ – 6 ७ – 7 ८ – 8 ९ – 9

The vowels are written as follows after a consonant:

ा ā ि i ी ī ु u ू ū ृ ṛ ॄ ṝ े e ै ai ो o ौ au

For example: क ka का kā कि ki की kī कु ku कू kū

कृ kṛ कॄ kṝ कॢ kḷ के ke कै kai को ko कौ kau

Generally two or more consonants in conjunction are written together in a special form, as for example: क्ष kṣa त्र tra
The vowel "a" is implied after a consonant with no vowel symbol. The symbol *virāma* (्) indicates that there is no final vowel: क्

The vowels are pronounced as follows:

a — as in but
ā — as in far but held twice as long as **a**
i — as in pin
ī — as in pique but held twice as long is **i**
u — as in push
ū — as in rule but held twice as long as **u**
ṛ — as in **ri**m
ṝ — as in **ree**d but held twice as long as **ṛ**
ḷ — as in happily
e — as in they
ai — as in aisle
o — as go
au — as how

The consonants are pronounced as follows:

Gutturals
(pronounced from the throat)
k — as in **k**ite
kh — as in Ec**kh**art
g — as in **g**ive
gh — as in di**g-h**ard
ṅ — as in si**ng**

Palatals
(pronounced with the middle of the tongue against the palate)
c — as in **ch**air
ch — as in stau**nch-h**eart
j — as in **j**oy
jh — as in he**dgeh**og
ñ — as in ca**ny**on

Cerebrals

(pronounced with the tip of the tongue against the roof of the mouth)

ṭ — as in **t**ub
ṭh — as in ligh**t-h**eart
ḍ — as in **d**ove
ḍh — as in re**d-h**ot
ṇ — as in si**ng**

Labials

(pronounced with the lips)

p — as in **p**ine
ph — as in u**p-h**ill
b — as in **b**ird
bh — as in ru**b-h**ard
m — as in **m**other

Sibilants

ś — as in the German word spre**ch**en
ṣ — as in **sh**ine
s — as in **s**un

Anusvara

ṁ — a resonant nasal sound as in the French word bo**n**

Dentals

(pronounced like the cerebrals but with the tongue against the teeth)

t — as in **t**ub
th — as in ligh**t-h**eart
d — as in **d**ove
dh — as in re**d-h**ot
n — as in **n**ut

Semivowels

y — as in **y**es
r — as in **r**un
l — as in **l**ight
v — as in **v**ine, except when preceded in the same syllable by a consonant, then as in s**w**an

Aspirate

h — as in **h**ome

Visarga

ḥ — a final h-sound: **aḥ** is pronounced like **aha**; **iḥ** like **ihi**.

There is no strong accentuation of syllables in Sanskrit, or pausing between words in a line, only a flowing of short and long syllables (the long twice as long as the short). A long syllable is one whose vowel is long (**ā, ī, ū, ṝ, e, ai, o, au**) or whose short vowel is followed by more than one consonant. The letters **ḥ** and **ṁ** count as consonants. Aspirated consonants (consonants followed by an **h**) count as single consonants.

INDEX OF SANSKRIT VERSES

This index constitutes a complete listing of the first lines of each of the Sanskrit poetry verses of this volume of *Śrīmad-Bhāgavatam*, arranged in English alphabetical order.

GENERAL INDEX

Numerals in boldface type indicate references to translations of the verses of *Srimad-Bhāgavatam.* Numbers in parentheses indicate approximate pages of long purports. References without periods indicate page numbers of the Introduction or Preface.

A

Abhijñaḥ, Lord as, 1.1(6)
Abhimanyu
as Uttarā's husband, 8.10
Absolute Truth
access to, devotion to Lord as, 2.12(1)
as aim of life, 1.10, 2.13, 2.14
as all-knowing, 1–2
aspects of, as qualitatively one, 2.11
aspects of, three described, **2.11,** 2.12(1)
as basis of reality, 1
Bhāgavatam reveals, **1.1,** 1.2(2), 1.2(3), 2.3
"body" of, as everything, 1.1(5)
defined, 1
demons reject, 8.19(1)
dependency of all on, 1.1(5–6)
duality as absent in, **2.11,** 2.11
energies of, as one with & different from, 2.11
full of opulences, 21
as goal of all works, **2.10**
as goal of Vedic literature, 21
goodness as needed to know, **2.24,** 2.24
hearing about, proper conditions for, 1.13
highest concept of, 21–22, 5.8
impersonal aspect of, 1.2(2), 2.12(1), 7.4
impersonal conception of, 21–22
knower & known identical in, 2.11
Kṛṣṇa as, 20, 31, 2.5, 2.12(1)
oneness & separateness of, with all, 1.1(5)
as paraṁ satyam, 1
personal aspect of, 2, 21, 1.1(8), 1.2(2), **2.11,** 2.12, 5.8, 7.4
realization of, imperfect & perfect, 2.12(1), 7.4
relativity absent in, 2.11
as reservoir of everything, 1–2
sexual nature in, 1.1(8)
as source of everything, 1–2
as substance of categories, 1.2(2)
as summum *bonum,* 1
as ultimate source, 1
as *varṇāśrama's* goal, 2.13

Ācārya Śaṅkara. *See:* Śaṅkara
Ācārya. See: Spiritual master
Activity (activities)
devotional service transforms, 8.42
goal of, 1.4(2)
in living beings, 6.34
purity in, 3.44
three material modes of, 1.1(9)
See also: Duty, occupational; Work, fruitive
Ādi-rasa, 1.1(8)
Administrators, 5.32
Advaita Prabhu, 11, 15, 16
Age of Quarrel. *See:* Kali-yuga
Aggressors
rules for killing, cited, **7.53**
types of, six listed, 7.16
Agriculturists, 5.32
Ahaṁ brahmāsmi, 1.19
Ahaṅkāra, 2.21, 3.1
See also: Bodily conception of life; Ego, false
Ahiṁsā, Buddha's teaching of, 3.24(2), 3.24(3–4)
Airplane of Vidyunmālī, 7.18
Air's being "dirty," analogy of, **3.31**
Ajāmila, 5.17
Ajita, 3.5(3)
Ajita & *jita,* Lord as, 28
Ajñāna, 2.28(3)
Akrūra-ghāṭa, 36
Akṣauhiṇī military division
defined, 8.48
Ākūti, **3.12**
Alarka, **3.11**
Amarakoṣa cited on meaning of *mūrti,* 5.38
Ambarīṣa Mahārāja, 1.1(8)
Amūrtikam, 5.38
Analogies
bird in cage & soul, 2.8
bird in tree & soul, 2.31
"blue" sky & universal form, 3.31
body & Supreme Lord, 5.20(1)
butter & Supersoul, 2.32
camel & materialist, 2.3

Caitanya quoted or cited (*continued*)
on Personality of Godhead as transcendental, 21–22, 23
on *praṇava oṁkāra* vs. *tat tvam asi,* 24
on qualifications for preaching, 3
on sacrifices, 10
on Śaṅkara's motives, 25
on *saṅkīrtana,* 33–34
on subject of *Vedas,* 5.24
on *Vedānta-sūtra,* 20, 33–34
on *Vedas* as unchallengeable, 20
on *Vedas'* three subjects, 25
on Vrajabhhūmī's residents, 8.21
Cakravartī. *See:* Viśvanātha Cakravartī
Cākṣuṣa Manu, 3.5(3), **3.15**, 3.15
Camel tasting his own blood, analogy of, 2.3
Caṇḍikā, 2.26
Candra, Lord, 8.18
Candraśekhara Ācārya, 15, 32
Cāpala (the *brāhmaṇa*), 11
Capital punishment, **7.37**–7.37
Cāraṇas, 1.4(2)
Car, identifying a man with, analogy of, 3.31
Caste system. *See: Varṇāśrama-dharma*
Caturbhuja, Kṛṣṇa as, **7.52**
Catuṣpāṭhī, 9
Chand Kazi. *See:* Kazi
Chāndogya *Upaniṣad* cited on *Purāṇas* & *Mahābhārata,* 4.19
Chanting holy name(s) of Lord
for all people, 6
as beneficial from start, 7.6
Caitanya as preacher of, 6, 9–11, 31–32, 33, 34, 39–40, 1.4(2–3)
Caitanya revived by, 18
at Caitanya's birth, 6
cleanses heart of all, 6
convenient nature of, 2.17
as cure for materialism, 7.7(1–2)
at death, 3.42
as devotee's concern, 6.26
disciplic line needed for, 5.38, 5.39
as duty of all, 11
elevation via, 5.39
humility for, 39–40
identical with Lord, 5.38, 5.39, 6.33
importance of, in this age, 6, 34, 1.4(2–3), 1.21
Kazi stopped, 9
liberation via, **1.14**
Lord as realized via, 34, 5.38, 5.39, 6.25
by materialists, 8.26
by materially impoverished, 8.26
for peace, 1.4(2)
proper method of, 5.38, 5.39
Chanting holy name(s) (*continued*)
purifying power of, 8.26
recommended by *Pañcarātra,* 5.38
revives senses transcendentally, 5.38
Śaṅkarācārya recommends, 3.42
for *sannyāsīs,* 6.13
singing meters for, 6.32
spiritual master directs, 5.38, 5.39
if unconsciously done, **1.14**
value of, 8.27(1)
Vedānta study vs., 34
See also: Hare Kṛṣṇa *mantra; Saṅkīrtana* movement of Lord Caitanya; Supreme Lord, glorification of
Chanting of hymns
as subtle material science, 7.27, 7.44
as Vedic military science, 7.44
Charity, 2.7
Chemistry, in service to Lord, 5.22
Chemists, 1.1(5)
Children, protection of, 8.5
China's attack on India, 5.11(2)
Cinema show, analogy of, 1.17
Cintāmaṇi-dhāma, Kṛṣṇaloka as, 8.21
Citraketu, 5.17
Civil disobedience, 9
Civilization, human. *See:* Society, human
Civilization, Vedic. *See:* Vedic culture
Cloudiness, analogy of, **3.31**
Cloud's existence in clear sky, analogy of, 3.1
Coal's (firewood) desirability, analogy of, **2.24**
Communism, spiritual, 1
Communist state, 1.2(2)
Competition, 1.2(1–2)
Conchshell, 20
Conditioned soul(s)
in all species, 1.1
Arjuna represented, 9.36
attributes of Lord in, 3.28, 5.20
benefit via Lord's pastimes, 6.34
Bhāgavatam satisfies, 5.11, 5.13
captivated by creation, 5.20
classes of, two described, 1.17
compared to prisoners, 7.5
compared with
devotees, 1.4
liberated souls, 4.4
covered
by material energy, 7.5
by mind & body, 2.8, 3.33
as degraded in this age, 3.43
Deity worship for, 8.22
as delivered by Lord, 3.33–34, 7.5
delivered by Lord's devotees, **1.15**, 5.24

Devotees of Lord
pure (*continued*)
tested by Lord, 7.40
tolerance in, 7.43
as transcendental as Lord, 7.12
varṇāśrama creates, 2.2
as vice-lords, 1.15
as purified by serving, 2.18
purifying effect of, **1.15**
qualifications of, 2.19, 5.36(2–3)
in quality one with Lord, 2.19, 5.36(2)
rarity of, 37, 5.16
remember Lord always, **5.36,** 5.36(2)
renunciation by, 8.27(1), 8.41
respected as much as God, 2.16
as *sātvatas,* 1.12
"secret treasure" of, 8.27(1)
second-class category of, 2.12(2)
as self-satisfied, 2.19
service to, **2.16,** 2.16, 5.23, 8.42
as spiritual master, 5.23
as spontaneous & unreserved, 3.38
submissively receive truth, 2.21
Śukadeva Gosvāmī as, 2.2
tested by Lord, 7.40
as *tīrthas,* 2.16
tolerance in, 7.43
as transcendental as Lord, 6.30, 7.12
transcendental to *karmīs* & *jñānīs,* 1.17
unauthorized type of, 2.12(2)
varṇāśrama system creates, 2.2
Vedānta studied by, 19
as vice-lords, **1.15**
See also: Ātmārāmas; Gosvāmīs; Liberated souls; *Paramahaṁsas;* Sages
Devotional service to Supreme Lord
as above liberation, 34, 5.9, 5.30
Absolute realized in, 2.12(1), 7.4
as access to Kṛṣṇa, 2.7, 2.20, 3.28(4)–3.29, 7.41
accumulates for many births, **6.24**
activities purified via, 8.42
as activity of soul, 2.19
affirmed by Caitanya, 25
in all activities, 27
for all men, 2.6, 2.7, 5.32
Arjuna changed via, 8.42
arts & science in, 5.22
associating with devotees for, **2.16,** 2.16, 2.18, 5.25, 5.28, 5.34, 6.16, 7.5(2)
as associating with Lord, 2.7, 6.22
attachment in divisions of, 7.10(3)
attracts liberated souls, **7.10**
Devotional service to Lord (*continued*)
basis of,
in authority, 2.12(2–3)
in hearing about Lord, 5.28, 7.5(2)
in Lord's omnipotence, 5.32
as satisfying Lord, 11
begins by service of devotees, 5.23
begins by temple worship, 6.21
benefits of, **6.23–6.24, 7.6,** 8.25
benefits all, 1.4(2)
Bhāgavatam invokes, **7.7,** 7.7(2)
bhāva stage of, 6.16
body & mind in, 5.27, 6.28
at *brahma-bhūta* stage, 5.9
Brahman realization inferior to, 5.30
Caitanya as teacher of, 24, 25, 39–40
caste system transcended by, 27
categories of, five reciprocal, 38
categories of, two described, 38
chanting process in. *See:* Chanting holy name(s) of Lord
classes in, 2.12(2)
classes of men against, 14
compared
to curd (yogurt), 3.8
flow of river, 5.28
touchstone, 6.28
complete satisfaction in, **2.6**
in conditioned life, 2.6
confidential
among devotees, **5.30,** 5.30
spiritual master bestows, 5.39
consciousness pure in, 1.2(3)
contrasted with impersonalism, 7.11
contrasted with material service, 6.22
control of senses in, 6.35
"creeper" of, protecting, 37–38
Deity worship in, 6.21
desire as outside of, 2.6
desire changed via, 8.42
desire in, 6.22
destroys false ego, **2.21,** 2.21
detachment via, 2.7, 2.12(1)
detriments to, 37–38, 2.17
development of, stages of, 5.34
disturbance eliminated in, 2.17
as disturbance if unauthorized, 2.12(2–3)
divisions & attachment in, 7.10(4)
divisions of, five described, 38
dormant in all, 5.28
doubt cleared by, **2.21**–2.21
duty relinquished for, **5.17**
dynamic nature of, 6.22

Hare Kṛṣṇa *mantra,* 6
See also: Chanting holy name(s) of Lord; Supreme Lord, glorification of
Harer nāma harer nāma
verse quoted, 34
Hari, 3.2, 3.26
Hari, 7.10(4)
Hari-bhakti-sudhodaya cited on *ātmārāma* verse, 7.10(3)
Haridāsa Ṭhākura, 12, 27, 2.2, 6.35
as *ācārya* of holy name, 2.2
Hari-kīrtana, 5.22
Hari-nāmāmṛta-vyākaraṇa, 8
Hastī, King, 4.6
Hastināpura, 4.6
as Pāṇḍavas' capital, 8.39
Haṭha-yoga, 37–38
Hayagrīva, Lord, 3.26
Hearing about Supreme Lord. *See: Śrīmad-Bhāgavatam,* personal reception of; Supreme Lord, hearing about
Hearing, as most important sense, 7.7(1)
Heart
"knots" in, **2.21,** 2.21
purified via service to Lord, **2.17**
satisfaction of, 4.27
Hiḍimba demon, 8.24
Hinduism. *See: Varṇāśrama-dharma;* Vedic culture
Hindus, customs of, 8.1
Hiraṇyakaśipu, 1.1(6), 1.14, 2.28(3)
as challenger to Lord's rule, 3.22
killed by Nṛsiṁhadeva, **3.18,** 3.28(2)
as materialist, 8.36
power & opulence of, 3.28(2)
History of world
modern & Vedic, 3.41
as repeated in all universes, 6.11
Hlādinī potency of Lord, 23
Hog's enjoying stool, 6.38
Horse sacrifice
as atonement, 8.51
by Indra, 8.6
purifying power of, 8.51
purpose of, 8.52
by Yudhiṣṭhira, **8.6**
Householders
sannyāsis' relation to, 4.8
sexual distinctions necessary for, 4.5
Hṛṣīkeśa, 5.13
Human beings
activities of, in all universes, 6.11
attributes of Kṛṣṇa for, 3.28(3–4)
austerity as duty of, 3.9
Human beings (*continued*)
bad, four classes of, 5.40
Bhāgavatam for, 5.11(2–4), 5.13(1–2)
as "branch" of Viṣṇu, 1.4(2)
chance for freedom for, 5.15
compared to animals, 2.20, 3.43
confused by Vedic literatures, 5.14–5.15
conversion of, to devotees of Lord, 5.36(2)
danger for, in this age, 1.22
degraded in this age, **1.10,** 3.43
delivered by Lord's devotees, 2.16, 5.24
delivered by Lord's grace, 3.33
dependent on Supreme Lord, 1.1(5)
as detached parts of God, 5.20(1–2)
devotional service for all, 2.15
disciplic line for, 1.22
divisions of, 37, 2.12(1)
duty of, as liberation, 5.15
duty of, to read Vedic literature, 5.21
energy of, sapped in this age, 1.10
enjoyment for. *See:* Sense gratification
equal God at no time, 2.26, 5.20(2)
exploited by mundane authors, 5.13(1)
food for, 8.40
foolish, worship Śiva, 2.23
four occupations for, in general, 2.14
good, four classes of, 5.40
happiness for, false & real, 3.13
"hearing" as qualification for, 2.32
ignorance & passion in, 2.20
inferior to Lord, 1.1(7), 5.20(2)
inquiry natural for, 1.1(2)
intellectual perfection in, **5.22**–5.22
liberation as opportunity for, 1.10
life span of, in all ages, 1.21
Lord in role of, **8.30**
Lord's qualities in, 3.28(3–4), 5.20(2)
love for Lord restricted among, 7.7(2)
material complexity of, 7.7(2)
miseries should be ended by, 1.10
modern. *See*: Kali-yuga
nature's laws control, 8.40
peace for, 1.16, 5.32
perfection for, 2.20, 3.28(3–4), **5.22**–5.22
religion for, 1.2(1)
self-realization for, 1.10, 1.22, 8.25
spiritualization of, 5.36(2–3)
Sūta Gosvāmī as guide for, 1.22
See also: Fruitive workers
Human society. *See:* Society, human
Humility, 2.28(2)
for chanting names of God, 39–40
Hymns, military chanting of, 7.27, 7.44

I

Living entity (entities) (*continued*)
as energy of lord, 21, 2.11, 5.20(2), 5.31
enlightened by Lord's grace, 3.33, 3.34
equal God at no time, 2.26, 3.28(3), 5.20(2), 7.5(2–3)
as expansions of Lord, 23, 2.22, 2.28(4), **3.5,** 5.8
false enjoyment by, 7.24
feeling, thinking & willing of, 7.5(1)
as "feminine," 7.7(2)
forgetfulness in, 2.31, 2.34, 3.33
form of Lord as goal of, 6.18
freedom for, 6.37
friends to, sages as, 1.4(2)
happiness for, in glorifying Lord, 6.34
helped by Supersoul, **2.34**–2.34
as helpless, 2.33
human life special for, 1.10
identify with matter, 2.11, **7.5,** 7.7(2)
ignorance in, 2, 23, 3.33
as individuals, 1.1(3)
inferior to Lord, 1, 2.26, 3.35, 5.20(2), 7.5(2–3)
knowledge limited in, 1–2
Kṛṣṇa as center for, 2.6
liberation of. *See:* Liberation from material world
Lord
activities of, inconceivable to, 8.16
as chief among, 1.1(3)
compared with, 2.26, 3.28, 3.35, 5.20, 7.5, 8.4, 8.18, 8.35
relationship of, with, 5.8
in material & spiritual worlds, 5.31
material energy covers, 21–22, 3.33, 7.5(1)
material nature reforms, 7.5(1), 5.9
misery for, 1.2(3), 5.18, 6.38, **7.5**
modes of nature afflict, 8.27(2)
as one with & different from Lord, 22, 1.1(5), 1.2(2–3), 7.5(3)
as parts of Lord, 21, 23, 2.6, 2.23
perfection for, 3.28(3–4)
as personal by nature, 21
as qualitatively one with Lord, 23, 1.1(5), 1.2(3), 5.20(2), 7.5(3)
rasas experienced by, 1.3(1–2)
relative existence of, 23, 2.11
as "renouncers," 8.27(1)
as separated forms of Viṣṇu, 2.23
as servants always, 8.35
as servants of Lord, 2.6, 3.38, 5.8, 5.20(2)
sexual distinctions absent in, 4.5
as sons of Lord, 2.33
as soul, 3.31, 3.32

Living entity (entities) (*continued*)
source of, **3.5**
struggle of, 2.4
surrender to Lord necessary for, 5.20(2)
symptoms of, 8.42
transcendental status of, **3.32**–3.33, 8.47
unification of, *xiii*
Viṣṇu as benefactor of, **2.23,** 2.23
as Viṣṇu's "branches," 1.4(2)
See also: Soul(s), conditioned
Lobha, 6.21
Locana dāsa Ṭhākura, 5
Lolārka, 7.18
Lotus feet of Supreme Lord. *See:* Supreme Lord, lotus feet of
Lotus flower
from abdomen of Viṣṇu, 3.2
Brahmā born on, 8.34
Lord compared to, **8.22**
Love
direct & indirect, 1.3(2–3)
of God, 7.7(2)
Lord conquered by, 8.45
as sum of *rasas,* 1.3(2)
See also: Supreme Lord, love for
Lunar eclipse, 6
Lust
destroyed by devotion to Lord, **2.19**
as diseased activity of soul, 2.19, 2.20
freedom from, artificial & true, 6.35
as perverted love of God, 2.8
See also: Passion, mode of

M

Machines, 1.1(7)
Madhvācārya, 1.17, 4.18, 8.19(1)
Mādhavendra Purī, 16
Mādhurya stage of devotional service, 36
Mādhyandina-śruti, cited on *Vedas,* 4.13
Māgha-melā, 37
Magician, Lord compared to, 3.37
Magnetism of touchstone, analogy of, 6.28
Mahābhārata
Bhagavad-gītā as essence of, 4.25, 5.15
chronology of compilation of, 7.8
cited on Kurukṣetra war, 8.46
as compiled for common people, **4.25,** 4.25, **4.28**
criticized by Nārada, 5.15
hearing from, as transcendental life, 7.12
history in, vs. modern version, 3.41
identical with *Vedas* in message, 4.13
Kṛṣṇa spiritualizes, 7.12
men as misdirected by, 5.15, 5.15

V

The International Society for Krishna Consciousness

CENTERS AROUND THE WORLD

Founder-*Ācārya:* His Divine Grace A. C. Bhaktivedanta Swami Prabhupāda

CANADA

Brampton-Mississauga, Ontario — 6 George Street South, 2nd Floor, L6Y 1P3/ Tel. (416) 648-3312/ iskconbrampton@gmail.com
Calgary, Alberta — 313 Fourth St. N.E., T2E 3S3/ Tel. (403) 265-3302/ vamanstones@shaw.ca
Edmonton, Alberta — 9353 35th Ave. NW, T6E 5R5/ Tel. (780) 439-9999/ edmonton@harekrishnatemple.com
Montreal, Quebec — 1626 Pie IX Blvd., H1V 2C5/ Tel. & fax: (514) 521-1301/ iskconmontreal@gmail.com
◆ **Ottawa, Ontario** — 212 Somerset St. E., K1N 6V4/ Tel. (613) 565-6544/ radha_damodara@yahoo.com
Regina, Saskatchewan — 1279 Retallack St., S4T 2H8/ Tel. (306) 525-0002 or -6461/ jagadishadas@yahoo.com
Scarborough, Ontario — 3500 McNicoll Avenue, Unit #3, M1V 4C7/ Tel. (416) 300 7101/ iskconscarborough@hotmail.com
◆ **Toronto, Ontario** — 243 Avenue Rd., M5R 2J6/ Tel. (416) 922-5415/ toronto@iskcon.net
Vancouver, B.C. — 5462 S.E. Marine Dr., Burnaby V5J 3G8/ Tel. (604) 433-9728/ akrura@krishna.com; Govinda's Bookstore & Cafe/ Tel. (604) 433-7100 or (888) 433-8722

RURAL COMMUNITY

Ashcroft, B.C. — Saranagati Dhama (mail: P.O. Box 99, VOK 1A0)/ Tel. (250) 457-7438/ iskconsaranagati@hotmail.com

U.S.A.

Atlanta, Georgia — 1287 South Ponce de Leon Ave. N.E., 30306/ Tel. & fax: (404) 377-8680/ admin@atlantaharekrishnas.com
Austin, Texas — 10700 Jonwood Way, 78753/ Tel. (512) 835-2121/ sda@backtohome.com
Baltimore, Maryland —200 Bloomsbury Ave., Catonsville, 21228/ Tel. (410) 744-1624/ contact@iskconbaltimore.org
Berkeley, California — 2334 Stuart Street, 94705/ Tel. (510) 540-9215/ info@iskconberkeley.net
Boise, Idaho — 1615 Martha St., 83706/ Tel. (208) 344-4274/ boise_temple@yahoo.com
Boston, Massachusetts — 72 Commonwealth Ave., 02116/ Tel. (617) 247-8611/ info@iskconboston.org
◆ **Chicago, Illinois** — 1716 W. Lunt Ave., 60626/ Tel. (773) 973-0900/ chicagoiskcon@yahoo.com
Columbus, Ohio — 379 W. Eighth Ave., 43201/ Tel. (614) 421-1661/ premvilasdas.rns@gmail.com
◆ **Dallas, Texas** — 5430 Gurley Ave., 75223/ Tel. (214) 827-6330/ info@radhakalachandji.com
◆ **Denver, Colorado** — 1400 Cherry St., 80220/ Tel. (303) 333-5461/ info@krishnadenver.com
Detroit, Michigan — 383 Lenox Ave., 48215/ Tel. (313) 824-6000/ gaurangi108@hotmail.com
Gainesville, Florida — 214 N.W. 14th St., 32603/ Tel. (352) 336-4183/ kalakantha.acbsp@pamho.net
Hartford, Connecticut — 1683 Main St., E. Hartford, 06108/ Tel. (860) 289-7252/ pyari108@gmail.com
Hillsboro, Oregon — 612 North 1st Ave., Hillsboro 97124/ Tel. (503) 567-7363/ info@iskconportland.com
◆ **Honolulu, Hawaii** — 51 Coelho Way, 96817/ Tel. (808) 595-4913/ hawaii.iskcon@gmail.com
Houston, Texas — 1320 W. 34th St., 77018/ Tel. (713) 686-4482/ management@iskconhouston.org
Kansas City, Missouri — Rupanuga Vedic College, 5201 Paseo Blvd., 64110/ Tel. (816) 924-5619/ rvc@rvc.edu
Laguna Beach, California — 285 Legion St., 92651/ Tel. (949) 494-7029/ info@lagunatemple.com
Las Vegas, Nevada — Govinda's Center of Vedic India, 7181 Dean Martin Dr., 89118/ Tel. (702) 434-8332/ info@govindascenter.com
◆ **Los Angeles, California** — 3764 Watseka Ave., 90034/ Tel. (310) 836-2676/ membership@harekrishnala.com
◆ **Miami, Florida** — 3220 Virginia St., 33133 (mail: 3109 Grand Ave., #491, Coconut Grove, FL 33133)/ Tel. (305) 461-1348/ devotionalservice@iskcon-miami.org
Mountain View, California — 1965 Latham St., 94040/ Tel. (650) 336 7993 / isvconnect@gmail.com
New Orleans, Louisiana — 2936 Esplanade Ave., 70119/ Tel. (504) 304-0032 (office) or (504) 638-1944 (temple)/ gopal211@aol.com
New York, New York — 305 Schermerhorn St., Brooklyn, 11217/ Tel. (718) 855-6714/ ramabhadra@aol.com
New York, New York — The Bhakti Center, 25 First Ave., 10003/ Tel. (920) 624-2584/ info@bhakticenter.org
Orlando, Florida — 2651 Rouse Rd., 32817/ Tel. (407) 257-3865/ info@iskconorlando.com
Philadelphia, Pennsylvania — 41 West Allens Lane, 19119/ Tel. (215) 247-4600/ info@iskconphiladelphia.com
Phoenix, Arizona — 100 S. Weber Dr., Chandler, 85226/ Tel. (480) 705-4900/ premadhatridd@gmail.com
Plainfield, New Jersey — 1020 W. 7th St., 07063/ Tel. (973) 519-3374/ harekrsna@iskconnj.com
◆ **St. Louis, Missouri** — 3926 Lindell Blvd., 63108/ Tel. (314) 535-8085 or 255-2207/ iskconstl@pamho.net
Salt Lake City, Utah — 965 E. 3370 South, 84106/ Tel. (801) 487-4005/ utahkrishnas@gmail.com
San Antonio, Texas — 103 Bernice, 78228/ Tel. (210) 570 7571/ Krishnatemplesatx@gmail.com
San Diego, California — 1030 Grand Ave., Pacific Beach, 92109/ Tel. (858) 429-9375/ krishna.sandiego@gmail.com
Seattle, Washington — 1420 228th Ave. S.E., Sammamish, 98075/ Tel. (425) 246-8436/ info@vediccculturalcenter.org
◆ **Spanish Fork, Utah** — Krishna Temple Project & KHQN Radio, 8628 S. State Road, 84660/ Tel. (801) 798-3559/ utahkrishnas@gmail.com
Tallahassee, Florida — 4601 Crawfordville Rd., 32305/ Tel. (850) 727-5785/ tallahassee.iskcon@gmail.com
Towaco, New Jersey — 100 Jacksonville Rd., 07082/ Tel. (973) 299-0970/ madhupati.jas@pamho.net

To save space, we've skipped the codes for North America (1) and India (91).
◆ Temples with restaurants or dining
*The full list is always available at Krishna.com, where it also includes Krishna conscious gatherings.

◆**Tucson, Arizona** — 711 E. Blacklidge Dr., 85719/ Tel. (520) 792-0630/ sandaminidd@cs.com
Washington, D.C. — 10310 Oaklyn Dr., Potomac, Maryland 20854/ Tel. (301) 299-2100/ info@iskconofdc.org
RURAL COMMUNITIES
Alachua, Florida (New Raman Reti) — 17306 N.W. 112th Blvd., 32615/ Tel. (386) 462-2017/ alachuatemple@gmail.com
Carriere, Mississippi (New Talavan) — 31492 Anner Road, 39426/ Tel. (601) 213-3586/ newtalavan@gmail.com
Gurabo, Puerto Rico (New Govardhana Hill) — Carr. 181, Km. 16.3, Bo. Santa Rita, Gurabo (mail: HC-01, Box 8440, Gurabo, PR 00778)/ Tel. & fax: (787) 767-3530 or 737-1722/ manonatha@gmail.com
Hillsborough, North Carolina (New Goloka) — 1032 Dimmocks Mill Rd., 27278/ Tel. (919) 732-6492/ bkgoswami@earthlink.net
◆ **Moundsville, West Virginia (New Vrindaban)** — 3759 McCrearys Ridge Rd., 26041/ Tel. (304) 843-1600/ mail@newvrindaban.com
Mulberry, Tennessee (Murari-sevaka) — 532 Murari Lane, 37359 Tel. (931) 759-6888/ murari_sevaka@yahoo.com
Port Royal, Pennsylvania (Gita Nagari) — 534 Gita Nagari Rd., 17082/ Tel. (717) 527-4101/ dhruva.bts@pamho.net
Sandy Ridge, North Carolina (Prabhupada Village) — 1283 Prabhupada Rd., 27046/ Tel. (336) 593-2322/ prabhupadavillage@gmail.com
ADDITIONAL RESTAURANT
Hato Rey, Puerto Rico — Tamal Krishna's Veggie Garden, 131 Eleanor Roosevelt, 00918/ Tel. (787) 754-6959/ tkveggiegarden@aol.com

UNITED KINGDOM AND IRELAND

Belfast, Northern Ireland — Brooklands, 140 Upper Dunmurray Lane, BT17 OHE/ Tel. +44 (028) 9062 0530/ hk.temple108@gmail.com
Birmingham, England — 84 Stanmore Rd., Edgbaston B16 9TB/ Tel. +44 (121) 420 4999/ iskconbirmingham@gmail.com
Cardiff, Wales — The Soul Centre, 116 Cowbridge Rd., Canton/ Tel. +44 (29) 2039 0391/ the.soul.centre@pamho.net
Coventry, England — Kingfield Rd., Coventry (mail: 19 Gloucester St., Coventry CV1 3BZ)/ Tel. +44 (24) 7655 2822 or 5420/ haridas.kds@pamho.net
Dublin, Ireland — 83 Middle Abbey St., Dublin 1/ Tel. +353 (1) 661 5095/ dublin@krishna.ie; Govinda's: info@govindas.ie
Leicester, England — 31 Granby Street, LE1 6EP/ Tel. +44 (0) 7597 786 676/ pradyumna.jas@pamho.net
Lesmahagow, Scotland — Karuna Bhavan, Bankhouse Rd., Lesmahagow, Lanarkshire, ML11 0ES/ Tel. +44 (1555) 894790/ karunabhavan@aol.com
◆ **London, England (city)** — 10 Soho St., W1D 3DL/ Tel. +44 (20) 7437-3662; residential /pujaris, 7439-3606; shop, 7287-0269; Govinda's Restaurant, 7437-4928/ london@pamho.net
◆ **London, England (country)** — Bhaktivedanta Manor, Dharam Marg, Hilfield Lane, Watford, Herts, WD25 8EZ/ Tel. +44 (1923) 851000/ info@krishnatemple.com; (for accommodations:) bmguesthouse@krishna.com
London, England (south) — 42 Enmore Road, South Norwood, SE25 5NG/ Tel. +44 7988857530/ krishnaprema89@hotmail.com
London, England (Kings Cross) — 102 Caledonian Rd., Kings Cross, Islington, N1 9DN/ Tel. +44 (20) 7168 5732/ foodforalluk@aol.com
Manchester, England — 20 Mayfield Rd., Whalley Range, M16 8FT/ Tel. +44 (161) 226-4416/ contact@iskconmanchester.com
Newcastle-upon-Tyne, England — 304 Westgate Rd., NE4 6AR/ Tel. +44 (191) 272 1911
◆ **Swansea, Wales** — 8 Craddock St., SA1 3EN/ Tel. +44 (1792) 468469/ iskcon.swansea@pamho.net; restaurant: govin-das@hotmail.com
RURAL COMMUNITIES
London, England — (contact Bhaktivedanta Manor)
Upper Lough Erne, Northern Ireland — Govindadwipa Dhama, Inisrath Island, Derrylin, Co. Fermanagh, BT92 9GN/ Tel. +44 (28) 6772 1512/ iskconbirmingham@gmail.com
ADDITIONAL RESTAURANTS
Dublin, Ireland — Govinda's, 4 Aungier St., Dublin 2/ Tel. +353 (1) 475 0309/ info@govindas.ie
Dublin, Ireland — Govinda's, 83 Middle Abbey St., Dublin 1/ Tel. +353 (1) 661 5095/ info@govindas.ie
Nottingham, England — Govinda's Nottingham, 7–9 Thurland Street, NG1 3DR/ Tel. +44 115 985 9639/ govindasnottingham@gmail.com

AUSTRALASIA

AUSTRALIA

Adelaide — 25 Le Hunte St. (mail: P.O. Box 114, Kilburn, SA 5084)/ Tel. & fax: +61 (8) 8359-5120/ iskconsa@tpg.com.au
Brisbane — 32 Jennifer St., Seventeen Mile Rocks, QLD 4073 (mail: PO Box 525, Sherwood, QLD 4075)/ Tel. +61 (7) 3376 2388/ info@iskcon.org.au
Canberra — 44 Limestone Ave., Ainslie, ACT 2602 (mail: P.O. Box 1411, Canberra, ACT 2601)/ Tel. & fax: +61 (2) 6262-6208
Melbourne — 197 Danks St. (mail: P.O. Box 125), Albert Park , VIC 3206/ Tel. +61 (3) 9699-5122/ melbourne@pamho.net
Perth — 155–159 Canning Rd., Kalamunda (mail: P.O. Box 201 Kalamunda 6076)/ Tel. +61 (8) 6293-1519/ perth@pamho.net
Sydney — 180 Falcon St., North Sydney, NSW 2060 (mail: P.O. Box 459, Cammeray, NSW 2062)/ Tel. +61 (2) 9959-4558/ admin@iskcon.com.au
Sydney — Govinda's Yoga and Meditation Centre, 112 Darlinghurst Rd., Darlinghurst NSW 2010 (mail: P.O. Box 174, Kings Cross 1340)/ Tel. +61 (2) 9380-5162/ sita@govindas.com.au
RURAL COMMUNITIES
Bambra, VIC (New Nandagram) — 50 Seaches Outlet, off 1265 Winchelsea Deans Marsh Rd., Bambra VIC 3241/ Tel. +61 (3) 5288-7383
Cessnock, NSW (New Gokula) — Lewis Lane (off Mount View Rd., Millfield, near Cessnock (mail: P.O. Box 399, Cessnock, NSW 2325)/ Tel. +61 (2) 4998-1800/
Murwillumbah, NSW (New Govardhana) — Tyalgum Rd., Eungella (mail: P.O. Box 687), NSW 2484/ Tel. +61 (2) 6672-6579/ ajita@in.com.au
RESTAURANTS
Brisbane — Govinda's, 358 George St , QLD 4000/ Tel. +61 (7) 3210-0255
Brisbane — Krishna's Cafe, 1st Floor, 82 Vulture St., West End, QLD 4101/ Tel. +61 (7) 3844-2316/ brisbane@iskcon.org.au
Burleigh Heads — Govindas, 20 James St., Burleigh Heads, QLD 4220/ Tel. +61 (7) 5607-0782/ ajita@in.com.au
Maroochydore — Govinda's Vegetarian Cafe, 2/7 First Avenue, QLD 4558/ Tel. +61 (7) 5451-0299
Melbourne — Crossways, 1st Floor, 123 Swanston St., VIC 3000/ Tel. +61 (3) 9650-2939
Melbourne — Gopal's, 139 Swanston St., VIC 3000/ Tel. +61 (3) 9650-1578
Newcastle — 110 King Street, NSW 2300/ Tel. +61 (02) 4929-6900/ info@govindascafe.com.au

Perth — Govinda's Restaurant, 194 William St., Northbridge, W.A. 6003/ Tel. +61 (8) 9227-1648/ perth@pamho.net
Perth — Hare Krishna Food for Life, NSW 2300/ Tel. +61 (02) 4929-6900/ info@govindascafe.com.au
NEW ZEALAND AND FIJI
Christchurch, NZ — 83 Bealey Ave. (mail: P.O. Box 25-190)/ Tel. +64 (3) 366-5174/ iskconchch@clear.net.nz
Dunedin, NZ — 133 London Street, Dunedin 9016/ Tel. +64 (2) 749-1369/ jambavati85@hotmail.com
Hamilton, NZ — 188 Maui St., RD 8, Te Rapa/ Tel. +64 (7) 850-5108/ rmaster@wave.co.nz
Labasa, Fiji — Delailabasa (mail: P.O. Box 133)/ Tel. +679 812912
Lautoka, Fiji — 5 Tavewa Ave. (mail: P.O. Box 125)/ Tel. +679 6664112/ regprakash@excite.com
Nausori, Fiji — Hare Krishna Cultural Centre, 2nd Floor, Shop & Save Building, 11 Gulam Nadi St., Nausori Town (mail: P.O. Box 2183, Govt. Bldgs., Suva)/ Tel. +679 9969748 or 3475097/ vdas@frca.org.fj
Rakiraki, Fiji — Rewasa (mail: P.O. Box 204)/ Tel. +679 694243
Sigatoka, Fiji — Sri Sri Radha Damodar Temple, Off Mission St., Sigatoka Town/ Tel. +679 9373703/ drgsmarna@connect.com.fj
Suva, Fiji — 166 Brewster St. (mail: P.O. Box 4299, Samabula)/ Tel. +679 3318441/ iskconsuva@connect.com.fj
Wellington, NZ — 105 Newlands Rd., Newlands/ Tel. +64 (4) 478-4108/ info@iskconwellington.org.nz
Wellington, NZ — Bhakti Lounge, 1st Floor, 175 Vivian St., Te Aro/ Tel. +64 (4) 801-5500/ yoga@bhaktilounge.org.nz/ www.bhaktilounge.org.nz
RURAL COMMUNITY
Auckland, NZ (New Varshan) — Hwy. 28, Riverhead, next to Huapai Golf Course (mail: R.D. 2, Kumeu)/ Tel. +64 (9) 412-8075/
RESTAURANT
Wellington, NZ — Higher Taste Hare Krishna Restaurant, Old Bank Arcade, Ground Flr., Corner Customhouse, Quay & Hunter St., Wellington/ Tel. +64 (4) 472-2233

INDIA (partial list)*

Ahmedabad, Gujarat — Satellite Rd., Gandhinagar Highway Crossing, 380 054/ Tel. (079) 686-1945, -1645, or -2350/ jasomatinandan.acbsp@pamho.net
Allahabad, UP — Hare Krishna Dham, 161 Kashi Raj Nagar, Baluaghat 211 003/ Tel. (0532) 415294
Amritsar, Punjab — Chowk Moni Bazar, Laxmansar, 143 001/ Tel. (0183) 2540177
Bangalore, Karnataka — Hare Krishna Hill, Chord Rd., 560 010/ Tel. (080) 23471956 or 23578346/ Fax: (080) 23578625/ manjunath36@iskconbangalore.org
Bangalore, Karnataka — ISKCON Sri Jagannath Mandir, No.5 Sripuram, 1st cross, Sheshadripuram, Bangalore 560 020/ Tel. (080) 3536867 or 2262024 or 3530102
Baroda, Gujarat — Hare Krishna Land, Gotri Rd., 390 021/ Tel. (0265) 2310630 or 2331012/ iskcon.baroda@pamho.net
◆ **Bhubaneswar, Orissa** — N.H. No. 5, IRC Village, 751 015/ Tel. (0674) 2553517, 2553475, or 2554283
Chandigarh, Punjab — Hare Krishna Dham, Sector 36-B, 160 036/ Tel. (0172) 601590 or 603232/ iskcon.chandigarh@pamho.net
Chennai (Madras), TN — Hare Krishna Land, Bhaktivedanta Swami Road, Off ECR Road, Injam- bakkam, Chennai 600 041/ Tel. (044) 5019303 or 5019147/ iskconchennai@eth.net
◆ **Coimbatore, TN** — Jagannath Mandir, Hare Krishna Land, Aerodrome P.O., Opp. CIT, 641 014/ Tel. (0422) 2626509 or 2626508/ info@iskcon-coimbatore.org
Dwarka, Gujarat — Bharatiya Bhavan, Devi Bhavan Rd., 361 335/ Tel. (02892) 34606/ Fax: (02892) 34319
Guwahati, Assam — Ulubari Chariali, South Sarania, 781 007/ Tel. (0361) 2525963/ iskcon.guwahati@pamho.net
Haridwar, Uttaranchal — Prabhupada Ashram, G. House, Nai Basti, Mahadev Nagar, Bhimgoda/ Tel. (01334) 260818
Hyderabad, AP — Hare Krishna Land, Nampally Station Rd., 500 001/ Tel. (040) 24744969 or 24607089/ iskcon.hyderabad@pamho.net
Imphal, Manipur — Hare Krishna Land, Airport Rd., 795 001/ Tel. (0385) 2455245 or 2455247 or 2455693/ manimandir@sancharnet.in
Indore, MP — ISKCON, Nipania, Indore/ Tel. 9300474043/ mahaman.acbsp@pamho.net
Jaipur, Rajasthan — ISKCON Road, Opp. Vijay Path, Mansarovar, Jaipur 302 020 (mail: ISKCON, 84/230, Sant Namdev Marg, Opp. K.V. No. 5, Mansarovar, Jaipur 302 020)/ Tel. (0414) 2782765 or 2781860/ jaipur@pamho.net
Jammu, J&K — Srila Prabhupada Ashram, c/o Shankar Charitable Trust, Shakti Nagar, Near AG Office/ Tel. (01991) 233047
Kolkata (Calcutta), WB — 3C Albert Rd., 700 017 (behind Minto Park, opp. Birla High School)/ Tel. (033) 3028-9258 or -9280/ iskcon.calcutta@pamho.net
◆ **Kurukshetra, Haryana** — 369 Gudri Muhalla, Main Bazaar, 132 118/ Tel. (01744) 234806
Lucknow, UP — 1 Ashok Nagar, Guru Govind Singh Marg, 226 018/ Tel. (0522) 223556 or 271551
◆ **Mayapur, WB** — ISKCON, Shree Mayapur Chandrodaya Mandir, Shree Mayapur Dham, Dist. Nadia, 741 313/ Tel. (03472) 245239, 245240, or 245233/ Fax: (03472) 245238/ mayapur.chandrodaya@pamho.net
◆ **Mumbai (Bombay), Maharashtra** — Hare Krishna Land, Juhu 400 049/ Tel. (022) 26206860/ Fax: (022) 26205214/ info@iskconmumbai.com; guest.house.bombay@pamho.net
◆ **Mumbai, Maharashtra** — 7 K. M. Munshi Marg, Chowpatty 400 007 / Tel. (022) 23665500/ Fax: (022) 23665555/ info@radhagopinath.com
Mumbai, Maharashtra — Shristhi Complex, Mira Rd. (E), opposite Royal College, Dist. Thane, 401 107/ Tel. (022) 28454667 or 28454672/ Fax: (022) 28454981/ jagjivan.gkg@pamho.net
Mysore, Karnataka — #31, 18th Cross, Jayanagar, 570 014/ Tel. (0821) 2500582 or 6567333/ mysore.iskcon@gmail.com
Nellore, AP — ISKCON City, Hare Krishna Rd., 524 004/ Tel. (0861) 2314577 or (092155) 36589/ sukadevaswami@gmail.com
◆ **New Delhi** — Hare Krishna Hill, Sant Nagar Main Road, East of Kailash, 110 065/ Tel. (011) 2623-5133, 4, 5, 6, 7/ Fax: (011) 2621-5421/ delhi@pamho.net; (Guesthouse) neel.sunder@pamho.net
◆ **New Delhi** — 41/77, Punjabi Bagh (West), 110 026/ Tel. (011) 25222851 or 25227478 Noida, UP — A-5, Sector 33, opp. NTPC office, Noida 201 301/ Tel. (0120) 2506211/ vraja.bhakti.vilas.lok@pamho.net
Patna, Bihar — Arya Kumar Rd., Rajendra Nagar, 800 016/ Tel. (0612) 687637 or 685081/ Fax: (0612) 687635/ krishna.kripa.jps@pamho.net
Pune, Maharashtra — 4 Tarapoor Rd., Camp, 411 001/ Tel. (020) 26332328 or 26361855/ iyfpune@vsnl.com
Puri, Orissa — Bhakti Kuti, Swargadwar, 752 001/ Tel. (06752) 231440
Raipur, Chhatisgarh — Hare Krishna Land, Alopi Nagar, Opposite Maharshi Vidyalaya, Tatibandh, Raipur 492 001/ Tel. (0771) 5037555/ iskconraipur@yahoo.com
Secunderabad, AP — 27 St. John's Rd., 500 026/ Tel. (040)

780-5232/ Fax: (040) 814021
Silchar, Assam — Ambikapatti, Silchar, Dist. Cachar, 788 004/ Tel. (03842) 34615
Sri Rangam, TN — 103 Amma Mandapam Rd., Sri Rangam, Trichy 620 006/ Tel. (0431) 2433945/ iskcon_srirangam@yahoo.com.in
Surat, Gujarat — Rander Rd., Jahangirpura, 395 005/ Tel. (0261) 765891, 765516, or 773386/ surat@pamho.net
◆ **Thiruvananthapuram (Trivandrum), Kerala** — Hospital Rd., Thycaud, 695 014/ Tel. (0471) 2328197/ jsdasa@yahoo.co.in
◆ **Tirupati, AP** — K.T. Rd., Vinayaka Nagar, 517 507/ Tel. (0877) 2230114 or 2230009/ revati.raman.jps@pamho.net (guesthouse: iskcon_ashram@yahoo.co.in)
Udhampur, J&K — Srila Prabhupada Ashram, Srila Prabhupada Marg, Srila Prabhupada Nagar 182 101/ Tel. (01992) 270298/ info@iskconudhampur.com
Ujjain, MP — Hare Krishna Land, Bharatpuri, 456 010/ Tel. (0734) 2535000 or 3205000/ Fax: (0734) 2536000/ iskcon.ujjain@pamhho.net
Varanasi, UP — ISKCON, B 27/80 Durgakund Rd., Near Durgakund Police Station, Varanasi 221 010/ Tel. (0542) 246422 or 222617
◆ **Vrindavan, UP** — Krishna-Balaram Mandir, Bhaktivedanta Swami Marg, Raman Reti, Mathura Dist., 281 124/ Tel. & Fax: (0565) 2540728/ iskcon.vrindavan@pamho.net; (Guesthouse:) Tel. (0565) 2540022; ramamani@sancharnet.in

ADDITIONAL RESTAURANT

Kolkata, WB — Govinda's, ISKCON House, 22 Gurusaday Rd., 700 019/ Tel. (033) 24756922, 24749009

EUROPE (partial list)*

Amsterdam — Van Hilligaertstraat 17, 1072 JX/ Tel. +31 (020) 675-1404 or -1694/ Fax: +31 (020) 675-1405/ amsterdam@pamho.net
Barcelona — Plaza Reial 12, Entlo 2, 08002/ Tel. +34 93 302-5194/ templobcn@hotmail.com
Bergamo, Italy — Villaggio Hare Krishna (da Medolago strada per Terno d'Isola), 24040 Chignolo d'Isola (BG)/ Tel. +39 (035) 4940706
Budapest — Lehel Street 15–17, 1039 Budapest/ Tel. +36 (01) 391-0435/ Fax: (01) 397-5219/ nai@pamho.net
Copenhagen — Skjulhoj Alle 44, 2720 Vanlose, Copenhagen/ Tel. +45 4828 6446/ Fax: +45 4828 7331/ iskcon.denmark@pamho.net
Grödinge, Sweden — Radha-Krishna Temple, Korsnäs Gård, 14792 Grödinge, Tel.+46 (08) 53029800/ Fax: +46 (08) 53025062 / bmd@pamho.net
Helsinki — Ruoholahdenkatu 24 D (III krs) 00180/ Tel. +358 (9) 694-9879 or -9837
◆ **Lisbon** — Rua Dona Estefânia, 91 R/C 1000 Lisboa/ Tel. & fax: +351(01) 314-0314 or 352-0038
Madrid — Espíritu Santo 19, 28004 Madrid/ Tel. +34 91 521-3096
Paris — 35 Rue Docteur Jean Vaquier, 93160 Noisy le Grand/ Tel. & fax: +33 (01) 4303-0951/ param.gati.swami@pamho.net
Prague — Jilova 290, Prague 5 - Zlicin 155 21/ Tel. +42 (02) 5795-0391/ info@harekrsna.cz
◆ **Radhadesh, Belgium** — Chateau de Petite Somme, 6940 Septon-Durbuy/ Tel. +32 (086) 322926 (restaurant: 321421)/ Fax: +32 (086) 322929/ radhadesh@pamho.net
◆ **Rome** — Govinda Centro Hare Krsna, via di Santa Maria del Pianto 16, 00186/ Tel. +39 (06) 68891540/ govinda.roma@harekrsna.it
◆ **Stockholm** — Fridhemsgatan 22, 11240/ Tel. +46 (08) 654-9002/ Fax: +46 (08) 650-881; Restaurant: Tel. & fax: +46 (08) 654-9004/ lokanatha@hotmail.com
Warsaw — Mysiadlo k. Warszawy, 05-500 Piaseczno, ul. Zakret 11/ Tel. +48 (022) 750-7797 or -8247/ Fax: +48 (022) 750-8249/ kryszna@post.pl
Zürich — Bergstrasse 54, 8030/ Tel. +41 (01) 262-3388/ Fax: +41 (01) 262-3114/ kgs@pamho.net

RURAL COMMUNITIES

France (La Nouvelle Mayapura) — Domaine d'Oublaisse, 36360, Lucay le Mâle/ Tel. +33 (02) 5440-2395/ Fax: +33 (02) 5440-2823/ oublaise@free.fr
Germany (Simhachalam) — Zielberg 20, 94118 Jandelsbrunn/ Tel. +49 (08583) 316/ info@simhachalam.de
Hungary (New Vraja-dhama) — Krisna-völgy, 8699 Somogyvamos, Fö u, 38/ Tel. & fax: +36 (085) 540-002 or 340-185/ info@krisnavolgy.hu
Italy (Villa Vrindavan) — Via Scopeti 108, 50026 San Casciano in Val di Pesa (FL)/ Tel. +39 (055) 820054/ Fax: +39 (055) 828470/ isvaripriya@libero.it
Spain (New Vraja Mandala) — (Santa Clara) Brihuega, Guadalajara/ Tel. +34 949 280436

ADDITIONAL RESTAURANTS

Barcelona — Restaurante Govinda, Plaza de la Villa de Madrid 4–5, 08002/ Tel. +34 (93) 318-7729
Copenhagen — Govinda's, Nørre Farimagsgade 82, DK-1364 Kbh K/ Tel. +45 3333 7444
Milan — Govinda's, Via Valpetrosa 5, 20123/ Tel. +39 (02) 862417
Oslo — Krishna's Cuisine, Kirkeveien 59B, 0364/ Tel. +47 (02) 260-6250
Zürich — Govinda Veda-Kultur, Preyergrasse 16, 8001/ Tel. & fax: +41 (01) 251-8859/ info@govinda-shop.ch

CIS (partial list)*

Kiev — 16, Zorany per., 04078/ Tel. +380 (044) 433-8312, or 434-7028 or -5533
Moscow — 8/3, Khoroshevskoye sh. (mail: P.O. Box 69), 125284/ Tel. +7 (095) 255-6711/ Tel. & fax: +7 (095) 945-3317

ASIA (partial list)*

Bangkok, Thailand — Soi3, Tanon Itsarapap, Toonburi/ Tel. +66 (02) 9445346 or (081) 4455401 or (089) 7810623/ swami.bvv.narasimha@pamho.net
Dhaka, Bangladesh — 5 Chandra Mohon Basak St., Banagram,1203/ Tel. +880 (02) 236249/ Fax: (02) 837287/ iskcon_bangladesh@yahoo.com
Hong Kong — 6/F Oceanview Court, 27 Chatham Road South (mail: P.O. Box 98919)/ Tel. +852 (2) 739-6818/ Fax: +852 (2) 724-2186/ iskcon.hong.kong@pamho.net
Jakarta, Indonesia — Yayasan Radha-Govinda, P.O. Box 2694, Jakarta Pusat 10001/ Tel. +62 (021) 489-9646/ matsyads@bogor.wasantara.net.id
Katmandu, Nepal — Budhanilkantha (mail: GPO Box 3520)/ Tel. +977 (01) 373790 or 373786/ Fax: +977 (01) 372976 (Attn: ISKCON)/ iskcon@wlink.com.np
Kuala Lumpur, Malaysia — Lot 9901, Jalan Awan Jawa, Taman Yarl, 58200 Kuala Lumpur/ Tel. +60 (3) 7980-7355/ Fax: +60 (3) 7987-9901/ president@iskconkl.com
Manila, Philippines — Radha-Madhava Center, #9105 Banuyo St., San Antonio village, Makati City/ Tel. +63 (02) 8963357; Tel. & fax: +63 (02) 8901947/ iskconmanila@yahoo.com
Myitkyina, Myanmar — ISKCON Sri Jagannath Temple, Bogyoke Street, Shansu Taung, Myitkyina, Kachin State/ mahanadi@mptmail.net.mm
Tai Pei City, Taiwan — Ting Zhou Rd. Section 3, No. 192, 4F, Tai

Pei City 100/ Tel. +886 (02) 2365-8641/ dayal.nitai.tkg@pamho.net
Tokyo, Japan — Subaru 1F, 4-19-6 Kamitakada, Nakano-ku, Tokyo 164-0002/ Tel. +81 (03) 5343- 9147 or (090) 6544-9284/ Fax: +81 (03) 5343-3812/ damodara@krishna.jp

LATIN AMERICA (partial list)*
Buenos Aires, Argentina — Centro Bhaktivedanta, Andonaegui 2054, Villa Urquiza, CP 1431/ Tel. +54 (01) 523-4232/ Fax: +54 (01) 523-8085/ iskcon-ba@gopalnet.com
Caracas, Venezuela — Av. Los Proceres (con Calle Marquez del Toro), San Bernardino/ Tel. +58 (212) 550-1818
Guayaquil, Ecuador — 6 de Marzo 226 and V. M. Rendon/ Tel. +593 (04) 308412 or 309420/ Fax: +564 302108/ gurumani@gu.pro.ec
◆ **Lima, Peru** — Schell 634 Miraflores/ Tel. +51 (014) 444-2871
Mexico City, Mexico — Tiburcio Montiel 45, Colonia San Miguel, Chapultepec D.F., 11850/ Tel. +52 (55) 5273-1953/ Fax: +52 (55) 52725944
Rio de Janeiro, Brazil — Rua Vilhena de Morais, 309, Barra da Tijuca, 22793-140/ Tel. +55 (021) 2491-1887/ sergio.carvalho@pobox.com
San Salvador, El Salvador — Calle Chiltiupan #39, Ciudad Merliot, Nueva San Salvador (mail: A.P. 1506)/ Tel. +503 2278-7613/ Fax: +503 2229-1472/ tulasikrishnadas@yahoo.com
São Paulo, Brazil — Rua do Paraiso, 694, 04103-000/Tel. +55 (011) 326-0975/ communicacaomandir@grupos.com.br
West Coast Demerara, Guyana — Sri Gaura Nitai Ashirvad Mandir, Lot "B," Nauville Flanders (Crane Old Road), West Coast Demerara/ Tel. +592 254 0494/ iskcon.guyana@yahoo.com

AFRICA (partial list)*
Accra, Ghana — Samsam Rd., Off Accra-Nsawam Hwy., Medie, Accra North (mail: P.O. Box 11686)/ Tel. & fax +233 (021) 229988/ srivas_bts@yahoo.co.in
Cape Town, South Africa — 17 St. Andrews Rd., Rondebosch 7700/ Tel. +27 (021) 6861179/ Fax: +27 (021) 686-8233/ cape.town@pamho.net
◆ **Durban, South Africa** — 50 Bhaktivedanta Swami Circle, Unit 5 (mail: P.O. Box 56003), Chatsworth, 4030/ Tel. +27 (031) 403-3328/ Fax: +27 (031) 403-4429/ iskcon.durban@pamho.net
Johannesburg, South Africa — 7971 Capricorn Ave. (entrance on Nirvana Drive East), Ext. 9, Lenasia (mail: P.O. Box 926, Lenasia 1820)/ Tel. +27 (011) 854-1975 or 7969/ iskconjh@iafrica.com
Lagos, Nigeria — 12, Gani Williams Close, off Osolo Way, Ajao Estate, International Airport Rd. (mail: P.O. Box 8793, Marina)/ Tel. +234 (01) 7744926 or 7928906/ bdds.bts@pamho.net
Mombasa, Kenya — Hare Krishna House, Sauti Ya Kenya and Kisumu Rds. (mail: P.O. Box 82224, Mombasa)/ Tel. +254 (011) 312248
Nairobi, Kenya — Muhuroni Close, off West Nagara Rd. (mail: P.O. Box 28946)/ Tel. +254 (203) 744365/ Fax: +254 (203) 740957/ iskcon_nairobi@yahoo.com
◆ **Phoenix, Mauritius** — Hare Krishna Land, Pont Fer (mail: P.O. Box 108, Quartre Bornes)/ Tel. +230 696-5804/ Fax: +230 696-8576/ iskcon.hkl@intnet.mu
Port Harcourt, Nigeria — Umuebule 11, 2nd tarred road, Etche (mail: P.O. Box 4429, Trans Amadi)/ Tel. +234 08033215096/ canakyaus@yahoo.com
Pretoria, South Africa — 1189 Church St., Hatfield, 0083 (mail: P.O. Box 14077, Hatfield, 0028)/ Tel. & fax: +27 (12) 342-6216/ iskconpt@global.co.za

RURAL COMMUNITY
Mauritius (ISKCON Vedic Farm) — Hare Krishna Rd., Vrindaban/ Tel. +230 418-3185 or 418-3955/ Fax: +230 418-6470

Far from a Center?
Call us at 1-800-927-4152
Or contact us on the Internet
http://www.krishna.com
E-mail: bbt.usa@krishna.com